Anthropological Linguistics

Language in Society

GENERAL EDITOR
Peter Trudgill, Professor in the Department of Language and Linguistics, University of Lausanne

ADVISORY EDITORS
Ralph Fasold, Professor of Linguistics, Georgetown University
William Labov, Professor of Linguistics, University of Pennsylvania

Anthropological Linguistics

An Introduction

William A. Foley
University of Sydney

BLACKWELL *Publishers*

First published 1997

Reprinted 1998

Blackwell Publishers Inc
350 Main Street
Malden, Massachusetts 02148, USA

Blackwell Publishers Ltd
108 Cowley Road
Oxford OX4 1JF, UK

Library of Congress Cataloging in Publication Data
Foley, William A.
Anthropological linguistics: an introduction/William A. Foley
p.   cm. — (Language in society; 24)
Includes bibliographical references (p.) and index.
ISBN 0–631–15121–4 — ISBN 0–631–15122–2 (pbk)
1. Anthropological linguistics. I. Title. II. Series: Language
in society (Oxford, England); 24.
P35.F64   1997   96–41302
306. 4'4'089—dc20   CIP

British Library Cataloguing in Publication Data
A CIP catalogue record for this book is available from the British Library

Typeset in 10.5 on 12pt Ehrhardt
by Graphicraft Typesetters Limited, Hong Kong
Printed and bound in Great Britain
by T. J. International Limited, Padstow, Cornwall

This book is printed on acid-free paper

In Memory of My Mother
Dorice Lelianne Brassard Foley
(1921–1993)

Advance praise for William A. Foley's *Anthropological Linguistics*

"An exceptionally wide-ranging, lucid and stimulatingly original presentation of key theoretical issues of interest to students and specialists alike." *John Gumperz, University of California*

"It really is an extraordinary job, a remarkable combination of encyclopedic coverage of the field with cutting-edge treatment of virtually every topic. The range of chapters is such as to make it very flexible, so that it can be adapted to many different approaches to a basic course in linguistic anthropology. In summary, this is a textbook worthy of its author, who is without question one of the foremost linguists of his generation." *Jane H. Hill, University of Arizona*

"It is a fine introduction to a very popular course, Anthropological Linguistics. Beyond his clarity and all his insights into the live issues of anthropological linguistics, Foley deserves special credit for shoring up the bridge from linguistics to biology. The numerous, detailed examples are fresh and engaging, and attest to Foley's wide knowledge of the languages of the world." *Alton L. Becker, Yale University*

"Here at last is an excellent textbook for the field of anthropological linguistics, and a necessary supplement to (or even a replacement for) those outworn sociolinguistics texts. Foley takes a broad definition of the field, covering essential background notions like the nature of culture and evolution, and specific topics as widely separated as the linguistic capacities of apes and hominids, the nature of semantic universals, the relation of language and thought, literacy, language and social interaction, and language change. Textbooks that cover such broad ground usually do so in woolly platitudes or false simplifications. Foley's text is in contrast rich in detail and deep in discussion. Some of the latest findings as well as the classic studies are covered, all nicely interwoven in sustained argument. Even experts will find interesting juxtapositions of fact and theories. Foley is an outstanding field-linguist and the leading authority on the languages of New Guinea, and he has brought his extensive first-hand experience to bear on the issues: the book combines a personal view with a dispassionate survey of the field. No thinking student of the role of language in culture and society will want to be without it." *Stephen C. Levinson, Director, Cognitive Anthropology Research Group, Max Planck Institute for Psycholinguistics, Nijmegen, The Netherlands*

Contents

Part III   Universalism: Innate Constraints on Mind   79

Series Editor's Preface

A number of books in the Language in Society series have dealt with anthropological linguistic fields such as the ethnography of speaking. This is the first book in the series, however, to deal with the important subject of anthropological linguistics as a whole. This is hardly surprising, since relatively few books at this level have ever been published on this somewhat neglected topic. This, too, is not particularly surprising, since adequate coverage of the field in its entirety requires expertise in both anthropology and linguistics of a type that rather few scholars, in this age of increasing specialization, actually have. In Bill Foley, however, the series is fortunate to have found a scholar who continues the tradition of Boas, Sapir and Whorf, and who can write expertly, and on the basis of his own researches, on anthropology from a linguistic perspective, and on linguistics from an anthropological perspective. This book will therefore make an excellent text for courses on anthropological linguistics of a type that many of us would have liked to teach before but have not been able to because of our own lack of the necessary depth and breadth of knowledge. This is not simply a textbook, however. Foley is very well known and admired as an original thinker and researcher in linguistics and anthropology, and the whole book is suffused with his exciting insights and his intellectual challenges to others working in the different disciplines that involve the study of language and society.

Peter Trudgill

Preface

This book is intended as a textbook in the field of anthropological linguistics for advanced undergraduate or graduate students. Anthropological linguistics is a crossdisciplinary field, with input from both linguistics and anthropology. This textbook is one written by a linguist, and as such, it presents what might be termed a linguistic "take" on this crossdisciplinary field (for a more anthropological "take" on many of the topics treated in this book, see Hanks (1995)). Over the last few decades, linguistics and anthropology have increasingly diverged from each other, linguistics with a largely positivistic, structuralist orientation toward its subject matter and anthropology with a more interpretivist, discursive one, so that it is often difficult for specialists in the two fields to talk to each other. This has also led to marginalization of anthropological linguistics in both disciplines. These developments are, in my view, to be deplored; it is vital, if we are to have a rich understanding of language, to have varied contributions from both disciplines. It is considerations like these that led me to write this book. Because I am a linguist by training and practice, this book may, perhaps, be more positivistic and structuralist than many anthropological colleagues may be happy with. I must beg their indulgence; I have tried to give a well rounded and balanced presentation of the field, but obviously I cannot completely escape my linguistic *habitus*. To my linguistic colleagues who may find the directions this book may take them in too alien, I can only say persevere; this is a wonderful expansion of one's understanding of language that ensues when one begins to appreciate the anthropologist's insights into this unique human skill.

A second important point about this book is that, while indeed intended as a textbook for the full range of anthropological linguistics, it takes a particular, coherent biologically based viewpoint to the topics covered. It is this which has guided the way topics are presented and explored. It is my view that textbooks most excite students when they engage them in re-evaluating their own, perhaps previously unexamined, beliefs about themselves and their world. I take very seriously the idea of "anthropology (and linguistics!)

as cultural critique" (Marcus and Fischer 1986), and I believe this is best done in a textbook context by providing students with a challenging, over-arching perspective within which various topics can be considered. The basic view here follows from the ground-breaking work of Maturana and Varela (1987). Humans are fundamentally biological beings, and their life processes and practices at base biological. Cognition, then, is not a disembodied mental process, but a biological process of the organism. So too, ultimately, is social life, cognition enacted in the public interactional realm. These contentions may seem simple, almost trivial, but, as we shall see, when taken seriously, they resonate with enormous power, challenging many of our most cher-ished beliefs.

Because anthropological linguistics is crossdisciplinary, it is necessarily a broad field, with many areas of research. I have tried to be reasonably comprehensive in my treatment of the field, addressing the relevant issues and current questions in each subfield, and this has resulted in a rather large book with many topics. Within a 15-week semester it is probably not poss-ible to cover all the topics presented. The book has been written with that in mind; each course instructor is invited to select that subset of topics which best fits her own pedagogical needs. The anticipated audience of the book is advanced undergraduate or graduate students who already have completed introductory courses in linguistics and anthropology. This back-ground is not absolutely necessary, however, for chapter 1 has been in part written to provide some background in the theory of culture and the struc-ture of language for students who do not have this preparation. Some readers may be surprised to find Part II, on the evolution of language, included in this book. I obviously do not find it out of place; I take very seriously the idea of the four fields of anthropology, physical anthropology, archeology, cultural anthropology and linguistics, and, therefore, I take as axiomatic the view that those subfields of linguistic anthropology that link to physical anthropology and archeology are as properly included in it as those linked to cultural anthropology.

Finally, the reader will no doubt note that the illustrative material of this book, while not exclusively so, is heavily drawn from Southeast Asia and the Pacific. The intention is certainly not to denigrate other areas; merely, as this is the area of my own expertise and one whose literature I am most familiar with, it seemed best to stick to something I know. I would cer-tainly hope that during their course of studies, students can be enriched with illustrative material drawn from a wide range of geographical areas.

Acknowledgments

During the course of nearly three years, I have been blessed with the help of many people and organizations. Thanks first to the Cognitive Anthropology Research Group at the Max-Planck Institute for Psycholinguistics led by Steve Levinson, for a productive, supportive and stimulating year in 1993, during which the first half of this book was written and to the University of Sydney for granting me sabbatical leave for that year. For useful comments on sections of this book, heartfelt thanks are due to Melissa Bowerman, Eve Danziger, Debbie Hill, Jane Hill, Steve Levinson, Paulette Levy, Gunter Senft, Jane Simpson, Dan Slobin, David Wilkins, and Steven Wilson. Especial thanks for detailed comments on the manuscript go to Pete Becker, John Gumperz, and two anonymous referees for Blackwell Publishers. Thanks for careful proofreading extend to Catherine Dunk and especially Andrew Ingram for his valiant efforts in the last two weeks of the final manuscript's preparation. Deeply felt thanks are also due to my Administrative Assistant, Virginia Mayger, and Administrative Officer, Diane Ferari, who put up with my moodiness and took on extra tasks over the last two years so that I could pursue my single-minded vision of completing this book. And to long-suffering Simon Barker, who typed the entire manuscript from untidy handwritten drafts, I can only say thanks for your enormous patience and diligence; I *really* couldn't have done it without you.

And, finally, and most importantly, a long hug, kiss and cuddle of thanks to my partner, Luke, who had to endure disruption and neglect over the last three years while I concentrated single-mindedly on this task. I can't bring back those lost years, but now it's time for you.

The author and publishers wish to thank the following for permission to use copyright material:

American Anthropological Association for figures from John B. Haviland, "Anchoring, Iconicity, and Orientation in Guugu Yimidhirr Pointing

Gestures," *Journal of Linguistic Anthropology*, 3:1 June 1993, fig. 1; and Brent Berlin, Dennis E. Breedlove and Peter H. Raven, "General Principles of Classification and Nomenclature in Folk Biology," *American Anthropologist*, 75:1 February 1973, fig. 1;

Blackwell Publishers and University of Pennsylvania Press for figures based on William Labov, *Sociolinguistic Patterns*, 1972, pp. 51, 54;

Cambridge University Press for material from J. Sachs, "Preschool boys' and girls' language in pretend play" in *Language, Gender and Sex in Comparative Perspective*, ed. Philips, Steele and Tanz, 1987, p. 182; Platt, "Social norms and lexical acquisition: a study of deictic verbs in Samoan child language" in *Language Socialization Across Cultures*, ed. B. Schieffelin and E. Ochs, 1986, pp. 143, 148; J. Irvine, "Strategies of status manipulation in the Wolof greeting" in *Explorations in the Ethnography of Speaking*, ed. R. Banman and J. Sherzer, 1974, p. 171; J. Lucy, *Grammatical Categories and Cognition: A Case Study of the Linguistic Relativity Hypothesis*, 1992, p. 138; and J. Lucy, *Language Diversity and Thought: A Reformulation of the Linguistic Relativity Hypothesis*, 1992, pp. 50, 52;

Chicago Linguistic Society for table from I. Mutsumi and D. Gentner, "Linguistic relativity vs universal ontology: Cross-linguistic studies of the object/substance distinction" in *What We Think, What We Mean, and How We Say It: Papers from the Parasession on the Correspondence of Conceptual, Semantic, and Grammatical Representations*, ed. Katherine Beals et al., 1993, table 1, p. 177;

Stephen C. Levinson for figures from S. Levinson, "Language and cognition: cognitive consequences of spatial description in Guugu Yimidhirr," Working Paper 23, Cognitive Anthropology Research Group, 1992, pp. 20, 28;

The MIT Press for extracts from B. L. Whorf, *Language, Thoughts and Reality: Selected Writing of Benjamin Lee Whorf*, 1956;

University of California Press for extracts from E. Sapir, *Selected Writings of Edward Sapir in Language, Culture and Personality*, trans./ed. David Mandelbaum, 1949. Copyright © 1949 The Regents of the University of California.

Every effort has been made to trace the copyright holders but if any have been inadvertently overlooked the publishers will be pleased to make the necessary arrangement at the first opportunity.

Part I
Introduction

Part I

1

Introduction

Meaning, Cognition, and the Domain of Anthropological Linguistics

Anthropological linguistics is that sub-field of linguistics which is concerned with the place of language in its wider social and cultural context, its role in forging and sustaining cultural practices and social structures. As such, it may be seen to overlap with another sub-field with a similar domain, sociolinguistics, and in practice this may indeed be so. But for my purposes in this book, I will make a distinction between these two sub-fields along the following lines. Anthropological linguistics views language through the prism of the core anthropological concept, culture, and, as such, seeks to uncover the *meaning* behind the use, misuse or non-use of language, its different forms, registers and styles. It is an interpretive discipline peeling away at language to find cultural understandings. Sociolinguistics, on the other hand, views language as a social institution, one of those institutions within which individuals and groups carry out social interaction. It seeks to discover how linguistic behavior patterns with respect to social groupings and correlates differences in linguistic behavior with the variables defining social groups, such as age, sex, class, race, etc.

While not insisting that this distinction is either sharp or absolute, I do believe it is useful and perhaps a few examples might help in establishing this. Consider the variable pronunciation of the progressive/gerundive ending, so that *running* can be pronounced [rʌnɪŋ] or [rʌnɪn] (informally described as "dropping the *g*," i.e. "runnin"). If we approach this variable from a sociolinguistic perspective, we will note the correlation between each pronunciation and particular social groupings, for example, the higher frequency of the [In] variant with male speakers, and [Iŋ] with female speakers; or, again, the higher frequency of the [In] variant with speakers of a working- or lower-class background, while higher frequencies of [Iŋ] are correlated with middle- and upper-class backgrounds. Such would be a typical sociolinguistic approach, see, for example, Labov (1972b). However, an anthropological linguistic approach, while taking note of all these correlations, would ask a further fundamental question: what do speakers mean when they use an [In] versus an [Iŋ] variant. Of course, the answer may vary in different contexts, but one possible answer, following Trudgill (1972), is that the use of [In], considering its link to the social variables of maleness and working class, could be an assertion of a strong masculine self-identity. Trudgill (1972) points out that male middle-class speakers in Norwich, Britain, often use variables like [In] to stake exactly this claim, regarding the values perceived to be associated with working-class life, like toughness, struggle against odds, and physical labor, as indicative of enhanced masculinity.

For another example, consider the choice between the two available languages, Yimas vernacular and Tok Pisin, in a contemporary Yimas village in Papua New Guinea. Again, a sociolinguistic study would reveal correlations: Yimas vernacular for older speakers, Tok Pisin for younger; Yimas vernacular for female speakers, Tok Pisin for male. But an anthropological linguistic description would probe further: given that any adult over forty can speak both languages, what determines the choice? The answer is that Yimas vernacular is viewed as uniquely tied to the traditional village way of life, while Tok Pisin indexes the modern world and the wider Papua New Guinea nation. When, say, a male speaker of forty-five uses Yimas, he could be making any number of claims: for example, the context is one of traditional Yimas cultural practices, like mortuary feasts, or he considers his self-identity as being mainly constructed around traditional Yimas beliefs and practices, rather than the modern economy of trade stores and outboard motors or the political life of local, regional and national governments, and so on. What is crucial here, as in the previous example, is the meaning of particular choices; it is this that is the subject matter of anthropological linguistics. And, ultimately, the distribution these choices have across various social groups is tied to the cultural meanings these choices have, leading particular social groups to statistically favor one choice. Hence, the statistical observation that Yimas vernacular is employed more frequently by women is connected to the fact that, in this community, women are the main sustainers of the traditional culture, engaging in the traditional economic areas of fishing and weaving and having fewer contacts outside the village, so that their self-identity is constructed in more traditional Yimas terms (for an exactly opposite situation, in which women are the leaders in linguistic innovations emphasizing the modern world over the traditional community, see Gal (1979) and chapter 15).

For a final example, let us consider the choice between speaking and not speaking at all, i.e. the strategic use of silence. Basso (1972) studied the uses of silence among the Cibecue Apache. Some social situations in which silence is conventionally observed include: a couple during early stages of courtship, on meeting strangers, on the return of an individual who has been away for a long time, when in the company of those in mourning, during a curing ritual, and when being insulted and abused verbally. These are the various social situations calling for silence, but what ties all of these together, what does silence among the Cibecue Apache *mean*? Essentially it indicates that a central participant in a social situation – e.g. the source of verbal abuse, the stranger, the partner in the courtship or the returned relative – is unknown to a greater or lesser degree, and hence unpredictable. Cibecue Apache culture valorizes predictability of social roles in ongoing social interaction, and unpredictability is taken as equivalent to "potentially dangerous." Silence is the culturally mandated sign in these contexts for "potentially dangerous," and an anthropological linguistic account of these phenomena, such as Basso (1972), seeks to disclose this core cultural belief within these diverse social practices.

The Nature of Meaning

As I claimed above and these examples reinforce, anthropological linguistics is a search for the meanings in linguistic practices within wider cultural practices. As such, it is clear that the concept of meaning is absolutely fundamental to the field. But meaning is a notoriously elusive concept; just what is it? One way to approach this problem, following a hallowed tradition, would be to look at some of the uses of the verb *mean* in ordinary English, such as:

1 Those clouds mean rain
2 Red means "stop!"
3 What does "thespian" mean?
4 I didn't mean what I said
5 I didn't mean to say it; it just slipped out

We seem to find two distinct broad senses of *mean* in these examples. The first of these is roughly "to be a sign or indication of; to signify," exemplified in 1 and 2. Of course, under this broad range of "signify" there are differences between 1 and 2. Example 1 is a case where the relationship between the sign (clouds) and what it signifies (rain) is an intrinsic fact about the natural world, a relationship between contiguity or cause and effect (clouds bring rain). There is nothing intrinsic or natural, however, between the color red and the instruction to stop, as in example 2. This is strictly a customary understanding among the members of a social grouping who agree to abide by this understanding; the relationship between the sign and what it signifies is strictly a convention. In the traditional terminology of semiotics, the study of signs, the kind of sign in example 2 is a *symbol*, while in example 1, it is an *index* (see pp. 25–7 and Peirce (1965–6)).

What about the other broad sense of English *mean*? This is clearly illustrated in examples 4 and 5. Here, *mean* roughly has the sense of "want" or "intend." Thus, in example 4 what I in fact did say was not what I wanted to say or intended; whereas in example 5, I had no intention of speaking at all, but I spoke nonetheless. Clearly, we can claim that "intend" is a good gloss for the uses of *mean* in these two examples.

But what about example 3? It seems that both senses of *mean*, "to signify" and "to intend" are operative here. A word like "thespian" means something by virtue of the fact that, by conventions of the language to which it belongs, it is a sign, i.e. its form /θespian/ signifies something like a concept, which we might paraphrase as "actor," or a referent, a real world entity like Laurence Olivier. Further, unlike clouds signifying rain, this sign takes on this signification when a speaker of the language has an intention to use this sign to signify exactly that, as when she uses it in a sentence like *he was the greatest thespian of this century*.

The complex dual sense of *mean* when used of linguistic acts was explicitly formulated in a now classic paper *Meaning* by the philosopher Grice (1971). Grice defines this sense of speaker A means X as "A intended the utterance of X to produce some effect in an audience by means of recognition of this intention" (Grice 1971:58). The notion of "intend" in *mean* is transparent in this definition, but "signify" is also implicit in that X can only produce an effect in an audience to the extent that X signifies something to it. This implicitness, however, is one of the weaknesses of Grice's formulation, for it fails to recognize the crucial conventionality of this signification. Consider a case in which a sanity test is administered to an irritable academic (Ziff 1971:61). In response to a particular question, the academic answers

Ugh ugh blugh blugh ugh blugh blugh

Now, by Grice's formulation, the academic clearly could have meant something by this utterance, namely, he intends to produce an effect in his audience, the man who posed the question. The intended effect was to show his impatience with the test and offend his questioner. But just as clearly, the utterance does not mean anything, for it fails to conform to conventional rules of signification of English or any other known language. The speaker may intend something with this utterance, but it completely fails to signify. We could appeal here to a common distinction (Harman 1971; Levinson 1983) between speaker's meaning (i.e. Grice's meaning, the meaning a speaker intends to ascribe to an utterance) and sentence meaning, the conventional signification assigned to an utterance by virtue of the linguistic practices of the community, embodied in its inventory of signs and their syntactic rules of combination.

But drawing the contrast in quite this way may be overly ethnocentric in privileging the speaker's intention too much and reflecting an "individualist" ideology of personhood typical of the industrialized West (see chapter 14). Duranti (1988b) argues that what an utterance means in a Samoan political debate is not what the speaker intends it to mean, but fundamentally what the powerful participants in the debate ultimately determine it to mean. It is the conventionalized social processes of negotiation and interpretation that fix its meaning. Contrary to Grice, in Samoa and elsewhere, meaning is not something one communicates to others, but rather something one *creates* with others. That this creation is heavily conventionalized in linguistic and cultural practices is the fundamental insight of Bakhtin (1981, 1986). As we create meaning in an ongoing relationship, we carry our history of linguistic and cultural practices from many other previous relationships. Our language is full of words, expressions, genres of our predecessors and our earlier relationships, which provide a vast pool of conventional linguistic practices to draw on in forging meanings. Examples are legion, but a simple case is how the mere presence of *once upon a time* immediately invokes a fairy-tale (see chapter 18).

The notion of meaning I am talking about here is not limited to linguistic practices, but has been highlighted by Geertz (1973) and other symbolic anthropologists as basic to cultural practices too. Consider the following example from Geertz (1973), who, in turn, drew it from the philosopher Gilbert Ryle (1949). Geertz draws our attention to the difference between a nervous twitch realized in the blinking of one's eye and a conspiratorial wink. While as acts of bodily behavior these two events are nearly if not exactly the same, i.e. the contraction of an eye, from another point of view there is a world of difference between them. A twitch is just that, nothing more and nothing less, a bodily action. But a wink is meaningful: it signals, perhaps, that you and I both know that I'm lying through my teeth, but that the person for whom I am spinning a yarn does not know this. It further signals that I would like you not to inform him of this. In short, it signals that I want us to enter into a conspiracy to conceal the truth. It is this meaning that I and you as members of American, British or Australian culture interpret from the physical contraction of the eye. This wink is a cultural act: we experience this physical contraction of the eye as meaningful and interpret it as such, as an invitation to a conspiracy.

Meaning as "Mental Representation"

But let us inquire further into the nature of this meaning that the signs of cultural and linguistic practices have. Where exactly can it be found? How exactly does one know how to interpret *thespian* as "actor" or a wink as an invitation to a conspiracy? The usual answer is through *concepts* "ideas, thoughts or mental constructs by means of which the mind apprehends or comes to know things" (Lyons 1977:110). In other words, the physical form of a sign such as its phonetic sequence or a contraction of the eyelids calls into play a concept in the mind of anyone who "knows" this sign; its physical form is merely a stimulus or gesture to bring to consciousness this idea or thought, or in modern parlance, this *mental representation*. This position entails postulating a pre-given natural world, the world out there, the source of perceptions, which is re-presented to the mind as concepts, *mental representations*, for the purposes of mental functioning, the analogy of the mind as the "mirror of nature" (Rorty 1979). Such a view necessarily postulates a rich inner world of mental constructions, which lies behind and provides the meaningful basis of signalling practices in the domain of language and culture.

Note that this approach sets up a dichotomy between a mental "internal" meaning and a physical "external" signal and raises a number of potentially serious problems. For example, what forges the link between the internal and the external? The external gesture is highly conventional, ultimately socially and publicly mandated. In this sense it gains a kind of objective existence, but the internal meaning is subjective, the functioning of an individual mind. What ties subjective experience to objective act? How can we derive public conventional meaning from the individual's private mental experience, or vice versa? And further, how can we know that a particular objective act is assigned the same meaning by two individual minds; in other words, what establishes the meaning as shared? Of course, this shared meaning is the basis of all cultural and linguistic practices, but, if meaning is the functioning of individual minds, what ensures that it is shared?

Meaning as Enaction

Questions like these suggest that equating meaning with internal mental representations may not be the most insightful direction for us to take. Let us consider an alternative, the enactive approach to meaning and cognition recently proposed by Maturana and Varela (1987) and Varela, Thompson, and Rosch (1991), which entails some quite radical breaks with most current views of knowing. Because of its unfamiliarity, it seems best to start with a simple example; consider first the behavior of a single cell protozoan, like an amoeba. If there is some food, say another protozoan, in its environment, this will generate certain chemical perturbations in the environment, which are registered on the amoeba's cell membrane and, in turn, trigger changes in the consistency of the protoplasm of the amoeba. These changes in protoplasm consistency cause part of it to extend in the direction of the food "quarry" rather like pinchers (called pseudopods). These then cause changes in the locomotion of the animal, ultimately resulting in it enveloping the food protozoan. What is crucial here is a correlation *internal* to the organism between the chemical changes affecting its cell membrane and the flow of protoplasm as pseudopods. More generally, there is a statable correlation in the organism between a sensory surface (in this case, the cell membrane) and a motor surface (in this case, the pseudopods). Note that the movement of the amoeba toward the food protozoan looks "intentional," but it clearly is not; merely, an internal correlation within the amoeba in the chemical changes throughout its protoplasm. Of course, no one would ascribe a mind or mental representations to a single cell creature like an amoeba, but to an external observer its behavior might be described (incorrectly, of course) as intentional, meaningfully directed to a goal.

With complex multicellular animals, when a nervous system enters the scene, the possibilities are more complex, but the same basic idea applies. The neurons provide contacts between physically widely displaced parts of the organism in precisely articulated ways, through the restricted pathways of the neurons. Without such a system, only the most diffused generalized contacts would be possible, through the unrestricted circulation of internal chemical signals, as in the amoeba. The neurons allow diverse sensory receptor cells and motor effective cells to be linked across the entire organism for example, the eye to the limbs, and the pattern of interaction between these can be, and, indeed with vertebrates is, quite varied. The possession of a nervous system expands the potential behavior of an organism dramatically.

For our purposes the most crucial property of a nervous system is its operational closure (Maturana and Varela 1987), i.e. the results of its internal processes are more of its own internal processes. Minsky (1986:288) expresses this very well:

> Why are processes so hard to classify? In earlier times, we could usually judge machines and processes by how they transformed raw materials into finished products. But it makes no sense to speak of brains as though they manufacture thoughts the way factories make cars. The difference is that brains use *processes that change themselves* – and this means we cannot separate such processes from the products they produce. In particular, brains make memories, which change the way we'll subsequently think. *The principal activities of brains are making changes in themselves.* Because the whole idea of self-modifying processes is new to our experience, we cannot yet trust our commonsense judgements about such matters.

Within the overall nervous system, the sensory receptor cells not only include those cells capable of responding to the environment, but also those capable of responding to changes in the organism itself. The nervous system acts like a thermostat; it maintains the possible internal changes in the organism within certain limits. In effect, the state of the nervous system determines the possibilities of any following states: "the nervous system functions as a closed network of changes in relations of activity between its components" (Maturana and Varela 1987:164). Perhaps one way to help visualize the operational closure of the nervous system is through the metaphor of a couple dancing. While dancing, the couple may be seen to be continually responding to the environment and altering their behavior according to its changes, for example, speeding up or slowing down in changes to the rhythm, adjusting their feet to bumps in the floor, etc. But, in fact, the range of behavior available to them is strictly constrained by the requirements on coordination of sequential movements during the dance; one cannot speed up and the other slow down or start a completely different dance routine, if the couple is to maintain this coordination. Like the dancing couple the nervous system is constrained by its present state to a range of possible subsequent states; not just any subsequent state is possible. Due to its status as a self-modifying system, the nervous system undergoes continuous structural changes. Thus, what counts as the "environment" for the purposes of the sensory receptor cells emerges from the world only through the present organization of the organism's nervous system, which, of course, is partly a function of its history of previous organizations. The "environment" does not exist as an object of cognition apart from the state of operational closure of the nervous system; it is not pre-given. The nervous system "affords" (see Gibson 1979) the world as "environment" its significance for present and possible subsequent states of organization, and, in turn, the world contributes to generating a history of the organism's states. This history of recurring interactions between organism and environment leads to the resulting congruence we have noted. This process is called *structural coupling* (Maturana and Varela 1987:75).

All interactions and structural couplings lead to structural changes in the neurons, and hence affect the operation of the nervous system. Further, every act of cognition depends on the operational closure of the nervous system, but for vertebrates and higher animals, with their greatly elaborated nervous systems, there can be a great deal of indeterminacy, often referred to as plasticity. The nervous system's plasticity results from its continuous transformation correlated to transformation of the environment, as each interaction affects it. We might view this as learning. But Maturana and Varela (1978:170) caution:

> What is occurring, however, is that the neurons, the organism they integrate, and the environment in which they interact operate reciprocally as sectors of their corresponding structural changes and are coupled with each other structurally: the functioning organism, including its nervous system, selects the

structural changes that permit it to continue operating, or it disintegrates. To an observer, the organism appears as moving proportionately in a changing environment; and he speaks of learning. To him the structural changes that occur in the nervous system seem to correspond to the circumstances of the interactions of the organism. In terms of the nervous system's operation, however, there is only an ongoing structural drift that follows the course in which, at each instant, the structural coupling (adaptation) of the organism to its medium of interaction is conserved.

We as observers, then, can speak of instinctive versus learned behavior simply in terms of their observable history. If the behavior is developed irrespective of the peculiarities of the organism's interactions, it is instinctive. If the behavior, however, arises only as the result of a particular history of interaction, then it is learned. Crucially, all cognition is an expression of structural couplings; to characterize it as an internal mental re-presentation of information from the environment is an extremely misleading way to describe this drift of recurring congruent structural changes in the nervous system. The "environment" cannot specify changes in the nervous system due to its operational closure; it can only trigger them. Remember how the "environment" triggers changes in the amoeba's shape. An observer of the amoeba engulfing a food protozoan might attribute intentionality to it, but he would be wrong. Animals with complex nervous systems and great plasticity of behavior are essentially the same. They live out their lives in ongoing drift of structural coupling with the environment. As observers we might attribute intentionality, mental representations or meaning to their behavior, but again we would be wrong. All that happens are correlations of changes of states in the nervous system and changes of states in the environment. Such living systems "do not operate by representation. Instead of *representing* an independent world, they *enact* a world as a domain of distinctions . . ." (Varela, Thompson, and Rosch 1991:140).

Social Phenomena

Humans live in social groups and as a result can engage in a particular kind of structural coupling – with each other. Because of the adaptive possibilities of the nervous systems of both organisms, the interactions in this social structural coupling can acquire a recurrent nature. This will result in congruent changes: codevelopment with mutual involvement through this reciprocal structural coupling, with each one conserving its adaptation and organization. Social phenomena, then, are those that arise in these types of reciprocal structural coupling. Note that the internal states of all organisms participating in such structural couplings directly reflect the network of understandings the organisms create in forging them. Any biological phenomenon is a social phenomenon when it arises in the context of recurring structural coupling between two or more organisms. This applies as much to a beehive as to the modern big city, the differences being due, in part at least, to other biological features of these organisms. A social system is the unity formed by social phenomena. What is crucial about them is that the drift of each individual organism involved is fundamentally a part of the whole network of mutual changes the organisms bring about in constructing the social system. Thus, the statuses of worker versus queen bee in a hive or lord versus vassal in a feudal kingdom are mutually determining, one constitutes the other in ongoing social structural coupling. The coordinated behaviors which trigger social structural coupling in a social system can loosely be called communication. For a beehive the form of communication is the circulation of chemicals; this determines a queen versus a worker. In a human city the most important forms of communicative behavior are linguistic practices. In both cases, it is this form, chemicals or language, which coordinates the behavior of the organisms in the social system, maintaining the ongoing structural coupling.

When these social systems and their patterns of communicative behavior have been stable for generations, though the individual organisms engaged in the structural couplings have changed, these patterns can be called cultural behavior. Cultural behavior is not essentially different from other forms of learned behavior; it is a consequence of the dynamics of social living over many generations, while individual members of the social system are replaced. As culture is a central concept in anthropology, let us now look at it in some detail.

Culture as Embodied Practice

As argued in the previous section, cognition is fundamentally a biological phenomenon, a relation of structural coupling between an organism and the environment, so that together they enact a world of significance. The earlier dichotomies of individual versus shared or inner mental experience versus outer public conventional action are seen to be misleading in the extreme; cognition is neither, but in a sense resides in both: in the organism's present state and its history of structural coupling. Ultimately, all knowledge is action in a given context, more specifically, *embodied* action. Because we are organisms of a particular biological type, i.e. our human bodies, cognition as action necessarily depends on those sensorimotor capabilities that our human bodies present. Further, as social beings, a fundamental type of structural coupling that our bodies engage in is with other organisms of the same biological type, so that our individual sensorimotor capabilities are transformed by this history of social interaction. In the final analysis, our biological being, as realized in our human bodies and their capabilities, is a social and cultural construction at least as much as it is an individual one. This is the basic insight behind Bourdieu's (1977, 1990) very influential idea of *habitus*. The habitus is a "set of dispositions which incline agents to act and react in certain ways. The dispositions generate practices, perceptions and attitudes which are regular without being consciously coordinate or governed by any 'rule'" (Thompson 1991:12). The habitus provides individuals with a "practical sense" of how to act in their lives, giving guidance for actions, but not strictly determining them. This "practical sense" is an embodied one; these dispositions that form the habitus and provide this practical sense are inculcated in the way the body acts, stands, sits, talks, cries, laughs, potentially even, copulates. The inculcation of these embodied dispositions occurs through histories of structural couplings with other beings throughout life, but especially in early childhood with parents, siblings, and peers. For example, boys are habituated to stand when they urinate, and girls, to sit (this is strictly not biologically necessary; boys could sit too, if habituated to do so). Such inculcated dispositions are generative of action, but these actions are accomplished unreflectively. These embodied action patterns, being preconscious, are highly durable and persist through life. The body, then, is the site on which the history of our structural couplings is inscribed; we are the product of that history, but at the same time, because the dispositions of the habitus are generative, we continually reproduce it. Ultimately, the grounding of our cognition of the world is embodied, and hence pre-reflective. For example, I know how to cycle from my house to my office, by left turn here, right turn there, straight for so many meters here; but if asked to describe it explicitly, I may find it quite difficult.

This is the reason why it is problematic to describe what we know explicitly through a system of rules. There is always some information which must be left out, which provides the grounding for the rules to operate, and fundamentally, what always must be taken for granted is the body and its sensorimotor capabilities (Taylor 1993). This claim can be fleshed out by supplementing it with some of Michael Polanyi's (1959, 1962; Polanyi and Prosch 1975) ideas about the distinction between tacit versus articulate knowledge. Articulate knowledge is that which is derivable from specifiable premises according to clear rules of logical inference. It corresponds to what can be explicitly stated and critically reflected on. We cannot so reflect on what we tacitly know, for this is a-critical knowledge with an essential personal commitment. Good examples of articulate knowledge are our knowledge of street names or the causes of the Russian Revolution. Good examples of tacit knowledge are how to drive a car or how to speak a language. Tacit knowledge does not take the form of logically connected chains of reasoning; its structure is perhaps most clearly manifested in the act of understanding: the creative grasping together of disjointed parts into a comprehensive whole.

Associated with the difference between these two types of knowledge are two different types of awareness: subsidiary versus focal. Consider one of Polanyi's examples: driving a nail down with a hammer. When we do this, we experience the hammer's head hitting the nail but in fact what we are actually perceiving are the vibrations of the hammer's handle in our hands. Without being aware of it, we use these vibrations to guide our manipulation of the hammer, all the while attending to the impact of the hammer on the nail. Thus, we are focally, explicitly aware of the action of driving the nail by being subsidiarily, tacitly aware of the vibrations in the hand. Ultimately, all human knowledge depends on this form; we know something explicitly and focally within a much wider background of subsidiary and tacit knowledge. Our bodies are the central locus of this background. Our body is certainly one thing in the world we normally know only by relying on our tacit awareness of it for attending to other things. We attend to external objects by being tacitly aware of things happening in our bodies; all cognition requires embodied understanding, which cannot be fully specified by explicit rules. This embodied understanding, including dispositions in the habitus, is tacit knowledge and hence one can only be subsidiarily aware of it; this accounts for why so much of the habitus is preconscious and unable to be reflected on or modified. This conservatism leads to the practices generated by the dispositions of the habitus being transmitted from generation to generation, in other words they are potentially *cultural practices*. Culture in this view is that transgenerational domain of practices through which human organisms in a social system communicate with each other. These practices may be verbal or non-verbal, but they must be communicative in the sense that they occur as part of ongoing histories of social structural coupling and contribute to the viability of continued coupling. It is through their effectiveness in continuing the viability of social structural coupling that we can describe these practices as meaningful. It is in this sense that cultural practices are meaningful, not in the more common sense of transmitting information, which, of course, may potentially lead us to the misleading presupposition of mental representations of the information in the transmitter's mind. Thus, a wink is a cultural practice because it occurs in the context of recurrent successful social structural coupling, a practice inculcated in the habitus over many generations as an acceptable and successful action in particular interactions. A twitch is not a cultural practice because it does not meet these requirements.

Culture, then, consists of the things people do to communicate in ongoing transgenerational histories of social interaction. Through its inculcation in the habitus it becomes embodied in the self and reproduces itself in future action. In this sense a human being is a thoroughly encultured being;

culture makes itself visible in all aspects of existence, down to the smallest routines of bodily hygiene. In fact, it may be in the little routines in which we enact bodily understandings of place and time that the most subtle workings of culture may be manifest (Giddens 1984).

Meaning in Cultural Practice – Symbolic Anthropology

But, perhaps, the most common thing people do in social interaction is making meanings with each other, again with language or non-verbally. People make meanings in relationships, structural coupling. One performs an action, say, calling out "Run!", and another person coordinates her behavior to it, either by running, replying "why?", or extending "to the house!". Thus, a meaning is forged in a communicative interaction by an action and its coordinated supplement. Actions by an individual do not mean in and of themselves. A relationship of structural coupling is required; another individual is necessary to coordinate herself to the action and supplement it (Gergen 1994; see also Urban's (1991) similar criticism of the methods of introspection to arrive at meanings in modern linguistics). Through patterns of action and coordinated supplement, whole histories of structural coupling and worlds of meaning are generated. Of course, meanings which are created in cultural practices are constrained to follow in the train of innumerable previous structural couplings over many generations. Thus, *run* as established by this history of coupling, means "move through a plane rapidly" not "blow one's nose." It is this which gives them their public conventional character, but, as noted by Bakhtin (1981), also ensures that any present meaning is always a reframing of the past, reworking things from past histories into the present relationship.

While perhaps not exhaustive of the domain of culture, meaning forging cultural practices are unquestionably the most salient ones, maybe due to the fact that some of these, like art and ritual, are those which encultured individuals seem to be most reflectively aware of (see Silverstein 1979, 1981). Not surprisingly, some highly influential theories of culture have seen it in exactly these terms – as a system of meanings, a human web of significance. Culture, in this approach, is an historically contingent network of signs, a linking of meanings with their outwardly expressed forms. A good example of a bit of culture is the English word "weed" (Shweder 1990). The *Shorter Oxford English Dictionary* defines a weed as "a herbaceous plant not valued for use or beauty, growing wild and rank, and regarded as cumbering the ground or hindering the growth of superior vegetation" (1973:2522). This definition shows a weed as a cultural creation through and through. What counts as a weed, "a plant not valued for use or beauty," is entirely in the practices of the beholder. One group's weed is another's cash crop. Thus, a plant is a weed only in certain understandings of it, particular dispositions toward it for particular human beings. There is nothing natural, impersonal or objective in calling a plant a weed. It takes on this label by virtue of the life practices of a certain culture which understands certain plants as useful and others as not, and the resulting dispositions toward those unuseful plants. Thus, culture in a sense is a network of habitual dispositions, different cultures being composed of different habitual dispositions, all embodied in the habitus.

The dispositions and practices are commonly expressed through symbols, that class of signs which bears a conventional relationship to their significations. Most words in natural languages are symbols in exactly this sense; building on ancient insights, Saussure (1959[1916]) pointed out the completely arbitrary relationship between the form of the French word *arbre* and its meaning "tree." This arbitrariness is amply demonstrated by the word designating this in other languages: German *Baum*, Tok Pisin *diwai*, Tagalog *kahoy*, Indonesian *pohon*, Yimas *yan*, Watam *padoŋ*. Understandings and practices are realized for humans through symbols. One view of culture, then, is really as a system of symbols by which a human being enacts his/her embodied understanding. This is the view propounded by the influential school of symbolic anthropology, the best known representative of this view probably being Geertz. He views culture as a system of public meanings encoded in symbols and articulated in behavior seen as symbolic action. These symbols are public expressions of shared practices and understandings among those who can be described as having the same culture. Cultural meanings are not in individual minds, but rather they are shared by the social actors. Cultural meanings are public meanings encoded in shared symbols, not self-contained private understandings. For Geertz, "they are things of this world" (Geertz 1973:10). Consider the earlier example of the involuntary twitch versus a wink. The latter counts as culture by virtue of it being symbolic action – a conventionalized gesture communicating a particular meaning. But it only does this by virtue of a public code in which doing so counts as a signal of conspiracy. Knowing what counts as winking is not the same as winking. Another example Geertz provides as an item of culture is a Beethoven quartet (Geertz 1973:11):

> that a Beethoven quartet is a temporally developed tonal structure, a coherent sequence of modified sound – in a word, music – and not anybody's knowledge of or belief about anything, including how to play it, is a proposition for which most people are, upon reflection, likely to assent.

Geertz's view of culture is thoroughly grounded in human embodied beings engaging in social action. This leads him to view thinking as primarily social and public and only derivatively as the private function of the individual mind: "Thinking as an overt, public act, involving the purposeful manipulation of objective materials is probably fundamental to human beings and thinking as a covert, private act and without recourse to such materials, a derived, though not unuseful, capability" (Geertz 1973:76) and "cultural resources are ingredient, not accessory, to human thought" (Geertz 1973:83).

The position that cultural meanings are encoded in public symbols expressed in social action in particular places and with particular histories and times leads Geertz to a strong position of cultural relativism. To paraphrase Becker (1995) he is interested in particularity, the deep understanding of the differences across cultures. The basic discipline of anthropology is translation – to gain access to the worlds of significance of those others that we study. Various descriptions of a cultural practice can provide different "takes" on it and thus yield alternative construals of these other worlds, but the understanding is always partial, some things always being omitted, as in any translation. We always strive for deeper and deeper understanding, with multiple perspectives. Given that the worlds of significance of members of different cultures are embedded in very diverse practices with generally separate histories, there is no reason to expect their complete commensurability across cultures. Indeed, our modern scientific ways of conceptualizing, our theories, are the products of our particular Western intellectual and social history, traceable back to the ancient Greeks, and may be very poor models for understanding the conceptual systems of other peoples widely separate from us in cultural tradition. Indeed, theories are no more than cultural tools for our intellect. They are culturally constructed tools of investigation, frameworks with which to interpret our experiences. Our knowledge of a theory lies in large part in our tacit use of it. Like all tools, theories amplify our human powers, but do so against a background of tacit knowledge much of which is tacit unquestioned cultural knowledge. Someone "testing" a theory is necessarily relying in an uncritical way upon other tacitly accepted theories and assumptions, of which they cannot, during this testing procedure, be explicitly aware; we cannot scrutinize our spectacles when we are using them to see with.

Geertz does not deny the possibility of human cultural universals, but he does believe that if such exist, they must be too abstract and insubstantial to provide much help in the deeper interpretation of the rich tapestries of meanings found in the world's cultures. For such a relativist, this diversity needs to be real and understood, but it need not result in complete chaos, with no intellectual or moral bearings. Becker (1995:420) perhaps says it best:

A relativist like me doesn't think anything goes. A relativist does think, however, that many things go, and that many different languages and their

cultures around the world have learned, over thousands and thousands of
years, to attune themselves to their worlds in much better ways than other
people tell them they must or should. Relativism doesn't mean anything
goes, but it means that the world the Balinese live in and that they shape
into understanding with their language is a valid, real, true, good world to be
in and doesn't have to be destroyed or replaced.

For Geertz, anthropology is tuning in with the natives, ("indwelling") so
that we can converse with them with increasing understanding. It does not
bear the hallmarks of detached objectivity, but of empathetic involvement.
Its goal is to "enlarge the universe of human discourse" (Geertz 1973:14).

The semiotic view of culture proposed by Geertz shares a number of
features with the embodied practices view proposed here. Descriptions in
Geertz's framework can provide rich sources of information about how social
agents can make meanings in social structural coupling. But ultimately it is
unsatisfying, because in Geertz's approach, ultimately there is no theoretical place for the organism, merely her public acts of meaning creation. The
core of the embodied practices view is the relationship in structural coupling of organism and environment, including other organisms in social interaction. There are necessarily two poles: organism and environment. But the
organism in the theory proposed by Geertz, specifically her nervous system
and its constraints, is nearly invisible. The uses to which public cultural
materials can be put are not limitless; they are quite strongly constrained by
the neurological constraints of the human brain, as it is realized in any particular individual human organism. This is a discipline no individual nor
indeed culture can escape, a point which Lévi-Strauss (1966) has forcefully
and repeatedly made. This again brings up the question of universals. Geertz
sees no point in pursuing these; if they exist, they would be too lifeless and
flimsy to inform deeply the thick description of a cultural practice. But this
is an empirical question which he and other symbolic anthropologists ignore
at the profession's peril.

Culture as Cognition – Cognitive Anthropology

Another popular view of culture does approach it from the point of view of
the organism and its neurological capabilities, but, conversely, undertheorizes
the contribution of the environment in structural coupling. This is the view
of the cognitive anthropologists, a key figure among them being Goodenough.
Goodenough and other cognitive anthropologists see culture not as a system
of public meaning bearing symbols, but, rather more all embracing, as a system of knowledge. There is a strong correlation in this school between culture
as knowledge and cognition, hence its name. Where, in symbolic anthropology, culture is public, located in shared codes of meaning realized in social

action, in cognitive anthropology, it is individual, found "in the minds and hearts of men" (Goodenough 1981:51). Goodenough (1964[1957]:36) provided the classic definition of culture within this school:

A society's culture consists of whatever it is one has to know or believe in order to operate in a manner acceptable to its members . . . Culture is not a material phenomenon; it does not consist of things, peoples, behavior, or emotions. It is rather an organization of these things. It is the form of things that people have in mind, their models for perceiving, reacting and otherwise interpreting them.

Crucially, then, culture is a mental phenomenon lying beyond actual social behavior, and as such, quite private and individual. Culture is the cognitive organization of material and social phenomena. Cognitive anthropology tries to determine what is significant for the members of a culture and how they mentally represent this knowledge in logical organizing principles (note that this view is clearly subject to all the criticisms of internal mental representations discussed above). The cognitive anthropologist then represents in some explicit fashion these organizing principles as a system of rules (again recall the earlier discussion of the problems inherent in approaches involving the use of explicit rules). What distinguishes various cultures from each other are the differing sets of organizing logical principles. Ultimately, within cognitive anthropology it is these mental representations that are the object of investigation. Culture is no longer found in the hustle and bustle of the everyday social world, but in the rarefied atmosphere of the individual's cognitive world. Language is often treated theoretically as a subsystem of culture within cognitive anthropology, but in practice the structure of language as revealed by modern linguistics has generally served as the paradigm for analyzing other aspects of culture. Indeed, linguistic methods and models are typically appropriated into other realms of culture, although more recent work also borrows heavily from artificial intelligence. Cognitive anthropologists pay great attention to the explicit models in which they cast their cultural descriptions, and debates may revolve around which representation is better for a given cultural domain, such as kinship. Various systems of formal representation invoked by cognitive anthropologists include taxonomies and componential analysis (from linguistics), and schemata, frames and scripts (from artificial intelligence); these will be discussed in greater detail in chapter 5. These methods of description all reflect the cognitive anthropologist's keenness to represent explicitly the way people have cognitively organized their cultural knowledge.

The basis of Goodenough's and other cognitive anthropologists' location of culture within the individual's mind is the fact that it is learned: "people learn as individuals. Therefore, if culture is learned, its ultimate locus must

be in individuals rather than groups" (Goodenough 1981:54). Goodenough
counters Geertz's arguments for the public nature of culture. On the example of the wink, Goodenough (1981) agrees with Geertz that knowing
how to wink is not the same as winking, but neither, Goodenough points
out, is knowing how to interpret winks as symbolic acts. It is the fact we
individual members of American culture *know* how to interpret them as
such that makes them symbolic acts. Goodenough (1981:59) summarizes:

> For Geertz, culture is both the acts as symbols and their meaning. He focuses
> on the artifacts – exposure to artifacts is what people share – and states that
> these artifacts as public symbols and the public meaning they have acquired
> in social exchanges constitute culture. We take the position that culture
> consists of the criteria people use to discern the artifacts as having distinctive
> forms and the criteria people use to attribute meaning to them. We address
> the problem of how these criteria, which are individually learned in social
> exchanges, can be said to be public at all, a problem Geertz does not address.

The strength of Goodenough and the cognitive anthropologists' approach
is in their close attention to the organism, her capabilities and the constraints on them. Therefore, for them, unlike Geertz, the question of universals should be one of abiding interest. Universals of human cognition
and universals of culture should mutually inform each other to provide
insightful and explicit descriptions of cultural forms, but this has in practice
been realized rather less than one might hope, although Goodenough (1970)
is an exemplary study. While the embodied practices approach taken here
might deplore Goodenough and other cognitive anthropologists' emphasis
on mental representations in the individual's cognitive world, their work
can be read as partial but potentially useful descriptions of the constraints
on patterns of structural coupling residing in the organism itself and the
potential range of states of its nervous system.

Clearly problematic for cognitive anthropology is how cultural practices,
localized as mental representations in the individual agent's mind, come
to be public. For Goodenough, the individual's cognitive world produces
appropriate cultural behavior; how it is shared is the theoretical problem:
"cultural theory must explain in what sense we can speak of culture as
shared or the property of groups . . . and what the processes are by which
such 'sharing' arises" (Goodenough 1981:54).

Thus, cognitive anthropology à la Goodenough theorizes the organism,
but problematizes the public environment; symbolic anthropologists à la
Geertz theorize the public domain of social action, but leave the organism
and her capabilities/constraints wholly untheorized. The intention of the
theory of culture as embodied practices developed here is to rise above this
dilemma. What is crucial about the concept of structural coupling and its

embodied history in the habitus is the mutual codetermination of organism and environment. The organism's state and trajectory is the result of its lived history of structural coupling with the environment including other organisms; the environment, on the other hand, is what the organism's state as a result of its history and its inculcated habitus takes it to be. Each negotiates changes in the other through interaction, especially through recurring social interaction. Knowledge and action are interdependent things. We know a plant as a weed by virtue of our cultural practices which remove unuseful plants; these cultural practices in turn lead us to label some plants as weeds. The idea that there is an abstract domain of cognition apart from acts of knowing is as nonsensical as the idea of a reified culture transcending individual human enculturations. Both knowing and acting are human practices, lived in an ongoing social environment, and, thus, seamlessly interconnected.

Cultural Practices and Social Differentiation

If culture is the domain of cultural practices, those meaning creating practices by which humans sustain viable trajectories of social structural coupling, it is obvious that culture should not be understood as a unified domain whose contents are shared by all. It follows in this view that it is totally inappropriate to speak of a finite domain that constitutes, say, American culture, for it is equally apparent that it is impossible for every American to engage in intensive recurring social coupling with every other (although certainly one of the effects of modern mass media is to greatly expand the possible reach of structural couplings; the effect of such media in diffusing cultural practices should not be underestimated; see Anderson (1983)). In a modern industrialized society, individuals engage in especially intense recurrent structural coupling with a small set of individuals, family, friends, workmates; sporadic structural coupling with a much larger group, acquaintances, service people, bureaucrats, etc.; but no direct structural coupling with the vast majority of people. In traditional small-scale societies, individuals may engage in daily structural coupling with all members, but even here some instances of structural coupling will be more recurrent and intense than others, for example, with closer kin relations, age mates, co-initiates, etc. Thus, within any collectivity or social system that we might designate, some networks of relations of structural couplings will be more dense than others; we might recognize those as groupings within the wider social system. These dense networks are both the cause and the result of those features we recognize as social phenomena *par excellence*: kin relations, class membership, language allegiance, etc. Thus, an individual is socialized into the working class by being born to members of that class and thereby engaging in particularly intense and recurring structural coupling with other members of that class. By engaging successfully in this ongoing history of structural coupling, the individual takes on the social behavior we recognize as diagnostic of working class, but it is also one's enactment of this behavior which is necessary to continue being a member of the network.

This idea can perhaps be made clearer by returning to Bourdieu's idea of the habitus. Because the networks of structural coupling that the individual engages in are structured into denser or more attenuated ones, the dispositions inculcated in the habitus are likewise structured, in that they must reflect the social characteristics of the particular relationship(s) of structural coupling in which they were acquired. Those inculcated dispositions which correspond to the densest section of an individual's relationships will generate the most experience-near (Geertz 1983), unquestioned pre-reflective aspects of his behavior, what we might consider his self-identity. Thus children socialized in a working-class family and neighborhood acquire a very different set of dispositions than children of a middle-class background. While working-class children from different families will obviously have individual differences due to the extremely dense network of relations within the family itself, the wider dense network of relations in the neighborhood, school, etc. will ensure a large shared set of dispositions appropriate to behavior which we identify with working-class culture. These dispositions generate such behavior and in turn are formed by it. This is beautifully brought out in Willis's (1977) classic study of a secondary school in a working-class district. Many of the boys in this school have internalized a view that their life choices for work are limited mainly to unskilled, industrial labor, the work of their fathers. They see no need for conformity to the norms of the educational system, because they deny its very premise: a good job in a valued world of work follows from educational success. As a result, their behavior in the school is highly disruptive and subversive of its authority, guaranteeing their own failure within the educational system and condemning them to the unskilled work of their fathers when they leave school, so that the cycle continues. The dispositions of the habitus are both generated by and generative of practice, social action, and cross a wide range of fields, as here where attitudes about the world of work carry over into the environment of school.

Examples like these demonstrate that social systems are anything but homogeneous domains. Nor are they closed and bounded; all are highly porous, for it is normally impossible to find a sharp point at which structural coupling ceases. This is obvious in the case of modern industrialized societies, in which many members have links around the world, but it is also true of small-scale, seemingly isolated societies. For example, Yimas village in the remote Sepik region of Papua New Guinea with 200 inhabitants might seem a promising candidate for cultural isolation, but one would be mistaken. The inhabitants engage in structural coupling with the odd foreign tourist, the resident linguist, missionaries, visitors from neighboring villages, and receive continuing radio broadcasts from Port Moresby with the latest national and international news and music hits. Even in traditional times before European contact, Yimas village was never a closed and bounded social system, as the inhabitants engaged in a long history of ongoing trade and exchange relationships with neighboring villages, and they in turn with other neighboring villages, building up a huge network of trading relationships across the island of New Guinea and beyond. This indicates that a geographical dimension needs to be added to the concept of a network of relations of structural coupling (see Giddens 1984). The denser relationships are likely to be centered around a physically restricted domain, a village, neighborhood, territory, etc. This locality corresponds to the local social system. The local social system is embedded in larger and larger social systems, marked by wider, but more attenuated networks of social interaction. These correspond to the super local social system and to units like the nation-state and, in the end, to the planet itself, our "global village" (see Wallerstein 1979).

Clearly, the local social system has the highest degree of shared cultural practices. It is this that has been traditionally described in ethnographies as "the culture" of a people. This is highly misleading, for no people, no matter how isolated, living together in an ongoing history of social structural coupling, in short, a social system, are completely homogeneous; some patterns of social interaction for an individual are always denser than others, for example, a woman to woman of her own kin group, to women of other kin groups, to men of other kin groups, etc. Because cultural practices are those meaningful practices which forge and continue ongoing histories of social structural coupling, it follows that knowledge of these will not be homogeneously distributed, but will reflect the patterns of the network of more or less dense social interactions. It would not be unexpected, therefore, to find some variations in cultural practices, for example, choices of linguistic forms, among the women of different kin groups in an isolated village. In modern complex societies, with people in a specific interaction potentially drawn from different classes and ethnic backgrounds, the distribution of cultural practices and knowledge of their meaning can become extremely complex. We no longer have a simple local social system, but a complex one, with elements from many different local social systems thrown in. This can be a source for very serious misunderstandings in interactions between people of different ethnic backgrounds. This insight has been the background for important work by John Gumperz (1982, 1993). In Gumperz (1993) he demonstrates how in a monolingual English conversation, different cultural practices between a native, British born, white, English as a second language teacher and an immigrant, Indian, second language speaker of English lead to a near total breakdown of communication. These differing cultural practices are a function of the speakers' respective ethnic backgrounds, British and Indian, and have been learned through structural coupling within the social groups in which they were socialized. The communication breakdown still occurs despite the fact that the conversation is exclusively in English, the formal norms of usage for which the ethnically Indian speaker controls well. It is the wider cultural expectations in which these norms are embedded that the Indian English speaker lacks and these, of course, are unreflectively inculcated during early socialization as part of the habitus of a competent actor of middle-class British background.

The Idea of Linguistic Practices

If cultural practices are those meaningful practices through which humans in relationships sustain ongoing histories of social structural coupling, then foremost among these must be linguistic practices. What people do incessantly in every known society is talk. Linguistic practices are the most pervasive way in which humans make meanings and sustain social systems; they do not exhaust human cultural practices, but are clearly primary among them. Humans could be succinctly defined as social beings encultured through language.

Just what is a linguistic practice? A possible definition is any communicative practice which promotes coordination of action between beings in ongoing social structural coupling through the meaning bearing capacity of signs drawn from a large system of signs and their combinatorial possibilities called language. Most commonly, the signs in this system are spoken, but in some cases they may be gestures, as in the sign languages of the deaf. The simplest idea of a sign consists of its form and an action it coordinates between interlocutors in the physical world, as when the pronunciation of the French phrase *à table* leads to the members of the family sitting down at the table to eat dinner. But signs in linguistic practices have the further unique and crucially defining characteristic that they can lead to coordination of behavior not just in the physical world, but in the domain of linguistic practices themselves: *Did you say "table"? No, I said "stable."* Ultimately, the signs of language are not about coordinating our behavior with regard to objects of the physical world, but with respect to the objects of the linguistic domain, the signs themselves, as even a casual study of any conversation between friends will demonstrate. The signs of linguistic practices are discriminations of distinctions already made in the domain of language; they are in no sense a mapping of the physical world into linguistic signals. Through their long ontogenic and phylogenetic history of viable structural coupling in linguistic practices, humans are thoroughly language-constituted beings.

For humans, the world has much of the character it has because it is a linguistically constructed reality (Grace 1987).

Linguistic practices, then, are those which coordinate our behavior through linguistic signs in the sense defined above. As we observe this coordination, we can see how the signs can be taken as descriptions of other descriptions already made in the linguistic domain. This is a core semiotic feature of linguistic practices – their potential metasemantics, the function of glossing: what is a "table"? "a piece of furniture with a flat top and legs." Note that "furniture" is itself already a strictly linguistic discrimination, a linguistic classification of a body of physical objects; the classification does not belong to the physical world, but resides in a world of linguistic discriminations. This metasemantic potential is at the base of much of our understanding of linguistic practices. We typically make use of rephrasing, paraphrasing, repeating, etc., whenever our linguistic practices fail to achieve coordination of behavior. This is most true of the scientific study of linguistic practices, the discipline of linguistics, which is absolutely dependent on metasemantics and glossing (and far too unreflectively, see Becker (1995)); what progress could be made in analyzing a language if its morphemes, words, and sentences could not be glossed into another analytical (usually Latinate) metalanguage, for example, Yimas *ama-wa-t* as first-person singular intransitive subject-go-perfective aspect?

The Nature of the Linguistic Sign: Icon, Index, Symbol

All linguistic signs consist of two poles: a physical form, such as a word's pronunciation, and a meaning, the discrimination it makes in the domain of language which sustains the coordination of behavior. Any sign, then, simple or complex, in any human language exhibits this dual structure; in the Yimas language the simple form *nam* corresponds to the meaning that can be glossed "constructed dwelling in which a family resides; house," while the complex form *mu-ka-tkam-tuk-mpun* corresponds to "I showed it (a plant of some sort) to them (more than a few) a while (more than 5 days) ago." All human languages exhibit this dual patterning, even sign languages like American Sign (ASL), in which a given configuration of the hand(s) is the form conveying a particular meaning. As described by Peirce (1965–6; see also Jakobson 1965; Silverstein 1976), signs can be classified into three types: icon, index, and symbol. An icon is a sign in which there is a perceptible likeness in its form and what its meaning describes. An example might be the verb *buzz off*, in which the verb's form [bʌ·z] bears a perceptible sound resemblance to the sound of a bee as it flies away. Iconicity plays an important role in language (Haiman 1985), especially in its poetic functions (Friedrich 1979, 1986), but I will have no more to say about it here.

An index is a sign whose meaning is interpreted from the context in which it is uttered. A non-linguistic example would be taking black clouds as a sign, an index, of coming rain. Linguistic signs which are indexes abound, but are often not recognized as such because of their context boundedness. When I speak Tok Pisin to an English-speaking Papua New Guinea friend, the language choice is an index of his ethnicity and an assertion of social solidarity between us. When I use *vous* to a stranger in a Parisian cafe, the pronoun is an index of our social distance. When Nootka Indians traditionally used special phonologically altered word forms to address certain classes of people, say, for example, hunchbacks or circumcised males, these abnormal speech forms are indexes of the addressee's condition (Sapir 1949). Finally, when Guugu-Yimidhirr speakers from Queensland used distinct lexical forms when speaking to their brother-in-law, the presence of these lexical forms is an index of this affinal kin relationship between interlocutors (Haviland 1979b). All of these are indexes, signs whose meaning comes from the context in which they are used. Note that there is a cline of creativity versus fixedness in the meaning bearing function of the indexes in these examples. The last example, the Guugu-Yimidhirr brother-in-law lexicon, is highly fixed and presupposed; it would be socially highly taboo to use anything else in this context. On the other hand, the first example, my use of Tok Pisin with Papua New Guineans, is not fixed, but a creative choice; I could use English, but I choose to use Tok Pisin to lay claim to a particularly solidary relationship between us. The choice of the language in itself stakes this claim. The more highly fixed and presupposed a choice is in a particular context, the less likely speakers are to be aware of the actual independent meaning signalling function of the index (see Silverstein 1976, 1979, 1981). The context boundedness of indexes, magnified in the cases of highly presupposed variants, makes them notoriously difficult to study and analyze. They are nonetheless central to the field of anthropological linguistics and will form the central topic of Part V.

A symbol is a sign in which the relationship between its form and meaning is strictly conventional, neither due to physical similarity or contextual constraints. This is the type of sign described by Saussure (1959[1916]), who emphasized the arbitrary relationship between the sign's form and its meaning, pointing out that the meaning "tree" is expressed by the form *tree* in English, but *arbre* in French. It is perhaps slightly misleading to overemphasize, as with Saussure, the arbitrariness of symbols; their conventionality, as in Peirce (1965–6), may be a better perspective to highlight, treating symbolic linguistic practices on a par with wider symbolic cultural practices (Geertz 1973; Turner 1967, 1969). The crucial effect of the conventionality of the relationship between form and meaning in symbols is that, unlike context bound indexes, it frees the domain of the symbol's meaning from the constraints of the immediate context. This is what it means to say that a word which is a symbol has a sense, a meaning which can be stated via paraphrase and holds across contexts of usage. Thus, a *woman* is an "adult female human being," and this holds across innumerable contexts, whether we are talking about giving birth, teaching a class, fixing a Ferarri or piloting a jet airliner. Paraphrase or metasemantics holds of all symbols via their conventionality; this is not, however, by and large true of indexes. There is a mixed class of signs, "shifters" (Jakobson 1957; Silverstein 1976) which partake of features of both indexes and symbols. Examples are first- and second-person pronouns, demonstratives like *this* and *that* and temporal adverbs like *now* and *tomorrow*. These have paraphrasable meanings like "the person who is now speaking this" or "the day after the day in which I am speaking," but this does not exhaustively describe them, for the actual context is necessary to do this: *I* "the person who is now speaking" is a different person in different contexts of speakers. Hence, shifters mix the paraphrasable property, drawn from the conventionality of being symbols, with the flexible context boundedness of indexes.

Language as Signs and their Combinations

Language is usually defined as a system of signs and their rules of combination. This is okay as far as it goes but it does often lead, especially in the practices of linguists analyzing languages, to an overemphasis on the systematicity of languages. The domain of symbols does exhibit high features of systematicity, drawn in no small part from the historicity of their conventionality (see Bakhtin 1981), but this is less true of indexes, which as pointed out above, may be highly creative of linguistic contexts. It may be better to abandon the reifying term "language," which tends to connote a closed discrete system, in favor of linguistic practices, which recognize talking as an activity in structural coupling, one with porous borders with other cultural practices, or even, "languaging" (Maturana and Varela 1987). For ease of expository purposes, however, I will stick to normal convention and use the term language.

All linguistic signs, be they icons, indexes or symbols, have a dual structure, a formal pole in relationship to a meaning. A good way to describe language is in terms of the constraints on these poles. The phonology of a language is the system of constraints upon the forms of its signs; its inventory of distinctive sound units and their rules of combination which produce the possible forms of symbols in the language. For example, in English /b/ is a distinctive sound or *phoneme*, as seen in the contrast between *pit* /pIt/ versus *bit* /bIt/. Further, this phoneme can be combined with other phonemes as the formal pole of signs in English; it can be immediately followed by /l/ or it can itself follow /m/: *blink* /blInk/ or *stumble*

/stʌmbəl/. Yimas contrasts with English in that the units /p/ and /b/ are not distinguished; the word *tamprak* can be pronounced either as [tamprak] or [tambrak]. Further, while as the above example shows, the sound [b] can follow the unit /m/, it may not be followed immediately by /l/; a vowel must occur between them, as in *tampaympl* [tambaymbɨl)]. Thus, English and Yimas contrast both in their inventory of distinctive sound units (phonemes) and their rules of combination which produce the forms of signs in the languages. The phonology of any language is the study of the principles which constrain the formal pole of the signs in that language.

The meaning pole also corresponds to particular domains of study, semantics, and pragmatics. Semantics uses the metasemantic devices of paraphrase and substitution to discover the basic units of meanings, the underlying semantic components, which, combined in varying ways, produce the various meanings of the symbols of the language. Some of these semantic units may be universal. Just as the phonologies of all spoken languages make use of the distinction between consonant and vowels, i.e. exploit this distinction for the formal pole of symbols in languages, all languages also employ the semantic units of male and female in meanings of contrasting symbols. English uses this contrast in the pair *uncle* versus *aunt*; "*male* sibling of parent" versus "*female* sibling of parent"; whereas Yimas opposes *away* "mother's brother" i.e. *male* sibling of *female* parent and *ŋaki* "father's sister" i.e. *female* sibling of *male* parent. The point is that both languages use the sex-based semantic units of female and male, although combined in overall quite different systems of kinship. Often, the semantic distinctions found with the meanings of symbols are quite language specific. For example, in the area of consumables, English has quite different verbs depending on the nature of the object consumed; *eat food*, *drink wine*, *smoke tobacco*. Thus, the meanings of these verbs must be specified with respect to the object consumed: e.g. *drink* "consume through the mouth a liquid substance." Yimas has none of this: a single verb *am-* covers all these acts; the verb simply means "consume." To specify "drink," we would have to overtly mention a liquid substance consumed, e.g. *arm am-* "water consume." Semantics, then, seeks to elucidate and represent the structure of the meaning pole of the symbols of a language by isolating the specific and general units of meaning employed and identifying the principles of combination.

Pragmatics tends to be currently defined as a residual discipline, which encompasses all aspects of meaning not delimited by semantics (Levinson 1983). As such, it includes the study of indexical meaning, how the choices of indexes presuppose or shape contexts. There are as yet few robust proposals for universal constraints in the domain of pragmatics – Grice's (1975) Cooperative Principle with its Maxims is one proposed; see also Brown and Levinson (1987), and Sperber and Wilson (1986) – but perhaps this is only to be expected, given its link to context, which is necessarily culturally embedded. Indeed, the boundary between pragmatics and anthropological linguistics or sociolinguistics is impossible to draw at present, as this book will demonstrate. Is code switching, i.e. using Tok Pisin to signal solidarity, which is clearly an indexical signal, properly in the domain of pragmatics or anthropological linguistics? Or is it ultimately the case that there is no meaningful distinction between these, as I would suggest?

A language is more than just an inventory of signs, their form and meaning. Ultimately, it is *a way of saying things*, and it accomplishes this by combining signs together to form larger units, specifically sentences. The principles of combination by which signs cohere to form a sentence is called the grammar of the language. The grammar of a language typically corresponds to two levels, morphology and syntax. Morphology involves the combination of units of a formal level smaller than a word. These cohere together to form a complex sign corresponding formally to a word. Examples include English *un-desir-abil-ity* or Yimas *ta-mpu-i-c-mpan-mpwi* NEG-3PL SUBJ-tell-PERF-3PL IND OBJ-talk OBJ "they didn't tell them." Syntax is the combination of units of a formal level of a word or higher (i.e. phrase or clause) to form a complex sign of yet a higher level. Again, an English example would be *my mother* or its Yimas equivalent *ama-na ŋayuk* 1SG-POSS mother "my mother." Most languages make use of both morphology and syntax to some extent, but the relative importance of the two may vary somewhat from language to language. For example, English is a language in which syntax plays a pronounced role; it is much less prominent in Yimas, and, as if to compensate, Yimas morphology is greatly elaborated.

In terms of how language uses grammar to go about saying things, a useful distinction was proposed by Chomsky (1980:54). He distinguishes between what he calls a "conceptual system" and a "computational system" in a language. The "computational system" corresponds to the strictly formal side of the grammatical possibilities for the combinations of signs. Taking the formal pole of signs, this is concerned with how these are combined to produce larger strings. The conceptual system, on the other hand, is concerned with meaning. It corresponds not only to the meaning pole of the signs themselves, but also to how the strings produced by the rules of the "computational system" are assigned meanings as sentences.

Grammar: The "Computational System"

Let us consider these in more depth, starting with the "computational system." The "computational system" is the source of the much discussed generative and creative power of language, its capacity to produce an infinite amount of linguistic forms. While this is an important point, it is often unduly highlighted at the expense of the more conventionalized aspects of the "computational system." While the rich morphological rules of Yimas verbal morphology are capable in principle of generating an infinite variety of complex verbal forms, the seeming output of such rules may often be known by Yimas speakers as conventionalized complex forms not unlike English compounds such as *bigwig*, though the Yimas forms are fully transparent. Thus, the Yimas roots *tay-* "see" and *yawra-* "pick up" combine morphologically to form the complex stem *tay-mpi-yawra-* "find"; the process is fully productive and transparent, but it seems that Yimas speakers often simply take it as a form meaning "find" (see also Pawley (1993b)).

The basic features of the "computational system" are often taken as definitional of human language itself, by Chomsky (1980) and many others, so they are commonly referred to as some of the "design features" of language (Hockett 1958, 1960). Some of these, like arbitrariness, that the form of each symbol bears an arbitrary, non-iconic relationship to its meaning, and duality, that each sign has two poles, a form and a meaning, have already been discussed. Closely related is the notion of hierarchy. This refers to the fact that language is structured hierarchically, with separate units of one level combining together to form a distinct, discrete unit of the next hierarchical level. For example, the phonemic units in English /t/ /æ/ /b/ together form the phonological word unit /tæb/ *tab*. The morphological units *un-*, *happy* and *-ness* go together to form the grammatical word unit *unhappiness*. This word in turn can be combined with other words, units of the same grammatical level, to form phrases: *his great unhappiness*. Phrases can then combine to form clauses: *His great unhappiness is a source of concern to us*; and in turn clauses can join together to form sentences: *His great unhappiness is a source of concern to us, but we can't do anything about it*. The great advantage of hierarchy in human language is that it allows us to make infinite use of a finite list of signs. By theoretically limitless combinations of a limited inventory of basic level units of phonemes, morphemes and words, a language permits infinite richness of expression (but note the reservations about this expressed above).

Related to hierarchy is the notion of order, which typically needs to be specified when units are combined. For example, the phonemic units /t/ /æ/ /b/ combined can result in /tæb/ *tab*, but in the opposite order they yield /bæt/ *bat*. In grammar, rather than phonology, languages typically only license a single order for the combination of units. In English *un-* must precede the root and *-ness* must follow: **ness-happi-un* is not an English word. Further, for English phrases, determiners and adjectives must precede their modified nouns; *his great unhappiness* is English, but *unhappiness great his* is not, although a word for word translation would be fine in Indonesian, for which the ordering rules in phrases are the opposite of English. Some languages may appear at first not to make use of order. For example, in Yimas both *numpran kpan* pig big and *kpan numpran* big pig are grammatical, but even in such languages order is a fundamental feature of the grammar, though it may be relaxed in some areas, such as the formation of phrases and clauses. Indeed, order is quite rigidly enforced in the formation of Yimas words by the combination of morphemes. In the complex Yimas verb *ta-mpu-i-c-mpan-mpwi* "they didn't tell them," the root is *i-* "tell," the two prefixes to its left and three suffixes to the right can only occur in the order found; the slightest deviation will produce an ill-formed word in the language. Thus, order is as relevant to Yimas as English; the domain of application is different.

A great deal of effort over the last 30 years or so has gone into developing explicit formalisms to represent the twin notions of hierarchy and order. Typically, these are represented in tree-like diagrams (1.1).

The branches of the tree, ADJ and N, represent the basic units which form a constituent together to compose the unit of the higher level, designated by the top category or mother node, in this case, NP. Their order is simply represented by the sequencing of base level units at the bottom of the tree. Such tree-like diagrams can be composed iteratively to represent multiple levels of structure within one diagram (1.2) in which the mother nodes label the category of which the branching nodes are unit constituents. Thus, the clause level constituent designated by S is composed of the phrase units NP and VP; the phrase level constituent VP is in turn composed of the word unit V and the phrase unit NP. A common feature of natural language is recursion, in which a unit of a higher level is intercalated with units of a

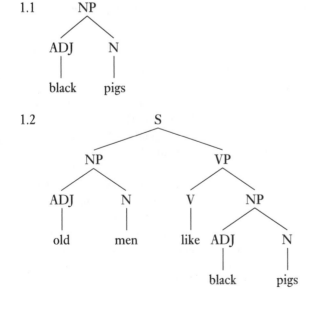

1.1   NP

ADJ   N

black pigs

1.2   S

          NP   VP

     ADJ   N   V   NP

     old   men   like   ADJ   N

                              black   pigs

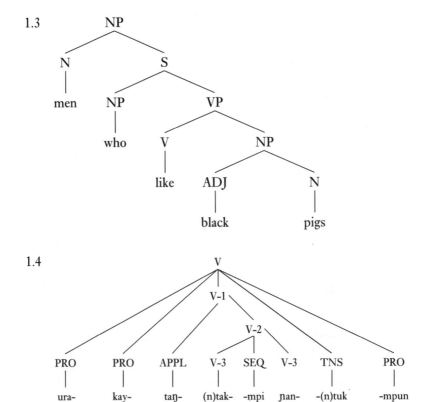

"We left those behind with them long ago"

lower level, theoretically infinitely, to form a constituent of a lower level.
This is the source of a great deal of the expressive flexibility of language. A
good example of recursion is the relative clause in which a clause level unit
is part of a noun phrase along with word level units (1.3).

Languages like Yimas with very complex morphology have hierarchical
word structures parallel to the English phrasal and clausal structures above.
Thus, we find word structures such as in 1.4. The verb roots *(n)tak-*
"leave" and *ɲan-* "stay" combine together with the marker of sequential
time relation *-mpi* SEQ to form a verb stem. This verb stem in turn composes with the applicative prefix *taŋ-* COM, adding an extra comitative
participant, "to do an action *with* someone." Finally, this constituent is
joined with the tense suffix and pronominal affixes to form a full verbal
word. Note that the hierarchical structure and fixed ordering of basic units
exactly parallel that of phrasal and clausal structures in English. This is

especially interesting in that Yimas has almost no constructions at the phrasal level, and clauses are extremely loosely structured, with fully free order of constituents. All languages make use of hierarchical structure and ordering of constituents, but they may do so in large degree at different levels.

In parallel fashion, while English employs recursion at the phrase level in relative clauses, Yimas does not, but it does exhibit something like recursion at the word level, in which word level units can be incorporated into other words:

maŋkaŋkl   kla-na-[kpa-ŋkl]-c-n
arm VI DL VI DL SUBJ-now-[big-VI DL]-become-PRES
"(His) arms are getting big now"

In the verbal word above, the inflected word *kpa-ŋkl* big-VI DL, which could occur as an independent clause level constituent, has in fact become a basic unit within the verbal word. This potentially independent word functions like a sub-word level unit, much like a bound morpheme such as the tense suffix *-n* PRES. This is somewhat like a clause functioning as a unit within a phrase (i.e. a relative clause), a pattern which, in fact, Yimas proscribes.

In spite of the enormous typological differences between Yimas and English, the basic properties of the "computational system," hierarchy, order, and recursion are present in both. This is to be expected, as they are universal-defining properties of human languages. The two languages differ largely in the areas of the grammar over which these properties are distributed. Yimas, in keeping with its status as a polysynthetic language, i.e. a language in which word level structures are the pivot of the grammar, exhibits them most fully in the building up of words. English, on the other hand, tends to illustrate these properties most clearly in syntactic constructions, like phrases, clauses, and sentences.

Grammar: the "Conceptual System"

Chomsky's "conceptual system" is concerned with the meaning of strings of signs, the "what is said" of sentences rather than the "how it is said" of the "computational system." It is highly unlikely there is any kind of unified "system" here, merely a number of domains of types and classes of meanings; their degree of integration is a matter for investigation. Perhaps the most basic is what could be called the "inventory," the basic level descriptions of objects and events that the language makes available in order to say things. The basic idea here is one we may call, following Grace (1987), a conceptual event. (The use of "conceptual" here may be misleading if it is taken to mean concepts in the sense of mental representations. That is

clearly not intended, rather the event as linguistically depicted and understood. Perhaps a better, less misleading, alternative would be "described
event," but I will stick to Grace's terminology, as it is already established
with a significance much as I have in mind.) A conceptual event is something the speaker reports as a simple event, to take Sapir's (1921) famous
example, *the farmer killed the duckling*. At the core of this conceptual event
is the verb *kill*. The verbs of a language are an inventory of the way humans
and other entities may be described to interact with each other and nature.
In essence, the verbs of a language provide a typology of the actions especially culturally salient for its speakers. This particular verb calls forth an
event in which one participant brings to an end the life of another participant; it is semantically complex, but nonetheless part of a unitary conceptual
event for speakers of English. However, for speakers of other languages, this
semantically complex notion may correspond to more than one verb. For
example, in the Watam language two verbs are needed to translate English
kill, a causing verb such as the general *mo-* "make, feel, do, become" or a
specific verb like *ruŋ-* "hit" plus a verb describing the resulting process of
dying *minik-* "die." Thus, "the man killed the pig" would be:

    namot markum mo   rugu-r   minik-rin
    man   pig   OBJ hit-DEP   die-PAST
    "the man clubbed the pig to death"

While Watam requires two verbs to English's one, the sentences in both
languages correspond to a unitary conceptual event. This is demonstrated
in that both describe the event in a single clause, with a single intonation
contour. If we wanted two separate events, both languages would require
two separate clauses: *because the man clubbed the pig, it died.*

    namot markum mo   ruŋ-tape (ma) minik-rin
    man   pig   OBJ hit-CONJ 3SG die-PAST
    "(Because) the man clubbed the pig, it died"

Thus, we can see that the natural packaging for conceptual events in English and Watam is the hierarchical level of the clause. Various grammatical
choices may skew this, but this is unquestionably the neutral case.

The basic lexicon of a language is the script by which speakers construct
linguistic descriptions. The basic classes of content words, nouns, adjectives
and verbs, are an inventory of descriptions available to speakers. Nouns
provide a descriptive inventory of entities of importance to speakers. Typically, they constitute the largest class of words; this is necessary to enable
the speaker to express herself effectively, given that the number of relevant

entities in any culture's experience is very large. Languages do classify entities differently, however, so that their range of meanings is quite variable. English has many words associated with the notion of "water": *water, river, stream, creek, brook, ocean, bay, lake, pond, pool, puddle*, where relevant semantic distinctions are liquid substance versus body of such substance, and among the latter whether it moves in one direction or not and their relative size. Yimas has only three: *arm, armpn* and *upŋk*, with similar semantic distinctions: *arm* means liquid substance, but includes *all* such substances, like petrol and kerosene in addition to water, while *armpn* versus *upŋk* contrasts moving body of water versus stationary respectively (note that size of such bodies is not a relevant semantic feature in Yimas). English makes a more finely grained system of distinctions than Yimas, its classification being more detailed, but the important point is that both languages impose a system of classification upon the description of bodies of water.

Verbs contrast with nouns in that they describe actions, events, or states. This entails a number of important differences between the two classes. Consider the difference between the English noun *rock* and verb *hit*. *Rock* is a noun and describes, as nouns prototypically do, an object locatable in the physical world, in this case a hard, solid mineral object of the natural world. As rocks are concrete objects, they are freely apprehensible by our senses; we can see them, touch them and, if they are small enough, manipulate them with our hands. Further, they are susceptible to changes in state: they can be moved, broken, crushed, or thrown. Finally, the boundaries of what is a rock and what is not are fairly sharp, both from the surrounding space and from other objects. As we can manipulate a rock, we can determine its boundaries in space, and, by noting the features of this object bound in space in this way, we are able to sort rocks from trees or mothers. Given all these properties of the objects called rocks and human perceptual and cognitive mechanisms, it seems warranted to hypothesize that a noun corresponding to *rock* is rather a predetermined category in the vocabularies of all languages. This would not exclude further nouns in a language to refer to types of rocks such as *boulder, pebble*, and *stone*. These may or may not be found, but all languages would have the core term *rock*. Note that the word "rock" in a language is not a mapping into language of the physical object in the natural world. It is a strictly linguistic description which bears only an indirect relationship to the physical object. Of course, for it to be an effective linguistic description the physical characteristics of the natural object must constrain the semantic properties of the word, but crucially they do not *inform* it. This is the nature of the semantic descriptions of language; they create a rich significant description of a linguistically constituted world, whose relationship to the physical world is strictly indirect, constrained by it but not informed by it. This is the nature of the human linguistic adaptation to its environment (see chapter 2).

Now let me contrast the English verb *hit*. This English word describes an action, prototypically that of a human lifting a hand, moving it through space toward some object, and bringing it into contact forcefully with the surface of that object. Note that actions are not apprehensible to our sense in the same way as objects; we cannot manipulate an action, in fact we cannot even really see an action. All we can see of an act of hitting are the participants engaged in it, the person raising his hand, moving it through space, coming into contact with a surface of an object, and then withdrawing from it. Obviously, there is no actual unitary action of hitting to be seen, but rather some participants engage in a series of actions which we interpret as a single act and describe with the label *hit*. Closely correlated with this property of actions is the fact that, unlike objects, they do not have discrete boundaries which separate them from other actions. Consider the actions described by the following additional English verbs of contact: *touch*, *grab*, *scratch*, *slap*. All four of these share many of the features of *hit*, but also contrast in some. *Touch* contrasts with *hit* in that for *touch* the contact is not forceful. *Grab* contrasts with *hit* in that the hand does not withdraw from the object contacted, but rather closes itself around it. *Scratch* adds the component that after coming into contact with the object the hand drags along the surface of the object, resulting in some damage to its surface. Finally, *slap* contrasts with *hit* in that slapping necessarily implies contact with an object with the flat palm surface of the hand, while *hit* has no such requirement; in fact, one need not contact the object with the hand at all in hitting: contact by an object held by the hand, such as a cane, is sufficient. It is important to note that the actions described by these five verbs are not really all that different from each other: all require the basic actions of raising the hand, moving it through space, and contacting the surface of an object. The boundaries distinguishing one from another are not sharp. If *touch* is distinguished from *hit* largely by the force of the contact, obviously there is no absolute boundary between touching and hitting. What one person might describe as "touching" might be labelled "hitting" by another.

The relationship between the set of verbs in a language and the description of conceptual events is much less clear-cut than the relationship between a noun and that which it describes. While both require a classification, the greater degree of abstraction involved in verbal meaning allows for much more leeway in interpretation. Thus, languages (and, within languages, speakers) exhibit a great deal of variation in the way verbs contribute to the description of conceptual events. We have already seen this difference in our comparison of English and Watam, but consider the extreme case of Papuan highlands languages, with about only 100 verbs. In such languages, conceptual events will typically require complex verbal exponence. Consider Kalam in which the conceptual event expressed in English by "I fetched firewood" requires no less than six Kalam verbs (Pawley 1993b:95):

yad am mon p-wk   d   ap   ay-p-yn
1SG go wood hit-break hold come put-PERF-1SG
"I fetched some firewood"

Such constructions are necessary in this language because of the paucity of basic verbs, but we need not go to such exotic places to see fundamental differences in the conventional expression of conceptual events. Consider the English clause *the bottle floated into the cave*, which describes an event of movement along a path into a cave in a manner of floating. Note that the main verb describes the manner and the adverbial modifier the path. As Talmy (1985) points out, Spanish has exactly the opposite convention: the main verb expresses the path, and the manner is described using a participle modifier:

la   botella entro   a   la   cueva flotando
the bottle   entered to the cave   floating

Interestingly, in this feature at least, Yimas is like English, the main verb being that of manner and the path expressed by bound directional affixes:

botel   antɲam-n   na-m(a)-ampu-pu-t
bottle V SG cave-OBLIQ V SG SUBJ-in-float-away-PERF
"The bottle floated away into the cave"

In summary, a conceptual event is an understanding by the speaker that what she is describing is a unitary whole. She represents this understanding by signalling it in a single clause, but the lexemic and grammatical devices the language makes available and the generally accepted conventions for their use determine how this conceptual event is to be signalled. At far extremes are English and Kalam. English with extremely rich lexical resources typically permits clauses with a single verb root. Kalam rarely does this, its small inventory of verb roots requiring chains or compounds of such roots to provide a full description.

Grammatical Categories

In addition to the lexical inventory, the "conceptual system" of language also consists of a number of subsystems corresponding to grammatical categories. Grammatical categories situate the conceptual event as described by the choice of lexical categories, either by modulating the meanings of the basic lexical categories or by locating the conceptual event in the continuum of time and space or some imaginary world. Again, languages show great variation in the kind of grammatical categories they employ and the number of subclassifications they make within that category.

Consider the grammatical category of number. This is typically applied to nouns discriminating between the number of tokens involved in the type described by the noun. Thus, English distinguishes one *basket,* from two or more *basket-s,* but Yimas distinguishes one *impram* "basket," from two, *imprampl* "baskets" from more than two *imprampat* "baskets." And just to illustrate an extreme development, Murik, a language related to Yimas, distinguishes four numbers in its nouns: one *iran* "house," two *irambo* "houses," a few, more than two, but less than about seven *iramoara* "houses" and many, more than seven *iranmot* "houses." Surprisingly, some languages lack the grammatical category of number entirely; Indonesian *rumah* "house, houses" may not be differentiated for number.

Fundamentally, those grammatical categories associated with the noun modulate the meaning of the lexical noun (although case is an exception here), while those associated with the verb modulate the conceptual event as a whole (as case may do as well). One set of verbal grammatical categories situates the conceptual event in time, i.e. aspect (ongoing event or finished event) and tense (took place before now, is happening now, will happen later). Some languages may have minimal elaboration here: for example, Thai has no category of tense, but does distinguish ongoing from completive aspect. Other languages may be gleefully exuberant. Yimas distinguishes not less than three past tenses (yesterday, up to five days ago, and past five days ago) and two future tenses (tomorrow and after tomorrow), as well as a host of aspectual contrasts. Some languages also have specific grammatical categories which situate the conceptual event in space, so called elevationals and directionals. For example, Yimas has a set of elevational prefixes which locates the conceptual event spatially with respect to the place of speaking: is it occurring above, below, etc., of where we are speaking. Finally, most languages have modal categories which describe the likelihood or probability of imaginary events actually occurring. This is indicated in English by auxiliaries like *must, might, could,* but in Yimas by verbal prefixes.

Tense is one of the so-called deictic categories in language. These allow the speaker to locate conceptual events in times and places remote from the here and now of the act of speaking itself. Tense locates events in a time removed from now. Other deictic categories like demonstratives or elevationals have similar functions; *that book* (near them over there) *fell* and Yimas *pu-na-l-am-n* 3PL SUBJ-now-down-eat-PRES "they are eating down there (away from us here)" both describe events and participants removed from the here and now of speaking. This illustrates another of the important "design features" of human language, displacement. This refers to the fact that human languages can talk about objects and events remote in time and place from the momentary act of the utterance itself. It is often claimed that this is again one of the features that distinguishes human languages from animal systems of communicating, a property made possible, as we have seen, by the presence of deictic categories like tense, elevationals, demonstratives. It is important to note that while some human languages may lack one of these deictic categories, as Thai does tense, all exhibit the property of displacement. Thai presses other categories such as demonstratives, aspect, modals, and classifiers into service to express notions of displacement.

Finally, there are the grammatical categories which express the kind of action the speaker is doing in signalling this conceptual event, what she is trying to do at the moment of speaking. This is the domain of speech act theory: is she merely reporting; is she asserting that the conceptual event has, is or will occur; is she asking whether it has, is or will occur; is she commanding that it occur, or wishing it so; is she warning, threatening or promising that it will occur; is she lying? Or indeed, by simply saying the conceptual event is she really making it occur, as in *I baptize you "Christopher,"* in which Christopher is baptized by uttering this sentence (among other actions). Languages typically have an enormous range of means for signalling these speech acts, ranging from intonation contours to independent or auxiliary verbs to bound verbal affixes or particles. For example, in English and Yimas, an assertion versus a question can be indicated by a difference in falling versus rising intonation. A command in English may be expressed by a tenseless verb root without a subject phrase, but in Yimas it is marked by a special verbal suffix and a unique set of subject pronominal prefixes.

Closely linked to the speech act grammatical categories of language is the final design feature of language, reflexivity. This refers to the fact that we can use language to talk about language itself, such as when we comment on its form, *the word "book" begins in the sound /b/* or verbally search out its meaning, *the meaning of the Yimas word* wakn *is "snake."* This is only possible because the speech act possibilities of language allow us to use language actually to perform actions other than merely to describe an event. So, for example, in definitions we actually employ language to describe a meaning we ascribe to a form. In puns, we use language to joke about and simultaneously report an act of linguistic analysis. Finally, in lying, we use language in an especially devious fashion. Rather than using language to describe something we believe to be at least potentially true about the world, we actually describe something we know to be untrue, but present it as if it were true. We do this by asserting a conceptual event but reflexively commenting to ourselves about this bit of language that "this is not true." This is a great feat of imaginative playing with language, a triumph of the creative forces let loose in the reflexivity of language, but perhaps this deceptive potential of language has not entirely been an unmixed blessing. In any case, for better or for worse, this feature of reflexivity is generally claimed to be a crucial defining feature of language and to be unique to human language among animal systems of communication (whether it is or not is at least now open to serious question; see Cheney and Seyfarth (1990)).

Summary

This chapter looks at the two fundamental concepts of anthropological linguistics, culture and language. Both concepts do not describe monolithic blocks of knowledge present in the minds of all members of the culture or speakers of the languages but rather are loosely structured domains of practices through which social actors navigate their way meaningfully in the world. Culture is simply the domain of cultural practices, those meaning creating practices through which humans sustain viable social couplings with each other. Linguistic practices are a sub-type of cultural practices, those communicative practices sustaining social coupling through the use of linguistic signs. Because these practices sustain ongoing social coupling, they are typically emblematic of social differences, neither culture nor language are bounded homogeneous domains; the knowledge of these practices is distributed along social lines.

Further Reading

On approaches to meaning see Devitt and Sterelny (1987), Grice (1989), Levinson (1983), Lyons (1977), and Taylor (1985a). For introductions to sociolinguistics see Holmes (1992), Romaine (1994), Trudgill (1983), Wardhaugh (1992), and the monumental survey by Fasold (1984, 1990). Maturana and Varela (1987) clearly lay out their theory of cognition.

Culture is a central concept in anthropology, and there is an enormous literature. For a good survey of various approaches try Alexander and Seidman (1990), Austin-Broos (1987), and Shweder and LeVine (1984). Bourdieu's concept of the habitus is developed in Bourdieu (1977, 1990). For a critical look at his work, see Calhoun, LiPuma, and Postone (1993). Geertz (1973), especially the first three chapters, is an excellent introduction to his views, as is Goodenough (1981) to his contrastive position. Keesing (1981) is a good discussion of both Geertz's and Goodenough's ideas. Ortner (1984) is a good survey of developments over the last 30 years.

Again, the literature on language is vast. Lyons (1977) is a good overview of semantics; another good source is Frawley (1992). Blakemore (1992), Levinson (1983), and Mey (1993) are all excellent introductions to the field of pragmatics. The rules of combination, syntax and morphology, are covered well in Bauer (1992), Brown and Miller (1991), Comrie (1989), Croft (1991), Kaplan (1995), and Spencer (1991). Berman and Slobin (1994) and Chafe (1994) are excellent crosslinguistic studies of conceptual events, associated grammatical categories and their realization in discourse. Silverstein (1976) is recommended for an introduction to Pierce's trichotomy of signs and its implications for linguistic and cultural description.

Part II
The Evolution of Language

2

The Evolution of Language

Evolution as Natural Drift

In the last section of the previous chapter I discussed and illustrated the properties of language, constraints to which all attested modern languages necessarily conform. It is highly unlikely that all these various properties arose simultaneously in the transition from ape calls to human language. Rather, they probably developed gradually and cumulatively during the course of human evolution. This chapter will look at a possible scenario for the evolution of language and will explore the different evolutionary developments in human physiology and behavior which made this outcome possible. But, first, it is necessary to look at the theory of evolution in general.

Evolutionary theory is currently undergoing significant changes from an earlier orthodoxy developed in the 1930s called neo-Darwinism, about which I will have more to say below. New developments emphasize the co-implicative role of both organism and environment in evolution, as both creatively influence the other in ongoing biological change. This theory can be called the "natural drift theory" of evolution, in contrast to neo-Darwinism. The distinctive features of the natural drift theory are best appreciated if one has an understanding of the basic tenets of neo-Darwinism, as it was developed in response to perceived weaknesses in this earlier theory, so I will turn first to a basic sketch of neo-Darwinism. Neo-Darwinism (see Dawkins 1986; Maynard Smith 1986, 1989) was developed in the 1930s as a synthesis between the classical tradition stemming from the views of Charles Darwin and the findings of modern genetics. There are significantly different versions of neo-Darwinism, but its central notion is the notion of adaptation, baldly stated, evolution functions through the adaptation of species to selected environmental pressures, increasing their fitness to the conditions imposed by the environment. The engine that drives this adaptation is reproduction through genetic mutation and recombination.

An organism in neo-Darwinism is essentially an ensemble of traits specified by the genes. The genetic code of this organism is, of course, the result of its individual reproductive ancestry, so that any population of a particular species will be genetically heterogeneous. These different genetic stocks within the population will lead to different degrees of success of reproduction, i.e. changes in the overall genetic makeup of the species' population. At its most fundamental, evolution is just the random shift in genes in a specific population.

But what determines the differential degrees of success in reproduction? This is the role played by, perhaps the most famous of Darwin's ideas, the mechanism of natural selection. This needs to be understood adaptationally, as the maximizing of fitness of certain genetic stocks to the pressures of the environment. Thus, genetic stocks which exhibit the highest fit to the demands of the environment will typically have the greatest degree of reproductive success. Genetic changes which increase this success are adaptive, in the sense that they improve the degree of fitness. Fitness can be measured through abundance, the absolute number of offspring produced, or the rate of population growth or persistence, i.e. the longer term survival of genetic lines of descent. In neo-Darwinism the central biological entity involved in adaptation and the maximization of fitness is not the organism nor the species' population, but the genes; to paraphrase E. Wilson (1980:3), the organism is just the genes' way of making more genes.

Opposition to neo-Darwinism along the lines of the theory of natural drift has emerged from a number of quarters in recent years (see Ho and Saunders 1984; Ingold 1990; Lewontin 1983; Maturana and Varela 1987; Ondling-Smee 1994). There is nowhere near complete agreement yet on this emerging theory of evolution as natural drift, merely some broad general axioms, and I will summarize this theory as presented in Maturana and Varela (1987) and Varela, Thompson, and Rosch (1991). Two crucial differences between the natural drift theory and neo-Darwinism are the central position of the notion of the organism and the active role of the environment, which is not relegated to a passive background against which genes randomly maximize their fitness. The interrelation between organism and environment is the basis of natural drift. Lewontin (1983:75–6) expresses this clearly:

> The organism and the environment are not actually separately determined. The environment is not a structure imposed on living beings from the outside, but is in fact a creation of those beings. The environment is not an autonomous process, but a reflection of the biology of the species. Just as there is no organism without an environment, so there is no environment without an organism.

To summarize, using Lewontin's title, the organism is both the subject and object of evolution. The central idea in these biological theories is the idea of a self-organizing network, already familiar from chapter 1.

Let us investigate this idea in more detail to see what it might mean. First consider the nature of an organism. The crucial defining feature is that they are unities, which are continually self-organizing. Consider a simple unicellular organism. Its internal components are continuously interacting; their interactions we term the cell's "metabolism" (Maturana and Varela 1987). What crucially defines this cell as living is the fact that this metabolism produces components, which, in turn, constitute the system of changes which produced them. And some of these components together will form an outer boundary, a membrane, to this network of interacting components. This membrane defines the borders of the unity which is self-producing, but is itself a part of the network which defines the entity. Thus, this organism could be represented as in 2.1 (Maturana and Varela 1987:46). Such is the fundamental structure of a living organism. Maturana and Varela (1987:46) remark on 2.1:

2.1
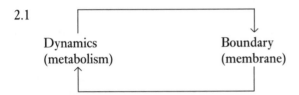

Dynamics   Boundary
(metabolism)   (membrane)

> Note that these are not segmental processes, but two different aspects of a unitary phenomenon. It is not that first there is a boundary, then a dynamic, then a boundary, and so forth . . . Interrupt (at some point) the cellular metabolic network and you will find that after a while you don't have any more unity to talk about! The most striking feature of an autopoietic [i.e. self-organizing] system is that it pulls itself up by its own bootstraps and becomes distinct from its environment through its own dynamics, *in such a way that both things are inseparable.* (emphasis added)

Fundamentally and in the most general sense, living organisms are self-organizing unities capable of reproduction. Reproduction is understood in the usual sense, the transfer of genetic information across generations, so that the organization of the original unity is conserved in the descendent unities. But unlike neo-Darwinism, genes are not viewed as an information "code" specifying the organism. They are components, essential components, but it is the network of interactions within the cell as a whole which specify its organization, not just some of its components.

Another factor which influences the network of interactions within the cell at any one time is the familiar concept of structural coupling, which occurs whenever there is a history of recurring interactions leading to structural congruence between two (or more) systems. All changes are reciprocal. The structure of the environment only triggers structural changes in the cell; it does not specify them, for the actual range of possible changes depends on the internal state of the cell. A history of reciprocal congruent changes in cell and environment is thus set up, resulting in a lineage of descent in which the structural coupling of previous cells is conserved. Thus, evolution through natural drift is the effect of both genes and structural coupling. Genes are an essential component in the network of interactions that constitute a cell, but so is the history of structural coupling which, through a lineage, is responsible for its present organization. The cell and its environment evolve together. Genetic changes are still random, just as in neo-Darwinism, but they interact as part of an organization which exists as a result of a history of congruent changes with the environment. Genetic changes which disrupt this history will lead to the disintegration of the organization, and hence be maladaptive. Otherwise, a wide range of genetic changes is acceptable. There is no maximization of fitness, merely a process of satisficing (Varela, Thompson, and Rosch 1991:196), taking a suboptimal solution that is satisfactory. Selection does not seek to increase adaptation, rather it operates as a "broad survival filter that admits any structure that has sufficient integrity to persist."

Multicellular organisms are not fundamentally different. At base, they are made up of single cell self-organizing unities, and, indeed, all reproduction of multicellular organisms is done through a unicellular phase. For a multicellular organism an important part of the environment of its component cells are other cells, with which they can form structural couplings. This leads to specialization of cell types, leading to tissues and organs. Most important among these are sensory cell groups and motor cell groups and, at least among many animals, those specialized cell groups which connect these two, neurons. But, of course, for any multicellular animal its history of structural coupling is not going to be determined by the individual interactions of its component cells, but by the full domain of interactions that it, as a complex self-producing unity in its own right, engages in. Its life as a self-organizing unity goes on in its component cells, but it transcends those components by being a coherent unity in itself. Any living organism engages in a continuing process of structural coupling with its environment, but it is essential to understand that the features of the environment do not determine any changes in the organism. Rather, the structure of the organism, as the result of its prior history of structural coupling, determines what changes are possible in it; the environment merely triggers an effect. Maturana and Varela (1987:96) state:

> The changes that result from the interaction between the living being and its environment are brought about by the disturbing agent but *determined by the structure of the disturbed system*. The same holds true for the environment: the living being is the source of perturbations and not of instructions . . .

environment and unity act as mutual sources of perturbation, triggering changes of state.

Evolution within this biological view is a process of random natural drift, within which this ongoing process of mutual and transformative structural coupling between organism and environment is conserved. The adaptation through satisficing of an organism to an environment is a necessary consequence of the organism's structural coupling with that environment. That this natural drift seems to have been "selected" by the environment is simply the viewpoint of the outside observer: all that really has occurred is the conservation of the viability of the organism as a self-organizing unity. We might summarize the basic claims of the theory of evolution as natural drift against those of neo-Darwinism as follows (Varela, Thompson, and Rosch 1991:196):

1   The unit of evolution is a network, capable of a rich repertoire of self-organizing configurations. For neo-Darwinism it is the gene, whose form is either fixed through heredity or may mutate into a derived, but fixed form.

2   Under structural coupling with the environment, these configurations generate selection, an ongoing process of satisficing that triggers changes in the form of viable trajectories. Crucially, conditions of satisficing prune trajectories which are not viable, but otherwise the organism is largely underdetermined. Many variations can survive in a given environment. This approach recognizes the richness of possibilities in biological systems. Neo-Darwinism contrasts by phrasing selection in terms of adaptation, the maximizing of fitness of the organism to the environment. This, in essence, claims that there are better, or maybe even unique, solutions to the problem of the fit between organism and environment, with the latter playing a highly deterministic role.

3   There is no one factor or system that determines which specific but non-unique trajectory will result. Rather the causes will be multiple. This leads to the consequence that many highly specific physiological or cognitive properties of an organism may be quite irrelevant to its survival, i.e. be completely non-adaptive in neo-Darwinian terms. This runs counter to usual neo-Darwinian assumptions that successful biological traits evolve to increase adaptation.

4   The opposition between inner (i.e. genes, mutations, etc.) and outer (environment) causal factors is replaced by a co-implicative relation, since organism and environment mutually specify each other through structural coupling. The environment cannot be separated from what organisms are or what they do, nor vice versa. Indeed, the so-called internal causes, genes, could be "conceived as elements that specify what in the

environment must be fixed for something to operate as a gene, that is, to be predictably correlated with a result" (Varela, Thompson, and Rosch 1991:199). The world, organism and environment, inside and outside, is all interconnected. For neo-Darwinism the environment is an independent, pre-given background which provides the selective pressures to which the organism, through internal random genetic change, successfully or unsuccessfully adapts. For this view, there is a clear contrast between internal and external causative agents in this process of adaptation.

5   Since every self-organizing system is a unity, it must undergo change as such. When any subsystem within it changes, this sets off correlative changes in other subsystems at the same time. It is not clear that neo-Darwinism would proscribe such developments, but given that the unit of evolution in it is the individual gene with its random mutations, it is not obvious how it could account for it naturally.

Human Evolution: From Apes to Modern Humans

It is well established by now that humans belong to the class of animals called apes, our closest living relative being the chimpanzee, with which we share some 98 per cent of our genes (Corballis 1991). Figure 2.2 illustrates the genetic relationships among primates based on DNA–DNA hybridization (Pilbeam 1988).

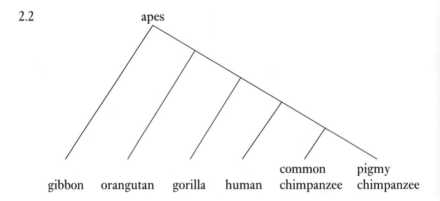

2.2   apes

gibbon   orangutan   gorilla   human   common chimpanzee   pigmy chimpanzee

This diagram indicates that humans are most closely linked genetically to the two species of chimpanzees, a bit more distantly (but still closely) to gorillas and yet more distantly to the orangutan and finally, the gibbon. Clearly, then, genetic evidence indicates that humans are apes, pure and simple and a case could be made (see Diamond 1991) for regarding them as nothing more than the third species of chimpanzee.

But what a different species it is when we compare a human being to a chimpanzee! Some of the very many contrasts are summarized below.

	Human	*Chimpanzee*
Habitat	Worldwide; adapted to different ecological zones, including extreme cold	Africa; basic adaptation to tropical forests, and marginally, adjoining savannas
Locomotion	Bipedal; upright stature	Walks on all fours; knuckle walking
Brain size	Large; mean endocranial capacity of 1350 cm^3	Smaller; mean endocranial capacity of 395 cm^3
Sexual patterns	Copulation independent of female oestrus; strong sexual dimorphism in secondary sexual characteristics, not body size	Copulation largely confined to periods of female oestrus; sexual dimorphism mainly in body size
Social life	Complex social patterns, often around monogamous pairing for rearing of offspring	Complex social patterns, but no monogamous pairing and offspring raised by mother
Culture	Enormously complex with many symbolic form clusters like art; very complex technology of tool making	Question as to whether culture is present, but if so, much less complex; very simple technology of toolmaking
Communication	By means of a complex vocal–auditory system of signs and rules of their combination, i.e. language	By means of a system of vocal–auditory calls, but not having evidence of internal structure

It would be hard to find any other instance of two closely related animals, either at the species or sub-species level, anywhere in the world which would demonstrate such extensive contrasts as these. How these differences arose in the course of the last 5 million years is the story of this section. As we shall see, it is a complex story with cause and effect constantly influencing each other, but it is clear that a primary factor is the threefold increase in brain size, undoubtedly a necessity for the enormous complexity of human social, cultural, and linguistic practices.

Apes are a relatively closely related group, and it is generally believed on genetic evidence that the earliest apes existed between 20 and 25 million years ago. Between 20 and 10 million years ago apes spread out from Africa to colonize the tropical and subtropical regions of Eurasia. The gibbon and orangutan are the modern descendants of these ancestral ape colonizers. Between 7 and 5 million years ago, the human and chimpanzee lineage diverged, so that our common ancestor dates from this time, with the split from gorillas no more than a couple of million years prior. Figure 2.3 represents these evolutionary developments (Kelley 1992).

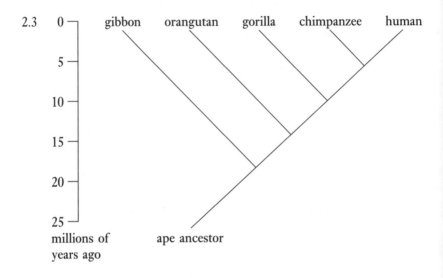

Australopithecines

The earliest ancestor of humans after our split from the line leading to the modern chimpanzee lived somewhere between 5 and 7 million years ago, probably in Africa, as this is where our closest genetic relatives, the gorilla and the two species of chimpanzee, live today, and also because the fossil evidence for the human lineage prior to about a million years ago also comes from this continent. We have few fossil remains from this period of 5 to 7 million years ago, and our oldest fossils on the hominid line (i.e. believed or conjectured to be directly ancestral to humans) are those of *Australopithecus afarensis* of East Africa, reliably dating from about 4 million years ago. Many believe this to be the ancestral hominid leading directly to humans through the genus *Homo* (Pilbeam 1988), but others dispute this claim, as the picture is complicated by no less than four closely related species of australopithecines in the fossil record. Basically, the four species of australopithecines can be divided into two types. "Gracile" australopithecines, typified by *Australopithecus afarensis* and a southern African form *Australopithecus africanus* from 3 million years ago, are light in build and rather ape-like with relatively long arms. They had mean brain sizes of about 400–500 cm^3, no more than 100 cm^3 larger than modern chimpanzees, so within the ape range. These "gracile" australopithecines were generally viewed as being on the direct lineage to *Homo*. The other two australopithecines, the "robust" forms, are *Paranthropus boisei* of East Africa and *Paranthropus robustus* of southern Africa. These date from 2.6 and 2 million years ago respectively, but are not believed to be ancestral to the *Homo* lineage and went extinct between 1.5 and 2 million years ago. These creatures were more heavily built, but again with relatively long arms like an ape. They had large crests at the top of their skulls and very thick jaws; it is believed these were associated with strong facial muscles needed for chewing, as they probably lived on coarse plant foods. Interestingly, the "robust" australopithecines had larger average brain sizes than the "gracile" australopithecines, up to 530 cm^3. What this indicates is not clear.

What about the behavior of these australopithecines? It is believed that they were more ape-like than human-like in this respect, with the "gracile" australopithecines favoring a more wooded habitat and the "robust" australopithecines a grassy savanna country (Wood 1992). They probably foraged mainly as vegetarians, with perhaps the odd opportunistic hunting like chimpanzees. They were moderately to strongly sexually dimorphic in size, so probably were not monogamous; the social arrangements were probably like chimpanzee or gorilla bands. They did not make stone tools, but again probably used tools of sticks, leaves, and stones at least as well as chimpanzees if not better, for their hands seem anatomically better suited to this type of manipulation than those of chimpanzees.

The crucial innovation of the australopithecines is that they were bipedal and stood upright, and in this respect their behavior was human-like and not ape-like. Evidence for this comes from a remarkable set of footprints made in volcanic ash discovered by Mary Leakey in Laetolil, Tanzania. They were made by three individuals of *Australopithecus afarensis* over 3.5 million years ago, demonstrating well-established upright bipedal locomotion on the ground, although their relatively long arms and other features suggest they had not entirely forsaken the trees (Wood 1992). Recent skeletal evidence from Ethiopia suggests bipedalism may date from 4 million years ago. What caused these animals to habitually walk upright on the ground? The general consensus is that it involved food and feeding behavior, probably in foraging for food over large distances on the ground, for which knuckle walking is not efficient. Australopithecines lived in more open woodland and, ultimately, savanna country than chimpanzees, where food and water resources were sparser and, hence, would need to have covered larger distances.

It may also be conjectured that this upright bipedal locomotion was also associated with preferential right-handedness, as found in all populations of the genus *Homo*, ancient and modern (Toth 1985), but not chimpanzees. MacNeilage, Studdert-Kennedy, and Lindblom (1987) argue that in arboreal primates foraging for food is done with the left hand, as this is linked to the right hemisphere, which is specialized for visual–spatial perception. The right hand is used for support, but, given body weight, would actually have been the stronger. As bipedalism developed and foraging for food on the ground replaced doing so in the trees, the right hand was freed from supporting the body. As the physically stronger hand it would have been used to exert force in the process of extracting food and, thus, would have become in time the skilled hand for manipulation. While preferential right-handedness remains a hypothesis for australopithecines, as we shall see, it has been clearly established for the next link in the human lineage, *Homo habilis*.

Homo Habilis

Between 2.5 and 2 million years ago a new hominid appeared in East Africa, *Homo habilis* ("handy man"), the first species of the genus *Homo* (although it is now believed by some that *Homo habilis* actually corresponds to two species of *Homo* existing around 2 million years ago). It probably evolved from the "gracile" australopithecines, but there is some contention about this. In any case, *Homo habilis* was a large brained species, with a brain of between 600–800 cm^3 (Pilbeam 1988), an increase of nearly 40 percent over *Australopithecus afarensis*. But as Bickerton (1990) points out, body weight also increased by approximately the same amount between *Australopithecus afarensis* and *Homo habilis*, so the increase in brain size, while still remarkable and requiring explanation, needs to be understood in this context. Recently, Dean Falk (1990, 1992, 1993) has proposed an intriguing theory for the constantly increasing brain size over the species lineage in the genus *Homo*. She notes that bipedalism occurred about 2 million years before a significant increase in brain size. Bipedalism was associated with diurnal foraging in the tropical savanna, an environment associated with great heat stress, and heat stress to the brain can cause death. Falk speculates that specific changes to that part of the circulatory system which controlled brain temperature released a physiological constraint on brain size, which permitted its large increase within the genus *Homo*. The trigger for this was the switch to bipedalism, which required the circulatory system to adapt to a vertical plane as well as a horizontal one, i.e. blood going to the brain has to work against gravity when someone is erect. This required a restructuring of the cranial blood vessels, but it is also these veins which cool the brain in cases of heat stress, rather like a radiator in a car (this is why Falk's theory is called the "radiator theory"). The efficiency of this increased cooling system released previous constraints on the size of brains, allowing them to increase in size.

The brain of *Homo habilis* is remarkable in other respects beside its size. Casts made by filling the interior of fossilized *Homo habilis* skulls with latex (endocasts) give us an idea of the structure of the brain of this species. It shows a number of anatomical features we associate with the brains of modern humans. First, both areas associated with language in modern humans, the posterior portion of the left frontal lobe and the inferior parietal lobe, exhibit anatomical patterns similar to those of modern humans (Tobias 1987). This has led some (Falk 1987; Tobias 1987; Wilkins and Wakefield 1995) to argue that *Homo habilis* was capable of rudimentary language. This evidence, while intriguing, is not conclusive, since the neural substrates of language are quite widely distributed throughout the left hemisphere, and the "language areas" of *Homo habilis* could have quite different functions only later co-opted to language. Further, the endocasts of *Homo habilis* show some significant asymmetries of structure between left and right hemispheres found in modern human brains: a forward projection in the right frontal lobe and differences in the angles of fissures in the inferior parietal lobe. These asymmetries are associated with preferential right-handedness in modern humans, and their presence in *Homo habilis* brains suggests a similar preference in this species, a finding well in accord, as we shall see below, with the archeological record.

In external anatomy, other than its large size, *Homo habilis* differed rather little from the "gracile" australopithecines, although it had shorter arms. Its teeth and face were similar, suggesting its diet was still predominantly plant food. There was still a large sexual dimorphism in size, with the male about twice the size of the female, indicative still of a non-monogamous social pattern like that of chimpanzees or gorillas (i.e. competition among males for females).

The major behavioral innovation of *Homo habilis* is the manufacture of stone tools. They are very simple, no more than chipped stones, flakes and broken bones, but they do represent a major break with all that has preceded them, in that they are the earliest form of technology, items made by the application of manufacturing techniques to transform some nonfunctional object. Chimpanzees and indeed other animals use tools, but they do not manufacture them; the limit of the chimpanzee's ability is the stripping of a twig. Toth (1985) has shown that the method of manufacture for these tools of *Homo habilis* shows that they were preferentially right-handed; indeed, a study of modern humans shows that hammering is the manual task which exhibits the strongest preference for right-handedness. Toth's (1985) finding is in accord with the neuroanatomical discoveries of Tobias

(1987) mentioned above on the lateralization of the brain, i.e. specializations of the hemispheres for diverse functions goes back in the hominid line at least 2 million years. Why did *Homo habilis* begin to manufacture tools? We can only conjecture, but one common suggestion, much disputed, is an increase in meat eating for this species over the australopithecines, although plant food still constituted the predominate part of the diet (as among modern humans). Tools would have been useful in butchering carcasses, whether hunted or scavenged. Calvin's (1983) proposal that the throwing of weapons with the stronger right hand led to lateralization and preferential right-handedness may also be tied to the rise of tools with *Homo habilis*.

Homo Erectus

After about 1.8 million years ago, a new hominid, *Homo erectus* appears in the fossil record of East Africa. The time frame indicates a relatively rapid transition from *Homo habilis* to *Homo erectus*. *Homo erectus* had only a marginal increase in body size of 10 percent over *Homo habilis*, but an increase of brain size of 45 percent, with a brain size of 800–1000 cm^3 (Pilbeam 1988), over half the size of modern humans and more than twice the size of chimpanzees. Anatomically, *Homo erectus* was more similar to modern humans than *Homo habilis* and less ape-like. Its teeth were smaller. *Homo erectus* was also taller, up to 182 cm (Corballis 1991), with overall human body proportions except that the hips were very narrow. Sexual dimorphism is much reduced in *Homo erectus*, suggesting a change in social organization to a more permanent pair bonding between male and female. This tallies with the narrow hips, suggesting a short gestation period, with consequentially a long and intense postnatal period of maternal care.

Homo erectus was probably the first hominid to migrate out of Africa and by 700,000 years ago had reached the far eastern edge of Asia (there are recent claims for australopithecines in China, but these are not yet well substantiated). The famous Java and Peking man are representatives of *Homo erectus*. *Homo erectus* appears to have been an enterprising and adaptive creature; this permitted it to colonize much of the Old World. Its tool kit was much more complex than that of *Homo habilis* and included handaxes and stone chopping and scraping tools, requiring imaginative and time-consuming methods of manufacture, although it is truly remarkable that the tool kit of *Homo erectus* survived unchanged for virtually the entire 1 million year long tenure of this species. They also probably used tools of wood and, in Asia, bamboo. The expanded tool kit corresponds to an increase in the importance of meat in the diet of *Homo erectus*, as this species was probably more adept at hunting than earlier hominids, although scavenging may still have contributed most of the meat. The bulk of the diet would have been plants. Finally, while still a matter of some debate, *Homo erectus* was probably the first hominid to use controlled fire; charred remains have been found in *Homo erectus* sites. This would have facilitated the colonization of temperate areas like the habitat of Peking man, and the hearth or campsite area where food was roasted may have become a focus of social interaction. Although late in the tenure of *Homo erectus*, the possibility of the controlled use of fire is important, it would demonstrate imaginative and symbolic powers of no mean order, as animals, including apes, typically fear fire and avoid it. The ability to manipulate and engage this source of energy also would suggest at least a rudimentary system of inter-individual signalling, a kind of language, the neural substrates for which were in place, it appears, by the time of *Homo habilis*.

Homo Sapiens

Somewhere between 400,000 and 200,000 years ago, *Homo erectus* is replaced worldwide by a new species, *Homo sapiens*. The earliest forms are usually referred to as "archaic" *Homo sapiens* to distinguish them from modern humans, as these earlier forms differ anatomically in many ways. The oldest clearly identifiable fossils of "archaic" *Homo sapiens* (400,000 years ago) again appear in Africa, so it is possible they developed there, although the alternative that *Homo erectus* developed independently through convergent drift into "archaic" *Homo sapiens* in a number of different areas cannot be ruled out. Anatomically, "archaic" *Homo sapiens* are midway between *Homo erectus* and modern *Homo sapiens*. Their basic skeletal structure and jaws and teeth were like *Homo erectus*, but they had a higher forehead like modern humans and a brain size (1100–1400 cm^3) well within the range of modern humans. The brain also had an expanded parietal region, and there were changes to the base of the skull that may relate to the presence of a larynx like that of modern humans (Stringer 1992). These two developments may be indications of speech.

"Archaic" *Homo sapiens* was found throughout the Old World; in Europe they are designated by the better known term Neanderthals, after a valley in Germany where the fossils of these hominids were first found. Neanderthals differ mainly from other populations of "archaic" *Homo sapiens* in their physiological adaptation to extreme cold, with short, stocky, extremely muscular bodies, in some respects not unlike those of peoples of the Arctic today. Their heads were very large, with an enormous projecting nose and prominent brow ridges. They had large front teeth, probably useful for gripping. Interestingly, they had a brain size, if anything, a bit bigger than modern humans, up to 1750 cm^3. They were found throughout Europe and western Asia up to about 30,000 years ago.

"Archaic" *Homo sapiens*, including Neanderthals, show a considerable cultural advance over *Homo erectus*. Evidence of symbolic behavior includes the application of color to artifacts (black and red ochre) and rituals involving the deliberate burial of the dead, although there is some debate over the interpretation of these (Gamble 1994). "Archaic" *Homo sapiens* may have understood the meaning of death, and this would reflect developed imaginative and symbolic powers. There has been some debate (Lieberman 1975, 1984, 1991) over the anatomy of the Neanderthal larynx, suggesting that they were incapable of anything like modern human language. This will be discussed more fully below, but in any case, it is hard to imagine symbolic behavior of the types mentioned above developing without some form of language, however incomplete in comparison to those of modern humans. The tool technology of "archaic" *Homo sapiens* was also extended beyond that of *Homo erectus* and involved a variety of functions: butchery, working of hides, woodworking, etc. Most important was the first attested appearance of composite tools, made from individual pieces put together and functioning as a single unit. These involved hafted tools, in which a blade or point was attached to a handle or stick.

By 30,000 years ago, "archaic" *Homo sapiens* was replaced everywhere in the Old World by "modern" *Homo sapiens*, humans essentially as we are today. How this happened has been the center of a great deal of debate since 1980, which still continues, but many specialists now favor the "Out of Africa" model. The other view, sometimes called the "candelabra model" claims that individual "archaic" *Homo sapiens* populations throughout the world evolved separately and locally into their descendent "modern" *Homo sapiens* populations. Proponents of this view argue that some anatomical differences among modern regional populations, especially those of East Asia, can be traced back to differences in the local populations of "archaic" *Homo sapiens* and, indeed, *Homo erectus*, demonstrating descent from these *in situ* regional ancestors (Wolpoff 1989). A clear weakness in this claim is the fact that all populations of "modern" *Homo sapiens* exhibit a marked "gracilization" (less robust skeleton and musculature) in comparison to their putative regional ancestors, and it is hard to believe this occurred independently in a number of widely separated areas. Indeed, this suggests that this development took place only once, in a single area, and this is the claim behind the "Out of Africa" theory. Just as it has been central stage throughout the history of the human lineage, according to this view, Africa was again the place where the most recent chapter in the evolution of humanity unfolded. The evidence for this view is now very strong and consists of two strands, archeological and genetic. First, the oldest fossils of fully modern *Homo sapiens* individuals are found in Africa, from East Africa from about 130,000 years ago and from South Africa from more than 100,000 years ago (McBrearty 1990). Outside of Africa the oldest dates are from around

90,000 years ago in the Mediterranean Middle East, suggesting a relatively rapid migration out of East Africa into Asia around 100,000 years ago. Interestingly, two Middle Eastern sites show coexistence of "archaic" and "modern" *Homo sapiens* for at least 40,000 years (Mellars 1989). Second, recent genetic studies of world populations of *Homo sapiens* (Cann 1988; Wainscoat, Hill, Boyce, Flint, Hernandez, Thein, Old, Lynch, Falusi, Weatherall, and Clegg 1986) contend that African populations of humans are indeed the most ancient, with the greatest degree of genetic diversity. It is generally the case in genetics, as in genetic linguistics, that high diversity indicates older occupation, more time for the original stock to diverge. Cann, Stoneking, and Wilson (1987) and Stoneking and Cann (1989) argue, on the basis of a theory of constant rate of change over time of mitochondrial DNA, that modern humans evolved in Africa sometime between 140,000 and 280,000 years ago, although there are some serious worries about the statistical soundness of their model (Templeton 1993). This date is in rough alignment with the fossil evidence (although we would probably expect to find still older fossils in Africa than the present ones dating from 130,000 years ago), but the theory of constant rate of change is itself highly controversial, so it is perhaps wise not to put too much faith in these dates.

"Modern" *Homo sapiens* has a brain size in the range of 1200–1760 cm^3, if anything a bit smaller than that of Neanderthals. We are much less robust in build than "archaic" *Homo sapiens*, with leaner musculature and slighter bone structure. It has been suggested that we are as custom built for warmth as the Neanderthals were for cold, a view in keeping with our proposed tropical or subtropical African origin. We also have a shorter and higher skull and a shorter jaw.

Cultural and technological organization undergoes an enormous explosion with the arrival of modern humans, with constant innovations leading right up to the present time. Already 70,000 years ago in Africa, there is evidence of a new stone blade technology, a quantum advance from previous flake technology (Gamble 1994), but the best archeological evidence comes from Europe from some 40,000 years ago. Over 130 different tools have been identified here (Corballis 1991), and new subsistence techniques involving projectile weapons and game traps indicate a growing sophistication in their use. Further, there is increasing standardization of stone tool types within a local area, but increasing differentiation outside it, suggesting a distinct consciousness of cultural groupings and transmission of cultural traditions. Correlated to this is the great outpouring in symbolic behavior including elaborate burials with grave goods, body ornamentation and cave art. All of this is cultural transmission and indicates a well-developed language.

As mentioned above, "archaic" *Homo sapiens* and "modern" *Homo sapiens* coexisted in the Middle East side by side for at least 40,000 years, probably following an early colonization of this area from East Africa. Outside of Africa, "modern" *Homo sapiens* was restricted to this area until about 40,000 years ago. Modern humans, adapted to the warmth of tropical and subtropical Africa, adjusted quickly and successfully to the similar ecological zone of the Middle East, but the colder climates of northern Eurasia, the domain of "archaic" *Homo sapiens* in the form of Neanderthals, resisted them until this date. The date of 40,000 years ago is an extremely important one in human evolution, the time of which has been called "the human revolution" (Mellars 1989). All over the Old World major changes appear in the archeological record. "Archaic" *Homo sapiens* and associated technology disappear from the Middle East (47,000–40,000 years ago). "Modern" *Homo sapiens* appears throughout large areas of Eurasia. Indeed, the first colonization of Siberia dates from this period (35,000–30,000 years ago) (Klein 1985) and may have even then extended into the Americas (Guidon and Delibrias 1986). Dates for the colonization of Australia and New Guinea are at least 20,000 years earlier – about 60,000 and perhaps over 100,000 years ago, suggesting perhaps a relatively rapid spread of "modern" *Homo sapiens* along the southern tropical and subtropical fringe of the Asian landmass. Reaching Australia and New Guinea required a sea crossing of at least 90 km (Jones 1989), necessitating rafts or boats, a tool kit and a cultural tradition and mental agility rich enough for the manufacture of these vessels. Modern humans appeared in Europe around 40,000 years ago and proceeded to replace Neanderthals, who disappear from the archeological record completely about 30,000 years ago.

Associated with this wide and rapid population dispersal is an abrupt shift in technology and cultural behavior. This is shown in a different and extended pattern of stone tool technology and the emergence of personal body ornaments, in new economic arrangements involving the trading of objects, and in enriched symbolic and representational behaviors, such as art. Indeed, major and innovative improvements in technology and subsistence practices, along with consequent developments in social behavior would be absolutely necessary for a less robust, tropically adapted species to so successfully and rapidly colonize such ecologically forbidding zones as northern Europe and Siberia. Some have seen the development of essentially fully modern language (Davidson and Noble 1989; Mellars 1989; Noble and Davidson 1991) as the crucial variable in this efflorescence of modern humans, driving a complex of behavioral changes. This is possible. Although it is likely that some form of language existed prior to modern humans, some development around 40,000 years ago may have led to its enrichment and hence its increased usefulness in symbolic and abstract thought, with a knock on effect on other forms of human cultural and social behavior. I will discuss this in much greater detail in the following sections.

Increase in Brain Size

On one, and very common, view, the story of human evolution can largely be reduced to one of incremental increase in the size of the brain. This has been seen as the logical and extreme outcome of a long process begun way back in the line of animal evolution, with increasing pace among vertebrates and, especially, mammals – encephalization. This is concentrating a greater volume of neurons in the head end of the animal. Humans, of course, with the highest ratio of brain size to body size, are the most encephalized of all animals. This concentration of potential neuronal interactions in one spot allows a tremendous increase in the functional open-endedness of the human nervous system, in biological terms, its plasticity, the ability to respond creatively and in non-preprogramed ways. Fundamentally, this entails an enormous increase in the ability to learn, which, in essence, is what distinguishes us from all other animals.

Besides its obvious difference in size, when one compares the human brain with that of the chimpanzee, our closest animal relative, we find some interesting differences, although the overall structure of both is in fact rather typical of primates (Deacon 1992b). Much of the gain in brain size in humans over chimpanzees is in the neocortex, that area associated with higher brain functions. Further, what is crucial about the human neocortex is the great enrichment of the interconnectivity of the neurons within it (Gibson 1988), which, as mentioned above, underlies the plasticity of human behavior. As Gibson (1991) points out, while the human is born with a full complement of neurons, postnatally, during brain growth, a massive restructuring occurs; there is a proliferation of neuronal interconnections and splitting within the neocortex. Such radical restructuring does not appear to affect the brain of chimpanzees. Further, since large brains have more widely spaced neurons, the density of neurons within the human brain would have decreased to a significantly greater extent than their overall number increased. This suggests greater flexibility in forging new neuronal interconnections. Ringo (1991) has developed a tantalizing model on the basis of these findings, one which accounts for the highly specialized nature of the human neocortex. As brain size and absolute neuron numbers increase, each individual neuron must be connected to a decreased fraction of the total number of neurons (otherwise the potential number of interconnections would simply overwhelm the brain's conductivity). But, as absolute connectivity, nonetheless, still increases with the enlarging brain, a partial resolution is decreased density of the neurons. More volume is available to each neuron in large brains, and short neurons, with resulting specialization of function, result. Ringo (1991:5) goes on:

One interesting possibility is that this increasing load from interconnectedness is avoided by utilizing specialization so that only within major groupings of neurons need there be full interconnection, while between major groupings only "results" need to be passed. This then suggests the argument that big brains need hemispheric specialization, because of interconnections getting out of hand, and further suggests that large hemispheres will be more specialized than small ones. This simply means that cortical areas will be more specialized.

Human brains, of course, are well known for their extensive hemispheric specialization, called lateralization; analytical processing, language, control of the right hand, etc. in the left hemisphere and holistic processing, musical ability, and control of the left hand in the right hemisphere. This is exactly as Ringo's (1991) model predicts. Hemispheric specialization among chimpanzees is more weakly developed; for example, as a population they do not exhibit strong preferential right-handedness, as humans do. Further, other aspects of open-ended human behavior which result from our increased neuronal interconnections in the neocortex are also absent in chimpanzees: inhibited emotional response, representative art forms, manufacture of composite tools and, finally, fully developed language (see pp. 75–8 for a discussion of this question).

With the increase in the size of the brain, the big story in human evolution, many people under the influence of neo-Darwinism have looked for a "prime mover," a basic environmental/behavioral causative force driving this development. Falk's (1990) "radiator" theory is not one of these; it merely accounts for how constraints on the size of the brain might have been removed, but does not in any way suggest mechanisms for its growth. But many "prime movers" have been suggested: warfare, hunting, tool production, throwing (i.e. rapid sequencing of the right arm, with consequent lateralization and strengthening of the left hemisphere), and social organization. Perhaps the one most in favor at the moment is language (Falk 1987, 1993), given that its neurological substrates seem to appear very early in the archeological record (2 million years) with *Homo habilis*, at the very beginning of the steep increase in the size of the brain. I believe that one should beware of such searches for a simple, all explanatory "prime mover." As mentioned earlier, evolution, as seen through the theory of natural drift, is a complex process of satisficing, preserving conditions of structural coupling between organism and environment, such that it is viable as a continuing self-organizing entity. Any genetic change which does not disrupt this history of structural coupling will be acceptable. There is no optimal fit between genetic change and maximal reproductive success, a broad range of possibilities are available. The trajectory of development is greatly underdetermined. Hence, we should not expect any one magic "prime mover." No one force determines which specific, but non-unique, trajectory will result;

the causes are multiple. In turn, this implies that many highly specific physiological or cognitive properties may be quite irrelevant to the survival of a species. It is a sobering thought that language might be one of these.

Language versus Speech

In discussing the evolution of language and speech, it is first of all important to emphasize that, contrary to popular usage and understanding, these two terms are not equivalent. For one thing, the particular bits of language presented before the reader now are clearly not spoken, but rather appear in a printed medium. As all languages can potentially be inscribed in such a visual medium, this demonstrates the independence of language from speech. One could object, however, that the written form of a language is nothing but a visual representation of its spoken form (Chinese logographic writing would, of course, be a problem for this objection), and so that language is really basically equivalent to speech after all. The answer to this objection is that there exists a class of fully developed and perfectly functional human languages which never use the spoken channel at all – the sign languages of the deaf, such as American Sign Language (ASL) and many others spread throughout the world. These languages are equivalent in every respect, save the use of the vocal/auditory channel, to spoken languages like English, Swahili, or Yimas. For obvious reasons, they employ the visual channel, but the linguistic units and grammatical constructions found in these languages parallel in every respect those of spoken languages (Klima and Bellugi 1979). Indeed, it is well known that deaf infants acquire a native sign language in the same way as other children acquire a spoken language (Goldin-Meadow 1993; Newport and Meier 1985), demonstrating there is a single language capacity for all linguistic behavior, be it realized in a vocal–auditory medium or a visual one. There is a very strong preference, though, that language be realized in the vocal–auditory medium; unless there is some very serious neural or sensory deficit in the vocal–auditory circuits, it is a spoken language which is acquired. This indicates that while language and speech are indeed distinct, there is a normal linkage between them; neurologically, it seems, humans are predetermined to acquire language and predisposed to acquire speech.

Lateralization and the Anatomical Bases of Language

What are the neurological and anatomical bases of language and speech? First of all, we know that for about 80 percent of all people, the language capacity is located in the left hemisphere (for 95 percent of all right handers and 70 percent of all left handers) (Corballis 1991). At birth, both hemispheres are available for the language capacity; if the left hemisphere is seriously damaged in childhood, language can appear in the right hemisphere, but this possibility is lost after childhood. The left hemisphere is consistently larger, suggesting specialization for some function as a whole. In the left hemisphere the language capacity seems to be located in a broad sweep around the region known as the Sylvian fissure (the main front to back convolution) from the motor areas of the frontal lobe to the auditory association areas of the temporal and parietal lobes. Thus, it is distributed from the prefrontal cortex far forward in the brain to the posterior half of the parietal lobe, about two-thirds of the length of the hemisphere. Neurologically, the language capacity is not a localized phenomenon within the brain. It is distributed over a number of areas, most of which serve other functions, such as auditory and tactile perception and motor control of the muscles of the face, mouth, and larynx. They are also closely associated with areas involving complex skilled manual behavior, the sequentialization of actions and organization of associations. All this suggests that the language capacity is not a unitary neural system, but a functional complex of previously discrete systems which have come to work together in language-bearing humans (in contemporary terms, it is modular).

The close association of the left hemisphere with language in humans is paralleled by another bit of behavior – handedness. About 90 percent of humans are right-handed, and the right hand is controlled by the left hemisphere. As mentioned in the previous section, preferential right-handedness in hominids appears in the archeological record about 2 million years ago with *Homo habilis* (Toth 1985). It can hardly be a coincidence that *Homo habilis* is also the first hominid to exhibit hemispheric asymmetry, with anatomical features of the left hemisphere of endocasts like those of modern humans (Tobias 1987). Clearly, then, all three, hemispheric asymmetry, preferential right-handedness and language capacity are interrelated. The source of this interrelationship will be pursued below.

The specialization of the left hemisphere in humans for language is part of a much broader pattern of hemispheric divisions of functions, termed lateralization. Besides motor control in which the left hemisphere directs the right side of the body and the right, the left side, much of our cognitive and perceptual functioning is also divided by the two hemispheres; for example, the right half of our visual field goes to the left hemisphere and the left half, to the right hemisphere. Cognitively, the left hemisphere is associated with analytical, sequential processing. Besides most of language processing, which is an analytical, sequential medium *par excellence*, time-sequencing processing is also done in this hemisphere. The right hemisphere performs global, holistic processing. It is associated with musical ability, spatial perception, imagery, recognizing people's faces and the emotions expressed there, and humor. Interestingly, it is not exclusively true to say that the language capacity is located entirely in the left hemisphere. While the analytical aspects of language such as phoneme recognition and the production, processing, and generation of sentence structure definitely are found in the left hemisphere, the more holistic or analogical aspects of language are, indeed, in the right hemisphere. For example, prosodic aspects of speech such as rhythm, emphasis, and intonation are strongly associated with the right hemisphere, as is the understanding of metaphors or jokes, which require an analogical rather than sequential type of reasoning for comprehension (Deacon 1992a).

In addition to the brain, the other major organs necessary to spoken language are those of the vocal tract (for sign languages it is the anatomy of the human hands and the eye, but I will not discuss sign languages further in this chapter). The human vocal tract is very different from the oral cavity of any other primate. First, our larynx is much lower in the throat than that of other primates (Lieberman 1991). This, plus the curvature of the oral cavity above the larynx, increases the size of the resonance cavity, allowing humans to articulate distinctly many vowels. The velum also can close off the passage to the nose, allowing humans to produce a contrast between nasalized and non-nasalized sounds. Our palate and lower jaw are reduced in length compared to other primates. Finally, humans have a tongue distinct from all other mammals (Lieberman 1991); it is round and forms both the floor of the mouth and the front of the pharynx. Chimpanzees, our closest relatives, have long thin tongues positioned entirely in the mouth. Interestingly, human infants have a vocal tract resembling that of a chimpanzee (Lieberman 1991). As they grow, their palates move backward along the bottom of the skull; this process begins at three months and continues rapidly until age five, but is only fully complete at adolescence.

Precursors of Language in Apes

As humans have evolved from apes, it is not an unreasonable expectation to seek precursors of human neural and anatomical structures for speech and language in other primates. These may be a guide in understanding the evolution of language and speech. While it was long thought that lateralization of functions was exclusively a property of the human brain, this view is now known to be mistaken; there is clear evidence for lateralization in other primates (Deacon 1992b; Falk 1987, 1992; MacNeilage, Studdert-Kennedy, and Lindblom 1987). The difference is one of degree, not kind; human brains are just more extensively lateralized than those of other primates. Preferential handedness, for example, appears to be widespread among nonhuman primates, but appears to differ from that of humans; across populations as a whole, there is a left-handed preference for visually guided movements, like eating or foraging, and a right-handed preference for skilled manipulation (MacNeilage, Studdert-Kennedy, and Lindblom 1987). The left-handed behavior has been interpreted as implying a right hemisphere visual–spatial specialization associated with eating and foraging – a clear precursor to the right hemisphere specialization for visual–spatial recognition in humans. The origin of right-handed preference is more complex. While primates were mainly arboreal, the right hand would have been used for support and this would have been linked to left hemisphere specialization for postural control (MacNeilage 1989). But as the apes began to increasingly forage on the ground, this was no longer needed; the right hand, which was physically stronger from previously supporting the body weight, took on the function of the skilled application of force to objects, and ultimately, became the skilled hand for manipulation. When bipedalism arrived in the hominid line, the hands were now completely freed, and this development was further accentuated, leading to the very strong preferential right-handedness we find in modern humans.

There are also precursors in primates for the human left hemisphere specialization for the language capacity. It is now well known that vocal communication in monkeys is lateralized to the left hemisphere; for example, studies of Japanese macaques (Petersen, Beecher, Zoloth, Green, Marler, Moody, and Stebbins 1984; Petersen, Beecher, Zoloth, Moody, and Stebbins 1978) demonstrate they exhibit a right-ear (connected to left hemisphere) advantage for recognizing the calls of their own species, but no such advantage when tested for other sounds. This shows that they have a left hemisphere specialization for processing vocal communication – a pattern of lateralization for vocal–auditory behavior parallel to that of human brains. Recent studies (Hopkins, Morris, Savage-Rumbaugh, and Rumbaugh 1989) also indicate a left hemisphere specialization in chimpanzees for the processing of coded symbols, a language-like behavior. All of this demonstrates that a left hemisphere specialization for "language" and "speech" is not unique to humans.

Deacon (1992b) has done extensive work comparing the neural circuits underlying primate calls with those of human language, and finds that, while there are many differences, there are also significant overlaps between them. For monkeys, the primary vocalization areas are in the deeper midbrain section. These are also involved in human spoken language, but so are parts of the left lateral frontal neocortex (the "language areas" discussed above). The role of these latter areas is negligible in primate vocalization, although anatomically they are present and exhibit patterns of neural connections corresponding to those in humans. Deacon (1992b) believes that language developed through reorganization of neural circuits, in which the midbrain vocalization area became progressively subordinated to the coordinated activity of prefrontal cortex and midbrain, and the frontal areas controlling motor programs for the face and mouth region. Deacon (1992b) emphasizes the continuity between primate and human brains; he says (Deacon 1992b:150) "I am not convinced that we need to postulate the appearance of novel connections as opposed to just shifted proportions among connections in the evolution of the human brain in order to account for human language abilities." He points out that size increases in areas of the brain during human evolution were not uniform; the human prefrontal cortex, which he identifies as the linchpin in human evolution, is twice the size one would expect in a primate of our proportions, whereas our visual area is only 60 percent of its expected size (Deacon 1992a). So, it seems that the basic neural organization of the language areas in the human brain has indeed been inherited from our primate ancestors; what is unique to humans is the relative size of these areas as compared to other parts of the brain and the connections between them.

We might well ask what might link posture control and vocalization together in the left hemisphere, as the above discussion proposes. MacNeilage (1989) suggests that they are directly interrelated; an arboreal animal would need to compensate posturally for the muscular expenditure needed to vocalize. Otherwise it may be thrown off balance, an unlucky result if the vocalization was to warn of a nearby predator.

All of the above discussion argues that the biological roots of language are to be found in primate vocalizations. Perhaps the most often cited contrast between primate vocalization and human language is the lack of intentional control in the former. Concerning chimpanzees, Jane Goodall (1986:125) noted:

> Chimpanzee vocalizations are closely tied to emotion. The production of a sound in the *absence* of the appropriate emotional state seems to be an almost impossible task for a chimpanzee . . . A chimpanzee can learn to *suppress* calls in situations when the production of sounds might, by drawing attention to the signaller, place him in an unpleasant or dangerous position, but even this is not easy. On one occasion when Figan [a chimpanzee at the Gombe Stream Reservation] was an adolescent, he waited in camp until the senior males had left and we were able to give him some bananas (he had none before). His excited food calls quickly brought the big males racing back and Figan lost his fruit. A few days later he waited behind again, and once more received his bananas. He made no loud sounds, but the calls could be heard deep in his throat, almost causing him to gag.

This contrasts sharply with the easy conscious control humans have over their language: when to speak or be silent, what to say and not to say. But even this difference seems to be one of degree and not absolute. Steklis (1988) studied the vocalization calls of monkeys and found that monkeys can learn to emit certain vocalizations in response to a certain arbitrary stimulus and to withhold vocalization to a second arbitrary stimulus in order to get food or avoid punishment. This demonstrates control of vocalization, but does not necessarily indicate intentional control. This, however, is independently confirmed by Cheney and Seyfarth's (1990) study of the use of predator signalling vocalizations by vervet monkeys. They noted that solitary vervet monkeys do *not* emit their signals when confronted with a predator. They appear to know that there is no potential recipient of the call, demonstrating understanding of the communicative intentions of such calls. Thus, drawing a distinction between human language and primate vocalizations on the basis of intentional control appears to be unwarranted.

Be that as it may, there is still a huge chasm between even the most elaborate of primate vocalization systems and human language. Indeed, Burling (1993) has recently suggested that these have much more in common with human non-verbal communication systems than human language. And Deacon (1992b) also points out the marked reduction of human pre-programed vocalization types in contrast to other primates and suggests the evolution of full human language may be responsible, so that one system is mutually exclusive of the other. Thus, while the biological roots of language are in these systems, the actual final result, due to human evolution over the last 5 million years, is quite different.

The Development of Human Language

What, then, were the processes by which language emerged from these earlier systems? A gestural theory of origin of language through manual signs, which has been under discussion for a number of years (see Hewes (1973) for example) seems unlikely from what we now know about the similar biological substrates of primate vocalizations and human language. It also leaves completely unaccounted for the proposed crucial transition to spoken language; how exactly would this have come about? Given what we now know, it seems economical to suggest that language started out in the same channel as we find it today – a vocal–auditory system of communication. But there is an important insight in the gestural theory, a close correlation between language and skilled manual activity, the dominant functioning of both for the great majority of the population being housed in the left hemisphere. How is this the key to language evolution?

Further, we must disabuse ourselves of the idea that language evolved suddenly *de novo* into a form much like it is today. From what has been said above this is most unlikely; language is a multilayered phenomenon, each of which may be of different origin and age. Further, it is likely, contrary to the views of some (Bickerton 1990), that language passed through many stages of increasing complexity during its evolution. Demonstrating that earlier hominids were incapable of language as we understand it today, as Lieberman (1984, 1991) claims to have done, does not prove that such hominids lacked language, merely the common, well-attested form of it today.

The key to the relationship between skilled manual manipulation and language seen by many observers (Corballis 1991; Greenfield 1991; Mac-Neilage 1992; Reynolds 1993) is that the same cognitive functions for analyzing and manipulating complex hierarchical information underlie both capacities. Recent work emphasizes the strong similarities in organization between these two abilities. MacNeilage (1992) notes three important similarities between manual actions and vocalizations. First, both are functions superimposed on anatomical features designed for other uses. Thus, the hands were originally claws or paws, used for locomotion. The lungs, mouth and other parts of the vocal tract also have other and *prior* uses, breathing and feeding. Second, these specialized functions of the hand and vocal tract, manipulation and vocalization, arose by a particular elaboration of their most distal components. Thus, it is the hand, the most distal part of the arm, which is fundamental in skilled manual actions. This is already well attested in monkeys, but is perhaps furthest developed in the great apes and humans. The vocal apparatus consists of three major components: lungs (expiration/sound), larynx (modulation), and mouth (resonance). Humans, in the phonetic properties of spoken language, show a remarkable extension of function of the most distal member of these three, the mouth, over all other primates. The resonance properties of the mouth are responsible for the production of the consonants and vowels which constitute the great bulk of the phonemic systems of languages. Other primates lack these. This difference, of course, is directly linked to the much greater volume of neurons given over to vocalization functions in the left hemisphere of the human brain than in that of the monkey. The third similarity between manual action systems and vocalizations concerns their overall structure. If we consider the vocalizations of apes, we discover that when a sound pattern is extended over time, this is done in a cyclically serial way: by simply repeating the sound (or pair of sounds, as in chimpanzees' pant-hoots) over time. This is found in human language as well, in the cyclical serial structure of syllables. However, superimposed on this is a hierarchical structure; within each syllable there can be subsyllabic components, for example a consonant and a vowel (2.4).

2.4

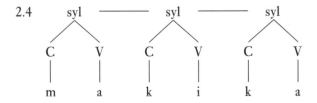

Primate vocalizations show no evidence for this cyclically serial, but internally hierarchical structure, in more formal terms, a syntagmatic–paradigmatic structure. But this is absolutely pervasive in all human languages; for example, clauses being composed of phrases, phrases of words, and words of morphemes. Human manual action shows the same serial hierarchical structure, as when one hand operates on an object supported by another. The hand grabs an object, and these then form a unit with respect to the action of the other hand. Human technological artifacts, even simple ones, betray this assembled, composite structure (Reynolds 1983, 1993). Consider hafted spears; the point and shaft are joined together and probably bound with twine. This is now a composite whole; it can be rotated in space and will remain intact. Primates, including our closest relatives, chimpanzees, are incapable of these kinds of actions. They can place nuts on a rock and then smash them with a second rock, but they do not hold a rock in one hand, put a nut on it and then smash this assembly with another rock. They can stack boxes together to reach a banana, but they cannot tie boxes together to move them as a complex to another point. In short, as expected, manual action and vocalization show parallelism in structure, but a divide separates human capacities in this area: humans are capable of serializing units, internally composed hierarchically of distinct sub-units; other primates are capable of serializing units, but these betray no internal structure. Greenfield (1991) has demonstrated that this human ability begins to appear about age 2 and traces it to neuronal developments in the frontal lobe cortex of the left hemisphere, a not unexpected finding. She, in fact, argues that the neural circuits controlling manual object combinations and grammar adjoin each other in this area, and, indeed, that such a pattern is found in other primates, particularly macaque monkeys. Again it appears what distinguishes a human from an ape and other primates is the much greater size and connectivity of the brain, not its basic structure. It is this which gives humans their enriched repertoire of behavior.

The Social Dimension to Language Evolution

Reynolds (1993) has added a new dimension to this argument. He notes that human tool using and artifact making activity have an essential *social* dimension. Actions between humans in doing these activities are complementary: each participant anticipates and coordinates with the actions of others in the activity. One man might prepare the point of a spear, while the other prepares the shaft. Other primates never do this: tool using is strictly an individual activity. Reynolds asserts that this social coordination of activities and the serial, but hierarchical, structure of action tasks and language are closely related, emerging together, synergistically, during human evolution.

He terms this the "complementation theory" and claims it is "a model of human evolution in which the ability mentally to represent reciprocal and complementary social relations is given equal status with the cognitive skills of causal inference and logical deduction, and with physical processes" (Reynolds 1993:423). Ultimately, the construction of complex assemblies, organized internally in a hierarchical way, such as a noun phrase in English or a complex predicate in Yimas, depends on this social organization.

And so must have the evolution of language and speech. Reynolds' theory highlights the important role social factors must have played in the evolution of language. Reynolds points out that the analog of this cooperative social behavior in primates is grooming, which is characterized by reciprocal, complementary roles in face-to-face interaction. Reynolds claims hominids diverged from apes when the social relations found in grooming were extended to organize technical skills like tool use.

And, we might add, vocalizations, for Reynolds' theory has found striking support in a very unexpected quarter in recent work by Aiello and Dunbar (1993) and Dunbar (1993). They note a close correlation between social-group size and brain size, and note that both of these were increasing significantly about the time of *Homo habilis* 2 million years ago. As the size increased, grooming behavior would have no longer sufficed to ensure group social cohesion. Aiello and Dunbar (1993) calculate that *Homo erectus* (Olduvai 9) with a cranial capacity of 1067 cm^3 and a mean group size of 116.39 would have needed to spend 33 percent of its time in grooming activity to promote social bonding. They posit that the function and complexity of vocalizations were extended to take on some of the load previously carried by grooming. They also point out that gelada baboons, living in the largest groups among primates excluding humans, with a mean group size of 115, have vocalization patterns with a number of features once considered unique to human speech: fricatives, stops and nasals, 3 places of articulation (labial, dental and velar), and prosodic melodies (Richman 1972, 1978, 1987). These vocal properties seem to supplement grooming as a mechanism for social bonding. Given the grooming time that would have been required for hominids, Aiello and Dunbar (1993) propose that vocalizations underwent a similar extension of function in the ancestral *Homo* lineage. Indeed, the importance of their role in promoting social cohesion has been emphasized continuously by many scholars, going back at least to Malinowski (1923); this, of course, is also central to the view of linguistic practices presented in chapter 1. This is often insufficiently recognized because speakers of written languages (and linguists!) often unduly overemphasize its propositional bearing function.

The evolution of human language seems to have been a multicausal process. These were the social factors identified by Aiello and Dunbar (1993) and Reynolds (1993), the cognitive interdependencies between manual action and language discussed by Corballis (1991), Greenfield (1991) and

MacNeilage (1992), and the neurological developments from a primate to human brain explored by Deacon (1992b) and Ringo (1991). All of these played a crucial part, and contrary to neo-Darwinist tenets and Bickerton (1990), there was no sudden and wondrous genetic mutation that gave rise to the language capacity. The distributed nature of the neurological developments and the diffuse nature of the features of the environment, both social and cultural, in which this development took place fully demonstrate the gross implausibility of a "language capacity" gene. Rather, language evolved gradually by co-opting structures from other domains of cognition, which became more and more attuned to their new linguistic function. Language is the composite result of many distinct tinkerings, but does not reside in any of them. Thus, there were many stages of linguistic systems before the modern languages we know today emerged – language was not a sudden catastrophic change. Taking the consensus of the scholars discussed above, the evolution of language involved a gradual and continuous transition from non-human primate communication systems, even if, today, following Burling (1993), these origins are so submersed that these ancestral forms bear a closer similarity to our non-verbal communication systems than modern language.

The Evolution of Language in the Genus *Homo*

So, the earliest linguistic systems emerged out of vocalizations like those of the great apes. The earliest innovation was probably an increase in the number of distinctive calls. Chimpanzees have about three dozen distinctive calls (Goodall 1986); we could expect this to triple or more before the auditory perceptive space became overloaded and processing problems would set in. These would be the earliest "words." Further extensions could be accomplished by combining these calls, a skill fully within the abilities of early hominids, as even chimpanzees can perform this with the signs of American Sign Language. Following Bickerton (1990), let us call this earliest linguistic system proto-language.

When did proto-language first appear? Aiello and Dunbar (1993) and Dunbar (1993) suggest the time burden for grooming would have already been costly by the time of *Homo habilis*, with mean grooming time aproaching 23 percent of its time budget. *Homo habilis* would have been under some pressure to augment grooming with vocal communication to promote social cohesion. Aiello and Dunbar's findings tally very well with what else we know of *Homo habilis*: preferential right-handedness (Toth 1985), indicating strong lateralization of the brain, and hemispheric asymmetry, with enlargement of areas in the left hemisphere associated with language in modern human brains. We can tentatively conclude, then, that proto-language was already well established with *Homo habilis* (see also similar conclusions in Wilkins and Wakefield (1995)).

From *Homo habilis* through *Homo erectus*, the lexical resources of proto-language probably continued to increase up to several hundred words. The length of sequences of signs also probably increased, for, on Ringo's (1991) theory, the significantly larger brain of *Homo erectus* would have been much more adept at framing and comprehending these longer sequences of signs. We would expect *Homo erectus* to have a significantly improved short-term memory capacity over *Homo habilis*. The fact that *Homo erectus* was the first hominid to colonize Asia, reaching as far as Java, developed a much more extensive tool kit, and possibly controlled the use of fire indicates symbolic capacities well beyond those of *Homo habilis*. This could only be accomplished so far by increasing the number of unique signs and lengthening their sequences. More signalling powers mean more signs, so it is likely that the first complex sign units, i.e. containing something like proto-phonemes, appeared with *Homo erectus*, although the exploitation of the use of internal phonological structure was probably not systematic. But, for all this, the evidence indicates that *Homo erectus* did not cross the bridge to fully modern language. Its tool kit, while extensive in comparison to that of *Homo habilis*, remains almost unchanged for nearly 1 million years. This would be unthinkable for modern humans and indicates that *Homo erectus* did not yet have the equivalent of our symbolic and linguistic abilities. It could be objected that the deficiencies of *Homo erectus* lie not in the capacity of language, but for speech; that it had many of the neurological components of the modern capacity for language, but that its vocal tract was insufficient for clear articulate speech (Lieberman 1991). This is possible, but we will never know. It seems unlikely, though, in view of the fact that some modern human larynxes made do with telescoped phonetic possibilities, a fact frequently overlooked in work of this type, such as Lieberman (1984, 1991). In Yimas, for example, 90 percent of all tokens of vowels are central vowels. There is no obvious reason why *Homo erectus* could not have had an analog of modern speech if the neurological components of the brain were fully developed. The archeological record suggests they were not.

Something equivalent to modern language probably did emerge with "archaic" *Homo sapiens*, less than 400,000 years ago. Interestingly, it is at this point that Aiello and Dunbar (1993) conclude that earlier hominids would have been under the same pressures of social bonding as that found in modern humans. There is no significant difference in proposed group sizes or percentage of time spent grooming among "archaic" *Homo sapiens*, Neanderthals, or modern humans. With "archaic" *Homo sapiens* the first semi-modern vocal tract appears, capable of producing the phones of modern languages, albeit with less stability (Lieberman 1991). This is found with a fossil skull from Africa, dating from about 150,000 years ago, and one from Europe, about 250,000 years old. It has been argued by Lieberman (1984, 1991) that one group of "archaic" *Homo sapiens*, the Neanderthals, dating from later than these two, had vocal tracts that were incapable of generating many of the fundamental phonemes of modern languages. This conclusion has been challenged by others, but, in any case, it is irrelevant to the question whether Neanderthals had speech. They need not have had the full phonemic inventory of many modern languages nor their typical phonotactic possibilities to qualify as having fully human language. Earlier full languages were probably quite different from modern languages, yet shared the crucial defining property of the serialization of composite units, composed internally of hierarchical structure. Evidence that "archaic" *Homo sapiens* did indeed have cognitive control of hierarchically structured composite units comes from their tool technology. For the first time, hafted tools appear. These are composite tools, made from individual pieces put together and functioning as a whole. This reflects the manual analog of hierarchical structure and, following the homology between manual action and language discussed above, is the first evidence in the hominid line for true syntax – the hierarchical organization of grammatical constituents in lower level units. Thus, we have the first appearance of the paradigmatic side of grammar; the syntagmatic (i.e. serializing of units) is much older, going back in the hominid line to *Homo habilis*.

How, then, did syntax arise? Largely, I believe, by having complex descriptions built up through the motor programs needed for phonological rhythm units. Suppose the system of signs available to us in the linguistic system already provides one sign for "small" and one sign for "lion." But what we want is not these two descriptions separately, but a composite one, combining both of them: "small lion." Simple serialization will not give us this. But, the phonology, much more concrete and tied to the phonetic motor patterns of rhythm probably already had ways of forming articulatory and auditory units, for example, a syllable timer (2.5).

Because syllable timing is a motor program, we fully expect homologies with other motor programs, like hand manipulation. This pattern of phonological unit timing was expanded beyond the syllable to the sign, so that two signs which formed a descriptive unit were formally treated as a phonetic unit: [[small]-[lion]], a proto-phrase. Later, as these became cognitively realized as formal structural units, the phonetic encoding constraints were

2.5

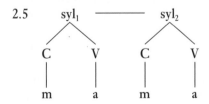

weakened (but never entirely lost; we see pervasive correlations between syntactic units and phonological ones in all modern languages). A similar origin also probably applies to the clause, involving a breath group unit. Complex words were probably later, with the relaxation of the phonetic constraints, and formerly independent words being realized as parts of words. Language as we understand it, then, was born about 200,000 years ago.

It would be a great mistake to believe that these earliest forms of modern human language were exactly like those of present-day middle-class English. Syntactic constructions were probably limited: phrases may not have consisted of more than two or three words (as in present-day Yimas), clauses rarely more than one argument (as in present-day Kalam), and clausal embedding avoided (as in the adjoined relative clauses of present-day central Australian languages). Yet all the basic formal properties which define contemporary human languages were in place.

If, by about 200,000 years ago, essentially modern language evolved, what, then, is the linguistic contribution to the "human revolution" of about 40,000 years ago? A number of scholars (Chase and Dibble 1987; Davidson and Noble 1989; Mellars 1989; Noble and Davidson 1991; White 1982) have attempted to link this to the first appearance of fully developed symbolic human language. But the contradiction between this position and the one taken here may be more apparent than real. It may only be around this period of 40,000 years ago or so that the propositional bearing function of speech, as opposed to its social bonding one, really came into its own. This would focus attention on the fit or lack of it between what was said and the physical world (the source of the linguistic function of reference). In short, we discovered the possibility of providing what Maturana and Varela (1987) term a semantic description of things. This also gave rise to a metalinguistic awareness, the idea in Davidson and Noble (1993:382) that "language arises from the discovery that meaning is conveyed by signs." Language certainly does not arise from this, but perhaps the "fully symbolic" kind of language that they and other scholars are talking about does. There is less need for this awareness when language is predominantly a kind of non-tactile social-bonding device. Further, the functions of reference and metalinguistic awareness in turn give rise to the idea of a "linguistic self": this person speaking conveys a meaning by using signs that bear a different fit to the sensible world than some other person does. And, finally, the enrichment of the proposition-creating function of language increases one's flexibility in imagining and describing states and events far removed from the cares and activities of the here and now. This is the displacement function of language, most notable in its use as a tool of cognitive reflection while talking to oneself, which Geertz (1973) described as a secondary function of language. This, again, is not a function of language likely to have been as highlighted in its earliest role as social glue.

The proposed elaboration and extension of the proposition creating role of language about 40,000 years ago amply explains the great explosion in symbolic and cultural behavior we find there. Art is closely tied to meta-linguistic awareness; the objects/feelings themselves can be conveyed by these depictions. The discovery of the linguistic self, the locus of intentional action, would lead to personal ornamentation and other indications of indi-viduality, as well as an increased understanding of the ongoing construct-iveness of social life. And the imagination involved in displacement would unleash tremendous new powers of creativity, greatly expanding the tech-nology. All of this, in turn, would have had cybernetic effects on the forms of language, enriching it lexically and in its combinatorial possibilities.

Summary

The claim in this chapter is that language did not evolve by neo-Darwinist adaptation – by a selection or linear series of selections to optimal fitness by random genetic mutations. No plausible genetic mutation could be the organizing principle behind the very complex neurological changes which gave rise to human language. Rather, language emerged from brain struc-tures which had been engineered for other functions, by co-opting them from their previous domains. In essence, language "colonized" the earlier hominid brain; the end result is the modern human brain, which is built for language, but not specifically genetically programed for it. In this view, language is not an optimal solution to the problem of human existence; it is a satisficing solution. But this satisficing solution has triggered fundamental shifts in the forms of viable trajectories for human beings. Some life traject-ories that were viable before we became language-bearing beings are no longer. Further, no one factor determined that becoming language-bearing beings would be a result of human evolution. The causes were multiple, "inner" (neurophysiological) and "outer" (social), co-implicating each other through continuous structural coupling. But, having followed this traject-ory, the end result, we modern humans, are now thoroughly language-constituted beings. To be human and to be language bearing is inseparable. Maturana and Varela (1987:234–5) express this most eloquently:

> It is by languaging that the act of knowing, in the behavioral coordination which is language, brings forth a world. We work out our lives in a mutual linguistic coupling, not because language permits us to reveal ourselves but because we are constituted in language in a continuous becoming that we bring forth with others. We find ourselves in this co-ontogenic coupling, not as a preexisting reference nor in reference to an origin, but as an ongoing transformation in the becoming of the linguistic world that we build with other human beings.

Epilog: Are Great Apes Capable of Language?

We have argued that within the hominid line a linguistic system, proto-language, goes back at least to *Homo habilis*, about 2 million years ago. The hominid line diverged from that of our closest living relatives, the two species of chimpanzees, about 5 million years ago. Chimpanzees do not naturally have any communication system similar to proto-language, but is there any reason to believe that they have a capacity for language approximating that of *Homo habilis*? Recent work in the teaching of symbolic systems to chimpanzees does indeed indicate that they do.

All three great apes, chimpanzees, gorillas and orangutans, have been the subjects of language-teaching experiments (Gardner, Gardner, and Van Cantfort 1989; Greenfield and Savage-Rumbaugh 1990; Miles 1990; Patterson and Linden 1982; Savage-Rumbaugh 1986; Savage-Rumbaugh and Lewin 1994), but the most intensive research has been with the two species of chimpanzees, so I will focus on these here. Because the vocal tract of chimpanzees differs so radically from that of humans, they are unable to master the phonemes of spoken language. Therefore, the linguistic systems taught to chimpanzees have used the visual medium rather than the vocal–auditory one. The earliest example of this was the well-reported case of Washoe, a common chimpanzee who was taught American Sign Language (ASL). She acquired well over a hundred distinct unit signs and combined these to produce complex messages like *Roger Lucy tickle*. This approach has since been used with other common chimpanzees with similar or better results. A second approach favored by those working at the Yerkes Language Research Center in Georgia is to use arbitrary geometric figures called lexigrams as linguistic signs. This approach has been used with both common chimpanzees and the rare pygmy chimpanzee or bonobo. Both species have acquired large vocabularies (upwards of 150) of lexigrams and combine these to signal complex messages. In particular, one individual of the latter species, Kanzi, shows a remarkable facility in the use of these lexigrams.

But do these lexigram sequences constitute sentences as used in language? To a certain extent, this depends on how one defines language. But it must be emphasized that the linguistic system mastered by a chimpanzee like Kanzi does not differ to any significant extent in formal complexity from those of a 2 to $2\frac{1}{2}$ year-old child. Whether this constitutes language is largely a matter of taste. It also should be pointed out that Kanzi demonstrates a quite high degree of competence in the comprehension of ordinary spoken English, even rather long sentences of fairly complex syntax. This strongly argues for his capacity for language: if an adult language speaker suffers brain damage and loses the ability to speak, but his comprehension is unimpaired, we do not hesitate to accord a language capacity to him. *Ceteris paribus*, the same judgment should be extended to Kanzi.

Let us inquire further into whether Kanzi and other chimpanzees have language by comparing their linguistic behavior with the features of human language discussed in chapter 1. The first question concerns whether the lexigrams are truly symbolic; do the chimpanzees really understand the basic arbitrary and abstract meanings these geometrical figures stand for? The answer to this question is clearly in the affirmative. Two common chimpanzees, Sherman and Austin, were able to look at lexigram symbols and answer questions that required understanding the meanings that these signified. For example, given the lexigrams for "key," "lever," "stick," "wrench," "apple," "banana," "pineapple" and "juice," they were asked to state whether each belonged to the class of "food" or "tool." To do this they needed to understand the semantic notions involved, and both performed this task with little difficulty (Savage-Rumbaugh and Rumbaugh 1993). Kanzi learned words by listening to speech, as do children; this was typically matched to the lexigram because his caretakers pointed to figures on his lexigram board when they spoke. He learned the word "strawberries" when he heard people mention the word as they came across wild strawberries in the forest. He soon learned to lead people to strawberries when asked to do so orally, as well as a number of other outdoor foods like wild grapes, honeysuckle, privet berries, blackberries and mushrooms, demonstrating he understood the distinct concepts for each of these words (Savage-Rumbaugh and Lewin 1994). This is interesting to note here and elsewhere, as with children, Kanzi's comprehension competence significantly outstrips his production.

This demonstrates that the notion of these lexigrams as symbols is well understood by these chimpanzees. Other parts of the "cognitive component" of language are also well within their abilities. For example, like a 2-year-old child, Kanzi seems to have a basic inventory of participant roles in sentences played by the meanings ascribed to lexigrams (Greenfield and Savage-Rumbaugh (1990) and Savage-Rumbaugh and Rumbaugh (1993)). Notions like agent, patient and location and, among location, sub-types like *in*, *on*, *to*, are all clearly understood and expressed in sentences produced by Kanzi. Sentences like *bite cherry* (patient) and *Penny* (agent) *tickle* illustrate the use of these notions in sentences produced by Kanzi.

When we come to the "computational component" of language, it is here that we find the greatest controversy concerning ape-language abilities. It has been claimed that apes do not make use of syntax, but this seems only partially true. Apes clearly do make extensive use, both in production and comprehension, of serial order of linguistic symbols. For example, a number of experiments were performed with Kanzi to see if he understood the syntactic function of serial order. He was instructed to carry out different actions distinguished only in the order of words, like *pour coke in the lemonade* versus *pour lemonade in the coke*. Kanzi was correct on 80 percent of such sentences, demonstrating a clear understanding of the syntactic function of word order in English. However, his capacities in production are significantly less, as expected. Serial order is still significant, but the principles governing order in Kanzi's sentence production are quite different from those of the model-language English. His productions are rarely more than two words, although they are novel and their meanings cannot be conveyed by single words (Savage-Rumbaugh and Rumbaugh 1993). The serial order is not rigid and potential ambiguity can result, but the basic principles are: (1) the action symbol precedes the patient symbol (in about 70 percent of all cases) and (2) the action symbol precedes a deictic gesture pointing to the agent (in over 90 percent of all cases) (Savage-Rumbaugh and Lewin 1994). There is some flexibility, especially in the first case, but the overall patterns are clear and demonstrate a productive use of word order in Kanzi's productions. It should also be emphasized that the importance of word order for syntactic relations in human languages has very frequently been greatly overblown by linguists trying to refute evidence of linguistic skills in apes. Not a few human languages have quite free word order, sometimes with great ambiguity in the encoding of syntactic relations and concepts like subject and object; for a good example, see Lisu (Hope 1974). Kanzi's production skills for serial order, while limited, do constitute behavior we could call language.

But serial ordering is only one side of syntax, the syntagmatic one. The other side, paradigmatic choices leading to hierarchically structured composite units like phrases or recursive structures, are largely lacking. This correlates with the earlier discussed inability of chimpanzees to produce tools of a composite form (Reynolds 1983, 1993). All that chimpanzees appear to be able to muster in this domain are compounds of two or occasionally three symbols, like Kanzi's *balloon water* to describe balloons filled with Koolaid (Greenfield 1991) or Washoe's *fruit drink* for "watermelon" and *food cry strong* for "radish." These are minimal composite units, but represent the upper bound for chimpanzees in hierarchically composed structures, a limit they share with children of around 2 years of age. Children, of course, go on to bigger and better things, but chimpanzees stop here, a fact probably due to their lack of specialized neuronal systems for language, although Kanzi appears to *understand* complex hierarchical structures when used in the spoken English addressed to him.

Whether the ability to produce hierarchically structured composite units is the crucial line which separates language from non-language is really a matter of taste; I prefer to take a more holistic view, treating this as just one of a number of defining features of language. However, if one does insist on this as the crucial feature of human language, then chimpanzees probably have not crossed this Rubicon. But, then again, probably neither had *Homo habilis* or *Homo erectus*, so possession of language could not be characteristic of the genus *Homo*, a rather counterintuitive result. Rather, it seems to me more preferable to state that chimpanzees, *Homo habilis* and *Homo erectus* do or did have a type of language, or proto-language to be more exact, which differs from all contemporary human languages in being lexically and structurally less elaborated. This is entirely what we would expect. Modern human languages are the result of 2 million years of social living, using language as a primary way of forging and preserving interpersonal relationships. This way of life generated ongoing social cooperation, linguistically mediated, with a continual increase in the ability to make distinctions in this realm. These distinctions in turn became a catalyst in the extension of the domains of social life, with the result of still more distinctions. And so on. Chimpanzees have not had the benefit of this process of social and linguistic development, and so we should not expect their linguistic behavior to match ours in every respect. Chimpanzees in the wild do not speak or sign or point to lexigrams; they have very different behavioral choices than humans, very different modes of life. Within their evolutionary trajectory, the conservation of their modes of life, language has not played a role, as it has for the hominid line. But Kanzi shows that maybe it could have, had different trajectories of satisficing been followed by chimpanzee ancestors. The important point is not whether chimpanzees and the other great apes are capable of language. That point can probably be debated interminably, with ever restrictive definitions of language. What is important is how much we share, how our linguistic capacities were already inchoate in our common ancestor more than 5 million years ago.

Further Reading

On theories of evolution, see Dawkins (1986) and Maynard Smith (1986) for good introductions to neo-Darwinism, and Ho and Saunders (1984), Maturana and Varela (1987), Oyama (1985) and Varela, Thompson, and Rosch (1991) for alternatives along the lines of the natural drift theory. Ondling Smee (1994) is also an interesting new approach to evolutionary theory.

For an introduction to human evolution and prehistory, one can do no better than Jones, Martin, and Pilbeam (1992), but also consult Mellars and Stringer (1989). Falk (1993) is very good on neurological evolution, as is Corballis (1991).

On the evolution of language, Bickerton (1990) is a good place to start. Other sources are Aiello and Dunbar (1993), Dunbar (1993), Lieberman (1984, 1991), Noble and Davidson (1991), and Pinker and Bloom (1990). Gibson and Ingold (1992) is an excellent collection of articles dealing with the interrelationship of language and skilled hand manipulation in tool making.

The linguistic capacities of apes have been the subject of much debate over the last 30 years; see Goodall (1986), Parker and Gibson (1990), Patterson and Linden (1982), and Savage-Rumbaugh (1994). Premack (1986) is a highly critical review of these claims for linguistic capacities in apes.

Part III
Universalism: Innate Constraints on Mind

3

Mind, Universals, and the Sensible World

Plato's Cave and the Theory of Universal Innate Ideas

As developed in chapter 1, anthropological linguistics is the study of how humans make meanings together in social interaction through conventional transgenerational cultural and linguistic practices. Part III looks at some potentially universal constraints on the kinds of meanings that humans can ascribe to signs and the systems that these might form. But first, I want to look at some of the typical forms that theories of universals have taken. Since at least the time of Boas (1966[1911]), but certainly before, it has been received wisdom among social sciences like anthropology and linguistics to assert the doctrine of the "psychic unity of humankind" – the equal capacities of all races of *Homo sapiens*. In practice this has largely involved asserting the fundamental unity in mental functioning of all humans. But even a cursory glance at the world reveals not unity, but diversity, at all levels of human cultural, social, and linguistic behavior. This apparent contradiction has been resolved by invoking a fundamental distinction between appearances and reality, behind the apparent surface diversity lies a deeper and more real unity, from which the surface diversity is generated, ultimately, it is hoped, in explicitly stateable ways.

This view is nothing if not venerable and traditional, being traceable back to Plato and reflected in the famous parable of the cave in his best known work, *The Republic*. A group of people are described as spending their entire lives in a cave. Chains shackle them so that they may only gaze upon a back wall of the cave. A fire behind them causes shadows to be cast on the wall; these are all they can see of the objects behind them. For Plato, this parable summarizes the nature of human understanding. Beyond the changeability and variety of sensible things in the world lies a transcendent timeless plane of pure and complete forms or ideas. Consider one of Plato's examples; the notion of Equality. No two sticks are ever exactly equal: and in any case no measurements could ever be exact enough to conclusively demonstrate this. The idea of equality exists beyond any physical manifestation of it in the material world. It exists in another world, that of ideas, in which it is perfectly, purely, and timelessly manifest only to the mind itself. Knowledge of these ideas is the only true kind of knowledge; only the timeless can truly be known, everything else is imperfect, contingent. Finally, the ideas are the explanation of the sensible world. Whatever reality there is in the material world comes from the ideas behind it; a particular material chair, for example, gets its reality as a chair from the idea "chair" beyond all its specific manifestations in the material world.

Plato's views have had an enormous influence in the history of Western thought and, under modern guise, they continue to do so today. They are usually articulated today in the modern form given them by the rationalist thinkers of the seventeenth century, such as Descartes, Spinoza, and Leibniz. The basic doctrine of rationalism is that knowledge of the world can be arrived at by pure reasoning, without any necessary appeal to experience of the material world. This is accomplished by the innate endowment within the human mind of the faculty of reason. The faculty of reason contains innately endowed concepts such as substance or causation, not derived from experience, but through which we understand experience. Because these are innate, they are given in essentially the same form to all humans, i.e. they are universal. In a rationalist framework it is these universals of reason which are of interest, not the unpredictable flux of sensible experience. Note again that it is a system of ideas located in the mind and the faculty of reason which are the fundamental reality; the experiential world of material things is of secondary importance (Descartes 1951[1641]:75):

> I cannot doubt that there is in me a certain passive faculty of perceiving, that is, of receiving and recognizing the ideas of sensible objects; but it would be valueless to me and I could in no way use it if there were not also in me or in something else, another active faculty capable of forming and producing these ideas.

The ancestry of rationalist thought in Plato's ideas could hardly be more striking. Because of the primacy given to the transcendent universal ideas in this intellectual tradition, it has long favored a deductive, theory centered, approach to the investigation of research questions, postulating fundamental innate mental concepts or principles from which actual behavior or experience is generated. Within current linguistics this view is pervasive. Thinkers as diverse as Chomsky (1980, 1988) and Wierzbicka (1980, 1992a) both propose theories of language with strong rationalist commitments. For example, Chomsky (1988) believes that the child is born with a rich innate endowment for the acquisition of language, with many highly specific facts about the nature of language to be acquired already set down in this endowment. Experience, in the form of the language of the speech community in which the child grows up, plays a strictly secondary and ancillary role, as a possible trigger for the acquisition process and as a guide in determining grammatical properties acquired when the innate endowment is underdetermined by permitting a choice, e.g. whether the grammar has VO or OV word order. Anna Wierzbicka's (1980, 1992a) postulated 30-odd universal semantic primitives from which all meanings of natural languages can be generated is similar in inspiration, although radically different in design. Both of these thinkers display robustly rationalist and Platonic agendas: behind the language forms observed exists an unobservable but generative system of purely mental and innate ideas.

The Kantian Synthesis

The rationalist agenda also plays an important role in other cognitive-oriented disciplines like anthropology and psychology, and Kant's (1958 [1781]) grand synthesis has been especially important here. Kant's great achievement was his reconciliation of rationalist/Platonic views with the opposing ideas of empiricist philosophy, which held that knowledge was acquired by practical sensible experience and not conferred by innately endowed reason. This school is represented in the Western tradition mainly by British philosophers such as Locke, Berkeley and Hume, and continues to be highly influential among English-speaking philosophers today. Kant himself was somewhat of rationalist stripe, but both rationalism and empiricism influenced him. Indeed, his *Critique of Pure Reason* is a valiant attempt at a synthesis of these two schools of philosophy, although the final result is clearly more of a rationalist treatise, in the positing of innate and universal mental concepts, than an empiricist one. Contrary to the rationalists, Kant claimed that knowledge was not simply reducible to innate principles, but on balance, contrary to the empiricists, he argued that knowledge is not the reflex of experience. We know the world through concepts, often innately given, but it is nonetheless independent of our concepts. Because our knowledge of the world is mediated by concepts, we can never have direct knowledge of it; we can only have knowledge of appearances. Here reappears Plato's contrast between sensible appearance and ideal reality, but Kant contradicts Plato by claiming that our knowledge is *only* through appearances. Direct knowledge of ideal timeless notions of reality is beyond our reach. Further, what is directly presented to the mind is not a holistic and prestructured appearance, but sensible impressions (perceptions, sensory data, such as sounds, smells, images, etc.) coming to the mind from the appropriate sense organs. These are a kaleidoscopic flux of changing unorganized impressions. This, thus far, is an empiricist position, but from where, then, comes our understanding of an ordered, predictable, and structured appearance of reality?

At this point Kant puts on his rationalist hat. The appearance of reality is due to the imposition of innate mental concepts upon the perceptual data from our sense organs. Our minds construct this order, as the rationalist would claim. These innate, universally pre-given categories are various. For example, we experience all things as embedded in space and time. These concepts are grounds of our existence, and formative of all our understanding of reality. Innate categories of the mind include mathematical ideas like quantity concepts (unity, plurality and totality), modality concepts (possibility, existence and necessity), and relational concepts (cause and effect). These categories are what the mind brings to sensation to organize it. Thus, our experience is a function of both the cognitive-organizing activity of the mind through its innate pre-given ideas and the distributed, data-acquiring functions of our sense organs. The links between the raw sensory data and the innate pre-given categories are provided by what Kant called schemas. These provide the principles determining how the pre-given categories are linked to a particular sense impression, for example, how "red color" is tied to a particular sensory impression of this color. This schema is activated by this particular sensory data, but calls into operation a mental category providing a coherent understanding of this data, hence an experience of it. In modern terminology, Kant has foreshadowed the idea of mental representations, a relationship between the physical, sensory world and the structure-giving categories of the mind (Gardner 1985). This is a crucially important idea that I will return to later.

The Kantian Legacy

It is important to emphasize that Kant's mental categories are innate, structure building and universal, all features they share with the earlier Platonic and rationalist views. In this sense, Kant follows within this tradition. Kant's work has been enormously influential in Western thought since his time. Not only philosophy, but behavioral and social sciences generally, such as psychology and anthropology, commonly conceive of issues within a framework largely set up along Kantian lines. Indeed, much of the current work in cognitive psychology would be inconceivable without the background understanding provided by the Kantian synthesis sketched above. This does not mean, however, that all psychological and anthropological theorizing is strictly Kantian. Far from it. It is just that Kant's thought is often the unacknowledged background for this theorizing.

Many of the theoretical positions we find in modern cognitive sciences like psychology, linguistics, or anthropology are amendments, extensions, or contradictions of Kantian views. For example, the positions of relativism, the topic of the Part IV, come from contradicting Kant's rationalist assumption that the mental categories are innate, substantive, and universal. We can contradict this view in both a strong and weak form, leading to two forms of relativism. The strong position denies all such mental categories and claims in a strong empiricist view that they are learned through experience, while the weak position argues that some more general and abstract categories might be innate, but that the actual substantive form in which they are realized in the mind is the result of experience. Consider the category of space. The strong view claims that we have no innate understanding of space at all, even as an abstract idea of being somewhere, but that it is learned through experience of being in the world. As such, this strong view is probably untenable. The weaker form argues that space as some abstract notion of being located somewhere is innate and universal, but beyond this many substantive and structure-building concepts within this domain are learned through experience. This is a potentially supportable view, and, indeed, positions like this will be my concern in Part IV.

Although not a necessary pairing, approaches arising from phenomenology are closely linked to relativism in much of modern thought. As pointed out above, Kant followed Plato in asserting a sharp contrast between the sensible appearance of things and the ultimate reality as things in themselves, and further claimed that our experience is forever restricted to the former. Phenomenology is concerned with gaining access to the things themselves by an ultimate reduction to the fundamental elements which make up experience itself. The irreducible *sine qua non* of all experience is consciousness. But there can be no consciousness unto itself; there must be consciousness of something. All consciousness is directed, and knowledge is arrived at in the context of this directed orientation toward the world. Shweder's (1990) proposed new subdiscipline of cultural psychology is a good example of a phenomenologically inspired cognitive and social science. For him human understanding is embedded in everyday practical activities in which human beings interact with each other and the things of the world. Thinking is embedded in these practical activities; in a sense they are "tools for thought" (Shweder 1990:23). As these practices are culturally constructed and thought is embedded within them, to this extent knowledge is culturally constituted. Thus, a phenomenological stance and a relativist view of mental functioning are a logically compatible, although not necessary, pairing, and one well exemplified in modern anthropology, for example, in the theoretical work of Geertz (1973, 1983). The view of culture as embodied practices developed in chapter 1 is also quite clearly a phenomenologically inspired one.

Contemporary linguistics and psychology contrast strongly with anthropology in aligning themselves much more closely with the rationalist stream in Kant's thought. The strongly rationalist views of Chomsky (1980, 1988) with his postulation of a rich and innate endowment of mental structures strictly targeted for the faculty of language was discussed above. Indeed, Chomsky's position is much more extremely rationalist than that of Kant. For Chomsky, the role of sensible experience in determining the form of language is quite marginal; its structure is mainly projected from the innate and universal mental structures. Other linguists may disagree with Chomsky about the nature of these mental structures, how richly their structure is specified or whether they are, indeed, unique to language, but given the many robustly attested universals of human language, few linguists today would dispute the need for some innate and universal structures underlying the forms of human language. Many would, however, argue that the role of experience, in the sense of being a child in a particular speech community, surrounded by others speaking a language with specific structural properties and uses, is quite central in the process and results of language acquisition.

It is within psychology that the Kantian legacy is probably at its most transparent. The subject matter of psychology is the psyche, and it is assumed within this discipline that this capacity is the same for all human beings. Psychology assumes a central-processing mechanism within all human beings, through which we think, experience, and learn. The aim of psychology is to describe this central-processing mechanism, which is assumed to be fixed, universal and abstract, in the most explicit terms possible. We must achieve access to this capacity by factoring out the various distorting effects of the culturally constructed environment. Hence, the practices of experimental psychology revolve around context free, novel, and often meaningless stimuli – all the better to reveal the formal universal central processor. When faced with significant cross-cultural differences in cognitive functioning (Cole and Scribner 1974), psychology takes refuge in its Kantian dogma: (1) either there is a problem in the test design, with unacceptable test materials of a culturally specific sort, so that the universal central processor has been unable to reveal itself or (2) the central processor is not yet fully developed in certain "primitive" peoples, due to cultural design, though the capacity is latent there (Hallpike 1979; see also Lévy-Bruhl 1926). In all cases, the basic idea is to transcend these vagaries of performance in order to unveil the true abstract forms and activities of the pre-given central-processing device common to all human beings.

The Use of Representations in Cognitive Studies

All cognitive disciplines following a rationalist approach to cognition share Kant's concern with epistemology – how is knowledge arrived at, experience understood? Many current approaches also favor invoking his solution of internal representations – forms or processes in the mind which re-present the objects or events in the sensory world. Knowledge then consists of acting on the basis of these mental representations. Thus, there is a crucial third level, a level of mental representations between the sensible world of things and physical world of chemical transference within neurons in the brain. The forms of these mental representations are commonly symbolic, in the sense discussed many times earlier, an abstract linking of a physical form with an arbitrary meaning. For example, the English phoneme /b/ may be one such mental representation. It is not reducible to the many varied articulatory events which may produce a voiced bilabial stop nor does it correspond exactly to the neurons stimulated in the brain when such a sound is received auditorily. Rather, it transcends yet links both of these. It is the organizing bit of the mind that knits the sensible events of the world and the neuronal activity of the brain together. In short, it is a mental representation.

In such a perspective, then, cognition is viewed as computations using these mental representations. The metaphor of the mind as a computer is very apt here. Some basic input in the form of sensory data is fed to the mind, which activates a set of mental representations. By manipulating these mental representations, the cognizer becomes aware of the mental experience corresponding to the sensory data. Modern grammatical theories provide good examples of these "information processing" – symbol manipulating – approaches to cognition. Consider the sentence *the farmer killed the duckling*. The articulatory sequence of events associated with *killed* calls up in a speaker of English a lexical entry for this word, which tells us that it is the past tense of a verb root *kill*. The lexical entry or mental representation for this verb provides a speaker with an enormous amount of information, e.g. that it means someone or something causes someone or something else to become dead, that both the causing participant and the affected participant are logically necessary to any sentence using this verb, and that the causing participant functions as the subject (before the verb) and the affected participant as the object (after the verb). This information from the mental representation for *kill* in turn is integrated with that from *the farmer* and *the duckling*, so that we know ultimately that *the farmer* is the causing participant and *the duckling* the affected participant. Such a model of sentence processing transparently illustrates the symbolic manipulation, or more commonly, information-processing approach to cognition.

Universals and Representations

The full rationalist thrust of the Kantian legacy to the symbolic manipulation approach to cognition emerges in the nature of the symbols themselves and the rules of their interaction. The usual strong claim is made here: the basic vocabulary of symbols and their rules of combination are claimed to be innate and universal, the manifestation of the psychic unity of humankind. Wierzbicka's (1980, 1992a) claim of 30-odd semantic primitives, which, through the use of simple but specifiable rules of combination, can be used to express the meanings of words in all languages, is a striking example of this approach to cognition. The fundamental ideas of Lévi-Strauss (1966) concerning paradigmatic binary oppositions, to be discussed in the next chapter, are another. Again, a linguistic example might clarify. Compare the Yimas close equivalent of the English example discussed earlier:

klaki   panmal   ya-n-tu-t
parrot V PL male I SG V SG OBJ-I SG SUBJ-kill-PERF
"The man killed the parrots"

Within these universal assumptions, we would claim that the Yimas verb *tu-* has the same mental representation as the English verb *kill*. However, the purported universal grammatical relations of subject and object are signalled in Yimas not by word order, but by verbal morphology; the first prefix is the object and the second, the subject. Yimas has ten gender classes for its nouns. The prefix *ya-* indicates that the object is gender class V and plural, while *n-* indicates that the subject is gender class I and singular. These gender and number specifications link *ya-* to *klaki* "parrots" and *n-* to *panmal* "man, male," so the sentence must mean "the man killed the parrots."

It is crucial to note that proponents of approaches like these can disagree strongly among themselves on the nature and richness of the universal innate endowment in mental representations. In the comparative English and Yimas example sketched above, I localized much of the shared universal mental structures to the semantic or lexical arena, the identical mental representations for English *kill* and Yimas *tu-*. The syntactic and morphological organization of the two languages was treated as a language-specific random fact. Other approaches may be much more universalizing than this, arguing that all languages have the same basic underlying syntactic structure as well. Present-day Chomskian linguistics (Chomsky 1988; Haegeman 1994) is of this type. In this view, one would argue that the English and Yimas sentences would have the same basic *underlying* structure, but certain superficial and language-specific processes operate in these two languages to produce the visible differences between them. Once again we find the same age-old invocation for explanation to a Platonic contrast between a superficial, random, contingent but visible, appearance and a deep, universal, necessary, but veiled, reality.

Challenges to Representations: Connectionism and Enactionism

Approaches invoking mental representations are dominant within all cognitive disciplines today, philosophy, linguistics, and psychology. And models within anthropological linguistics which link a cognitive theory invoking mental representations to strong universalist claims about them will be the subject of the remainder of this Part. But first, I want to mention recent challenges to the theory of mental representations in the forms of alternative theories which dispense with them. These alternative theories are important in that they have informed previous chapters of this book, specifically the embodied practices theory of chapter 1, and will reappear in following chapters. These theories go by the name of connectionism (Bechtel and Abrahamsen 1991; Smolensky 1988) and enactionism (Maturana and Varela 1987; Varela, Thompson, and Rosch 1991). Both deny the necessity of mental representations as a kind of halfway house between the sensory world and neuronal activity. In connectionism, knowledge inheres in the connections between the neurons themselves (hence this school of thought's name); it is in neural networks, the connections among neurons and systems of neurons. These networks exhibit many thousands of connections among hundreds or thousands of units. A percept or concept, then, can be viewed as a consequence of changes in the strengths of certain connections among others in the network. An input is processed when a stable arrangement of values in the connections in the network sets in. Note that knowledge is emergent in this system, by hitting upon some global organization of the neural net that satisfies the task set by the sensory data. Thus a phoneme /b/ is cognized whenever the neural network for processing it is called up; the basic patterns of this network are said to be stable across all instances of its emergence. Note, further, that meaning and understanding are not located in particular symbolic mental representations; they are distributed, a function of the global state of the network and linked to its overall satisfactory performance in a task domain set by sensory data. No one cluster of neurons "codes" /b/; it resides in the emergent neural network.

Enactionism follows much of connectionism's agenda, but argues that it has not gone far enough. It claims that connectionism still suffers from the cognitivist hangover; i.e. cognition only happens in the head. Enactionism highlights the fundamental role of lived *embodied* action in all cognition. Connectionism still operates with a rationalist split between the sensible world and knowledge as neural networks in the head. Enactionism expands the network to our embodied being in a sensible, but *interactive* environment. "Mind and world arise together in enaction" (Varela, Thompson, and

Rosch 1991:177). The knower is in constant structural coupling with her world, and this interaction is neither mental nor strictly cognitive, but is fully embodied. "Furniture" is not some notion understood simply through a distributed neural network in the brain; it is something our bodies use, sit on, or sleep in. Knowledge is perceptually guided action in this view, bringing forth a meaningful world in which continued structural coupling is possible. This coupling is not optimal; as with evolutionary change, it is simply viable. Knowledge is a kind of lived history.

It is an interesting question to inquire about the position of universals in connectionism and enactionism. This question has been little discussed in connectionism. Universals could be stated as global formal constraints upon the arrangements and activation patterns of neural networks. If that is the case, then connectionism may face serious problems in capturing some of the many rich universals of patterns in human languages and cultures discussed in the rest of this Part. Enactionism is a more promising alternative. Given the nature of our human biology, universals can represent constraints derived from this realm in the possible choices of drift in structural coupling. This provides a much wider frame of interpretation for universals than does connectionism, as our universal human biology is not restricted just to our neurons and their connections, but includes the whole realm of our embodied existence as reflected in our interactions with each other and the world. The importance of this view will be apparent in later chapters of this Part.

Summary

The Platonic–Rationalist tradition of universal innate ideas underlying an apparent superficial diversity of experience is a hallowed one. Much modern work in the social and cognitive sciences assumes this tradition as an often unquestioned background assumption within which theorizing is done, especially in its Kantian articulation which assumes an intermediate level of mental representations between our sense experience and its neurological realization in the brain. Cognition is understood as computations using these mental representations. Universals of human cognition are put down to innate constraints on the properties of these mental representations, the debate in much of modern work in the cognitive sciences revolving around where to localize and how to state these innate constraints. Recent approaches, connectionism and enactionism, challenge directly this centrality given to mental representations in cognition, arguing that there is no need for this intermediate level of representation between the sensory world and neuronal activity, and that cognition should be seen as the result of networks of activity, either of neurons (connectionism) or the entire embodied organism and its environment (enactionism).

Further Reading

On the debate between rationalism and empiricism and Kant's resolution, see Anderson, Hughes, and Sharrock (1986) and Gardner (1985), and the many references therein. Chomsky (1968, 1980) and Wierzbicka (1980) are good introductions to rationalist approaches to universals in linguistics; for more empiricist approaches see Comrie (1989) and Hawkins (1988). Brown (1991) is an important source on putative anthropological universals. Connectionism is well summarized in Bechtel and Abrahamsen (1991), while Smolensky (1988) is an important new trend in this framework. Varela, Thompson, and Rosch (1991) introduce the enactionist alternative.

4

Structuralism

Saussure

The Platonic and rationalist legacy finds perhaps its strongest articulation within anthropology as structuralism, a school of thought closely tied to the work of French anthropologist Lévi-Strauss. The basic ideas, however, are not completely original with him, but go back to developments within linguistics in the first half of this century, particularly European structural linguistics. Indeed, linguistics and its methods of analysis was and continues to be the reigning model for much of the anthropological study of cognitive categories across cultures. This is perhaps even more true of the American school of cognitive anthropology to be discussed in the next chapter than it is for Lévi-Strauss, since in this school the analysis of cognitive categories within cultures depends almost entirely on a semantic analysis of the words and phrases used to label those categories in the native language. What attracts both Lévi-Strauss and these American cognitive anthropologists are the formal structural features of human languages; they try to extend these features to culture, construing cultural categories like the words of language. Culture is like a grammar, a formal code consisting of symbols and their logical relationships, and the job of the anthropologist is to crack this code, to unveil the logical workings of the human mind.

The structural linguistics which influences Lévi-Strauss stems from three sources: Saussure, a Swiss linguist whose posthumous *Course in General Linguistics* (1959[1916]) was highly influential; the Prague School, specifically through the work of Jakobson; and American descriptive linguists, mainly Boas, discussed in greater detail in Part IV. The first two influences are much stronger as structural anthropology as developed by Lévi-Strauss and his followers exhibits a markedly European-flavored type of structuralism; henceforth in this section structuralism refers to this particular European incarnation. The basic doctrine of structuralism is that the true nature of things lies not in the things themselves, but in the relationships between them. No element has any significance in itself, but only in relation to all elements in the system, so that it is the entire system with its axes of contrasts and comparisons which defines each and every element within it. Consider an example adapted from Saussure. What ultimately defines the daily 17.30 train from Sydney to Woy Woy? Clearly, it is nothing material nor substantive, not the individual cars nor passengers, for these change every day and so could not be the defining criteria. The defining features are not inherent in the train itself, but emerge from the system of daily train schedules which timetables this train with respect to all others. It is not the 17.15 train from Sydney to Katoomba nor is it the 18.30 train from Sydney to Woy Woy. It is the relational character of this train with respect to all other trains in the schedule which is its defining feature. And it remains the 17.30 Sydney to Woy Woy train even if it is an half-an-hour late. This is not important; what is crucial is that it be distinguished from the 18.30 Sydney to Woy Woy train. The system of contrasts as set up in the train timetable defines this train, not its actual real world realization as a particular string of cars with particular passengers departing at a particular (sometimes, later) time.

Structuralism Illustrated: The Phoneme

Ideas of contrast and structure inherent in systems are well known in the analysis of language and were pioneered by Saussure. They are perhaps easiest to illustrate in phonology. Consider the English word *bat*, which consists of three segments arranged in a particular sequence (*tab* is different from *bat*). *bat*, when pronounced, is a continuous burst of sound, not composed of a sequence of clearly segmentable discrete units. How do we know there are three segments? Further, each pronunciation of *bat* is somewhat different from every other pronunciation of the same word by different speakers and by the same speaker on different occasions (say, when under the influence of alcohol). How do we identify these physically different forms as the same word? What is the nature of the constancy behind this diversity?

The answer, of course, is the concept of the phoneme, a fixed identity within an overall structure of contrasting units. The pronunciation of *bat* may exhibit wide diversity, but each is contrastive with every other word in English, for example, *pat, mat, cat, sat, fat, vat, bit, bet, but, boat, beat, bought, back, bag, bad, bass, badge, batch*. We claim that English has a /b/phoneme, a /p/ phoneme, an /I/ phoneme, a /k/ phoneme, and so on because of the distinctness of these words. These words are distinct because different forms (*bat* versus *cat*) correspond to different meanings (a flying winged insectivorous or fruit-eating mammal versus a commonly domesticated ground-dwelling carnivorous mammal). Phonemes like /b/ and /p/ function as linguistically significant distinctive elements in English because of the overall system of phonological contrasts in this language, but they do not do so, say, in Yimas. In this language there is a single phoneme corresponding to these two, which varies between them, so that the word for "they two" can be pronounced as either [imban] or [impan]. For [p] and [b] in Yimas, substitution of one for the other causes no change in the discrimination of the word (a different form, but same meaning); a Yimas speaker hears both [imban] or [impan] as "they two." There is but one phoneme, here realized either as a [b] sound or a [p] sound.

This example illustrates general principles in the theory of structuralism. What counts is whether differences in form (in this case phonetic form) stand in a functioning system of contrast. Each language draws upon a different and in principle unique set of distinctions in the formal continuum of sound and makes them functional by employing them to make meaningful distinctions. What defines each unit, then, is its place in a specific system of contrasts. Consider the definition of the phoneme /ə/ in the vocalic phoneme inventories of Iatmul of New Guinea and Trukese:

Iatmul	Trukese		
ɨ	i	ɨ	u
ə	e	ə	o
a	ɛ	a	ɔ

The value of /ə/ in Iatmul and Trukese is very different. In Iatmul it is contrasted only along an axis of vowel height, with the other central vowels /ɨ/ and /a/, but in Trukese, not only is it contrasted along an axis of height, but also one of frontness and backness of vowels with /e/ and /o/. The phonetic quality of /ə/ in Iatmul and Trukese may be very close, but their values as phonemes are very different. A phoneme is not a physically identifiable unit; it is an abstract theoretical construct, postulated as a locus for the axes of functioning contrasts in the system of forms. These relations of contrast are prior to the forms which encode them. Such are the tenets of structuralism.

Contributions of the Prague School

This notion of functioning contrast was given a great boost in formal rigor with the ideas of the Prague School. They noted that these functioning contrasts formed sets of oppositions defined through phonetic features (4.1). Using these phonetic features set up through the contrastive oppositions, one could actually uniquely define the phonemic units themselves (4.2).

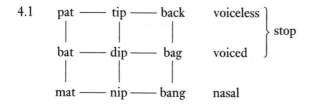

4.1
$$
\begin{array}{ccc}
\text{pat} \text{---} & \text{tip} \text{---} & \text{back} \\
| & | & | \\
\text{bat} \text{---} & \text{dip} \text{---} & \text{bag} \\
| & | & | \\
\text{mat} \text{---} & \text{nip} \text{---} & \text{bang}
\end{array}
\qquad
\begin{array}{l}
\text{voiceless} \\
\\
\text{voiced} \\
\\
\text{nasal}
\end{array}
$$

$\left.\begin{array}{l}\text{voiceless}\\\text{voiced}\end{array}\right\}$ stop

bilabial   alveolar   velar

4.2 /b/ $\begin{bmatrix}\text{stop}\\\text{voiced}\\\text{bilabial}\end{bmatrix}$ /n/ $\begin{bmatrix}\text{nasal}\\\text{alveolar}\end{bmatrix}$ /k/ $\begin{bmatrix}\text{stop}\\\text{voiceless}\\\text{velar}\end{bmatrix}$

Jakobson (1968) pushed this structural thesis one step further. Noting the metaphysical thesis behind the concept of opposition, he attempted to restate all oppositions as binary, i.e. two poles of contrast along a single dimension. He devised universal binary features, where the two poles could be defined as the presence (+) versus absence (−) of a feature. Jakobson's phonetic features were based on acoustic parameters, and we can state the defining properties of phonemes in terms of these features. Consider how this would apply to the phonemic system of stops in Yimas:

p   t   c   k

The Yimas stops are all voiceless, but contrast in the place of articulation: bilabial, dental, palatal, and velar. The phonemic features Jakobson would have used to describe these phonemes are: (1) grave versus acute: low–high frequency of sound waves (pitch) and (2) diffuse versus compact: low–high noise energy (loudness) (in more recent phonology, the phonetic features used might differ, but the basics of the analysis would remain the same). Now, the Yimas stop phonemes can be represented in binary features as shown in 4.3. Each unit can then be described in terms of its component features (4.4) (this is a type of componential analysis, discussed in the next chapter).

English, of course, contrasts with Yimas in lacking a palatal stop phoneme, so its voiceless stops would be represented as in 4.5. Note, again, that /k/ in Yimas and English, while phonetically quite similar, are phonemically distinct due to the sorts of contrastive oppositions in the system. Jakobson also introduced the notion of markedness into the system. This is ultimately a claim that one of the two poles in the opposition is more basic and is used in defining the nature of the opposition. The other pole is expressed as the absence of this defining feature. Thus, for [grave]–[acute], [grave] is the unmarked member of the pair; [grave] is therefore stated as [+grave] and

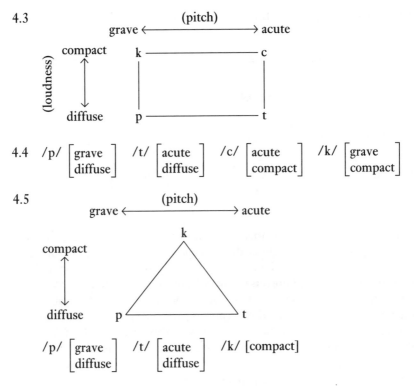

4.3

4.4 /p/ $\begin{bmatrix} \text{grave} \\ \text{diffuse} \end{bmatrix}$ /t/ $\begin{bmatrix} \text{acute} \\ \text{diffuse} \end{bmatrix}$ /c/ $\begin{bmatrix} \text{acute} \\ \text{compact} \end{bmatrix}$ /k/ $\begin{bmatrix} \text{grave} \\ \text{compact} \end{bmatrix}$

4.5

/p/ $\begin{bmatrix} \text{grave} \\ \text{diffuse} \end{bmatrix}$ /t/ $\begin{bmatrix} \text{acute} \\ \text{diffuse} \end{bmatrix}$ /k/ [compact]

acute as [−grave]. The English voiceless consonants can then be restated using the +/− notation (4.6).

Structuralism and the Meaning of the Sign

I have spent the last several paragraphs outlining the structural approach to analysis of the formal, phonological pole of the linguistic sign, but structuralism has not neglected the meaning pole, and it is its labors in this area which are probably more germane to the field of anthropological linguistics. The same basic structuralist tenets are applied to the analysis of meaning. Saussure himself was a strong relativist in this domain, although more rationalist, universalist themes emerge in later work, notably Lévi-Strauss. For Saussure, the meanings arbitrarily attached to the forms in the overall structure of the sign are *not* preexisting concepts. Meanings and concepts like phonemes only emerge in a system. The meanings of signs are contingent and vary across languages and, within languages, across historical ages. There is no essential core of meaning, contrary to Kant, no fixed universal concepts. As is typical of structuralism, the meaning of a sign is defined

4.6 /p/ $\begin{bmatrix} + \text{ grave} \\ - \text{ compact} \end{bmatrix}$ /t/ $\begin{bmatrix} - \text{ grave} \\ - \text{ compact} \end{bmatrix}$ /k/ [+ compact]

grave

+   −

+   k

compact

−   p   t

relationally. Each language sets up a different set of meanings, a distinct and arbitrary way of organizing the world into concepts and categories; this is essentially an empiricist approach to cognition. Meanings are arbitrary divisions of a continuum, and the meanings of a sign are therefore determined by those of other signs dividing up the same continuum. Consider the meaning of the color term *orange*, an issue we will have cause to return to in chapter 7. How do we know the meaning of this color? With Saussurean structuralism, only by virtue of the fact that it contrasts with a whole set of color terms which divide up the color-spectrum continuum: *red, yellow, green, blue, violet, black, white*, etc. Only when we understand the relationship between *orange* and these other color terms do we know the meaning of *orange*. *Orange*, then, is not an independent concept defined by some essential property, but one term in a system of color terms, defined by its relations with other terms which delimit it; *orange* is what is not-*red*, not-*yellow*, etc. To understand it, we must understand them; it is the product of a system of distinctions, just as a phoneme is.

And just as phonemes have different values in different languages depending on the system of functional oppositions, the meanings of superficially synonymous words in different languages are construed as distinct, constructed from varying semantic oppositions. Saussure's example concerns English *sheep* versus French *mouton*. He asserts that these two words are distinct in meaning, because English *sheep* contrasts with *mutton*, as animal to edible meat, while French *mouton* covers both of these. For Saussure, each language is a unique system, whose system of meanings, like its phonemic system, must be understood in its own terms. Cognitively, this has strongly relativistic implications, as the categories encoded in natural language only rarely have exact crosslinguistic equivalents. As such, Saussure's strong position is untenable, as the next chapter will demonstrate. For example, English contrasts *river* with *stream* (both moving bodies of water, with an idealized linear shape) and *pond* and *lake* (both stationary bodies of water, with an idealized round shape) along a dimension of size. Yimas makes no use of this size opposition, but does of the other one, *armp* "river, stream" versus *upŋk* "lake, pond." For Saussure, the meanings of English *lake* and Yimas *upŋk* are utterly distinct, because they participate in different systems of semantic contrast. If we hold Saussure's position, however, it is difficult to account for why Yimas *upŋk* enters into the same opposition with *armp* that English *lake* does with *river*. It seems more profitable to argue that the meanings of English *lake* and Yimas *upŋk* are actually very close, with just an additional semantic contrast inherent in English *lake* to distinguish it from *pond*. This also suggests that Saussure's strong relativism in the domain of linguistic concepts is misguided, but that some universal organizing principles may be at work here, a view Lévi-Strauss propounds with vigor.

Lévi-Strauss's Innovations

The crucial innovation of Lévi-Strauss to structuralist theory was to extend the Prague School notion of defining oppositional features to the analysis of meaning and, ultimately, cultural categories. As these Praguean phonetic features are drawn from a smallish, presumably universally available set, similar expectations could be held for the semantic oppositions which generate the basic meaningful categories of languages and cultures. Hence, Lévi-Strauss abandons Saussure's empiricism for a strongly rationalist position. The human mind is everywhere the same; what distinguishes French culture from, say, Yimas culture are the particular arrangements of the culture generating semantic oppositions. The surface differences are stripped away to reveal the underlying similarity of organization of all cultures (a Platonic perspective), generated by an innately endowed human mind which is everywhere the same (rationalist assumptions). Contrary to much of European anthropology prior to him (see, for example, Lévy-Bruhl (1921)), Lévi-Strauss denies significant differences in the thought processes of so-called "primitive" or non-Western peoples and the modern scientific Western culture. Rather, it is due to the nature of the materials they "think with" that the differences emerge. Traditional non-Western peoples have an inductive "science of the concrete" (Lévi-Strauss 1966:1), making generalizations from primary sensible data, an approach opposed to our scientific paradigms, which emphasize abstract measurements and deductive formal principles, but the same basic thought processes inform both.

Lévi-Strauss (1966:269) writes:

> Certainly the properties to which the savage mind has access are not the same
> as those which have commanded the attention of scientists. The physical

world is approached from opposite ends in the two cases: one is supremely concrete, the other supremely abstract; one proceeds from the angle of sensible qualities and the other form that of formal properties. But if, theoretically at least and on condition no abrupt changes in perspective occurred, these two courses might have been destined to meet, this explained that they should have both, independently of each other in time and space, led to two distinct though equally positive sciences: one which flowered in the neolithic period, whose theory of the sensible order provided the basis of the arts of civilization (agriculture, animal husbandry, pottery, weaving, conservation and preparation of food, etc.) and which continues to provide for our basic needs by these means; and the other, which places itself from the start at the level of intelligibility, and of which contemporary science is the fruit.

The basic method of the "science of the concrete" is classification; indeed, for him, the principle function of all minds is to classify. True to his rationalist credo, Lévi-Strauss claims that all individuals, "primitive" or "civilized," classify along the same lines and use the same methods. The "science of the concrete" differs from Western science in that its practitioners classify things in terms of their everyday, overt sensible features, rather than the underlying abstract features that the scientist uses. The classifications and categories resulting from these two systems, of course, are often quite different, but the basic thought processes that gave rise to them remain the same.

What are these thought processes? They are distinctive features of semantic oppositions, very much like the phonetic features of structural linguistics. In parallel to these too, the number of semantic oppositions which generate cultural categories are limited, drawn from a universal set of potentiality. The systems thus generated are therefore not unlimited; indeed, some can be viewed as no more than formal permutations of others. Lévi-Strauss illustrates the ideas most extensively in his analysis of the phenomenon of totemism (Lévi-Strauss 1964, 1966). Totemism is common among many traditional peoples; it involves beliefs linking certain local animals, plants, or other objects with certain social groupings, typically a clan. The members of the crocodile clan may believe themselves descended from this animal, have certain rituals associated with it, and perhaps have a taboo on eating it or speaking the name. The phenomenon has long puzzled anthropologists, but Lévi-Strauss sees it as a prime example of his "science of the concrete." Totemic classifications reflect a system of oppositions through which the Native organizes the social units of his culture. These oppositions relate these social units to each other, isomorphically to the ordering in the natural world among the totemic objects. A set of natural objects organizes a set of cultural ones.

In deciding how to order the totemic objects, for example, animal species, again the principles of the "science of the concrete" are applied. The

4.7

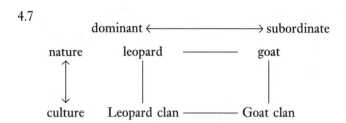

Native chooses classificatory features that reflect the sensible qualities unique to each species. These distinguishing classificatory features serve, by analogy, to organize the culture's social units, for the two are connected by the same logical principles, mere formal transformations of each other. Lévi-Strauss (1966:61) provides a telling example in the Luapula of Zambia. For example, they have a Leopard and Goat clan. Culturally, these clans stand in a joking relationship, a social metaphor of the natural relationship in which leopards eat goats. This could be represented as 4.7.

The point for Lévi-Strauss is that oppositions like this which generate these systems of classification are good to think with. It is these structure-building thought processes which distinguish humans from animals, culture from nature. As nature is an always given datum through our sensible experience, humans imitate our understanding of nature in the cultural categories we construct. The products of our cultures are ordered in the same way as we understand the products of nature to be ordered. This is always the case with human thought; totemism is merely an especially transparent example. The object of ethnography is to discover how the relations we apprehend in nature are used to generate cultural products. Ultimately, then, ethnography is a study of the processes of human thought. But Lévi-Strauss is a strong rationalist: the structure of human thought is everywhere ultimately the same, the product of an innate, universal endowment. Therefore, the systems which generate cultural categories are underlying everywhere the same; universals of human culture are at the level of deep underlying structure, not superficial fact. It is the principles of binary opposition and analogical transformation which structure the systems in which all cultural categories are generated. Ethnography as a science needs to study these principles, bracketing the cultural context so these pristine principles of structuring can emerge. A structure which appears at one level with given cultural content may reappear elsewhere with entirely different content. The structure is the goal; the observed differences in content are irrelevant. Further, because of the axiom of absolute universality of these principles, what can be discovered by analyzing cultural categories and products in one culture is merely a formal transformation of those in completely different cultures.

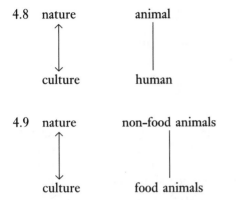

4.8 nature animal

  culture human

4.9 nature non-food animals

  culture food animals

An Example of Structural Analysis in Anthropology: Taboo in English

To understand what all this entails in practical cultural and linguistic description, it is best to work through in some detail an example of structuralist analysis in anthropological linguistics. I have chosen a particularly clear and interesting study by Edmund Leach (1964) concerning taboo and animal terms of abuse in English. The themes here are similar in some respects to those of totemism, so it is a particularly apropos choice. We are interested in explaining why *you swine* is an effective epithet in English, but *you polar bear* induces only laughter. The basic distinction between animals and humans is that animals belong to nature and humans to culture (4.8). This is the basic opposition responsible for totemism as discussed above. However, other than functioning as objects good to think with in totemic classifications, the other basic concern of humans with animals is as food. Of course, what counts as food is a cultural construct. Yimas people regard snakes as inedible and find the idea of eating them revolting, yet they are a delicacy among the neighboring Arafundi people. So, to the whole domain of animals, humans apply a further opposition of nature ↔ culture, so that animals customarily eaten belong to the domain of culture and animals that are not recognized as potentially food at all belong to the domain of nature (4.9).

Poles of oppositions can be expressed by positive or negative values, p or not p, or with Jakobsonian distinctive features, so human equals not animal and not human equals animal. Leach's theory of taboo revolves around the residual, ambiguous category between the two poles of the opposition, in this case human–animal, i.e. pets. That these are of special note follows from his empiricist (Leach is British, not French like Lévi-Strauss, hence,

4.10

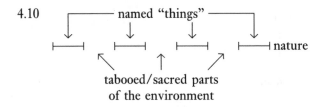

tabooed/sacred parts
of the environment

this empiricist flavor) theory that we arbitrarily segment the continuum of the world presented to us through our senses into separate named "things," reflexes of our language categories. These discriminations are clear-cut and unambiguous (we will have cause to question all this in the next chapter). But between these separately named discriminated things lie parts of the natural continuum which remain unnamed and undiscriminated, the realm of the sacred and the tabooed. Leach's (1964:35) diagram (4.10) will perhaps clarify.

To Lévi-Strauss's idea of strict binary oppositions, Leach has added the powerful idea of the borderline, liminal category, partaking of both poles of the opposition, but belonging completely to neither. We need not accept his empiricist theory of their acquisition to see the power of such categories, for they are omnipresent in human culture: initiation rites in the passage from child to adult; mortuary rites in the passage from life to death; sorcery materials focused on body exudations like semen, milk, hair, reflecting a passage from self to other (they themselves reflect a transition from clean to dirty); and incarnate deities like Jesus and Krishna, much more emotively powerful than the abstract gods they incarnate, because they are ambiguous between human and divine. The list can go on and on. Clearly, it is these ambiguous liminal categories that attract the maximum cultural interest and arouse the strongest taboos.

The two fundamental oppositions in the area of taboos and epithets associated with animals are nature–culture and self–other. The liminal category nature–culture for animals (animal–human) is pets, as already mentioned. Note that pets are highly tabooed as food. The English (and cultures derived from them such as Australian and American) do not eat their pets like dogs and cats and regard the culinary practices of East Asians, who do eat dogs in some cases, with horror. Note, however, that because these animals are tabooed, their names make effective epithets: *you son of a bitch, pussy*. The other use of the nature–culture opposition already mentioned are food animals–non-food animals. The liminal category here, animals simultaneously food and non-food, are what we might call game animals, rabbits being especially good exemplars. The name of the humble rabbit has been subjected to especially heavy taboo during the history of English, the old name *coney*, being replaced by *rabbit* because of its similarity to the common

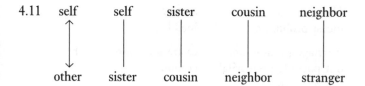

4.11   self   self   sister   cousin   neighbor

         other   sister   cousin   neighbor   stranger

4.12   self ⟵————————————⟶ other

       self : sister : cousin : neighbor : stranger

4.13   self ⟵————————————⟶ other

       self : sister :   cousin   : neighbor : stranger

       self : home :   farm   :   field   : remote

       self : pet : livestock :   game   : wild

name for female genitals. The choice of the name for Playboy *bunny* clubs
was surely no accident (nor, indeed, were Penthouse *pets*!).

The other basic opposition, self–other, is highly generative of cultural
systems. The social order is generated by applying it recursively (4.11).
These recursive relations can then be represented linearly in a somewhat
simplified fashion (4.12). Following Lévi-Strauss's principles of analogical
transformation, this opposition of self–other can be extended to the domains of geographical space and animals (Leach 1964:36), as demonstrated
in 4.13.

A sister, home, and pet bear analogous relations to self as do a neighbor,
field and game animal. Thus, a pet is tabooed for food, while a sister is
tabooed for sexual intercourse (the areas of eating and sexual intercourse are
themselves common areas of taboo, being liminal categories in their own
right between nature and culture: humans as cultural beings engaging in
activities that nature ordains for survival and procreation). Game animals
are those humans control, not tame, but not truly wild, like our fields and
meadows are in comparison to truly wild, inhospitable areas. They are killed
at set times of year, in accordance with set hunting rituals. Neighbors are
not kin, but potential affines, as well as potential enemies. When we take
them as spouses, we do so in accordance with set marriage rituals. The set
of analogical equivalents across this opposition in the social and animal
domains can be summarized, as in 4.14 (Leach 1964:44). The whole system
can be summarized in structuralist formalism as in 4.15.

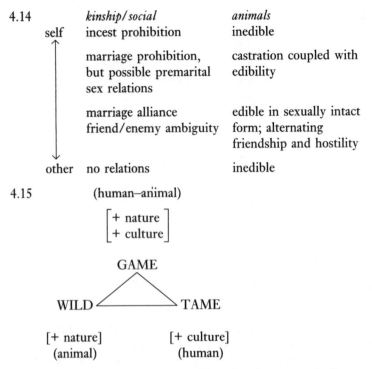

4.14

	kinship/social	animals
self	incest prohibition	inedible
	marriage prohibition, but possible premarital sex relations	castration coupled with edibility
	marriage alliance friend/enemy ambiguity	edible in sexually intact form; alternating friendship and hostility
other	no relations	inedible

4.15   (human–animal)

$$\begin{bmatrix} + \text{ nature} \\ + \text{ culture} \end{bmatrix}$$

GAME

WILD — TAME

[+ nature]   [+ culture]
(animal)   (human)

As we have come to expect with cultural systems built up of polar oppositions like these, it is the ambiguous, liminal categories which are the focus of the greatest cultural elaboration. Consider the case of the fox in English culture; the cult of the fox is certainly a salient feature of the culture of certain social classes. The fox is a strongly liminal category. It occupies a borderline position between edible field animals (GAME) and inedible wild animals (WILD). As such it is categorically problematic, and the barbarous practice of the hunting and killing of foxes in Britain is an elaborate ritual surrounded by extraordinary taboos. Even the language used is extraordinary, marked by special words for familiar objects, an avoidance feature so typical of the language of sacred rituals in countless other cultures. The fox itself must not be spoken of as such: it is referred to as a *dog* (the dogs themselves are *hounds*), its head as a *mask* and its tail as a *brush* (Leach 1964:52). These features are all hallmarks of the highly problematic status of this liminal category.

Structuralist analyses like this one by Leach and similar work on myth and totemism by Lévi-Strauss (Lévi-Strauss 1963, 1966, 1969) and other anthropologists attempt to lay bare the basic semantic oppositions which generate the many diverse cultural forms attested. Of necessity the work is highly abstract, invoking a Platonic and rationalist other world of innate universals informing this very diverse apparent world of contingent facts. One finds these analyses convincing to the extent one accepts the necessity of such a level of abstraction. Geertz has probably spoken for many when he said (Geertz 1973:355):

> For what Lévi-Strauss has made for himself is an infernal culture machine. It annuls history, reduces sentiment to a shadow of the intellect, and replaces the particular minds of particular savages in particular jungles with the Savage Mind immanent in us all.

But, if one is a committed rationalist, this, of course, is exactly what one wants anthropology to do.

Summary

Structuralism is a school of thought within the social sciences which holds that the elements of a system have no significance in themselves, only in relationship to the other elements of the system. Thus, /b/ is an element of the English phonemic system because it contrasts with other such elements; *bat* contrasts with *cat* as distinct English words. This idea of functioning contrast was developed into the formal idea of opposition in the work of the Prague School, defining elements in a system as the points of intersection of multiple axes of opposition, represented as the +/− poles of binary features. This idea of binary features was taken up by Lévi-Strauss and wedded to a strong rationalist agenda as the basis for his structural anthropology. The function of human minds everywhere is to classify, and they do this in terms of a finite, universally available series of semantic oppositions which underlie all cultural categories, such as nature versus culture. Because all human minds are ultimately the same, due to the doctrine of the psychic unity of humankind, all cultures are underlyingly organized in the same way, via the universal set of semantic oppositions, the apparent differences being due simply to varying arrangement of these oppositions.

Further Reading

Structuralism has been enormously influential in this century, and there are many sources. Sturrock (1986) is an excellent introduction, while Culler (1976) summarizes Saussure's contribution. Lévi-Strauss's own work is voluminous, but the most relevant for purposes here are Lévi-Strauss (1963, 1966). Leach's (1974) short book on Lévi-Strauss is an excellent place to begin to explore this important thinker, but Pace (1986) is also very useful.

5

Cognitive Anthropology

The Intellectual Background of Cognitive Anthropology

Unlike continental structuralism as promulgated by Lévi-Strauss, the American bred school of structural anthropology, known as cognitive anthropology, exhibits a more attenuated position, at least in its earlier incarnations, with respect to claims of strong innate universals of the human mind. While influenced by continental structural linguistics, American cognitive anthropologists also drew strongly from American structural linguistics, a tradition founded by Boas in the early part of the century and developed by such eminent linguists as Sapir, Whorf, and Bloomfield. Boas, Sapir, and Whorf are the pivotal characters within American anthropological linguistics of the theory of relativism, i.e. that lived practical experience molds categories of thought, and this relativist strain of thought is an important background in the early formulation of cognitive anthropology. Boas, the key figure in both American anthropology and linguistics at the beginning of the twentieth century, with a background in German post-Kantian philosophy of the nineteenth century, is pivotal here, for he imported these philosophical ideas into his framing of theoretical concepts in both linguistics and anthropology. The German post-Kantians of the nineteenth century were strongly influenced by the ideas of the Romantics (this will be discussed in more detail in the chapter 8), and, as such, were much taken with racial differences and cultural diversity. This created tension with Kant's postulation of universal, innate mental categories. They resolved this conflict when they introduced a degree of relativism into the theory: the nature of the categories were to some degree informed by the individual's experience in the world. Humans constructed the world through the categories, but the experience of the world could modify the categories, which, in turn, determined their construction of the world: a cybernetic interactive view of constructed mind and sensible world – in short, the position of relativism to be discussed in detail in Part IV. For Boas (and Sapir and Whorf behind him), this post-Kantian position was a given: culture, then, was the setting in which these adjustments to mind through practical experience were carried out. Note that this type of relativism does not contradict the doctrine of the psychic unity of humankind: the categories given to humans at birth are identical for all; the diversity of human mental categories is due to the molding effect of experience upon these given categories.

How does experience mold these given categories? The mechanism Boas proposes is classification: from the infinite flux of sensible experience we abstract common and related elements and assign these to the same category of thought, typically labelled linguistically. These experience-derived categories modify and interact with the innately given categories of the human mind. Boas, and even more so his successors Sapir and Whorf, emphasized the social and conventional (Boas termed it "unconscious") nature of this process of category formation; these classifications are habitual within a particular cultural and linguistic system. The Boasian approach to linguistic categories (and by extension cultural categories) differs radically from later Bloomfieldian views in being unashamedly mentalistic: these classifications are mental categories of meaning, socially embedded. The linguist Bloomfield, following the behaviorist school in psychology, rejected all appeals to mentalism. For him the only theoretical constructs possible were completely observable physical phenomena; only directly observable behavior was to be studied. As meaning does not obviously have these properties, it was regarded as largely outside the purview of rigorous linguistic analysis.

Cognitive anthropology differs from European-inspired structural anthropology mainly in the greater weight given to the Boasian heritage in its formulation. The history of cognitive anthropology can conveniently be divided into two periods. The first from about 1950–70 (so-called "ethnoscience") is closely tied analytically to American structural linguistics and favors a relativistic reading of the Boasian heritage. The second period from 1970 to now was ushered in by the publication of Berlin and Kay's *Basic Color Terms* (see chapter 7). Much more strongly universalist and innatist readings of the Boasian theory of classification now emerged, influenced no doubt by the rise within linguistics of a strongly universalizing innatist theory of grammar, Chomsky's generative grammar (Chomsky 1968). Because rationalism and a universalist theory of mental concepts is the focus of this Part, I will focus in this chapter (and the next two) on work of the second period, providing a briefer survey of the first.

Work in cognitive anthropology of either period shares some basic assumptions. Culture is a mental phenomenon, "cognitive organizations of material phenomena" (Tyler 1969:3). Goodenough's early, but classic definition is a succinct a statement as any: "a society's culture consists ·of whatever one has to know or believe to operate in a manner acceptable to its members." (Goodenough 1964[1957]:36). Note the clear parallel to ongoing work in linguistics salient in all structuralist approaches to anthropology. A culture is a mental system which generates all and only the proper cultural behavior. Culture, then, is the cognitive anthropologist's analog of the linguist's notion of grammar. As with the analysis of grammar, the goal of the cognitive anthropologist is to define principles underlying the organization of culture in the mind. Further, as linguists like Chomsky typically invoke logical and mathematical models in which to cast their descriptions of grammatical phenomena, cognitive anthropologists do the same. "A culture consists of a set of logical principles which order relevant material phenomena. To the cognitive anthropologist these logical principles rather than the material phenomena are the object of investigation" (Tyler 1969:14). Note that like Lévi-Strauss's this agenda is clearly Platonic; we want to go beyond mere material phenomena to the underlying logical components. One possible difference is that at least in early cognitive anthropology, in which the relativist flavor of the Boasian heritage is strong, there is no necessary assumption that the underlying components were the same in all cultures: "a culture consists of many semantic domains organized around numerous features of meaning, and no two cultures share the same set of semantic domains or features of meaning, *nor do they share the same methods of organizing these features*" (Tyler 1969:11, emphasis added).

Componential Analysis

The main formal logical methods adopted by cognitive anthropologists in their analysis of cultural domains are, as in Lévi-Straussian structural anthropology, those of structural linguistics. Indeed, if anything, the paradigmatic role of language in cultural analysis is even more central in cognitive anthropology, for it is believed, following Boas, that language categories are the most transparent guide to the cultural categories, classifications which emerge by the imposition by the Native people of order on their sensible environment. The methodology typically followed by cognitive anthropologists in their analysis of culture systems is to collect all the words in the native language denoting various categories within a particular semantic domain, for example, all the words referring to kin relations in the kinship domain or all the words for types of plants in the ethnobotanical domain. Such a domain of terms is called a *folk classification*. To elucidate the cognitive organization informing a folk classification, cognitive anthropologists performed a type of linguistic analysis highly derivative of the techniques of structural linguistics. The terms within the folk classification are analyzed semantically into their meaning components. Borrowing heavily from Jakobson's ideas of distinctive features, cognitive anthropologists claim to uncover the cognitive organization of the folk classification through *componential analysis*, representing the meanings of the terms through a set of semantic oppositions.

This is all best understood by working through an example, one modelled on Conklin's (1969) well-known componential analysis of Hanunoo pronouns; I will use Tagalog, a language with which I am familiar, but exhibiting the same pattern in this respect as Hanunoo. Consider the system of pronouns in Tagalog with their English glosses:

ako	"I"
ka	"you (SG)"
siya	"he/she"
kata	"I and you (SG)"
tayo	"I, you (SG) and he/she/they"
kami	"I and he/she/they"
kayo	"you (SG) and he/she/they"
sila	"they"

We could represent this system in the categories of the metalanguage of modern linguistics, drawn largely from the system of linguistic classifications developed by the ancient Latin and Greek grammarians:

		SG	DL	PL
1	INCL	—	kata	tayo
	EXCL	ako	—	kami
2		ka	—	kayo
3		siya	—	sila

But the gaps in this representation suggest that this system of semantic components of person, number, and exclusivity drawn from the Western grammatical tradition might not be the most insightful into the Native Tagalog categories used to generate the pronoun system. What we, as cognitive anthropologists, want to know are the Native Tagalog dimensions of semantic contrasts which organize this system of pronouns. Note first that the dimensions of number are rather different in Tagalog than English; there is a dual number, referring to two people, not just a singular and plural. Further, the notion of person is clearly different in Tagalog than English; there are three words *kata*, *tayo* and *kami*, all of which we would translate by English "we," two of these being true plurals. Clearly, then, we must go beyond categories like person and number to deeper, but simpler semantic components, out of which these concepts are constructed. Let us tackle person first. Note that Tagalog, like many languages of island Southeast Asia and the Pacific, has a fundamental opposition as to whether the speaker "I" is included or not. Let us call this the speaker included (S) feature. If the speaker "I" is included in the meaning of the pronoun, it is specified + for this feature; otherwise, it is −:

> S+:   *ako, kata, tayo, kami*
> S−:   *ka, siya, kayo, sila*

The second feature in this componential analysis of the semantic domain of Tagalog pronouns is whether the addressee "you (SG)" (A) is included (+) or not (−):

> A+:   *ka, kata, tayo, kayo*
> A−:   *ako, siya, kami, sila*

These two features together give us the following partial analysis:

S+	*kata, tayo*	S−	*ka, kayo*
A+		A+	

S+	*ako, kami*	S−	*siya, sila*
A−		A−	

This system can also be represented in a paradigm similar to the representation used in structural anthropology, notably by Lévi-Strauss, a chart rather like a graph, in which the two features intersect and determine the forms by the proper cluster of features at each point (5.1).

5.1

		S	
		+	−
	+	*kata*	*ka*
		tayo	*kayo*
A			
	−	*ako*	*siya*
		kami	*sila*

Already, we can see some formal properties of the words by labelling the categories corresponding to the semantic contrasts revealed by the componential analysis. Clearly, the form *si-* in *siya* and *sila* is associated with the features [S− A−].

What simple feature will do for the remaining differentiation of the pronominal forms? Clearly, the English number categories, singular–plural, are not adequate because they will not distinguish *kata* from *tayo*, both meaning "we." We could invoke a three-way opposition, singular–dual–plural, but this is counter to the usual choice of binary oppositions in structuralist

5.2

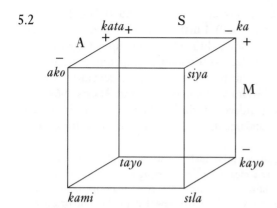

analyses like these, and furthermore is problematic in that the dual category has only one member *kata*, the [S+ A+] pronoun. Where are the dual pronouns for the [S– A+], [S+ A–] and [S– A–] groups? The language has none, and this suggests we are on the wrong track.

Note carefully the category in which the dual pronoun *kata* is found: [S+ A+]. Note further that these features require that both a speaker and an addressee be included; unlike the other categories which have at least one [–] specification, i.e. a person is excluded, this category cannot possibly be singular: at least two persons must always be included, [S+ A+]. Thus, dual is the equivalent of singular for this group of features; it is the minimal number of individuals in the group [S+ A+]. We can therefore define a feature of minimal membership in which singular and dual (+) contrast with plural (–). All eight pronouns can be defined uniquely in terms of these three features:

kata	S+A+M+	*tayo*	S+A+M–	*ka*	S–A+M+
kayo	S–A+M–	*ako*	S+A–M+	*kami*	S+A–M–
siya	S–A–M+	*sila*	S–A–M–		

Because there are now three semantic features of opposition, there are three axes of contrast, and a paradigm laying out the organization of this domain can be set out in the form of a cube (5.2). Again, this analysis reveals formal correlates not previously obvious; *-yo* is associated with [A+ M–] and *ka* with [S– A+].

The purpose of this type of structuralist semantic analysis in cognitive anthropology is to reveal the cognitive organization of this domain for the Tagalog Native speaker. The strong cognitivist view claims such a close correspondence between the results of such formal analyses and the Native's cognitive organization. This is impossible to verify without independent psychological tests of competing formal analyses, as undertaken, for example, by Romney and D'Andrade (1969). Further, competing formal analyses of a semantic domain are by no means difficult to come up with. Even with a simple eight-term system like Tagalog pronouns, competing analyses with other features are possible, but with much more complex semantic domains like kinship (Romney and D'Andrade 1969; Wallace and Atkins 1969), the possibilities become daunting indeed. Burling (1969:426) in an important paper neatly summed up this fundamental dilemma in cognitive anthropology:

> students who claim that componential analyses or comparable methods of semantic analysis can discover a means for "discovering how people construe their world" must explain how to eliminate the great majority of logical possibilities and narrow the choice to the one or few that are "psychologically real" . . . I doubt whether any single analysis tells us much about cognitive structure, even if it enables us to use terms as a native does.

This suggests a more modest goal for cognitive anthropologists: simply to produce an explicit formal statement of the semantic features underlying the folk classification which will allow the non-Native to use it correctly. The logical principles underlying it, then, are those of the Western ethnographer, not the Native; to get at the latter, independent psychological testing is necessary.

Taxonomy

As mentioned above, cognitive anthropology follows a Boasian agenda in its interest in how diverse systems of classification of nature are encoded in Native languages. Componential analysis is a method to get at the semantically primitive concepts behind the classification provided by the Native terms in a given semantic domain. These are all relationships of contrast, as English *she* contrasts with *he* in the semantic feature of sex. The other type of semantic relationship of interest to cognitive anthropologists is that of inclusion, how particular terms are organized into larger groups to provide a more encompassing system of classification. Hierarchical relationships of inclusion like this form what is called a *taxonomy*. Terms are hierarchically related so that the meanings of more specific terms are included within the meanings of higher level/more general terms. According to Wierzbicka (1985), the more specific terms are "a kind of" the higher up more inclusive general terms. On the same level terms are in contrast, the semantic terms of the contrast to be arrived at by componential analysis. Thus, in English, *poodle* contrasts with *dachshund*, which contrast with *Labrador*, but all are included in the higher level term *dog*. Dog in its turn contrasts with *cat* and

5.3

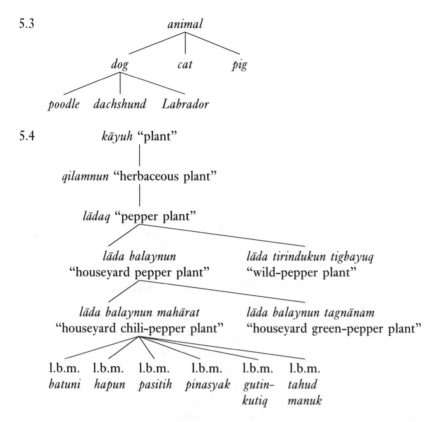

5.4

pig, but these are all included in the term *animal*. Using a familiar tree representation, this taxonomy can be represented as in 5.3.

A more extensive taxonomy can be illustrated by Conklin's (1969) analysis of Hanunoo chilli-pepper plants. All pepper plants are known as *lādaq*, but these belong to the more inclusive class of herbaceous plants (*qilamnun*), which in turn are included in the general class of plants (*kāyuh*). Pepper plants are divided into houseyard cultivated plants (*lāda balaynun*) and wild-pepper plants (*lāda tirindukun tigbayuq*). Houseyard pepper plants in turn are divided into houseyard chilli-pepper plants (*lāda balaynun mahārat*) and houseyard green-pepper plants (*lāda balaynun tagnānam*). Finally, there are no less than six types of houseyard chilli-pepper plants, for example, the "cat's penis" houseyard chilli-pepper plants (*lāda balaynun mahārat gutin-kutiq*). The taxonomy can be represented in tree form (5.4).

Taxonomies are generated by the logical relationships of contrast on the same level (*lāda balaynun* and *lāda tirindukun tigbayuq* are contrastive types of pepper plants), but inclusion on the next hierarchical level (both are types of *lādaq*). Occasionally, the same Native term may function at more

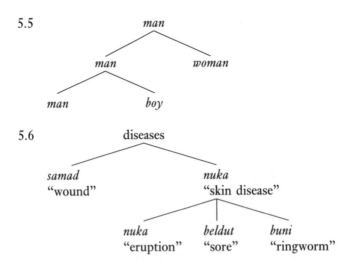

5.5

5.6

than one level. English *man* (Frake 1964) is a good example, as in the taxonomy shown in 5.5. The widest most inclusive sense of *man* includes all humans, but on a lower level it contrasts with *woman* according to sex. This second level, however, is also an inclusive category, for it contains at still a lower level yet another sense of *man*, which contrasts with *boy* according to maturity. Frake (1964) provides a parallel example in the Philippine language Subanun with the form *nuka*. At the most inclusive level it means "skin disease" contrasting with "wound" and including all pathological skin conditions. At a lower level, it means "eruption" contrasting among others with *beldut* "sore" and *buni* "ringworm" (5.6).

Universalist Trends in Cognitive Anthropology

While the earlier period of cognitive anthropology was somewhat empiricist and relativistic in its interest in the different systems of classification revealed in Native languages, there was a rationalist undercurrent in the claim that innate universal properties of the human mind provided the logical principles like contrast and inclusion which underlay the organization of these cultural systems (Tyler 1969:14). This rationalist and Kantian stance is very close to that of Lévi-Strauss (1966); it is also very clearly Platonic in its insistence on underlying logical concepts which generate sensible classificatory behavior. It is these strands of the cognitive anthropologist's endeavor which really come to the fore in its second universalist period from around 1970. Cognitive anthropology in its transition to this view was clearly guided by strongly universalizing theories in Chomskyan linguistics (Kay 1970) and developments in artificial intelligence (D'Andrade 1981). In common with other disciplines in the cognitive science cluster like linguistics, cognitive psychology and neuroscience, cognitive anthropology became strongly enamored by the pervasive metaphor of the human mind as being like a digital computer. As a computer processes data fed into it according to the steps specified for it by the particular program running, the human mind was seen as an opportunistic information processor, doing so along the lines of psychological processes largely specified by innate universal human endowment (D'Andrade 1990). Culture, as the shared symbolic information transmitted through social groupings, is then to be studied from this psychological viewpoint. Cognitive anthropology is concerned with how cultural content interacts with psychological processes, how cultural information is constrained by the way the mind processes information (D'Andrade 1981). This agenda displays a marked kinship with that of Lévi-Strauss: "in the process of repeated social transmission, cultural programs come to take forms which have a good fit to the natural [read 'innate'] capacities and constraints of the human brain" (D'Andrade 1981:182). Strong rationalist or Platonist ideas now emerge to take central stage in cognitive anthropology: by deep investigation of the constraints on cultural systems of meaning, particularly as revealed in the comparative study of the terms and expressions of particular semantic domains in natural languages, the cognitive anthropologist can uncover the general psychological processes employed by the innate central-processing mechanism of the human mind in generating these cultural systems. Paradigmatic ground-breaking examples of such investigations are Lounsbury's (1965, 1969) kinship studies, discussed in detail in chapter 6, and Berlin and Kay's (1969) comparative study of color terminology, discussed in chapter 7. Both of these important studies claim to reveal universal constraints of patterning in the semantic domains of kinship and color, which had previously been thought to be randomly structured, according to a culturally and linguistically defined arbitrary classification – a strong blow for the rationalist, Platonist cause.

Biological Taxonomies: Berlin's Approach to Ethnobiological Classification

Berlin's (1992) work in folk systems of biological classification (ethnobiology) is yet another example of this type of work. Berlin (1992) claims to have uncovered universal constraints on the forms of the taxonomies representing ethnobiological knowledge. According to him all ethnobiological-classification systems are organized into a shallow taxonomic structure, with no more than six mutually exclusive ranks. The top level is the unique beginner or kingdom level, labelled as *plant* or *animal* by English, but often unlabelled in other Native systems. Next are the life-form taxa which, while labelled, are typically few in number, from ten to fifteen. English examples under the unique beginner *animal* include *bird*, *snake*, *fish*, etc. Taxa included within a particular life-form taxon usually exhibit a high degree of diversity, for instance *ostriches*, *peacocks*, and *magpies* are all included in the life-form *bird*, but are markedly different.

The next level of taxa, generic rank, are for Berlin the core of any ethnobiological classification. The largest number of taxa in any classification system is found at this rank, but these rarely exceed 500 items in each kingdom. According to Berlin and work by Rosch (1977, 1978), taxa at the generic rank are the most salient for the Native: they are simple lexemes, most frequently used, learned early by children acquiring the Native language, and most easily elicited from informants. English examples of generic level taxa are *magpie* or *kookaburra* under the life-form *bird* in the *animal* kingdom or *eucalyptus* or *pine* under *tree* in the *plant* kingdom. It is possible to have generic taxa directly affiliated to a unique beginner without being a member of a life-form taxon; an example might be *octopus*, which, while clearly an animal, is also clearly not a fish, nor any life-form taxa (it is important to note that we are dealing with folk concepts here, not scientific ones; while *octopuses* are *molluscs*, this latter concept is a scientific one, not part of the folk biological knowledge of English speakers). As Wierzbicka (1985) convincingly points out, the inclusion relationship between generic taxa and life-forms can be paraphrased as "a kind of" (as, of course, can all relations of inclusion in taxonomies); so a *kookaburra* is a kind of *bird* and a *eucalyptus* is a kind of *tree*. The relationship between generic taxa is one of contrast, different kinds of the general type of thing denoted by the label for the life-form taxon. Unlike a life-form taxon like *bird* the membership of a generic taxon like *dog* is relatively homogeneous, corresponding approximately to biological genera, that is, natural groupings with many attributes in common (see also Wierzbicka 1985). Berlin claims that they are the basic level for all systems of ethnobiological classification, but this has been challenged (Dougherty 1981; Hunn 1985), and I will return to this presently.

Generic taxa are commonly monotypic i.e. terminal units of the taxonomy dominating no further taxa. However, some generic taxa are polytypic, inclusive of specific subgeneric taxa. These are typically few in number and for a given generic taxon are labelled by complex polynomial lexemes. Thus, the generic taxon *eucalyptus* in Australian English might have as included specific taxa: *snow gum*, *blue gum*, *stringy bark*, *yellow box*, and others. An exception to this principle is the English generic taxon *dog*, which, due to centuries of close human interest and carefully controlled breeding, has many specific taxa. Finally, a specific taxon may dominate varietal taxa; these are rare and have polynomial labels. The full taxonomy may be represented as in 5.7 (Berlin, Breedlove, and Raven 1973:215).

5.7

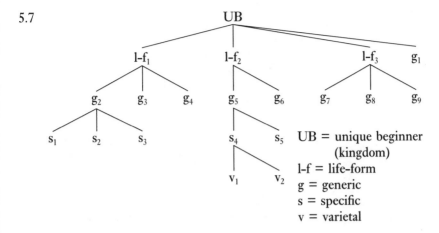

UB = unique beginner
(kingdom)
l-f = life-form
g = generic
s = specific
v = varietal

5.8

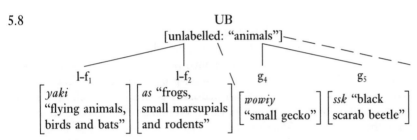

As an illustration of an ethnobiological system of classification let us consider Bulmer's (1967, 1968, 1970; Bulmer and Tyler 1968) work on the enthnozoology of the Kalam, a people of New Guinea. As with many languages, Kalam lacks a label for the unique beginner of the ethnozoological taxonomy, i.e. no word corresponding to English *animal*. Kalam has five life-form taxa and no less than 89 unaffiliated generic taxa, i.e. generic taxa not included in any life-form taxa and coordinate to them in being directly dominated by the unique beginner. Part of the system thus far could be represented as in 5.8. The life-form *as* in turn includes 25 generic taxa. These are labelled by simple monomial lexemes and all but three are monotypic (i.e. are not divided into specific taxa). Those which are polytypic have between two and four specific taxa; for example *jejeg* (tree frogs) includes four specific taxa (5.9). Bulmer and Tyler (1968) report that the specific taxa of the generic *jejeg* (tree frog) contrast only in a single dimension of color.

The crucial claim of Berlin's (1992) work with respect to the innatist universalist agenda of cognitive anthropology is his insistence that innate and universal perceptual and cognitive faculties underlie these organizations of biological forms, *independent of any cultural mediation*. The basic idea is

5.9

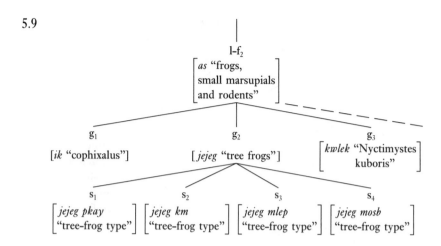

that humans come biologically preprogramed to create biological categories along lines dictated by natural similarities and discontinuities. This bears a family resemblance to the innatist Chomskyan theories of language acquisition discussed earlier. Human information-processing abilities lead them to spontaneously know the world as it naturally is, and this is reflected in the commonalities of organization found in ethnobiological classification systems the world over. There is a universal human cognitive structure that reveals itself in ethnobiological classification, as it does in kinship terminology and color term systems. Humans everywhere distinguish *dog* from *cat*, and they do this on the basis of innate cognitive capacities, not human interests; "ethnobiological systems of classification are based primarily on the affinities that humans observe among the taxa themselves, quite independent of the actual or potential cultural significance of these taxa" (Berlin 1992:31) and "human beings are drawn by some kind of *innate* [emphasis added] curiosity for those groupings of plants and animals that represent the most distinctive chunks of biological reality" (Berlin 1992:290).

This is a strong claim and one, as we shall see, that has not gone unchallenged, but let us explore its implications first. The crucial atom of all ethnobiological classification is the level of the generic taxa and the relationship some of these have to their more inclusive life-form. For Berlin, generic taxa constitute a "specifiable and partially predictable set of plant and animal taxa that represent the smallest fundamental biological discontinuities easily recognized in any particular habitat . . . its members stand out as beacons on the landscape of biological reality, figuratively crying out to be named" (Berlin 1992:53). Generic taxa are the basic level categories in any ethnobiological system. As in his joint work with Kay on color terminology (Berlin and Kay 1969), Berlin argues that certain exemplars of a generic taxon are more representative, more focal, than others. This is the basis of prototype theory, well known from the work of Rosch (1977, 1978). The idea behind this theory is that categories are fuzzy, with some exemplars being prototypical members, close to the focal centre of the category, and others less prototypical examples, more toward the vague border of the category. Meaning in prototype theory is not represented in terms of a critical list of defining properties, as in the classical Aristotelian tradition, but in a cognitive schema to which a given exemplar fits more or less well (see chapters 6 and 7). Thus, to use a famous example (Fillmore 1975) we might define *bachelor* as "unmarried male human." But although the Pope and a 55-year-old man in a coma since age 12 meet these criterial features, do we want to label them bachelors? Clearly not, for they are so far from the prototype we have for this concept in contemporary cultural schemas of courtship and marriage. Berlin invokes the idea of prototypes to explain the nature of generic taxa; the discontinuities of the natural world represented by these taxa are cognitive foci of human-processing mechanisms.

Generic taxa are configurational categories, nearly immediately apparent; whether something is a tiger or not is not normally a matter of debate (a generic taxon), but whether it is a Siberian, Bengal, or Sumatran tiger (specific taxa) might very well be. A generic taxon can be described by a large cluster of distinctive attributes (Wierzbicka 1985), something we might describe as an object schema (Casson 1983), but in Berlin's view and in keeping with prototype theory, this description is not its meaning. For him generic taxa "elude linguistic definition" (Berlin 1992:61); they are ostensively defined terms for perceptually salient foci in the natural world. The meaning of a word like *tiger* is its reference, the object in the natural world or the sensible experience thereof labelled by this term. In this sense it is exactly parallel to a word like *red*, which simply identifies a color but which cannot reasonably be said to be definable by a list of criterial features; again, however, some shades of red may be more prototypically *red* than others (see chapter 7 and Berlin and Kay 1969).

A life-form taxon contrasts with a generic taxon in being conceived of as a supercategory, one with many different categories, each of which is an exemplar of it, prototypical or not. It is thus a category composed of many different kinds, the generic taxa included in it. A generic taxon, on the other hand, is simply a category, a thing, not normally understood as being composed of subcategories. Wierzbicka (1985:228–9) explains clearly:

> While concepts such as *animal*, *bird*, *tree* or *flower* [i.e. life-form taxa] are thought of as having many different kinds, concepts such as *cat*, *lion*, *parrot*, *swallow* or *spruce* [i.e. generic taxa] are not. When they give the matter some thought, native speakers of English will no doubt agree that there are different kinds of cats, parrots or spruces, and that there might even be different

kinds of lions and swallows. But this differentiation is not essential to their understanding of the concept *lion*, *swallow*, *parrot* or *cat*. On the other hand, if someone doesn't know that there are different kinds of . . . birds or flowers then I think he doesn't really understand the full meaning of the words *bird* or *flower*.

Life-form taxa commonly group together generic taxa which seem biologically highly diverse: Kalam *as* covering frogs, small marsupials, and rodents is an example. This has led some researchers (Hunn 1985; Randall and Hunn 1984) to argue that life-form taxa are "biologically arbitrary" and "artificial" (Hunn 1985:124–8). Contrary to generic taxa, it is claimed that life-form taxa do not encode clearly discriminable foci in the natural world; "there is no perceptual discontinuity motivating the recognition of *tree*" (Hunn 1985:126). Berlin strongly disagrees: "life-form taxa form rather large *groupings of perceptually similar* folk genera . . . based on a *small number of biological characters*" (Berlin 1992:189). For example, Kalam *as* "frogs, small marsupials, and rodents" could be perhaps defined as "small four-legged foraging animals with more hind leg strength than fore leg." Although defined by a set of characteristics, Berlin claims that such groupings are no less perceptually salient than a generic taxa like *wowiy* "small gecko." He claims, then, that life-form taxa are formed on the basis of the same innate universal cognitive faculties as are generic taxa: by labelling biological foci, salient perceptual discontinuities in the natural world.

Classification and "Hidden Nature"

Recent work by other investigators (Atran 1985, 1990; Gelman and Coley 1991; Wierzbicka 1992b), while concurring with Berlin's view of strong innate and universal constraints underlying ethnobiological classification systems, has questioned his use of prototype theory in describing taxa, especially generic taxa. These researchers claim that generic taxa are characterized by distinct boundaries, not fuzzy ones, as prototype theory would hold. They argue that a generic taxon contrasts with a life-form taxon in having a hidden underlying "nature" manifested in the sensible properties of the category, but distinct from them. Human categorizers presume this hidden underlying nature to be present equally in all exemplars of the category; thus, the boundary of the category is sharp, and the claims of prototype theory are refuted. This hidden underlying nature is what is held responsible for the characteristic form and behavior of the taxon, and it is by this nature that humans assign variant forms to a particular generic taxon. For example, Wierzbicka (1992b) provides the example of a purple cow which does not give milk or say "moo," but which English speakers still categorize as "cow" because it can be thought of, through this hidden underlying nature, as an animal of the type which does do all these things. Atran (1990) notes that it is again this presumption of a unique hidden underlying nature that allows English speakers to fit juvenile forms like tadpoles to a taxon like *frog*. Although the relationship is perceptually not obvious, we do so by a process of inference based on the presumption of an underlying nature. This presumed underlying nature is what causes organisms of a particular kind to develop in a set way and display the traits they do. This presumed underlying nature appears to be linked to living beings and is due, no doubt, to the fact that they reproduce among themselves along *genetic lines* – by passing the underlying nature from one generation to the next. This discontinuity between natural entities and artificial ones created by human culture and technology is a universal perceptual focus of human cognition (see Wierzbicka 1985, 1992b), and as such, is the basic organizational principle of ethnobiological classification. Further, because the underlying nature is passed by reproduction, we may safely infer non-obvious, but pervasive similarities between genetically related living beings. For example, if we believe that snakes are genetically related to monitor lizards by a process of evolutionary change we may be led to seek traces of legs in snakes (and we will find them among those most "primitive" of snakes, pythons and boas). It is processes of inference like these which are the basis of all systems of classification of living beings, ethnobiological or modern scientific.

Life-form taxa probably lack hidden underlying natures, but rather are characterized by diagnostic semantic features which define them. Consider an example adapted from Wierzbicka (1992b). If I see a kookaburra, I will probably quickly identify it as belonging to that generic taxon. But if my companion, a habitual bird watcher, insists that it is not really a *kookaburra*, that it just looks like one, I will probably defer to her judgment, assuming that the hidden underlying nature of this living being was not that of a kookaburra, a move aided no doubt by the fact that this nature is both underlying and *hidden*. But if I have identified the creature I saw as a *bird*, a life-form taxon, and my companion similarly insists otherwise, I am very likely to put up much stronger resistance. Why? Because there is a list of criterial diagnostic features which I can appeal to in assigning a given exemplar to a life-form taxon, and in this case the creature sighted meets all requirements for the taxon *bird*. Various generic taxa are assigned to a particular life-form taxon by meeting these diagnostic requirements, as life-form taxa are inclusive groupings that generic taxa are *kinds* of. To determine whether something is a kind of something else, explicit classificatory criteria are needed, but note that the fit of particular generic taxa to these may be more or less good, with possible resultant prototypicality effects in life-form taxa.

Challenges to Berlin's Approach

The strong claim by Berlin and others that the principles underlying the organization of systems of ethnobiological classification are universal has not gone unchallenged. Berlin argues that the basic, most perceptually salient taxa are those of the generic level in all systems. Dougherty (1981) has challenged this on empirical grounds. Which are the most salient categories can be established by psychological testing and observation: the most frequently used in talk, most easily recalled or identified, and first learned by children. In a comparison of Tzeltal with English, Dougherty demonstrated that, while generic rank categories were indeed the most salient for Tzeltal speakers, it was the life-form taxa which were in general most salient for English speakers. For English speakers, the life-form taxon *tree* scored higher on all these dimensions than did its included generic taxa, *oak*, *maple*, or *birch*. On face value this refutes Berlin's claim of a universal perceptually driven basis for the salience of generic taxa in natural discontinuities. Rather, it introduces a strain of relativistic thinking into studies of ethnobiological classification. The fundamental level of classification, the most salient categories, are not fixed by innate, universal predispositions. They vary with human interests, the way the members of the culture interact with the entities in the semantic domain. In horticultural societies like the Tzeltal, with close links to the natural world, certain natural discontinuities of that domain are highly apparent to them, so that the generic level is the most salient. But for modern urban speakers of English, interaction with the natural world is highly attenuated (many urban speakers of English would be hard put to identify an *oak*), so that the more inclusive life-form level is the most salient. Salience in ethnobiological classification reflects human interests, not panhuman psychological constraints.

The work of Hunn (1985) and Randall (1987; Randall and Hunn 1984) also builds upon this relativistic idea of categorization as reflecting human interests. They highlight this function: "the fact that cultural knowledge of the natural world might also be of use practically has been treated as beside the point, almost as an embarrassment" (Hunn 1985:117). This view argues that biological taxonomies only lexicalize a small portion of the available flora and fauna, but what is lexicalized is of special importance to the Native. Thus, we find many residual life-form taxa, like *bush* in English, which label entities that we have little interest in dividing further, but many generic taxa like *cat*, *dog*, *pig*, etc. which reflect the special importance these have for us. Further, in some languages, the word for a well-defined life-form taxon may be polysemous, reflecting human concern with it. For example, the Watam word *padoŋ* "tree" also means "wood" indicating the function this life-form serves in the human economy. Functional human concerns may be primary over biological features: "vegetables" and "farm

animals" may yet turn out to be more psychologically salient and evolutionarily important than "bushes" and "snakes" (Randall and Hunn 1984:346).
Berlin (1992:184–5) challenges this assertion, arguing that the direction is
the other way around: trees are known by innate human psychological processes to possess certain physical properties, i.e. woodiness, to which secondary functional attributes are attached. For Berlin, innate rational human
information-processing capacities are primary over any relativistic concern
with human interests. But the position of Hunn and Randall is closely
parallel to the view of Rosch (1978) and the enactionist or embodied practices view of cognition discussed previously. Rosch demonstrates that disin-
terested intellectualist human processing does not uniquely inform the basic
level categories, but that they are where "biology, culture and cognitive
need for informativeness all meet . . . the basic level of categorization, thus,
appears to be the point at which cognition and environment become simultaneously enacted. The object appears to the perceiver as affording certain
kinds of interactions and the perceiver uses the objects with his body and
mind in the afforded manner" (Varela, Thompson, and Rosch 1991:177). I
will return to these issues with the discussion of relativism in the next Part.

Hunn and Randall also argue for replacing Berlin's taxonomic model
of ethnobiological classification, with its relations of contrast and inclusion,
with what they call a "natural core model," in which this domain is composed of a dense central core of multipurpose complex-linked taxa, mostly
Berlin's generic taxa, and a special purpose periphery consisting of unaffiliated generic taxa and residual life-forms. In this model inclusive taxonomic
relations, kinds of *trees*, kinds of *birds*, are actually very atypical, and the
taxonomic relationship is greatly downplayed; "(inclusive life-forms) are
simply core taxa of exceptional heterogeneity [so contrasting with the usually simple core generic taxa], and their developmental priority is due to
their perceptual salience, the same cognitive principle that underlies the
recognition of folk generic taxa" (Hunn 1985:198). Hunn's view suggests
a flexible use of inclusive taxa like life-form taxa, which may arise spontaneously and creatively in the dense core area for particular perceptual or
functional needs, whereas Berlin's more rigid taxonomic model does not easily
accommodate this (Berlin 1992). The phenomena of intermediate taxa argues for Hunn's view. These typically occur between life-form and generic
rank, and are largely *ad hoc* classifications of generic taxa into a mid-level
ranking under the life-form taxon. To take Dougherty's (1981) example,
the generic taxa *pine*, *spruce*, and *fir* may be classed in the intermediate taxa
"needle-bearing" (*evergreen*), contrasting with "leaf-bearing" (*deciduous*) and
"frond-bearing" (*palms?*), all under the life-form taxon *tree*. This reflects
an *ad hoc* classification of generic taxa in the dense-core area, either on
perceptual or functional (garden needs, Christmas trees?) grounds. Within
Hunn's flexible, constructive core–periphery model such *ad hoc* intermediate

5.10   *furniture*

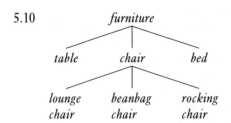

categories make perfect sense; within Berlin's rigid taxonomic model invoking contrast and inclusion, they do not.

Taxonomies in Other Domains?

Taxonomies have been invoked to organize other semantic domains, particularly those of artificial human creations, but recent work (Atran 1987; Gelman and Coley 1991; Wierzbicka 1985, 1992b) now indicates that this move was probably misguided, as taxonomies, if valid at all, are probably restricted to the biological realm. Rosch (1977; Mervis and Rosch 1981; Rosch and Mervis 1975; Rosch, Mervis, Gray, Johnson, and Boyes-Braem 1976) undertook research to investigate the cognitive organization of humanly created artifacts and detected what she took to be a taxonomic structure like that of ethnobiological classification. On the basis of a battery of psychological tests she isolated a *basic level category*, parallel to generic taxa, which refers to classes of intrinsically separate things, with many common attributes, highly similar motor sequences for human manipulation and interaction and strong similarities in shape. Examples of such basic level categories in English are *table, chair, knife,* and *fork.* The basicness of such categories for speakers of English in American culture again is a reflection of the fundamental tenet of enactionism; they realize grounds in which environment and cognition are simultaneously enacted. It was noted that these basic level categories have specifics: e.g. *lounge chair, rocking chair, beanbag chair, dining chair, desk chair,* each with a distinct subset of attributes. There are also inclusive supercategories, like *furniture* or *cutlery,* that the basic level categories were believed to be *kinds* of, generating the now familiar taxonomic organization (5.10). Rosch (1977; Rosch, Mervis, Gray, Johnson, and Boyes-Braem 1976) and others (Kempton 1981; Kronenfeld, Armstrong, and Wilmoth 1985) claim strong prototype effects (a *lounge chair* is a core exemplar of *chair,* as opposed to a *beanbag chair*), with the usual fuzzy boundaries of these categories (is a *refrigerator* a kind of *furniture* or not?).

Recent work (Atran 1987; Wierzbicka 1985, 1992b) strongly argues against taxonomic organizations, like that above, in any area besides ethnobiology.

This claims that there are no true inclusive "supercategories" like *furniture* or *cutlery*. A chair is not a kind of *furniture*, nor a knife a kind of *cutlery*. These are not taxonomic inclusive categories like *bird*; a kookaburra is really a kind of *bird*. Rather, *furniture* labels a kind of function in a particular location (Wierzbicka 1985); objects to which this label can be applied can be humanly created artifacts designed for ease of living and found in places where humans live. A chair can serve this function, but that is not what it is. Consider *cutlery*, which labels humanly created objects which are used to eat food. A knife can serve this function, but it can just as easily serve the function of being a weapon, an object used to harm living things. An object cannot be both a *kind* of *weapon* and *cutlery* at the same time, for the true notion of *kind of* is inherent to the object itself: a *kookaburra* cannot be both a kind of *bird* and a kind of *snake*. This is ruled out because true taxonomic relationships are exclusive, defining characteristics. But a knife is not in a taxonomic relationship to *cutlery*. It is a functional, attributive relationship: a knife can function as *cutlery*, but also as a *weapon* and perhaps even a *tool*. Wierzbicka (1992b) argues that the fuzziness and prototypicality effects of artificial "supercategories" like *furniture* and *cutlery* is due to the fact that they are not taxonomic; the uses to which things are put is much less sharply defined than the kind of thing that something is.

Partonomy

Another type of cognitive organization studied by cognitive anthropologists is the part–whole relationship, sometimes called a partonomy. Similar formal principles are invoked to structure this relationship as with a taxonomy (Andersen 1978; Brown 1976; Burton and Kirk 1979), but such a representation ignores the critical semantic difference: a taxonomy is built on the notion of *kind* of – a kookaburra is a kind of bird, while a partonomy is predicated on the notion of *part* of – the hand is part of the arm. Recognizing this, however, there are still some parallelisms; for example, a higher level category can be inclusive of a lower one, generating occasionally a complex hierarchy (5.11).

5.11

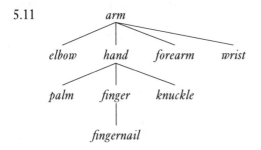

5.12

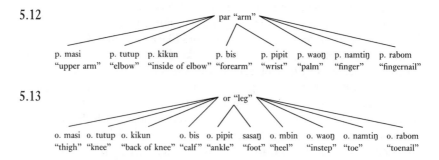

p. masi	p. tutup	p. kikun	p. bis	p. pipit	p. waoŋ	p. namtiŋ	p. rabom
"upper arm"	"elbow"	"inside of elbow"	"forearm"	"wrist"	"palm"	"finger"	"fingernail"

5.13

o. masi	o. tutup	o. kikun	o. bis	o. pipit	sasaŋ	o. mbin	o. waoŋ	o. namtiŋ	o. rabom
"thigh"	"knee"	"back of knee"	"calf"	"ankle"	"foot"	"heel"	"instep"	"toe"	"toenail"

Note that for English speakers, while the hand is part of the arm, it is lexicalized separately. Yimas is the same, contrasting *nŋkwara* "hand" with *maŋkaŋ* "arm." Watam, however, has a single word *par* "hand, arm" covering the entire domain, so its partonomy of the arm would look like 5.12. Note the reduced hierarchical structure in the Watam partonomy as opposed to that for English. Interestingly, the partonomy for *or* "leg" shows close parallels, usually using the same modifying lexemes (5.13). Note that in Watam nails, fingernails, and toenails are conceived as part of the whole arm and leg, *par rabom* "fingernail" and *or rabom* "toenail," not the hand or foot, as in English, in spite of the fact that Watam has a distinct lexeme at least for "foot," *sasaŋ*.

It has been claimed (Andersen 1978; Casson 1983) that partonomies are also like taxonomies in possessing basic level, high salience categories (similar to generic taxa) dominating specific categories and being dominated by inclusive "supercategories." Examples of the basic level categories are said to be *hand, foot, eye*, etc., with *arm, leg*, and *face* inclusive supercategories and *finger, toe*, and *pupil* specific ones. While English supports such claims, Watam at face value refutes it, since there is no evidence for a basic level category *hand* as part of an inclusive supercategory *arm* and having a specific subordinate category *finger*. There is no unitary category *hand* at all; rather, it is analyzed into areas designated as parts of *par* "arm." Further, while Watam does possess a lexeme *sasaŋ* "foot," none of its parts are described in terms of it. They are named as parts of *or* "leg," exactly parallel to the situation for *par* "arm." The Watam data suggests there may be much more language-specific relativity in partonomies of the body-part domain than some current strong advocates of universal principles underlying systems of ethnoanatomy would care to admit.

Scripts and Cultural Practices

As mentioned above, much of the later work in cognitive anthropology has been inspired by ongoing developments in the field of artificial intelligence.

One of the most pervasive ideas imported from artificial intelligence is that of scripts (Casson 1983; Schank and Abelson 1977). Scripts are cognitive-event schemas, how actions are intended to unfold in the normal course of things. They represent the standardized knowledge a Native has of how to accomplish things in the culture. In this sense, they are not typically claimed to be strongly underlain by innate universal principles and represent a partial return to earlier goals within cognitive anthropology: "culture consists of whatever one has to know or believe in order to operate in a manner acceptable to its members" (Goodenough 1964[1957]:36). A commonly cited example for American and other Western cultures is *Eating Out at a Restaurant*. All of us by being socialized as members of these cultures have clear expectations of how this should unfold, from the process of getting seated, ordering, eating, paying, and leaving. Even variations from the most stereo-typical enactment of this script is standardized: e.g. getting the waiter's attention for sending undercooked food back to the kitchen. The script concept, then, is a powerful idea for thinking about the cognitive organization of cultural information, and not surprisingly has been enthusiastically embraced by cognitive anthropologists (Agar 1972; Dougherty and Keller 1985; Holland and Skinner 1987; Lutz 1987).

Some earlier ethnographic work can profitably be recast in the script frame-work, and for illustration purposes, I will do just that, rephrasing Frake's (1972) well-known study of Subanun drinking practices. The Subanun engage in drinking bouts of a beer-like alcoholic beverage *gasi* as part of particular festivities. Just as Americans have clear standardized expectations as to how dining in a restaurant should proceed, the Subanun have set idealized cognitive representations, a script, for these drinking bouts. An analysis in terms of the concept of script hopes to lay out clearly the cognitive understanding the Subanun have of these occasions.

The drink, *gasi*, is drunk through bamboo straws from a Chinese jar. The source of the beer is a mash made of rice, manioc maize and/or Job's tears mash. Water is added to this mash filling the jar to the brim to produce a drinkable liquid. Each drinker takes a turn in drinking from the straw, after which the jar is filled again to the brim. A round is completed when all drinkers in the group have had a turn; a new round then commences. The drinking bout is divided into three periods, each with its own distinctive expected behavior, especially verbal behavior. The first period is the tasting stage. The drinking behavior consists of brief turns with little attention to gauging individual consumption. The verbal behavior at this stage is concerned with setting up social rank. The provider of the jar with *gasi* invites someone to drink first, thereby signalling that the recipient is the person to which he and his kin in the group owe the greatest deference. The recipient asks permission of the others one by one to initiate drinking. The term of address, kin terms or otherwise, that he uses to address each member of the group delimits his view of their social relationship. After drinking, the initial drinker normally invites the person who invited him to drink first to go next. This is the normal expectation, the most stereotypical script, but he may do otherwise, in this case signalling a particular kind of marked social relationship.

After the preparatory stage one, the drinking bout proceeds to the major phase, stage two of competitive drinking. The drinking behavior consists of much longer turns, with careful gauging of individual consumption. Each drinker keeps a mental record of each other's consumption in a round, and successive drinkers must equal the consumption of the initial drinker of the round. As the brew gets weaker, the required mark of consumption gets progressively raised. Some individual drinkers may retire from the group at this stage. Further, other types of non-linguistic behavior may now co-occur with drinking, such as music, dancing, and singing. The verbal behavior associated with competitive drinking is more varied than at stage one. Drinkers exchange information and discuss the quality of the brew, and their individual drinking performance is evaluated by others. The amount of verbal responses a drinker can elicit from the others indicates the amount of drinking and talking time the others will give him. If he feels discouraged he will drop out, and typically the group gets reduced to less than half-a-dozen men.

At this point a second substage of verbal behavior, which we might call discussion, emerges within stage two of competitive drinking. The face-to-face verbal interaction intensifies, with gossip being freely exchanged. At first confined to relatively trivial topics, it shifts in many cases to more weighty ones, concerned with what we might see as legal questions, as there is no organized juridical system in Subanun society. Drinkers compete with each other in effective legal decisions, but this requires commanding a dominating role in the drinking bout, both verbally and drinking wise. He who succeeds by cogent argumentation in getting his legal arbitration accepted thereby increases his social status.

Finally, the drinking bout proceeds to stage three, game drinking. Turns become shorter again, drinking games occur and opposite-sex pairs team up for drinking together. The verbal behavior too signals this change to a less serious and more jocular vein of interaction, although competition among drinkers is still central. The phonological form of the utterances may be creatively played with through verbal games, using stylized song and verse patterns. Verbal duelling occurs and unfinished legal questions may be settled in this manner, replacing cogent argumentation with displays of verbal artistry. The whole point of stage three is to conclude the drinking bout on a note of conviviality, and drinkers who displayed hostility during earlier stages of the bout may receive special attention to minimize rancor.

The script for Subanun drinking may be summarized as follows:

Subanun Drinking

		Drink	Talk
Stage 1:	Tasting	Brief turns; don't gauge consumption	Invitations: set up social rank
Stage 2:	Competitive drinking	Longer turns; gauge consumption closely; some drinkers retire; sing, dance	1. Exchange information: brew, performance, "light" topics 2. Discussion: gossip, "serious" topics, legal questions. Winning argumentation in resolving disputes
Stage 3:	Game drinking	Shorten turns. Engage in drinking games	Engage in language games: verbal duelling used to resolve disputes

This is the idealized cognitive script that a Subanun Native has for drinking bouts of *gasi*. Individual bouts may diverge somewhat from the stereotypical script, but if they diverge too far, they will no longer be recognized as appropriate bouts of *gasi* drinking in Subanun culture (see the discussion of genre in chapter 18). It is in this sense that such a script may be claimed to represent the cognitive organization of this behavior for Subanun Natives. And it is the determination of such Native cognitive representations which at base is the goal of all cognitive anthropology. Those who claim robust innate and universal ideas within the human mind simply argue further that these function to constrain severely the form of any such Native cognitive representation. Two semantic domains where such robust innate and universal constraints have been posited are kinship and color terminologies. The next two chapters will present case studies of each of these domains.

Summary

Cognitive anthropology is an American school of structuralism that developed out of earlier Boasian work in linguistic anthropology. It holds that culture is to be reduced to cognition and is interested in the mental representation of cultural practices, rather than the behavior itself, a clear Platonic position. Various analytical procedures and systems of representation drawn from structural linguistics or cognitive psychology, such as componential analysis, taxonomies and scripts, are employed to represent explicitly this cognitive organization of cultural phenomena. In its earlier period, cognitive anthropology exhibited relativist tendencies, but ultimately became thoroughly rationalist and universalist. This is clearly illustrated in Berlin's and others' descriptions of systems of ethnobiological classification. All ethnobiological classification systems are organized in the same way, a shallow taxonomy of no more than six mutually exclusive ranks. Further, Berlin claims that these classifications are determined by universal perceptual and cognitive faculties, with no mediation of cultural practices. Others have traced this putative universal basis of classification to a "hidden nature" universally apprehensible by all human cognizers, while some have challenged the strong universalist claims for the basis of ethnobiological classifications and argue that cultural practices do indeed have a role in their framing. Other areas in which cognitive anthropological research has been productive are in partonomies, the relations of parts to whole and the application of the artificial intelligence idea of scripts as a way to describe culture practices.

Further Reading

The history of cognitive anthropology up to the present is well reviewed in D'Andrade (1995). Tyler (1969) anthologizes key articles in its earlier relativist period. For more recent developments, see Casson's (1983) and Dougherty's (1985) collections of articles. Berlin (1992) is a thorough treatment of his work on ethnobiology, while Atran (1990), Gelman and Cooley (1991), and Wierzbicka (1992b) develop the theory of natural hidden essences and its implications.

6

Kinship

The Terms of Kinship Analysis

Of all topics within anthropological linguistics, kinship has probably attracted the keenest and most sustained interest. It is also a favorite semantic domain in which cognitive anthropologists like to demonstrate the usefulness of their approach. Like many other semantic domains, the analysis of kinship has been studied from two perspectives, universalist (Goodenough 1970; Lounsbury 1965, 1969; Murdock 1949) and relativist (Leach 1958, 1962; Needham 1971; Schneider 1980, 1984). On the face of it, kinship would seem to be a good domain in which to demonstrate universals, for mating and reproduction is a necessary feature of any viable society. Surprisingly, then, the kinship systems of the world's languages, the way Natives classify their kin, while falling into a number of types, are quite variable. The purpose of the work of cognitive anthropologists has been to argue that beneath this apparent variation is a system of universal categories to which any kinship system can be reduced. In keeping with the theme of this Part, I will confine myself mainly to analyses of kinship systems based on universalist assumptions, turning at the end to a brief consideration of relativist critiques.

An approach to the analysis of kinship systems based on strong universalist assumptions is a venerable tradition in anthropology, clearly traceable at least to Malinowski (1929), if not Morgan (1871). Malinowski (1929, 1930) saw the genesis of kinship within the nuclear family, with its primary kinship relationships being the basis of all kinship, the wider kinship relations in the society being derived from these by a process of extension. This view was reiterated by Murdock (1949:92–3), who sees the nuclear family as a cultural universal:

> The point of departure for the analysis of kinship is the nuclear family. Universally, it is in this social group that the developing child . . . learns to

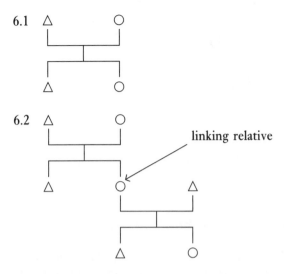

6.1

6.2

linking relative

respond in particular ways towards his father, his mother, his brothers and sisters, and to expect certain kinds of behavior in return.

Thus, the units of analysis for kinship systems are to be terms based on the universal categories of the nuclear family: parents, spouses, children, and siblings (6.1) (△ indicates a male person and ○ a female; ⌊____⌋ a marriage bond; | a descent parent–child relationship; and ⌈____⌉ a sibling relationship). More complex kinship relations are based on these units through extension via a linking relative. Figure 6.2 indicates two nuclear family units knitted together into a larger kinship grouping through a female-linking relative, a daughter/sister within one nuclear family, but a mother/wife in the other.

Universals of Kinship

The kinship terms of the nuclear family can be said to be the universal salient foci of any kinship system as well as its fundamental building blocks. In a sense, then, they are somewhat parallel to the focal colors of color terminologies (see chapter 7) or the generic taxa in ethnobiological classification, but just how parallel? The universal principles underlying these other two systems can reasonably be claimed to lie in biological constraints – panhuman, universal, and innate perceptual and cognitive faculties underlie categorizations in these domains, recognizing natural discontinuities, but do this *independently of any cultural mediation*. Clearly, any presumed universals of kinship systems cannot lie in perceptual universals, for our kin are not different in any obvious perceptual way from non-kin. Rather, any universals of structure must be due to biological constraints on the arrangements of human reproduction and our cognitive understandings of these constraints. While universals of ethnobiological classification and color terminology have reasonable claims to being innate, this is not likely to be true of universals of kinship systems; following Murdock's (1949) comments above, they are probably due to universal human experiences in the process of socialization. Is it reasonable to claim that kinship systems, at least in their fundamental outlines, are organized in terms of these biological constraints and independently of any cultural mediation? Sahlins (1977) claims that it is not, but Wierzbicka (1992a) claims that it is, at least in part. She wants to argue that mother and father are the most primitive units in all kinship systems and these are to be defined in their most basic senses in strictly biological and hence universal terms: mother as the person that bore one and father as the person who provided the needed wherewithal for the mother to bear one (genitor). If kinship systems were based on this formula, an exposition of them in universal terms would indeed be straightforward, but the anthropological literature provides many contraindications to it, especially with the concept of father, for while who bore me is readily apparent, who provided the wherewithal for this event is, as thousands of paternity blood tests demonstrate, not so.

Many ethnographic descriptions show that the genitor is not the primary designation of the term father in many languages. Consider the case of the Nayar of southern India (Gough 1959, 1961). In this society before a girl has her first menstruation she undergoes a ceremony which forms a permanent union with a young man. He leaves the girl after a few days, having had sexual relations or not, but all rights of sexual access cease on his departure. The girl is now free to enter into liaisons, even multiple ones, with other men and may bear children from these men, who could then acknowledge paternity by the bestowal of gifts. The children concerned, however, do not refer to their genitors by the term for father *appan*; that is reserved for the young man with whom she formed a permanent union in the premenstrual ceremony, someone with whom their mother may never have had sexual relations. The Nayar case clearly demonstrates the unviability of Wierzbicka's position on the centrality of universal, biological notions for the term father, and supports Sahlins' (1977) of the crucial mediation of culture in the construction of meaning in a kinship system.

Wierzbicka (1992a) is probably much closer to the mark in the case of mother. It is rarely, if ever, the case that the Native term for mother does not necessarily include the bearer of the child, for obvious biological reasons (for one interesting possibly problematic case, that of Mota in Vanuatu, see Rivers (1914)). Goodenough (1970) makes the important and, I think, valid point that it is really the relationship between the mother and child

6.3

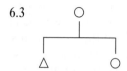

that defines the nuclear family. This is really the fundamental unit for the genealogical reckoning of kinship. The father, then, is simply the marriage partner of the mother at the onset of her pregnancy who is responsible for the personhood of the child within the society, with the consequent duties toward it and the rights over it (anthropological notion of *pater*). The notion of personhood is important here, for it indicates why the Nayar father is not the genitor, but the young man in the premenstrual ceremony: it is he and only he, who by engaging in this ceremony, made her eligible to engage in sexual relations and ultimately bear new social persons, although his rights and duties with respect to these persons are negligible. David Wilkins (personal communication) provides further evidence for the father as the marriage partner who is the social person maker. Among the Arrernte of central Australia, if a woman who is married to a man of one kin group bears a child by a man of another kin group, the kin group classification of the husband will be used to reckon that of the child; he will be the father and determine what kind of person this child is, i.e. which kin group he belongs to.

The basic atom then of kinship systems is the bond between mother and child (6.3). This is clearly a biologically based universal, but may have particular cultural constructions, for example, in Mota (Rivers 1914), and certainly will be associated with culturally specific symbolic elaborations (Bean 1978, 1981; Lakoff 1987; Turner 1987). The link between mother and child is the basis of genealogy, a basic axis of structure in all systems of kinship. Father is not a concept grounded universally in biology; rather, it is culturally constructed: the man who the culture regards as responsible for the social personhood of the child. Malinowski's (1929, 1930) naturalist approach to kinship boils down in this perspective to a claim that genealogical levels defined in this way through the mother–child link, plus other naturally given biological categories, will be sufficient to generate all kinship systems. The person using any kinship term or the reference point for any reckoning of a kinship relation is called *ego*; any kinship system is always seen from the perspective of a particular ego.

An Analysis of Watam Consanguineal Kin Terms

The basic structure underlying a kinship system is typically approached through an analysis of the Native terminology used by someone to refer to kin categories, as all kinship systems are built up by joining together different nuclear family atoms through linking relatives. Thus, the English word *mother* refers to just this, ego's mother, while ego's mother's sister is called *aunt*. In Watam, both of these categories would be covered by a single term *aem*. Clearly, if we are to arrive at an understanding of the structure of a kinship system through an analysis of the categories denoted by the Native terms, a metalanguage in which to cast these denotata is necessary. Typically, those of English for the nuclear family are used: father (F), mother (M), brother (B), sister (Z), wife (W), husband (H), son (S), and daughter (D). ♀ and ♂ indicate female and male egos and o and y, older and younger relative age. A large subset of the Watam kinship terminology, that of blood relations or consanguines, can be glossed using this system as follows:

bijir	FFFF (i.e. ego's father's father's father's father), MMMM, FFFFB, FFFFZ, MMMMM, FFFFF, MMMMZ, MMMMB, SSSS, SSSD, BSSSS, ZSSSS, BDSDD, ZSDSS, SSSSS, DDDDD, etc.
ŋgamar	FFF, MMM, FFFB, FFFZ, MMMB, MMMZ, SSS, SSD, BSSS, ZSSS, BDSD, ZSDS, etc.
nenkai	FF, FM, MF, MM, FFB, FMB, FMZ, FFZ, MFB, MMZ, MMB, MFZ, FFFBZ, MFFZD, MMMZS, MMMZD, etc.
aes	F, FB, FFBS, FMZS, etc.
aem	M, MZ, MMZD, MFZD, FFZD, etc.
akwae	MB, MFS, MMS, MMZS, etc.
namkwae	FZ, FMD, FFD, FFZD, FFBD, etc.
yakai	♀eZ, ♀FBeD, ♀FZeD, ♀MBeD, ♀MZeD, ♂eB, ♂FBeS, ♂FZeS, ♂MBeS, ♂MZeS, etc.
yap	♀yZ, ♀FByD, ♀FZyD, ♀MByD, ♀MZyD, ♂yB, ♂FByS, ♂FZyS, ♂MByS, ♂MZyS, etc.
ondaŋ	♀B, ♀FBS, ♀FZS, ♀MBS, ♀MZS, etc.
mbi	♂Z, ♂FBD, ♂FZD, ♂MBD, ♂MZD, etc.
itiŋ	S, BS, ♀ZS, FBSS, FZSS, etc.
namoŋ	D, BD, ♀ZD, FBSD, FZSD, etc.
amuk	♂ZS, ♂ZD, ♂MZDD, ♂MZDS, etc.
rumbun	SS, SD, DS, DD, BSS, BSD, ZSS, ZSD, etc.

The "etc." at the end of the lists of referents for each term indicate that these terms in principle apply to an infinite list of kin relationships. This is not very helpful in elucidating the cognitive principles underlying the kinship system, nor, indeed, is such a simple listing of referents. Anyone familiar with the literature of kinship can work out from this listing the basic structure of the system, but, of course, an explicit logical analysis laying all this out is our ultimate goal, and one, given our universalistic focus in this chapter, employing universal biological categories.

The first of these, already mentioned, is genealogical, defined as the mother–child link. The Watam kinship terminological system ranges over no less than nine genealogical levels. Taking ego's generation as zero, we can recognize the outermost genealogical level in the Watam system represented by *bijir* as four levels removed from it in either ascending generations (ego's MMMM) or descending (ego's DDDD). Thus, there are four mother–child links separating ego from any kin relation denoted by *bijir* (6.4). There are no other semantic dimensions relevant to the meaning of *bijir* and so it can be simply defined as:

bijir   Kin G^4

The next kin term *ŋgamar* is parallel: it covers three generational links in ascending or descending order from ego (MMM and DDD), with no further semantic contrasts:

ŋgamar   Kin G^3

With two genealogical levels removed from ego, the symmetry between ascending and descending generations disappears. We find distinct terms for the ascending and descending generations, but no further semantic differentiation:

nenkai   Kin G^{+2}
rumbun   Kin G^{-2}

As we come closer to ego's generation, the symmetry between ascending and descending generations disappears and more semantic features become relevant to an explicit description of the meaning of the terms. Let us consider the first ascending generation, which contrasts four terms: *aes*, *aem*, *akwae*, and *namkwae*. *aes* refers to "father," but it also covers all male (S^M) blood relatives of father's generation (G^{+1}) related to ego, *not* linked to him through his mother, the parent of opposite sex to these male relatives. The semantic feature referring to the linking relative as being the same or different sex to the kin category is known as parallel (same sex) or cross (different sex). This may be explicitly represented with a feature P(arallel), specified + or −.

6.4 △   ○ MMMM (*bijir*)

```
+4
+3
+2
+1
EGO △
−1
−2
−3
−4
```

○ DDDD (*bijir*)

aes   Kin $G^{+1}P^+$ S^M

aem is similar to *aes*. It denotes all female (S^F) consanguineal relations linked to ego through a parent of the same sex (parallel), i.e. his mother:

aem   Kin G^{+1} P^+ S^F

The other kin terms of the first ascending generation refer to the consanguineal cross kin categories (P^-). *akwae* refers to male relatives of the first ascending generation linked to ego through the opposite-sex parent, mother, i.e. prototypically MB, while *namkwae* covers the other case, female relatives of G^{+1} linked to ego through the male parent, e.g. FZ. The former, as we shall see, is especially important in the system with a reciprocal G^{-1} term *amuk*. These two terms are defined then as:

akwae   Kin G^{+1} P^- S^M
namkwae   Kin G^{+1} P^- S^F

In ego's own generation (G^0), the Watam kinship system reveals itself as being basically of Hawaiian type, with no contrast between siblings and cousins. The basic dimensions of semantic contrast in G^0 are the intrinsic sex of the kin referred to, its sex relative to that of ego, and their relative ages. If ego and her sibling/cousin are of opposite sex, different terms, undifferentiated for age, are used than if they are of the same sex. Thus, a male speaker calls his sister/cousin *mbi*, while a female speaker calls her brother/cousin *ondaŋ*. We can extend the use of the parallel feature introduced above to cover this as well: same sex siblings/cousins being P^+, opposite P^-:

mbi   Kin G^0 P^- S^F
ondaŋ   Kin G^0 P^- S^M

If ego's sex and that of the sibling/cousin are the same, the kin terms are not differentiated for sex, but for relative age, one term *yakai* for those kin older than ego and another *yap* for those younger:

yakai   Kin G^0 P^+ A^O
yap   Kin G^0 P^+ S^Y

Finally, we come to the first descending generation, which has three terms: *itiŋ*, *namoŋ*, and *amuk*. The crucial fact here is that *amuk* is the reciprocal of *akwae*: whoever categorizes a particular kin relation as an *akwae* is in turn referred to by this kin as *amuk*. Members of the kin category *amuk* can be of either sex, but the labelling ego must always be male, i.e. an *akwae*, G^{+1} S^M P^-. What crucially defines *amuk* then is that the male ego is linked to the referent by an opposite-sex sibling, his sister. Thus, the relationship is a cross one (P^-), but this alone is insufficient because it would also include the relationship FZ and BS and BD. We also need to specify the sex of the linking relative, in this case, the mother, who is female. Note the differences shown in separate diagrams in 6.5. Clearly, two features are needed: P^- to distinguish the relations in (b) from (c) (MB versus MZ), and sex of linking relative as female to distinguish (b) from (a) (MB versus FZ). *amuk* can then be defined as:

6.5

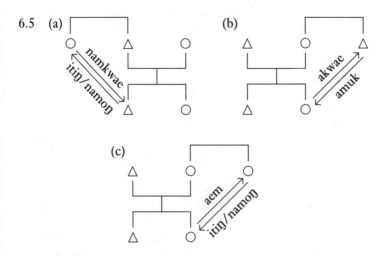

amuk   Kin G⁻¹ P⁻ SLRᶠ

Note that the sex of the referent is *not* relevant to *amuk*, covering both ♂ZD and ♂ZS. In this it differs from *itiŋ* and *namoŋ* which do contrast according to inherent sex. The meaning of these terms can be represented as:

itiŋ   Kin G⁻¹ Sᴹ
namoŋ   Kin G⁻¹ Sᶠ

The delimitation of the respective semantic domains of these three terms can be established by invoking a rough analog of the linguistic elsewhere principle (Andrews 1990; Kiparsky 1973), that is, the most highly specified term is preferentially applied first. If that is inapplicable, then less specific terms are available. For kin relations of G⁻¹, *amuk* is the most highly specified term; if its semantic features are met, the kin relation falls under the category labelled by that term. If this is not the case, then either *itiŋ* or *namoŋ* is applicable, depending on the referent's sex.

Lounsbury's Reduction Rules and Universals of Kinship

This analysis of the semantic dimensions of consanguineal kin terms in Watam reveals kinship relations in this culture to be structured entirely in universal biologically given terms like generation, sex and age, in line with Malinowski's (1929, 1930) views. Pursuing this further, can the Watam data be used to support Murdock's (1949) even stronger constraint that the fundamental atom of kinship is the universal nuclear family, the mother and her children and her associated spouse, the father? Prima facie, the Watam data seem to contradict this, with, for example, *aem* "mother" extending to MZ, MMZD, MFZD, FFZD, etc., i.e. all kin of G^{+1} P^+ S^F. Lounsbury (1965, 1969), however, has developed pioneering ideas reconciling systems like those of Watam with Murdock's claim. Lounsbury argues that kin categories are structured in terms of a focal member, i.e. within the nuclear family or having the closest link to it, and non-focal members more distantly linked. Thus, for the kin category denoted by Watam *aem* the focal member is M and non-focal members of increasing distance are exemplified by MZ, MMZD, FFZD, etc. The use of focal and non-focal membership by Lounsbury (1965, 1969) was an early precursor of Rosch's (1977, 1978) development of prototype theory. Lounsbury captures the relationship between the focal and non-focal members of the category through a small set of reduction rules which assimilate the latter to the former, claiming in essence that the latter are a special kind of extended case of the former. A simple example of this is the half-sibling rule, operative even in the English kinship system. It states that any child of either of one's parents is one's sibling. Thus, the English term *brother* applies to our half brothers as well as our full brothers. This can be explicitly written as PCh → Sb (parent's child equals sibling); a summary of the following more specific cases:

> FS → B
> MS → B
> FD → Z
> MD → Z

This rule is operative in Watam as in English; thus, *ondaŋ* ♀B also covers ♀FS and *mbi* ♂Z applies to ♂MD.

The next rule, the merging rule, is not found in the English kinship system, but is central to that of Watam. It applies to parallel siblings and states that a person's parallel sibling as a linking relative is equivalent to that person herself. Parallel siblings are equivalent as long as *one of them is a linking relative*. Thus, a woman's sister as a linking relative to a more distant kin relation is equivalent to the woman herself. Considering both sexes, we can state this more abstractly as:

> ♂B ... → ♂ ...
> ♀Z ... → ♀ ...

The reciprocals of these last two rules also hold: any parallel sibling of a linking relative is equivalent to the linking relative:

> ... ♂B → ... ♂
> ... ♀Z → ... ♀

The merging rule is of paramount importance in understanding the extensions of Watam kin categories beyond the nuclear family. Consider, first, the extension of *aem* M to MZ. MZ reduces to M by a simple application of the merging rule ♀Z . . . → ♀ . . . , my MZ → my M. This is extended to MMZD by application of the merging rule and half-sibling rule: my MMZD → MMD (merging rule: ♀Z . . . → ♀ . . . ; MZ . . . → M . . .), MMD → MZ (half-sibling rule: PCh → Sb; MD → Z), MZ → M (merging rule: . . . ♀Z → . . . ♀; MZ → M).

The merging rule is of wide provenance in Watam. As expected, it applies to a man's brothers as well: FFBS → FFS (merging rule: ♂B . . . → ♂ . . . ; FB . . . → F . . .), FFS → FB (half-sibling rule: PCh → Sb; FS → B), FB → F (merging rule: . . . ♂B → . . . ♂; FB → F). So the Watam kin term *aes* has the focal member F and the non-focal extended membership FFBS. The G⁰ terms are also subject to it. For example, the focal member of the term *yakai* is ♀eZ. But the merging rule extends this to ♀FBeD as well: ♀FBeD → ♀FeD (merging rule: . . . ♂B → . . . ♂; . . . FB → . . . F), ♀FeD → ♀eZ (half-sibling rule: PCh → Sb; FD → Z). For an example on G⁻¹ level consider *amuk* which has the focal member ♂ZD, but non-focal ♂MZDD: ♂MZDD → ♂MDD (merging rule . . . ♀Z → . . . ♀; . . . MZ → . . . M), ♂MDD → ♂ZD (half-sibling rule: PCh → Sb; MD → Z).

The straightforward application of Lounsbury's ideas to Watam data is further vindication of Malinowski's (1929, 1930) and Murdock's (1949) position on the universal basis of kinship systems, using biologically given dimensions, like genealogy, age, and sex. But Watam is a rather easy case because it adheres to natural generational differences very strictly. Much more problematic cases would be systems of kinship terminology which obscure natural genealogical levels by throwing together into one kin term category relations of more than one genealogical level. Such systems, well attested in the cultures of the world, are known as Crow-Omaha systems of kinship terminology. I will restrict my attention to Crow systems in this book and will illustrate with the Crow-type kin terminology of the Trobriand Islanders of New Guinea (Lounsbury 1965; Malinowski 1929).

Crow-type Kinship Systems

Crow-type kinship terminological systems are commonly, but not exclusively, found in societies which have descent rules with a matrilineal bias, i.e. membership in a central social category is decided by one's mother's group. This is in contrast to patrilineal descent in which one's membership is fixed by that of one's father. Membership in this social grouping may determine many aspects of one's social life: where one may live, who one may marry, and many other rights and duties pertinent to the individual. Crow-type

6.6

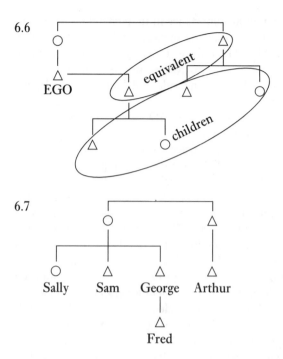

6.7

systems are commonly associated with matrilineal societies (Trobriand society, for example, is one) because they associate males of the same matriline. The basic principle of a Crow-type system is to equate a woman's brother (G^0) with her son (G^{-1}). They are treated as equivalent in certain respects for the purposes of kinship reckoning, although individual Crow systems differ slightly in the way they treat this equivalence. What is common to all, however, is a rule which equates MBCh with BCh, which, for a man, due to the merging rule equates them to his children: δBCh $\rightarrow \delta$Ch. This relation is shown in 6.6.

In such systems, MB and B are equivalent as linking relatives, so that their children are classified with the same term.

This categorization also operates reciprocally, consider 6.7 (drawn from Keesing 1975:114). Sam will classify both Fred and Arthur as S by the above principle because they are the children of his B and MB respectively. They, in turn will call him F, even though Arthur is of the same generation as Sam. Thus, because a man classifies this MBCh as Ch, they in turn classify their FZS as F. This is the effect for male egos, muddling of the generational reckoning. What about female egos? Consider Sally. To her, Fred is BCh, a cross "nephew," as is Arthur, due to the equivalent MB = B. For both Arthur and Fred, Sally is a cross "aunt," but note that Arthur is of the same generation as Sally, so again generations are conflated.

6.8

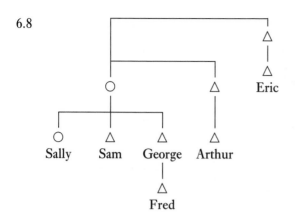

In most Crow systems, this equivalence of a woman's brother with her son spreads out across the generations, so that relations of dispersed generations may be categorized with the same kin term. For example, MMBCh may be equated with BCh (MMBCh = MMSCh (because a woman's brother is equated to her son) = MBCh (by half-sibling rule) = BCh (muddling of generations)). Consider this in 6.8 (also from Keesing 1975:144). Sam classifies Eric with Arthur and Fred as BS and, as a male ego, ultimately as S (merging rule: $\male B \ldots \rightarrow \male \ldots$). All of them then categorize Sam as F, in spite of that Eric is one generation above him. Sally, as a female ego classifies Eric as BS, a cross "nephew," as established above; he categorizes her as FZ, a cross "aunt," again even though he is one generation higher.[3]

Trobriand Kinship and the Skewing Rule

Lounsbury (1965, 1969) attempts to account for this generational muddling of Crow-type systems with a third type of reduction rule, a skewing rule, which in essence states the equivalence of a woman's brother and her son. Slightly different versions of this rule are needed for different Crow-type systems. In the Trobriand case considered here, the rule is restricted to the two males as linking relatives. Thus:

$$\female B \ldots \rightarrow \female S \ldots$$

Let any woman's brother, as a linking relative, be regarded as equivalent to her son as a linking relative. This equivalence is recognized in the Trobriand kin terminology with the term *kada* which is used reciprocally to refer to one's MB and to a $\male$ZCh (6.9).

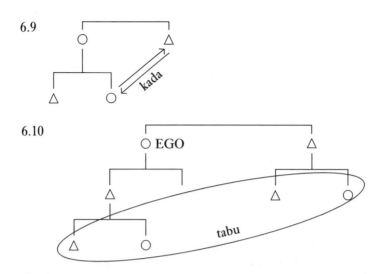

6.9

6.10

This skewing rule results in the expected equivalence as shown in 6.10. Thus, my (♀ ego) brother's children are equated to my son's children and categorized under the single term *tabu*. Crucially, and most strikingly, a parallel equivalence must hold between the reciprocals of these two kintypes. FZ is the reciprocal of BCh and FM is the reciprocal of ♀SCh. So:

FZ → FM

or any person's father's sister is also to be regarded as equivalent to that person's father's mother. And, although FZ and FM are of different generations (G^{+1} and G^{+2} respectively), they are again categorized under the same kin term *tabu*, which now spans four generations: FM (G^{+2}), FZ (G^{+1}), BCh (G^{-1}) and SCh (G^{-2}); see 6.11.

This Trobriand version of the Crow-type generation skewing rule operates in concert with the earlier discussed half-sibling and merging rules to categorize non-focal more distant kin relations under those of closer focal or basic meanings of the terms. The basic or focal meanings of the kin terms are those closest to the collateral line of the nuclear family. Thus, for *tabu* it is G^2, grandparent and the reciprocal grandchild, i.e. FF, FM, MF, MM, SS, SD, DS, DD. FZ is a less close non-focal extension of *tabu* due to the skewing rule: FZ → FM. Sample reductions to account for the extensions of the kin terms to more distant kin relations follow (Lounsbury 1965:172–3):

$$♂MBS \quad \rightarrow \quad ♂MSS \text{ (skewing rule: ♀B} \ldots \rightarrow ♀S)$$
$$\rightarrow \quad ♂BS \text{ (half-sibling rule: MS} \rightarrow B)$$
$$\rightarrow \quad ♂S \text{ (merging rule: ♂B} \ldots \rightarrow ♂ \ldots)$$
$$\therefore \quad \textit{latu} \text{ "child" } G^{-1}$$

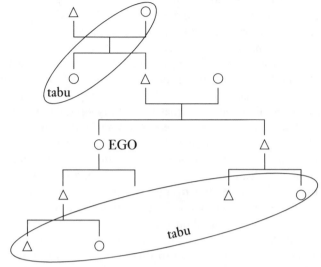

♀MBS	→	♀MSS (skewing rule: ♀B ... → ♀S)
	→	♀BS (half-sibling rule: MS → B)
	→	♀SS (skewing rule: ♀B ... → ♀S)
	∴	*tabu* "grandchild" G^2
FZS	→	FMS (skewing rule: FZ → FM)
	→	FB (half-sibling rule: MS → B)
	→	F (merging rule: ♂B ... → ♂ ...)
	∴	*tama* "father" $G^{+1}S^M$
FZDD	→	FMDD (skewing rule: FZ → FM)
	→	FZD (half-sibling rule: MD → Z)
	→	FMD (skewing rule: FZ → FM)
	→	FZ (half-sibling rule: MD → Z)
	→	FM (skewing rule: FZ → FM)
	∴	*tabu* "grandparent" G^2

Universals and Variation in Kinship Systems

Lounsbury's work in reduction rules and, in particular, their operation in Crow-type systems is of fundamental importance in the understanding of the systems of kinship terminologies and their relevance for studies of universal constraints in categorization. These reduction rules, especially the half-sibling and merging rules, are remarkably widespread and show sur-prisingly little variation from system to system. This can be read to support the claim that universal and innate processes of human cognition underlie the structure of kinship systems from culture to culture. The operation of particular reduction rules may allow some variation in kin classification, but this is strictly constrained. For example, MZ can be classed with M (merging rule: Watam) or not (English), and FZ can be classed with FM (skewing rule: Trobriand) or not (English), but there are strict limits to this. No known system classifies MZ with FM and opposes both to FZ. It is universal constraints of this type that Lounsbury's reduction rules seek to capture by determining possible extensions from focal members to non-focal ones. There seems little doubt that many heavy constraints inform possible systems of kinship terminology, for all attested systems fall into a very small number of distinct types, with relatively minor internal variation, not unlike the possible vowel systems of languages.

The basic standpoint of reckoning for these postulated universally constrained processes of kin classification are the focal kin terms of the nuclear family and its collateral line of ascending and descending generations. Focal members are those closest to this line. In Rosch's (1977, 1978) terms, these are the basic level of categorization. From an enactionist or embodied practices perspective, the focal members are prototypically associated with culturally defined, highly salient styles of interpersonal interaction. Within the most focal set of kin terms, those of the nuclear family members, especially mother and child, the biological bedrock of the focal membership of kinship categories most clearly emerges. Kinship systems are cultural constructions, no doubt, but the scaffolding of such constructions are, to a large extent anyway, the universal biological categories given by nature, sex, age, and genealogy. Humans observe these biological features in the persons around them, and they are used to inform the structuring of social reality we call kinship (see Gellner 1973). But the possible structures are heavily constrained, and these biological features are important universal variables in these constraints. Lounsbury's importance lies in his demonstration that, contrary to appearances, biologically reckoned genealogy is central to Crow-type systems. In these systems, generational skewing is the result of a principle of equivalence which depends upon the prior specification of the genealogical level of focal members of the kin terms. In the Trobriand terminology, *tabu* is specified focally as G^2; this is prior to its extension through skewing to $FZ(G^{+1})$ and $\female MBS(G^0)$.

Relativist Responses to Universalist Approaches to Kinship

The universally constrained biological basis of kinship systems, upheld by Goodenough (1970), Lounsbury (1965, 1969), Malinowski (1929, 1930) and

Murdock (1949), has not gone unchallenged by those of a more relativist persuasion. Indeed, Lounsbury's (1965) analysis of the Trobriand system was itself a response to one such description of this system by Leach (1958, 1962). Other figures with relativist views include Needham (1971) and Schneider (1980, 1984). Leach and Needham, inspired by Lévi-Strauss's (1969) alliance theory, see kinship terminologies as not being structured in mainly biological, and particularly genealogical, terms, but, rather in social ones. Individuals then are not classified into particular kin categories according to their genealogical connections, but because of their membership in certain social groupings, especially those defined by descent or marriage prescriptions. Thus, the Watam term *aes* kin $G^{+1}P^{+}S^{M}$ or with Lounsbury's prototype theory F, extending out to FB by the merging rule ($\male$B ... → $\male$ ... : FB → F), has, in Leech and Needham's conception of kin terms as marking social categories, the meaning "man of father's clan." All relations within each social category denoted by a kin term are reckoned as equivalent members; there is no focal versus non-focal membership distinction.

Kin terms often have much wider uses than just reference to persons related through kin-type (i.e. biological) relationships. Kinship as a clear-cut semantic domain is commonly claimed to be an ethnocentric imposition of our cultural categories on those of the local culture, for which kinship is not neatly separable from other aspects of social organization. Schneider (1984) argues that the anthropological construction of a domain of kinship demarked by kinship terminologies is no more than an elevation of a local common-sense western European theory of relatedness through biology to a position of a scientific theory. He calls this the "blood is thicker than water" assumption, which, he claims, has in an unquestioned and unreflective manner motivated the scientific theory of kinship. Like all such local theories it needs to be recognized as such. The theory of kinship, then, is a chimera: "there is no such thing as kinship and it follows that there can be no such thing as kinship theory" (Needham 1971:5). Further, because the wide social categories expressed by the kin terms are their meanings in this view, the role of the nuclear family declines. Indeed, it is claimed that it is not universally relevant as an element in social organization. Because of this, the basis of the reckoning of genealogical connection, the mother–child link, is necessarily weakened, reinforcing the claim of the centrality of social categories, rather than biological ones, in kinship.

Because the categories of social personhood in different cultures are in no obvious way subject to biological constraints, Leach's (1958, 1962) and Needham's (1971) position is a relativistic one and should predict that kinship terminological systems should vary widely in the same way that social categories, i.e. priests, doctors, witches, etc., vary. But this prediction is false. The systems of kinship terminologies found in the world's languages are, as discussed above, quite constrained, falling into a small number of well-defined types, with relatively minor variation internal to each type. It must be admitted, however, that this claim assumes that kinship terminologies or distinct systems can be delimited unproblematically, an assumption that most relativists will reject (see Schneider 1984). What criteria, a relativist might inquire, would I use to include Watam *aes* within the class of kin terms, but *rondamot* "exchange partner" without? This is a tricky question to answer, but a number of approaches are possible; for one fruitful line, see Danziger (1991:57–85). Gellner (1973), for instance, argues that the domain of kinship can be isolated specifically by establishing the web of biological relations among persons (recognizing, of course, the culturally constructed nature of these relations) and then noting the terms used to label these relations. In any case, a universalist like Lounsbury (1965, 1969) would insist that, by whatever approach, a clearly delimited semantic domain of kin terms can be established, and that for a linguist it is not clear why this task should be any more difficult than for any other word class. This is certainly a debatable point, but if the variation among the types of systems isolated in this way can be stated rather precisely, largely in biological terms, then a strong relativist position is difficult to defend, for it has no obvious way to account for this. Having said this, however, it does need to be conceded that many systems of kinship terminology, for example, those in central Australia, do make use of sociocultural semantic dimensions like moiety, subsection, etc. But, universalists would counter, those are always used in addition to biologically defined dimensions like sex and age. The latter could then be reasonably claimed to be the primary universal givens in kinship, which may be supplemented, *but not supplanted*, by socially defined categories. In this view, human cultures first and foremost employ universal biologically given dimensions in kin terms to symbolize social meanings. They may not be the only dimensions, but, it is insisted, universally they are the most basic ones.

Summary

Kinship has long been a cultural domain within which anthropological linguists have sought to identify universal constraints, for the cultural practices which kinship seeks to label, namely mating and reproduction, are features of all human societies. The debate has revolved around whether these universals can be stated in the strictly biological terms of mating and reproduction without recourse to social and ultimately cultural categories. The core of kinship has been identified as the reproductive mother–child relationship and only secondarily the mating husband–wife relationship. Kinship is built on complex chains of linking of these two types of relationships, but the actual labels for individual relatives within this elaborate kinship network, the local kinship system, will vary across languages. Componential analyses of kinship systems seek to identify the fundamental building blocks which structure them, e.g. to identify why Watam *aes* "father" includes father's brothers, but English *father* does not, having a separate term for these relatives. Lounsbury's work makes a strong claim for the universal biological basis of kinship systems by reducing their terms largely to the universal core and biologically based notion of the nuclear family. He does this by a series of reduction rules which equate more distant relatives to genealogically (and biologically) closer ones and ultimately those of the nuclear family. He argues that such universal constraints even apply in systems which wreak havoc on the basis of genealogy through the terminological merger of relatives of diverse generations. To the extent that this is demonstrable, a strong case has been mounted for biologically based universals in kinship systems. Relativist critiques may challenge these conclusions, but are confronted with the inescapable fact of the relatively small number of well-defined types of kinship systems found in the languages of the world, a fact which strongly suggests robust universal constraints in this domain.

Further Reading

Kinship is perhaps the most studied area in anthropology. Barnard (1994), Fox (1967), Harris (1990), and Keesing (1975) are good introductions to the issues, while Bohannan and Middleton (1968), and Graburn (1971) are anthologies of pivotal articles in the history of this field. On universalist approaches to kinship systems, see Gellner (1973), Goodenough (1970), Lounsbury (1965, 1969), and Scheffler and Lounsbury (1971). For relativist critiques try Needham (1971) and Schneider (1980, 1984).

7

Color

The Neurophysiology of Color

Undoubtedly the most influential and possibly the most robust claims of universal innate constraints on the semantic structure of certain cognitive domains have been made in the area of color terminology, starting with the landmark study of Berlin and Kay (1969) and extended with subsequent work by them and associates (Berlin and Berlin 1975; Kay 1975; Kay, Berlin, and Merrifield 1991; Kay and McDaniel 1978; MacLaury 1987, 1991, 1992). The crosslinguistic study of color terminologies has become something of the paradigm case for demonstrating the effects of universal innate biological constraints on human categorizations of the world. Color has long been a favored semantic domain in which to investigate issues of the relationship between language and thought (Brown and Lenneberg 1954; Lantz and Stefflre 1964; Lenneberg 1953; Lenneberg and Roberts 1956; Stefflre, Castillo Vales, and Morley 1966). This is a tradition that Berlin and Kay (1969) build on, but crucially they are attempting to show universal constraints in this domain, rather than relativistic effects linked to language differences, as is the aim of the earlier work. The whole thrust of work in color terminologies stemming from Berlin and Kay (1969) is to demonstrate that universal design features of the human visual perceptual system strongly constrain the systems of color terminologies found in the world's languages to a very small and largely predictable subset of the very large set of theoretically possible, but actually unattested, types:

> basic color categories can be derived directly from the neural response patterns that underlie the perception of color. (Kay and McDaniel 1978:130)

> predicting the composite color categories of the world's languages from properties of color vision that are independent of culture and of language, biological properties which are in fact independent of human experience *per se* being widespread in genera other than *Homo*. (Kay, Berlin, and Merrifield 1991:18)

Thus, universal constraints in color categorization are directly based in (primate) neurophysiology, and this is reflected in the color-naming systems found in the world's languages. Cultural practices and human interests, according to this view, play no role in the actual sensible experience covered by a given basic color term in a language, as this is informed strictly by biological constraints. This, of course, is a claim already made familiar by the work in ethnobiological classification and kinship already discussed, but it can be made more strongly here and tested more rigorously, given the clearly restricted perceptual basis of the domain and the greater knowledge we have of the human visual system, particularly the physiology of color vision. Ethnobiology, by contrast, is a much more open-ended domain, with probably many more perceptual features relevant to a given classification than just color, and not even the most extreme upholder of the pivotal role of genealogy in the reckoning of kinship relations would argue that this could be reduced to simple perceptual universals. Of these three domains, then, color is quite unique and provides a particularly good arena to study the effect of universal innate constraints, biological ones of human physiology, on human categorization as revealed in linguistic systems of basic color terms.

Before considering the actual linguistic and categorization results of this work, it is best to summarize what is presently known about color and the physiology of human color vision (Davidoff 1991; Thompson, Palacios, and Varela 1992). The physiology of human vision is constant across all races and populations of present-day members of the genus *Homo*, provided, of course, there is no individual pathology. All of the colors that we see are a combination of six basic colors: red, yellow, green, blue, white, and black. For example, turquoise is a combination of blue and green; orange, of yellow and red. Perceivable color varies along three dimensions: hue, saturation, and brightness. Hue is the "coloredness" of a color, its redness, yellowness, greenness, or blueness. These are the fundamental hues, defined as oppositions of red to green and blue to yellow. Combinations are possible across these oppositions, but not within them, as typically within a binary opposition, one pole excludes the other. Thus, turquoise is a combination of green and blue (across the oppositions), but there is no hue that is a combination of yellow and blue. Not all colors have hue; white and black do not, nor do their intermediate shades of grey. Colors with hue are known as chromatic colors; those without hue, achromatic colors. Saturation defines the strength of hue within a given color. Saturated colors have vivid hues, while desaturated colors are like pastels, closer to grey. Finally, brightness indicates the light reflectance of a color, from dazzling to barely visible.

Why is color perceived along these dimensions? Simply because the human visual system is structured in such a way as to reveal these dimensions, according to the now widely accepted opponent-process theory, proposed in modern form by Hurvich and Jameson (1957), but traceable back to nineteenth-century work by Hering. In this theory, the human visual system consists of three subsystems. The first subsystem signals differences in brightness and is achromatic. The other two signal differences in hue; one for the red–green opposition and one for yellow–blue. The relation between these subsystems and actual neuronal connections is not yet settled, but something like the following is generally accepted. The retina contains clusters of cone cells which respond to contrasts in "hue," by differential responses according to the wavelengths of the received light. There are three clusters of cone cells: long wave, middle wave, and short wave. The output of the three cone types is reorganized at neurological levels higher than the retina so that their signals can be additively or subtractively compared. The difference between the signals from the long- and medium-wave receptors constitutes the red–green subsystem, while the difference between the sum of the signals from long- and medium-wave receptors and the signals from the short-wave constitutes the yellow–blue subsystem. The achromatic brightness subsystem is the result of the summed activity of the long- and medium-wave cones. As the two chromatic subsystems are made up of oppositions, one pole always excludes the other; an increase in blue is always at the expense of yellow. This system of oppositions explains in neurophysiological terms the difference between pure hues and secondary "mixed" colors. Pure blue results when the yellow–blue subsystem signals "blue" (i.e. whatever neuronal firing pattern that realizes "blue" is occurring) and the red–green subsystem is neutral, signalling neither "red" nor "green." Turquoise, on the other hand, results when the yellow–blue subsystem again signals "blue," but the red–green subsystem signals "green." Purple, in like manner, is the result of "blue" from the yellow–blue subsystem and "red" from the red–green. Such secondary, "mixed" colors are thus cognitively "computed" from inputs from the two subsystems (this process is modelled formally in Kay and McDaniel (1978)) and are not the responses to neuronal stimulation in only one subsystem, as are the pure, primary opposing hues of the two subsystems. Slight differences in hue of, say, turquoise reflect differences in the relative contributions of "blue" and "green" from the two subsystems. Finally, white, black, and grey result when both the yellow–blue and red–green subsystems are neutral, and the third subsystem of brightness is operative; neurological-firing patterns for high brightness signals "white" and its relative absence, "black," with "grey" in between.

Color Categorization

With this background in the neurophysiology of human color vision in mind, let us return to issues of anthropological linguistics, specifically the constraints this physiology has upon the color categorization reflected in languages. All of this work in universals of color categorization inaugurated by Berlin and Kay (1969) uses the Munsell set of color chips, a set "of 320 color chips of forty equally spaced hues and eight degrees of brightness, all at maximum saturation, and nine chips of neutral hue (white, black and greys)" (Berlin and Kay 1969:5). These represent the controlled stimulus for the required and evaluated responses of color naming. Speakers of languages are asked to provide the basic color term for each stimulus chip, and to date well over 100 languages have been investigated using this methodology, with from two (Dani) to eleven (English) basic color terms. A basic color term is defined on the basis of a number of criteria such as: (1) it is monolexemic, not composed of composite parts, excluding, for example, *bluish* in English; (2) is not included, hyponymically, within another color term, excluding, for example, English *scarlet*, which is *a kind of red*; (3) is attributively not restricted, excluding English *blond* which is restricted to hair and wood; and, perhaps most problematically, (4) is salient psychologically, for example, listed first among terms in the given domain or most widely known. Commonly, these criteria converge, but in individual cases they may conflict, requiring additional criteria or creative decisions on the part of the analyst.

Using these criteria to establish basic color terms and investigating their usage as names for particular stimuli of colored chips, noticeable patterns emerge. First, it is generally the case that regardless of the number of color terms in a language, the focal hue, the best exemplar of a named color, is remarkably consistent across languages. Thus, a speaker of a language with three basic color terms like Watam will identify as the best exemplar of "red" about the same hue as will speakers of English of eleven basic color terms, essentially "fire-engine red." The boundaries, however, of what hues count as "red" is much less stable, but surprisingly, within languages (i.e. variation among speakers of the same language), as much as across them. These prototypical effects are claimed by Kay and McDaniel (1978) to lie in the universal neurophysiology of color vision. Membership in the category labelled by "red," for example, is established by the proportion of "red" response in the neurons of the red–green subsystem. Pure or focal red occurs when the yellow–blue subsystem is neutral. Similar definitions apply to the other focal hues: yellow, green, and blue. Less focal hues have more partial responses in their own subsystem and greater or less contribution from the other subsystem. This neurophysiological description accounts for our perception of primary colors through what Kay and McDaniel call "fundamental neural responses," but is extendable to secondary, "mixed" colors. For example, those hues labelled "purple" by English speakers are the intersection of the neurophysiology underlying "blue" and "red," i.e. a "blue" pattern of neuronal firing in the yellow–blue subsystem and a "red" pattern in the red–green subsystem. In this way, the neuronal and cognitive underpinnings to all the colors subsumed by the eleven basic color terms of English can be modelled. Second, universal patterns of color-naming systems emerge across languages. No language, for example, has a word for "green," unless it also has a word for "red." The maximum number of basic color terms seems fixed at around a dozen, but a language may have much less. If so, a given color term will be a composite category, covering a range of stimulus colors, for example, the native Trobriand color terminology has four terms (Senft 1987); one of these *digadegila* covers the spectrum range of yellow–green–blue, although its prototypical focus seems to be "yellow" (Senft 1987:329). The patterns of such composite categories seems largely, but not completely, predictable on neurophysiological grounds.

Types of Basic Color Terminologies

The simplest system of color naming found in any language consists of two terms (considering the basis of the color domain in oppositions, it is impossible to conceive of a simpler system and still call it "color"). This is exemplified in Papuan languages of New Guinea like Dani (Heider 1972a) and Australian languages, such as Burara (Jones and Meehan 1978). There is some debate as to whether the contrast in such systems is truly one of color (hue), rather than brightness. Dani has been extensively studied by Rosch (Heider 1971, 1972a, b). This has two basic color terms – *mili* and *mola*: *mili* contains black and darker browns and all the cooler colors, greens and blues; *mola* covers white and the warmer colors, reds, yellows, orange, reddish-purple, pink and lighter browns, like European skin colors. The foci of these color terms were highly variable across speakers: for *mili* ranging from black to pure blue or pure green and for *mola*, burgundy, red, pink, brown, or pastel shades. Some speakers chose pure black and pure white as the foci for *mili* and *mola* respectively. On the basis of these findings, Rosch argued that these terms denoted both hue and brightness, glossing them as *mola* DARK/COOL and *mili* LIGHT/WARM, where COOL and WARM described the cool (green, blue) and warm (red, yellow, orange) hues. Interestingly, in spite of Dani's only having two basic color terms, Rosch has been able to demonstrate prototype focal effects for a range of hues lacking unique names in the language. Made-up names for focal hues can be learned more rapidly and recalled more easily than those for more peripheral ones. Thus, made-up names for pure green and pure blue are more accessible than for turquoise (i.e. "mixed" blue–green), in spite of the fact that Dani lacks unique basic color terms for all three of these. This is evidence for Kay and McDaniel's (1978) claim for the universal innate basis for focal colors in the human color vision system.

Jones and Meehan's (1978) evidence suggests that brightness is indeed the basic dimension of contrast for the two Burara basic color terms, *gungaltja* and *gungundja*. *Gungaltja* refers to light, bright colors, like white, pastels, and red. Its focal prototype is reflective aluminum foil, certainly suggesting high brightness as its basic feature. All other colors are covered by *gungundja*. The Burara system, then, is a more transparent brightness-based two-term system than the mixed brightness–hue system of Dani. In fact, MacLaury (1992) suggests two parallel paths of development of basic color terms, one based on hue and one on brightness, with crossover relations between them. Burara is probably the most likely example of a basic color system grounded in brightness contrasts, Dani exemplifying the more common crossover between the two dimensions.

When a language has three basic color terms, the warm colors red–orange–yellow split from LIGHT/WARM to form the following three-way contrast: LIGHT, WARM, and DARK/COOL. A true hue contrast now definitely emerges. The focal hue for LIGHT is white, and for WARM, red but DARK/COOL continues to have variable foci in black, pure blue, or pure green. Watam is a good example of this type of language, with *wawar* LIGHT: white, greyish, *mbukmbuk* DARK/COOL: black, dark brown, green, blue, and *yaup* WARM: red, orange, yellow, red-brown. This early emergence of RED fits well with Sahlin's (1976) claim of its psychological salience and emotional attractiveness.

With four basic color terms, the possibilities now become quite complex, with no less than five-attested systems (Kay, Berlin, and Merrifield 1991). The two most common of these were uncovered as early as Berlin and Kay (1969). In one, the WARM category, previously covering from red through yellow, but focused on red, splits into two distinct terms: RED and YELLOW. This system is found in traditional, pre-Spanish Bisayan of the Philippines (Berlin and Kay 1969:68): *mabosas* LIGHT/WHITE, *maitum* DARK/BLACK, *mapula* RED, and *madurag* YELLOW. In such systems orange is divided between RED and YELLOW.

The other commonly attested four-term system separates the cool colors, green and blue, from the DARK/COOL category, resulting in DARK/BLACK and GRUE, a composite category made up of green and blue. In such systems the focal hue for GRUE is either blue or green or bifocal in both, never turquoise, i.e. the secondary "mixed" hue composed of these two primaries. This again is said to vindicate Kay and McDaniel's (1978) universal neurophysiological account for basic color terminologies. Ibibio of Nigeria is one such four-term system: *àfíá* DARK/BLACK *èbúbít* LIGHT/WHITE, *ńdàídàt* WARM, *àwàwà* GRUE/focus in green (Berlin and Kay 1969:64).

The other three systems are more problematic. In one, GRUE separates from DARK/COOL and RED emerges as a distinct category from WARM, but "yellow" rejoins the LIGHT category. A neurophysiological account for this is not apparent, nor is a diachronic mechanism which would yield this four-term system from the previous three-term one of DARK/COOL, LIGHT, and WARM. Most problematic of all are systems which have as a basic color term a YELLOW/GREEN composite category, in which YELLOW again splits from WARM, but this time merges with GRUE. How can YELLOW be simultaneously LIGHT/WARM and DARK/COOL? Once previously thought to be rare, YELLOW/GREEN is now attested on four continents: Asia (Hanunoo), Australia and Oceania (Gugu-Yalanji, Trobriand), North America (Salish, Wakashan, Creek, Natchez, Karok), and South America (Chacobo). There are two types of such systems. One has a YELLOW–GRUE category and is exemplified by the traditional Trobriand color terminology (Senft 1987): *pupwakau* LIGHT/WHITE, *bwabwau* DARK/BLACK, *bweyani* RED, and *digadegila* YELLOW/GRUE. Other languages with this system include Karok (Bright 1952) and Gugu-Yalanji (Berlin and Kay 1969:70; Rivers 1901). This grouping of YELLOW/GRUE poses formidable problems for Kay and McDaniel's grounding of generalities of basic color terms in innate perceptual properties of the human color vision system, specifically, the subsystems based on opposing colors. Yellow and blue (member of the composite GRUE) are opposing poles of the same subsystem and if these subsystems based on oppositions are the universal grounding for human color categorizations, it is hard to see how yellow and blue could be conflated in a single named category. This serious problem is clearly seen by MacLaury (1992), who tries to solve it by claiming this category is actually informed by a brightness dimension, not one of hue, these colors occupying a range of middle brightness. This is in keeping with his postulation of the pivotal role of a brightness dimension in the sequence of development of basic color terms, but it rather does contravene the strict Kay and McDaniel universalist interpretation in terms of hue, and poses the question what favors the mediation of the brightness dimension in addition to hue in certain color terminologies. Culture?

The other four-term system involving YELLOW/GREEN actually divides GRUE into BLUE and GREEN, merging the former with BLACK and the latter with YELLOW. Hanunoo of the Philippines (Conklin 1964) is one such system: *bi:ru* DARK/BLACK/BLUE, *lagtiq* LIGHT/WHITE, *raraq* RED, *latuy* YELLOW/GREEN. Other languages with this system are Creek (Kay, Berlin and Merrifield 1991) and Shuswap (MacLaury 1987). Given that these languages assign yellow and blue to different named categories, they do not pose the quite same problems for the universal neurophysiological basis of basic color terms in color oppositions like yellow–blue; they do, however, pose problems of their own, such as how would they arise from a previous three-term system of DARK/COOL, LIGHT, and WARM? Again the role of yellow is pivotal; it must migrate out of the WARM category to join with the green focus of GRUE, a composite category already separate from DARK/COOL. Thus, the ancestor of four-term systems with YELLOW/GREEN may be the common type with the four terms LIGHT/WHITE, DARK/BLACK, WARM and GRUE, as in Ibibio. MacLaury (1987) proposes something like this for the history of the color terminology of Shuswap, a Salish language of Canada in which the WARM term extended to the green focus of GRUE (due to an operative brightness dimension?) and simultaneously retracted from red. Blue then merges with DARK/BLACK. Halkomelem, another Salish language (MacLaury and Galloway 1988), shows the opposite trajectory: GRUE is extended to the yellow focus of WARM, isolating red and simultaneously retracting from blue, which again merges with DARK/BLACK. While not ruled out on a neurophysiological account of opposing color hues, yellow–blue and red–green, such an account certainly provides no straightforward explanation of such migrations of yellow or green. MacLaury's (1992) theory of a co-emergent brightness dimension, with YELLOW/GREEN a category of medium brightness, seems to offer the only avenue of explanation here.

Languages with five basic color terms exhibit fewer possibilities than those with four, there being three-attested types. The most common arise from the two most widely attested four-term systems, either by splitting WARM into RED and YELLOW or by dividing DARK/COOL into DARK/BLACK and GRUE, again with variable focus of GRUE in either blue or green, or bifocal in both. All such languages have DARK/BLACK, LIGHT/WHITE, RED, YELLOW, and GRUE and are illustrated by Tzeltal, a Mayan language of Mexico (Berlin and Kay 1969:82); *ʔink'* DARK/ BLACK, *sak* LIGHT/WHITE, *cah* RED, *k'an* YELLOW, and *yaʃ* GRUE. Uncommon, but attested, systems include those in which only GREEN is separated from DARK/COOL, leaving blue to remain in the latter along with black: DARK/BLACK/BLUE, LIGHT/WHITE, RED, YELLOW, and GREEN. Chinook Jargon, a pidgin previously spoken in the Pacific north-west of the United States and Canada, is an example of this five-term system (Berlin and Kay 1969:75): *liʔeɬ* DARK/BLACK/BLUE, *tkʔup* LIGHT/WHITE, *pəl* RED, *ptcɔh* GREEN, and *kawakawak* YELLOW (with pale greens). And there is at least one reported language (Kay, Berlin, and Merrifield 1991) in which green migrates from GRUE to merge with yellow to form a YELLOW/GREEN composite category, isolating BLUE as a new uniquely named color category: DARK/BLACK, LIGHT/ WHITE, RED, YELLOW/GREEN, and BLUE. Kwak'wala (Saunders 1992), a Wakashan language of Canada, may also illustrate this last system: *zutla* DARK/BLACK, *mela* LIGHT/WHITE, *tlakwa* RED, *lhenza* YELLOW/GREEN, and *zasa* BLUE.

The possibilities for systems of basic color terms from the minimum of two members up to five can be seen in 7.1.

Beyond five basic color terms, there appears to be far less order. Berlin

7.1

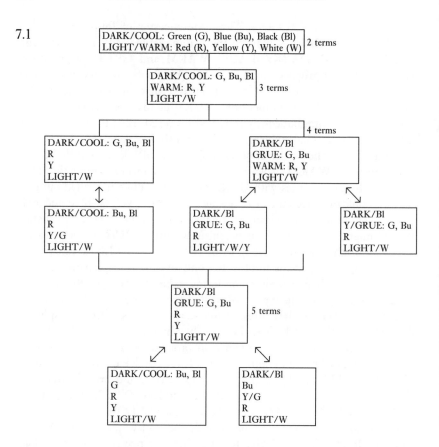

and Kay (1969) in their early phase of the theory proposed the strong constraint that GRUE necessarily splits into GREEN and BLUE, followed by the addition of BROWN, and then the emergence of PURPLE, GREY, PINK and ORANGE in any order, but later research has shown this to be false. Evidence above shows that GREEN and BLUE may already emerge as distinct in a five-term system. It is also now well established that, contrary to Berlin and Kay (1969), GREY, BROWN, and PURPLE appear as basic color terms in no fixed order. Indeed, GRUE may persist undissolved into GREEN and BLUE well after GREY, BROWN, or PURPLE have been labelled with their own basic color terms (Kay, Berlin, and Merrifield 1991).

It is important to note that MacLaury (1991, 1992) has found that prior to their emergence as basic color terms both purple and brown show conflicting categorizations in different languages. Thus, in a typical five-term system, purple may be assigned completely to the GRUE category or to the boundary between GRUE and RED. Similarly, brown can be included in the YELLOW or DARK/BLACK category. Variable categorizations like these may be the source of the largely unpredictable pattern for their emergence as basic color terms. PINK and ORANGE do generally appear to be distinctly late, though see Saunders (1992:151) for a claim that ORANGE is a basic color term in Kwak'wala, otherwise a language with a five-term system, as mentioned above. Finally, some languages may have more than one basic color term corresponding to a single one in English: for example, Russian has two basic color terms for BLUE, *goluboj* for LIGHT-BLUE (i.e. "sky-blue") and *sinij* for DARK-BLUE, and Hungarian has two words for RED, *piros* LIGHT-RED and *vörös* DARK-RED (Wierzbicka 1990).

Universal Constraints on Basic Color Terminologies

Much of the early enthusiasm in the research tradition inspired by Berlin and Kay (1969) lay in a belief that this work uncovered strong universal constraints in one linguistic and cultural domain, contrary to the received wisdom of relativism current in the mid-1960s. However, as sketched above, the current findings in this field represent a significant retreat from the early strong universals proposed in Berlin and Kay (1969), with multiple possibilities now available to languages in their basic color terminologies especially in four- and five-term systems. Still, it is equally apparent that constraints are operative, for not all possibilities are attested: for example, there is no four-term system with ORANGE, LIGHT/WHITE, YELLOW, and GRUE. And for three-term systems only one possibility exists: DARK/COOL, WARM, and LIGHT/WHITE. Why not, COOL/GRUE, DARK/BLACK, and LIGHT/WARM? In other words, why does WARM split from LIGHT before COOL splits from DARK? Phrased in a different way, why does the presence of a distinct COOL/GRUE term always imply the prior emergence of a WARM term, but not vice versa? Such questions demand answers and do argue for universal constraints on the structuring of this linguistic domain. The source of these constraints is quite possibly neurophysiological, to be found in the structure and functioning of the human color vision system, but Kay and McDaniel's (1978) account in terms of Hurvich and Jameson's (1957) opponent-process theory of color vision, with systems of opposing hues, yellow–blue and red–green, is clearly not completely adequate, failing especially in the case of languages with the composite category YELLOW/GREEN/BLUE, like Trobriand (Senft 1987). The neurophysiological account requires opposing colors in the same subsystem, like yellow and blue, to be in separate labelled categories, yet clearly they are not. The future success of the neurophysiological explanation of findings of this research tradition may founder on such cases. As the opposing hue hypothesis is what is contradicted here, MacLaury (1992) tries to account for such systems in terms of brightness, arguing that this represents a second universal, neurophysiologically based, dimension in color terminologies. This move appears necessitated by the data, but if it should turn to be unmotivated, then the findings of this research tradition will no longer be supported by a neurophysiological base. And if this is the case, what is the source of the discovered constraints on basic color terminologies? Culture? This, contrary to the whole intent of this tradition, right back to Berlin and Kay (1969), opens the door to relativism, a point not lost on MacLaury (1992:137):

> Inserting a category of *yellow–green–blue* into the sequence casts doubt upon the presumed connection between panhuman visual physiology and the widely observed regularities of color categorization; it calls into question the very notion of color-category universals.
>
> Since the *yellow–green–blue* category represents the extreme, dropping it into the universal sequence concedes the debate to the relativists.

Relativist Responses to Proposed Universals of Color Terminologies

So what is the relativist response to this imposing body of work and how do they account for the universal constraints on basic color terminologies already mentioned? It is perhaps best articulated in Sahlins (1976), but see also Lucy (1996), Saunders (1992), and Tornay (1978). The basic point, of course, is that cultural practices are a crucial mediating force in color naming and the systems of basic color terms. They argue that culture must be the crucial autonomous intermediary between any innate and hence universal neurological perception of color stimuli and the cognitive understanding of these. This point is echoed linguistically by Wierzbicka (1990) who notes that the meaning of a color term in a language cannot possibly be a neural response to a color chip, but rather the cognitive understanding the Native speaker of the language has of that term: "language reflects what happens in the mind, not what happens in the brain" (Wierzbicka 1990:163).

The basic thrust of the relativist critique of the Berlin and Kay (1969) inspired tradition is to invert its determinism: "it is not, then, that color terms have their meaning imposed by the constraints of human and physical natures; it is that they take on such constraints in so far as they are meaningful" (Sahlins 1976:3), i.e. meaningful in a culturally constructed symbolic system; symbols for practical public action, as in Geertz (1973). Herein lies the rub; Berlin and Kay (1969) and associates regard a particular color as a label given in response to a controlled stimulus, a Munsell color chip, an act of naming an objective sensible difference. The language of color, thus, is reduced to a nomenclature of objective pure color referents in a controlled sensible world. The basic color terms in a language are separated semantically from other words denoting color on essentially this principle: they denote color and nothing else, whereas secondary color terms have additional denotations and connotations. But to relativists like Sahlins (1976) and Lucy (1996), it is exactly this strict separation which is at issue. And where is the meaning of the color terms in all this? The meaning of a color term is its cognitive understanding, the culturally defined relations it engages in and activates, not its mere recognition and labelling. Color terms in a given culture do not mean Munsell chips. And from this point of view, there is no basis for a *semantic* separation of basic and secondary color terms.

The relativist critique thus rejects the strictly referential/behaviorist theory of meaning, that words are simply labels for perceived stimuli, implicit in the methodology of Berlin and Kay (1969), and subsequent work. This assumes an objective pre-given reality which language simply labels. In the tradition of basic color terminology, this pre-given reality is the separate domain of color, embodied in the contrastive dimensions of the Munsell color chips. Relativism challenges this assumption and claims that any such domain is not a pre-given, easily isolatable piece of reality, but is culturally constructed, seamlessly linked to other parts of that culture's symbolic order and meaningful practices. By isolating color as the only dimension in a pre-given domain of reality, Berlin, Kay, and associates create a completely artificial situation, parallel across cultures and languages, which, *by definition*, should result in their universal findings. Combined with their rejection of secondary color terms and the connotative, non-"color" meanings of basic color terms in languages, Berlin and Kay's (1969) findings are virtually assured (Lucy 1996). Lucy (1996) discusses how different the color terminology of Hanunoo looks from its presentation in Berlin and Kay (1969:64), if the full detail of Conklin's (1964) ethnographic description is systematized. Berlin and Kay (1969) characterize Hanunoo simply as a four-term system, now known to be *bi:ru* DARK/BLACK/BLUE, *lagtiq* LIGHT/WHITE, *raraq* RED and *latuy* YELLOW/GREEN. But Conklin (1964) provides much fuller information. Besides this four-fold contrast in hue/brightness, "this classification appears to have certain correlates beyond what is usually considered the range of chromatic differentiation, and which are associated with nonlinguistic phenomena in the external world" (Conklin 1964:191). Thus, the four terms contrast according to semantic dimensions other than color ascribed to their typical referents. There are three of these (Conklin 1964:191):

First, there is the opposition between light and dark, obvious in the contrasted ranges of meaning of *lagtiq* and *bi:ru*. Second there is an opposition between dryness or desiccation and wetness or freshness (succulence) in visible components of the natural environment which are reflected in the terms *raraq* and *latuy* respectively. This distinction is of particular significance in terms

of plant life. Almost all living plant types possess some fresh, succulent, and often "greenish" parts. To eat any kind of raw, uncooked food, particularly fresh fruits or vegetables, is known as *pag-laty-un* (<*latuy*). A shiny, wet, brown-colored section of newly-cut bamboo is *malatuy* (not *mararaq*). Dried-out or matured plant material such as certain kinds of yellowed bamboo or hardened kernels of mature or parched corn are *mararaq*. To become desic-cated, to lose all moisture, is known as *mamaraq* (<*paraq* "desiccation" . . .)
. . . A third opposition, dividing the two already suggested, is that of deep, unfading, indelible, and hence often more desired material as against pale, weak, faded, bleached or "colorless" substance, a distinction contrasting *mabi:ru* and *mararaq* with *malagtiq* and *malatuy*. This opposition holds for manufac-tured items and trade goods as well as for some natural products (e.g. red and white trade beads, red being more valuable by Hanunóo standards; indigo-dyed cotton sarongs, the most prized being those dyed most often and hence of the deepest indigo color – sometimes obscuring completely the designs formed originally by *white* warp yarns; etc.).

Conklin concludes by alternatively glossing the four terms as DARKNESS, LIGHTNESS, DRYNESS and WETNESS, respectively, and notes that (Conklin 1964:192):

> what appears to be color "confusion" at first may result from an inadequate knowledge of the internal structure of a color (sic) system and from a failure to distinguish sharply between sensory reception on the one hand and per-ceptual categorization on the other.

Relativists like Lucy (1996) and Saunders (1992) charge that Berlin and Kay, and subsequent workers, only get the results they do by bracketing out such rich cultural information about the meanings of the basic color terms and by focusing solely on the chromatic information they denote. Lucy notes that adequate Native knowledge (the goal of any truly cognitive anthropo-logy) of the Hanunoo system could never be achieved by codifying labelling responses in the Hanunoo language to color stimuli provided by Munsell chips. The thrust of the relativist critique is to claim that basic color terms stand in meaningful relationships to each other not only according to chro-matic contrasts, but many other culturally defined dimensions, and, further, they individually and as a group may enter into relations with many other terms and semantic domains, as part and parcel of the wider meaningful practices which make up the culture. Colors as perceptual structures are merely raw materials of cultural production, the handmaiden of meaningful practices: virginal white versus promiscuous red. Colors, too, are good to think with. Saunders (1992:219) summarizes this view nicely:

> I propose to relocate colour semantics out of the psychophysical domain of nomologically necessary "pure" perception into the domain of *value*, as

that which most fully characterises the mental (or psychological). Instead of evolutionarily emerging neuro-based epistemological primitives (fundamental neural responses/basic color terms) I propose to locate a quality like Kwak'wala *lhenxa* [YELLOW/GREEN] . . . in "intentional space" and characterise it in terms wedded to an intentional view of the world, i.e. in purposive, indexical, and interactional terms. Then *lhenxa* . . . have meaning only in the normative setting of the customs, regular beliefs and desires, and appropriate behaviour of a Kwakiutl . . . community [i.e. embodied practices], as components of vistas only discernible from their intentional points of view. Categorisation in terms of "colour" or whatever, would then be inextricably bound up with having states of mind which cannot be understood except by those who enjoy the appropriate kind of intentional liaison with the world [i.e. structural coupling], that is, by people who have the skills to use terms like *lhenxa* . . . *mauve*, or *Prussian blue* in the appropriate contexts – an intentional liaison only secured when one is part of (or becomes part of) a community for which *it is utterly natural* to identify features of the world with these notions.

Exactly parallel comments are found in relativist critiques (Schneider 1984) of proposed universals of basic kinship term categories discussed in the previous chapter. *Mother* is not just collateral, first-ascending generation female, contrasting to *aunt, daughter* and *father*; she is the bearer of semantic dimensions that account for expressions like *necessity is the mother of invention*; *she was like a mother to me*; maybe even *that storm was a real mother*. Similar questions apply to extensions of the Kannada word for "mother," *amma*, to cover "woman," "goddess," "pox," and "help!" (Bean 1981). Only a culturally sensitive reading, in which particular embodied practical engagements with the world are appropriate, can truly account, a relativist would claim, for the semantics of basic kinship terms.

If we concede all this, then, what explanation is available for the universal constraints on basic color terminologies unearthed by Berlin and Kay (1969) and others? Why does WARM always precede COOL/GRUE, for example? If such constraints really are valid (see Lucy (1996) for some serious doubts), then an explanation is required, and simple neurophysiology, for reasons discussed above with regard to the YELLOW/GREEN/BLUE composite category, may not provide a complete answer. Sahlins (1976) does, however, localize the strongest constraints in universals, albeit culturally mediated, of human experience, underlain by biology. WARM precedes COOL/GRUE because "red is to the human eye the most salient of color experiences. At normal light levels, red stands out in relation to all other hues by virtue of a reciprocal, heightening effect between saturation and brightness . . . Red, simply, has the most color; hence its focal position in the contrast of hue to achromaticity (lightness/darkness)" (Sahlins 1976:4–5). Sahlins cautions that the fact that the early emergence of WARM is rooted in biologically based human experience does not imply, however, that WARM *means* this experience. The meaning of WARM is in the oppositions it shares with DARK/COOL and LIGHT/WHITE, and these are culturally constructed. Thus, in a language with a three-term system, WARM is a difference that makes a difference. Like all differences, such as between day and night, WARM versus DARK/COOL must be perceptually discriminable, and WARM emerges early because it scores so highly here on several dimensions. Sahlins (1976:12) summarizes:

> No less than any other code, a system of color meanings must be grounded in a corresponding set of distinctive perceptual properties. Hence, the natural correlates of color words: they comprise the minimal distinctions on the object plane – of lightness/darkness, hue/neutrality, uniqueness/admixture, and the like – by which differences in meaning are signalled.

The members of a culture infuse these distinctions with meaning and employ them in the course of embodied practices in the service of their own symbolic ends, as they do with phonetic distinctions, such as voiced–unvoiced. As mediums of symbolic ends, color categories are cultural notions, enacted in the sense of Varela, Thompson, and Rosch (1991:171): "experiential, consensual and embodied: they depend upon our biological and cultural history of structural coupling."

Summary

The systems of color terminologies among the languages of the world present a promising case for the establishment of universals in human categorization, due to the panhuman neurophysiology of human vision. The thrust of work in the tradition stemming from Berlin and Kay (1969) has been to prove exactly this claim, locating established universals in the systems of basic color terminologies in the mechanisms of human color vision and arguing further that cultural interests and practices play no role. They have determined a typology of basic color terminologies varying from a minimum of two terms up to a maximum of eleven, with the actually attested systems restricted to a very small and mainly predictable subset of the very large set of theoretically possible, but actually unattested, types, a finding strongly in support of universal constraints in this domain. Further, the focal hue of a basic color term like "red," for instance, remains the same across languages, regardless of whether it comes from a three-term system, where the term covers the range from red through yellow, or an eleven-term one, more evidence that universal perceptual biologically based constraints are operative. Relativists respond by claiming that this research tradition gets the results it does almost by definition, by bracketing out all the cultural information in the meaning of color terms, so that only the non-cultural perceptual components can reveal themselves. They argue that the meaning of a color term is not a labelling response to a color stimulus, but the full culturally defined relations it engages in and activates, its role in the ongoing social coupling of a people.

Further Reading

Color has also been much written about. Davidoff (1991), Hardin (1988), Lamb and Bourriau (1995), and Ottoson and Zeki (1985) are good introductions to the field, but see Thompson (1995) and Thompson, Palacios, and Varela (1992) for an alternative. There is a large amount of literature in the Berlin and Kay tradition, but the basic sources are Berlin and Kay (1969), Kay and McDaniel (1978), Kay, Berlin and Merrifield (1991), and MacLaury (1992). Important relativist responses are Lucy (1996) and Sahlins (1976).

Part IV
Relativism: Cultural and Linguistic Constraints on Mind

8

On Relativist Understanding

The Idea of Relativism

Relativism is a philosophical position which claims that experience in the form of culturally mediated human interests plays a crucial and determinative role in cognitive functioning; it is to be contrasted with universalist rationalism, which contrarily emphasizes innate biological and psychological determinism. Relativism claims that knowledge is obtained through culturally mediated conceptual schemes, i.e. historically situated, contingent frameworks of meaning and understanding (of course, individual personal differences can also lead to relativities of understanding, but as this is outside the conventional transgenerational domain of cultural practices, it does not really fall within anthropological linguistics). These are made up of folk and scientific theories, linguistic and cultural categories, and social practices which we acquire as a result of the trajectory of our life experience, situated in a particular culture, language, space, and time. As a result, these schemes may be relative to that life trajectory and not shared with others of a different history. In its extreme form, relativism may claim that nature, in the form of human biology, may place no constraints on the possible trajectories of human life experience and interpretive conceptual schemes, but there would be few researchers today who would accept such an extreme formulation, preferring instead to foreground the claim that nature greatly underdetermines the course of human lived experience, giving great rein for the play of culture and hence, relativist understanding (Geertz 1973, 1983; Tambiah 1990). One of the most influential forms of relativism within both linguistics and anthropology is that of neo-Kantianism; by holding to Kant's view that mental categories impose order on sensible experience, but by dropping his insistence that such categories are innate and universal, a relativistic neo-Kantian doctrine is arrived at. This claims that the organizing mental categories arise from different theories, languages or cultural systems which, reflecting human interests, in turn impose order on sensible experience. Like Kantianism in general, this theory assumes an unorganized, but still pre-given reality, which, however, only takes on a coherent form by the imposition of the mental categories supplied by the language, culture, or theory. Because the categories found in various languages or cultures obviously differ, it then follows that each language or culture will impose different coherent orders, resulting in contrastive ranges of sensible experiences for the Natives of these languages and cultures. Experience, then, is a common activity, a social fact, inscribed in the linguistic or cultural categories of the community, and an obvious question presents itself: how comparable are these categories across communities?

The Problem of Translation

This is generally known as the incommensurability problem, namely, the degree of comparability of conceptual categories across knowledge systems, be they theories, languages or cultures. This really boils down to a problem of translation, how the meanings expressed in one system of signs (i.e. theory, language, or culture) are expressed in another. A great deal has been written about the limits of translation within philosophy over the last half century or so (Davidson 1980, 1984; Gadamer 1975; Kripke 1980; Putnam 1975, 1981; Quine 1961, 1969), and this discussion had direct relevance to our considerations here. Quine's work concerning the indeterminacy of translation is the starting point; Quine is a realist, accepting the reality of an external pre-given and knowable world, rather than a neo-Kantian one, but fundamental to all of his philosophy is the idea that our sensible experience of the world underdetermines our response to it, in the form of those conceptual schemes we construct to understand it. Our theories of the world, embodied in linguistic and cultural categories are rather autonomous from, and in rather loose fit with, our sensible experience; we can deal with our experience in conceptual terms in different ways. It is not the case, of course, that just *any* conceptual scheme will fit our experience, but it is also equally not true that just *one* will. As all understanding of experience is couched in some chosen conceptual scheme or other, there is by necessity a limit to the certainty of our knowledge due to this underdetermination, in essence, a relativist conclusion.

This conclusion has obvious implications for the theory of translation between any conceptual scheme, be it mediated in linguistic or cultural practices. Because we are always understanding from within some conceptual scheme or folk theory, or another, we will have to understand some other theory in terms of our own, i.e. translate it into the terms of our own (or translate both into the terms of a third, *meta*-language, but this too consists of its own particular categories underdetermined by experience; in this relativist view, there is no uniquely determined system with a complete optimal fit to sensible experience). Because translation requires moving the categories of the alien system into those of our own, this imposes constraints on how radically different the alien system can be. If completely incompatible, even partial translation should be impossible. The fact that a fair degree of translation between conceptual schemes across languages and cultures does seem possible indicates that at least some minimal communalities do exist. But this should not blind us to the wide gulf between them. Quine emphasizes that languages are systems; we are not trying to match the meanings of words across the systems, but the conceptual schemes these belong to – a much taller order, as this implies aligning the systems as wholes. Let me illustrate with Quine's famous example of *gavagai*, a word of some alien language. Suppose the Native speaker consistently supplies this as a response to passing rabbits. The linguist would probably confidently translate this as "rabbit." But how do we know this is right? In English the class of nouns to which *rabbit* belongs is associated with semantic sense properties of the object they describe as being "bodies," coherent wholes with sharply defined borders; this is part of the semantic system to which the word belongs. But the alien language, like some human languages such as Yucatec (Lucy 1992a) or Japanese (Imai and Gentner 1993), might employ a different semantic system for its nouns. *Gavagai* might belong to a class more like English mass nouns in which things are manifested fragments of substances, so that *gavagai* is more like "rabbit stuff." It may be that there is little in the linguistic behavior of the speakers of English and the alien language to betray this difference in the basic semantic systems. Hence, the meaning of a word is underdetermined and so is the task of translation. The latter always requires the translator to make underdetermined guesses about matches between the systems which cannot be completely resolved. And inevitably the kinds of guesses she is likely to make are those embedded in the categories and practices, the conceptual systems, of her Native language.

The "Bridgehead" of Understanding

The indeterminacy of translation due to different underlying conceptual schemes is the basis of the incommensurability problem, but we must beware of jumping to too radical conclusions; indeterminacy does not mean impossibility. Putnam (1981) and Davidson (1984) point out the background of shared, rough, working assumptions about the world which is necessary for even indeterminate translation. Some rough, at least partial, translation is always possible between any two languages (and between any two cultures, otherwise anthropology as a discipline could not exist); if the conceptual schemes of another language or culture were truly absolutely incommensurate at any level we could never hope to understand it at all. If the goal of the discipline of linguistic anthropology is "the enlargement of the universe of human discourse" (Geertz 1973:14), "rescuing the 'said' of such discourse . . . and fixing it in perusable terms" (Geertz 1973:20), radical incommensurability signals total defeat for this discipline, because it implies the impossibility of ever understanding, even partially, alien discourse, never mind, fixing it in "perusable," i.e. scrutinizable, terms. To avert this undesirable consequence, we must abjure radical incommensurability in favor of less extreme views. Putnam (1981) and Davidson (1984) may point the way here. They invoke a "bridgehead" of comparability across different languages and cultures, but unfortunately are vague indeed in substantive claims about the content of this "bridgehead." But they do propose the (unfortunately and rather condescendingly named) interpretive Principle of Charity which states that our basic strategy in interpreting any alien system is to assume that the speaker or actor who we do not yet understand is consistent and correct in her beliefs. In the context of actual translation, this implies that we proceed by "treating not just our present time-slices, but also our past selves, our ancestors, and members of other cultures past and present, as *persons*; and that means . . . attributing to them shared references and shared concepts, however different the conceptions that we attribute" (Putnam 1981:119). This quote is not unproblematic; first, it assumes a clear universal concept of person, an issue addressed in chapter 14; and second, how do we arrive at this contrast between shared concepts, but different conceptions? Putnam tries to establish this through illustration, for example, our modern scientific understanding of temperature versus that of seventeenth-century scientists. Given the difference between our present scientific understanding of heat and that of the seventeenth century, we can certainly claim that they and we have different conceptions of temperature, different sets of beliefs about it and its nature. However, Putnam asserts that we could not state that these conceptions differ and how they differ without being able to translate between them, an act based in a shared concept. The intelligibility of the translation between the two different conceptions is predicated on the shared concept.

Unfortunately, explication by illustration is not always clear and the notion of shared concept here is still rather vague. What could temperature as a shared concept be between these two eras – the experiential understanding of heat or cold? If this is the case, then some shared concepts may be based in universal bodily experiences, a rather functionalist viewpoint (Johnson 1987; Lakoff 1987; Malinowski (1960[1944])). Those which lack a bodily base are more difficult. Consider the difference between two concepts of "god," that of the monotheistic Bible versus the *devas* of the polytheistic Hindu Vedas. We translate Sanskrit *deva* as "god," but how do we do this, given the radical differences in conception? We do so by *assuming* that they are somewhat parallel concepts, sharing some commensurabilities, such as perhaps universal beliefs in beings outside the everyday world and having extraordinary powers, and then lay out their distinctive features, their culturally based conceptions. The commensurable beliefs are not in this case rooted in bodily experience, but derive from being plausible candidates for conceptual baggage that a human person can be expected to carry, and so this assumption is warranted by the Principle of Charity, i.e. suppose, in the face of the absence of evidence to the contrary, that a great many of the aliens' beliefs are the same as ours.

The Principle of Charity, then, asserts that there is a broad background of shared beliefs and understandings common to us all by virtue of being a human person. Obviously, the wider the range of common experiences one shares with another, the easier the application of the Principle of Charity. This is the idea behind Clark's (1992) notion of "common ground"; he demonstrates its cognitive force in his Schelling tasks, such as when a subject is asked to choose one from a set of three balls, a basketball, a squashball, and a baseball with a reward in the offing if she chooses the same as the next respondent. If she does not know who the next respondent might be, the choice is likely to be relatively random, but if she is told that it will be her squash partner, then odds increase greatly that the choice will be the squashball. This reflects the "common ground" they share, a restricted application of the Principle of Charity, i.e. assume the other has similar beliefs to yourself. "Common ground" provides ample reasons for assuming these beliefs. Some such beliefs are necessary for the success of any even very partial project of translation, linguistic or cultural. We are, thus, forced to accept this axiom. This broad background is the "bridgehead," the base of agreement, but the parameters within this remain almost completely unspecified. How wide is this "bridgehead"; is the shared background much less significant than the differences that are not shared? We do not yet even have the tools with which we could begin to answer this question, but the differences in the languages and cultures of the world are certainly not trivial. And further, can the bridgehead be widened by "enlarging the universe of human discourse" (Geertz 1973:14)? Can the gradually deepening understanding of another conceptual system broaden our understanding of our own and human potentiality? This is, indeed, the hope of any linguistic anthropology and a job for which the tools of the discipline called hermeneutics are particularly well suited.

Hermeneutics

Translation, as we have seen, is an interpretive task, an indeterminate reading of the categories of one conceptual system in terms of another. This will be guided by the "bridgehead," but will still largely consist in particular cases of interpretive guesses attributing quite specific beliefs to the Natives of the alien system, for example, that Yimas *tuakaca-* means "causing something to split open along its length," an act for which the vague categories of the "bridgehead" will provide little help. Hermeneutics is specialized to this type of work (Bauman 1978; Bernstein 1983; Dilthey 1976; Gadamer 1975; Hiley, Bohman, and Shusterman 1991; Ricoeur 1981; Taylor 1985b). This discipline arose in the context of the great difficulties involved in the translation and interpretation of written texts from distant ages, most typically Biblical texts, but quickly broadened into an endeavor to uncover the meanings of all human activities and creations. This broadening was facilitated by input from Romanticism, which emphasized the free, creative aspects of human actions and the subjective meanings these had for their creators. The outward forms of human cultures, their social organization, political institutions, and especially art and history, reflected the inner meanings of its members, their subjective understandings of living. The role of hermeneutics was to penetrate behind the outer forms to the subjective inner meanings, and this was done by treating them like texts to be read (for a modern exemplar of this methodology see Geertz's famous interpretive analysis of the Balinese cockfight (Geertz 1973:412–53)). The same meanings can be expressed in very different outward forms, and it is the task of hermeneutics to disclose what these are. But meanings do not exist entirely independently of their knowing subject, who attributes and responds to them. This applies crucially to the hermeneutic interpreter himself, situated in his own spatially and temporally bounded, culturally defined system of meanings. This is the bedrock, the basic given of all hermeneutic interpretation, from which we proceed to understand any other system. We proceed from this starting point in the methodology known as the hermeneutic circle. We thoroughly acquaint ourselves with the behavior we wish to interpret, be it language text or ritual process, trying to determine its basic categories by acquiring evidence, if possible, from first-hand reports of Natives. We establish a rapport with these, trying to empathize with their viewpoints about the relevant behavior. We try to gather a more objective focus on the behavior by gathering as many first-hand reports as we can and reconciling their viewpoints as much as possible. This allows a gradual movement from the understanding of components toward an understanding of the whole. As our grasp of the meaning of the whole becomes more focused, this throws the components into greater relief, allowing a "thicker" interpretation of their significance. This, in turn, broadens our conception of the whole. This continual movement back and forth between component and whole results in ever "thicker" interpretations on a widening hermeneutic circle, within which we do the interpreting. Note that the basis of all this is empathizing with the other, by recreating in our own imagination what their experience might be like. This is the essence of any relativist under-standing – taking the other seriously as other, not just an exotic, or worse, substandard version of self. However, any interpretive act of imaginative recreating is fundamentally constrained, of course, by our powers of ima-gination. What we interpret cannot be entirely alien to us and our point of view; hence the important role of some analog of the Principle of Charity in hermeneutic interpretation. But our viewpoint and our powers of ima-gination can be extended by conscious good-faith engagement with hermen-eutic practice and the continual widening of the hermeneutic circle. Such an engagement should constantly throw up the interpreter's own beliefs for critical evaluation, revealing our own deep-seated historically bound assumptions. Hopefully we will respond to this by revising these beliefs when need be, with a concomitant increase in our powers of imagination and empathetic understanding.

Hermeneutics and Translation of Grammatical Categories

One of the foremost practitioners of the hermeneutic method within an-thropological linguistics is A. L. Becker; for my purposes here I will be concerned with a recent paper in which he focuses upon the interpretation or glossing of grammatical categories in an alien language (Becker 1993, 1995). This should not be interpreted to mean that he or I intend to claim that translation is simply a matter of matching grammatical categories. On the contrary, translation requires deft interpretive handling of all aspects of language including crosslinguistic problems in understanding of style, reg-ister and genre types, as well as meaningful paralinguistic phenomena like pauses, overlaps, hesitations, etc. (see Gumperz (1982) for a discussion of the meaning signalling potential of these). Ultimately, it is a world of sig-nificance, bound in contextualized, communicative, cultural and linguistic practices (of which, say, genre types (see Bakhtin 1986) and their fram-ing devices (see chapter 18) are especially good exemplars), which must be translated, not isolated sentences or words inflected with grammatical cat-egories. Nonetheless, grammatical categories are a convenient place of entry into these interpretive problems and are particularly interesting in that it is hard to see what outside of the world of language they can correspond to. What, for example, is aspect but a linguistic partitioning of experience (see also Grace 1987)? The matching up of the meanings of grammatical cat-egories across languages is particularly problematic, for there is no obvious interpretation of the Principle of Charity which provides a "bridgehead" of comparability, at least one which is non-linguistic and hence not bound to a specific language.

The task of interpretation is difficult here. Becker takes up this point. He notes that when we try to understand the grammatical categories of a distant language we always err by assimilating them too closely to those of our own. By "thicker" description and wider hermeneutic circles we can get closer and closer fits, but, he argues, complete understanding will always elude us. The confusions of interpretation due to our own systems of grammatical categories are of two kinds: exuberances, when we add information to the interpretation because our Native system requires it, for example, supplying plural number to translations from Southeast Asian languages; and deficiencies, when we omit information intended by the distant system, but missing from our Native one, for example, far past tense from translations of Yimas into English. Becker emphasizes that much of the real interpretive work in anthropological linguistics is done in the act of glossing from the distant language into the metalanguage of description, usually a European language like English, French, German, Spanish, or Russian. We do this by matching the grammatical categories of the distant language to those of the metalanguage in the translations of examples. This act of glossing is typically done with less than full critical awareness, and as much of the real interpretive work of grammatical categories is really done in the glossing, we might legitimately conclude that Becker's worries about the confusions of exuberances and deficiencies might be significantly understating the problem. In any case, the entire question of the relativity of grammatical categories across languages is a topic we will explore in great depth in chapter 10.

Relativism and Enactionism

Fundamental to much current relativist thinking is an unquestioned neo-Kantian epistemology, a view that an unstructured, but pre-given world is apprehended by imposing order upon it, an order encoded in the conceptual schemes of our linguistic and cultural categories: "'objects' do not exist independently of conceptual schemes. We cut up the world into objects when we introduce one or another scheme of description" (Putnam 1981:52). The categories are purely mental, as is sensible experience, and there is a posited sharp distinction between the subjective knower and the objective world, with epistemological primacy being given to the former. This epistemology has recently been presented with a formidable challenge in the form of enactionism (Johnson 1987; Maturana and Varela 1987; Varela, Thompson, and Rosch 1991), with earlier roots in the philosophy of Merleau-Ponty (1962, 1963). As mentioned several times earlier, this school of thought holds that epistemology is not about how a pre-given mind knows a pre-given world, but is rather the enactment of a world and a mind together on the basis of a history of actions that an embodied being takes in the world, a history of structural coupling. Knowledge is not *encoded* in mental categories, be they linguistic or cultural, but is *embodied* in the lived histories of organisms, their communicative, cultural and linguistic *practices*, demonstrating their continued viability (see the earlier discussion of evolution as natural drift in chapter 2). Knowledge simply facilitates the preservation of this viability in the structural coupling of organism and environment, leaving wide possibilities of choice. Biology specifies the principles of sensory and motor systems for structural coupling; cognition as embodied means having constraints imposed by having a body of particular design specifications, but these are embedded in a much more inclusive biological, cultural, and linguistic context. The embodied actor guides her actions by preserving structural coupling within the constraints imposed by all these contexts, but as these constantly change, not least due to her previous actions, there is no pre-given, knower/actor independent world, but one enacted by the history of her actions.

Knowing as embodied action is always grounded in biology, but as encultured beings, we always live it in a cultural tradition, and hence, relativist understanding is crucial to its full interpretation. Further, the history of our structural coupling, the generation of explanations for our behavior (see Boas 1966 [1911]:63–9), is largely reported to ourselves and each other through language, another source of relativist understanding. For it is through language that we humans exist in a network of structural coupling with other humans and bring forth a shared world of significance with each other. For enactionism and a relativism consonant with it, biology proposes, but culture and language disposes.

Summary

Relativism holds that cultural practices play a crucial and determinative role in cognition. In any explicit formulation this leads to the problem of incommensurability: if different cultures lead to differences in understanding, how are shared understandings possible? Ultimately, this becomes a question about the possibilities of translation. How can the meanings expressed in one system of signs be communicated in another, and what is the nature of indeterminacies in translation across such systems? One answer to these questions is the idea of the "bridgehead," a broad background of shared beliefs and understandings common to all by virtue of being human persons. This is unfortunately vague and one approach that has attempted to flesh this proposal out is hermeneutics, a widening circle of disciplined interpretation of texts and practices leading to hopefully ever deepening understanding, tying guesses derived from the "bridgehead" with knowledge of the individual case under study. Ultimately, it is often unacknowledged interpretive guesses like these that guide us in translating grammatical categories in exotic languages, for there is little outside of the world of language itself that they can correspond to. Relativism is highly compatible with enactionism or the embodied practices approach to cognition: cognition is not encoded in knowers' minds, but is embodied in their lived history of communicative cultural or linguistic practices. Understanding is the result of one's interactive history; to the extent that this differs, relativism is the result.

Further Reading

On relativism generally as a philosophical position see Margolis (1986), Rorty (1979, 1989, 1991), and the articles in Hollis and Lukes (1982), and Krausz (1989). For classic anthropological studies taking relativism as axiomatic, one cannot do better than Geertz (1973, 1983, 1995), especially his paper specifically on this issue (Geertz 1984); also Tambiah (1990) is a good discussion of this issue. On the indeterminacy of translation and the bridgehead, try Becker (1995), Davidson (1984), Quine (1960, 1969), and Putnam (1975, 1981). Hermeneutics has an enormous literature, but good sources include Bernstein (1983), Gadamer (1975), Taylor (1985b), Thompson (1981), and the valuable collection of articles in Rabinow and Sullivan (1979), and Hiley, Bohman, and Shusterman (1991). Duranti (1993) is a good discussion of the application of these ideas to anthropological linguistics.

9

Models and Metaphors

Models for Understanding

If we live out our lives largely in mutual linguistic coupling, the systems within language must be powerfully compelling for our understanding. Further, if the idea of a pre-given, knower independent world is a fantasy, then the related idea that language simply maps that world and is a straightforward reflection of non-linguistic reality (Grace's mapping view, see Grace (1987:7–10)) is simply mistaken: "language was never invented by anyone only to take in an outside world. Therefore, it cannot be used as a tool to reveal that world" (Maturana and Varela 1987:234). As noted above, in our mutual linguistic coupling we use language to report our history of structural coupling and in turn generate explanations about our present state and beliefs. These explanations in language become theories or models about the world through which we project successive viable histories of structural coupling. These may need to be revised, but they do provide constructed models of possible realities we can expect to encounter in our lives.

A great deal of work in anthropological linguistics since 1980 has been concerned with this issue of the construction in language of models for construing experience. We might think of these as folk theories about the world, carried in our everyday, ordinary language, in contrast to scientific theories, which employ specialized forms of language. Lakoff (1987) is a basic compendium of much of the research about these language-transmitted folk theories (he calls them *idealized cognitive models*). As an example of what these might be like, let us consider a classic study by Gentner and Gentner (1982), which deals with people's models or folk theories of electricity. Because the mechanisms of electricity are essentially invisible, people employ explanatory models to try to understand its properties. The Gentners studied students in their late teens and found that they understood electricity in terms of two models, the flowing water and the moving crowd model. In each of these the properties of electricity are mapped onto features of more familiar experiences of the physical world. When electricity is modelled as flowing water, it is conceived of as like water flowing through a hydraulic system. Thus, the following table (Gentner and Gentner 1982:110) illustrates the mappings from a basic hydraulic system to an electric circuit:

Hydraulic system	*Electric circuit*
pipe	wire
pump	battery
narrow pipe	resistor
water pressure	voltage
narrowness of pipe	resistance
flow rate of water	current

Because of these mappings, the following implications hold: whenever something would cause the flow rate or pressure of water within a hydraulic system to increase or decrease, its mapping equivalent in an electrical circuit should have an analogous effect on current or voltage.

The moving crowd model of electricity conceives of it as a teeming mass of electrons, all trying to pass along the wires. The mappings in this model are as follows (Gentner and Gentner 1982:120):

Moving crowd	*Electric circuit*
course/passageway	wire
crowd	battery
people	electrons
pushing of people	voltage
gates	resistance
passage rate of people	current

The mappings of this model have the following implications: what might cause the force of people moving to alter, either due to increased or decreased concentration, or their rate of passage to change (i.e. number of people passing a given point in a set interval) will, in its analogical equivalent in an electrical circuit, have similar effects on voltage or current.

The Gentners performed some ingenious experiments to test the actual cognitive effects these models might have for those who profess them. These experiments revolved around the interpretation of serial versus parallel circuitry. The subjects, late-teen students, were asked to solve problems involving different layouts of serial and parallel connections. Interestingly, the two models make different predictions in different components of the circuits. Consider first the case of batteries. Batteries connected in serial form result in more current, whereas those connected in parallel do not. In the flowing water model this conclusion is a logical deduction, for in its conceptualization batteries are pumps. Pumps connected serially, i.e. one after the other, should produce a higher water flow by incrementally increasing the pressure, each pump adding its contribution to the output of its predecessor. Pumps connected in parallel should not obviously have this effect. In the moving crowd model, batteries correspond simply to the crowd itself and a meaningful contrast between serial and parallel connection is even hard to imagine in this context.

The second test components of the circuitry are resistors, again connected in serial and parallel fashion. These also have different effects on the current, serial resistors halving it, but parallel resistors doubling it. In this case, the moving crowd model is the superior one for interpretation. In this framework, resistors are like gates. Serial gates, one following the other, should have no effect on the crowd flow of, say, soccer fans milling out of a stadium after a match, but parallel gates, i.e. a number of simultaneously open gates around the perimeter of the stadium, should definitely increase the flow, and do so largely in proportion to their number, two gates being twice the crowd flow as one. On the other hand, in the flowing water model, resistors correspond to the narrowness of pipes, so that any increase in the degree or number of narrow pipes would lead to a concomitant decrease in the water flow, exactly the opposite of what actually occurs with parallel resistors.

The Gentners' experimental results were generally as predicted by their hypothesis that the subjects' cognitive models would guide their interpretations of the novel circuitry. Those subjects who claimed to hold the flowing water model performed better on batteries than resistors, while those who professed the moving crowd model did better on resistors, particularly in parallel, than batteries. The Gentners claim that these models are truly the source of their subjects' behavior; it is they that guide their inferences, resulting in correct or incorrect responses. They are not merely after the fact rationalizations of things they do not understand, but the actual framework with which they seek to grasp and structure this invisible and unfamiliar domain. In Lévi-Straussian terms, these models are "good to think with."

The moral of the Gentners' landmark study is that such folk theories or models constitute people's understanding of phenomena. Far from being applications, or conventional expressions, of knowledge structured in other ways, they are in fact constituent of that knowledge, and thereby constrain people's inferences about phenomena, especially novel phenomena, for instance, parallel resistors. Further, these models are largely encoded and understood in *linguistic* terms. While water flowing through pipes and crowds milling out of soccer stadiums are sensible experiences of the physical world, the fact that electricity is *like* these is not of this world; it is strictly a linguistic construction. The construal of electricity as like one of these is not just done through language, but is *of* language, for this equivalence holds in no other epistemological domain. And, further, any inferences about the behavior of electricity due only to this linguistic equivalence also belongs to the domain of language.

Metaphor as Constitutive of Understanding

Models such as electricity is like a teeming crowd are fundamentally metaphors, and all metaphors are the construal of something as partaking in part of the features of something else. If, for example, I say that "Ed is a jellyfish," I do not want to assert literally that Ed belongs to the class of beings, coelenterates, that contains jellyfish. Rather, I want to assert that Ed and jellyfish are alike with respect to a smallish and delimited set of features; the most important of these may be that they float about with little strenuous self-induced locomotion, are helpless on land, and, that, being almost prototypical invertebrates, they lack a backbone or indeed any skeletal structure at all. When these features are transferred to Ed, construing him in terms of them, the assertion can be meaningfully read as an indictment of his force of character: that he has no strong guiding vision or moral direction and that he is weak and indecisive, or, in further metaphorical terms, lacks a backbone, for we associate bone generally, and especially the backbone, with strength and firmness, as it provides our body with its distinctive structure and further allows us to stand up straight and face the world to act within it decisively. Still other properties of jellyfish might be appropriate, given an individual's personal experiences of them and Ed, such as sliminess or coldness (D. Wilkins, personal communication). Thus, what is basic about a metaphor is that we use the information we have about one known domain, in this case, jellyfish, to structure an assertion about the properties of another less well-known domain, here, Ed's character. This whole process is known as metaphorical extension and consists of mapping features from a source domain (in our examples thus far, flowing water or teeming crowds and jellyfish) to a target domain (electricity or Ed's character). Source domains are typically well-known everyday experiences or things, commonly those of the physical world. They are good to think with, in that their component elements and their interrelations are non-problematic with respect to everyday sensible experience. Target domains are typically more abstract, more removed from the everyday physical world of experience (see Fernandez 1986). They often correspond to theoretical ideational domains (i.e. a person's character) or invisible and only indirectly known components of the physical world (i.e. electricity). By mapping certain salient features of the source domain onto the target domain, metaphor allows us to construe the more abstract, less directly knowable in terms of the more concrete and directly experienceable. The choice of the metaphor tells us what features to transfer, how to understand the target domain; note the difference between "Ed is a jellyfish" and "Ed is a lion"! The importance of choice among metaphors is crucial and introduces a degree of relativist understanding, the role of culture, into this domain. As Quinn (1991) points out, the choice of metaphors for some domains is not totally random, but reflects some basic cultural understandings individuals have of that domain. In her example, the metaphors that Americans use to describe marriage are drawn from a small set of eight basic types, reflecting a cultural scenario of marriage. The choice of metaphors, however, while not random, is nonetheless also not predictable and, thus, reflects the constitutive understanding one wishes to place upon marriage in any given context. Further, in areas for which, unlike marriage, there is likely to be little or nothing in the way of a cultural scenario, for example, electricity, the role of metaphor in constitutive understanding is likely to be nearly or absolutely total.

Metaphor and Embodied Experience

Lakoff (1987, 1990) and Johnson (1987) argue that the source domain is largely centered in embodied experience. Human understanding of any target domain is structured first and foremost in terms of the human body and its everyday practical interaction with the physical world; this is the pre-eminent source domain of metaphor. This statement is well in accord with the claims of the enactionist school that embodied practical understanding in structural coupling is the nature of cognition. The features of the human body and its orientation with the physical world provide many of the basic dimensions for source domains in metaphorical extensions. Lakoff (1987) and Johnson (1987) call these *kinaesthetic image schemas*. A simple example is that when the human body stands upright, it presents to the world a vertical axis drawn from the head to the feet. This axis defines a dimension of UP–DOWN, experienced bodily as things moving from the ground in the direction to where the head is and beyond (UP) or the opposite (DOWN). This is extended metaphorically to anything whose movement can be understood as a movement of an object along a vertical line such as prices (movement along a line of monetary values: *prices went UP/DOWN*), temperatures (movement along a line of degrees: *the temperatures soared/plummeted*) or even emotions (movement along a range of feeling states: *I'm feeling really UP/DOWN today*). Because a higher position on these dimensions often means more of the object, i.e. higher on the price line means more pricey, secondary metaphors of MORE IS UP and LESS IS DOWN have developed: *Lewis and Clark opened up the country*; *they shut down the Parliament*. This leads to yet another extension GOOD

IS UP, BAD IS DOWN: *Sam looks up to Mary; Fred looks down on the proletariat.* Many more extensions from the UP–DOWN dimension are pervasive in English and many other languages; the reader should have no difficulty in providing further examples (see also Casson 1983:451–2).

Let me turn now to still another pivotal kinaesthetic image schema, the so-called CONTAINER schema, discussed in detail in Johnson (1987:30–40). The basic bodily experience of the CONTAINER schema is the body itself: things are either inside it or outside it. Containers that humans create and use have the same opposition, IN/OUT, with the components: interior, boundary, and exterior (for the human body these could be internal organs, muscles, and bone versus skin versus the external world). Equally salient is the movement of our bodies in space as we move in and out of containers: *she jumped into/out of the swimming pool.* Extending from our bodily experience, we can think, therefore, of a delimited volume of space as a container which a given object may be inside or outside of and, through movement, can change its position, for example, *she squeezed toothpaste out of the tube.* *IN* and *OUT* on both their stationary and movement meanings can be schematized (9.1).

9.1   Stationary   Motion

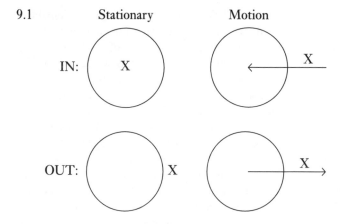

My main focus of interest here is the metaphorical extension of the CONTAINER schema to the non-physical world; for example, events as CONTAINERS (*I'm trying to get into/out of the contest*), emotional states (*he's fallen in/out of love*), narratives and other verbal acts (*John tells an ok story, but he puts in too many embellishments/leaves out too many details; Mary was included in/left out of the conversation; the actor wants to get into a new contract/out of his old contract*), relationships (*Fred's looking to get into a deep and meaningful relationship/get out of his marriage*), and perceptual and knowledge fields (*the bird flew into/out of my field of vision; that's beyond/within my comprehension*). In each case the subject domain is a container that one can be "inside" or "outside" of. The inferences to be drawn depend on the nature of the particular domain: what is implied by treating the state of being in love as a container is quite different from treating a conversation in this way.

The Conduit Metaphor and the Understanding of Meaning

One of the most interesting of all uses of the CONTAINER schema is with respect to meaning. The relationship between a word and its meaning is like a container and its contents; thus, a word or sentence HAS meaning, like a glass has water in it. This is illustrated in metaphorical extensions like *that sentence was beyond my comprehension*; *he defined his terms too narrowly*; *the words he used didn't really fit*. This metaphor is part of the large CONDUIT metaphor (Reddy 1993), a folk theory of language form and use in Western culture. Its basic components are (Johnson 1987):

1 ideas or thoughts are objects
2 words and sentences are containers for these objects
3 communication consists in finding the right word–container for your idea–object, sending this filled container along a conduit (e.g. writing) or through space (e.g. speech) to the hearer, who must then take the idea–object out of the word–container

This metaphor or folk theory of language molds our understanding of the phenomenon (to the point that it is sometimes taught as a scientific theory of language to beginning linguistics students!). Its guiding force is pervasive in English: consider, for example, Kay's (1987) study of hedges like *loosely speaking*: *loosely speaking, the first humans lived in Kenya*. The point of the hedge here is to assert that the FIT between the speaker's full thoughts and her actual words is LOOSE, not exact. First of all, given gradual evolution there is no clearly delimitable time of the *first* humans, rather, a gradual succession of species and varieties leading to *Homo sapiens*. Second, at the time of this gradual evolution there was no Kenya, it being only a modern political development. And finally, the archeological sites are not restricted to Kenya, but are also found in adjoining areas of Ethiopia, Uganda, and Tanzania. The speaker is well aware of all this and employs a hedge like *loosely speaking* to indicate that the words used to communicate her ideas are not fully inclusive of them, there is only a loose fit between what she thinks (the idea–object) and what she says (the container).

A slightly different perspective is provided by *technically speaking*: *technically speaking, frogs are amphibians*. In this case, the hedge expresses that the fit between the words and the thought is one mediated by a set of experts, those who have the technical expertise to propound this linkage. In this case, it is professional herpetologists who have the requisite knowledge to define the class of animals called amphibians through a set of distinctive properties and establish that frogs are *properly included* in that class. It is they who mandate the fit between the idea–object (class of amphibians defined by distinctive properties) and the words–containers (*frog, amphibian*).

The CONDUIT metaphor plays the constitutive role in the usage of both hedges; thoughts/ideas are objects that fit into containers, either loosely or strictly, a fit that may be mediated by technical knowledge beyond that of everyday understanding. In the Western cultural tradition of the theory of language, the conduit metaphor is sometimes reified even further, so that the object-likeness of meanings contained within words is often taken as a theory of meaning, i.e. that the meaning of a word is that object in the common everyday world that it maps (Grace's (1987) mapping view). The fit, then, between the container and its object contents is one mediated by the objectness of the common pre-given world of experience. All languages are analogous in that they are maps of this world, although they may differ in the alignments and overlappings of their individual mappings and the precision with which their word–containers fit the objects of the pre-given world, for example, a three-term basic color terminology versus a five-term one. Such a view is the base of our common Western folk theory of language, as witnessed in the usage of hedges, but also largely our current scientific understanding.

Other cultural traditions, however, may not construe language in these terms. Rumsey (1990), in an important paper, demonstrates on the basis of linguistic evidence from an Australian language, Ungarinyin, that Aboriginal cultural ideology does not understand language in this way, i.e. meaning as simply a mapping of a concept or words as standing for/containers of things. In this language, Rumsey points out that there is no distinction between direct discourse (exact reporting of what was said) versus indirect discourse (reporting what was "meant"), suggesting that the contrast between saying and meaning is not highlighted in this culture, a contrast which is the foundation of the CONDUIT metaphor. In the Aboriginal view, saying *is* meaning; speaking a word brings forth a world in which meaning is enacted and validated. The meaning of a word is not exhausted by what it refers to in some objectively known, pre-given world, but also includes the world of cultural and social understandings it brings into being when used. Ultimately, those cultural understandings are its meaning, a local view rather close to that of Wittgenstein's (1953) notion of "forms of life." Such a linguistic ideology applies with equal force to the cultures of the Middle Sepik and can be illustrated with the meanings and usages of totemic names (Harrison 1990; Wassman 1991). In these cultures, tens of thousands of totemic spiritual names are associated with animals and places, with different social groupings having distinct names to refer to what appears to us as observers to be the same objectively given real-world object. For example, in Manambu (Harrison 1990:55), different subclans have different names for the male Eclectus parrot; *Kwarulukən, Waiyakəndu, Wapilaw*, and *Apakwaru*. The meanings of these terms, however, are *not* equivalent, for they express different understandings depending on the social groups to which they are linked, distinguishing among them, for example, as ceremonial groupings in ritual. In Aboriginal and Sepik cultures, meaning is not primarily something a word *has*, it is something a word *does*.

Cultural Models and Metaphors: Emotions in American English

Let me turn now to a discussion of another cultural model based on metaphors in American English, that of anger (Lakoff and Kövecses 1987) and love (Kövecses 1986). This model first of all employs the CONTAINER scheme with the metaphor, THE BODY IS A CONTAINER FOR THE EMOTIONS (see above). Secondary to this is the metaphor EMOTIONS ARE CONTAINED LIQUIDS. This last metaphor may be due to ancient and medieval theories about bodily humors, but applies in modern English to both negative emotions like anger (*you make my blood boil*) and positive ones like love (*she overflowed with love*). The final metaphor is EMOTION IS HEAT (*don't get hot under the collar; it was a torrid love affair*). The three of these together give us a basic cultural model for anger: ANGER IS THE HEAT OF A FLUID IN A CONTAINER, shown in examples like *simmer down; let him stew in his own juices*. Because of the nature of this metaphor, what we understand about the behavior of heated fluids in containers is transferred to understanding the feeling of anger. For example, as water increases in heat to boiling point it produces steam, so intense anger behaves like steam (*he's steaming in the corner*). Fluids in a closed container like a thermometer rise when heated, as does anger (*we got a rise out of him*). When fluids are heated in a closed container, the pressure within the container builds up, just as anger may (*I'm trying to bottle it up*). Pressure may be released (*I gave vent to my anger*) or build up to explosion point (*I just blew up*). When explosions occur, things go up in the air (*I blew my top*) or come out (*she had kittens*). Interestingly, the most salient physiological sensation we have of pressure building up in the body is pressure of urine in the bladder, giving rise to *she's really pissed off*.

Love shares some of the basic metaphors of anger, as illustrated above, but contrasts in others. It can be hot (*there were sparks between them*) or a fluid (*he poured out his feelings for him*). Unlike anger, for which the fluid is inside us, love is often taken as a fluid which we are inside (*he swept me off my feet*). Features of large external bodies of water are then often used to describe the feeling of love (*waves of passion overcame him; he was engulfed by these feelings for him*). And as such bodies are salient to humans according to their depth, this is a salient feature of metaphors for love in this cultural model (*she fell deeply in love with her; she was profoundly moved*). Finally, because the currents within seas often move us about beyond our control, this feature too is salient in describing love (*I was swept away by him*). The important point about these cultural models of both anger and love is that they and the metaphors that make them up are constituent of our under-standing of these concepts. They are in the main inaccessible to our under-standing except through these and other, possibly competing, models, in the same way that the understanding of electricity to non-specialists is not avail-able except through systems like the flowing fluid or teeming crowd models.

Models, Metaphors, and Grammatical Categories

Finally, I want to close this chapter by demonstrating the central import-ance of the idea of metaphor to the grammatical organization of a language, especially through the phenomenon of grammatical extensions. This occurs when previously independent lexical words become reanalyzed as gram-matical morphemes, often through a process of metaphorical extension. An excellent example is the use of body-part terms in Native Meso-American languages; we will illustrate with Copala Trique, a Mixtecan language of Mexico (Hollenbach 1990). In this language, as in English *head of the bed, foot of the mountain*, body-part nouns can be used to denote parts of inan-imate objects, but in a much more thorough-going fashion than English:

takun^5 kuchri$^{3?}$ tako^5 ki^{32h}
nose of vehicle   foot of mountain
"nose of the airplane"   "foot of the mountain"

But note:

takun^5 mi^{3}shte$^{4!}$ shra^5 we$^{3?}$
nose of machete   back of house
"handle of the machete"   "roof of the house"

The latter two, because of their startling difference from English, strike us as more clearly metaphorical (the roof of a house is like the back of an animal), but all are in fact metaphors. Body-part terms are also extended, in this case sharply metaphorically, to abstract nouns:

tako⁵ yo³ʔ ra³ˈ yawi³²
foot of year head of month
"beginning of the year" "end of the month"

The basis of this metaphorical extension is the vertical idea of stacking things up, beginning at the bottom (foot) and ending at the top (head).

Body-part nouns are also used in Copala Trique in functions analogous to English prepositions (the language lacks case marking or any overt marking of syntactic functions, save these body-part nouns/prepositions). Examples of such prepositional usage are:

katu^{5h} gwa^4 rike$^{3!}$ nuwi^4 a^{32}
entered John stomach of church DECL
"John entered inside the church"

nikun$^{1!}$ gwa^4 rian^{32} sha^{3}na$^{1!}$ a^{32}
stands John face of woman DECL
"John is standing in front of the woman"

These examples are cases of grammatical extension, the use of body-part nouns rather like prepositions by extension from a particular part of the body or object to the immediate area projected out from that part (e.g. "stomach" → "inside," "face" → "front," "side" → "next to," "back (of animal)" or "head (of human)" → "above," "feet" → "bottom"). These are metonymic extensions, based on part–whole or spatial–temporal adjacency associations (e.g. *crown* for the state), rather than metaphor proper, but the same basic principles of extension from some shared features or associations are at work here. Because of the dearth of syntactic function words in Copala Trique, these body-part nouns are also used for expressing temporal and logical relations:

ka^{ʔ}an^{2h} zo^{3ʔ} rike$^{3!}$ wa^{ʔ}nu^{1h} gwi^3 a^{32}
will go he stomach of three days DECL
"He will go within three days"

ka^{ʔ}an^{2h} zo^{3ʔ} shra^5 ko^{3ʔ}ngo$^{2!}$ a^{32}
will go he back of Monday DECL
"He will go after Monday"

kawi^{3h} zo^{3ʔ} she^{ʔ}e$^{4!}$ shi^{ʔ}i$^{3!}$ za$^{1!}$ a^{32}
died he feet of sickness good DECL
"He died from a real illness"

The extension of *rike*$^{3!}$ "stomach of" is the most straightforward: body part to space within body where body part is found (metonymic) and then to analogous space in an object, metaphorically treating a given time span as just such an object. The extension of *shra*^{5} "back of" is through the concept of the adjoining space "above." The Trique apparently conceive of temporal elapsing as an uphill journey, so the future is "above" you. Finally, the extension of *she*$^?e^{4!}$ "feet of" is through adjoining space, "base" or "bottom," with now a metaphorical extension similar to English *basis*, *ground* to "(be)cause of." Fascinatingly, this form also functions as a conjunction in:

kawi$^{3?}$ ni^{3}ka$^{2!}$ zo$^{3?}$ a^{32}
died   spouse he   DECL
"His wife died"

she$^?$e$^{4!}$ dan^{32} nano$^{4!}$ ra$^{4!}$ zo$^{3?}$ a^{32}
feet-of that   tells   inside he   DECL
"therefore, he's sad"

Finally, even what would appear to be a strictly syntactic marker for indirect objects and human or pronominal direct objects, probably modelled on Spanish *a*, is in origin a body part, in this case *man*$^{3!}$ "body of":

go$^{3?}$ gwa^4 sa$^?$an^{32h} man$^{3!}$ pe^{3}dro$^{4!}$ a^{32}
gave John money body of Peter   DECL
"John gave the money to Peter"

kene$^?$e$^{3!}$ gwa^4 man$^{3!}$ pe^{3}dro$^{4!}$ a^{32}
saw   John body of Peter   DECL
"John saw Peter"

The extensions are obscure here, and undoubtedly the effect of Spanish is hard to isolate from the Native system. But the basic idea seems to originate in the first example, giving something to someone usually means the object comes into space associated with that person (body of person is metonymically extended to space surrounding that body). The crucial point about these examples is that they demonstrate how pervasive the metaphorical and metonymic extension of body parts has been in the grammatical organization of Copala Trique, for *man*$^{3!}$ "body of" can hardly be much more than a syntactic marker here. The central role that such extensions play in the formation and reanalysis of grammatical categories will reappear when I discuss the ideas of Benjamin Lee Whorf in the next chapter.

Summary

Relativities of understanding are often couched in terms of models constructed in language for construing sensible experience outside of it. These models are often more than just models, but are the very terms by which we comprehend the phenomena so modelled; this is particularly so for phenomena not immediately visible to our senses, such as electricity. Competing models for this domain have been shown to be the actual frameworks which cognizers used to understand the phenomenon and draw inferences concerning possible behavior. These frameworks, which guide inferences, such as, electricity is like a teeming crowd, therefore that q, is a construction of language, a metaphor, a statement construing one, often less familiar, thing in terms of the properties of another more familiar one. Metaphors are often constructed around the particulars of our embodied experience as we interact with the world, statements in language of beliefs embodied in practical activities. Highly abstract domains, such as theories of meaning, are commonly understood in these metaphors drawn from embodied practices, and their terms are compelling for us, often showing up in the theories, folk and even scientific, we might propose to describe such domains. The effect of metaphor is pervasive in language, even the scope of grammatical categories does not escape it.

Further Reading

The literature on models and metaphor is also vast. For a good philosophical overview, try Black (1962). Recent work on models in anthropology is presented in Holland and Quinn (1987). For an excellent introduction to theory of metaphor, see Ortony (1993) and, for anthropological applications, Sapir and Crocker (1977). Fernandez (1986, 1991), Friedrich (1979, 1986), Lakoff (1987), Johnson (1987), and Lakoff and Johnson (1980) are important sources for the application of metaphor theory to anthropological linguistics.

10

Linguistic Relativity and the Boasian Tradition

The Boasian Tradition and its European Precursors

The Principle of Linguistic Relativity is a descriptive and theoretical axiom of the Boasian tradition, an American school of anthropological linguistics which flourished during the first half of the twentieth century. Contrary to its usual understanding by later scholars and some current reformulations, it was not seen by researchers in this tradition as an hypothesis, something to be proved or disproved by experimental procedures involving the usual distinction between dependent and independent variables (Hill and Mannheim 1992). Rather, it is more like a mathematical axiom, a shared postulate or assumed background of understanding, within which significant questions can be asked and valuable research work proceed. This is most clear in the work of Whorf, undoubtedly the most famous proponent of the Principle of Linguistic Relativity, who defined it as such (Whorf 1956:221):

> the "linguistic relativity principle" . . . means, in informal terms, that users of markedly different grammars are pointed by their grammars toward different types of observations and different evaluations of externally similar acts of observation, and hence are not equivalent as observers but must arrive at somewhat different views of the world.

Whorf, as a trained natural scientist, was thoroughly familiar with Einstein's Principle of Relativity and, thus, he chose its terms as metaphors in which to formulate his version of the Principle of Linguistic Relativity, namely, how an observer's frame of reference affects his observation of experience. For example, according to Einstein, two observers travelling at very different velocities, one close to the speed of light and one not, will have very different observations about the passage of time. Whorf's Principle of Linguistic Relativity is deliberately phrased in similar terms: speakers of languages of very different grammatical constructions, what Whorf called "fashions of speaking" (Whorf 1956:158), are led by these linguistic frames of reference to different observations of the world and interpretations of observations. This, without the metaphorical appeal to Einstein's theories, is also the force of Sapir's famous statement (Sapir 1949:162):

> Human beings do not live in the objective world alone nor alone in the world of social activity as ordinarily understood, but are very much at the mercy of the particular language which has become the medium of expression for their society. It is quite an illusion to imagine that one adjusts to reality essentially without the use of language and that language is merely an incidental means of solving specific problems of communication or reflection. The fact of the matter is that the "real world" is to a large extent unconsciously built up on the language habits of the group. No two languages are ever sufficiently similar to be considered as representing the same social reality. The worlds in which different societies live are distinct worlds, not merely the same world with different labels attached.

The Boasian tradition derives its name from Franz Boas. He was born and trained in Germany and, not surprisingly, many of the distinctive ideas of the Boasian tradition, including linguistic relativity, have precursors in German thought of the nineteenth century. All German thought of this period was, of course, within the shadow of Kant's great philosophical synthesis, so that his epistemological stance (i.e. that mental categories were imposed upon sensible experience) was widely accepted. But Kant's legacy was tied to a Romantic emphasis on free, individual creativity and its subjective meaning, leading to a heady neo-Kantian relativist mix, arguing for diversity among the mental categories of peoples according to culture, race, nation, with consequent differences in their experiences and expectations.

The earliest clear exponent of this neo-Kantian relativist mix is Johann Herder, a contemporary of Kant and the Romantic writers, Goethe and Schiller. Herder believed that language and thought stood in a relationship of mutual dependence and called language "a natural organ of the understanding." Human cognition is limited and mediated through one's language. For Herder, humans' experience and understanding differ to the extent that their languages do, each language and each culture reflecting the world in a particular way. Herder phrased this last idea in typically Romantic fashion in terms of an irreducible spiritual individuality of each language.

Herder's ideas were further developed by Wilhelm von Humboldt, one of the great intellectual titans of the nineteenth century. Humboldt's thought is a sophisticated blend of universalism and relativism. True to a relativist neo-Kantian vision, Humboldt held that language is an *a priori* framework of cognition, imposing organization on the total flux of sensations presented to our senses. As each language differs from any other, the resulting shape of the experienced world is altered. Indeed, following Herder, Humboldt believed that a nation's and culture's mental quality determines the sort of language its people have; therefore, language determines the way they think and experience reality. However, Humboldt also believed that all languages share universal properties and therefore had to express *some* universal grammatical notions like parts of speech, case, mood, etc. If a given language overtly lacks these features, they would have to be added conceptually (Manchester 1985:77): "when a grammatical form possesses no designation in a language, it is nevertheless still present as a guiding principle of the understanding of those who speak the language." Each language, then, expresses only a part of the total possible thought available; it is a foray (*Versuch* "attempt") into the total potentiality of the world. All languages are such attempts and thus, ontologically incomplete, although Humboldt did believe that some languages, notably the classical inflecting languages like Greek, Sanskrit and Latin, were more successful attempts than others (for his reasons why, see Humboldt 1988[1836–9]:140–68).

Boas

Boas, trained in Germany, imported the German intellectual tradition of Herder and Humboldt to the United States, where he is a central figure in the American tradition of anthropology and anthropological linguistics. Boas, however, received his Ph.D. not in these disciplines, but in psychophysics, and had a strong feel for the necessity of grounded empirical work in anthropology and linguistics, parallel to the role of experimentation in the natural sciences. He found this in the comparative study and analysis of the manifold cultures and languages of the Native inhabitants of North America, the American Indians. He grounded anthropology and linguistics in fieldwork among these cultures and languages and, thus, really for the first time, the ideas of Herder and Humboldt were investigated on the basis of solid empirical facts.

As with earlier Kantian approaches, Boas pointed out the function of language in organizing our experience of the sensible world, emphasizing particularly its classificatory function. Because the range of individual personal experience is infinitely varied, but expressed by a limited number of lexemes and grammatical formatives, an extended classification of experience must underlie all speech. This is a rather straightforward version of structuralist thinking (see chapter 4). Furthermore, these classifications vary dramatically across languages, e.g. English verbs of consumption contrasting along a dimension of object ingested, *eat, drink, smoke,* versus a single Yimas verb root *am-* to cover all three. Boas, inaugurating a tradition followed by his successors, liked especially to emphasize the variability of grammatical categories across languages, especially contrasting Indo-European languages like English with those of Native America. Consider his example *the man is sick* (Boas (1966[1911]:39). In English a number of grammatical categories are necessary: definiteness, number, tense, etc., so that the English sentence could perhaps be paraphrased as "a single man that I believe you can identify is at present sick." Kwak'wala, a Native language of British Columbia, on the other hand, requires some different categories like visibility and deixis, so that the English sentence would be rendered vaguely as "definite man near him invisible sick near him invisible" or more idiomatically, employing the locative grammatical categories common in Kwak'wala as "that invisible man lies sick on his back on the floor of the absent house." By comparisons such as this, Boas developed Humboldt's idea of language as *Versuch*: in each language only a part of the complete thought we have in mind is expressed. Linguistic variability entails that each language has a tendency to select only some of the individual concepts in the whole idea for expression. In other words, the relationship between language and thought is one way; linguistic categories may express (at least partially) those of thinking, but never the other way around: linguistic categories do not determine thought.

This position was strongly bolstered by Boas's lifelong commitment to the doctrine of the psychic unity of humanity. He believed the range of individuals' abilities do not vary across cultures. Apparent differences in linguistic sophistication do not reflect cognitive differences, merely different emphases of their cultures (Boas 1966[1911]:63). Thus, the fact that some Papuan languages of New Guinea have few basic numerals, *one*, *two*, and maybe *three* reflects nothing about the cognitive abilities of speakers of these languages, merely the lack of need for higher numerical expressions because there are not many things they need to count. That Boas is undoubtedly correct in this assertion is demonstrated by the ease with which these peoples borrow or innovate complex numerical systems when culture contact makes them necessary, for example, counting kina (the national currency in modern Papua New Guinea) in bride price payments. Boas, forever the anti-racist, continually argued that all languages are equally viable vehicles for the expression of thought, in spite of their formal differences, which might reflect differences in cultural interests (see his famous discussion of words for "snow" in Eskimo (Boas 1966[1911]:21–2)). There is in this vision a clear role for linguistic universals as the result of the psychic unity of humanity, but an equally strong rejection of Humboldt's view of some languages as being more successful attempts (*Versuch*) than others.

The final important point that Boas made about linguistic classifications is their unconscious and automatic character; the principles of a language's construction remain largely unknown to its speakers. This is generally not true of other ethnographic phenomena, and Boas argued that this gives linguistic classifications a uniquely privileged position in gaining access to the symbolic world of culture. Boas argued that because many types of ethnographic behavior can rise to consciousness, they may be subject to secondary reasonings and reinterpretations. Boas (1966[1911]:64–5) provided the example of the variability of table manners across cultures versus that of grammatical categories across languages; the rationale for the propriety of the former is subject to conscious reasoning within a culture, e.g. if we stick meat on the end of our knife and put it into our mouth, we might cut our tongue. Therefore, it is not proper. But the categories of language are not subject to explanations of this type. What average speaker is even aware of the anomaly, much less able to provide an explanation, of why the causative of *ripe* is *ripen*, but *large* is *enlarge*, not **largen*. Boas argued that the unconscious formation of categories, linguistic or ethnographic, is a fundamental fact about human life, but that the investigation of linguistic categories is of foremost importance because they always remain unconscious and can be studied for what they reveal about the culture's symbolic constructions (see, for example, the earlier discussion of the cultural models of anger and love expressed in the metaphors used in American English) without too great a distortion from secondary explanations.

Sapir

Edward Sapir was Boas's most brilliant linguistics student and probably the most illustrious American linguist of the twentieth century. He continued many of Boas's themes, but added a structuralist vision of language as a coherent system of interlocking sets of subsystems to his teacher's Kantian ideas of linguistic categories as classifications of experience. As such, each language is a formally complete system, the diversity of which makes languages incommensurate with each other to some degree (Sapir 1964:128):

> Inasmuch as languages differ very widely in their systematization of fundamental concepts, they tend to be only loosely equivalent to each other as symbolic devices and are, as a matter of fact, incommensurable in the sense in which two systems of points in a plane are, on the whole, incommensurable to each other if they are plotted out with reference to differing systems of coordinates.

Further, in contrast to Boas, Sapir emphasized the conventional, social function of these shared and systematized linguistic classifications, arguing, as the quote from him at the beginning of this chapter does, that linguistic classifications are not labels applied by an individual knower/speaker to a pre-given objective world (Grace's (1987) "mapping view"), but that the experienced world is socially and culturally mediated, one "to a large extent unconsciously built up on the language habits of the group" (Sapir 1949:162) (Grace's (1987) "reality-construction" view). Indeed, possibly through influence deriving from Durkheim and the Année Sociologique and Saussurean structuralism, Sapir viewed linguistic classifications as systematic collective representations, "social facts," in contrast to the individualist focus of Boas, for whom they were basically mental ideas.

Sapir closely followed Boas in upholding the latter's doctrine of the psychic unity of humanity. Although Sapir did claim that languages were systematically incommensurable to each other (see above quote), so that passing from one to another requires a major shifting of the coordinates of experience, he also believed that such shifting is well within the abilities of all humans, a version of psychic unity. The basic psychological processes of humans everywhere are identical, thereby making such shifting possible (Sapir had a keen interest in the "personality psychology" of his day, an area from which he hoped for insights into these basic universal psychological processes (Sapir 1949:507–97)). Like Boas, Sapir viewed variation across languages as indicative, not of cognitive deficiencies, but of cognitive predispositions. An excellent example is found in his famous paper *The grammarian and his language* (Sapir 1949:150–9), in which he discusses the problems of translating Kant's *Critique of Pure Reason* into Eskimo or Hottentot. The reasons, he points out, that these languages lack terms to translate Kant's abstruse philosophical concepts are not in the languages themselves, but in the speakers, whose interests are not oriented in the direction of this particular type of intellectual culture. Having had no occasion to speculate on the nature of causation, the speakers of these languages simply lack a term for it. But, Sapir emphasizes, the gap is strictly lexical; both languages have the notion of causation strongly developed in their processes of lexical derivation or syntactic construction formation, such as *the ice melted* versus the causative forms *fire melted the ice* or *the fire made the ice melt*. They both also have processes that derive abstract nouns from verbs, *speech* < *speak*, *laughter* < *laugh*, so there is absolutely no reason why the languages cannot derive *causation* < *cause*; it is simply that the speakers have no interest in such a word. Thus, the expression of causation is independent of both an intellectual understanding of the concept and the possession of a word for it. Indeed, in a typically Boasian vein, Sapir argues that our own intellectual understanding and use of the word is an example of secondary reasoning and interpretation, developed late in our own intellectual tradition; how many English speakers actually use the word?

Having dutifully asserted and argued for the psychic unity doctrine, Sapir also defended a version of the Principle of Linguistic Relativity. While all languages can do the same work of symbolic expression, the different techniques of expression are salient and indicate relativities of understanding. This led him to reverse Boas's view, drawn from Humboldt, that language reflects thought, each language through its categories reflecting only a part of the complete thought in mind, in favor of a position that language categories guide thought, but not absolutely. Lucy (1992b:19) uses the verb "channels" to describe Sapir's position, i.e. language channels thought, and this seems a good choice to capture the open-endedness and non-determinism of the relationship between them in his formulation. For Sapir, it is only in language that the full potential of thought is unfolded; true conceptual thinking is impossible without language because it is symbolically mediated and not a simple mapping of sensible experience, a position remarkably prescient of Geertz (1973:76). Because grammatical categories vary across languages, resulting in mutual incommensurability, different languages must channel conceptual thinking in different ways (Sapir 1949:159):

> The upshot of it all would be to make very real to us a kind of relativity that is generally hidden from us by our naïve acceptance of fixed habits of speech as guides to an objective understanding of the nature of experience. This is the relativity of concepts or, as it might be called, the relativity of the form of thought . . . For its understanding the comparative data of linguistics are a *sine qua non*. It is the appreciation of the relativity of the form of thought which results from linguistic study that is perhaps the most liberalizing thing about it. What fetters the mind and benumbs the spirit is ever the dogged acceptance of absolutes.

It is important to emphasize that the relativity here is of "concepts" or "the form of thought," not the process of thinking, which is neurological in base and hence universal, part of the psychic unity of humanity. What is relative is the interpretation of sensible experience in conceptual terms, such as viewing electricity as a flowing fluid. Different "concepts," as reflected in contrasting "habits of speech" of languages, have crucial effects on the inferences their speakers draw from sensible experience, in the same way that those who hold the flowing water or teeming crowd models of electricity draw different inferences about batteries and resistors.

Sapir illustrated his Principle of Linguistic Relativity in typically Boasian fashion with contrastive examples; his own exposition is clearer than anything I could hope to write, so I will just quote it at length (Sapir 1949:157–9):

> This brings us to the nature of language as a symbolic system, a method of referring to all possible types of experience. The natural or, at any rate, the naïve thing is to assume that when we wish to communicate a certain idea or impression, we make something like a rough and rapid inventory of the objective elements and relations involved in it, that such an inventory or analysis is quite inevitable, and that our linguistic task consists merely of the

finding of the particular words and groupings of words that correspond to the terms of the objective analysis. Thus, when we observe an object of the type that we call a "stone" moving through space towards the earth, we involuntarily analyze the phenomenon into two concrete notions, that of a stone and that of an act of falling, and, relating these two notions to each other by certain formal methods proper to English, we declare that "the stone falls." We assume, naïvely enough, that this is about the only analysis that can properly be made . . . In the Nootka language the combined impression of a stone falling is quite differently analyzed. The stone need not be specifically referred to, but a single word, a verb form, may be used which is in practice not essentially more ambiguous than our English sentence. This verb form consists of two main elements, the first indicating general movement or position of a stone or stonelike object, while the second refers to downward direction. We can get some hint of the feeling of the Nootka word if we assume the existence of an intransitive verb "to stone," referring to the position or movement of a stonelike object. Then our sentence, "The stone falls," may be reassembled into something like "It stones down." In this type of expression the thing-quality of the stone is implied in the generalized verbal element "to stone," while the specific kind of motion which is given us in experience when a stone falls is conceived as separable into a generalized notion of the movement of a class of objects and a more specific one of direction. In other words, while Nootka has no difficulty whatever in describing the fall of a stone, it has no verb that truly corresponds to our "fall."

This illustration of the Principle of Linguistic Relativity is obviously very close, if not identical to, Grace's (1987:10–11) "reality-construction" view of language; indeed, it would be hard to find a better case exemplifying the latter. Speakers of English and Nootka experience the world differently because their contrastive grammatical categories provide them with distinctive understandings and beliefs about the nature of things in that world (a strongly Quinean point about ontological relativity (Quine 1969)). English construes this event as involving an object, an entity, which undergoes displacement in space, but this view of the world is not shared with Nootka. For Sapir, a language was a constraining channel through which its speakers construe experience, analogous to one of the models of electricity, not a reflection of some independent pre-given reality, either physical or mental.

Whorf

And so we come to Benjamin Lee Whorf, undoubtedly the most unusual of the great triumvirate of the Boasian tradition. Unlike Boas and Sapir, Whorf was not a professional academic; having received a degree in chemical engineering, he worked as an investigator for an insurance company and studied linguistics as an avocation in his spare time. He came into contact with Sapir after the latter came to Yale University in 1931 and kept up intensive contact with professional linguists from then until his death in 1941. Whorf is the name most intimately associated with the Principle of Linguistic Relativity, although much of his thought was directly inspired by Sapir. However, Whorf's training as a natural scientist and his own unusual interests led him to develop it in his own way. He followed Boas in viewing linguistic categories as inherently classificatory and Sapir in his insistence on the systematicity of these categories, but he introduced a new and important distinction between two types of categories: overt and covert. An overt category is one with ever present formal markers, for example, plural in English, for nearly every plural noun in English takes some morphological marking for its number status. Covert categories are those without an ever present formal marker, but are indicated by their possibilities of combination with other words in various constructions. Intransitive verbs are a covert category in English because they bear no formal marking but as a group may not occur in the passive construction: *the stone was fallen.* Covert categories are of especial relevance to Whorf because, lacking any overt marker of their membership, they must be organized around some common feature, typically semantic, which will be revealing of some organizational principle of the language's grammar. Covert classes with such subtle elusive meanings, only detectable by their combinations with other words in constructions, Whorf called *cryptotypes.* He illustrated some cryptotypes in English by their failure to occur with *up,* otherwise freely combinable with mono- or disyllabic verbs (Whorf 1956:70–1): dispersion without boundary (*scatter/spread/smear it up*), oscillation without agitation of parts (*rock/wave/wriggle it up*), or non-durative impact with a psychological reaction (*tap/strike/stamp/stab it up*). Cryptotypes were especially important to Whorf because they uniquely reveal the guiding force of semantics in linguistic categorization: "as outward marks become few, the class tends to crystalize around an idea – to become more dependent on whatever synthesizing principle there may be in the meanings of its members" (Whorf 1956:80). Semantic organization is central to the Principle of Linguistic Relativity, because it is really in alternatives of meanings or interpretations that diverse languages differ.

Like Boas and Sapir, and contrary to the beliefs of many later commentators, Whorf had a strong commitment to universals and the psychic unity of humanity: "there is a universal, *Gefühl*-type way of linking experiences, which shows up in laboratory experiments and appears to be independent of language – basically alike for all persons" (Whorf 1956:267). But also like Boas and Sapir, he was not interested in this type of controlled, highly self-aware type of thinking, but the unconscious, automatic, habitual thinking of people in everyday life. Like Sapir, Whorf believed that thought, inasmuch as it is a cognitive understanding of the world, is linguistically mediated: "thinking . . . contains a large linguistic element of a strictly patterned nature" (Whorf 1956:66). Because linguistic patterns differ, the Principle of Linguistic Relativity naturally follows, as in this famous quotation (Whorf 1956:212–13):

> It was found that the background linguistic system (in other words, the grammar) of each language is not merely a reproducing instrument for voicing ideas but rather is itself the shaper of ideas, the program and guide for the individual's mental activity, for his analysis of impressions, for his synthesis of his mental stock in trade. Formulation of ideas is not an independent process, strictly rational in the old sense, but is part of a particular grammar, and differs, from slightly to greatly, between different grammars. We dissect nature along lines laid down by our native languages. The categories and types that we isolate from the world of phenomena we do not find there because they stare every observer in the face; on the contrary, the world is presented in a kaleidoscopic flux of impressions which has to be organized by our minds – and this means largely by the linguistic systems in our minds.

In some ways, the interpretation of this passage within Whorf's corpus is rather problematic. Some of the sophistication of Sapir's vision of linguistic categories as conventionalized understandings, symbolic guides to social reality, is lost in favor of a neo-Kantian appeal to linguistic systems as the organizer in the mind of the kaleidoscopic flux of impressions presented to us through our senses – overall, a view quite reminiscent of Boas. But Whorf himself is rather unsure of this neo-Kantian commitment; in the lines immediately following the previous quotation he presents a view much more in sympathy with that of Sapir:

> We cut nature up, *organize it into concepts, and ascribe significances* [my emphasis] as we do, largely because we are parties to an agreement to organize it in this way – an agreement that holds throughout our speech community and is codified in the patterns of our language.

Whorf's vacillation in this regard probably reflects tension between his professional training as a natural scientist and his apprenticeship with Sapir as a social scientist; the methodologies and assumptions of these two types of sciences are commonly seen as being quite different (see the discussion in Part I of Hiley, Bohman and Shusterman (1991), and Taylor (1985b)).

Whorf's is the most explicit formulation of the Principle of Linguistic Relativity (Whorf 1956:221):

> the "linguistic relativity principle" . . . means, in informal terms, that users of markedly different grammars are pointed by the grammars toward different

types of observations and different evaluations of externally similar acts of observation, and hence are not equivalent as observers but must arrive at somewhat different views of the world.

A formulation carefully phrased, as pointed out at the beginning of this section, in terms similar to Einstein's Relativity Theory. Whorf was primarily interested in how large scale systems in individual languages, his "fashions of speaking," have effects on the understanding of concepts, especially the equivalents of our Western scientific concepts of "matter," "space," and "time" (again his natural scientist predilections suggest themselves). He approached the empirical demonstration of his Principle into two ways: firstly, the typical Boasian method of contrastive analysis of individual examples in particular languages, already illustrated in the earlier discussion; and second, and highly innovatively, a detailed comparison of a set of linguistic systems, fashions of speaking, in two languages, with a view to drawing global conclusions about the differences in habitual thinking, the conceptualization of experience, for their speakers.

As an example of the first, consider his contrast between Shawnee, an Algonkian language of eastern North America, and English. Shawnee has two verbs, *ni-kwaškwi-tepē-n-a* and *ni-kwaškwi-ho-to*, both based on the same root *kwaškwi-*, meaning roughly "condition of force and reaction." The two words translate into English as "I push his head back" and "I drop it in the water and it floats," respectively, two sentences which seemingly have nothing in common because they are organized around different verbs, "push" and "drop." According to Whorf, because of these differences in verbal selection, English speakers are not likely to conceptualize these events as having much in common, a view well in accord with most native speakers' intuitions. However, in Shawnee, the same verb root *kwaškwi-* is used, predisposing Native speakers to conceptualize these events as quite similar. The differences are provided by the meanings of the other co-occurring morphemes:

ni – kwaškwi   – tepē – n   – a
I – force and reaction – head – by hand – act on animate object
"I act with force with my hand on an animate object, a head, followed by its reaction"
"I push his head back"

ni – kwaškwi   – ho   – to
I – force and reaction – on water – act on inanimate object
"I act with force on an inanimate object on the surface of the water followed by its reaction"
"I drop it in the water and it floats"

According to Whorf's Principle, the grammatical differences in the way these events are talked about will actually predispose speakers of Shawnee and English to conceptualize them in different terms, Shawnee as alike, English as unlike: "facts are unlike to speakers whose language background provides for unlike formulation of them" (Whorf 1956:235).

Whorf's Theory of "Cognitive Appropriation"

The most thoroughgoing example of Whorf's second approach to demonstrating the viability of the Principle of Linguistic Relativity, a global comparison of linguistic systems in two languages and habitual ways of thinking demonstrated in cultural practice, is found in his essay, *The relation of habitual thought and behavior to language* (Whorf 1956:134–59), written for the Sapir memorial volume and originally published in 1941 (Lucy (1992b) sees this paper as central to Whorf's corpus). In this paper Whorf contrasts the linguistic patterns and habitual thought or experience of Hopi with what he calls Standard Average European (SAE), regarding the differences among English and other European languages as trivial with respect to the features he is investigating. The semantic domains he is concerned with are those of mass and time. The gist of Whorf's argument is that these abstractions are not cognizable directly, but only through experience, and experience, as per the Principle of Linguistic Relativity, is interpreted through categorizations ultimately derived from the grammatical systems at work in the language. Just how Whorf makes this argument is especially ingenious.

He makes use of what Lucy (1992b:46) calls "cognitive appropriation," "the use in thought for its own ends of a structure of relations deriving from some other domain." This reads remarkably like metaphorical or metonymic extension, discussed in the previous chapter. Whorf's natural scientist vocation led him to look for physicalist source domains for cognitive appropriation, and his job as a fire insurance investigator provided him with no shortage of good examples (Whorf 1956:135–7). Perhaps his most famous example concerns empty gasoline drums. Full gasoline drums are handled with great care, but empty ones are not, people are sometimes found smoking around them, tossing cigarette butts about, etc. But empty drums are possibly the greater hazard, containing highly explosive vapor. Physically, the situation is dangerous, but, Whorf points out, speakers of English are led astray by the polysemy of the word *empty*: (1) "applied in analysis of physical situations without regard to, e.g. vapor, liquid vestiges, or stray rubbish, in the container" (Whorf 1956:135) and (2) "null and void, negative, inert" (Whorf 1956:135). The "empty" label on the drum is meant in the sense of (1), but is understood by speakers through metaphorical extension in the polysemous sense of (2), with potentially disastrous consequences. Lucy

10.1   Linguistic form

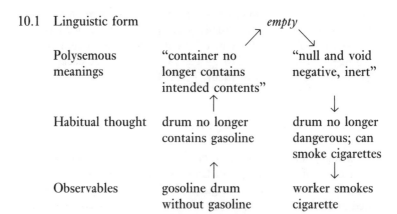

		empty
Polysemous meanings	"container no longer contains intended contents"	"null and void negative, inert"
Habitual thought	drum no longer contains gasoline	drum no longer dangerous; can smoke cigarettes
Observables	gosoline drum without gasoline	worker smokes cigarette

(1992b:50) diagrams this example, shown in 10.1. Whorf's point is that the organization of this whole is determined by the meanings residing in the descriptive term *empty* applied to the drums; people behave to the world as their linguistic categories predispose them to do. They "shape" thought in that the metaphorical and metonymic extensions implicit in them guide us in our interpretation of experience, exactly as discussed in chapter 9.

Whorf argues that very similar extensions apply within grammatical categories and that global differences in the way these extensions occur or do not occur across languages are responsible for differences in habitual conceptualizations of experience for speakers of these languages. Lucy (1992b:50–62) presents an especially clear summary of Whorf's arguments in this regard. Whorf contrasts English (for SAE) and Hopi with respect to the grammatical category of number, pointing out that the plural category in English applies to both perceptually tangible objects, like *men* and imaginary groupings, such as cycles, like *days*, which are never perceptually tangible. Whorf's discussion of this is clear (Whorf 1956:139):

In our language . . . plurality and cardinal numbers are applied in two ways: to real plurals and imaginary plurals. Or more exactly if less tersely: perceptible spatial aggregates and metaphorical aggregates. We say "ten men" and also "ten days." Ten men either are or could be objectively perceived as ten, ten in one group perception – ten men on a street corner, for instance. But "ten days" cannot be objectively experienced. We experience only one day, today; the other nine (or even all ten) are something conjured up from memory or imagination. If "ten days" be regarded as a group it must be as an "imaginary," mentally constructed group. Whence comes this mental pattern? Just as in the case of the fire-causing errors, from the fact that our language confuses the two different situations, has but one pattern for both. When we speak of "ten steps forward, ten strokes on a bell," or any similarly described cyclic sequence, "times" or any sort, we are doing the same thing as with "days". CYCLICITY brings the response of imaginary plurals. But a likeness of cyclicity to aggregates is not unmistakably given by experience prior to language, or it would be found in all languages, and it is not.

Note Whorf's invocation of cognitive appropriation to account for the use of the plural category to express the repetition of cycles: they are seen as being like plural groupings of a physical object – an extension, however, that is neither objectively grounded in the physical world nor found in all languages. This process of extension is very like the process of grammatical expansion illustrated in chapter 9, in which Trique body parts become spatial prepositions. Here cycles of time are quantified in parallel fashion to multiple tokens of the same physical object. This has cognitive consequences for speakers of European languages like English in that they will conceive of temporal intervals like days in terms rather like concrete objects and be predisposed to experience time in this way (Whorf 1956:140):

> Habitual thought then assumes that in the latter the numbers are just as much counted on "something" as in the former. This is objectification. Concepts of time . . . are objectified as counted QUANTITIES, especially lengths, made up of units as a length can be visibly marked off into inches.

Whorf's description presents Hopi as being fundamentally different. The grammatical category of plural is only used with nouns referring to object-like entities, denoting groupings of such entities. Words denoting time intervals belong to a special word class called tensors, which never pluralize. Rather, the counting of tensors is done by ordinals: "first day," "second day," "third day," etc. According to Whorf, this is not the counting of tokens of an object in a group, but counting successive *reappearances* of the same thing, which cannot cohere into a group. This use of ordinal numbers applies to nouns as well as tensors. Whorf summarizes the situation thus (Whorf 1956:140, 148).

> In Hopi there is a different linguistic situation. Plurals and cardinals are used only for entities that form or can form an objective group. There are no imaginary plurals, but instead ordinals used with singulars.

> Time is mainly reckoned "by day" . . . or "by night" . . . which words are not nouns but tensors, . . . The count is by ORDINALS. This is not the pattern of counting a number of different men or things, even though they appear successively, for, even then, they COULD gather into an assemblage. It is the pattern of counting successive reappearances of the SAME man or thing, incapable of forming an assemblage. The analogy is not to behave about day-cyclicity as to several men ("several days"), which is what WE tend to do, but to behave as to the successive visits of the SAME MAN.

10.2

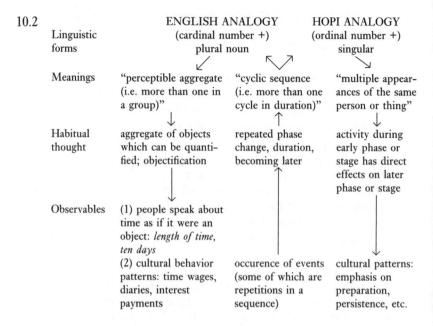

	ENGLISH ANALOGY (cardinal number +) plural noun		HOPI ANALOGY (ordinal number +) singular
Linguistic forms			
Meanings	"perceptible aggregate (i.e. more than one in a group)"	"cyclic sequence (i.e. more than one cycle in duration)"	"multiple appear-ances of the same person or thing"
Habitual thought	aggregate of objects which can be quanti-fied; objectification	repeated phase change, duration, becoming later	activity during early phase or stage has direct effects on later phase or stage
Observables	(1) people speak about time as if it were an object: *length of time, ten days* (2) cultural behavior patterns: time wages, diaries, interest payments	occurence of events (some of which are repetitions in a sequence)	cultural patterns: emphasis on preparation, persistence, etc.

Lucy (1992b:52) summarizes Whorf's exposition (10.2). Note that the crucial difference between English and Hopi concerns the assimilation with respect to grammatical categories of the words denoting temporal intervals, marking the occurrence of events. How these are to be conceived is not straightforwardly given in the physical world, and their assimilation/classification with other grammatical categories is virtually assured due to the necessary classificatory function of language so highlighted by Boasians. In English the grammatical class of countable nouns is extended to include time words, with one set of cognitive consequences for the way time is experienced, while in Hopi, they belong to the class of tensors, which are counted with ordinal numerals, and this has different cognitive and experiential results.

Whorf presents a cluster of evidence to argue that speakers of English conceive of units of temporal intervals as countable tangible objects. He notes that the "fashions of speaking" (i.e. metaphors) that English speakers use to talk about time clearly exhibit this conceptualization (Whorf 1956:152–6): we *spend/save/lose/buy* time; *time is money* (i.e. dollars, cents); I never *have enough* time; a *long/short* time. Further, Whorf argues that our very conception of history is due to our conception of objectivized time, derived from our linguistic categorization (Whorf 1956:153):

> But OUR objectified time puts before imagination something like a ribbon or scroll marked off into equal blank spaces, suggesting that each be filled with an entry. Writing has no doubt helped toward our linguistic treatment

of time, even as the linguistic treatment has guided the uses of writing. Through this give-and-take between language and the whole culture we get, for instance:

1. Records, diaries, bookkeeping, accounting, mathematics stimulated by accounting.
2. Interest in exact sequence, dating, calendars, chronology, clocks, time wages, time graphs, time as used in physics.
3. Annals, histories, the historical attitude, interest in the past, archaeology, attitudes of introjection toward past periods, e.g. classicism, romanticism.

Hopi culture embodies a different conceptualization according to Whorf. Remember that their view of time intervals is of cycles repeating the same essence. Thus, each day is not inherently different from the last (contrast English: "tomorrow is another day!"). The culture emphasizes continuity and persistence, rather than change. Given this view, it is not surprising that Hopi show little interest in careful documentation of past ages, e.g. our history with its necessarily detailed record of change through the ages. Because each day carries the essence of those before, one can affect the future by careful preparation here and now ("Well begun is half done" is one English proverb the Hopi would understand, Whorf asserts). But this idea of preparation always applies within a backdrop understanding of cultural persistence and constant repetition.

On the basis of his comparative study of English and Hopi linguistic and cultural patterns, Whorf is led to the following conclusion (Whorf 1956:158):

> Concepts of "time" and "matter" are not given in substantially the same form by experience to all men but depend upon the nature of the language or languages through the use of which they have been developed. They do not depend so much upon ANY ONE SYSTEM (e.g. tense, or nouns) within the grammar as upon the ways of analyzing and reporting experience which have become fixed in the language as integrated "fashions of speaking" and which cut across the typical grammatical classifications, so that such a "fashion" may include lexical, morphological, syntactic, and otherwise systemically diverse means coordinated in a certain frame of consistency.

It is vitally important to understand correctly Whorf's claim of linguistic appropriation in this quote. First of all, he is not talking about thought *per se*, but about concepts, i.e. the kinds of conceptual systems used to construe experience are created in the way people talk, not in some pre-given pre-linguistic reality (as also, in his "empty" drum example). Second, the conceptual systems do not reside in any particular grammatical category, but are a result of the entire organization of the grammatical systems of the language and its metaphorical/metonymic extensions, "the fashions of speaking." It is configurations within the grammar which frame the conceptual systems of the language's speakers, resulting in particular construals of

10.3   linguistic patterning as fashions of speaking

↓

conceptual systems/construal of experience

↓

cultural practices and beliefs

experience and resulting cultural practices and beliefs. We could summarize this as shown in 10.3 (see Lucy 1992b:64). Note that in Whorf's formulation there is an implicit neo-Kantian assumption that communal knowledge (cultural practices and beliefs) is underlain by individual acts of knowing (conceptual systems/construal of experience), although the latter are in fact at least in part acquired through a communal resource (grammatical systems). There is a certain degree of tension in this formulation (as there is generally in Whorf's thought in this regard), but it can be profitably reinterpreted in an enactionist framework so that conceptual systems and cultural practices and beliefs are a unitary knowledge network, with individual and culture joined in indissoluble structural coupling. There is no statable boundary between individual knowing and cultural knowledge. The systems of linguistic patterning in this reformulation are as Sapir viewed them: a public sedimentation and unfolding of this knowledge, through which it is transmitted across generations (see chapter 17). Ultimately, Whorf is of central importance not so much for his formulation of the Principle of Linguistic Reality (Sapir's is probably more insightful), but for the ground-breaking empirical study he did of the relationship between the linguistic patterns of a people and their habitual conceptual systems of interpretation. Indeed, until very recently, no one had even progressed as far as he in this regard.

Neo-Whorfianism: The Empirical Studies of Lucy

Boas, Sapir, and Whorf all died within five years of each other. This, plus the disruption of World War II, led to the decline of the Boasian tradition as a dominant integrative research agenda within American anthropological linguistics. During the 1950s and 1960s some individual research projects investigating the role of the Principle of Linguistic Relativity (Bright and Bright 1969; Brown and Lenneberg 1954; Carroll and Casagrande 1958; Hoijer 1964; Lenneberg 1953; Lenneberg and Roberts 1956; Mathiot 1964, 1969) were undertaken, often under somewhat different assumptions from those of Sapir and Whorf (Lucy 1992b). It was during this period and through these studies that the Principle of Linguistic Relativity was reformulated as a hypothesis, to be *tested* by experimental methods, involving the usual understanding in terms of dependent and independent variables. This was not Sapir and Whorf's view, for whom this Principle was an axiom; the language of experimental science, such as independent and dependent variables, is *never* found in Whorf's corpus (Hill and Mannheim 1992), demonstrating that he did not view Linguistic Relativity as a hypothesis whose validity could be determined by these methods. The rephrasing of Linguistic Relativity as a hypothesis led to rather disappointing research results, and its vitality as a guiding principle of intellectual discovery gradually declined. This was aided and abetted, no doubt, by the rise of strong universalist theoretical trends in anthropological linguistics, inspired by the work of Chomsky, and Berlin and Kay. However, since around 1980, tentative new growth has begun to emerge in the Boasian tradition, especially at the University of Chicago around Paul Friedrich and Michael Silverstein, and their students. Silverstein's papers (Silverstein 1976, 1979, 1981, 1985, 1987, 1992) articulate a sophisticated re-working of Sapir and Whorf's ideas, but the most extensive study of the Principle of Linguistic Relativity since Whorf appears in important work by John Lucy (1992a, b), in which he offers a revised and more psychologically rigorous reformulation for it.

Lucy diverges from Sapir and Whorf and follows later researchers in viewing Linguistic Relativity as a hypothesis to be tested. He parameterizes the hypothesis by separating language and thought as autonomous domains and then determines how systems in the former have detectable effects in the latter, chiefly through psychological cognitive testing administered to speakers of different languages. It is not clear that this operational separation of language and thinking is consonant with Whorf's own views, for whom the relationship between language and habitual thought was apparently much more direct and unmediated, but in any case, Lucy's work can stand on its own as a valuable contribution in its own right. Lucy's (1992a) work revolves around a contrastive study of the grammatical category of number in English and Yucatec Maya, a language of Mexico. Both English and Yucatec mark plural on nouns, but they differ with respect to the distribution of the inflections. English contrasts count nouns like *man* and *book* with mass nouns like *milk* and *rice*. All count nouns are pluralizable, and this inflection is obligatory, if semantically called for; mass nouns may not be inflected for plural; so: *men*, *books*, but **milks*, **rices*. In Yucatec, pluralization is optional and, even then, is only available for nouns denoting animate beings. Using the features [± animate] for animacy and [± discrete] for the count/mass noun distinction, the three classes of nouns in the two languages can be defined as in 10.4. Note that the crucial group of nouns is class B, whose behavior contrasts in the two languages: like group A in English, but like group C in Yucatec. Globally, pluralization is more salient in English: a wider range of nouns is pluralized (groups A and B) than in Yucatec, and pluralization is obligatory when semantically required, whereas group A nouns in Yucatec are only optionally pluralized. Under the general

10.4

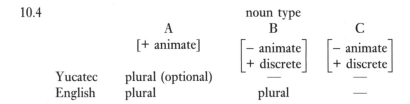

	A [+ animate]	noun type B $\begin{bmatrix} -\text{ animate} \\ +\text{ discrete} \end{bmatrix}$	C $\begin{bmatrix} -\text{ animate} \\ +\text{ discrete} \end{bmatrix}$
Yucatec	plural (optional)	—	—
English	plural	plural	—

rubric of the Linguistic Relativity Hypothesis, this implies a number of specific hypotheses about the habitual cognitive functioning of English as opposed to Yucatec speakers: (1) English speakers should attend to the number of various objects perceived more often than Yucatec speakers; (2) they should attend to the number of more sorts of objects (those referred to by both groups A and B) than Yucatec speakers (only group A); and (3) speakers of the two languages should differ in the way they attend to the number of objects denoted by nouns in group B, English speakers being more attentive than Yucatec speakers.

Lucy administered a number of cognitive experiments to test these predictions and found that they were indeed confirmed. In a range of non-verbal experimental tasks, involving the sorting and recall of pictures of scenes of everyday Mexican village life, English speakers and Yucatec speakers performed differentially as expected: English speakers attended to the number of objects more frequently and did so more saliently for those referring to animate beings (group A) and objects (group B) than those referring to substances (group C); Yucatec speakers were mainly sensitive to number for objects denoted by animate nouns (group A) and this less consistently. Furthermore, the differential for group B nouns was also detected: the salience of number for objects denoted by this group was significantly higher for English speakers than Yucatec speakers.

A second important linguistic difference between English and Yucatec concerns enumeration. English nouns can be counted and indefinitized directly: *three men, a man*, but Yucatec, being a numeral classifier language (see chapter 12), requires a classifier '*óoš-túul máak* three-classifier man "three men." Numeral classifiers typically provide information about the shape or other perceptual qualities of the referent of the noun. This is rather like the treatment in English of nouns denoting substances (group C), *three bottles of milk, two kilos of rice*; note that the counting words here tell us about the shape, amount, or other perceptually bounding qualities of the substance denoted by the mass noun. Lucy suggests that Yucatec contrasts with English in that its nouns are all semantically rather like mass nouns, denoting a substance, some stuff, rather than an object, and that the classifier provides materially bounding criteria for this stuff in any particular physical manifestation. If English nouns predominantly denote objects but Yucatec nouns, stuff, then the following hypothesis about the habitual cognition of the speakers of these languages presents itself: English speakers should have a relative preference for classifications based on shapes, but Yucatec speakers should have one for materials. Again Lucy performed some cognitive experiments and found the hypothesis confirmed. For example, speakers of the two languages were presented with a cardboard box usually used to hold cassette tapes and asked whether it was more like a plastic box of similar shape or a small piece of cardboard. English speakers consistently opted for the former, and Yucatec speakers for the latter.

Silverstein's Reformulation

Lucy's (1992a) study is important empirical work which will hopefully help to reinvigorate research within the Boasian tradition. He has forged a new rigor into the study of Linguistic Relativity by his careful joining of thorough linguistic analysis and contrastive typology with experimental cognitive psychology. Silverstein's work represents a return to probably more traditional understandings of Linguistic Relativity in the Boasian tradition. In contrast to Lucy's psychological slant, with its deductive hypotheses for testing through the standard metrics of dependent and independent variables, Silverstein's pursuit is an interpretive, rather hermeneutic one, that envisages the Principle of Linguistic Relativity as a guiding framework within which the interaction between linguistic form and function and wider cultural beliefs and practices can be profitably investigated. Silverstein broadens the Principle of Linguistic Relativity beyond its normal focus on the propositional, referential function of language, the domain of semantics, to its indexical functions in the enaction of discourse contexts, the domain of pragmatics. Silverstein sees Whorf's most valuable insight to be the proposal of a principled relationship between the systems of grammatical categories in a language and "an ideology of reference, an understanding at the conceptual level of how . . . language represents 'nature'" (Silverstein 1979:202), in other words, the propositional referential function of language. But Silverstein's aim is to go beyond this, to generalize Whorf's claim "from the plane of reference to the whole of language function" (Silverstein 1979:194). Silverstein claims that Western theoretical treatments of language have tended to reduce all meaning to reference, but that this is an impoverished view of language functions. Indeed, as Rumsey (1990) has argued (discussed in chapter 9), this Western emphasis on reference may be a Whorfian effect itself, due to our linguistic "fashions of speaking" distinguishing wording from meaning and the cultural model of the conduit metaphor, an understanding not shared with other cultures, such as Australian Aboriginals, with different linguistic conventions.

Thus, Silverstein's project is fundamentally the broadening of the Principle of Linguistic Relativity beyond the referential value of grammatical categories to include their indexical pragmatic properties. He combines this with another theme inherited from earlier work in the Boasian tradition, the relative inaccessibility to conscious awareness of linguistic categories and any consequent secondary explanations. Silverstein (1981) develops a typology of grammatical categories in terms of their accessibility to conscious awareness. Silverstein claims that speakers can more readily become aware of bits of speech which have a high referential component (i.e. relative ease in metasemantic glossing) to their meaning, for example, nominal and verbal root lexemes. Bits of speech whose meaning is more pragmatic and indexical, for example, particles like *there*, pronouns with politeness differences such as French *tu* and *vous*, or grammatical categories like subjunctive mood, are much more opaque to speakers' conscious awareness. A second parameter is segmentability; units which are coherent when segmented are more accessible than those which are not. So, discontinuous morphemes like Yimas near future *na-* . . . *-kiak* or grammatical categories whose exponents are not clearly segmentable, such as case signalled by mutating the initial phoneme of a noun root (in Nias, a language of Indonesia), should be less accessible than the English plural category, e.g. *book-s*. Still a third parameter concerns the degree to which the linguistic forms transparently carry their contextual presuppositions. Deictic forms like *this* or *that* are highly transparent in that the context for their usage is readily apparent in the external world, "close/near self" versus "distant/near other." This contrast should be relatively accessible to awareness, but not that between French *tu* and *vous*. In that case the context for their use is actually dialogically created by their ongoing usage; their presuppositions are not particularly transparent contextually, so this contrast will be relatively opaque to awareness. Silverstein (1981) also proposes two further parameters which are mainly concerned with the ease with which the speaker may restate the indexical value and conditions of the linguistic form; the greater the ease, the higher the conscious awareness. Note that in many ways, Silverstein's ideas about parameters of conscious awareness of grammatical categories are a development and more rigorous formulation of Whorf's (1956) concept of covert categories and cryptotypes. He states it as follows (Silverstein 1981:1):

> the point I wish to make is that it is extremely difficult, if not impossible, to make a native speaker take account of those readily-discernible facts of speech as action that he has no ability to describe for us in his own language.

The notion of limits of awareness is crucial to Silverstein's work because the higher the conscious awareness of a form and its functions by speakers the more likely it will be seized upon as a locus for conscious reflection and hence a source for Boas's (1966[1911]) secondary explanation and ideological refashioning, especially ideologies and folk theories or cultural models about the nature of language. For example, because nominals and, in particular, proper names are maximally referential, segmentable and transparently presuppositional, it is no surprise that they have served as the basis for our Western ideologizing about language, in particular, Western philosophical theories about language which are predicated on referential theories of meaning, for example, truth conditional semantics. Rumsey's (1990) work demonstrates that such ideologies, however, may not be universal. Further, because of constraints of awareness on grammatical categories, the outcome of conscious reflection on language will be skewed in favor of those which are more accessible: they will be more likely sources for conscious reflection than those less accessible. This has far-reaching implications for Whorf's principle of cognitive appropriation, the structuring or construal of a given domain in terms of a more familiar one. In the context of Silverstein's thought, this entails that more accessible grammatical categories will be the structuring domains through cognitive appropriation for those less accessible. Because semantic (more accessible) and pragmatic (less accessible) meanings are parcelled out among grammatical categories in different ways in different languages, the sources of cognitive appropriation will differ correspondingly. The Principle of Linguistic Relativity then turns out to be a statement about how these different parcellings of meaning among grammatical categories (and other parameters such as segmentability) in various languages lead to different patterns of cognitive appropriation and ultimately different systems of ideologizing about the "world," i.e. the construal of experience. The fact that cycles of time are linguistically treated with respect to the grammatical category of number like objects in English leads both cycles and objects to be understood through cognitive appropriation to be alike meaningwise in certain ways. This is then projected from conscious reflection into ideologies and conceptualizations that model recurring intervals of time in ways like multiple tokens of a kind of object (see Whorf 1956:134–59). The crucial contribution of Silverstein here is to outline a theory of linguistic structure and meaning that can be parameterized with respect to the likelihood and direction of such processes of cognitive appropriation; note that plural in English scores highly in terms of the parameters of accessibility to awareness. Ultimately, Silverstein's ideas boil down to another claim that features of structure within language lead to concepts about the structure of the "world" – a wholly Whorfian outlook.

Summary

The Boasian tradition in anthropological linguistics is intimately associated with the Principle of Linguistic Relativity, the idea that speakers of different languages, of diverse structures and systems of grammatical categories, are led by these linguistic frames of reference to differing construals of experience of the world. While having sources in German Romantic thought of the nineteenth century, the Boasian tradition was inaugurated by Boas and carried on by Sapir and Whorf and is characterized by demonstrating this axiom of linguistic relativity by careful contrastive studies of how languages of diverse structural types might describe the same objective event in the physical world. For Sapir and Whorf these differences in expression were indicative of actual differences of interpretation of these events, different conceptualizations, but all the while they emphasized the doctrine of the psychic unity of humanity, i.e. that the fundamental cognitive abilities of humans are everywhere the same. Whorf's detailed studies of Hopi and English, comparing the different extensions in the two languages of grammatical categories through cognitive appropriation, shows how these contrastive systems of metaphorical extension can lead to different construals of experience and ultimately different cultural practices. After a hiatus of some 40 years, the Boasian tradition has been recently revitalized in the work of Lucy and Silverstein, Lucy, by adding psychological-testing matrices to the familiar contrastive linguistic studies of the Boasian tradition and Silverstein, by extending the domain of the Principle of Linguistic Relativity into the study of indexicals and other pragmatic phenomena, and by articulating a richer typological theory paramaterizing the likelihood of certain linguistic units being the source for the modelling of others in terms of their accessibility to conscious awareness.

Further Reading

For the Boasian tradition it is essential to read the primary works of the three main participants: Boas (1966[1911]), Sapir (1949), and Whorf (1956). Important secondary sources are Darnell (1990), Gumperz and Levinson (1991), Hill and Mannheim (1992), and Lucy (1992b). Lucy's own work is presented in Lucy (1992a), and Silverstein's, in a series of papers (1976, 1979, 1981, 1985). Other important sources include Friedrich (1986) and Witherspoon (1977). Humboldt's influence on this tradition can now be traced through a new translation of his major work (Humboldt 1988).

11

Space

Proposed Universals of Space

Whorf (1956:158–9) had the following to say about space:

> But what about our concept of "space," which was also included in our first question? There is no such striking difference between Hopi and SAE about space as about time, and probably the apprehension of space is given in substantially that same form by experience irrespective of language. The experiments of the Gestalt psychologists with visual perception appear to establish this as a fact.

Surprisingly, Whorf's ideas about space tally fairly closely with much of the received wisdom within current linguistics and cognitive psychology (Clark 1973; Lyons 1977; Miller and Johnson-Laird 1976; Talmy 1983). Basically, this view is the following. Spatial conception is strongly informed by innate, presumably biologically based, universals, so that it is essentially the same in all languages and cultures. Given these universal conditions and our ecological niche as terrestrial, diurnal creatures, it is claimed that we are predisposed to conceive of space in relativistic and egocentric terms, projecting out from the anatomical patterns of our bodies. Thus, the coordinates through which spatial orientation are established are projected from ego, the deictic central reference point for all spatial reckoning, along two horizontal axes and one vertical. The vertical one, drawn from our upright position or, perhaps, the experience of gravity establishes the UP–DOWN axis; the horizontal axes are FRONT–BACK, derived from the anatomically asymmetric division of the body into two halves, and LEFT–RIGHT, from the symmetrical division. The location of objects in space then is always determined relative to the orientation of the speaker: if we are standing eye to eye across from each other, my left is your right. There are no fixed, absolute angles used in human spatial orientation. Thus, the universal terms of spatial conception in this hypothesis are like those of English and familar European languages. Terms like LEFT–RIGHT, FRONT–BACK should not only be lexical universals among the languages of the world, but their actual usage should closely parallel that of the English terms.

Relativities in Spatial Conceptualization: The Case of Guugu-Yimidhirr

Recent work by researchers associated with the Cognitive Anthropology Research Group at the Max-Planck Institute in Nijmegen, the Netherlands (Brown and Levinson 1992, 1993, 1994; Haviland 1993; Levinson 1992, 1994a, b; Levinson and Brown 1994) poses a serious challenge to these strong universalist claims about the bases of spatial conception and, contrary to the surprising claim of Whorf's above, rather suggests findings more consonant with the Principle of Linguistic Relativity. It now appears that different languages have fundamentally different ways of describing spatial orientation and that these differences correspond systematically to differences in cognitive behavior, suggesting, along Whorfian lines, a correlation between linguistic patterns and habitual thought. It now appears that sensible experience, in the form of the categories of the native language that one learns, has an important role in molding one's spatial cognition, contrary to strong universalist and rationalist assumptions now current within the cognitive sciences like linguistics and psychology. This is not to claim that there are no universal innate conditions in this area. There almost certainly are. It is simply to claim that they greatly underdetermine the range of possible cognitive systems, leaving wide latitude for contingent human experience, in the form of languages and cultures, to play a guiding role in spatial cognition.

Perhaps the most surprising finding of the Nijmegen research group is the discovery of languages (and speakers!) for whom space is conceived of not relatively, using concepts like LEFT, RIGHT, FRONT, BACK, which have no fixed designation and depend on the speaker's viewpoint, but *absolutely*, with axes fixed in geographic space, rather like our cardinal directions, north, south, east, and west. Such languages have been found in Australia, South Asia, Oceania, and Mesoamerica. A particularly striking example is Guugu-Yimidhirr, of north-eastern Australia. This language completely lacks all spatial terms which are relative to body orientation; in particular there are *no* terms for locating the position of objects in space equivalent to FRONT, BACK, LEFT, RIGHT (e.g. the latter two terms can only be used to refer to the left and right hands and perhaps other symmetrical body parts like eyes, legs, etc.). Rather, the language heavily employs four roots, corresponding roughly to the four cardinal directions as shown in 11.1 (Haviland 1993). The Guugu-Yimidhirr terms do not

11.1

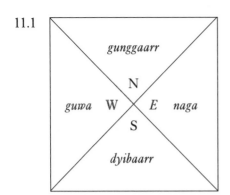

describe compass points, as do their English equivalents, but, rather, quadrants of a hypothetical horizontal plane. Further, it is rotated slightly clockwise
from the corresponding European compass points so that the median of the
north quadrant is actually oriented slightly north-east (about 15°) according
to our compass point equivalents.

Note that these spatial categories are absolutely fixed, due to the geogra-
phy of the earth, and are not subject to variation according to the spatial
orientation of the speaker. If something is to my north, it is to my north
regardless of whether it is in front of me, to the back of me, to my left, or to
my right. Its spatial position is absolutely fixed with respect to mine, regardless of my relative viewpoint. The astounding thing about languages like
Guugu-Yimidhirr is that it is these absolutely based terms that are habitually used by speakers to describe location or motion. It is as if in response
to a question "where's the salt?," I responded "it's there, to the east." In the
relativistic, egocentric spatial universe of the English speaker, this is likely
to provide little enlightenment and lead to a puzzled look or worse, but this
is exactly how a Guugu-Yimidhirr speaker would respond. All horizontal
spatial information is described in these terms: the sun doesn't go down, it
goes west; the fork isn't at my left, it lies south; the tide doesn't go out, it
goes east. Note that while English speakers can use such an absolute system
for large, global distances (i.e. Africa lies south of Europe), Guugu-Yimidhirr
uses it for all degrees of spatial distance, from the knife, a centimeter to the
south, to Sydney, 2000 km to the south. All movement is also described in
these terms; I don't just go to the store, I go north to the store.

It is unlikely that the differences in spatial orientation for English and
Guugu-Yimidhirr speakers are restricted just to verbal description; the
thoroughgoing differences between the absolute and relative systems suggest real differences in speakers' experience and conception of space. Brown
and Levinson (1993) provides a nice illustration of what these differences
in experience might be like. Consider a table of four, dining in the revolving

restaurant at the top of the Centrepoint Tower in Sydney. I am sitting facing the Prime Minister, who is at the head of the table, with Madonna to my left and Hillary Clinton to my right. This is the relative, egocentric construal of their location in space. At 8.00 p.m., when we all sit down to dinner, the table is aligned so that the Prime Minister is at the north, I, to the south, and Madonna and Hillary Clinton to the west and east respectively; this is the absolute reckoning of spatial location. However, at 8.30 p.m., due to the revolving of the restaurant, the Prime Minister is now east, I, west, and Madonna and Hillary Clinton, north and south respectively. But from an egocentric, relativistic point of view, nothing has changed at all; everyone is in the same position they were half an hour ago. The differences do not stop there; consider the layout of cutlery at any individual place setting: fork to the left of the sitter, knife to the right. But for a Guugu-Yimidhirr speaker, no such general rule is possible: at the northern end of the table, fork to the east, and knife to the west, but with a complete reversal on the southern end, never mind the complexities of the east and west edges.

Clearly, the potential cognitive consequences of the difference in the geocentric absolute system for spatial reckoning of Guugu-Yimidhirr and the egocentric relative one of European languages like English are manifold. Exquisitely simple and straightforward in design, the Guugu-Yimidhirr system does always require an amazing ability to determine the exact lay of the four quadrants in any geographical space. In open country and daylight conditions, this may not be too taxing, using the sun as a guide, but it is also commonly done in thick rainforest conditions and at night! What this does appear to require is that Guugu-Yimidhirr speakers carry about a kind of mental map of their country, aligned for the quadrants and allowing them to fix the location of any object within it with respect to their own position. Indeed, given their ecological conditions, the Guugu-Yimidhirr absolute system seems especially suited to navigation within their country, always providing fixed coordinates for the speaker's own position and any landmark he wishes to describe. The egocentric, relative system of English is actually much less suited to these conditions, as anyone lost in a forest will testify. Directions like "go 3 km to the left, then 6 km to the right, and finally 2 km to the right again" are highly unlikely to get one home for dinner time! Guugu-Yimidhirr directions like "go 3 km to the east, then 6 km south, and finally 2 km to the west" probably would.

Testing for Relativities of Understanding

Levinson (1992) has investigated the cognitive consequences of the absolute spatial reckoning system of Guugu-Yimidhirr speakers and contrasted them with a control group of Dutch speakers, whose linguistic system is the egocentric, relativistic equivalent to English. He approached this question experimentally, devising a few non-linguistic tasks that should reveal the cognitive functioning of this system. First, he attempted to test the ability of ten Guugu-Yimidhirr speakers to indicate the directions of particular locations beyond the range of vision, ranging from a few kilometers as the crow flies to a couple of hundred. They were driven through the bush by various circuitous routes and, on halting at a place with restricted visibility (e.g. dense rainforest), asked to perform this task. The results were amazing: the average error was 13.9° or less than 4 percent. This shows a remarkable facility of Guugu-Yimidhirr speakers in using this absolute system. In order to determine the location of these landmarks it was not sufficient to simply know the direction of north, south, east, and west; a particular landmark might be south of one part of Guugu-Yimidhirr territory, but north of another. Thus, the Guugu-Yimidhirr speaker must be absolutely sure of his location, so that any landmark can be located with respect to it and assigned to the proper quadrant. This is evidence that Guugu-Yimidhirr speakers do indeed carry about some type of mental map of their territory with a proper alignment of quadrants. The Dutch sample shows no such comparable ability; preliminary results suggested that they can probably not even achieve a 90° average error in related tasks.

Levinson's (1992) experiments further probed the cognitive consequences of this absolute system by systematically testing the recognition and recall of spatial orientation of objects for Guugu-Yimidhirr men. In one recognition test, speakers facing north were shown two cards, each with a red square and a blue rectangle toward an edge. On one card the red square was to the viewer's left and the blue rectangle to his right; the other was reversed (of course, they were identical cards, just rotated 180°). The speaker was asked to choose one card and remember it. He was then led into another room, with another table with the same two cards lying on it, but now facing south. Note that Guugu-Yimidhirr speakers and Dutch speakers should behave differently here. If a Dutch speaker chose the card with the red square to his left (in the west quadrant), when rotated south he should still choose a card with the red square to his left (but this time in the *east* quadrant). The Guugu-Yimidhirr speaker should show no such switch; having chosen the card with the red square to the west, he should stick with this choice, regardless of the fact that the square is now on his right when previously it was on his left, see 11.2 (Levinson 1992:20). The results were exactly as predicted: 9 out of 10 Guugu-Yimidhirr speakers chose the card with the red square in the same quadrant regardless of whether they were looking north or south, demonstrating that they were clearly identifying the cards on the basis of absolutely aligned quadrants. All 15 subjects of a Dutch control group contrasted in identifying the cards on the basis of a relativistic egocentric LEFT–RIGHT axis.

11.2

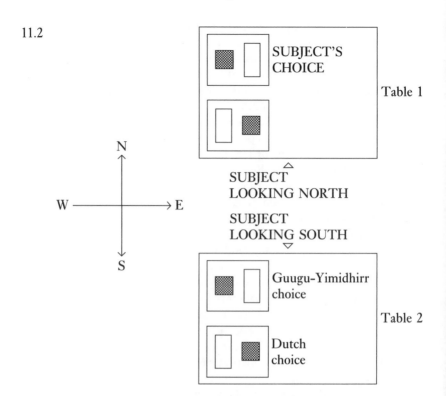

A simple recall experiment showed similar results. A table facing north was laid out with a lineup of three toy animals, all facing one direction, say east and to the right. The subject was asked to remember it, and it was then destroyed. He was then led into another room, with a table facing south and asked to reproduce the alignment. If he does this task absolutely, he will set up the line facing east, but this time to the left. If, on the other hand, he does it relatively, the line will be set up facing right, but to the west. Results for this test were not as strong as the previous one, but were in line with predictions: 9 out of 15 of Guugu-Yimidhirr subjects preserved the absolute eastward alignment of the array, while 13 of 15 Dutch control subjects preserved the relative rightward alignment.

A final experiment tested both memory and inference. A subject facing south was shown a route map diagrammatically indicated by arrows, such as 11.3 (Levinson 1992:28). He was then led to another room, where, now facing north he was asked to choose from three cards to complete the route, see 11.4 (Levinson 1992:28). Note that A and C are identical cards, just rotated 180°. If the subject rotates the map along with himself 180° along a relative LEFT–RIGHT axis, he should choose C. If, on the other hand, he holds the original map in fixed absolutely aligned axes, he should select A,

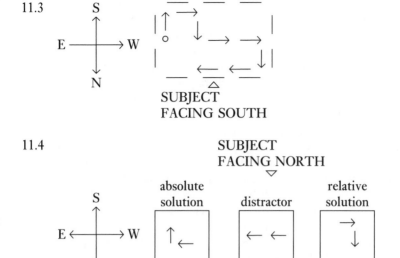

11.3

SUBJECT
FACING SOUTH

11.4

SUBJECT
FACING NORTH

absolute solution   distractor   relative solution

A   B   C

which completes the map without rotation. 8 out of 12 of Guugu-Yimidhirr men chose A to complete the map, while all 15 of a Dutch control group chose C, as predicted.

Levinson's (1992) findings with Guugu-Yimidhirr speakers are powerful support for the Principle of Linguistic Relativity. These experiments suggest that the expressive devices of the Guugu-Yimidhirr language do seem to have direct effects on the habitual thought processes, in recognition, memory and inference, of its speakers. Guugu-Yimidhirr speakers must store spatial information in memory in a distinct way from English or Dutch speakers – any object is always anchored in a kind of concrete space, already aligned according to the axes of the four quadrants. Astounding confirmation of this is provided by Haviland (1993). Guugu-Yimidhirr speakers typically gesture to indicate direction when they tell narratives, and these gestures preserve absolute orientation, so that if an event occurs to the east in the narrative, the narrator will gesture to the east, regardless of his personal orientation. Haviland videotaped the story of a capsized boat in 1980; two years later Levinson serendipitously also videotaped the same story. In the 1980 rendering, the narrator is seated facing west, while in the 1982 version, he is facing north. However, in both renditions his gestures are absolutely oriented, so that when he gestures south to indicate a southerly direction in the story's events in the 1980 version he gestures to his left, but in the 1982 version over his shoulder. Throughout both renditions of the story, gestures to indicate orientation and motion in the story's events are accurately given, but due to the different orientation of the story's narrator, they are necessarily differently oriented gestures in each case. This strongly supports the contention that the participants, places, and events in this story are known by the narrator with their orientation and motion coordinates already specified according to the fixed absolute axes of the quadrants. This is no mean mental feat and seems to be linked to the expressive needs of the Guugu-Yimidhirr language which require it. It is strong support for the Principle of Linguistic Relativity: the channelling effect of language categories on habitual thought.

It is vital to note that claiming the effects of linguistic relativity for spatial cognition for Dutch versus Guugu-Yimidhirr speakers does not vitiate the claim of the psychic unity of humanity. Cognitive abilities, independent of language, of both types, relative and absolute, are available to any cognizer. This is why speakers of English with a relative strategy can learn Watam, which employs an absolute one. Note that there is not infinite variation in the choice of strategy; the choice is restricted to absolute or relative strategies (or a third, intrinsic strategy that I will not talk about here (see Levy 1994; Levinson 1994a)). Subjects may fall back on these when presented with unfamiliar cognitive tasks, such as some of these experiments, hence the lack of 100 percent statistical consistency in the above examples (i.e. only 67 percent of Guugu-Yimidhirr speakers chose the absolute card in the map completion test, rather than 100 percent). However, the language categories of Dutch versus Guugu-Yimidhirr privilege only one of these strategies as a way of talking about space. This may have a channelling effect on cognition through an impulse to have isomorphism among the various systems which store spatial information in memory, specifically the visual and linguistic ones (see Levinson (1994a) for an argument suggesting this might be so). This pressure for isomorphism in the categories used for the storage of a given bit of information in memory is a likely source for the Principle of Linguistic Relativity; it would seem that linguistic categories are somewhat more weighty than others. This is perhaps not surprising, given the discussion in chapter 2 on the extent to which we are language-constituted beings.

Another Example: Tzeltal of Mexico

The cardinal points or quadrants type of the absolute spatial-reckoning system found in Guugu-Yimidhirr is not the only kind attested around the world. Many coastal Indonesian and Pacific island communities have absolute systems consisting of an axis contrasting seawards with inland/mountainwards and roughly an east–west axis derived from the path of the sun or the seasonal monsoonal winds. Longgu of the Solomon Islands is one such language (Hill 1993). In mountainous country absolute systems typically

11.5   uphill (*ajk'ol*)

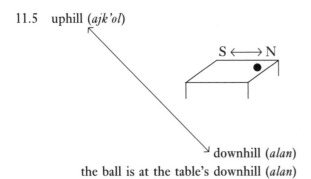

downhill (*alan*)
the ball is at the table's downhill (*alan*)

consist of a dominant uphill–downhill axis with a weaker side axis. Tzeltal, as spoken in a Mayan community of southern Mexico, illustrates this latter system and has recently been described in some detail by Brown and Levinson (1992, 1993, 1994), and Levinson and Brown (1994). The Tzeltal speakers of Tenejapa area live in mountainous country ranging from elevations of 2800 metres to 900 metres. The land falls from highland south to lowland north, so that the downhill/uphill axes correspond roughly to our north/south. The terms are downhill/north *alan* and uphill/south *ajk'ol*. Orthogonal to this is a transverse axis, *jejch*, with the poles unnamed. As in Guugu-Yimidhirr, this absolute system is used for all scales of spatial location, from millimetres to hundreds of kilometres, the terms *left* and *right* being restricted to the designation of hands only.

Unlike Guugu-Yimidhirr, the Tzeltal system is not a cardinal point or quadrant system. Rather, it is a single 45° inclined axis (*alan/ajk'ol*) with locations orthogonal to it (*jejch*), although the actual direction orthogonal to the main axis (east/west or left/right) remains undiscriminated. In the steeply inclined country of the Tzeltal, the downhill/uphill meaning of *alan/ajk'ol* predominates, but what happens on a horizontal surface, say, a table? In this case, the north/south reading emerges; a ball may be described as being at the north end (*alan*) of the table, for example, if the alignment of the table within the room is more or less consonant with the downhill/uphill layout of Tenejapa country (11.5). In addition to this extension of the 45° inclined (*alan/ajk'ol*) axis to the 0° horizon, there is also an extended use to the 90° vertical axis, so that locations can be described as being above here or some point X with *ajk'ol* and below with *alan* (11.6).

Finally, the *alan/ajk'ol* axis can be used to indicate the relative nearness of two objects with respect to an observer's position. The close object is called downhill (*alan*) and the further one, uphill (*ajk'ol*). This occurs regardless of the geographical orientation of the observer, say, facing north (11.7). Note that this last use of the axis is a relative one: which object is uphill (*ajk'ol*) or downhill (*alan*) depends on the position of the observer.

11.6   *ajk'ol*

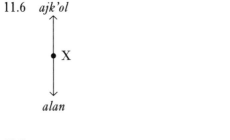

alan

11.7

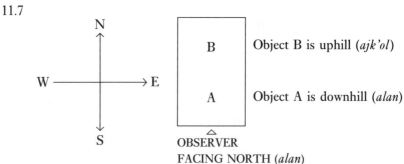

Object B is uphill (*ajk'ol*)

Object A is downhill (*alan*)

OBSERVER
FACING NORTH (*alan*)

If, in the above diagram, the observer was at the north end of the table facing south, B would be downhill (*alan*) and A uphill (*ajk'ol*). The reason for this seeming aberrant usage seems to be that when we look at two objects lying in front of us from a standing position, the closer one actually projects onto our two-dimensional visual field as being below the one farther away. This suggests that this relative usage of the downhill/uphill (*alan/ajk'ol*) axis actually derives from the previous up–down use of it in the 90° vertical dimension.

Brown and Levinson (1992, 1993, 1994) have experimented with giving Tzeltal speakers similar cognitive tasks as administered to Guugu-Yimidhirr speakers and, not surprisingly, given the similarity in absolute systems of spatial orientation, have achieved roughly parallel results. In the memory experiment involving the alignment of the three toy animals, nearly 80 percent of Tzeltal speakers performed absolutely, while almost 100 percent of a Dutch control group did so relatively. In the incomplete map test of memory and inference, again, Tzeltal speakers tended to perform absolutely, with Dutch speakers overwhelmingly (nearly 100 percent) relatively. Finally, the recognition test involving the red square and the blue rectangle affixed to a card aligned in a particular way showed the same result: Tzeltal speakers tending toward absolute reckoning, Dutch speakers contrastively nearly always performing relatively. Indeed, on the card recognition task and the map memory and inference test, Dutch speakers *never* performed

11.8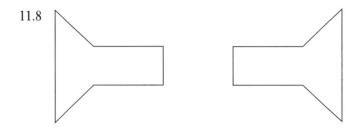

absolutely, and only one did on the toy animal alignment test for memory. As with the Guugu-Yimidhirr results, these findings support the claim of an interference of linguistic systems, in this case, the *alan/ajk'ol* axis and its semantic parameters, on the contents and processes of habitual thought: Tzeltal speakers and Dutch speakers behave differently in these tasks because their languages are systematically different in exactly that area which the tasks are designed to probe. Again, the claims of the Principle of Linguistic Relativity seem substantiated.

An interesting difference between Tzeltal and Guugu-Yimidhirr is an unequal salience of the two axes. In Guugu-Yimidhirr all four named quadrants seem equally so, but in Tzeltal the main downhill/uphill (*alan/ajk'ol*) or north/south axis seems much more developed than the transverse (*jejch*). Correlated to this is the fact that, as pointed out by Levinson and Brown (1994), the whole notion of 180° asymmetry associated with the relative LEFT–RIGHT axis (my left and right hand are not identical, but are 180° flops of each other – figures related in this way are called enantiomorphs) seems curiously missing in Tzeltal. Presented with figures which differed in being enantiomorphs of each other (11.8), Tzeltal speakers generally simply failed to recognize the difference. They typically failed to recognize such left–right inversions in pictures of inanimate objects; indeed, subjects were quite adamant there was no difference. Tzeltal speakers seem largely to ignore differences in shape due solely to rotation around 180° (in contrast to their keen and abiding interest in other details of shape, see Brown (1991) and Levinson (1994b)). This is undoubtedly connected to the lack of a LEFT–RIGHT axis for the plane of rotation and, further, the weak development overall of the *jejch* axis transverse to the dominant 45° incline downhill/uphill (*alan/ajk'ol*) axis.

Topological Properties of Space

Continuing on with the notion of space, let us look at some other systematic linguistic differences in the description of space across languages and their possible cognitive correlates. In many cases an object (figure) is located with respect to some place or object (ground) by specifying some topological properties of the ground. If we say the *cat is on the mat,* the figure (cat) is located at a place with respect to the mat (ground) by specifying with the preposition *on* some of the topological properties of the mat (it is a surface plane capable of supporting an object, in this case, the figure, the cat). It is the function of spatial adpositions (English, Korean), case endings (Finnish, Hungarian), or locative adverbials (Yimas) to specify the topological properties of the ground, so that the figure can be located with respect to it. The topological properties of the figure are not so specified. Thus, if I say *Rose is waiting at/on/in the corner,* the choice of the different prepositions reflects a difference in the spatial topological properties of the ground and, hence, where the figure could be located: *at* the corner is a place without extension, the figure is located there; *on* the corner is a surface capable of supporting the figure, the figure is located there; *in* the corner is viewed as a container, the figure is contained within it.

These spatial particles like English prepositions carry the crucial semantic information for locating the figure with respect to the ground. However, the semantic information carried by such particles varies widely from language to language; could these linguistic differences correspond to cognitive ones in accordance with the Principle of Linguistic Relativity? Even in closely related languages there may be interesting semantic contrasts. Bowerman (1993, 1994) points out that the semantic range of English *on* corresponds to three distinct prepositions in Dutch, *op, aan,* and *om.* Crucially, English *on* requires that the figure is in contact with the exterior surface of the ground and is supported by it. The corresponding Dutch prepositions break this up into three categories in the following way: a figure is described as *aan* the ground if it resists gravity by being attached to it (*handle aan pan, picture aan wall*); as *om* the ground for encirclement relations parallel to English *around* (*ring om finger*); and as *op* the ground for natural relationships of support, like a flat plane below the figure (*cup op table*), or sticky legs or a magnetic strip (*fly op wall, sticker op refrigerator*), or other natural situations (*boil op leg*). Clearly, if a child is learning English or Dutch, she will have to pay attention to different types of topological relationships to master the correct use of these prepositions.

That this is true is demonstrated by further work by Bowerman, jointly with the Korean-speaking linguist S. Choi (Choi and Bowerman 1992). English expresses motion with a general manner verb followed by a preposition indicating the spatial information about the path (*John walked into/ out of the theater; the bottle floated up/down-stream*). Korean, like Romance languages, has the main verb in transitive clauses expressing the path, with the manner an optional constituent (rather like *John entered the theater walking*). With intransitive inchoative verbs, motion, path and, optionally, manner are all separate constituents (like *the bottle went/up-stream floating*). In both cases the path information is essentially expressed by the verbs.

There are two further important differences between English and Korean. First, English uses the same path preposition for causative or inchoative events (*the snake crawled into the stove; Harry put the snake into the stove*). Korean does not, using distinct verb roots for these two syntactic frames: *tule kata* enter go "go in" versus *nehta* "put in." Second, English prepositions contrast with Korean path verbs in their semantics; for example, there is no global Korean equivalent to *in* and *on*, requiring instead more specific verbs that vary according to the properties of the figure and ground. Finally, there are some systematic differences in the meanings of roughly equivalent verbs; English uses *put on* for clothing of all types, whereas Korean has different verbs for putting clothes on different parts of the body.

Relativities of Spatial Conception and Language Acquisition

The Principle of Linguistic Relativity would predict that systematic linguistic differences such as these should be reflected in the process of language acquisition, suggesting cognitive correlates for the speakers of the two languages. Specifically, if the particular properties of the languages in question are found early in the language acquisition process, this indicates that any universal constraints for the organization of spatial information are not bindingly strong (although clearly present as in the earlier discussion) and that experience in the form of the language being learned actually plays a crucial role in the structuring of this domain. This is exactly what Choi and Bowerman (1992) found. By 20 months both English- and Korean-speaking children betray clear evidence of using linguistic elements expressing spatial information in the way found in the corresponding adult language. For example, English children freely use prepositions like *in, out, on, off* in both causative and inchoative syntactic frames, saying *out* for climbing out of a bag or taking something out of it. In contrast, Korean children make a strict distinction between these two usages, in the fashion of the adult language, saying *kkenayta* for taking something out of a loose container, but not for getting out of the bathtub. English children early master the distinction between *in* for containment and *on* for support, using these creatively, like English-speaking adults: *in* for containment within containers regardless of a tight or loose fit and *on* for both surface attachment (i.e. Lego pieces) and surface contact (climbing on a chair). Korean children like adult speakers of the language have no global semantic categories of containment or surface contact and support. By 20 months Korean children use the proper specific verbs; *nehta* "put into a loose container," *nonta* "put on a loose surface," *ipta/ssuta/sinta* "put clothing on trunk/head/feet." In summary, by 20 months the linguistic output of English and Korean children in this domain of spatial expressions is more like that of adult speakers of the same language than like each other. This is further evidence, this time from the area of language acquisition, for the operation of the Principle of Linguistic Relativity in the domain of spatial language and conception: experience in the form of expressive devices for spatial information provided by the language one learns and speaks plays a critical channelling role in the way one habitually thinks about, recognizes, and remembers spatial concepts.

But why should this be? Why should we expect spatial conceptualization to be informed by experience and not simply dictated by innate and universal psychological structures? Simply because our spatial conceptualization provides the wherewithal by which we navigate through the world, and we would thereby expect that our history of structural coupling, our experience, will then play a role in molding this conceptualization. The environment talked about in spatial language is practically known to us; it exists for and through our active engagement with it in structural coupling. The spatial understanding of the world is not arrived at by some passive bird's eye mapping of our environment, but by understandings of it worked out by practical interaction with it and in it, through knowledge stored in labor, myth, ritual, kinship, and other activities. The different linguistic systems for talking about spatial information in English, Guugu-Yimidhirr, Tzeltal, and Korean, are not the result of minor embroidery on a universal base, permutations on a foundational psychological algorithm, but the end result of thousands of years and millions of human beings' life histories in structural couplings, and "languaging" ideas about space within this coupling. They reflect no more and no less than the life world of the speakers of these languages in this domain.

Summary

Whorf, along with much of current cognitive science, argues that spatial conception is strongly informed by innate, probably biologically based, universals and is therefore essentially the same in all languages and cultures, making use of axes like UP–DOWN, FRONT–BACK and LEFT–RIGHT. Recent work argues that these claims are false, that languages have fundamentally different ways of describing spatial information and that these differences are systematically related to cognitive effects, evidence for the operation of linguistic relativity. It has been demonstrated that not all languages describe spatial information in relative, egocentric terms like FRONT–BACK or LEFT–RIGHT, tied to body orientation, but that many use absolute terms, fixed in geographical space, like EAST–WEST or UPRIVER–DOWNRIVER. These variations in linguistic description are systemically related to differences in cognition, speakers of languages with relative terms regularly perform differently in psychological tests than do speakers of languages with absolute terms. This conclusion is supported by findings in the field of language acquisition: even very young children learning languages with contrastive systems for expressing spatial relations use spatial terms rather like adult speakers of the target language, arguing against a strong binding influence of universal constraints in the structuring of this domain and supporting a claim for the powerfully relativizing effects of the categories of the language being learned. How we talk about space is not solely, nor perhaps even primarily, a result of our innate biological endowment, but also our history of engaging with our spatial environment and sedimented in our linguistic practices.

Further Reading

The work on space is mainly recent research from the Cognitive Anthropology Research Group at the Max-Planck Institute of Psycholinguistics; see Brown and Levinson (1992, 1993, 1994), Haviland (1993), Levinson (1992), and Levinson and Brown (1994). Bowerman's work is found in Bowerman (1993), and Choi and Bowerman (1992). Other sources on space include Ingold (1986), Landau and Jackendoff (1993), and Pinxten, van Dooren, and Harvey (1983).

12

Classifiers

Ontological Relativity

From his standpoint as a relativist, Quine (1960, 1969) raises crucial questions about the semantic structure of language, in particular with respect to nouns. He is concerned with the inscrutability of the meaning of a noun when trying to translate it into another language. The problem is perhaps best exemplified with Quine's own example (Quine 1960:51–7, 73–9). Imagine someone trying to translate the word *gavagai* of an alien language into another, say English. On noting that this word is prompted by the appearance of the animal rabbit, he translates it as "rabbit," i.e. the sense of the alien term is "rabbit." But, counsels Quine, this move is wholly unmotivated and perhaps misleadingly guided by the ontology of the world reflected in the English language. The alien term could mean "rabbit stuff," "rabbit stage" or, indeed, simply "rabbitness," and no obvious methodology is available for distinguishing among these alternatives as the proper translation of *gavagai*. Thus, the proper translation of *gavagai* is radically underdetermined by the available data, and the English speaker's translation is guided by her understanding of the ontology behind the meaning of prototypical nouns in English, i.e. they refer to "bodies," objects with fixed boundaries and fairly discrete permanent shapes (e.g. humans, animals, cups, tables, houses, etc.). "Bodies," for Quine, are rather prominent in our ontology and, as such, this is reflected in our linguistic patterns, but this is no guarantee of their playing a similar function in the ontology of the speakers of the alien language. For them, material or stuff may be the major ontological category, so that "rabbit stuff" may be a better translation for *gavagai*, but again, it must be emphasized, available empirical data is always insufficient to be conclusive about this – hence Quine's axiom of the indeterminacy of translation. This in turn is linked to his principle of ontological relativity (Quine 1969).

Quine's example may not be so fanciful after all. It has long been believed and recently reiterated (Imai and Gentner 1993; Lucy 1992a) that differences in linguistic patterning for nouns in varying languages reflect differences in the ontological beliefs their speakers hold about the referents of nouns. The difference can best be grasped by looking at the contrast between count and mass nouns in English. Consider the difference between a noun like *book* and one like *rice*. *Book* may be pluralized directly (*books*), enumerated directly (*seven books*), is interrogated with *how many* (*how many books are there?*) and takes the indefinite article *a* in the singular (*a book*). In contrast, the mass noun *rice* cannot be pluralized (**rices*), cannot be enumerated without a measure word specifying quantity (**seven rices* but *seven cups of rice*), is interrogated with *how much* (*how much rice is there?*) and takes the indefinite article *some* rather than *a* (**a rice*; but *some rice*). This sharp difference in grammatical behavior correlates with a clear difference in semantics: count nouns refer to entities which by and large are "bodies," objects with clear specifiable shapes and fixed discrete boundaries, while mass nouns refer to "stuff," substances or materials, not corresponding to a discrete unitary object. Note that English mass nouns require unitizers to refer to a specifiable unitary object of the material (*one bag/ cup/ pot of rice*). Any part or amount of stuff referred to by a mass noun is more of the stuff, but a part of a body referred to by a count noun is not equivalent to the body; a chapter of a book is not a book.

There are many languages of the world in which all or the great bulk of nouns behave like the mass noun *rice* and few or none like the count noun *book*; these are languages with numeral classifiers, good examples of which are Yucatec Maya of Mexico (Lucy 1992a) and Thai (Hundius and Kölver 1983). In such languages, nouns are not inflected for plural (Thai *rôm* "umbrella/ umbrellas"; Yucatec *há'as* "banana/bananas") and cannot be enumerated directly, but require a classifier to accompany the quantifier (Thai *rôm sǎam khan* umbrellas three classifier "three umbrellas"; Yucatec *kan-p'éel há'as* four-classifier banana "four bananas"). In addition, these languages lack distinct indefinite articles. Rather, the numeral *one* plus the classifier is used to unitize their nouns, the combination often functioning to indicate indefinite reference (Thai *rôm khan niŋ* umbrella classifier one "an umbrella"; Yucatec *um-p'éel há'as* one-classifier banana "a banana"). These facts indicate that the semantics of these nouns in numeral classifier languages are like those of mass nouns in English; they refer to stuff, substances, or material without definite shape or a determinable unit in its own right. This further suggests Quine's idea of ontological relativity; the ontology of speakers of numeral classifier languages may be systematically different from that of English speakers. Rather than an ontology which gives prominence to "bodies," reflected in English and other European languages, theirs might be weighted toward substances. Cognitive evidence which indicates that this indeed may be the case for the speakers of at least some numeral classifier languages will be presented in this chapter, but first let us look in greater detail at this phenomenon of classifiers generally.

The Nature of Classifiers

The basic function of classifiers is to build up a descriptive referring expression for the noun. Typically, nouns in classifier languages on their own are very vague in their reference, as the following Thai example demonstrates (Hundius and Kölver 1983:181):

> plaa wâay yùu nay mêɛnáam
> fish swim stay in   river
> a. "fish swim in rivers" (generic/habitual reading)
> b. "the fish (SG/PL) swim(s) in a river/rivers"
> c. "a fish/fish (SG/PL) swim(s) in the river/a river" etc.

In keeping with its semantics as a substance concept, the noun gives only a vague clue as to what body or object it is intended to denote. In order to be appropriately determined, a classifier is used to provided sufficient information to narrow this down. Hence, it is not uncommon to find a particular noun co-occurring with different classifiers to highlight different aspects of its meaning, e.g. Burmese (Becker 1975:113):

noun	numeral	classifier	
$myi^{?}$	tə	$ya^{?}$	river one place (e.g. destination for a picnic)
$myi^{?}$	tə	tân	river one line (e.g. on a map)
$myi^{?}$	tə	hmwa	river one section (e.g. a fishing area)
$myi^{?}$	tə	sîn	river one arc (e.g. a path to the sea)
$myi^{?}$	tə	θwe	river one connection (e.g. tying two villages)
$myi^{?}$	tə	pa	river one sacred object (e.g. in myth)
$myi^{?}$	tə	$khu^{?}$	river one unit (e.g. in discussion on rivers in general)
$myi^{?}$	tə	$myi^{?}$	river one river (neutral unmarked)

Yucatec (Lucy 1992a:49–50):

Numeral-classifier	noun	
'un-ts'íit	há'as	one-1 dimensional banana (e.g. the fruit)
'un-wáal	há'as	one-2 dimensional banana (e.g. the leaf)
'un-p'éel	há'as	one-3 dimensional banana (e.g. the fruit)
'un-kúul	há'as	one-plant banana (e.g. the tree)
'un-kúuch	há'as	one-load banana (e.g. a bunch)
'un-p'íit	há'as	one-bit of/some banana

Ulithi (Sohn and Bender 1973:270):

Classifier-possessive	noun	
lawa-yi	*yixi*	property-my fish (I'm keeping)
xala-yi	*yixi*	cooked food-my fish (I'll eat)
xocaa-yi	*yixi*	raw food-my fish (I'll eat)
xolo-yi	*yixi*	caught-my fish (I caught and will eat later)

Thai (Hundius and Kölver 1983:188–9):

noun	numeral	classifier	
ríisǐi	*sǎam*	*ʔoŋ*	hermit three sacred (e.g. holy man)
ríisǐi	*sǎam*	*ton*	hermit three ghost (e.g. warlock)

Clearly the choice of the classifier is determined by the kind of descriptive speech act the speaker wishes to perform. In very many cases, perhaps most, a noun is associated with a default classifier that highlights certain aspects of its shape, consistency, or function (the actual parameters will be discussed below). Generally, the noun will appear with this assigned classifier. However, when the speaker wishes to highlight some other particular semantic features of the noun in a given context, then a different classifier which particularly attends to these features can be used. So, in the Burmese example given above, *myiʔ* is the usual default classifier for *myiʔ* "river" (a so-called "repeater" form because the classifier is the same as the noun). However, in the contexts mentioned, where other semantic features of rivers, even sometimes idiosyncratic ones, are relevant, a different classifier can be used to foreground these features. It must be emphasized that classification of nouns in a particular language through the use of classifier morphemes is specifically linguistic and therefore used as a linguistic resource in various types of speech acts. It does not reflect directly a classification of physical reality, but only one for linguistic purposes. It is, as Becker (1975) claims, a "linguistic image of nature," not a map of nature. Classifier semantics may appeal to perceptually salient features of the typical referents of the nouns they classify, as we shall see below, but this is not their primary function. Rather, it is to provide sufficient descriptive information for the communicative purposes of human speakers in ongoing social discourse.

This point is clearly brought out in recent work on Arrernte of central Australia (Wilkins 1993a). In common with many Australian languages (Dixon 1982), Arrernte typically constructs nominal expressions consisting of a generic classifier plus a specific noun, such as (Wilkins 1993a:1–2):

thipe "flying, fleshy creatures"　　*thipe angepe* "crow"
arne "igneous plants"　　*arne ilwempe* "ghost gum"

ure "fire-related things"	*ure kwerte* "smoke"
kere "game animals"	*kere aherre* "kangaroo"
merne "edible food from plants"	*merne langwe* "bush banana"
tyerrtye "person"	*tyerrtye Peltharre* "person of Peltharre subsection"
pmere "(socially significant) place"	*pmere Mparntwe* "Alice Springs"

The social and context sensitive use of these classifiers in the ongoing linguistic construction of an intersubjective communicative reality, a social structural coupling, is well exemplified. Classifiers are an important linguistic resource for Arrernte speakers to convey salient semantic information in a given context. Consider the specific noun *arlkerrke* "meat ant." This word denotes a large black ant that lives in the ground under a mound, can inflict a very painful bite and eats meat, often stealing small bits of meat from people. This will commonly be associated with the generic classifier *yerre* "ant," and the speaker's use of this form invites the addressee to consider *arlkerrke* as having the discourse-salient semantic properties of ants in general, i.e. living in the ground, biting people and stealing food. *Arlkerrke*, however, can also be combined with the classifier *awelye* "medicine" and in this case the entire noun phrase *awelye arlkerrke* denotes a culturally significant practice of the Arrernte people in which they stomp on the nest to make the ants come out so that they can gather them up. They then either crush the ants to get the juice inside which they apply directly to sores and cuts, or they crush the ants in hot water and use the water to rinse the cuts and sores to ease the pain. The combination of *awelye* "medicine" with *arlkerrke* invites one to contextualize the ants within a particular discourse as having the relevant semantic properties of medicine. Finally, *arlkerrke* can also be combined with the classifier *pmere* "(socially significant) places." This classifier selects places which are important to the Arrernte people. For them, like most Australian peoples, places have proper names like people, classified as kin and closely tied to the ancestors who caused these places to come into existence through their actions in the Dreamtime (see Wilkins 1993b). When *pmere* combines with *arlkerrke*, the nominal expression names a place associated with meat ants due to their being connected through the same ancestors, because for the Arrernte, all living things are linked to a particular Dreamtime ancestor. The place expression *pmere arlkerrke* invites one in a particular discourse context to think of this place in terms of the Dreamtime meat-ant ancestor who created it. Clearly Arrernte speakers creatively use classifiers as a linguistic resource to evoke a rich culturally specific tapestry of meanings in particular contexts; they do not reflect a straightforward one-to-one mapping of the physical world into linguistic categories.

Thai provides one final illustration of this point, for it commonly uses classifiers to reflect social status or stylistic differences among the interlocutors in a discourse rather than a simple expression of particular semantic properties of the nouns being classified (Juntanamalaga 1988). For example, in formal, polite speech, tame elephants take the unique classifier *chîak*, but in casual speech it is subsumed with other animals in the general animate classifier *tua*. Similarly, *bay* or *lûuk* are the classifiers for eggs and fruit in normal speech, but in high formal styles, especially used in the presence of royalty, *fɔɔŋ* is correct for eggs, while *phŏn* is used for fruit. Like Burmese and Arrernte, Thai shows that speakers use classifiers as a linguistic resource to create and sediment meanings, in this case, transparently social meanings.

Typology of Classifier Systems

The languages of the world exhibit a range of types of classifier systems and a diversity of semantic parameters expressed with them. Craig (1992, 1994) is a good summary of the various types. The most prototypical is that of numeral classifiers already exemplified by Yucatec, Thai and Burmese, in which a classifier is necessary to unitize the noun (remember it denotes substance, not a body) before it can be enumerated, although in many languages, such as Thai, classifiers may be used with other modifiers of the noun phrase like determiners or adjectives (Hundius and Kölver 1983). In a sense, the classifiers function is to "em-body" the noun, so that it can be discretely quantified or modified like the object it denotes. Because the most salient perceptual property of objects or bodies are their shape, it is not surprising that shape is perhaps the most common semantic feature expressed by classifiers. Denny (1976) points out that shape is specified according to the overall salience of a particular dimension. So, if no dimension is saliently extended over the others, the object is round or three dimensional. Many languages have a classifier for round or unspecifically three-dimensional objects: Thai *lûuk*: *krasŭn săam lûuk* "three bullets"; Yucatec -*p'éel*: *kam-p'éel há'as* "four bananas" (Lucy 1992a); Trukese -*féw*: *e-féw maas* "one eye" (Benton 1968); Indonesian *buah*: *tiga buah kapal* "three boats." In many languages, the classifier for round or three-dimensional objects is the neutral or unmarked choice, e.g. Yucatec; in many versions of colloquial Indonesian, for instance, it is the only classifier based on shape.

Classifiers for shape with a single salient dimension, i.e. long, are also common. Examples are Yucatec -*ts'iit*: *'un-ts'iit che'* "one stick" (Lucy 1992a) and Tarascan *itʃá*: *itʃá-ndi-ti-ni* "long object on shoulder" (Friedrich 1970). Many languages with rich systems distinguish among saliently one-dimensional objects according to their consistency: whether they are rigid or flexible. Denny (1976) claims this distinction is due to the differences in manipulation of such materials in human technologies; in any case it is a common distinction exemplified by Trukese *-foc* 1-dimensional rigid versus *-sen* "1-dimensional flexible" (*e-foc nuu* "one coconut palm" versus *e-sen oo* "one fishing line") (Benton 1968). Thai, with its rich classifier system, makes even more distinctions with saliently one-dimensional objects (Hundius and Kölver 1983:195–7):

ʔan	long, narrow	*krabɔɔŋ sǎam ʔan*	"three clubs"
tôn	long, plant-like	*suŋ sǎam tôn*	"three logs"
lêm	long, pointed	*khěm sǎam lêm*	"three needles"
khan	long, handled	*rôm sǎam khan*	"three umbrellas"
lam	long, hollow	*ria sǎam lam*	"three boats"
sǎay	long, curved	*thanǒn sǎam sǎay*	"three streets"
sên	long, flexible	*phǒm sǎam sên*	"three hairs"

Finally, classifiers with two salient dimensions, a plane or flat objects, are well attested, as in Yucatec *-wáal*: *'un-wáal há'as* "one banana leaf" (Lucy 1992a), Tarascan *itfú-*: *itfú-hpa-ni* "to make tortillas (flat pancakes)" (Friedrich 1970), or Trukese *-cé*: *fa-cé simpuŋ* "four newspapers" (Benton 1968). Again a contrast between rigid two-dimensional objects and flexible ones is common, the latter classifier often homophonous with the noun for "leaf": Thai *phèn* "2-dimensions rigid" versus *bay* "2-dimensions flexible" (also "leaf"), (*caansǐaŋ sǎam phèn* "three phonograph records" versus *tǔa sǎam bay* "three tickets"), although Thai makes further, more specific distinctions among saliently two-dimensional objects (Hundius and Kölver 1983:197–8).

Animate and human "bodies," i.e. animals and persons, often get special attention in classifier systems due to the attention they have for us and the empathetic understanding we hope we share with them. Shape is not the basic semantic parameter here, as this is not what is salient to us as humans when we interact with other humans or animals, although, as we shall see, similarity of shape may be the basis for the metaphorical extension of these classifiers into other domains. Some languages may have a single classifier for humans and animals, as with Yucatec *-túul*: *'un-túul maak* "a man" and *'un-túul k'eek'-en* "a pig," but this is unusual. More common is to distinguish people from animals as with Indonesian *orang* versus *ekor*: *tiga orang perempuan* "three women" versus *tiga ekor kuda* "three horses." On the other side, the languages of the highly stratified societies of Southeast Asia, like Thai and Burmese, often have many classifiers for persons, reflecting their spiritual or social function and status. The basic Thai system is shown in 12.1 (Hundius and Kölver 1983:193–4). Because animals are quadrupeds with limbs, the Thai animal classifier *tua* is also extended to things of similar shape: tables, chairs and even shirts, as they have sleeves (i.e. like arms)

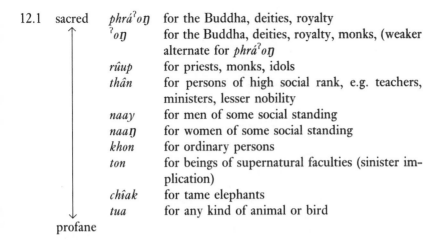

12.1 sacred   *phrá²oŋ*   for the Buddha, deities, royalty

                ²oŋ   for the Buddha, deities, royalty, monks, (weaker alternate for *phrá²oŋ*

                rûup   for priests, monks, idols

                thân   for persons of high social rank, e.g. teachers, ministers, lesser nobility

                naay   for men of some social standing

                naaŋ   for women of some social standing

                khon   for ordinary persons

                ton   for beings of supernatural faculties (sinister implication)

                chîak   for tame elephants

                tua   for any kind of animal or bird

    profane

(Hundius and Kölver 1983). Burmese is similar, but less complicated (Becker 1975:116):

hsu   for Buddhas relics, idols

pâ   for deities, saints, monks, royalty

û   for people of high status, e.g. teachers, scholars

yau²   for ordinary people

kauŋ   for animals, ghosts, corpses, depraved people, and children

In European culture we often conceive of social distinctions metaphorically along a vertical dimension, with those of more social status as *higher* than those of less (we speak of *upper* versus *lower* classes). Becker argues that such a conceptualization is incorrect for Burmese and, indeed, finds this unable to account for the extension of the *hsu* classifier used for Buddhas, relics, and idols to common objects like fishing and mosquito nets, gardens, and staircases. Rather, Becker suggests that the Burmese language, following a received tradition of Buddhist philosophy and speculation, conceives of the cosmos of being ordered not hierarchically, but in terms of concentric circles (12.2), with the Buddha (*hsu*) in the center, progressively moving away toward those beings most removed from the wisdom and sacredness of the Buddha (interestingly, the world *pâ* means "close" in Burmese). It is this circular cosmological model which explains the usage of *hsu* with fishing and mosquito nets, gardens, and staircases: in traditional Burmese culture such objects were similar in shape to the above model. Nets were conical in shape, staircases, spiralling, and gardens laid out as a wheel. Again, we find a metaphorical extension to the inanimate world on the basis of shape, much as with Thai *tua*, but in this case in terms of an

12.2

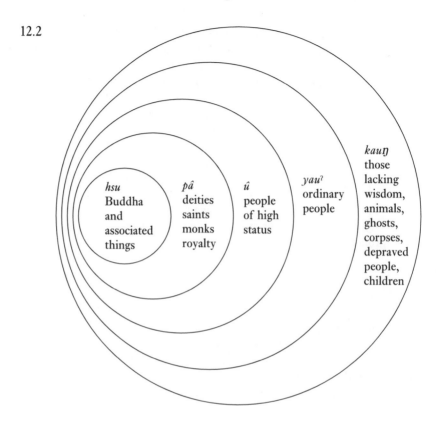

abstract conceptual model of the cosmos. The Burmese data further demonstrate the rich linguistic resources classifiers provide for speakers in communicating culturally salient meanings.

Other kinds of classifiers are those used with possessive constructions;
these are particularly common in the Oceanic languages of the Pacific region. The classifiers specify the use, or lack thereof, that is intended for the
possessed object. A simple example is provided by Fijian:

na   no-gu   maqa   "my mango" (as property, e.g. for sale)
DET CLF-my mango
na   me-gu   maqa   "my mango" (to suck)
DET CLF-my mango

Micronesian languages like Trukese or Ulithi are the most elaborated in this
respect. Trukese has something over two-dozen possessive classifiers, expressing a range of different functions that an object can be put to, such as
food (cooked or raw), personal property, clothing, footwear, vehicles, eyewear,

dishes, etc. A given noun can co-occur with a range of possessive classifiers to specify the different uses an object may be put to, as in these Ulithi examples involving *yixi* "fish" (Sohn and Bender 1973:270):

Classifier-possessive	noun	
lawu-yi	*yixi*	"my fish" (property)
xala-yi	*yixi*	"my fish" (cooked food)
xocaa-yi	*yixi*	"my fish" (raw food)
xolo-yi	*yixi*	"my fish" (just caught)

As with similar earlier examples in Burmese or Arrernte, the choice of classifier is a linguistic resource available to the speaker to highlight particular meanings associated with *yixi* "fish" in various discourse contexts.

Cognitive Consequences of Ontological Relativity

Now let us return to the Quinean questions of ontological relativity with which we began this section. Classifying languages have been claimed to contrast with languages like English systematically in the semantics of their nouns. Nouns in classifier languages denote materials or substances, non-discrete and unbounded, while in English and other European languages, they denote objects with discrete boundaries and defining shapes. More widely, in Quinean terms, this can be held to reflect ontological relativity for the speakers of these languages: prominence given to material or substance for the speakers of classifier languages, but bodies for speakers of English.

This claim has recently been investigated by Lucy (1992a), and Imai and Gentner (1993). Lucy (1992a) performed a series of cognitive tests with speakers of English and Yucatec Maya to detect if the linguistic differences between these languages could be correlated to cognitive ones. Yucatec, as we have seen, is a canonical numeral-classifier language, while English lacks such constructions. Interpreting this difference in the light of its implications for Quinean ontological relativity suggests the following prediction: English speakers will give prominence to the form or shape of the object denoted by a given name, in keeping with their ontological commitment to the primacy of "bodies," while Yucatec speakers will, in contrast, focus on the substance or material composition of the same object. This means that in performing various cognitive tasks English speakers should attend relatively more to the shape of objects and Yucatec speakers relatively more to their material composition. This hypothesis was tested in the following way.

Subjects were presented with a triad of objects. Each triad consisted of an original object and two alternative objects. For example, one triad consisted of a cardboard box as the original, with either a plastic box or a piece of

12.3   *Triad objects*

Triad number	Original	Shape alternative	Material alternative
1.1	sheet of paper	sheet of plastic	book
1.2	strip of cloth	strip of paper	shirt
1.3	stick of wood	candle stick	block of wood
1.4	cardboard box	plastic box	piece of cardboard
1.5	length of vine	length of string	woven ring of vine
1.6	grains of corn	beans	tortilla
1.7	half gourd	half calabash	gourd with opening
1.8	ceramic bowl	metal bowl[a]	ceramic plate

[a] A plastic bowl was used with the English sample

12.4   *Preference*

Group	Shape	Material
English	12	1
Yucatec	2	8

cardboard as the alternatives. Note that the first alternative resembles the original object along a dimension of shape, while the second is like it in terms of material composition. The prediction is that English speakers would consistently prefer the first alternative and Yucatec speakers, the second. The full set of triads are set out in 12.3 (Lucy 1992a:138).

Note that there are eight triads in all; speakers who chose the shape alternative four or more times were scored as preferring to classify on the basis of shape, the remaining speakers, on the basis of material. Table 12.4 shows the results, which are strongly in the predicted direction: English speakers overwhelmingly classifying objects on the basis of shape, while Yucatec speakers overwhelmingly doing so on the basis of material. The response patterns are clearly distinct for the two groups and are not random. The evidence strongly points in the direction of the Principle of Linguistic Relativity: the different linguistic patterns with respect to enumeration/ unitization of English and Yucatec are directly correlated with habitual thought patterns or, more formally, with processes of categorization of their speakers. What seems visually salient for classificatory purposes for English speakers is shape, but for Yucatec speakers it is material, as in the linguistic subsystems. This again suggests the function of isomorphism across patterns of classification discussed earlier. Quine's ontological relativity may not vary randomly, but may indeed be connected, in a very Whorfian fashion, with systems of linguistic patterning.

Universal Ontology versus Ontological Relativity

Confirmation an extension of Lucy's findings have been provided in Imai and Gentner (1993), who investigated the cognitive behavior of Japanese children in the light of earlier work by Soja, Carey, and Spelke (1991). Soja, Carey and Spelke argue that, contrary to Quine's view of ontological relativity, children universally know the conceptual distinction between "bodies" and substances and, further, that this knowledge exists prior to language acquisition, constraining the possible meanings of new words being learned. They came to this conclusion from the results of a word-learning task for 2-year-old English-speaking children. These children, who showed no evidence of an awareness of the count/mass grammatical distinction for English nouns, were taught new words in a syntactic frame neutral for this grammatical distinction (e.g. "this is my *blicket*," not "this is a *blicket*" (count: body) or "this is some *blicket*" (mass: material). In one case, the word was given in the presence of a novel physical object, say, a pyramid made of wood. Like Lucy's methodology, the children were then presented with two alternatives: one was an object of the same size and shape, but made of different material (e.g. a pyramid made out of sculpting material); the other was pieces of the same substance that constituted the object (e.g. pieces of wood). The children were asked to choose which of the alternatives was the *blicket*. When asked to do so, the children typically chose another object of the same shape rather than pieces of the same substance, suggesting they took the new word learned to be a name of some object, not a label for the material constituting it.

In the second case, a new word was presented in the presence of some non-solid substance (e.g. Nivea skin cream arranged into a distinctive shape). Again, the children were shown two alternatives: a different kind of substance (e.g. hair-styling gel) arranged into the same shape or the same substance placed into piles. And, again, the children were asked to choose among the two alternatives, but, interestingly, this time they did so on the basis of constituent material, choosing the alternative of the same substance, not the same shape.

On the basis of these findings, Soja, Carey, and Spelke propose a thesis of universal ontology in contradistinction to Quine's (1969) ontological relativity. Fundamentally, this asserts that children are endowed natively with the conceptual distinction between objects or "bodies" and substances. This does not vary across languages, nor do children have to learn it on the basis of the grammatical distinctions in their languages, as Quine (1960) had asserted.

12.5   *Standard Object/Substance*

	Shape	Material
Complex Object		
1 clear plastic clip	metal clip	a clear plastic piece
2 ivory plastic T	copper T	an ivory plastic piece
3 porcelain lemon juicer	wood lemon juicer	porcelain pieces
4 wood beater	black plastic beater	wood pieces
Simple Object		
1 cork pyramid	white plastic pyramid	a chunk of cork
2 dylite UFO	wood UFO	a dylite piece
3 red Super Sculpy half egg	gray Styrofoam half egg	red Super Sculpy pieces
4 orange-wax kidney	purple-wax kidney	orange-wax pieces
Substance		
1 lumpy Nivea (reverse C)	Dippity-Do (Reverse C)	a Nivea pile
2 Crazy Foam (Gamma)	clay (Gamma)	a pile of Crazy Foam
3 sawdust (Omega)	leather (tiny pieces, Omega)	two piles of sawdust
4 decoration sand (S-shape)	glass pieces (S-shape)	three piles of sand

Imai and Gentner (1993) contend that Soja, Carey, and Spelke's results may be due, at least in part, to the fact that these tasks were administered to children speaking English as a first language, a language whose grammatical distinction between count and mass nouns transparently signals a conceptual distinction between objects and substances. To truly test the validity of the principles of universal ontology or ontological relativity, a language which lacks a straightforward linguistic system for making this contrast is needed. In short, a language employing numeral classifiers, and, in the case of Imai and Gentner's study, it is Japanese. Imai and Gentner replicated Soja, Carey, and Spelke with Japanese speaking 2-year olds. They also made a slight modification to the earlier experiment; instead of two types of triad groups, objects versus substances, they employed three: complex objects, made of clear separable parts; simple objects, with no obvious separable parts; and substances. Table 12.5 shows the stimuli used (Imai and Gentner 1993:177). Other than this, the methodology of Soja, Carey, and Spelke's (1991) experiments were followed closely, except of course that the instructions were in Japanese and the nonsense novel words obeyed Japanese phonotactic patterns.

The results were extremely interesting and mixed: evidence for both universal ontology and ontological relativity. In the trials involving complex objects, Japanese 2-year olds behaved much like English-speaking American ones: they showed a strong object bias and consistently paid attention to shape as a distinctive cue to learning the denotata of new words, albeit with a weaker preference than American 2-year olds (mean percent response: American English children 93 percent; Japanese children 79 percent). With the substance trials, the Japanese children behaved similarly to the English-speaking ones, although the preference was again weaker. The Japanese children at age 2 did not choose the substance alternative significantly differently from chance in this case (their performance here significantly contrasting with that for complex objects), but those of age $2\frac{1}{2}$ showed a statistically significant material bias on these trials, parallelling the responses of the American English speaking children.

The findings thus far demonstrate support for the universal ontology hypothesis, but the findings with simple objects dispute this. Here a marked crosslinguistic difference between the Japanese children and the American English children was found: Japanese children (both 2- and $2\frac{1}{2}$-year olds) responded at chance (50 percent shape, 50 percent material), in sharp contrast to Soja, Carey, and Spelke's (1991) findings that American English speaking children of the same age show a strong shape bias for such objects (93 percent), equivalent to the rating for complex objects). This is evidence in that domain for ontological relativity, and Imai and Gentner (1993:182) suggest the following:

> The ontological status of entities may be better characterized as a continuum that has a gradient structure with prototypical objects on one end and prototypical substances on the other end. In this case, when children's determination of whether a given entity belongs to the object category or substance category is based on the nature of the entity itself, we may expect graded effects: children may have an easier time deciding whether the novel name is an object name or a substance name when the entity is a prototypical object or substance than when its ontological status is in the middle of the object/substance continuum. Thus, the fact that Soja et al's American 2- and 2.5-year-olds showed a very strong object bias for simple objects while Japanese subjects did not is evidence for Quinean linguistic relativity. It is interesting that, given no linguistic apparatus to flag a given entity as an object or substance, Japanese children's performance on simple objects was just in between the Complex Object and Substance trials.

These findings indicate that the extremes of the continuum are governed by principles of universal ontology, "bodies" versus substances, but the middle area is subject to ontological relativity. In this domain the Principle of Linguistic Relativity may obtain: language patterns lead the cognitive assessment of these cases. English-speaking children, because of the salience of the count/mass distinction, regard them as being like complex objects, while Japanese children lacking such linguistic channelling respond at random.

These differences in response patterns seem to solidify with age and language facility, not merge. Imai and Gentner (1993) extended the study to fourteen American English speaking children of 4 years of age and an equivalent number of Japanese 4-year olds. In addition, eighteen American English speaking adults and eighteen Japanese adults also were tested. With complex objects, American English and Japanese 4-year olds and adults continued to project novel word meaning onto shape (4-year olds, English 96 percent, Japanese 80 percent; adults, English 94 percent, Japanese 90 percent). For older Japanese speakers, the response pattern with substances showed a stronger bias than that of 2-year olds, 4-year olds choosing the material alternative 91 percent and adults 85 percent of the time. On the other hand, American English speakers show an increase in bias toward *shape* according to age; in contrast to the significant material bias found in Soja, Carey, and Spelke's 2-year-old children, Imai and Gentner (1993) found that both American English speaking children of age 4 and adults do not perform significantly differently from chance with the substance trials. Finally, the large difference between American English and Japanese 2-year olds with simple objects is still found with older subjects. American English speakers exhibit a strong *shape* bias (4-year olds 91 percent, adults 74 percent), but Japanese subjects show a *material* bias that increases with age. As with Japanese 2-year olds the response of 4-year olds was random, but adult Japanese speakers exhibit a reliable material bias here (63 percent material response), a result completely consonant with Lucy's (1992a) findings with Yucatec speakers. Generally, Japanese speakers become more substance oriented with age, and English speakers, more shape oriented, a finding well supportive of Quine's (1969) theory of ontological relativity.

Imai and Gentner's (1993) work explores borders within which any principle of relativity, including linguistic relativity, must be situated. Japanese speakers, like American English speakers, identify complex objects on the basis of shape. Differences in linguistic patterning play no role here; this is determined by universal cognitive processes, presumably innately endowed. Ontologically, such entities are universally "bodies." However, there are many other entities whose ontological status is less clear-cut, such as *water*, *corn*, *rice*, *glass*, *gel*. In these cases, the ontology assigned to these entities by subjects is correlated with the linguistic patterns of their languages. Adult English and Japanese speakers differ significantly in their assessment of both substances and simple objects, a difference probably tied to their contrastive linguistic systems for nouns, a count/mass grammatical distinction versus numeral classifiers for enumeration/unitization. Thus, the ontology these entities have is projected from the meanings their corresponding nouns have in their respective linguistic systems. Meanings, then, are determined by an interplay of cognitive and semantic universals (universal ontology, e.g. complex objects) and language-specific constraints (ontological relativity, e.g. simple objects). The latter is the domain of the Principle of Linguistic Relativity. As Becker (1995:420) has so eloquently put it, relativity does not mean that anything goes; however, it does mean that many things go. What we have just seen are some of the kinds of constraints that prevent randomness of the type that anything goes. What is now needed is more effort and greater precision in spelling out some of the many things that do go.

Summary

The crosslinguistic parameter of presence or absence of classifiers is a good feature within which to investigate the validity of the Principle of Linguistic Relativity. The presence of the grammatical category classifiers is prototypically taken to be diagnostic of an ontology of substance, with the classifier needed to embody the denotation of the noun into the corporeal properties of shape and discreteness, while their absence is viewed as evidence for a governing ontology of bodies, with the corporeal properties of shape and discreteness already inherent in the noun. Classifiers then correspond to a descriptive speech act by the speaker, ascribing discoursally relevant properties to the otherwise semantically vague noun. The most common such property, not surprisingly in view of the hypothesis of an ontology of material inherent in classifier languages, is shape, so that classifier languages commonly make distinctions in their classifier system along the lines of the number of salient dimensions of the object described by the nominal expression, but other properties such as texture or salient accessory features may be highlighted. Psychological testing of speakers of classifier languages does indeed show that they attend to the natural substance of objects more saliently than speakers of classifier-less languages, who focus on shape. But this does seem to be parameterized according to age and the nature of the object categorized: for complex objects with parts, very young speakers of both types of languages seem to attend to shape, but for substances, they attend to the composite material, indicating the operation of cognitive universals of ontology. With older speakers and for simple objects, on the other hand, the structural differences in the languages do affect object categorization, arguing for ontological and linguistic relativity.

Further Reading

For classifiers, a good overview is provided by Craig (1992, 1994) and the articles in Craig (1986); see also Dixon (1982). Ontological relativity is propounded in Quine (1969). Lucy's (1992b), and Imai and Gentner's (1993) studies are well worth reading carefully for their methodology and implications.

Part V
The Ethnography of Speaking

Part V
The Ethnographic Interview

13

Speaking as a Culturally Constructed Act: A Few Examples

Communicative Relativity

In the introduction to the first volume of collected papers on the topic of this Part, the ethnography of speaking, we find the following statement (Hymes 1972b:32–3):

> it is essential to notice that Whorf's sort of linguistic relativity is secondary, and dependent upon a primary sociolinguistic relativity, that of differential engagement of languages in social life. For example, description of a language may show that it expresses a certain cognitive style, perhaps implicit metaphysical assumptions, but what chance the language has to make an impress upon individuals and behavior will depend upon the degree and pattern of its admission into communicative events . . . Peoples do not all everywhere use language to the same degree, in the same situations, or for the same things; some peoples focus upon language more than others.

Hymes's point here is to relativize further Whorf's Principle of Linguistic Relativity by pointing out that Whorf's view presupposes a commonality across the linguistic communities being compared in the basicness of the function of language as a referring device, a means for classifying experience (see also Silverstein (1979)). Hymes contends this is by no means obviously the case (see also Rumsey (1990)); he wishes to extend the Principle of Linguistic Relativity beyond the view of language as a device for denotation to its full indexical powers to enact a world of lived experience. The uses of language across cultures is in fact highly variable. Different cultures often impose quite different conventions for the use and form of language in comparable social situations, as we shall see below, and appropriate linguistic practices in line with these conventions is a definite characteristic of a speaker's membership in the linguistic community as a competent member (Hymes's (1972a) *communicative* competence as opposed to a more narrow notion of grammatical competence). For example, English speakers in America, Britain, and Anglo-Celtic Australia follow a convention that in a meeting normally one person holds the floor, i.e. speaks, at a time. This convention, however, is not part of the communicative competence of English creole speakers of Antigua in the West Indies; conversations there may seem quite anarchic to us, with several speakers holding or trying to hold the floor simultaneously (Reisman 1974). Thus, such social meetings in America and Antigua are not superficially similar events employing somewhat divergent linguistic practices; they constitute different types of linguistic events. Because linguistic practices are the primary communicative behavior through which humans sustain ongoing histories of social structural coupling, different systems of such practices entail different trajectories of lived history, embodied in the habitus and its practices in the sociocultural world. As Hymes (1966:116) put it, paraphrasing Sapir (1964:128):

> people who enact different cultures do to some extent experience distinct communicative systems, not merely the same natural communicative condition with different customs affixed. *Cultural values and beliefs are in part constitutive of linguistic reality.* [My emphasis]

The remainder of the section will draw up the implications of Hymes's claim by contrastive cultural studies of linguistic practices in two areas: social events of litigation and the settling of disputes within the community, and the rituals by which social contact is established among interlocutors, better known as greetings.

Language in Litigation: The Courtroom

The most obvious kind of social event of litigation and the settling of disputes in American, British, and Australian society is the institution of the courtroom. Note that the courtroom as a social event seen through a linguistic perspective is governed by a large number of very strict conventions for the use of language. A courtroom includes a number of distinct participants: judge, lawyers or barristers, defendant(s), plaintiff(s), witnesses, jurors, court officials, and onlookers. The rules of speaking are strictly enjoined according to the participants' role in the courtroom. Onlookers are never permitted to speak at all, under legal punitive measures labelled contempt of court. The judge has the widest latitude in speaking, she even controls the speaking roles of the other participants, but she too is bound by fairly defined conventional limits. If during the cross examination of a witness, the judge should start spouting stanzas from Spenser's *The Faerie Queen*, her behavior would be regarded as extremely odd by all assembled, to say the least. The judge's statements must focus on topics germane to the particulars of the case being heard.

Other participants may have other roles with respect to speaking imposed on them. Jurors, like onlookers, must observe silence, but unlike onlookers who can take any pose with respect to the proceedings, including boredom, jurors are constrained to appear interested and follow the proceedings keenly. Witnesses, on the other hand, are allowed to speak, but only in response to questions put to them by the lawyers or the judge. The forms of their responses are rigidly codified: they must be concise and directly relevant to the topic of the question. Extraneous asides are not permitted. Witnesses can be verbally admonished by the judge if their responses are not fully satisfactory, again under the legal sanction of contempt of court. The defendant(s) and plaintiff(s), like jurors, must observe silence during the proceedings, unless, of course, they are called as witnesses, in which case they talk under the conventions pertaining to witnesses.

The most elaborate conventions are those enjoined upon the lawyers or barristers. Next to the judge, they have the widest latitude in speaking, but, again, within quite set limits. The lawyers of the defendant(s) and plaintiff(s) speak in set turns established by the rules of the court or by the license of the judge. They give opening and closing statements during the proceedings and, with the judge, conduct questioning of the witnesses. The lawyers of the defendant(s) and plaintiff(s) may, during the questioning of the witnesses, interrupt each other with objections to the pattern of questioning. The validity of such objections is determined by the judge and judgment is pronounced by the formulaic use of the words "sustained" or "overruled." The crucial factor determining this outcome, is the judge's decision concerning the relevance of the topic of the questioning to the particulars of the case. Questioning on topics not deemed relevant will be thrown out, so that lawyers must constrain the topics of the speaking within a narrow range. If one lawyer continues to interrupt another without license of the judge, she too is subject to the punitive sanction of contempt of court (as we can see from these examples, contempt of court is nothing more than failure to obey the conventions of speaking proper to courtroom proceedings). Finally, the style of speaking expected of lawyers is different from all other participants: they are expected to speak aggressively and forcefully, and to openly display emotional responses to the unfolding of events in the courtroom. This is in especially marked contrast to the judge, who should remain calm, detached, and impartial during the proceedings.

It is clear from the summary above that an American, Australian, or British courtroom is a linguistic event of a highly specialized and marked kind, with numerous well-defined roles and conventions with respect to speaking for a successful outcome. It is also a particular type of cultural event, a ritualized forum within these societies for the settling of social disputes. Other cultures have different ways of settling such disputes. Commonly this consists of discussion between the disputing parties in the presence of the assembled members of the camp or village. I will discuss such a case among the Ilongot people of the Philippines (Rosaldo 1973) in detail below, but first I want to discuss what happens when such a traditional system comes in contact with the linguistic conventions of the modern courtroom.

Talking Among Australian Aboriginals

Australian Aboriginal people have settled disputes through traditional methods of camp discussion and sanctions for tens of thousands of years before the intrusion of the courtroom ritual with the European invasion of 200 years ago. Australian Aboriginals have long established conventions for speaking in groups which differ widely from Australians of European descent (Walsh 1994). White Australians, especially of the middle class, typically direct their talk to another individual. Even in public speaking, a speaker is expected to cast his eye over the audience, looking briefly at one individual and then another in order to establish this directionality of his talk. In a conversation all members should be included; it is felt to be a serious social gaff if someone is left out of a conversation. A conversation is ideally organized in terms of turns, with each participant taking on a turn as speaker; indeed in some conversations, participants could be said to vie for the role of speaker at certain times. A conversation with only one speaker throughout its duration would certainly be regarded culturally as a "failed" conversation. Finally, if one wants to terminate or withdraw from a conversation, this must be signalled explicitly (*"bye now, I've got to run"*), even if the withdrawal is only temporary (*"wait a second, I've left the tap running"*).

The conventions informing speaking in groups among Australian Aboriginals are radically different (Walsh 1994). Talk is not projected to any individual, nor is any response expected (hence eye contact is not important). Talk is simply broadcast generally, there being no mandated pattern of turns among speakers, and any response is up to an individual hearer. Further, participants in the conversation can freely tune in or out. Walsh describes the following typical scene (Walsh 1994:220):

A group of men is sitting on a beach facing the sea. They are there for some hours and little is said. After a long period of silence someone says: "Tide's coming in." Some of the group murmur "Yes" but most remain silent. After another very long pause someone says "Tide's coming in". And there is some scattered response. This happens many times until someone says: "Must be tide's going out."

Another crucial factor determining differences between middle-class white Australian and Aboriginal conventions for speaking is what might be called the Aboriginal "knowledge economy." For European-derived cultures, the economy is concerned largely with material property, but in Aboriginal society, the emphasis is on intellectual property (what Bourdieu (1984) might call "cultural capital"; see chapter 16). The dissemination of information is tightly controlled and restricted: only through kinship and initiation does someone gain the right to know some bit of information or traditional lore, and this right is carefully guarded. This is in marked contrast to our modern European-derived culture where copious amounts of information are freely available; just look at the institution of the *Encyclopedia Britannica.*

These radical differences in conventions in cultural practices have serious consequences when Aborigines encounter the institution of the courtroom, which, we have seen, imposes very strict conventions for speaking. Unaware of these, Aboriginal people may behave according to their own conventions for speaking in groups. For example, in response to a question put to an Aboriginal witness, a number of Aboriginal spectators in the audience may respond simultaneously, with serious legal consequences for them if the judge is unaware of the distinct Aboriginal conventions for speaking. Further in response to a question, an Aboriginal witness may launch into a long monolog, undirected to any particular participant, including the questioning lawyer, in keeping with his conventions. This runs counter to the intention of the questioning lawyer, who, true to his own conventions for speaking, wants to break up the answer into a set of short, paired question and response utterances, determined by his preplanned array of questions. Finally, the principles underlying the Aboriginal restricted "knowledge economy" can preclude a particular Aboriginal witness from divulging certain information in answer to a question, even if he knows it. This follows from the fact that he may not have the right to such knowledge and may face severe social or supernatural sanctions if he should divulge it. Failure to do so, of course, may leave him open to the legal sanction of contempt of court, leaving the witness with a potentially very difficult choice. The Aboriginal practice also runs counter to that of the questioning lawyers, who, by asking the same questions of a series of witnesses, hope to arrive at a clear understanding of the "truth" of the matter. Not all witnesses have a right to the same answer; our received legal concepts of truth and perjury are simply not relevant here.

Language and Disputes Among the Ilongot
of the Philippines

The Ilongot people of the northern Philippines (Rosaldo 1973) also traditionally settled social disputes through discussions in public groups. Like traditional Aboriginal society, Ilongot culture is egalitarian in outlook. They value consensus rather than privilege, and no decision is totally binding. They claim that no person can coerce another, and even though some people can wield considerable influence, this is no guarantee that their arguments will be heard. Note that this egalitarian anarchic structure is in marked contrast to the formal hierarchic structure implicit in a courtroom and points up the problem of social control in this culture: how are disputes settled and the partners reconciled?

Basically, Ilongot litigation is resolved through linguistic events, specifically a meeting between the disputing parties involving a special oratorical style called *qambaqan*, "crooked" speech. Fellow Ilongot adults cannot be coerced or fooled; rather they must be persuaded by this more subtle mode of speaking, "crooked" speech, which is artful and charming. The Ilongot say it permits a man to "hide" behind his words; the graceful use of this style of speaking within an oratorical performance allows a man to persuade another and resolve a conflict by finding terms for agreement that satisfies both parties. The conventions for speaking in "crooked" speech are very different from those of ordinary talk. "Crooked" speech is characterized by a number of structural features: altered stress patterns, phonological elaboration of words like reduplications, metaphors, repetitions and paraphrases, and puns. These devices allow the speaker to "hide" or distance himself from his words, for example, speaking of "rice" when he means marriage (metaphor).

Typically, Ilongot oratory effaces details of facts of individuality: participants may refer to themselves as "tongues" or "voices," acting on behalf of someone else, even someone whose position they may disagree with. It invokes shared cultural understandings or appropriate social behavior in terms of a person's responsibilities and rights. In this sense it resembles our legal practice, including courtrooms, for both evaluate a person's behavior in terms of more general publicly agreed, social categories and understandings. Ilongot oratory is subject to a number of conventions for speaking which function to enforce this distant, generalizing, and controlled tone (Rosaldo 1973:210–18) (see also Irvine's (1979) discussion of the features of formal speech, which this effacement of individuality plus other properties of Ilongot oratory and our courtroom procedures clearly illustrate). The orator sits in a tense posture. Gestures are limited to movements of the shoulders and eye contact with his opponent is avoided; rather he looks sideways beyond him in a gesture of distance and control. Names of people are avoided; they are referred to through their social position. Differences and conflict are signalled through labels of local origin and descent (*sikin qirumyad* "you of the descent category Rumyad"), while agreement and resolution are marked by kin terms (*sikin qamak* "you, my father"). The use of these labels highlights the shifting attitudes toward the parties in the dispute during the course of the oratorical event, but always in terms of general social categories. Oratorical exchanges are demarked by a great deal of "mirroring," i.e. an orator answers and echoes back his opponent's speech. This is accomplished by established conventions for tying an orator's speech to what was said before; this ensures that the speakers orient themselves to the topic at hand, and that the speech be orderly and not readily interrupted. Conventions for accomplishing this include simple phrases demarking the beginning and ending of an orator's speech, like "I am through now," to which the next speaker will begin with "okay, are you finished there?" Also within a particular speech there is a great deal of repetition, both of the opponent's points during his speech and points previously made by the speakers.

Finally, some particular formal features of "crooked" speech are used to make an orator's speech effective, and at the same time artful and indirect. Indirection is marked by the free use of hedging words like *qamuŋa* "kind of," *legem* "just" or *kaw* "maybe." Uncertainty is also marked grammatically by reduplication: *sibe·sibera* "just, kind of, answering." This is necessary to efface potentially insulting or threatening remarks. Metaphors and other linguistic devices like puns allow the orator to convey his purpose, but again to "hide" behind the surface form of the utterance (Rosaldo 1973:217).

> *qaŋgen nu quyunanmu ma deweta salagumqagume bandi* . . . "Even if you took the handle of the truly piled up treasures . . ." (i.e. even if you get everything"; the pun involves a contraction of *salagusag*, the name of a tree whose bark is used in making handles, and *qagum* which means to "pile up, to collect").

The point of "crooked" language is not deviousness or deception; rather it reflects a belief that only through the careful and artful use of language can one resolve a fractious relationship with another man. Men are all equal, different, difficult to understand, and importantly, prone to violence and the taking of offense, so that language must be used gently to understand another man's feelings. There is no quick, straightforward way to this understanding, only by working through language in ways which are as highly conventionalized as those of an American courtroom. The different conventions in the two societies, as we shall see in the next chapter, reflect quite different conceptions of the idea of personhood.

Greetings: Australo-American and African Style

For a second example of culturally defined conventions for speaking in particular social events, I want to consider the situation of greetings. Greetings are used to establish social contact among interlocutors; as such, the kind of routines used to perform this ritual can be expected to vary along with different cultures' understandings of social positions of any given interlocutors. Greetings in Australia and America are used commonly to create an impression, however unreal, of social equality between the interlocutors, as befits the professed ideology of social structure in these cultures. The information expressed in these greetings is often completely beside the point, rather the focus is the establishment of social contact between interlocutors and the claim of a professed equality. Laver (1981:301–2) points out that the small talk in greetings typically groups into three categories:

1   speaker oriented (factors personal to speaker):
    Hi, big job I'm doing, isn't it?
2   addressee oriented (factors personal to addressee):
    Hi, what's a nice boy like you doing in a place like this?
3   neutral (factors common to both speaker and addressee):
    Good day, beautiful snowstorm we had, wasn't it?

While the ideology of greetings in American and Australian culture is egalitarian (for example, the ubiquitous Australian vocative term, *mate*), there are still some obvious social differences that are recognized. For example, children are unlikely to greet an unfamiliar adult without some vocative term indicating the latter's higher social status like *Mr*, *Mrs*, *sir*, or *lady*. Even in more relentlessly egalitarian Australia, a 10-year-old boy is highly unlikely to address a well-dressed unfamiliar man of 50 by the term *mate;* *Mr* or *sir* would be more appropriate. There are interesting differences between America and Australia in this area, though. In Australia, a male customer and a mechanic are likely to greet each other reciprocally with the term *mate* or first names, suggesting an affirmation of equality. In America, on the other hand, Brown and Ford (1964) indicate that the customer is likely to be greeted with his surname, but the mechanic with his first name, suggesting a different social position of the interlocutors, at least in this particular social interaction.

   The enaction of social inequalities among interlocutors is highly elaborated in the greeting rituals of the Wolof people of Senegal in West Africa (Irvine 1974). Wolof is a stratified Muslim society, and greeting rituals are used as a way of negotiating relative social status among the interlocutors. The basic dichotomy in Wolof society is between nobles and commoners. The local ideology associates lower status with both physical activity, i.e. movement, and speech activity. Higher status people are associated with passivity. Because of this, it is the lower status person who initiates the greeting encounter, by moving toward the higher status person and beginning the ritual greeting. As a consequence, any two persons in a greeting encounter *must* place themselves in an unequal ranking and must come to some understanding of what this ranking is; the simple choice of initiating a greeting is a statement of relatively lower status. Opting not to engage in a greeting ritual at all is not an available choice; cultural norms dictate that a greeting must occur between two parties making contact, even if one party must make a wide detour (perhaps a couple of hundred meters in the fields). Within the village center, a greeting is mandated for all those that pass within 30 meters of oneself.

The form of a greeting encounter is highly conventionalized. It consists of salutations, questions about the other party and his household, and praising God. Irvine (1974:171) provides an illustration (13.1) of a typical Wolof greeting, in which person A has moved toward person B and extended his hand.

In this greeting, person A has assumed the role of the lower ranked person and B, the higher rank. Note that the more active, lower status, A poses questions to the higher status B, who in a typical higher status passive role simply responds, but poses none of his own. In addition to the typical speech acts performed and their roles in turn taking, A and B are also ideally distinguished in terms of the non-segmental phonological features of their speech. Correlated to the activity associated with lower status, A will speak a lot, rapidly, loudly, and with a higher pitch. Higher status B, on the other hand, being more passive and detached will be terse, responding briefly and slowly to questions posed in a quite low-pitched voice.

It should not be taken for granted that all interlocutors would be happy to assume the higher status role, for, while that role implies respect and power, it also obliges one to support those of lower status, most typically, a financial obligation. One may very well wish to avoid this. As the greeting encounter is a typical way to establish relative ranking, a person must carefully choose his strategies during the encounter to position himself where he wants to be. There are a number of strategies of self-lowering available, besides initiating the greeting. For example, one can assume the role of questioner oneself. Thus, when the Initiator reaches the stage of Praising God, the Respondent can begin to launch his own round of questions, so switching roles and the assignment of relative ranking. A prolonged contest for roles and relative ranking could now ensue. The other possible strategy for self-lowering is to ignore the Initiator at his first salutation *salaam alikum* "peace be with you"; instead of responding *malikum salaam* "and with you be peace," the other interlocutor immediately jumps to saying his own name, thus claiming the role of Initiator for himself. It is also possible that an interlocutor might want to elevate himself through the greeting. The easiest

13.1

Salutations	1. A.	*Salaam alikum.*	Peace be with you. [Arabic]
	B.	*Malikum salaam.*	With you be peace. [Arabic]
	2. (A.	A's name)	[A gives own name]
	(B.	B's name)	[B gives own name]
	3. A.	B's name	[A gives B's name]
	B.	$\begin{cases} \text{A's name} \\ \textit{Naam, A's name} \end{cases}$	$\begin{cases} \text{[B gives A's name]} \\ \text{Yes, A's name} \end{cases}$

Questions			
Q1	1. A.	*Na ngga def?*	How do you do?
	B.	*Maanggi fi rek.*	I am here only.
	2. A.	*Mbaa dyamm ngg' am?*	Don't you have peace?
	B.	*Dyamm rek, naam.*	Peace only, yes.

Q2 (a)	1. A.	*Ana waa kïr gi?*	Where/How are the people of the household?
	B.	*Nyu–ngga fa.*	They are there.
	2. A.	*Ana* [name]?	Where/How is X?
	B.	*Mu–ngga fa.*	He/She is there.
(b)	1. A.	*Mbaa* $\begin{cases} \textit{tawaatu} \\ \textit{feebaru} \end{cases}$ *loo?*	Isn't it that you aren't sick?
	B.	*Maanggi sant Yalla.*	I am praising God.
	2. A.	*Mbaa kenn* $\begin{cases} \textit{feebarul?} \\ \textit{tawaatul?} \end{cases}$	Isn't it that anyone isn't sick?
	B.	*Nyu–nggi sant Yalla.*	They are praising God.

Praising God	1. A.	*H'mdillay.*	Thanks be to God. [Arabic]
	B.	$\begin{cases} \textit{H'mdillay.} \\ \textit{Tubarkalla.} \end{cases}$	$\begin{cases} \text{Thanks be to God.} \\ \text{Blessed be God.} \end{cases}$ [Arabic]
	2. A.	$\begin{cases} \textit{H'mdillay.} \\ \textit{Tubarkalla.} \end{cases}$	$\begin{cases} \text{Thanks be to God.} \\ \text{Blessed be God.} \end{cases}$
	B.	$\begin{cases} \textit{H'mdillay.} \\ \textit{Tubarkalla.} \end{cases}$	$\begin{cases} \text{Thanks be to God.} \\ \text{Blessed be God.} \end{cases}$

way to do this, of course, is to avoid initiating the greeting, but, if both parties are following this self-elevating strategy, a quite awkward situation arises: the greeting *must* take place. Even after the greeting has been initiated, there are still a few ways to indicate self-elevation. For example, one can pass rapidly through the greeting, posing few questions and repeating nothing, so as to get to a new topic of conversation quickly.

The contrast between the cultural meanings implicit in the Australian/American greeting encounter and that of the Wolof greeting could not be more glaring: the former is assertion of social *equality*, real or imagined, highlighted in these cultures' ideologies, while the latter is nothing less than the enaction of social *inequality*, implicit in this culture's local ideology and the basis of its social organization (Irvine 1974).

Summary

The case studies reported illustrate the enormous extent to which the linguistic practices of a people are determined by wider cultural practices and beliefs. Communicative relativism in the way languages are used to forge communicative relationships of social coupling is at least as pervasive as the more familiar Whorfian linguistic relativity concerned with the way they express semantic and grammatical categories. A greeting is not simply a greeting; it is a forum in which to enact through linguistic practices the cultural ideologies of equality in Australia or inequality in West Africa. The communicated meaning is radically different. The way language is used in American courtrooms or Ilongot village disputes reflects different beliefs about human nature and how truth and social harmony can be most advantageously arrived at. Similar considerations apply to American one-on-one turn-taking conversations versus Antiguan simultaneous multi-speaker ones versus Aboriginal Australian broadcast conversations directed to no one in particular. Ultimately, these different linguistic practices reflect different trajectories of lived experience for their speakers and consequently are emblematic and creative of wider cultural practices and beliefs, in short, the habitus.

Further Reading

On crosscultural differences in the beliefs and practices surrounding speech, see the classic collection of articles in Bauman and Sherzer (1974), as well as Sanches and Blount (1975), and the overview articles by Bauman and Sherzer (1975), and Duranti (1988a). Hymes's early (1972b[1964]) statement of the field is also important, as is the collection of articles to which this is the introduction (Gumperz and Hymes 1964). Book length studies of individual cultures include Basso (1990), Bauman (1983), Duranti (1994), and Sherzer (1983).

14

Politeness, Face, and the Linguistic Construction of Personhood

Linguistic Practices, Person and Habitus

What is behind these distinct uses of language among American, Australian Aboriginal, Ilongot, and Wolof cultures? A clue is provided by an insightful Wolof proverb about greetings: "When two persons greet each other, one has shame, the other has glory" (Irvine 1974:175). Thus, the distinct linguistic practices associated with the interlocutors in a Wolof-greeting encounter are linked to the kinds of persons they are; indeed, considering the way relative ranking can be manipulated during the encounter through the verbal strategies of self-lowering and self-elevating, these linguistic behaviors are *constitutive* of what kinds of persons they are. Their understanding of what kind of person they are *vis-à-vis* the other interlocutor is embodied in their habitus. To the extent they rate of higher rank, the habitus will enact that proper demeanor in bodily and linguistic practices; so too, if of lower rank. The proper demeanor is embodied in the habitus through countless previous such rituals, the lived history of the individual's social structural coupling, in which he has been both higher and lower ranked. The mandated behavior is thus inculcated in the habitus, which, in turn, reproduces it. Note importantly that this formulation is not deterministic; the habitus of the organism is the result of its history of structural coupling, but, crucially, structural coupling is a relationship of an organism and its environment, including other organisms. Due to the great plasticity of the human nervous system, the human organism may react in an unspecifiable number of ways to a given environmental stimulus; this is what we recognize as free will and is as applicable to the strategies employed in the Wolof ritual greeting as to any other form of human behavior. The embodied practices of the habitus are, if you like, the more tacitly known ones (for further elaboration on free will or agency and a cline of awareness of social practices from fully conscious to unconscious, see Giddens (1984)). Further, due to the unique ability to monitor and ultimately reflect on one's practices through the descriptions made available through language, humans are capable of constructing further descriptions or explanations of these practices, which commonly cohere into local *ideologies*. In the current context, the claim is that the repertoire of linguistic practices in a culture, embodied in the habitus of that culture's members, are both indicative and constitutive of its conception or local ideology of personhood – what is a person and what are the types of persons there can be? Thus, the differences we found above in American, Ilongot, and Wolof understandings and uses of language are all emblematic of their local ideologies of personhood. Through competent linguistic usage in a range of contexts, the speaker comes to enact these local beliefs and, in so doing, the linguistic practices are both significant and constituent of them (Bourdieu 1977, 1990; Giddens 1979, 1984). Thus, the differences in linguistic practices between the interlocutors in the Wolof greeting encounter do not simply signify relative social inequality among persons, as per the local ideology; but by engaging in the linguistic practices available, for example, those of self-lowering and self-elevating, the interlocutors actually create the terms out of which this local ideology can be constructed (this is at base Giddens's (1979, 1984) idea of the duality of structure, his concept of structuration, which is the mutual dependence of structure – in this case, inequality and the institutions which embody it – and agency).

The Construction of Personhood

Since the early 1980s or so a large amount of work in cultural anthropology has focused on crosscultural differences in the conception of the person (see Carrithers, Collins, and Lukes 1985; Geertz 1973, 1983; Gergen 1991; Gergen and Davis 1985; Harris 1989; Kohut 1977; Kondo 1990; Marsella, DeVos, and Hsu 1985; Myers 1986; Read 1955; Rosaldo 1980a, 1984; Shweder and Bourne 1984; Spiro 1993; Taylor 1989; White and Kirkpatrick 1985; Wierzbicka 1993). Not surprisingly, given the volume of all this research, a complete consensus on the issues involved has not yet emerged, but some basic differences in various cultures' beliefs about personhood do seem apparent. The bedrock of these cultural differences seems to lie on how the self is "inscribed" in social relationships (see Gergen 1990). According to this view, the avenue to understanding the nature of the self is not through the individual or the contents of her mental states, i.e. beliefs, feelings, intentions, but rather through social collaborations or structural couplings in the social environment. Each person is dependent on others; their survival cannot be separated from their relationships with others, and, in turn, relationships depend on the mutual coordination of actions among social actors. Gergen (1990) calls such a network of coordination a relational nucleus, "a self-sustaining system of coordinated actions in which two or more persons are engaged" (Gergen 1990:584–5). Such a notion is highly reminiscent of Maturana and Varela's (1987) biological notion of self-organizing systems engaged in structural coupling. How this relational nucleus is formed is largely through speech (Gergen 1990:584–5):

> The individual's well-being cannot be extricated from the web of relationships in which he/she is engaged. The character of the relationship depends, in turn, on the process of adjusting and readjusting actions. In effect, forms of relationship depend on the mutual coordination of actions . . . Thus, for example, as we encounter each other from day to day, our actions tend toward coordination. The movements of the eyes, hands, and feet, for example, or the number of words we speak, their volume and speed, and so on, are all in the process of becoming mutually coordinated . . . As this coordination takes place – taking turns in conversation, adjusting the tone of voice so that the other may hear without discomfort, speaking in mutually acceptable patterns of words, walking together at similar speeds, and so on – we come to form a relational nucleus.

Note that this occurs through the coordination of our individual embodied habitus.

Given this view of social functioning, the person emerges simply as the point of intersection of multiple relational nuclei, a lived history of structural couplings. Each of us carries within us in the habitus a great number of relational patterns developed through our history of structural couplings with others. When we and someone else meet, this interaction now becomes the meeting point of the various patterns of relationships within which we are and have been enmeshed. The unfolding pattern of our relationship will be channelled to a large extent by the wider system of structural couplings that each of us brings to this meeting. The Wolof greeting encounter is an excellent example of this: how the status differential will emerge in the encounter is strongly conditioned by our own discernment of our social status as we have established it in previous encounters, both with the present interlocutor and innumerable others.

Self versus Person

Anthropologists, following Mauss (1985[1938]), commonly make a distinction between the notion of self and that of person (Fitzgerald 1993; La Fontaine 1985). The self refers to a proposed universal human awareness of one's own individual embodiment, while the person is a social concept made up of local notions of one's rights and obligations, and hence varies crossculturally. Harré and Mühlhäusler (1990) make a similar distinction, referring to the former as "numerical identity" and the latter as "qualitative identity." This is phrased in terms of their thesis of the Double Location of the self (Harré and Mühlhäusler 1990:88):

> We come to appreciate that we have location as embodied beings amongst the material things of a temporally continuous physical environment [anthropological notion of "self"]. But we also come to appreciate that we have, at any moment, a more or less well-defined location amongst other people in a social environment of rights and obligations, so acquiring for that moment a certain set of responsibilities [anthropological notion of "person"].

This thesis has a corollary: that of the Double Indexicality of the pronoun "I." This pronoun indexes both notions of location, so that the speaker of an utterance presents herself as having a bounded location in time and space and also a certain set of social responsibilities. Stated in this bald form, the sharp contrast between self and person may be difficult to maintain. First, it is not clear how such putative characteristics of individual embodied selves, like kindness or cruelty, can be meaningfully talked about, except in terms of dyadic social relationships (see Gergen (1994)). Rosaldo (1984) argues that the Ilongot have no ideology of a sharp distinction between the private individual self and a public social presentation of the person. She asserts that what Ilongot individuals think and feel is mainly the result of public social activities, realized through the dyadic interaction of persons, suggesting a blurring of the proposed universal contrast between individual self and social person. Ilongot claim that there is usually no gap between what one feels and what one does. As an egalitarian society, individuals do not have a strong experience of social constraint, which would reinforce a strong boundary between a private, bounded individual self and a social person of rights and responsibilities: "there is no social basis of a problematic that assumes needs for controls, nor do individuals experience themselves as having boundaries to protect or as holding drives and lusts that must be held in check if they are to maintain their status or engage in everyday cooperation" (Rosaldo 1984:148).

A further difficulty in maintaining a sharp distinction between self and person lies in the severe problems in getting a clear fix on this mental awareness of individual embodiment, which is the very basis of the notion of self. This awareness is a very peculiar one, for it is highly diffuse, neither bounded nor stable. It seems largely a linguistic construction: a localization in our bodies through the use of *I* of the intersection of the various patterns of recurring structural coupling that we engage in, and further, a report through linguistic description of the enaction of these couplings (for related ideas see

Mead (1934)). The self is that organism whose actions we report by using *I*. Recent work (Minsky 1986; Varela, Thompson, and Rosch 1991) on the architecture of the mind has claimed that the mind consists of many little "agents," each of which has only a small-scale domain of functions. These "agents" can be organized into larger systems for more inclusive tasks, and these, in turn, can be organized into still larger systems, and so on, all on an analog of social structure, hence the Society of Mind (Minsky 1986). What counts as a collection of agents at one level is simply one "agent" at a higher level. Minsky (1986) illustrates with the example of the "agent" which builds towers out of toy blocks – the Builder. But at a lower level, Builder is composed of other "sub-agents" Beginner, Adder, Finisher, etc., and these, in turn, require further "sub-agents," Finder, Lifter, Mover, etc. The point is this: where, if this indeed is the structure of the mind, could the global, diffuse awareness of the self as individual embodiment be located? Only, as Varela, Thompson, and Rosch (1991) point out, in the series of mental events and formations, i.e. actions of "agents" and "sub-agents," that have coherence and integrity over time. Our understanding of this coherence and integrity is, of course, our memory, or especially what Becker (1971:77–9) calls our "inner-newsreel," what we constantly review in our mind's eye as our life experience, particularly those experiences that give us self-esteem, make us feel good and positive about ourselves (in other words, a selective replay of our history of structural coupling). But, of course, these life experiences, both positive and negative, mainly occur in dyadic interactions, joint configurations of persons, again forcing us to the conclusion that a sharp contrast between individual self and social person is just untenable. (But see Cohen (1994) for a contrary argument. He argues that accounts like Rosaldo's of the Ilongot simply are not tenable. Like Harré and Mühlhäusler, he asserts that individual self-consciousness as a bounded embodied being is a universal property of humans, to argue otherwise is to exoticize the other and deny them desirable traits we claim for ourselves. He notes that in any shared social event like a ritual, each participant has different understandings and interpretations of the event, and this demonstrates the consciousness of a self. Individual experience of any public event is undoubtedly true; to deny it would be to negate the centrality of the human organism and her great plasticity of the nervous system in any instance of structural coupling. Individual experience, however, does not a self make, for there is no evidence for any universal-bounding properties underpinning this experience.)

Local Conceptions of Personhood

Having sketched some of the boundaries of the concept of the person, let me now turn to some of the crosscultural differences in its articulation, the local ideologies of personhood. Let me start with one familiar to most readers – the Western European concept of person. The local ideology may be summarized in one word, individualism, which perhaps reaches its greatest emphasis in American culture. The basic premise of this ideology is egocentric personal autonomy, summarized well in a classic definition by Geertz (1983:59):

> The Western conception of the person as a bounded, unique, more or less integrated motivational cognitive universe, a dynamic center of awareness, emotion, judgement, and action organized into a distinctive whole and set contrastively both against other such wholes and against its social and natural background . . .

In this egocentric individualist ideology of the person, society becomes subordinated to the individual; in a fashion not unrelated to the ideas of philosophers like Hobbes and Locke, society is imagined to have been created via a "social contract" to protect the interests of idealized autonomous individuals, independent of society, yet living within it. These individuals are themselves more important than any constituent grouping. Indicative of this is the importance Western cultures place on privacy and private property; this asserts the centrality of the individual and his wants and needs.

What is the nature of these individuals? Freedom from constraint and autonomy in action seems to be criterial for our ideology of person as individual. Note that the catchcry of the feminist movement, "a person in her own right" implicitly associates personhood with individual rights to action and freedom from constraints. Each person is viewed as having inalienable rights to these individualist claims of autonomy. Each individual is unique, but all, ideologically at least, have equal claims to these rights; a common ethical system governs all our social relations, undoubtedly a result of the universalist morality in the Christian base of Western culture, for, according to Christian teaching, the spiritual component in all persons confers upon them an immeasurable value which must be recognized before all humanly or socially created values. This leads us properly to view a person as an individual, an embodiment of absolute value in her own right, and not simply in terms of her position in any social pattern. Actual inequality among persons is ideologically interpreted as the result of free competition for status rewards among theoretically equal individuals, safeguarded through the rule of law as set out in the "social contract." But the ideas of the unequal status differentials and the equal opportunities of individuals are sharply distinguished. This is the principle behind our current pervasive systems of bureaucratic organization, as so insightfully pointed out by Max Weber (1968[1922]) long ago. The defining characteristic of bureaucracies is a distinction between office and office holder or unequal social role and equal individual. The allocation of these offices to particular persons is determined, ideologically at least, by their *individual* capabilities, not their social connections. Thus, inequality and hierarchy are features of society; persons are free and equal individuals.

The egocentric individualist concept of the person in Western culture is in marked contrast to that of many traditional cultures. These cultures have a sociocentric, context dependent conception of personhood (Shweder and Bourne 1984). In these cultures the individual and his autonomy are not singled out as the local understanding of person, rather his embeddedness in the social context is the stuff of his definition as a person. Personhood is, thus, defined in sociocentric terms, according to the social position a particular human being occupies. The sociocentric conception of personhood regards the good of the social grouping as fundamental and subordinates individual wants and needs to the collective good. (Note the point here is not to argue that these sociocentric cultures have explicit articulated ideologies of personhood parallel to the ideology of individualism of the West (though whether all members of Western societies are explicitly aware of a coherent ideology made up of the principle of individualism noted above is itself open to serious debate); rather, the claim is that their understanding of personhood, whether tacit or not, is enacted in, indeed, constructed through, linguistic and other cultural practices and thereby, inculcated in the habitus. Certainly with one's beliefs thrown into relief through culture contact, they may become articulated: as one of my Balinese students said after two years residence in Australia, trying to articulate his Native understanding, "We (i.e. the Balinese) have a communal culture.") Such a local conception of the person is widely held, for example by such otherwise highly divergent cultures as that of Bali and the Gahuku of highlands New Guinea:

Bali (Geertz 1983:62):

> a persistent and systematic attempt to stylize all aspects of personal expression to the point where anything idiosyncratic, anything characteristic of the individual merely because he is who he is physically, psychologically or biographically, is muted in favor of his assigned place in the continuing, and, so it is thought, never-changing pageant that is Balinese life. It is dramatis personae, not actors, that endure; indeed it is dramatis personae, not actors, that in the proper sense really exist. Physically men come and go – mere incidents in a happen-stance history of no genuine importance, even to themselves. But the masks they wear, the stage they occupy, the parts they play, and most important, the spectacle they mount remain and constitute not the facade but the substance of things, not least the self.

Gahuku (Read 1955:276):

> To the Gahuku-Gama, the palpable differences between people, the idiosyn-
> cratic variations in their natures, are like a shimmer which overlies their social
> identity. They are not unaware of these variations: they do not ignore them;
> but they do not distinguish, as clearly as we are accustomed to, between the
> individual and the status which he occupies. They tend, in other words, to
> categorize, to see men largely in terms of their position in a system of social
> rights and obligations . . . the more outstanding a man is the more he is held
> in, and the more pronounced his own esteem the more closely he identifies
> himself with his status. Individual identity and social identity are two sides of
> the same coin. We ourselves are accustomed to distinguish between them . . .

Because of this radically different understanding of personhood, members of such cultures do not typically talk of other human beings in terms
of individual characters or personality traits like kindness or humility as we
do, but rather talk about typical actions of people in particular social contexts. Read (1955:255–6) is quite explicit about this in the case of the
Gahuku: "people do not normally appeal to abstract principles but rather
emphasize the practical consequences of moral deviation. Instead of saying
it is 'good' or 'right' to help others, they state quite simply that 'if you don't
help others, others won't help you.'" Shweder and Bourne (1984) point out
systematic differences in the language of description for moral and social
behavior between American English and Oriya of India. Whereas Americans are likely to say of someone in abstract terms of individual character
that "she is friendly" or "he is hostile and aggressive," Oriyas in similar
situations are likely to report them as context dependent actions like "she
brings cakes to my family on festival days," or "he shouts curses at his
neighbors." Americans describe personality by individual traits, but Oriyas
do so by reference to social actions, a "cases and contexts" approach (Shweder
and Bourne 1984:188). Americans describe what is true of a person's behavior
(friendly, hostile, etc.) but overlook the dyadic social interactional contexts
in which these are played out (see earlier discussion of Gergen (1990)),
while Oriyas focus their attention on the particular social contexts in which
the behavior occurred, and do not provide abstract general labels for individual character traits or the inner feelings and intentions of the actor.
Shweder and Bourne link these differences to the contrastive American
egocentric versus Oriya sociocentric understandings of personhood: in
American culture a person is a unique individual transcending any particular social interaction, while the Oriya ideology holds that the person is
a point in a network of social patterns of hierarchy and exchange, the sum-
mation of social roles.

Sociocentric conceptions of personhood do not preclude a strong sense of one's own individuality (*not* equivalent to individualism), a feature of Gahuku culture emphasized by Read (1955). Rosaldo (1984) makes a telling point of the necessarily different articulations of sociocentric ideologies in hierarchical versus egalitarian societies. In societies where social statuses and, hence, persons are unequal and ascribed through caste, as in India or Bali, constraint on individual action is the order of the day, in order to ensure the inheritance of the traditions' order of ascribed social privileges. This entails proscriptions on individuals' social actions, tying them closely to what is emblematic of their social position and, thus, curtailing much of their individual expression. Bali, as described in Geertz (1973, 1983) is a good example of such a culture; see the earlier quote from Geertz (1983:62–4) on page 266. The Balinese have a large inventory of labels for describing persons in terms of their position in the hierarchical caste-based social structure: birth order names (first-born, second-born, etc.), kinship terms and names based on these (mother of X, sister of Y), caste titles, and so on. These ascriptions when applied to someone define him in terms of the fixed pattern of Balinese social life and prescribe the proper social behavior between him and you. This fact finds perhaps its most striking articulation in the complex rules of linguistic etiquette, for which Bali and its neighbor Java are justly famous: given a particular status differential between interlocutors only certain forms of language are acceptable and others strictly proscribed, as will be discussed in detail in chapter 16.

Such extensive and rigid prescription of appropriate behavior is quite alien to Gahuku culture, a culture with an aggressively egalitarian ideology, if ever there was one. There are no inherited societal offices which confer authority, such as chiefdoms elsewhere in Melanesia. Authority is earned, through physical and economic power. In such a flexible egalitarian society, it is not surprising that the local ideology of personhood, while sociocentric, emphasizes the transient physical incarnation of persons as embodiments. It is through the physical powers of the body that one achieves authority, power and esteem, be it the male power of aggression and dominance or the female power of procreation. Hence, Gahuku are keenly aware of themselves as embodied individuals and lavish attention on their bodies, especially their skin, a key term in the local ideology of person (Read 1955:266). All of this is in keeping with the open egalitarian nature of Gahuku society which does not prescribe different social behavior among social unequals, as in Bali, and therefore encourages the play of individual differences in reaping social rewards: "the majority of social rewards go to the physically strong and self-assertive; to the proud and the flamboyant and to the extroverted warrior who demands, and usually obtains the submission of his fellows" (Read 1955:254). The concept of the person, however, is still sociocentric; it derives its meaning from the complex of social obligations one has (Read 1955:276):

There is no real dichotomy between man and society, no essential separation of the individual from the social pattern. Of course it does not follow that idiosyncratic differences are unimportant. Age-mates, for example, are expected to be the closest of friends, but although the formalities of friendship are generally maintained with all of them, it is clear that men have a greater affection for and feel a closer bond with some than others. People are probably very well aware of this, but it is only to an outsider, such as the anthropologist, that they can express their personal preferences. The same could be said for most other relationships, but even when we have made every allowance for the manner in which differences in temperament and character may modify a formal bond, the fact remains that, to his fellows, status – his position in the system of social rights and obligations – is a basic and inseparable constituent of each man's identity. Indeed, it is possible to conclude that for most purposes and in most situations social identity is more important than idiosyncratic individuality.

The kind of person someone is and the rights and obligations one has toward them is still, as in Bali, a function of the social position occupied: a mother's brother is a different kind of person than a brother-in-law; a kinsman, different from an enemy; and a big man different from a poor man. Gahuku individuality is not individualism of the Western kind. People are persons of a type or non-persons because of their social position, not because of an inalienable and intrinsic value. The ideology of personhood in Gahuku like Bali is sociocentric, the palpable differences result from it being an egalitarian society with largely open competition to win positions of social status, in contrast to the relatively closed caste system of Bali in which positions of social status are largely ascribed through inheritance, and so competition for these positions is more muted and effaced. In both societies the persons are largely understood to *be* their social positions, while in Western societies the social position is just that, an office that the person as an autonomous individual occupies.

The Linguistic Construction of Personhood and the Concept of Face

How are these differing local ideologies of personhood learned and enacted? How do they become embodied in the habitus? Largely, as Gergen (1990:585) so clearly points out, through the use of language (see the quote on page 262). As we converse in a dyadic relationship, thereby forging a structural coupling, our verbal actions become coordinated as communicative practices in sustaining the structural coupling. It is through this coordination that particular structural couplings are fashioned, and it is the summed lived history of these which constitute the person. Maturana and Varela

(1987) highlight the central role that talking plays in our social structural coupling by terming it "linguallaxis," a kind of linguistic trophallaxis, the biological term for the structural correlation that takes place between organisms through exchanges of food or chemical secretions, as when the organization of a beehive is determined by a particular balance of hormonal secretions. The idea of linguistic practices as linguallaxis is supported by Aiello and Dunbar's (1993) claim for the evolution of language essentially as a kind of social glue, supplementing grooming as human bands increased in size: bodily practices as communicative in social coupling (trophallaxis: grooming) are supplemented by linguistic practices (linguallaxis), which gradually supplant the former during the course of human evolution. For a beehive, alter the hormonal balance and you alter the organization of the hive; for a human social grouping, a change in patterns of verbal behavior (linguallaxis) can have equally dramatic effects on social positioning; just consider the case of the Wolof greeting encounter. Further, as Shweder and Bourne (1984) point out, the local ideology of personhood is constituted by what people say while talking, for in a profoundly Whorfian way, the metaphors speakers use to describe persons and their behavior are both derived from and constructive of their local understanding of personhood.

Goffman (1967, 1971) takes a more fine grained look at how the coordination of linguistic behavior in a dyadic relationship enacts our particular cultural understandings of personhood. He points out that it is the goal of interactants in a social encounter to protect the fragile self-esteem they have of themselves; at the very least, to minimize damage to this esteem, at best, to increase it. This self-esteem is termed face by Goffman (1967), defined as "the public self-image that every member wants to claim for himself" (Brown and Levinson 1987:61). Face is largely enacted linguistically between interactants (although other modalities are also possible; see Goffman (1956) for a classic exposition). Through the words we and others choose and use, our face and those of the other interactants in the social interaction are subject to modification and possible undermining. Face is linguistically constructed, and the ability to use verbal skills with facility is how we can manipulate a social encounter to maximize our face gains and minimize our losses; again, the Wolof greeting encounter is a paradigm exemplar of this fact.

Politeness, and Positive and Negative Face

Brown and Levinson (1987), in a now classic monograph, develop a rich theory of linguistic politeness or linguistic etiquette around Goffman's concept of face. Politeness is, of course, a battery of social skills whose goal is to ensure everyone feels affirmed in a social interaction, so its link to a theory of face is transparent (for other views on linguistic politeness, see Lakoff (1973, 1977) and Leech (1983)). Brown and Levinson (1987) break Goffman's concept of face into two aspects, positive and negative face. Positive face is what we typically understand by the concept of face and that which was highlighted by Goffman: one's positive self-esteem, "the positive consistent self-image or 'personality' (crucially including the desire that this self-image be appreciated and approved of) claimed by interactants" (Brown and Levinson 1987:61). Negative face is one's freedom to act, "the basic claim to territories, personal preserves, rights to non-distraction – i.e. to freedom of action and freedom from imposition" (Brown and Levinson 1987:61). Brown and Levinson see the two aspects of face as the basic wants of any individual in a social interaction – to be affirmed in her positive self-esteem by at least some others and to be unimpeded in her action. Social interaction is viewed as cooperative activity (see Grice 1975), in which interactants work to maintain each other's face. However, it is inevitable in the course of human social interaction that certain acts need to be done which threaten others' face. Some verbal acts like promises or orders threaten one's negative face by interfering with one's unimpeded freedom of action: an order certainly curtails this. Others, like apologies or disagreements threaten positive face; disagreeing with someone's view suggests there is something wrong with that view and, potentially, themselves, a clear challenge to their self-esteem or positive face. Speech acts like orders or warnings, which threaten a person's sense of face, both positive and negative, are called face-threatening acts or FTAs for short.

Linguistic politeness is basically the redressing of the affronts to face posed by face-threatening acts to addressees. Connected to the two aspects of face, we find both positive and negative politeness. Positive politeness, as expected, seeks to redress the affront to the hearer's positive face. The speaker (S) indicates his recognition that the hearer (H) wishes to have his positive-face wants honored; typically S asserts that he wants at least some of H's wants. Positive politeness strategies include statements of friendship, solidarity, compliments. Examples of utterances employing positive politeness strategies include (for full details, see Brown and Levinson (1987: 101–29)):

1 Attend to H's interests, needs, wants
   You look sad. Can I do anything?
2 Use solidary in-group identity markers
   Heh, mate, can you lend me a dollar?
3 Be optimistic
   I'll just come along, if you don't mind.
4 Include both S and H in activity
   If we help each other, I guess, we'll both sink or swim in this course.

5 Offer or promise
   If you wash the dishes, I'll vacuum the floor.
6 Exaggerate interest in H and his interests
   That's a nice haircut you got; where did you get it?
7 Avoid disagreement
   Yes, it's rather long; not short certainly.
8 Joke
   Wow, that's a whopper!

Note all of these strategies are to make H feel good about himself, his interests or possessions. Negative politeness is oriented to H's negative face, his desire for autonomy. Typically, negative politeness strategies emphasize avoidance of imposition and so S maintains she will only minimally interfere with H. They include apologies or other distancing styles. Examples of utterances employing negative politeness strategies include (Brown and Levinson 1987:129–211):

1 Be indirect
   Would you know where Oxford Street is?
2 Use hedges or questions
   Perhaps, he might have taken it, maybe.
   Could you please pass the rice?
3 Be pessimistic
   You couldn't find your way to lending me a thousand dollars, could you?
4 Minimize the imposition
   It's not too much out of your way, just a couple of blocks.
5 Use obviating structures, like nominalizations, passives or statements of general rules
   I hope offense will not be taken.
   Visitors sign the ledger.
   Spitting will not be tolerated.
6 Apologize
   I'm sorry; it's a lot to ask, but can you lend me a thousand dollars?
7 Use plural pronouns
   We regret to inform you.

All of these strategies have the effect of trying to gloss over or minimize the imposition on H.

Finally, an S may consider the potential affront of an FTA to be potentially so serious that he regards neither positive or negative politeness as sufficient redress. In this case, he may do the FTA "off the record" with a hint (*it's cold in here*, as a request to close the window) or some other indirect strategy, such as irony (*Harry's so successful in his intimate relationships!!*) or

14.1   Circumstances determining
choice of strategy:

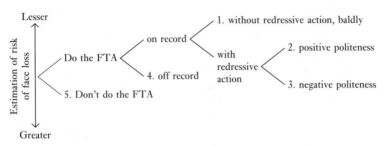

vagueness (*Perhaps, someone went to the casino last night*). Brown and Levinson (1987:60) show the available range of verbal behaviors to redress loss of face (14.1), the greater potential for loss of face requiring greater redressive action of the FTA, culminating in the extreme case to avoidance of the FTA completely.

Crosscultural Differences in Politeness and Face

Brown and Levinson present this model with its concept of the dual aspects of face and associated strategies of politeness as a universal one, and their monograph provides copious evidence and examples drawn from three widely disparate languages, English, Tzeltal, and Tamil. They use it to develop a typology of cultures according to the types of politeness dominant and their distribution across social groupings. In egalitarian societies in which social distance, and status and power differentials between interactants are minimal, like the Ilongot, positive politeness strategies will be favored, whereas in hierarchical status-conscious societies, like Bali, negative politeness strategies will be much in evidence. Thus, in Bali a low caste rice farmer supplicating to a high government official will use extensive strategies of negative politeness, but be addressed baldly with no politeness redressing. Brown and Levinson conjecture that in hierarchical societies powerful high status groups have negative politeness cultures (recognizing such groups have power, i.e. freedom to act as they will, and redressing the imposition on this freedom), while dominated groups have positive politeness cultures (recognizing the need to assert solidarity and mutual regard for positive self-esteem in view of the obvious restrictions on power; see chapter 16). These differences indicate and inform a view of the person in such groups as autonomous, free, and powerful or dependent, bound, and weak respectively. Given these correlations, it is not surprising to find in gender studies that female speech is said to be characterized by more positive politeness, and male by negative politeness (see also chapter 15).

In a similar vein, in a comparative study of politeness in England and Greece, Sifianou (1992) notes a difference between those two cultures in the significance accorded to the two aspects of face. The English place a higher value on privacy and individuality (negative face), while the Greeks emphasize group involvement and ingroup relationships (positive face). The limits to personal territory among Greeks include all those who belong to the same ingroup, defined as someone concerned with one's welfare. Positive face extends to cover these, so that there is a strong desire that one's companions are also liked and approved. Positive face is, thus, defined over the group of ingroup associates, not on isolated individuals, as is largely the case in England. Members of an ingroup will employ positive politeness or no politeness amongst each other and restrict negative politeness to outsiders. It is the duty of each ingroup member to help all others, so members see no need for thanking or apologizing (negative politeness) for services requested or rendered. Hence, requests and wishes are expressed much more baldly, without redressive action, than in English. In English culture a much more distant and indirect form of behavior is normative, where aid is seen as depending on an individual's discretion. Thank yous and apologies are required for even relatively minor impositions, even with an ingroup, reflecting the more individualist ethos associated with face (prominence of negative face).

A more serious objection to Brown and Levinson's formulation is presented in Matsumoto (1988) and Gu (1990), dealing with East Asian cultures, Japanese and Chinese respectively. They argue that Brown and Levinson's division of face into positive and negative face is untenable for these cultures, and particularly that the weight given to negative face, freedom to act, and negative politeness, avoidance of imposition on the freedom to act, derives from the importance given to individualism in the Western European concept of the person. Matsumoto (1988) points out that what is most important to a Japanese person is not her right to act freely, but her position in a group in relationship to all others, her acceptance by these others and the duties it entails. This, of course, is transparently a difference between an egocentric individualistic conception of personhood and a sociocentric, context bound one. Face as positive self-esteem (positive face) is indeed operative in Japanese culture, but again must be understood in sociocentric, rather than the individualistic terms in which Brown and Levinson frame it: "a Japanese generally must understand where s/he stands in relation to other members of the group or society, and must acknowledge his/her dependence on others. Acknowledgment and maintenance of the relative position of others, rather than preservation of an individual's proper territory, governs all social interaction." (Matsumoto 1988:405).

This view of face and consequently personhood has clear linguistic manifestations. Japanese is a language typified by expressions of deference, for example, honorifics (see chapter 16). An English deferential expression would be *Excuse me, sir, could you please close the window.* Deference in English is associated with the avoidance or downplaying of an imposition; the more we feel we might be imposing, the more deferential we might be. It is clearly a strategy for negative politeness, redressing a threat to negative face. In keeping with her contention of the lack of a relevant idea of negative face in Japanese culture, Matsumoto (1988) argues that deference in Japanese culture does not function to minimize imposition (negative politeness), but rather to represent a positive relationship between the interlocutors (positive politeness). A good example (Matsumoto 1988:409) is:

Doozo yorosiku onegaisimasu
"I ask you to please treat me well"

An expression like this is employed when someone is introduced to someone and expresses a wish that the relationship will be a beneficial one. Formally, as a speech act, it is an imposition, and through its expression, the speaker places himself in a lower recipient position and is clearly deferential. But just as clearly it acknowledges interdependence, a virtue in Japanese culture. It is an honor in this society to be asked to take care of someone, and this confers status on the person being so asked. It enhances the addressee's positive face, but by using this expression and putting himself in a positively valued relationship of interdependence, the speaker has also enhanced his own positive face. It is not negative versus positive face which is relevant in Japanese culture, but just face, viewed as positive self-esteem. Linguistic acts enhance it or threaten it; one can "lose face" in the sense that one's positive self-esteem as a valued member of a group with assigned rights and duties has been diminished. The differences between the Japanese and Western European concepts are indicative and constitutive of their respectively sociocentric versus individualist conceptions of personhood.

While giving due to such crosscultural variations, Brown and Levinson emphasize the universal bases of the model and the constraints it imposes; they note, for example, in "no society will members use positive politeness for big FTAs and negative politeness for small ones, or positive politeness only to superiors and negative politeness only to inferiors." (Brown and Levinson 1987:253). Both of these unattested patterns will be in contravention of the model.

The Cooperative Principle and its Conversational Maxims

Crucial to Brown and Levinson's model of politeness is a principle of cooperation among interlocutors in the mutual maintenance of face in conversation;

ideally speakers perform various types of speech acts more or less politely to preserve each other's face. An important linguistic analog of this (and a basic inspiration for Brown and Levinson) is found in the work of the philosopher, Grice (1975; 1989). Grice attempts to unravel the logic or basis for rational behavior behind human linguistic interactions in conversations. The fundamental principle involved here is called by Grice the Cooperative Principle, which means that people engaged in a particular linguistic interaction will say things appropriate at every point in the interaction. For example, if I come running down the street to you, yelling "Help! My house is on fire" and you respond "OK, don't panic. I'll call the Fire Brigade," this is an appropriate response and obeys the Cooperative Principle. If, on the other hand, you respond "Do you think my lawn needs cutting?", we have a clear violation of the Cooperative Principle, and this would get me to try to figure out the cause of your lack of cooperation. The Cooperative Principle reflects a rational plan to coordinate our contributions during conversations, a cultural game plan for our mutual structural coupling in linguallaxis. Grice (1975:45) describes the Cooperative Principle as "making your conversational contribution such as is required, at the state at which it occurs, by the accepted purpose or direction of the talk exchange in which you are engaged." This is quite vague and leaves open the possibility for a significant deal of crosscultural variation: for example, what type of information and how much is required, who or what determines the talk's purpose and direction, etc. As we shall see, the possibilities of variation are indeed attested in various cultures.

To flesh out the vagueness in his Cooperative Principle, Grice (1975:45–6), further proposes a number of conversational maxims which guide communicative interaction in conversations. There are four of these:

1　The Maxim of Quantity – don't give too much or too little information for the current purposes of the interaction. If I ask you how your son is doing and you answer, "Fine, he's in University now and doing well," the information provided is about right and reflects an appropriate use of the Maxim of Quantity. If, however, you answer "Alive," this is a clear violation of the Maxim by providing too little information, or if you answer "Fine, he's in University now, got a new boyfriend and a great new haircut, bought a couple of new CDs yesterday, a new bed last week, and is planning a trip to Canberra next week,' this too is a clear violation of the Maxim by providing too much information.

2　The Maxim of Quality – don't say things you believe to be false or for which you lack adequate evidence. Telling the truth is mandated by this Maxim, and lies are clear violations. This Maxim reflects the speaker's sincerity and responsibility not to mislead others.

3　The Maxim of Relevance – don't say things which are not germane to the topic under discussion. This Maxim ensures that the conversation be coherent. The earlier example of response to my cries for help because my house is on fire reflects its operation well. A response like "Okay, don't panic, I'll call the Fire Brigade" is appropriate, but "Do you think the grass needs cutting?" is a clear violation.

4 The Maxim of Manner – don't be ambiguous or obscure, long-winded, or incoherent. This Maxim refers to the form of the contribution to the conversation: it should be brief and clear in expressing one's ideas. If in writing a review of a performance of Shakespeare's *Macbeth*, I write "Ms X provides a less than inspired characterization of Lady Macbeth" I have obeyed the Maxim of Manner. If, on the other hand, I write "Ms X enunciated fairly distinctly the lines written by Shakespeare for his character Lady Macbeth," I have violated the Maxim.

In ongoing conversational interactions, speakers violate or flout Grice's four Maxims regularly. They do this for a particular purpose; the hearer, assuming the operation of the Cooperative Principle, tries to reason why the speaker has flouted a particular Maxim, what she is implying by doing so, and so comes to a conclusion about her intentions, an implicature. Thus, in the immediately preceding example of the overly long and obscure review, the reader is asked to infer why the Maxim of Manner has been violated; the implicature is, of course, a negative review of Ms X's performance. In the case of the flouting of the Maxim of Relevance by responding "Do you think the grass needs cutting?" to my cries of help because my house is on fire, the most obvious implicature is that the neighbor does not want to help me, either because he is a nasty selfish person or I have offended him grievously in the past, or perhaps because he is mentally ill.

Flouting Grice's Maxims is a very common way of politely performing face-threatening acts "off the record" (Brown and Levinson 1987:214). Hints, for example, flout the Maxim of Relevance. So a very polite request to close the window through "Gee, don't you find it's a bit cold and drafty in here?" accomplishes its purpose by generating an implicature through violating the Maxim of Relevance. If the answer is a simple "yes" with no redressive action, the hearer has not realized that the Maxim has been flouted and generation of the implicature will have failed. If, on the other hand, the hearer does realize the Maxim has been flouted and asks why, then he will probably conclude that the speaker wants some action taken to redress the situation of the cold room and will rise and close the window; the implicature was successfully generated. Understatement as a way of being polite is a flouting of the Maxim of Quantity: too little information has been provided, thus generating implicatures in the hearer as to why the flouting has occurred. A good example might be a statement by a house guest to a host, "Oh, the house needs just a little bit of work, doesn't it?", when, in fact, it is so badly ridden by termites that it is under imminent threat of collapse or condemnation by the local council. Finally, floutings of the Maxim of Manner also very effectively perform polite "off record" face-threatening acts. Vagueness or ambiguity of expression, both of which are direct violations of the Maxim, are especially common when making particular face-threatening acts like requests or accusations, for example, "Looks like someone partied a bit too much last night," said to a partner suffering a severe morning hangover. The obscurity of the expression flouts the Maxim of Manner and causes us to ask why. The implicature generated, of course, is criticism of the partner's behavior last night, but, as this is a particularly potent FTA against one's positive face, the criticism is muted and stated indirectly through flouting of the Maxim.

Crosscultural Variation of the Cooperative Principle: The Malagasy Case

As mentioned above, Grice's articulation of the Cooperative Principle was vague enough to allow for significant crosscultural variation. The four Maxims were an attempt to set down more explicit sub-principles, but evidence from other cultures tentatively suggests that these reflect more an ethnographic description of conversational behavior in Western European derived cultures than absolute universal constraints. The crosscultural variation is so significant and generally so unrecognized in discussion of Grice's Maxims that Hymes (1986:78) has been led to criticize their "ethnocentric enormity." As noted above, areas where crosscultural variation might be expected include the nature and amount of information expected in conversations in particular cultures and who or what determines the conversation's purpose and direction. The kind and amount of information expected in conversations is regulated by the Maxim of Quantity; in short, be properly informative. But what counts as properly informative is clearly culturally determined, as Keenan (1976) brilliantly demonstrated by a study of conversational practices among Malagasy peasants. Malagasy peasants, especially men, are typically much less informative in their information exchanges than are Americans or Australians. They see information as a valuable commodity, something which confers prestige within the context of the largely egalitarian village, and so they are reluctant to share it freely. In small close-knit villages like this, where everyone is related to everyone else, where little contact with the outside world is possible, where there are few secrets and less privacy, information that is not publicly available is highly prized for the temporary status it confers. Hence, when someone is asked a question, it is unlikely that the information required by the questioner will be immediately and fully provided; rather vague, partial answers are the norm. So if someone is asked where they are going, they are not likely to respond, "to the store to buy some beer; we're planning a party this evening." A more typical Malagasy answer would be "oh, maybe, just a little to the north," hardly an informative response, as the questioner can clearly work out for himself the direction of the person's walk.

Another, and maybe even more significant factor affecting the operation of the Maxim of Quantity in Malagasy conversations is a cultural reticence to commit oneself publicly to any particular claim, for fear of damage to one's face if the claim should turn out false or fail to eventuate. Malagasy want to avoid taking responsibility for information communicated, so the information provided is kept to a minimum and often presented in a round-about or obscure fashion, at least to our ears (a violation of the Maxim of Manner). So, people avoid committing themselves to some future event, in case it should fail to occur. If asked when a festival will occur, proper responses will be uninformative or vague, like "I'm not sure" or "around June," even if the respondent is fully cognizant of the exact date which has been set. The same potential loss of face causes people to be extremely careful when giving advice or warnings, so as to leave open the other possibilities that could occur. Asked when a particular Mr X might be home, a typical response would be, "Well, if you don't come after sunset, then you won't see him." This seems curiously roundabout and uninformative to our ears, but given Malagasy cultural values, it is a perfect way to provide some information in reply, but avoid a commitment to a future event.

Vagueness and lack of informativeness are also typical of the expressions used to refer to people. People avoid identifying particular individuals in their utterances, as this may expose the person to retribution. It is also in keeping with the sociocentric, context dependent understanding of persons in this culture, in contrast to the individualist West. Consequently, individual persons are referred to by expressions that note their position in the social collective. Often all traces of individuality are effaced, so that villagers may refer to each other as *olona* "person," *zazalahy* "boy," or *ray aman-dreny* "elder." Thus, a woman might say "Is the person (*olona*) still sleeping?" to her son, when the "person" referred to is her husband (Keenan 1976:73). Note in our usage and in accordance with Grice's (1975) Maxims, such a usage of "person" would only be appropriate when the speaker was unaware of the sleeper's identity. In Malagasy, one could even appropriately say "someone is looking for you" when that someone is your brother (Keenan and Ochs 1979:153).

Given Malagasy cultural beliefs, one area that presents especial problems in verbal interactions are speech acts of requests or orders, not so much because, as in Brown and Levinson (1987) they impose on one's freedom to act or negative face, but because they threaten Malagasy positive face values of equality and non-confrontation, and also, if accepted, commit the addressee explicitly to some future event. The former explanation is reasonable in an egocentric, individualist culture like those of the West, but is largely inappropriate for a sociocentric culture like Malagasy (as argued also by Matsumoto (1988) for Japanese). Requests are typically presented indirectly in the form of hints. Further, people will not proceed directly to the hint in a social encounter, even if the main purpose of the interaction from their point of view is to make a request. Keenan and Ochs (1979:154) provide the following striking example to illustrate this point. One day, a group of boys arrived at their house for an unannounced visit. After some twenty minutes or so of small talk, the topic of cut feet was introduced, a common injury in the volcanic country in which this village is situated. Some time after this, one of the boys in the back of the group showed Keenan and Ochs a badly cut foot, which needed immediate attention. It would be hard to imagine a more indirect, open-ended and vague way of performing requests than this!

The Cooperative Principle and the Determination of Meaning

Another area in which there appears to be significant differences across cultures in the interpretation of the Cooperative Principle and the associated Maxims concerns who or what determines the conversation's purpose or direction at any point, or more precisely, who assigns interpretations to speaker's utterances during an ongoing speech event. The normal Western understanding, following Searle's (1969) path-breaking work on speech acts, is that this is done by the speaker himself. This reflects an encoding or mapping conception of language: the speaker has particular intentions in his mind and by choosing his words and a particular speech act conveys these intentions to his hearers. The meaning of the speech act is the speaker's intentions; it is he as an individual who properly assigns interpretations to his utterances; the audience is merely a passive spectator who guesses at these intentions, either rightly or wrongly.

Again recent work (Duranti 1988b; Rosaldo 1982) suggests that this conception of meaning and interpretation implicitly reflects the West's individualist ideology of personhood and does not generalize straightforwardly to cultures whose ideologies are of a more sociocentric bent. Duranti (1988b) argues that in Samoan culture, the meaning of utterances, at least in formal speech events involving political and judicial oratory called *fono*, are constructively arrived at by the participants, a task viewed by all as a cooperative one, albeit hierarchically structured along the lines of the society generally: "Rather than taking words as representations of privately owned meanings [as in Searle's analysis of speech acts], Samoans practice interpretation as a way of publicly controlling social relationships rather than as a way of figuring out what a given person 'meant to say'" (Duranti 1988b:15). Meanings are thus dialogically constructed in the ongoing speech event and do not reside in any person's intentions or psychological states. Reflecting this, Samoans do not say, "you mean x?", but "is the meaning of your words x?", focusing on a view of meaning as interpretations arrived at in context, rather than the intentions of the speaker. Further, in a *fono* speech event the meanings of utterances are debated by the orators, who both cooperatively and competitively work toward a public interpretation of statements and events. In a *fono* opinions are often phrased by orators as if being delivered for a group, rather than just an individual, such as the chief, for whom the orator is speaking. Therefore, speakers often shift between the singular pronoun "I" or the plural exclusive "we" (for a similar phenomenon of "segmentary person" in highlands New Guinea languages, see Rumsey (1989)). The speech acts, then, are not of the individual, but the group and, hence, the entire group can be seen as sharing responsibility for the implications of the utterance. This again reflects a sociocentric ideology in which the values of a person is understood in terms of his position in the group.

A similar story is presented in Rosaldo's (1982) account of speech acts among the more egalitarian Ilongot of the Philippines. Rosaldo argues that the Ilongot do not regard speech acts as the achievement of individualist selves coding their intentions in linguistic expressions, but most prominently as ways of invoking cooperative bonds among people, and cooperation is fundamental to social interactions in this egalitarian society. It is the social cooperative bonds and the interactive meanings created through these which are paramount to the Ilongot, not the intentions within an individual's mind, which, indeed, hold little interest for them (they say "we can never really know what is in a man's heart"). Rosaldo demonstrates her point by an analysis of the directive speech acts or *tuydek*, which are seen by Ilongot as the exemplary acts of speech. Directives are used by adults to children or by a man to a woman. They are significant to the Ilongot because they are seen as a way to instruct others in their proper cooperative and complementary social roles and in this function are seen as paradigmatic for language generally. Rosaldo (1982:379) states this clearly:

> *Tuydek*, then, were seen as the exemplary act of speech. As significant in ordering domestic life as in the socialization of the young, directive utterances were, for my Ilongot friends, the very stuff of language: knowing how to speak itself was virtually identical to knowing how and when to act.

Further, directives are not seen as a threat to the overall egalitarian ethos of the culture. They value sameness, but do not disregard differences, assigning them merely to their proper social places. If men especially failed to use directives, then Ilongot society would fall apart for lack of vitality and direction. Directives are commonly issued baldly without any redressive action, but Ilongot do not regard these as an affront to their equality and dignity, because, as Rosaldo points out, they are viewed as expressing reasonable social expectations, relationships nurtured in continuing social interactions, rather than impositions of the other's prerogatives of action. Again, Rosaldo's (1982) data suggest along with Matsumoto (1988) a revision of the claims by Brown and Levinson (1987) on the universal importance of negative face.

Local Constructions of Personhood and Linguistic Relativity

The Boasian tradition with its Principle of Linguistic Relativity, as discussed in Part IV, links crosscultural differences in formal linguistic systems to differences in habitual thought patterns, so the above crosscultural differences in the pragmatics of linguistic usage pose an obvious question: can these too be linked to a Principle of Linguistic Relativity? In other words, do crosscultural variations in the pragmatic conventions for speaking languages lead to different meanings and interpretations being exchanged in the communities that speak the languages and ultimately, in the perspective being proposed here, in different understandings of personhood being constructed and inculcated linguistically in the habitus? Recent work (Gumperz 1982, 1993; Ochs 1990) indicates that this may very well be the case. The crucial notion here is context and the various indexical linguistic elements (Silverstein 1976, 1979). As pointed out in chapter 1, a given context not only regulates the meaningful interpretation of indexical elements, but equally important is the crucial fact that indexical elements themselves actually creatively shape the meaningful background of the context. Ochs (1990) notes, for example, that the affective dimension or background feeling tone of a context can be carefully crafted by the use of particular indexical elements, and these in turn can forge particular types of social identities or understandings of personhood in the culture. She provides a Japanese example; this language has a number of sentence final particles *ze*, *zo* or *wa* to signal the speaker's affective disposition. *Ze* and *zo* indicate a coarse and intense style of speaking, while *wa* indicates softness, and a delicate and hesitant presentation. She claims that these are the primary meanings of these indexical elements; however, it is necessary to know that *ze* and *zo* are mainly associated with male speakers, and *wa*, with female speakers. The use of these sentence final particles both indicate and constitute local understandings of engendered persons in Japanese culture: men are forceful while women are soft and hesitant. Thus, Ochs argues, the direct indexing of affect via these particles indirectly indexes gender, and competence in their use constitutes a framework for an enaction of the local ideology of engendered personhood (see also chapter 15). There may be universal principles at work here in the linking of affect to gender (for example, the opposite linking, forcefulness to female and softness and hesitancy to male, is probably much rarer crossculturally), but the basic point is a wholly relativistic one: the meaning of particular forms, i.e. indexical elements, depends on who says them in what context (e.g. a Japanese woman could use *zo* to signal a specific meaning in some context, perhaps she is angry with her son). The interpretation of indexicals depends upon particular conventions of language use in a given culture. This, then, is a second Principle of Linguistic Relativity: if the pragmatic conventions of linguistic usage for two languages differ, this *may* entail differences in the interpretation of indexical elements, and hence, the meanings of utterances (Silverstein 1976, 1979).

The work of Gumperz (1982, 1993) since 1980 or so has been an attempt to articulate this type of linguistic relativity. The basis of his idea is the concept of a "contextualization cue," a particular type of indexical, which in combination with other cues and structural features of the utterance leads to a particular interpretation of the utterance in the given context. Examples of particular contextualization cues might be high-falling pitch, as in $\hat{I}$, *didn't do it*, pauses, low volume, etc. Contextualization cues will differ according to the conventions for language usage, leading to relativities in the interpretation of utterances. Even if speakers speak prima facie the same language, the rules for its usage may differ according to age, gender, ethnicity, class, etc., predisposing each to differing interpretations of utterances. Gumperz (1993) presents a case study of how differences in the usage and understanding of contextualization cues between a native speaker of British English and a fluent English speaker of Indian background combine with differing cultural expectations to cause a serious breakdown in understanding between the interlocutors. For example, the speaker of Indian English foregrounds constituents by speaking with high pitch or loudness over the entire constituent, while the British English speakers do so with only a syllable receiving high-falling pitch. This causes confusion in the information structure for the interlocutors: what is important to the speaker? Further, the British English speaker sees the social encounter as an interview to screen qualifications or establish rights, in keeping with her individualist view of personhood, while the Indian English speaker, true to a sociocentric conception of personhood, views the interaction more as a petition to someone who is *in a position* to grant his request.

These differences in interpretation can accumulate in a conversation, ultimately leading to a breakdown in communication, as eventuated in the interaction mentioned above. Gumperz (1993) claims that the knowledge of contextualization cues is distributed unevenly across a culture reflecting the density of networks of social relationships. The speaker of Indian English in the above example, although a fluent English speaker, has not mastered the contextualization cues proper to British English because his ethnicity denies him full immersion in the middle-class white culture in which these cues are culturally transmitted. Gumperz emphasizes that economic and political forces are barriers to the easy transmission of the knowledge of contextualization cues, as with other types of cultural knowledge, and, further, that linguistic relativity of the type exemplified here is in fact an outgrowth of complex social stratification and its associated differences in language uses (see chapter 16).

In many ways Gumperz's position reiterates that of Gergen (1990): effective meaning is created in the mutual coordination of action among social actors. Gumperz's work tries to uncover the linguistic barriers to this effective coordination (for a summary of such work, see Scollon and Scollon (1995)). Remember that Gergen (1990:585) too emphasizes speech as the primary way in which this coordination is achieved (see also Maturana and Varela's (1987) notion of linguallaxis). As all societies, no matter how simple and egalitarian, contain people of obvious differences, even if only in age and sex, the patterns of mutual coordination among social actors, which define social relationships, will also necessarily differ somewhat across the society: that the way a typical American male interacts with other males is different from the way he interacts with females is clear for all to see. Because speech is the primary way that mutual coordination with others is achieved, we would therefore expect to find linguistic differences correlated to social ones, along the lines of sex, status, ethnicity, age, etc. This is indeed the case, and such differences will occupy us for most of the remaining chapters of this Part.

Summary

The understanding we have of ourselves and others as persons is largely constructed through the diverse linguistic practices we engage in. Through social couplings sustained by ongoing linguistic practices we enact and construct the terms in which the concept of person is conceived, the local ideology. These terms are not everywhere the same; a basic dichotomy of local beliefs about personhood is between egocentric, which emphasizes the individual and her autonomous rights and perogatives of action, and sociocentric, which highlights the embeddedness of the individual in the wider social collective and ascribes value to her in terms of her position in this collective. This contrast in local ideologies of personhood is clearly enacted in the linguistic practices of different cultures. The concept of face has been proposed as a useful concept to understand human social interaction, the goal of which is to enhance or at least minimize loss to the sense of face. Face has been divided into two types: positive, one's self-esteem, and negative, freedom from imposition or constraint. Diverse linguistic practices, combined under the rubric of politeness, are employed to minimize threats to both types, but it has been claimed that this analysis is at least partly ethnocentric; in sociocentric societies like Japan, the concept of negative face, individual autonomy of action, is marginal. Other proposed crosscultural principles of linguistic interaction, like the Cooperative Principle, the idea that people will say appropriate things at each point in an interaction, and its associated four Maxims of Conversation, are subject to significant variation. While clearly important in constructing meaningful conversations in American or Australian English, their importance and function is much less obvious in others, for example Malagasy society, which contrarily emphasize indirectness and vagueness. Similarly in individualist societies, the meaning of an utterance is usually taken to be what the speaker intends, but in sociocentric ones, meaning is constructed by participants and often reflects the contributions of varying participants depending on their social position. All these different conventions for linguistic practices across cultures suggest that actually different meanings are exchanged in these communities, another type of linguistic relativity, and that access to these meanings will be differentially distributed according to social positions.

Further Reading

Person and self are currently hot topics in anthropology and the literature is voluminous, but see Carrithers, Collins and Lukes (1985), Cohen (1994), Geertz (1973, 1983), Gergen and Davis (1985), Myers (1986), Poole (1994), Rosaldo (1980a), Rosenberger (1992), Shweder (1991), and Taylor (1989). Brown and Levinson (1987) present their theory of face work and politeness, based on earlier work by Goffman (1956, 1967, 1971) and Grice (1975, 1989). Matsumoto (1988) is a Japanese-inspired criticism of Brown and Levinson's proposals. Gumperz's path-breaking approach is summarized in Gumperz (1982).

15

Language and Gender

The Cultural Construction of Gender

The sexual contrast in physique between male and female is an obvious one in all human societies; it is a biological given. (Or is it? For serious doubts over such a bald, perhaps Eurocentric statement, see Errington (1990), Foucault (1984), Moore (1988, 1994), and Yanagisako and Collier (1987); perhaps even the "biological given" of physical sex is a cultural construction.) But what is made of this difference culturally, what significances are ascribed to it, is anything but an obvious given; indeed, if sex is a biological fact, then gender is a cultural construction. This contrast in sex typically provides a powerful basis for constructing opposing cultural categories of masculine versus feminine, but the content of these categories is not permanently set, but rather is constructed in an ongoing fashion through the daily practices of social interaction. In line with the above discussion, the notions of gender daily inform cultural behavior in the understandings we bring to social relationships and in turn are constructed by our practices in these relationships; in short, our habitus is engendered.

Although the categories of gender are culturally constructed and hence their content is variable across cultures, one aspect of this opposition which does seem extremely widespread, if not universal (as claimed, for example, in Rosaldo (1974, 1980b)) is the fact of the greater status or prestige granted to the masculine. Rosaldo (1974, 1980b) labels this as the universal fact of male dominance across cultures and describes it as follows (Rosaldo 1980b:394):

> a collection of related facts which seem to argue that in all known human groups – and no matter the prerogatives that women may in fact enjoy – the vast majority of opportunities for public influence and prestige, the ability to forge relationships, determine enmities, speak up in public, use or forswear the use of force are all recognized as men's privilege and right.

This thesis of the "*universal* asymmetry in cultural evaluation of the sexes" (Rosaldo 1974:17) has not gone unchallenged (see Errington and Gewertz 1987; Leacock 1978; Moore 1988; Sacks 1979; Sherzer 1987), but, regardless of its universal status, such an asymmetry between the sexes is indeed very widespread. The question is: why should this be? Rosaldo (1974) argues that the basic delegation to women of childbearing and early rearing has resulted in a fundamental separation in all societies between a domestic, home sphere of influence and a public realm. Because of women's childbearing and rearing responsibilities, their roles are foregrounded in the domestic sphere of influence, but because men are to a large extent free of these responsibilities, especially in the early years of child rearing, they have a much wider scope to engage in the public realm, engaging in social interactions that forge political alliances, economic ties, religious sects, etc. But why should this lead to such a widespread asymmetric evaluation of these two realms, with those of women typically viewed as inferior, and why would this be found in otherwise egalitarian hunter-gatherer societies? It is well known that in most such societies it is the women, constrained by child rearing responsibilities, that provide the great bulk of food through gathering. But the men, who are free of these responsibilities, are able to engage in the potentially more risky activity of hunting, which in turn results in the more higher valued food, meat. Young men typically use this valued food, as well as other labor, to solicit the favor of older men in competing for their daughters as wives or lovers. The younger men's labor and especially the meat they provide is a medium of exchange in marital politics, but the vegetable food gathered by women, in spite of it usually providing the bulk of the diet, lacks such a high valuation and plays no role in such politics. Women, then, are effectively excluded from the politics of marital exchanges, and, because these typically form the basis of wider political and economic relations in these small-scale societies, from the public realm generally. And it is through these relations in the public realm that the power to control and distribute resources in the society is determined; hence the positive evaluation of the public realm over the domestic (although a question which really needs to be asked here is whether the judgment is an effect of our own local Western ideology; is the public realm really evaluated as being more prestigious than the domestic in all cultures?).

Chodorow (1974) adds another important plank to this argument about the universal asymmetry of the sexes through a developmental perspective. As noted above it is women in their domestic sphere of responsibilities who raise children of both sexes. A girl has a clear role model present to follow; femininity seems to be acquired through this model in a relatively easy and straightforward manner. The domestic sphere in which she is reared provides the little girl with a clear model of what her lifetime responsibilities and privileges will be like. Not so for the little boy. He must *learn* to be a man. The characteristic public male activities of hunting, political debate, farming, etc. are largely unavailable to him as he grows up in the household. He finds he must sever these household ties and establish his maleness as separate from them. Hence, little boys seek play outside the household with other boys and jostle for position within these groups in order to establish their identity. Because characteristic adult male activities are largely unavailable, boys typically know of masculinity only as abstract rights and duties and therefore see their identity in terms of the formal roles that these entail. Male childhood play typically concerns games in which boys compete for the prestige associated with these imagined formal roles (i.e. competition who will be the doctor and who will be the patient in familiar childhood games). The developmental differences discussed by Chodorow (1974) reinforce the sociological ones highlighted by Rosaldo (1974, 1980b): women are from birth channelled to a domestic sphere of influence, but men are almost compelled to jockey for prestige in the political games of the public realm, and consequently, power.

Rosaldo and Chodorow's interpretation are not supported by all scholars in this field. Some (e.g. Leacock 1978; Sherzer 1987) wish to argue that in some cultures the categories of masculine and feminine are complementary: separate, but equal. Errington and Gewertz (1987) is an especially sophisticated statement of this view. They argue that in societies like our own modern industrialized societies, in which immersion in the domestic sphere of influence entails exclusion from the public domain of paid work, separate can never mean equal. For in such societies it is work which confers status, prestige and interest, and, most importantly in these highly individualized societies, money, which confers independence and the power to appropriate resources. To the extent that commitment to the domestic sphere involves limited access to this highly valued public realm of work, women are both separate and unequal. However, Errington and Gewertz argue that this does not apply to the Chambri, a sedentary hunter-gatherer group of New Guinea. In this sociocentric culture, in which a person is defined by her social and kin position in the village, one's value is not determined individually, through a job or the patterns of personal consumption it permits. Rather, one's worth is directly linked to the network of one's social connections, in Chambri terms, largely the kinship categories one has with others. The positional identities of Chambri men and women within the society are completely different and not in competition. The strategies that Chambri men and women use to validate their sense of worth in their social position, generally through manipulation of kinship links, are also exclusive of each other: women through having babies and thus forging new kinship links and men in patriclans competing politically over power, secular and spiritual. Men do not dominate women in Chambri society, according to Errington and Gewertz, because they do not deprive them of the ability to make and enact decisions validating their socially defined self-worth. Chambri men and women are by and large able to allow each other to pursue their separate strategies to validate self-worth; separate, but equal.

Whether this interpretation of the Chambri case is in fact warranted is at least debatable. Scholars sympathetic to Rosaldo and Chodorow's position would point to the fact of women's exclusion from most ritual life, sacred lore, and political debating as evidence of their secondary status within Chambri society, although the degree of economic independence enjoyed by Chambri women is certainly remarkable when compared with that of their Western sisters. Perhaps a safe conclusion to be drawn from this is that while male public activities do attract a more prestigious evaluation in all societies, this does not necessarily entail a devaluation of women's activities.

Gender Differences in Linguistic Practices: Three Cultures

The ideology of gender categories is typically enacted in linguistic practices; indeed, it is through language that the individual cultural understandings of gender categories are learned (see chapter 17 and Ochs 1990) and the coordination of gender roles achieved. Commonly, highly valued styles of speaking are associated with men's activities in the public realm, and this skill is ideologically denied to women. A good example of this is Malagasy speech norms. As mentioned earlier in chapter 14, the Malagasy value indirectness in their speech, and this norm is most clearly articulated in the public ceremonial *kabary* speech, which only men are expected to cultivate. *Kabary* are ritualized dialogs between two men, which frequently involve mutual criticism, but, as direct confrontation is strongly negatively valued in this culture, the criticism is couched in very indirect terms, using proverbs, allusions, and innuendo. Further, before criticism begins, the speaker typically comments positively on his rival's talk, setting the stage for his own comments, as in this example (Keenan 1974:129):

Thank you very much, sir. The first part of your talk has already been received in peace and happiness. I am in accordance and agreement with you on this, sir. You were given permission to speak and what you said gave me courage and strength. You said things skillfully but not pretentiously. You originate words but also recognize what is traditional. But as for myself I am not an originator of words at all but a borrower. I am more comfortable carrying the spade and basket. You, on the other hand, have smoothed out all faults in the speech; you have woven the holes together. You have shown respect to the elders and respect to the young as well. This is finished. But . . . [criticism begins].

Kabary speech is associated most prominently with public male activities and is very highly valued culturally, conferring high status on those who use it with great skill.

Malagasy women are not permitted to engage in *kabary* displays. They are thus barred from garnering prestige through skillful use of this highly valued speech style. Further, women are expected, indeed, in some circumstances, encouraged to violate the norm of indirectness, which is generally the hallmark of high status speech. Thus, their direct style of speaking identifies Malagasy women as being of secondary status and in fact is partly what constitutes them as such. Women perform all sorts of verbal activities which Malagasy cultural ideology negatively evaluate: berating others in public, expressing anger, arguing, haggling at the market. Men often find this directness a useful trait to exploit; when a man experiences a public injury to himself or his property, it will likely be his wife who makes accusations for him in public. Because of their latitude in speaking directly, it is they who sell produce in the market and buy necessities there. Ferocious haggling is often required in this situation, one for which the female norms of directness are much more suited than the male ones of indirectness. In the markets, men typically sell things that have fixed prices, like meat, abrogating the need for haggling. It is important to note that regardless of the useful ends that women's norms for speaking serve, their direct style of speech is devalued by both sexes. Thus, the respective linguistic behaviors of the two sexes is assigned differential prestige: the indirect male style, prototypically exemplified by the *kabary* language of male public encounters, is status bearing, but the everyday direct style (should we call it *domestic* language?) is not. Through these linguistic differences and ascribed status, cultural concepts of gender are constructed and transmitted.

For a related but somewhat different case, consider gender differences in speech in Javanese (Smith-Hefner 1988). Javanese is a language with an extremely developed system of speech styles reflecting politeness and relative status of speaker and addressee, as well as that of the topic under discussion (more fully discussed in chapter 16). As expected, Javanese society is highly stratified along caste or class lines, but status distinctions along gender lines are not strongly in evidence. In fact, ethnographic studies emphasize the relatively high status of women in Javanese society (Keeler 1990). Javanese women are free to work in the rice fields, markets, or business. They do the shopping and bargaining and generally deal with money matters. They interact freely with men, have wide economic independence and participate extensively in religious, political, and social life. Since Indonesian independence in 1949, boys and girls have been equally educated.

When we turn to linguistic practices, however, significant differences emerge between men and women's speech. Both sexes use the system of speech styles for politeness, but not in identical fashions. Within the family, wives typically use a more polite form of speech to their husbands than their husbands do to them, reflecting and declaring a somewhat higher status of the man. For example, she may call him *mas* "elder brother," but he will call her by her first name, a nickname or *dhik* "younger sibling," this difference in seniority emblematic of a difference in status.

Outside of the domestic sphere, there are even more significant differences in linguistic usage between the sexes. While both may use the highly deferential polite speech styles, men use them with greater art and to more effect. In a pattern highly reminiscent of the previous Malagasy case, to which, of course, Javanese culture is historically related, Javanese women have a local reputation of being more talkative than men and doing so with less skill. They are said to speak off the top of their heads without reflection; this often results in a less appropriate or even incorrect choice of linguistic form. Typically, this involves using a polite form which is too polite, leading to embarrassment on the part of the addressee, as it exalts them beyond what they feel is proper (humility, as we shall see, is positively valued in Javanese culture). Javanese men, again in common with their Malagasy brothers, are much more circumspect and controlled in their use of speech. They are more taciturn than women, and this increases with age. They are highly preoccupied with status distinctions and sensitively attuned to the proper use of polite speech styles. The artistic use of polite speech forms signals one's refinement and status. The proper use of these styles requires a fine attunement to the relative status of oneself and one's addressee. As humility is positively evaluated culturally, so actually higher status men may creatively use polite forms to their lower status addressees, but in so doing, subtly convey their great skill in the use of the extremely complex system of these forms and, hence, their superiority. He may express deference, but actually hint at social superiority. As Javanese grow older, they may become increasingly engaged in these subtle games of linguistic etiquette to enhance their status.

The linguistic differences in the use of polite speech forms of Javanese men and women reflect their differential engagement in the domestic and public realms of life. While possessing a strong local ideology of relative equality between the sexes, Javanese society is nonetheless highly stratified. This stratification is most prominently played out in the public political realm, and men excel in this realm through the artful use of polite speech form to enhance their status. Women, on the other hand, are focused on the home and the economic chores associated with its well being. The use of polite forms intrude a bit on this sphere, but not in any way parallel to their importance in the public male status arena. This is also reflected in women's less overall skill in using the polite speech styles. Again, the different cultural understandings of the two gender categories is articulated in and constructed through language.

A final case is provided by the Kuna, a group of Native Amerindians in Panama. Sherzer (1987) describes Kuna society as basically egalitarian, both in its sociopolitical structure and its gender relations. Positions of leadership may, theoretically at least, be occupied by either men or women. The Kuna view the gender categories of masculine and feminine as complementary; separate, but equal. Men hunt and farm; women perform domestic chores. Economically, women have significant independence in that they produced the appliqued cloth blouses for which the Kuna are noted and sell these in markets as a source of cash for themselves and their families.

This complementarity in sociopolitical roles is carried over, according to Sherzer, into the types of linguistic behavior associated with each sex. Each has a characteristic set of speech genres, associated with both public and domestic contexts. Each genre has specific linguistic features. Public speech genres for men include political oratory and ritual incantations, especially curing chants. Political meetings commonly consist of debates among village leaders and ritualized chanting by chiefs; these speech genres are performed by men, because it is men who typically fill these roles. Public speech genres for women also include political speeches and debates, this time in the cooperatives for the marketing of their appliqued cloth blouses, and ritual chants. But the most important speech genres for women are those of the domestic sphere: lullabies and ritual wailing for dying and deceased relatives. Very significantly, however, Sherzer reports no speech genres distinctive to men for the domestic sphere, a fact no doubt which must buttress Rosaldo's (1974) claims. Kuna do not positively evaluate the speech of either men or women more highly; skilled speakers of either sex are equally lauded. Further, both men and women are equally loquacious and state their views directly and confidently. Thus, according to Sherzer's description, the egalitarian, but complementary ethos of gender roles in Kuna society generally finds expression in linguistic behavior. Styles appropriate to the public political domain of men are equally available to women, although the genres might differ (note that, however, this does not apply the other way around: the domestic styles of women are not taken up by men). As men and women perform complementary economic and social roles in Kuna society, their characteristic speech genres are also complementary: separate, but equal.

What do the patterns of language usage and gender in these three societies have to tell us about Rosaldo's (1974, 1980b) claim about the universal fact of male dominance, "the universal asymmetry of cultural evaluation of the sexes" in favor of the male and his public realm over the female and her domestic sphere. Malagasy and Kuna society are basically egalitarian, while Javanese is highly stratified: Malagasy and Javanese societies have highly salient differences in linguistic behavior between the sexes, while Kuna does not. But, nonetheless, the evidence from all three societies suggests that male dominance is expressed and constructed through language. Eckert and McConnell-Ginet (1992:483) see dominance as being "sustained by privileging in community practice a particular perspective on language, obscuring its status as one among many perspectives, and naturalizing it as 'neutral' or 'unmarked.'" How language sustains male dominance in both Malagasy and Javanese society is clear, for the indirect norms of Malagasy males are canonized as "properly" speaking Malagasy, rather than just one way, and the obsessive concern of Javanese males with the artful use of polite speech to enhance status becomes the avowed aim of all in speaking Javanese "well" (Smith-Hefner 1988). The Kuna case is more subtle and potentially misleading. Note that men and women equally participate in characteristic speech genres for their sex in the public realm, but only women have distinctive domestic speech genres. The public realm is ungendered, available to persons of either sex, but the domestic sphere is stamped linguistically to be engendered as feminine, the domain of women. Masculine is, thus, the unmarked gender; feminine, the marked. The masculine is the unmarked perspective and thereby a privileged one, while the feminine with its specific domestic responsibilities (and speech genres) in Kuna society is a less privileged one. Thus, while Kuna society is much more egalitarian in its engendered speech norms than Malagasy or Javanese, there is nonetheless a weak form of male dominance.

Male Linguistic Dominance in American English

These case studies now lead us to ask how is male dominance in the norms for speaking reproduced in modern Western societies? A number of studies of cross-sex conversational interactions in American English indicate that generally men do indeed assume a more dominant role; in McConnell-Ginet's (1988:98) words, conversation turns out not to be "an equal-opportunity activity." For example, the usual stereotype is that women talk more than men in this culture, but actual quantitative studies show the opposite to be the case. Swacker (1975) asked cross-sex dyads of college students to describe some pictures as thoroughly as they liked with no time constraints on their statements. The mean time in this task for males was 12.0 minutes, while it was only 3.17 for females (the males out-talked the females by a ratio of 4 to 1!). Edelsky (1981) observed conversations in university faculty meetings and again discovered that the speaking turns of the men ranged between 25 percent and 400 percent longer than those of the women. Further, the more formal the topic, the greater the difference.

Interruption between interlocutors in cross-sex conversation is one area that has attracted a great deal of study. Zimmerman and West (1975) recorded cross-sex conversations in different public places between acquaintances.

They tallied the number of interruptions, which they defined as "an incursion into the current speaker's talk prior to the last lexical constituent that could define a possible terminal boundary" (Zimmerman and West 1975:114), contrasting this crucially with *overlaps*, "simultaneous speech where a speaker other than the current speaker begins to speak at or very close to a possible transition place in a current speaker's utterance (i.e. within the boundaries of the last word)" (Zimmerman and West 1975:114). Zimmerman and West viewed overlaps as mistakes in timing to the next speaker's turn, but interruptions as deliberate challenges to the speaker's right to hold the floor. They found a strong difference in patterns of interruptions and overlaps in the same-sex versus cross-sex dyads. In same-sex conversations, overlaps and interruptions were about evenly distributed between the two speakers, regardless of the sex of the dyad, but in cross-sex dyads men produced 96 percent of the interruptions to the women's 4 percent and also 100 percent of the overlaps! Further in same-sex dyads most of the breaks into talk were overlaps (22 overlaps as opposed to 7 interruptions), while in cross-sex dyads they were interruptions (48 interruptions as opposed to 7 overlaps), with all but 2 of these interruptions coming from men. Zimmerman and West's work demonstrates a clear asymmetry in speakers' rights to hold the floor in conversations; men are far more likely to usurp women's rights than the other way around. By the sheer control they exercise in the development of a conversation, male domination must be seen as basic to conversational norms in American society.

Most significantly, the greater conversational power of males emerges even in contexts in which the female conversation partner has stronger claims to higher status and power in a wider domain, demonstrating that this is indeed an asymmetry in engendered norms for speaking, inculcated tacitly in the habitus. Woods (1988) recorded triadic conversations in work settings, involving both male and female supervisors and subordinates. She found that gender was the most significant factor determining speech behavior, more important than status. With respect to patterns of interruption, higher status people were more likely to interrupt successfully (i.e. gain the floor, switch the topic, etc.) than lower status conversational partners, but men of lower status were still usually successful in interrupting a higher status female speaker. For example, a subordinate male was successful in interrupting nine times and only unsuccessful once, while his female supervisor successfully interrupted six times and was unsuccessful three times. When status and masculine gender go together, the dominance of men in these conversations is pronounced indeed: a male supervisor interrupted successfully four times and never unsuccessfully, while his female subordinate interrupted successfully once and unsuccessfully four times. Not surprisingly, a male subordinate to this woman still fared better than she did in this interaction; he interrupted successfully four times and only twice unsuccessfully. Woods' data again demonstrate male dominance in conversational interaction: men hold and snatch the floor more successfully than women, regardless of their relative status.

The conclusion of this work on gender asymmetries in the control of conversational interactions through interruptions has recently been challenged (James and Clarke 1993; James and Drakich 1993; Tannen 1989, 1990). One argument assumes the "two cultures" model of engendered speech styles to be discussed below, but the basic point is that it is difficult to distinguish true interruptions, bidding for the floor, from statements trying to support the speaker's turn and her contribution to the conversation. In other words, what counts as an interruption is really a matter of an analyst's interpretation of the interactions, requiring a great deal of background knowledge about the interlocutors. Given this background, could we view the interruption as a reinforcement of what is being said or as a bid for control of the floor? Such questions also imply there may be great difficulty in imposing a sharp methodological distinction in the functions of overlaps and interruptions, especially across different types of conversational contexts. For example, Edelsky (1981), the study of speech in university faculty meetings discussed earlier, found that if the one speaker at a time rule, which usually applies in formal meetings, was relaxed, women spoke just as much as men, using overlapping to reinforce the contributions of others. Finally, the view of interruptions as a bid to control the floor may not be a universally correct interpretation of its function, even in white middle-class American society. Tannen (1990) argues that speakers from different sub-cultures may have "high-involvement" styles of speaking, which display short pauses, fast pacing, and what are read as interruptions, but these are often used to reinforce the speaker's point, rather than contradict him or snatch the floor. Interruptions in such sub-cultures are not necessarily claims to dominance, but rather assertions of interest and solidarity.

Indeed, quite the opposite, the refusal to speak very much at all, can often be an effective claim to dominance. Pamela Fishman (1983) tape-recorded many hours of conversations between the husband and wife of three white middle-class graduate student couples. In interpreting her material she hit upon the idea of *conversational work*: a conversation is produced by the active participation of at least two participants, paying attention and responding to the remarks of the other. The conversation is successfully maintained as long as this goes on; failure to do so subverts the conversation. Fishman's work revealed a number of strategies to initiate, maintain, or subvert conversation. Maintenance strategies include: (1) attention getters, like *this is interesting*, which attempt to legitimize interest in the following topic; (2) questions, which set up a required answer, thereby insuring some response from their interlocutor; and (3) ritualized rhetorical questions, like *do you know what?*, which requires a further question *what?* in response, and then an answer, setting in train the development of a topic. Fishman found that all three strategies were used overwhelmingly more frequently by women than men: attention getters twice as often, asking questions two-and-a-half times more frequently, and ritualized rhetorical questions again twice as often. Fishman claimed that this asymmetry demonstrates that women shoulder much more of the burden than men in conversational work. Indeed, she argues further that women actually aid men in developing their topics in conversation, especially through the strategy of asking questions, but also through generally encouraging responses. Men, by contrast, often behave in quite the opposite fashion, commonly providing minimal responses like *hmm* or *yeah* following the woman's speaking turn. These act to discourage the woman in her development of the topic, displaying little interest and no explicit picking up of the woman's topic, so that her contribution to the conversation quickly fades out. In this case male dominance of the conversation, in determining where it will and will not go, is realized through asymmetrical speech norms typified by the male's lack of speech, rather than his hogging the floor.

The "Two Cultures" Model

What could be the source of these strikingly asymmetrical norms for speaking between men and women? Remember the theories of Chodorow (1974) discussed above. Unlike girls, who have clear role models in their mother and the other women of the domestic sphere, boys have to learn how to be men. He must sever his ties with the feminine sphere of the home and establish his identity in the world outside, jostling with other boys for position and status to establish their claims of masculine identity. Male childhood play consists of games in which players compete for status-bearing roles. The play of girls, on the other hand, tends to model the cooperative connections among women in the household. Chodorow's ideas have found their way into work on language and gender in what is sometimes called the "two cultures" model (Maltz and Borker 1982; Tannen 1990). This model argues that men and women inhabit two different cultural worlds as far as the understandings they bring to conversational interactions; men see conversations as status contests in which they can be one up or one down, while women see them as a means of forging interpersonal connections. These different views of the ends of conversation lead to communicative misunderstandings not too dissimilar to those highlighted by Gumperz (1993) in his work on crosscultural communication, hence the name, "two cultures" model.

Maltz and Borker (1982) trace these differences to the styles boys and girls develop in childhood during play. Boys typically play in larger groups than girls and these groups are structured hierarchically according to status. Status is relative and ever changing so the main point of boys' play interactions is to manipulate their peers to enhance their status. In these competitive attempts to enhance status, speech has three roles: (1) to assert one's dominance, (2) to attract and hold an audience, and (3) to assert oneself when others have the floor. The styles of speech used will reflect these functions: orders, threats, and ridicule (asserting one's dominance), boasting or other types of display of verbal skills (attracting and holding an audience), and refusals to listen to others or interruptions of their turns (asserting oneself when others have the floor). The world of girls is utterly different. Their play groups are smaller, often just pairs, and their games are cooperative and organized in non-competitive ways. Differentiation among girls is not established in terms of status differentials of power, but in terms of relative closeness. Friendship is construed in terms of intimacy, commitment, and loyalty. The goal of interaction is to reinforce these feelings of connection. To put it baldly and oversimplistically in terms of Brown and Levinson's (1987) theory, boys are more focused on their negative face, in that status gives them independence and freedom to act, including coercing others to act as they want (i.e. power), while girls are more concerned with positive face, the positive evaluation they give each other through mutual closeness. Of course, conflict necessarily arises sometimes in all human groups, even those exclusively of girls. Boys typically resolve conflict through displays of dominance, often involving physical force, but in the more egalitarian cooperative groups of girls this option is not easily available. Girls must learn to use interactive strategies which attend to the positive face needs of the other, but at the same time effectively criticize them for their behavior. Girls, then, are necessarily more "polite" than boys. Speech for girls must serve both these ends: (1) to create and maintain relationships of equality and closeness and (2) to criticize others effectively without rupturing a desired relationship. Their typical styles of speech will emphasize hortatives rather than commands and exhibit a high proportion of modal constructions and emotional terms (marking close, equal relationships), and be relatively polite and indirect (acceptable criticism).

Goodwin (1980) is a study of play activities among black children in an urban neighborhood of Philadelphia that is often cited as confirming Maltz and Borker's proposal. In a task of making slingshots in preparation for a fight, the boys consistently gave each other orders, often in a bald form: *Gimme the pliers!*; *Man, don't come in here where I am!*; *Get off my steps.* Or they refused to perform as directed, posing a direct challenge to the status of the person who ordered them: *No. I'm not going in there. I don't feel like it; I'm not getting "out" of nowhere.* Or they ridiculed the person who gave the order: *You shut up you big lips.* The whole point of the verbal

interchanges in these tasks is to negotiate for relative status: each boy post-
ures, challenges, and counterchallenges until a hierarchy for this activity is
settled. Of course, hierarchies in boys' groups are fluid; what emerged in
this task may have been quite different in another task domain. The girls
studied engaged in a task of making glass rings out of bottle necks. Instead
of commands, the girls typically used hortatives or modalized expressions:
Let's go around Subs and Suds: come on; *Let's go find some*; *Maybe we can slice
them like that*; *We gonna paint em and stuff.* Also, rather than refusing the
suggestions of others, the girls typically agreed to them: *Hey, let's go in there
and ask do they have some cases*; *Yep Okay? Yep let's go and ask them.*
Further, if a conflict emerged, rather than regarding it as a challenge to
status, girls typically reacted with requests for further information (Goodwin 1980:169):

> (on reaching a city creek)
> *Pam*:   Y'll gonna walk in it?
> *Nettie*: Walk in it, You know where that water come from? The toilet.
> *Pam*:   So I'm a walk in it in my dirty feet. I'm a walk in it and I don't
>   care if it do come.
> *Nettie (overlaps)*: You could easy wash your feet *(to investigator)*. Gonna
>   walk us across? Yeah. I'll show y'all where you can come.

Note that at the end of this interaction each of the participants has given a
directive and countered the other's action; neither is one up or one down,
as would be the typical end goal of an equivalent conversation involving
point scoring.

  Tannen (1990) elaborates Maltz and Borker's proposal, developing a full
model of male and female conversational practice along the lines of the "two
cultures" model. She interprets the various findings of research in language
and gender, such as the above asymmetries in interruptions and conversational maintenance, in the light of this model. She argues that women
emphasize connection and intimacy with others and use language to establish and maintain these connections. They avoid direct confrontation and
use language to suggest actions, rather than ordering them, hence what is
commonly noted as the greater politeness of women, both positive and negative. Males, on the other hand, continue the status games learned in boy-
hood into adulthood. Language is a weapon for asserting themselves and
their status and power. It is a major arena in which men can compete with
each other for the much desired one-up position. They use language to
display their power and skills and to defend themselves from the kind of
verbal attacks they typically launch on others' claims to status and power.
In short, the type of status games that Javanese men engage in with the
artful use of the system of speech levels is just one exemplar of a much

more pervasive male perspective on language. If, for women, language is the means to forge connection, for men, it is the way to establish position, and ultimately, power.

The "two cultures" model is not without its critics. Some argue that it greatly exaggerates the real differences in the engendered norms for speaking. Indeed, in one of the very studies commonly cited to support the "two cultures" model discussed above (Goodwin 1980; 1991), the author actually argues against such an interpretation of her findings. She claims that girls are just as skillful in countering the status claims of others as boys, rather they simply choose to use these resources less frequently. But if need be, girls can maintain their position just as effectively as boys (and probably, if restricted to just verbal means, more effectively than boys). The "two cultures" model's emphasis on the separateness of the two cultures as learned in childhood does not square with these findings, nor does it really account very well for the great deal of clear and understood communication that does occur across the sexual divide. After all, men and women do spend a great deal of their time together and often *do* communicate effectively, interpreting the other's utterances in the way they intended (or sometimes deliberately in a way they did not intend, due to an understanding of the other's speech norms, as when a man correctly interprets a woman's indirect wh-imperative like *why don't you leave your shoes outside* as a command, but feels he can safely choose to ignore it since it is cast in the form of a question. He would be unlikely to do so if a male buddy said *leave your shoes on the doorstep*). The "two-culture" model claims that misunderstandings arise when shared norms for speaking between the sexes are mistakenly assumed. But a close look at the ethnographic and sociological literature demonstrates that much more typically some differences in the engendered norms are in fact taken for granted (see Malagasy and our own folk culture beliefs about "speaking like a lady" and the above wh-imperative example). Finally, the nature of the separation of men and women is *not* equivalent to that between, say, Australian and Yimas culture; but the "two cultures" model has not come to terms with this.

Gender Deixis

Another side to the relationship between gender and language might be called *gender deixis*, in which some actual linguistic elements are indexicals of some fact about gender, maybe that of the speaker or that of the addressee, or both. Such gender deixis is well attested in languages and has been so since at least the sixteenth century, during which the Spanish conquistodores commented that the Native inhabitants of the Caribbean islands had distinct languages for men and women. This was somewhat of an exaggeration; in actuality there were some differences in grammatical forms in the language depending on whether the speaker was male or female. Since this time, such differences indicative of gender deixis have been reported for many languages, especially the Native languages of North America (e.g. Bogoras 1922; Ekka 1972; Flannery 1946; Sapir 1949:206–12; Taylor 1982). I will consider here the case of Koasati, a Native language of the south-eastern United States, as described by Haas (1964). In this language the speech of men and women differ in certain verbal forms, so the choice of one set of forms as opposed to the other can be said to point directly to the speaker's sex. Here are some of the basic differences in the verb, summarized by Haas (1964:228) in three basic rules:

1   If the women's form ends in a nasalized vowel, the men's form substitutes an *s* for the nasalization:
    W   M
    lakawwą· lakawwá·s "he will lift it"
    ką·   ká·s   "he is saying"
2   If the women's form has final falling pitch and ends in a short vowel followed by *l*, the men's form substitutes high pitch and *s* for the *l*:
    W   M
    lakawwîl lakawwís "I am lifting it"
    molhîl molhís   "we are peeling it"
3   If the women's form has final falling pitch and ends in a short vowel followed by *n*, the men's form retains the falling pitch, but substitutes an *s* for the *n* and lengthens the preceding vowel:
    W   M
    lakawčîn lakawčî·s "don't lift it"
    tačilwân tačilwâ·s "don't sing"

Haas thus analyzes the women's forms as basic and the male speakers' forms as derived from them. This entails a claim that the historically older, conservative forms are those of the women, while the male forms have arisen by a series of phonological changes to these over time.

    Koasati exhibits gender deixis in which the forms involved specifically signal the gender of the speakers, regardless of the addressee. In other such cases, the male forms may be restricted to only the situation when the addressee(s) is exclusively male, with the female form used elsewhere (in Yana; Sapir 1949), or more complexly, as in Kūrux (Ekka 1972) in which the forms basically signal same-sex dyads, male to male and female to female, but the male forms are used with cross-sex dyads, except for the third-person singular in which a specific form exists for males speaking to females.

Gender Markers

Cases like Koasati, with specific language forms which signal gender deixis, are relatively rare across the world's languages. Much more common, indeed if not universal, is a pattern of *gender markers* (McConnell-Ginet 1988), in which particular linguistic features are commonly, if not prototypically, associated with one or the other of the sexes, but this association is *statistical*, not mandatory. Another way to conceive of the contrast between gender deictics and gender markers may be in terms of Silverstein's ideas concerning the "limits of awareness" (Silverstein 1981; see chapter 10). The indexical elements of gender deictics are commonly grammatical formatives or allomorphs of formatives, hence relatively segmental and presupposing of fixed contexts, i.e. gender of speaker and/or addressee. As such, the form and function of gender deictics are fairly amenable to explicit awareness and articulated explanation. Gender markers, on the other hand, are often not segmentable morphemes or allomorphs, but more importantly, they are not presupposing of fixed contextual backgrounds; rather it is their very usage which frames the meaning of context, as, for example, when my actual usage of Tok Pisin to a Papua New Guinean forges a contextual background of solidarity which may not exist if English were chosen as the language of communication. It is this relatively creative force of gender markers which renders their form and function comparatively opaque to explicit awareness and articulated explanation (see also Giddens (1984) on the contrast between discursive versus practical awareness, one closely parallel to Silverstein's). Gender markers are sociolinguistic variables of the type made famous in the work of Labov (1972b). Most of the research in English on the correlations between gender and linguistic forms has focused on gender as one of the parameters, such as class or ethnicity, governing the distribution of particular sociolinguistic variables. For example, one variable Labov investigated in his New York study was the variable realization of the initial consonant in words like *there*. Pronunciation in New York City varies from the standard [ð] to the substandard [d], (making *there* sound like *dare*). Horvath (1985), reanalyzing Labov's data, shows that a higher rate of standard [ð] pronunciation is associated with women than with men. For example, 100 percent of middle-class women used this [ð] pronunciation, as opposed to 69 percent of men, and 80 percent of lower- and working-class women do, as opposed to only 47 percent of lower- and working-class men. Clearly, then, a high rate of [ð] pronunciation is a gender marker for women in New York City English, especially middle-class women.

Peter Trudgill (1974) in his study of sociolinguistic variation in Norwich in England discovered a similar pattern. Considering the pronunciation of the final /ŋ/ in words ending with -*ing* (it is well known this varies from [ŋ]

15.1

| | Middle Class | | | Working Class | |
	Middle	Lower	Upper	Middle	Lower
male	4	27	81	91	100
female	0	3	68	81	97

to a more casual, "substandard" [n]), he found the distribution of the [n] pronunciation across the classes according to sex shown in 15.1 (Trudgill 1983:86). Note, again, that in all classes, women use the more standard [ŋ] pronunciation more frequently; indeed, among the middle-class women, the [n] pronunciation hardly seems to exist at all.

Women and Linguistic Conservatism

The findings from Koasati, New York City, and Norwich English all demonstrate women to be more conservative than men linguistically, sticking to speech forms less innovative than those of men. Because older, less innovative forms tend to be more prestigious and more "standard," women are typically described as speaking in more statusful styles than their male counterparts. Indeed, women seem to be at least subliminally aware of this tendency. In a brilliant study, Trudgill (1972) investigated the normative judgments men and women made toward their own speech. He considered a number of variables, and I will focus on the variable pronunciation of the final vowel in *ear, idea, here*, which varies from the standard pronunciation [Iə] to the local [ε·] (making *ear* homophonous with *air*, and *here*, with *hair*). Trudgill tape-recorded interviews and noted the actual distribution of pronunciations for each interviewee. He then asked each of them how they thought they pronounced these words, noting that some self-reports were accurate, some overestimated their use of the standard varieties (over-reporting) and some underestimated it (under-reporting). The results, which are very instructive are set out in 15.2 (Trudgill 1983:92). There is a marked gender asymmetry in the figures. Well over half the women (68 percent) claimed to be using the prestige standard pronunciation [Iə], when in fact they were *not*, but half of the men claimed to be using the local, less prestigious and more working-class variant [ε·], when, in fact, they were using the standard! What could be the cause of this asymmetry? Following Labov (1972a), Trudgill called the source of the male behavior, *covert prestige*, in that the speech forms typical of working-class speech have an appeal to middle-class men, associated, as it seems to be, with masculinity

15.2

	male	female
over-reporting	22%	68%
under-reporting	50%	11%
accurate	28%	18%

and toughness, reflecting clear articulations of gender understandings in British culture. If covert prestige is really operative in the speech of men, then we would expect male speech to be more innovative, to articulate claims of class and gender affiliation.

But what about the women? Why are they sticking to the more prestigious forms, indeed, over-reporting their use of them? The work of Milroy (1987a) points to an explanation. In her study of Ballymacarrett, a Belfast neighborhood, she found that men had a large network of social connections within the neighborhood, while women did not (remember Rosaldo's (1974) contrast of the male public realm versus the female domestic sphere). Men live their lives mostly in this neighborhood network and use the local linguistic features to signal this affiliation (covert prestige). Women, on the other hand, either stay within the home, a circumscribed domestic sphere, or work outside the immediate neighborhood. In order to claim connection with this wider world and to function effectively within it, prestige standard linguistic features are more valued.

That something like this explanation is necessary is shown by cases like that described by Gal (1978), in which women are the vanguard in language change, rather than the conservative custodians they are usually portrayed as. In a bilingual Hungarian–German speaking part of Austria, women are choosing to give up speaking Hungarian in favor of German, while their male compatriots are clinging to Hungarian. This reflects an ambit claim by women in favor of the wider industrial world in which German is spoken, with its greater possibilities for careers and life choices, especially as they increasingly choose German-speaking husbands from this world. Hungarian is the language associated with the farming life of the local community. Most of the young men in the community are still selecting this farming life-style as their preferred life choice, so they maintain Hungarian as their primary language. In this case, women are the linguistic innovators, although in favor of the more prestigious language in terms of the wider world.

Similar findings are reported by Nichols (1980, 1983), concerning a transition, on a small island in rural south-eastern United States, from an English-based creole called Gullah to Standard American English. The original language of the island was Gullah, but as industrialization has come to the adjoining mainland, islanders have migrated out and have adjusted their speech accordingly. Women migrants have typically taken up service jobs, such as sales clerks or even professional jobs like teachers, while the men usually have jobs in the construction industry, often several islanders working together. The jobs held by the women clearly require some facility in varieties of spoken English close to standard, but this is not the case with those of the men. Not surprisingly, the women are switching from Gullah to Standard English much more quickly than the men. The island forms an interesting contrast with a nearby coastal community with far more limited employment opportunities, the men holding laboring jobs in plantations or unskilled factory work and the women at most domestic laborers or seasonal farm workers. The much more restricted access to the wider world for women in this community results in their being linguistically conservative, exhibiting a higher rate of creole English linguistic features in their speech than do men. The case is probably an analog of the Ballymacarrett one discussed above, but in this situation the linguistic norms conserved are substandard ones, rather than prestigious standard forms. Another similar case is that of Yimas village, in which younger males are rapidly switching to Tok Pisin, indicative of communication and action in the wider world, while the women continue to favor the local vernacular, with its local domestic connotations. Thus, women tend to be conservative linguistically when their worlds of action are circumscribed and restricted, especially to the domestic sphere, but to the extent that women may make a greater claim to a wider public world of action than men, their linguistic usage will be innovative. How this last point squares with Rosaldo's (1974) claims remains to be clarified.

Women and Politeness

Finally, one stereotype of women's speech is that it is more polite than men's. Studies at least since Lakoff (1975) have made this claim, but is it true? Lakoff (1975) mentions a number of linguistic features which she believes is associated with women's greater politeness. One of these is tag questions, in which the subject and verb of the preceding statement is repeated in a question of typically reversed polarity, such as *Bill took Luke to the party last night, didn't he?* or *Louise and Lucille didn't leave together last night, did they?* Lakoff claims that female speakers tend to make use of tag questions as a consequence of their reluctance to make direct assertions, to avoid potential conflicts with addressees, a type of negative politeness in Brown and Levinson's (1987) terms. Tag questions have come under intensive study since Lakoff, and most of this work contradicts her claim of a gender asymmetry in their use (Dubois and Crouch 1975). An especially interesting study was done by Holmes (1984). She argues first of all, that tag questions serve two types of functions: modal tags, which request information from an addressee or indicate that the addressee confirms the truth of a statement (*Luke and Bill went to the party, didn't they?*) and affective tags, which display the speaker's concern for the addressee (*You didn't go there, did you?*). Affective tags are themselves of two types: softeners, which mitigate a request or criticism (negative politeness) (*Wash the car for me, would you, son?*) and facilitative, which demonstrate the speaker's desire to continue the conversation (positive politeness) (*still at the same old job, are you?*). When tags are classified according to function, Holmes found a clear gender asymmetry in their usage, a large majority of male speakers' tag questions are modal (61 percent), but most of women's tag questions are affective (65 percent), especially facilitative (59 percent). This shows that men typically use tag questions to gain or confirm information, while women use them to develop and encourage conversation. Interpreted in a "two cultures" framework, it may be taken to mean that men use tag questions to get information that may be valuable in relative status competitions, while women use them to establish connections. What this would mean about the relative politeness of men's and women's speech is, however, not obvious, but for a very interesting study, see Brown (1980). Further, cases like Java demonstrate the difficulty of any direct link between gender and relative politeness, for in this society men are linguistically more polite than women, as men compete in the more artful use of the highly deferential polite speech levels to enhance their own status. A case like this poses new problems: is using highly polite linguistic forms to gain one up on one's addressee really being deferential and "polite"? Ultimately what is the relationship between linguistic reflexes of politeness and politeness in a wider sense? These are questions that demand answers before any real progress on the relationship between gender and politeness can be made.

Summary

Unlike sex, gender is a cultural construction, and part of this construction seems to be that women everywhere and their domestic sphere of influence are accorded inferior valuation as opposed to men and their world of public action. This differential evaluation finds articulation in the regard accorded to women's versus men's typical linguistic practices in many cultures: men's indirectness and taciturnity in Malagasy culture are the valued norms in speaking Malagasy, as opposed to women's directness and talkativeness. Similarly, men's artful use of high speech forms and honorifics is the "proper" way to speak Javanese. Patterns of dominance are also apparent in male and female patterns in speaking American English: men hold the floor longer than women, interrupt more frequently or even refuse to respond, all indications of greater male power in conversations. A recent model to explain these differences, the "two cultures" model, traces these asymmetries in speaking norms back to early socialization; girls in cooperative tasks, modelling the connections among women in the household, but boys in competitive games and sports, jostling for status and position, learning how to be men. From this early socialization, women look to verbal interactions as ways to forge connections, but men as a way of competing for status. The modelling is not without its critics, who argue that it greatly exaggerates the real differences in male and female norms. Gender deixis and gender markers are formal indexes in language of the gender assignments of speech act participants, such as special verbal forms for male or female speakers as in Koasati or particular formal features statistically favored by one sex or the other, e.g. higher uses of the [Iŋ] variant for female speakers of American English. The fact that women typically use more prestigious variants is often attributed to their greater linguistic conservatism, but this conservatism is really a fact about their social connections in the community, and in some cases this can result in their being the linguistic innovators.

Further Reading

The material on language and gender has grown enormously since the late 1970s. For basic anthropological thinking in this arena see Moore (1988, 1994), Strathern (1988) and the articles in Collier and Yanagisako (1987), Ortner and Whitehead (1981), and Rosaldo and Lamphere (1974). Excellent overview articles in the specific field of language and gender are Eckert and McConnell-Ginet (1992) and McConnell-Ginet (1988). Other materials in this area include Baron (1986), Cameron (1990, 1992), Coates (1993), Goodwin (1991), Philips, Steele and Tanz (1987), and Tannen (1990, 1993).

16

Language and Social Position

Social Inequality: Class, Power, and Prestige

For obvious reasons all human societies have a sex-based distinction among their members, a biological distinction typically elaborated, as we saw above, into culturally significant asymmetries of gender in various spheres of behavior, not the least of which being linguistic practices. There are two other biologically given attributes of individuals that are also obviously universal – age and kin relationship – which may also be culturally elaborated in societies of even the simplest social organization; I will return to this below. But those societies most familiar to us, such as the urban-based societies of Europe, the Americas, Asia, and Australasia are clearly much more complex than these. These are all societies exemplifying extensive *social stratification*, in which people are grouped into strata of higher or lower prestige and, often, concomitant power, power being the ability to realize one's wants and interests even against resistance. The criteria for assigning people to these various strata or classes vary; in our familiar Westernized societies it is primarily occupation and the amount and kind of property owned, but what is germane to our discussion here is that people typically behave in ways consonant with or viewed as appropriate to their class position, for example, in where they live (upmarket versus downmarket suburbs), how they play (polo versus soccer), how they dress (expensive Italian business suit versus overalls) and, most importantly for our purposes, how they talk (posh versus substandard). This complex system for classifying people is mainly a way of controlling access to "scarce goods," those things, not necessarily material, which are highly desired in the society, so that people seek these out and compete with each other to gain them. Besides obvious goodies, like houses, money, cars, these include more abstract, but probably even more highly sought after things like power and respect (positive face (Brown and Levinson 1987)). The class system, like cultural constructions of gender, positions people so that access to these scarce goods is either facilitated or hindered; people in higher classes possess more of these "scarce goods" and have greater ease in acquiring still more of them than people in lower classes. Put bluntly, the class system functions to reward those in the higher classes over the lower classes; from this, predictable conflicts of interest emerge between the various classes.

A person's class position is determined primarily by their economic power. We classify people by occupation and income, housing, educational level, etc. Ultimately, all these variables relate to their position in the economic system, their position in the production of wealth and its distribution, especially the distribution of property. Social classes, then, are aggregates of people who have similar overall positions in the economic system, i.e. they have roughly equivalent amounts of wealth and property at their disposal, and the effective means of power that this brings. In modern industrial societies the variables which most consistently indicate a person's social class position are occupation and educational level. The latter generally provides a professional apprenticeship for occupation, and one's occupation provides the main source of income for the great majority of us, which provides us with wealth and property. Further, one's history of education inculcates in one the proper behavior and demeanor, in short, the habitus, expected of one's class; hence, members of particular classes tend to behave differently according to their class positions, e.g. the dress styles of middle-class professionals like doctors and lawyers versus working-class laborers like garbage collectors or street sweepers. The inculcation of these attitudes and practices in the habitus through education and other processes of socialization (see chapter 17) confers on them a kind of naturalized status, an authority so that they seem to legitimate the way the world is meant to be. Of course, the range of acceptable practices in the lower ranked classes is constrained by the power of the upper ranked ones, and to the extent that these are read as natural and legitimate, the lower ranked classes could be said to be complicit in their domination by the elites (although there may be resistance to this reading by some dominated subgroups). This is Gramsci's (1971) notion of hegemony: domination of oppressed classes through their complicity in the system of cultural practices which dominate them, not through the use of naked force. The role of a standard language is a good example (see chapter 20). There is nothing about the standard variety of a language, say Standard American English, that makes it any better than any other variety, say Vernacular Black English. Yet people accept the standard variety as *standard*, that to be emulated, and thereby may denigrate their own varieties. Standard languages are hegemonic in exactly Gramsci's sense: people are complicit in devaluing their varieties of speech and accepting the legitimacy of the standard. It is no accident that Standard American English is the speech of the middle and upper classes in America, that the educational system labors tirelessly in its inculcation, and finally, that those who fail to acquire it are restricted to the lower classes, all the while in most cases accepting the prestige of the standard (resistance, however, is not unknown; note the high prestige Vernacular Black English has for inner city Blacks and see the discussion of covert prestige (Trudgill 1972)). Finally it is important to note that one's social behavior is determined at least as much by one's, and other's, beliefs about one's class position, as it is by any objective ranking (e.g. according to income) in the economic system. A number of skilled working-class jobs today, like plumbers, electricians etc., may have a considerably higher income than middle-class professions like teachers, but their social behavior, their habitus, is still often that characteristic of the working class, demonstrating that concepts of class position are at least as much social creations as they are objective realities. Indeed, even the class ranking of a doctor over a plumber is partially a value judgment of the society's members, especially the elites, as to the importance of their respective contributions to their interests. We generally regard the quality maintenance of our bodies as more important than that of our toilet. Levels of remuneration could be seen to follow from these considerations.

The German sociologist, Max Weber (1968[1922]), argued that the notion of class was insufficient in understanding the complex stratified system of modern societies. So, while sticking to a definition of class in economic terms, i.e. the ownership of property, he argued that social inequalities also arise due to differences in *status*. Status is the hierarchical ranking of individuals along a dimension of social prestige, which leads to differentials in power and access to scarce goods. Thus, other people are seen as inferior or superior to oneself in terms of social honor (this is what Bourdieu (1984, 1991) refers to as "symbolic capital"). Marx had conflated class and status, and they normally do coincide in that one's occupation, which is the source of wealth, is also ranked according to its social prestige, doctor versus plumber, as in the above example, but they do vary independently. The *nouveau riche* are people whose class position may be high, but whose status, at least in the eyes of some, old long-established wealthy families, is not commensurate with it. One's status entitlement is not a fixed constant quality; rather it is something one endorses, negotiates, or indeed even creates (e.g. Wolof greeting ritual) in a given social interaction. Because status refers to a position on a hierarchical scale of social prestige, people are often highly attuned to their relative ranking *vis-à-vis* someone else in any interaction. This leads to culturally mandated patterns of deference/ avoidance between inferiors and superiors, e.g. one bows or curtsies to a monarch, but the monarch does not respond similarly (see the discussion of status contests in the Wolof greeting in chapter 13).

The overall system of status entitlements in Western culture depends on a number of criteria: mainly, occupation, educational level (i.e. class properties; Bourdieu's (1984) "economic capital"), cultural pursuits (Bourdieu's "cultural capital"), or accomplishments (Bourdieu's "social capital"). Status normally goes with particular class backgrounds, but they are *not* equivalent: for most people, a doctor in American society is of high status, regardless of income earned. A common finding in sociological studies is that people on the margins of classes and related status entitlements are most sensitive to relative status distinctions; they strongly attempt to assert their distinctiveness and status in the face of what they perceive as threats from below, those mobile groups of people whose class positions and relative status they fear might be rising.

Social Roles

Status entitlement is clearly a subjective judgment, dependent on the beliefs, strategies, and feelings of the interactants; there is no objective yardstick for status entitlements, but the single most important variable is a decision as to who has the most power in the sense of ensuring their interests will be met; normally, deference (status entitlements) will be granted to those with the most power. The actors which come to any social interaction are not blank slates, but come to it with a habitus inculcated with particular attitudes and practices due to their life trajectory, especially class position and educational history. Their habitus leads them to have certain interests which they will seek to realize in any interaction. However, different contexts or fields (Bourdieu 1990) will necessarily make different demands, so actors are called upon to present themselves in different ways; in other words they take on *roles*. The way these roles will be enacted will be constrained by the dispositions in the habitus; for example, middle-class and working-class weddings are typically quite different due to the manner in which the individual actors enact expected roles. Ultimately in any social interaction all actors want to realize their interests, but due to real differences in power among them, mainly because of their class position, not all can do so to the same degree. This is recognized by all participants, resulting in status accruing to those who can most effectively enforce their own interests. Status entitlements can also be strategically manipulated by lower ranked actors, as in the Wolof greeting; by publicly recognizing status entitlement and giving deference, one can further one's own interests and gain a desired resource. Clearly, then, different roles attract differing status entitlements; doctor–patient, teacher–student, clergyman–parishioner are all socially codified role dyads with asymmetrical power and differential status entitlements. We typically function in multiple roles because of the different fields of interaction we find ourselves in: male, father, husband, teacher, airline passenger, parishioner, all of which may have different status entitlements accruing to them due to power differentials: e.g. fathers have power over sons, teachers over students, etc. These differential status entitlements are cultural conventions learned by all adequate actors during socialization and thereby inculcated in the habitus.

Society, then, is a network of fields of conventionalized interactive relationships of differential power, reward, and prestige. A person becomes a social actor, acquires a habitus, through engaging in these interactions (Gergen 1990). Interactions between actors proceed smoothly to the extent that they share these tacit conventions for interactions, complementary expectations of how particular roles should be enacted; this is why social relations break down with those who, for some reason or another, lack the knowledge of or refuse to follow the proper conventions, especially in the highly complex urbanized societies of the industrialized world (as in Gumperz's (1993) illustration of the breakdown in communication between the Indian English student and his British teacher; see the discussion in chapter 14).

Roles vary enormously in the degree to which they are vague and openly negotiable or highly conventionalized and fairly rigid, e.g. man → male friend versus man → doctor. How openly negotiable a role might be tends to be closely correlated with the extent of power asymmetry between the actors: lower power asymmetry means more openly negotiable, as in the case of a man with his male friend. Different societies too may vary in the degree of conventionalized behavior prescribed and proscribed for similar roles, e.g. the role of priest in Australian society versus its equivalent, *pedanda*, in Balinese society. Thus, some occupational roles involve quite clear and fairly exact requirements of conduct and prescribe an elaborate code of behavior for the actor (e.g. priest); as we shall see in chapter 18, a defining characteristic for such heavily prescribed roles is often the control of a set of genres (e.g. Christian liturgy). Others are more open-ended and non-specific (e.g. public servant). Roles also differ in the extent to which they have an overall effect on a person's life. Some are highly pervasive (e.g. father, mother, professional occupations like doctor or professor) and have manifold effects on an actor's life. Indeed, highly pervasive roles are very likely to become central definitional aspects of a person's identity (e.g. mother, doctor) indelibly etched on her habitus; she is likely to see herself quite largely in terms of it and in turn to be identified by others in the same way.

Other Types of Social Structure

Societies organized into class divisions comprise all familiar industrialized societies, but this is not the only type of social structure possible. Another type of hierarchical social structure is exemplified by *caste societies*. Class is something one can earn through life through economic activity: one can change one's class position through increased wealth. In contrast, *caste* is a social rank ascribed to one through birth and permits little or no alteration through life, regardless of one's economic success or lack thereof. Social stratification is more rigid in caste societies, unlike the upward or downward mobility typical of class-based social systems (at least in their ideology). All dimensions of a person's life are affected by their caste position, not just their occupation: for example, where they may sit in temples, what food they can eat, where they can live, who they can marry, etc. Status entitlements are very closely linked to caste in caste societies; members of a given caste are distinguished from superior and inferior grades and accorded different amounts of honor. Fundamentally, a caste-based social structure is one of institutionalized inequality of social prestige and power. Social actors are assigned to hierarchically linked caste groups by parentage, and one's own group defines the limits for interactions with others of equivalent status entitlements. Interactions with actors of other castes are inherently hierarchical, either one is in a higher caste, deserving of deference in recognition of one's higher position, or in a lower one, in which situation one gives deference to one's higher caste interactant. Generally, one's life horizons are strongly circumscribed by one's caste position, even one's choice of spouse, for caste societies are typically endogamous in caste. Caste typically also determines class or economic position because membership of caste is occupationally specialized, as in India, in which tanners or butchers belong to particular castes. The most complex caste societies are those of India or derived from these like Hindu Bali or medieval Java. Bali has four basic castes, in descending order: priests, nobles, merchants, farmers. Each caste is recognized by distinctive titles, prescribed social behavior, residence patterns and even funeral rites, amongst many other variables. The feudal societies of medieval Europe were another example of a caste society, although a sub-type best approached through Weber's notion of *estates*. The division there was between a small powerful landowner caste, the estate holders, and a vast laboring folk of landless peasants. Again, membership of each was determined by birth. The landowner caste exercised authority and enjoyed wealth and power through the revenue it collected from the peasants who worked its lands. The characteristic social tie in feudal societies was the dependence of the inferior landless peasant on the superior local landowner, who collected revenue from the peasant, but who, in turn, was expected, in theory at least, to provide the peasant with protection from depredations of other landowners. The landowner was the immediate source of law within his domain. The landowner caste itself was subdivided hierarchically, from lower to higher, mainly according to the amount and richness of land owned. More or richer land could support a higher density of peasants, from which the landowner could raise larger armies to field in the event of disputes with neighboring landowners. Thus, higher ranked landowners had more power, which could be nakedly displayed as military power if need be.

Caste and class societies are both typified by the hierarchical sorting of people according to ascribed and differentially distributed social features. Age-set societies contrast to these two in that the only features which are relevant to social stratification are biological: age and sex. Age-set societies are those typical of "simpler" hunter-gatherer groups, like those of Australian Aborigines or Amazonian Indians. They usually lack any system of central administration; the office of chief may be present, but usually involves more ritual power than political clout, and succession to this office may often not be hereditary. In age-set societies, people are assigned to hierarchical groupings, age grades, according to their age, and move from one to another as they age. Political power is concentrated in the highest age grades, the elders (commonly, the group of elders consists of men only, but this is not universally the case). Because an important part of social structure in these societies, especially that determining the distribution of political power, consists of the ranking of age grades, transitions from one age grade to the next is commonly marked by initiation rituals (these of course, may be found in more complex societies as well). The elder age grades hold the power to determine the running of the society; the younger age grades mainly effect their decisions and defend the village or horde. The elders settle disputes, decide who marries whom, play the major roles in rituals. Because power accrues to the older members of society, so does the great bulk of status entitlements; the younger must defer to the older in various patterns of behavior. However, for all the power and prestige differentials in age-set societies, in contrast to caste and class societies, many of these are egalitarian, for, ideally in such societies, the pattern of social development is identical for all members of a given age grade. The process of aging will in time advance them into the higher age grades, the group of elders, with its associated power and prestige.

Social Deixis: The T/V Phenomenon

As I have exemplified extensively in previous sections of this chapter, there is typically an indexical correlation between the social context of a given linguistic interaction and the linguistic forms used. This principle is probably realized most notably in the way the variables of social stratification, class, caste, status, role, ethnicity, age, etc., are given concrete expression in the linguistic choices of actors. In line with my discussion of gender deixis in the previous chapter, I will define *social deixis* as the overt expression, in the actual indexical linguistic forms used, of some parameters of the relative social position of one or more of the linguistic interactants, be it speaker, addressee, or even a bystander in the interaction. It is also possible, as we shall see, to indicate something about the relative social position of a non-interactant, namely some third-person participant referred to in an actual linguistic utterance. Due to the more abstract interactionally constructed basis of social position opposed to the more concrete biologically based variable of sex, social deictic forms tend to be relatively more creative of contextual value than presupposing: by using *madam* to someone we may establish her claim to higher status, rather than merely signify it. In Silverstein's (1981) framework this would indicate that gender deictics should be more accessible to conscious awareness than social deictics: whether this is true or not remains to be determined.

Undoubtedly, the best known type of social deixis is the T/V phenomenon, first insightfully described in Brown and Gilman (1972). This refers to the phenomenon, almost universal in European languages, but also attested elsewhere in the world (Old Javanese, Fijian), of two second-person singular pronouns, a T form, named after Latin *tu*, for informal, relaxed usage and a V form, from Latin *vos*, for formal polite contexts. The V form, which in usual usage marks plurality, i.e. second (French) or third (German) person plural, comes to be used for second-person singular in a distancing deferential mode. Brown and Levinson (1987) describe this as an impersonalizing strategy to redress an addressee's negative-face wants, their desire to act unimpeded: the utterance is not in formal terms addressed to a singular addressee *per se*, but to a larger inclusive group, hence mitigating any direct threat to his negative face.

Brown and Gilman described the use of the T/V pronouns along two dimensions: power and solidarity. One has power over another to the degree to which one can control or influence the behavior of another (Brown and Levinson's P variable). The dimension of power is inherently asymmetrical; that X has power over Y entails that Y lacks power over X. The solidarity dimension (Brown and Levinson's D variable) declares a claim of closeness and common interests between interlocutors, an assertion of at least some shared lived history. It is basically an assertion between potential equals; either they are solidary (common background/interests) or not, but there is no significant asymmetry of power between them. The power dimension basically asserts an inequality in economic or political power, and the different degrees of status this inequality entitles one to; it is, thus, largely linked to class or caste positions. Because the power dimension is asymmetrical, it is transparently characterized by non-reciprocal T/V pronoun usage. The powerful superior person says T to a powerless inferior, for given the power differential, she has no need to attend to the latter's face needs. But the inferior powerless person needs to say V, the distancing impersonal form, to the powerful superior in order to acknowledge his face wants. So in eighteenth-century France, a noble would address a peasant with T, but receive V in return. Or a master would speak T to his servant and receive V.

The attributes which may form a basis for an assertion of solidarity

16.1

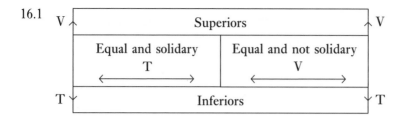

include political party membership, family background, religious affiliation, gender or sexual orientation, roughly equal age, etc. Even a continued frequency of social contact, some lived history together (itself typically a function of shared interests or background), may suffice for an assertion of solidarity. Solidarity, then, is closely related to social roles, and their relative status entitlements, that the two interactants find themselves in. If these are roughly equivalent in status, there is a strong likelihood that, after becoming acquainted, the interactants will assert solidarity between themselves. Claiming or disclaiming solidarity is a way of differentiating address among interlocutors who rate each other as equal in power. Hence its usage is symmetrical, asserted solidarity being indicated by T and lack of solidarity marked by V.

Brown and Gilman (1972:259) summarized the usage of T and V forms along the dimensions of power and solidarity (16.1). The chart accurately describes the general system of address forms in European languages, until roughly around 1800. In this earlier period, European social structure was feudal or closely approximated a caste society. Social stratification was rather rigid; one's social position was largely determined by one's conditions of birth (i.e. nobility versus peasantry), and there was almost no mobility. With the Industrial Revolution of about 200 years ago this began to change and a class society based on one's economic position and increased possibilities of mobility began to emerge. Related to this, the dimension of solidarity came to take on greater importance and became potentially applicable to all persons, so that now mutual T and V forms can be used between inferiors and superiors, depending on the degree of solidarity being asserted: customer–waiter, employer–employee, with reciprocal V (low solidarity), but parent–child, master–servant, with reciprocal T (high solidarity). Brown and Gilman (1972:259) summarized modern usage as shown in 16.2.

The outer vertical lines in 16.2 represent the power dimension, the rest, the solidarity dimension. Note that the upper left and lower right boxes represent the problematic cases, in which the power and solidary dimension conflict: superior in power, suggesting V, but solidary, claiming T, and inferior in power, marked by T, but not solidary, indicated by V. In such cases, as just mentioned, in modern European usage, the solidarity dimension wins,

16.2

(V)	Superior and solidary T	V Superior and not solidary	V
	Equal and solidary T ← ——————— →	Equal and not solidary V ← ——————— →	
T	Inferior and solidary T	V Inferior and not solidary	(T)

requiring mutual T in the first instance and mutual V in the second (hence I have added the parenthesis around the stigmatized power-based options in these cases of conflict). Since solidarity has been established as the primary dimension, the domain of T has progressively expanded in European societies; this reflects a pervasive ideology to play down rigid social boundaries in European societies and to emphasize a principle of equality among people that goes back to the Enlightenment, and given rigorous articulation in the French Revolution, and also to highlight the general ideological view that economic mobility is potentially available to all in these industrialized class-based societies. So, more and more social relations have become solidary enough for mutual T, although the parameters which determine this do vary among the different European societies. But potentially any sort of camaraderie from a common task or fate to shared sexual orientation may be sufficient for mutual T. Those with radical socialist political ideologies, which advocate the abolition of class-based power and status differentials between people, and who would rather stress their equality, may use T to everyone they address. On the other hand, those of more conservative political persuasions, for example, an upper-class descendent of the French nobility, may maximize the use of V. It is also interesting to note that in colonial situations in which the colonizers had clear power over the colonized, the power dimension seemed to be highlighted in interactions between colonizer and colonized. For example, in Africa, French colonial officers always used T to the local people, but received V from them in turn.

English, of course, is the one obvious European language which lacks a T/V contrast in its second-person singular pronouns of address. Does this mean English does not have any linguistic reflexes of the dimensions of power and solidarity? Far from it. It just indicates them in a different way, in the system of titles and names (other European languages do this as well, of course, in addition to the T/V pronouns). Brown and Ford (1964) studied the system of address using titles and names in American English. In this dialect of English the principle choice is between first name (FN), e.g. *Bill* or title plus last name (TLN), e.g. *Mr Wilson*. FN is roughly equivalent to the T pronoun, and TLN, the V pronoun. The three possible patterns identified by Brown and Ford are (1) reciprocal FN, (2) reciprocal

TLN, and (3) one interlocutor gives FN, but receives TLN. Roughly, these usages parallel those with T and V pronouns: reciprocal FN indicates high solidarity; reciprocal TLN, low solidarity and asymmetrical FN–TLN indicates a marked differential in class position and status entitlement. As might be expected in an industrial society stratified by class, in which occupation is the primary determinant of class position, a marked discrepancy in the status of occupation is the major factor in the choice of asymmetric FN–TLN. So, one addresses one's employer with TLN, but will likely receive FN in return (this is in interesting contrast with more egalitarian Australia in which mutual FN would be likely here). A student might address his professor as *Professor Wilson*, but receive *Luke* back in response, if he is well known to the professor (again, Australia would more likely use mutual FN or TLN). The other factor favoring the asymmetric usage is a large differential in age. Typically, if someone is twenty or so years older than one there is a significant tendency to use TLN, but receive FN back (this is especially expected with children, but often continues into adulthood). So a 6-year old calls the next door neighbor *Mrs Smith*, but in turn is addressed as *Jimmy*. This usage occurs because older people have higher status in American culture than younger people, especially children. In cases where the occupation factor and age factor are in conflict, so that the younger person has the more prestigious occupation, the occupation factor wins out. So a young executive will probably address an elderly building custodian as *Harry*, but be called *Mr Barrett* in return.

Mutual FN is the most common form of address in American English; Americans try to get on a "first name basis" as soon as sufficient common interests and background are established to make a reasonable assertion of solidarity. Mutual TLN is typically used only between newly introduced adults (although even here the relationship may start with mutual FN if the interactants are roughly equal in age and occupational background so as to suggest a presupposition of common interests). Newly introduced American adults will try to find a basis for solidarity in common interests and background in the early stages of their interaction so as to switch as quickly as possible to mutual FN. Interlocutors of the same generation and sex find this easiest to do, so they are the most rapid in their transition to mutual FN, but any variable based on shared life history and values, like religious affiliation, kinship, school or university attended, nationality or ethnicity, and even common experiences may do. If, on the other hand, two newly introduced people have a clear differential in occupation and status entitlement, like a doctor and his male patient, quick transition to mutual FN may not occur. Rather, the superior may address the inferior with FN, but continue to receive TLN. So, when the doctor and the patient first introduce themselves mutual TLN are used: *Doctor Wilson – Mr Barrett*. After the professional relationship has been established, the superior may shift to FN

16.3   ← TLN →
        FN ↓ ↑ TLN
            ← FN →

to indicate increased common background and familiarity, in short, solidarity, but continue to receive TLN (such shifts to solidary forms are properly the initiative of the superior person; initiatives from the inferior person may be rebuffed, if the superior feels solidarity is not sufficiently established, causing embarrassment to both parties). Only later, if ever, will mutual FN be adopted, when the inferior feels the relationship is sufficiently solidary. Brown and Ford (1964:241) illustrate this pattern of transitions (16.3).

Although FN and TLN are the most common forms of address in American English they do not exhaust the repertoire of individual Americans. For example, in addition to TLN, T alone is also an option: *Doctor, Professor, Captain, Mister, Madam*. This is typically used with occupations or positions of high status or when the last name is unknown, so that extreme social distance is needed. The generalized title has an impersonalizing effect on the addressee (see Brown and Levinson 1987:190–205), so that absolutely no claim of solidarity based on shared personal interests is possible. At the opposite extreme, there are many alternatives to FN to express claims of extremely high solidarity. Thus, with very close friends, nicknames are commonplace; *Scotty, Geordie, Will*. And with our intimates, the options are truly amazing: *sweetheart, honey, darling*, among hundreds of other, often very idiosyncratic, forms.

It is worthwhile pointing out the similarities between this discussion of T/FN and V/TLN address forms and Brown and Levinson's (1987) concern with positive and negative face/politeness. The T/FN forms are associated with positive face/politeness, suggesting closeness and solidarity between the interlocutors. The V/TLN forms, on the other hand, are linked to negative face/politeness, expressing a lack of intrusion on the individual's space and rights, in a word, social distance. The asymmetrical usage indicates that the inferior attends to the superior's negative face by using V/TLN, indicating his perceived higher status and consequent power, but receives from the superior the T/FN forms, not so much to suggest closeness and solidarity, but as a suggestion of dependence – of the inferior to the superior's discretion in his use of power to pursue his own interests.

Social Deixis and Honorifics: Japanese

Many languages have immensely more complex systems of social deixis than the T/V pronouns of European languages or the FN/TLN of American

English. Many languages, especially of South and East Asia but including others (Duranti 1992; Hill and Hill 1978), have a special class of words or grammatical morphemes, whose sole function is to indicate social deixis among the interlocutors or the referent of some participant in the utterance. These grammatical units are called *honorifics*. Japanese (Inoue 1979; Shibatani 1990) is an especially rich example of a language like this. Basically, Japanese has two concurrent systems of honorifics, one which registers the relative status entitlements of addressee against speaker and one which signals the relative higher status of a participant in the speaker's utterance *vis-à-vis* the speaker himself. The first is equivalent to T/V and FN/TLN phenomena, but the latter is not present in European languages.

Japanese speakers indicate deference to an addressee of higher status or with whom one has no claim to solidarity through the use of V-like pronoun forms (but not restricted to just second person as in European languages) and special verb forms suffixed with the polite suffix -*mas*. Thus, the following example (Shibatani 1990:377) is equivalent to a T form, asserting an equivalent, solidary relationship with the addressee:

    boku kare ni   au   yo
    I   he   DAT meet PRTCL
    "I'll see him"

If the addressee is a stranger or a superior with whom solidarity cannot be claimed, the first person pronoun changes to a V form and the verb takes the suffix -*mas* (Shibatani 1990:378):

    watakushi kare ni   ai-mas-u
    I   he   DAT meet-POLITE-NONPAST
    "I'll see him"

Such V pronouns and -*mas* can profitably be viewed as addressee honorifics (Levinson 1983:96), as they indicate deference by the speaker for the addressee, due to his perceived superiority or, more likely, lack of solidarity.

The other type of honorific in Japanese is called referent honorifics, in which deference is accorded by the speaker to the referent of a nominal participant in her utterance. Consider the following example (Inoue 1979:287):

    Sakai ga   Suzuki no   tame ni   chinzu o   kai-ta
    Sakai NOM Suzuki GEN sake DAT map   ACC draw-PAST
    "Sakai drew a map for Suzuki"

This is a neutral, non-deferential form, used to a solidary or inferior addressee. If the addressee is not solidary or especially if superior, then the polite verb form *kaki-mashi-ta* draw-POLITE-PAST would be used. The lack of any honorific markers indicates that Sakai and Suzuki are at least equal in status to the speaker, but probably inferior. If the two are equal to the speaker, the basic level honorific, the respectful title, *san* Mr would be added to their names (Inoue 1979:287):

> Sakai san ga   Suzuki san ni   chizu o
> Sakai Mr NOM Suzuki Mr DAT map   ACC
> kai-ta/kaki-mashi-ta
> draw-PAST/draw-POLITE-PAST
> "Mr Sakai drew a map for Suzuki"

If the speaker is considerably lower in status than Sakai, say, significantly younger, then special subject honorific forms must be used to indicate the relative high status entitlement of Sakai *vis-à-vis* the speaker (Inoue 1979:288):

> Sakai san ga   Suzuki san ni   chizu o   o-kaki-ni
> Sakai Mr NOM Suzuki Mr DAT map   ACC HON-draw-DAT
> nat-ta/nari-mashi-ta
> become-PAST/become-POLITE-PAST
> "Mr Sakai came to draw a map for Mr Suzuki"

If there is a significant status differential between Sakai and Suzuki, such that the recipient, Suzuki, is of higher status than the subject, Sakai, then special "object" honorific forms are required to show the higher status entitlement of Mr Suzuki (Inoue 1979:288):

> Sakai san ga   Suzuki san ni   chizu o   o-kaki
> Sakai Mr NOM Suzuki Mr DAT map   ACC HON-draw
> shi-ta/shi-mashi-ta
> do-PAST/do-POLITE-PAST
> "Mr Sakai did the drawing of a map for Mr Suzuki"

The effect of "object" honorification is to show respect to Mr Suzuki through humbling Mr Sakai, hence the local Japanese name for this construction *kenjoo go* "humbling language." Finally, when Suzuki has lower status than Sakai, but the speaker wants to assert solidarity with Suzuki, special honorific forms of the verbs of transfer are employed. One is *kudasai-* "give" which honors the subject, Sakai, and the other *itadaki-*, which humbles the recipient, Suzuki (Inoue 1979:289):

> Sakai san ga   Suzuki san ni   chizu o   kai-te
> Sakai Mr NOM Suzuki Mr DAT map   ACC draw-ing
> kudasai-ta/kudasai-mashi-ta
> give-PAST/give-POLITE-PAST
> "Mr Sakai gave Mr Suzuki the drawing of a map"

Sakai san ni   Suzuki san ga   chizu o   kai-te
Sakai Mr DAT Suzuki Mr NOM map   ACC draw-ing
itadai-ta/itadaki-mashi-ta
receive-PAST/receive-POLITE-PAST
"From Mr Sakai, Mr Suzuki received the drawing of a map"

In these examples the addressee honorific and referent honorific axes are operating independently. Quite often, however, they are used in concert, as in the following examples (Shibatani 1990:376):

itu   o-kaeri   ni   nari-masu-ka (addressee = subject)
when HON-return DAT become-POLITE-Q
"When are (you) coming back?"

Taroo wa   sensei o   o-tasuke   shi-mashi-ta (addressee = object)
Taroo TOP teacher ACC HON-help do-POLITE-PAST
"Taroo helped (you) teacher" (*sensei* is used as a second person singular polite pronoun)

While traditional Japanese society, which was the original context of these forms, was feudal, modern Japan is an industrial, largely middle-class based society. There are, however, very significant differences to European societies, differences reflected in the uses of honorific forms. While both dimensions of power and solidarity are operative in the choices of Japanese honorific forms, these notions, especially the latter, must be understood here in particularly Japanese terms. Crucial to Japanese society is a contrast between ingroup versus outgroup. This contrasts members of a family and organizations conceived in terms of a family, like corporations (the ingroup), with people outside the family or organization. For example, when speaking about one's father within the family unit (ingroup), one may optionally use honorifics, reflecting his seniority in age and power/status differential. However, when speaking about one's father to someone who is not a (extended) family member (outgroup), honorifics must not be used, but just general polite forms with *-mas* and probably humbling forms (Inoue 1979:292):

chichi wa   genki de   ori-mas-u
father TOP health INSTR be(HUM)-POLITE-NONPAST
"(My) father is healthy"

In speaking about the addressee's father (outgroup) honorifics are necessary, either with or without the polite *-mas* verb forms (Inoue 1979:293):

```
o-too        san wa   o-genki      des-u         ka
HON-father  Mr TOP   HON-health  be-NONPAST   Q
o-too        san wa   o-genki      de
HON-father  Mr TOP   HON-health  INSTR
irasshai-mas-u                      ka
be(HON)-POLITE-NONPAST            Q
"Is (your) father healthy?"
```

Similarly, within a corporation, colleagues would use honorifics in referring to the company president when talking among themselves (ingroup),
but when speaking to an outsider (outgroup), no honorifics would be used.
Thus, if a colleague within the company calls the company president's secretary asking to speak to him, the secretary would answer with full honorifics
(Shibatani 1990:379):

```
shatyoo  san wa   ima o-dekake ni   nat-te
president Mr TOP   now HON-go DAT   become-ing
i-mas-u
go-POLITE-NONPAST
"The president has gone out now"
```

But in answer to a call from an outsider, she would say (Shibatani 1990:379):

```
shatyoo   wa    ima dekake-te ori-mas-u
president TOP   now go out-ing be(HUM)-POLITE-NONPAST
"The president has gone out now"
```

with simple polite *-mas* forms and the humbling form of the copula, *ori-*,
but no honorifics. Thus, within the ingroup, one may use honorifics to
signal differences of status and power within it, but this is not proper when
addressing someone outside of it. Rather the whole ingroup needs to be
presented as a unit of equals and probably humbled with respect to the
addressee, who must be addressed minimally with the polite forms in *-mas*,
reflecting his social distance and potential power. When talking about members of the outgroup, however, honorifics are necessary, again reflecting
their social distance.

Of course, not all Japanese engage in occupations, such as corporation
members, which would cause them to regard themselves as belonging to a
family-like ingroup. For instance (Inoue 1979), university professors regard
their students as belonging to their group, but do not consider the wider
university to be part of their group. So a university professor answering a
call from an outsider concerning one of his colleagues, would answer with
full honorifics and polite *-mas* forms (Inoue 1979:294):

Mori sensei wa   gaishutsu shi-te
Mori teacher TOP go out   do-ing
irasshai-mas-u
be (HON)-POLITE-NONPAST
"Professor Mori has gone out"

Compare this with the company secretary's response in similar circumstances; the professor would not use humbling forms like *ori-*, even if the colleague were a very junior member of the faculty. The colleague is simply not a member of the professor's ingroup, thereby requiring honorifics in referring to him.

Social Deixis and Honorifics: Javanese

Undoubtedly the most complex systems of honorifics, humbling expressions and polite speech forms indicating deference to the addressee are found in the Javanese language (Errington 1985a, b, 1988; Geertz 1972; Gonda 1948; Poedjosoedarmo 1968; Uhlenbeck 1978). Traditionally, Java was a caste society, with the king at the center, having the most power and the highest rank and status; there was decreasing power, rank, and status as one moved away from him, as measured by genetic rules of descent. Thus, the king's grandson held a higher rank than his second cousin. Traditionally Javanese society was greatly concerned with the minutiae of determining precise ranking among the various members of the nobility. This was important because it was these fine gradations of ranking which determined a whole range of appropriate social behavior, including linguistic behavior.

Describing the Javanese repertoire of deferential linguistic forms is made complicated by the fact that the same system is not shared across all groups in society; specifically, nobility have different conventions than commoners, some of whom may have only the vaguest control over the system, and older conservative members of the nobility again retain different conventions from younger, more innovative members. Here I describe a simplified version of usage among more traditional nobility. The system involves a basic contrast between two speech levels, *ngoko* and *krama*, which exemplify contrastive lexical items for most items of basic vocabulary and other things (Errington 1985b:290):

ngoko: apa   kowé   njupuk sega semono
krama: menapa panjenengan mendhet sekul semanten
       Q   you   take   rice that much
       "Will you take that much rice?"

The two sentences have the same referential meaning, but they index very different social meanings. The *ngoko* forms are the basic language; all vocabulary items in the language have at least a *ngoko* equivalent. *Ngoko* is the "basic," spontaneous, natural, somewhat cruder manner of speaking to intimates and inferiors (Errington 1985a:292). In terms of Brown and Gilman's dimensions of power and solidarity, it functions like a T pronoun: reciprocal *ngoko* indicates intimacy and familiarity among the interlocutors, while asymmetrical *ngoko* indicates the *ngoko* speaker as being of higher rank and power than his interlocutor. *Krama* items in opposition to *ngoko* number in the many hundreds, and it is the "common standard polite address" (Errington 1985b:292). In terms of Brown and Gilman's dimensions, it is like a V pronoun, properly spoken reciprocally between non-intimates or asymmetrically by a lower ranked person in speaking to a higher ranked one. As with Japanese, strong co-occurrence constraints hold among the lexical items of the sentence as to speech level, either all *ngoko* or all *krama*.

Javanese is unique in having yet a third intermediate level, called *madya* "middle." The *madya* equivalent of the above two sentences is (Errington 1985b:290):

$$\text{napa sampéyan} \begin{Bmatrix} \text{mendhet sekul} \\ \text{njupuk sega} \end{Bmatrix} \text{semonten}$$

Q　　you　　　　take　　　rice　　　that much
"Will you take that much rice?"

The *madya* vocabulary is small, composed mainly of indexical items like deictics or pronominals and some grammatical elements like the question marker *napa* above. In the absence of specific *madya* forms, either *ngoko* or *krama* equivalents are used in a *madya* level sentence, as with *njupuk sega* (*ngoko*) or *mendhet sekul* (*krama*) above. *Madya* is mainly disliked by the nobility, viewed as commoner speech, for whom it is often the highest level they can muster, lacking competence in proper *krama*. So the nobility use *madya* mainly as an outgroup code in speaking to commoners. Since at least the 1930s an egalitarian ethos has proscribed asymmetrical *ngoko–krama* speech with non-intimate commoners, the outgroup for the nobility, so that reciprocal *madya* is used in this situation, a good solution, for, as already noted, *madya* is typically the only form of non-*ngoko* speech controlled by most commoners. This association with outgroup commoner usage, a social group of low rank in the view of nobles, also accounts for the nobility's general devaluation of this speech level.

In addition to these three speech levels, Javanese also has a rich system of honorifics and range of humbling expressions. Like the Japanese *-mas* forms, the three speech levels, *ngoko*, *madya*, and *krama*, express deference or lack thereof to the addressee, while the honorifics and humbling expressions, again like their Japanese equivalents, express deference to the referent of a nominal participant in the speech event, which, of course, could be the addressee. Honorifics, locally called *krama inggil* "high *krama*" can be used to express deference to a participant, regardless of whether the overall style is *ngoko* or *krama*. They are not used with the *madya* speech level, probably due to its stigma among the nobility, who are the only group that effectively control the honorifics (Errington 1985b:290):

> *ngoko* with honorifics:
> apa sliramu   mundhut   sega semono
> Q   you (HON) take(HON) rice that much
> *krama* with honorifics:
> menapa panjenengandalem mundhut   sekul semanten
> Q   you (HON)   take(HON) rice   that much
> "Will you take that much rice?"

Honorifics in Javanese, like Japanese, as a word class typically refer to persons, their bodies and their parts, their possessions, bodily acts and exchanges and transactions. Errington (1988) describes the physical domain and the psychosocial domain as the major areas with honorific lexemes, all denoting deference to a person through his body or actions, and identifies some 100 lexemes as honorific terms in these domains, many of which are now falling out of use. Honorifics function to mark the high status of the referent *vis-à-vis* one or both of the speech act participants. When they refer to the addressee, as in the above examples, they may complement or augment the basic meaning of the chosen speech level. When used with *krama*, they augment the deference shown by the speaker to the addressee through his choice of *krama*, but when used in *ngoko*, they complement the speech level choice, marking respect for a familiar, intimate addressee and asserting a reasonable claim of some status for him.

Finally, there is a small set of humbling lexemes, called locally *krama andhap* "low *krama*." These lexemes are mostly verbs of exchange, either possessions or speech, and indicate that the initiator of the exchange is typically inferior in status to its addressee or recipient. So, we could substitute the honorific form *mundhut* in the above examples with the humbling *krama andhap* lexeme *nyuwun* "request" (Errington 1988:175):

> apa sliramu   nyuwun   sega semono
> Q   you(HON) request(HUM) rice that much
> "Will you request that much rice?"

This sentence indicates the relatively low status of the addressee in relation to the unspecified recipient of this act of requesting (although the use of an honorific pronoun *sliramu* in an overall *ngoko* style still indicates a modicum of deference by the speaker to his familiar, solidary addressee). Another example (Errington 1988:176):

> aku nyuwun   buku karo Pak Har
> I   request(HUM) book from Mr Har
> "I requested a book from Mr Har"

This sentence is in *ngoko*, indicating a solidary, familiar relationship with the addressee. However, the humbling lexeme *nyuwun* "request" is also used, indicating that the speaker is showing deference to a higher ranked Mr Har. If the same status ranking were to hold, but Mr Har were to do the requesting, then the honorific *krama inggil* verb for "request," *mundhut* must be used to express the requisite deference by the speaker to this referent (Errington 1988:175):

> Pak Har mundhut   buku karo aku
> Mr Har request(HON) book from I
> "Mr Har requested a book from me"

Exactly the same inversion is found in the following two examples in the *krama* speech level for a deferred to addressee (Errington 1988:183):

> Bapak mundhut priksa kaliyan kula
> Father asked(HON)   to   I
> "Father asked me (a question)"

> Kula nyuwun priksa kaliyan Bapak
> I   asked(HUM) to   Father
> "I asked Father (a question)"

Both examples express deference to Father as of higher rank and power in relationship to the speaker.

Social Deixis in Egalitarian Societies: Age and Kinship Relations

Java and Japan are both complex societies where caste or class play vital roles in ascribing one's overall social position, and linguistic forms are directly emblematic for this position, so that by their appropriate usage one is able to identify and construct oneself as a person of a particular type and standing. What about societies which are not stratified in this way? Do simple egalitarian age-set societies have analogs of these types of specialized linguistic uses? The straightforward answer is yes. In age-set societies, the basic building blocks of social structure are kinship links and age ranks, and both of these variables can serve as the basis for differential linguistic behavior. For example, among the Tunebo, an egalitarian Native people of Colombia in South America (Headland 1986), requests addressed to members of the older age rank in the society (approximately over 40 years old), should be expressed in a different linguistic form than those addressed to the younger: they are hedged, explicitly state the purpose of the request to the advantage of the speaker, and necessarily omit mention of the ability of the addressee to comply. Indeed, even in highly stratified societies, age may be an important variable in determining appropriate linguistic forms. Brown and Ford (1964) noted that a large difference in age (20 years or more) may determine that TLN is appropriate over FN. And in Bali, with a social structure and system of speech levels much like Java, a large age differential can be a complicating factor. For example, a conversation between a young high-caste person and an old low-caste person will be in asymmetrical high–low speech levels, as expected. However, the younger person will address the older in low speech level, but with teknonyms (i.e. "father/ grandfather of X"), whereas given first names are normal usage in the low level (Wayan Arka, personal communication):

Ida Bagus: Pekak   Putu lakar mas kija (low level)
(high caste) Grandfather Putu will go   where
             "Where are you (Grandfather of Putu) going?"
Pekak Putu: tiang jagi lunga ka pasar (high level)
(low caste)   I   will go   to market
             "I'm going to the market"

Kinship can also be an important variable in determining appropriate linguistic usage. In many traditional Australian Aboriginal languages, there are special avoidance lexemes expressing deference, which are typically used in the presence of tabooed in-law relatives (Dixon 1971; Haviland 1979a, b). In Guugu-Yimidhirr (Haviland 1979a, b), one is prohibited completely from speaking to one's mother-in-law, while with one's brothers-in-law, a special set of lexemes, so-called avoidance language, must be employed. This brother-in-law avoidance language involves replacing lexemes of the everyday language with special avoidance forms, much as *krama* forms replace basic everyday *ngoko* in the higher speech level of Javanese. For example, the everyday Guugu-Yimidhirr sentence (Haviland 1979b:221)

nyundu buurraay waami
you(SG) water   find
"Did you find water?"

becomes in brother-in-law language:

yurra   wabirr yudurrin
you (PL) water find
"Did you find water?"

in which the second person plural pronoun *yurra* is used with singular reference much like the V pronoun form in European languages. The use of such a sentence is a social deictic; an indexical of a deferential social relationship of brother-in-law as the addressee.

This linguistic usage is paralleled by other types of avoidance behavior in Guugu-Yimidhirr society. One avoids touching or looking at tabooed in-law kin. One does not joke or curse in their presence and always restrains emotional displays. Indeed, even when speaking in brother-in-law language, talk is highly mediated and indirect: a man directs messages to his in-laws via his wife, while speaking with avoidance lexemes. Correlated with the prohibition on cursing and emotional displays, all potential "swearing words" such as those for genitalia or bodily acts are shunned; even those words which could suggest such referents are proscribed in brother-in-law language. For example, one should not say *warrbi* "axe" because it could suggest "penis," or *nambal* "stone" which might be interpreted as "testicle." Thus, the specific social deictic function of the avoidance lexemes is mirrored in wider conventions of appropriate social behavior of muted individual emotional display, again very similar to the conventions for speaking in the *krama* speech level in Javanese or high addressee honorifics in Japanese. All these linguistic systems are social deictics of deference indicating what kind of person you are to me or how you or I feel about the person we are speaking about, and not surprisingly this deference, the enaction of personhood, has non-linguistic analogs as well, as embodied as they are as practices of the habitus.

Social Markers: Sociolinguistic Variables

In parallel with the markers of gender discussed in chapter 15, social deictic forms like T/V phenomena, honorifics, or avoidance language can be contrasted with other indexical linguistic features which function as *social markers*, present in most, if not all, languages. Classic examples of social markers are *sociolinguistic variables*, investigated insightfully in the pioneering work of Labov (1972b). Sociolinguistic variables are linguistic features that show statistically significant variation along the lines of social variables, like class positions, ethnicity, age, sex, etc. The most commonly studied involve phonological variation, but in principle the method can be extended to study any linguistic feature, be it morphological, syntactic, lexical, or even discoursal.

One clear sociolinguistic variable, or social marker in my sense, is the phonetic realization of the phoneme /r/ in postvocalic position among speakers of New York City English, the topic of one of Labov's most ingenious studies (Labov 1972b). In New York City, postvocalic /r/ is either realized as retroflection of the vowel (/r/-ed variety) or is absent (/r/-less variety). The /r/-less variety was the standard prestigious pronunciation prior to World War II, but following that and with the rise of national television with a standard /r/-ed variety, the /r/-less pronunciation has become increasingly stigmatized and regarded as substandard.

New York society, like elsewhere in the United States, is strongly stratified by class. As discussed above, class is mainly determined by economic position, and hence a good indicator of people's relative class positions is their consumption patterns (see also Bourdieu (1984)). Labov wanted to study the distribution across classes of the /r/-ed versus /r/-less varieties, and to do this he hit upon the clever idea of studying the pronunciation of salespersons in three different New York City department stores, selected according to the class of the typical customers (class as measured by their consumption patterns). The assumption here of course, is that the speech of salespeople in each department store would harmonize with that of the typical customers, so that their distribution of /r/-ed versus /r/-less varieties would be indicative of wider class-based patterns.

The three stores in which Labov undertook his study were Saks Fifth Avenue, Macy's and S. Klein. On a number of objective criteria, i.e. price of goods, layout of goods for sale, Labov ranked the three stores in the above order from "most classy" to "least classy," the hypothesis being that the workers in the three stores would be aware of these prestige rankings and manifest social and linguistic behavior consonant with their relative standing. Labov's technique in determining salespeople's realization of /r/ was simple, but ingenious. On entering the store, he determined from the store directory a department which was located on the fourth floor (note the presence of two postvocalic /r/s in this phrase). He then approached a salesperson, inquiring "Excuse me, where are the __?", filling in a department from the fourth floor. The answer, of course, would be "fourth floor." The investigator would then lean forward and repeat "Excuse me?," resulting in a more carefully and emphatically enunciated "fourth floor." He then transcribed both responses. Note that using this methodology, Labov was able to get four instances of postvocalic /r/, in ordinary and careful articulation, and preconsonantally and word finally.

Labov's findings are displayed in table 16.4 (Labov 1972b:51). Note that the percentage of speakers always pronouncing postvocalic /r/ is highest in the store with clientele drawn from higher classes, Saks, and lowest in that with predominantly working- and lower-class clientele, S. Klein. Conversely, the percentage of speakers who never pronounce postvocalic /r/ is greatest

16.4

	Saks	*Macy's*	*S. Klein*
all [r]	30%	20%	4%
some [r]	32%	31%	17%
no [r]	38%	49%	79%
number of subjects	68	125	71

in the lowest ranked store, S. Klein, but lowest in the highest ranked store, Saks. Macy's, the medium ranked store, draws its clientele most widely, from middle class to working class and, not surprisingly, exhibits scores for this variable in an intermediate range between the two. Thus, Labov was able to demonstrate a correlation between the sociolinguistic variable of the pronunciation of postvocalic /r/ and social class, as measured by the expected clientele of these three stores, in short, a clear social marker of class. In an even more emphatic demonstration of this fact, Labov discovered variation for this variable in the Saks store itself. In the quieter exclusive upper floors of Saks, with the most expensive goods, and therefore well-heeled clientele of the highest classes, the percentage of all or some [r] realization of this sociolinguistic variable was significantly higher than on the less expensive and exclusive ground floor! A social marker, *par excellence.*

Sociolinguistic variables are not restricted to phonological phenomena, although these are generally the most commonly studied. The third-person singular present tense indicative verb suffix /-s/ is a sociolinguistic variable, a social marker of class, in the speech of Norwich, England. In this dialect, this suffix is often absent, resulting in sentences like the following (Trudgill 1983:43):

She like him very much.
He don't know a lot, do he?
It go ever so fast.

Trudgill demonstrated that this sociolinguistic variable is closely correlated to rankings of social class, as in table 16.5 (Trudgill 1983:44). We see a clear break in the distribution of this sociolinguistic variable for class: middle-class speakers almost never fail to use it, while working-class speakers almost always do (there are minor variations among the divisions within these two main class strata). Again we find a sociolinguistic variable as a clear social marker of class.

Speakers seem to be well aware, at least tacitly, of the meaning of class affiliation tied to the various social markers. Remember the gender-based

16.5

	% verbs without /-s/
Middle middle class	0
Lower middle class	2
Upper working class	70
Middle working class	87
Lower working class	97

16.6

Lower class	50%
Working class	53%
Lower middle class	86%
Upper middle class	75%

differentiation of covert prestige for male speakers of Norwich discussed in the previous chapter. In that case, middle-class male speakers typically claimed to use features of working-class speech with a much higher frequency than they actually did. While these features are indeed social markers of working-class affiliation, these middle-class men are at least tacitly aware of this meaning and are thereby using these forms to assert solidarity with this class, or at least some perceived social norms of this class which they admire, like toughness, unaffectedness, masculinity. Labov (1972b) demonstrates a similar awareness of the meaning of social markers in his study of the distribution of the pronunciation of postvocalic /r/ in New York City. He found that speakers were highly sensitive to this sociolinguistic variable when asked to rate tape-recorded speech on a scale of occupational suitability, be it television personality, executive secretary, receptionist, factory worker, etc. Scores for sensitivity to this sociolinguistic variable are shown in 16.6 (Labov 1972b:131). Note again the sharp break between these scores of the middle classes and those below, with the middle classes being most aware of the class affiliation meaning of this social marker, especially the lower middle class. Labov takes their particularly high score as evidence of their *linguistic insecurity*. They are seen to be particularly aware of and attuned to the meanings of such social markers, because they regard their own class position and perhaps their control of middle-class norms appropriate to it as especially insecure, with a threat of downward mobility, leading to strong censure of any social markers that may mean links to lower class strata and perhaps overemphasis on those associated with higher strata.

Findings like these, in which particular linguistic features are markers of social meaning, particularly claims of class affiliation, are to be expected in class societies with their fluidity and the prominence given to economic position and consumption patterns, but what about societies structured according to caste, with social position ascribed by birth? Gumperz (1958) discusses the case of Khalapur village in northern India. This village is mainly comprised of Hindus divided into four major ranked caste groupings or *varna*: priests, nobles, merchants, and untouchables (highest to lowest). Within each *varna* are further ranked sub-divisions according to traditional occupation, called *jati*, with associated customs and ritual practices. The untouchable caste is sharply distinguished from the other three by ritual status and also residential patterns. The untouchables are comprised of three *jati* and these lived in geographically separated parts of the village with their own water sources, which, further, are enclosed by walls, emphasizing their isolation from the remainder of the village. The untouchables mostly stay in these neighborhoods, and their children only play with their caste-mates.

This cleavage between the untouchables, and the other castes is marked in their respective linguistic behavior. For example, villagers of the higher castes make a phonemic contrast between /ə/ and /u/, but many untouchables use /ə/ everywhere. Thus, higher castes say /dutɔil/ "blanket," while many untouchables say /dətɔil/. Thus, the lack of a /u/–/ə/ contrast is stereotypical of untouchable speech, a social marker of the untouchable caste, while its presence is a marker of higher status touchable caste speech. Further, like sociolinguistic variables as social markers in class societies, villagers are well aware of the meaning of this social marker, so much so that some untouchables substitute /u/ for /ə/ in various words, but often where it is not justified by the standards of touchable speech, a process called hypercorrection. So the word for a type of village building /dəlán/ is pronounced by some untouchables as /dulan/. This is rather like the linguistic insecurity of the lower middle class in New York City and reflects the untouchables' perception of their inferiority in many social and ritual respects *vis-à-vis* the other three castes, leading to their emulating incorrectly the linguistic habits of these castes, taking this phonemic contrast as a social marker of superior caste position and its associated secular and spiritual attributes.

Even within the untouchable caste there are linguistic differences. The sweeper *jati*, for example, fails to contrast certain simple vowels and diphthongs in non-final position, while the other two untouchable *jati* and the touchable castes do so. Sweepers say /bal/ "ear of corn" and /lal/ "red," so that these two words rhyme, while all others say /bali/ and /lal/ respectively. Finally, the shoemaker *jati* of untouchables pronounce the low front vowel word finally as [ʌ], but all others, untouchables and touchable castes alike, pronounce it as [æ]. All of these linguistic differences are social markers, indicative of the sharp social contrast in Khalapur between untouchables and the other touchable castes, and within the untouchable caste, social distinctions among its *jati*. Such relatively fine-grained distinctions are perhaps to be expected in a caste society with its more rigid social divisions tied to one's birth origins, rather than one's economic position, although in caste societies these are typically closely correlated. With modernization and education, they may become less closely correlated, so that a corresponding correlation between sociolinguistic variables as social markers of caste position may be more tenuous; more recent studies in Indian sociolinguistics appear to support this (Krishnamurti 1979; Schiffman 1973; Zvelebil 1964).

Social Markers: Code Switching

Sometimes whole languages or varieties of languages can be used as social markers; these are the phenomena of code switching and diglossia. The phenomenon of code switching, or shifting from one language or variety of language to another in the course of a verbal interaction, is very complex and can signal a range of distinct meanings, from a change in the topic under discussion to the formulating of the setting. I will only be concerned here with code switching as an index of the relative social relationships of the interlocutors. Perhaps the most prototypical case of code switching is alternating between distinct languages, a phenomenon associated with bilingualism (Romaine 1995), in which speakers have fluency in two (or sometimes more) languages. Situations like this are widespread throughout the world. Yimas village provides an apt example. Almost all adult Yimas are bilingual in Yimas vernacular and Tok Pisin, the major lingua franca of Papua New Guinea. The former carries social connotations of traditional cultural patterns, intimate relations and local conditions, while the latter means modernity, the power associated with it, and the wider world. Most Yimas men in their thirties and forties conduct a large part of their conversations in Tok Pisin, liking to appear modern sophisticated men of the world. Consider the case of the village councillor, Andrew Andikapan, a man of mid forties who in the 1980s and 1990s served as president of the Karawari Council, the local government body in the area. As the Karawari area is linguistically highly diverse, with about a dozen languages spoken within it, all affairs and meetings of the local government council are conducted in Tok Pisin. Because of his position, Andrew Andikapan must conduct most of his verbal interactions in Tok Pisin, but, even when not strictly necessary, as when talking with fellow Yimas villagers, he will speak in Tok Pisin, as a statement of his important high status and powerful role as a political man of the wider world (in fact, Tok Pisin is generally the language of politics even within Yimas village). However, when he is speaking with his mother, he will normally use Yimas vernacular, even though she herself speaks and understands Tok Pisin. This is because his relationship with her, the role of son, is an especially intimate, traditional one, for which Yimas vernacular is appropriate; Tok Pisin as an outgroup code of modernity would put distance between them (he might, of course, employ Tok Pisin if he was speaking angrily to her, using the language emblematically of his powerful position and temporary emotional distance from her).

Sankoff (1972) describes a similar multilingual situation of code switching among Buang villagers, also of Papua New Guinea. The languages of choice here are Buang vernacular, Tok Pisin and Yabem, an Austronesian language of the area north of Lae town, spread as a lingua franca for education by Lutheran missions during the twentieth century. The factors which condition the choice of code are complex (Sankoff 1972:39), but, for example, in speaking to anyone associated with the missions, in a role like pastor or teacher, Yabem would be used, while to a Buang villager, Buang would probably be spoken, depending on the topic under discussion. Business and government or community affairs have a high likelihood of being conducted in Tok Pisin, as in Yimas village. Tok Pisin is also the code of choice to strangers, who could not be expected to know Buang. The overall situation is highly reminiscent of Yimas village; the choice of language carries social meaning, being a social marker; "Buang represents an identification with the people, shows that the speaker considers himself a part of the local community and is accepted as such . . . use of Neo-Melanesian [i.e. Tok Pisin] is regarded as appropriate for people of power and authority, in contexts having a relationship to the . . . broader society, especially the domains of business and government" (Sankoff 1972:48).

Yet another well-known example of code switching comes from the South American nation of Paraguay, which has two national languages, Spanish and Guarani, the latter being a Native Amerindian language of the area (Rubin 1968). About half the population of the country is bilingual in the two languages, and code switching among these bilinguals is extensive. As in the two cases from New Guinea, the Native or indigenous language, Guarani, is the solidary one, used when speaking to friends or making confessions to a priest. It is obviously also the language of intimate family life used with siblings and spouses. Besides carrying a social meaning of solidarity, Guarani is also the language of choice when speaking to social inferiors, like servants and members of the peasantry and lower classes; this is the semantic dimension of power. This double meaning for Guarani, solidarity or power asymmetry of superior to inferior, as a social marker is not unique; clear parallel cases are the earlier uses of T pronouns in European languages or *ngoko* forms in Javanese. The intrusive language of wider communication, Spanish, like Tok Pisin for New Guinea, is the non-solidary language. It is used in formal contexts like schools, businesses and government offices, and to those with whom one is not on intimate terms, like strangers or foreigners. At the outset of courting, one typically speaks to one's sweetheart in Spanish, reflecting lack of intimacy and distance, but as the relationship progresses and deepens, the lovers switch to Guarani. The other usage of Spanish is in asymmetric power relationships, as in speaking to one's social superiors, like high government officials; Spanish is viewed as the language of those who have power and dominance. This double social meaning for Spanish, non-solidarity and power asymmetry, is again well attested in earlier usages of V pronouns in European languages and *krama* forms in Javanese.

It is important to note that the dual social meanings of the languages in Paraguay, non-solidarity and power (Spanish) and solidarity and powerlessness (Guarani) are not straightforwardly paralleled in the two New Guinea cases presented. Both Yimas and Buang villages are strongly egalitarian with no hierarchical class or caste divisions. Hence the choice of vernacular versus intrusive Tok Pisin is mainly a statement of a solidary versus non-solidary relationship. However, in the association of Tok Pisin with business or government activities, we can see a development of an alignment of Tok Pisin with those who have power.

Not all cases of code switching involve the alternation between distinct languages; sometimes the choice is between varieties of one language. Blom and Gumperz (1972) is an excellent case study of one such situation of code switching in a rural northern Norwegian town, Hemnesberget. Hemnesberget, like Norway generally, is a class-based society, but one overwhelmingly middle class, lacking both extremes of wealth or poverty. Norway is a European country with a particularly complex linguistic situation with no less than two standard languages (see a good summary discussion of how this came about in Trudgill (1983:161–8); also chapter 20). The inhabitants of Hemnesberget have a choice of two codes, Bokmål, the standard Norwegian language current in northern Norway, and Ranamål, the local dialect of Norwegian. These are two different varieties of basically the same language, but divergent in areas of phonology, morphology, syntax, and lexis. As in the previous case studies, the local variety, Ranamål, is solidary, emblematic of the unique identity and egalitarian values of the locally descended residents. Hence, these people use it in the home, with friends and neighbors in casual conversation and generally to others to express sympathy for local values and affiliation to this "local team." The version of the standard language, Bokmål, on the other hand, is linked to non-local, pan-Norwegian values and associated with wider political and economic concerns. Bokmål was in fact introduced into the area by the former landowning, commercial and administrative elite, who have since departed the area. Hence, it is generally regarded by most of the locally descended inhabitants as tainted with connotations of inequality of status. However, many individuals who now fill the roles of the departed elite are of non-local descent and associate the standard Bokmål with higher standards of education, influence, and prestige. They therefore prefer it and regard the local Ranamål as indicating lack of education and sophistication. Locally descended residents, on the other hand, take refusal to speak the local dialect as a declaration of non-solidarity and contempt for the "local team" and its egalitarian community spirit. If a locally descended resident were to use Bokmål forms to other local residents, he would be regarded as *snakk fint* "putting on airs." Again, the choice between these two codes has a clear social meaning; these codes function as social markers of a speaker's origin and social affiliations.

The choice between Bokmål and Ranamål in Hemnesberget is similar in some respects to a phenomenon first identified by Ferguson (1972:244–5) as *diglossia*:

> diglossia is a relatively stable language situation in which, in addition to the primary dialects of the language (which may include a standard or regional standard), there is a very divergent, highly codified (often grammatically more complex) superimposed variety, the vehicle of a large and respected body of literature (written) either of an earlier period or in another speech community, which is learned largely by formal education and is used for most written and formal spoken purposes but is not used by any sector of the community for ordinary conversation.

The situation in Hemnesberget in the choice between standard Bokmål and local Ranamål differs from Ferguson's description of diglossia in that both varieties are regularly used by some townspeople in ordinary conversation, but in other features resembles diglossia. Ferguson discusses four cases of diglossia in depth: standard High versus Swiss German, Standard Parisian French versus Haitian Creole, *Katharévusa* versus *Dhimotikí* Greek and Classical versus colloquial Cairene Arabic. In each case the former is the high (H) form, and the latter, the low (L). I will illustrate diglossia here with a discussion of the Arabic situation. The differences between the H form, Classical Arabic of the Koran, and the L form, the everyday language of Cairo, are very considerable as shown in these following examples (Trudgill 1983:117):

	H	L
"I say"	[agu·l]	[aʔʌ·l]
"I cannot"	[laʔastətiˤ]	[maʔdarʃ]
"many"	[kaθirah]	[kətir]
"that"	[ða·kə]	[da]

Diglossia is basically the result of the early codification of a language in a written form, and for Arabic, that is the classical language of the Koran.

However divergent the modern dialects have become throughout the Middle East and North Africa, the classical language has always retained its prestige, for it is widely believed that the words of the Koran constitute the actual words of God (a similar belief surrounds the use of Classical Sanskrit in India). Thus, while there are books written in Colloquial Arabic, important high status documents are still always written in Classical Arabic (this also facilitates communication across the Arab world, for while the modern colloquial Arabic dialects actually comprise several mutually unintelligible languages, Classical Arabic is universally known by the well educated). Classical Arabic is predominantly a written language, and Colloquial Arabic, a spoken one. But just as Colloquial Arabic can be written in novels and letters, Classical Arabic can be spoken. Ferguson describes its typical spoken uses as sermons in churches or mosques, speeches in parliament, university lectures, and news broadcasts. Its use therefore can fairly be summed up as being proper to situations of some formality (Irvine 1979), with highly restricted possibilities of mutual interaction (or none at all, i.e. sermons or news broadcasts) and very conventionalized or stylized social roles (i.e. mullah, priest, parliamentarian, or professor). Interestingly, in universities in Arabic-speaking countries, the formal lectures of a course may be delivered in H, but the more interactive sections or tutorials may in large part be in L. Again this reflects a difference from the code switching of Hemnesberget. There both the situation and the social position of the interlocutors determine the choice of code; in the diglossic situation of Arabic, only the social situation is relevant. Indeed, Ferguson emphasizes that the H variety is *never* proper in a normal conversational situation, unlike Bokmål in Hemnesberget. To do so would make the person an object of ridicule. Thus, diglossia is not normally a social marker in the sense I have used this term here. The use of H or L varieties does *not* typically characterize the social position of the speaker or her interlocutor. What it does do is construct and identify particular types of formal social situations.

Social Markers and Ethnicity

So far, I have looked at a number of different variables of social differentiation, class, caste, age, gender, which could be the basis for differential linguistic practices, learned through repeated histories of structural coupling in language with persons associated with these variables. There is at least one more important variable: ethnicity and/or race. Language and ethnicity/race are very closely tied together in very many societies. Labov (1972b) identified a sociolinguistic variable in Martha's Vineyard, an island off the south-east coast of Massachusetts which appears, at least in its early stages, to be a clear social marker of ethnicity or a claim to ethnic identification.

Labov found that many speakers of English on Martha's Vineyard had a marked centralization of the vocalic nucleus in the low rising diphthongs: [wəIf] and [əbəʊt] instead of [waIf] and [əbaʊt] for "wife" and "about" respectively. This centralization appeared to be strongest among younger islanders of native Yankee ethnic descent, who had occupied the island for a couple of centuries as fishermen and whalers. Labov concluded that the sound change [aI]/[aʊ] to [əI]/[əʊ] originated as a social marker for these Yankee fishermen to differentiate themselves ethnically from the small Indian population and immigrant Portuguese fishermen, but has since spread to all permanent island residents, regardless of ethnicity, to distinguish themselves as true islanders from the hordes of tens of thousands of tourists who descend on the island each summer.

Perhaps the most common way in which ethnicity/race makes itself felt as a variable in construing linguistic choice is in code switching. Indeed, in the many multilingual and multiethnic countries of Africa, Asia, the Americas, and the Pacific, language and race/ethnicity are so closely tied together as to be almost interchangeable as a label of one's social identity. For example, the word in Tok Pisin for someone of one's own ethnic group or village is *wantok*, literally "one language." In these multilingual multiethnic countries, use of a shared local ethnic language is a claim to solidarity, while use of the standard or official language asserts non-solidarity or an asymmetry in power. Myers-Scotton (1993) presents some telling examples from Kenya, in which the standard lingua franca is Swahili. Consider the following conversation between a brother and sister in the brother's store (Myers-Scotton 1993:144), in which the languages used are the local vernacular Luyia and Swahili:

Brother (Luyia):	Good morning, sister.
Sister (Luyia):	Good morning.
B (Luyia):	Are you alright?
S (Luyia):	Yes, just a little.
B (Swahili):	Sister, now today what do you need?
S (Luyia):	I want you to give me some salt.
B (Swahili):	How much do you need?
S (Luyia):	Give me sixty cents worth.
B (Swahili):	And what else?
S (Luyia):	I would like something else, but I've no money.
B (Swahili):	Thank you, sister. Goodbye.
S (Luyia):	Thank you. Goodbye.

Note that the opening greetings and pleasantries are connected in Luyia, the shared ethnic language of solidarity, but when he opens the business part of the transaction he switches to Swahili, making it a more distant impersonal exchange. The sister continues in the solidary code of Luyia, possibly in the hope of a handout, but the brother rebuffs her, continuing his use of Swahili, so that his sister knows she is being treated as a customer, not a sibling.

In another example, a visitor approaches the headquarters to IBM in Nairobi and is stopped by the entrance security guard (Myers-Scotton 1993:88):

Guard (Swahili): Who do you want to see?
Visitor (Swahili): I would like to see Solomon I.
G (Swahili): Do you really know him. We have a Solomon A. I think that's the one [you mean].
V (Swahili): That one who comes from Tiriki – that is a Luyia person.
G (Luyia): Will Solomon know you?
V (Luyia): You see him and tell him Shem L. wants to see him.
G (Luyia): Sit here and wait.
Another visitor, just appearing (Swahili): Is Mr K. here?
G (Swahili): Yes, he's here – he is doing something right now. He can't leave until he finishes. Therefore you will wait until he comes. You will wait about five or ten minutes.
Guard goes to look for Solomon A.

Note that at the beginning of the exchange, when no ethnic connection is established, it is conducted in Swahili, the lingua franca. But when the visitor asks for someone from the Luyia area, the guard assumes that the visitor is also Luyia. Since the guard himself is Luyia, a claim of shared ethnicity and solidarity is now warranted, so he switches to Luyia. The visitor knowing that he is likely to get favorable treatment now encourages this claim of solidarity by also switching to Luyia. When a second visitor arrives on the scene, he is addressed in Swahili and told to wait, while the guard acts on the responsibilities incumbent as a result of the claim of ethnic brethren implicit in the mutual use of Luyia. In this exchange, the exchange of Luyia is a straightforward social marker of this ethnic-based solidarity, as Swahili was used earlier in the transaction as a statement of social distance.

Trudgill (1983:134–6) reports on similar research findings in Kampala, the capital of Uganda, also a highly multiethnic multilingual city. The city has many immigrants with distinct ethnic languages, but the language of the local ethnic group, the Baganda, is Luganda. English is the official language, but in addition Swahili is widely known, and especially used by Kenyan immigrants. In one interaction, two immigrant Kenyans of distinct unrelated ethnic languages were discussing problems faced by Kenyans in

Uganda, as the first had just lost his job. The interaction could have been conducted in English or Swahili. But as the topic under discussion was shared problems facing them as Kenyans in Uganda, the proper and actual choice was the Kenyan national language Swahili. This was symbolic of their status as equals, Kenyan brothers in this difficult alien land. English as a prestigious language of power would be inappropriate; but if the conversation had been a competitive one, say over money, then English would have been the likely choice.

Later that evening, the unemployed Kenyan struck up a conversation with his Ugandan neighbor, who held a rather high post. The Kenyan wanted to induce the Ugandan to help him get a new job, so he spoke to him in Luganda, which, being the local Ugandan language of the capital, was a move signalling solidarity, but also deference, recognizing that power in this country was in the hands of Ugandans. It also in this case stressed a certain degree of shared ethnicity in spite of their different nationalities, for both Luganda and the Kenyan's native ethnic language belonged to the Bantu group of languages, whereas more than half of the languages spoken by Uganda's inhabitants are Nilotic. The Kenyan's Luganda not being particularly good, the Ugandan switched the conversation to English, which in this context could be seen as both neutral and distancing, i.e. non-solidary. The conversation continued in this language, but when the time came to ask the favor to help him to find a job, the Kenyan again switched back to Luganda, for reasons outlined above. We are not told whether the request was accepted or declined, but if declined, was probably done so in English, again for reasons discussed above.

In the cases discussed thus far, ethnicity/race has been a primary independent variable in linguistic choice. However, in many modern class-based societies this is not the case, because, due to attitudes of racism or other historical circumstances, ethnicity/race and class are very closely intertwined, so that one's ethnic or racial membership has a major determining role in one's class position. Such social patterns are readily apparent in America or Australia, so that Blacks, for example, in both countries mainly belonged to the lower classes. Such examples could be multiplied many times, for example, people of Turkish ethnicity in Germany or detribalized, acculturated Native peoples of Brazil also mainly belong to the lowest classes in those societies. Again, this is typically marked linguistically. Blacks in many American cities have realizations of sociolinguistic variables like those of the lower classes. In his study of the three New York City department stores, Labov (1972b) found that black employees had the lowest rates of all /r/ pronunciations and the highest rates of no /r/, see 16.7 (Labov 1972b:54).

Because of their low, somewhat marginal class position in modern class stratified industrialized societies and their obvious differences via ethnicity/ race, some ethnic/class groupings are often strongly set off in their social

16.7

	Saks	*Macy's*	*S. Klein*
All [r]	50%	12%	0%
Some [r]	0%	35%	6%
No [r]	50%	53%	94%
number of subjects	2	17	18

behavior, including linguistic practices, from the rest of the society. Indeed, the varieties of English spoken by many Blacks in America or Australia, Vernacular Black English or Aboriginal English respectively, may be so different from the standard languages of each country that these varieties themselves could be regarded as social deictics of the race of the speaker. It is also the case, of course, that many Blacks have control of both their vernacular varieties of English and varieties closer if not equivalent to the standard and, therefore, have the option of code switching, to express various kinds of social and situational meanings.

Vernacular Black English in the United States is marked by a large number of pervasive systematic structural differences from Standard American English, some of which it shares with other lower class dialects, but some of which are unique to it. Like working-class dialects of a number of east coast areas of the United States, Vernacular Black English lacks postvocalic /r/: [kʰa·t] *cart*. But it also often lacks intervocalic [r], [pʰæ·t] *parrot* and postvocalic /1/: [tʰoω] *told*. Again in common with some working-class dialects, the interdental fricatives are merged with stops: [dɪs] *this*. And finally, there is often wholesale reduction of certain final consonant clusters: [los] *lost*, [wɛs] *west*. This has morphological implications: because such words now end in /s/, they take the proper plural allomorph /-əz/: /dɛs/ from *desk*, plural /dɛsəz/, /tɛs/ from *test*, progressive /tɛsɪn/ (above examples from Labov 1972a).

There are still more radical grammatical differences. For example, the third-singular present tense indicative ending -*s* may be missing: *he go, it run*, etc. (Baugh 1983:94–7). The copula is also pervasively absent, leading to sentences like (Trudgill 1983:64):

She real nice
He not American
If you good, you going to heaven.

In fact, the verb *be* appears in Vernacular Black English in an aspectual function, to express habitual or durative aspect (Baugh 1983:70–1):

Why you be running in the street so much?
Them brothers be playing . . . they be blowin they souls out

do in past participle form *done* functions similarly as a completive aspect marker (Baugh 1983:74):

The teacher done lost her keys
He done busted his lip

Finally, *been*, the past participle of *be*, when stressed, expresses a kind of mixed aspectual-tense category, marking an event which began in the past, but which may have finished or could continue into the present (Baugh 1983:80):

We been lived here
I been had that job

In addition to these structural differences there are significant contrasts in the linguistic practices of American Blacks. How they use Vernacular Black English pragmatically is quite distinct from the general American norms for Standard American English. There are a number of speech genres (see chapter 18) and styles of speaking which are unique to Vernacular Black English and representative of cultural attitudes toward language and its use which are very different from mainstream America (Abrahams 1976; Kochman 1972, 1981). *Rapping* is a rapid fluent way of showing off one's verbal skills, often a competitive verbal game between the interlocutors. *Signifying* and *sounding* are more aggressive verbal presentations, the former teasing or boasting to goad the interlocutor into an aggressive act, while the latter is a direct verbal insult, resulting in a rather stylized slanging match of hurling insults back and forth called *playing the dozens*. The onlookers are likely to keep *signifying* to encourage the opponents to continue *playing the dozens*. Such competitive and skillful verbal displays are a far cry from norms of speaking for white Americans, who could almost be described as being verbally deprived by comparison.

Summary

Societies are structured in a number of ways, but the commonest in the experience of most of us in the industrialized world is the class society, in which social inequality, differential power and prestige is ascribed to individuals largely through their economic position. Systems of social inequality are ways of restricting people's access to scarce goods, not just material ones, but also social esteem or status; those of higher classes have greater access than those in lower classes. Various social roles are linked with the concepts of class and status, in that these reflect the ways such concepts are primarily instantiated and enacted. One central way to enact social roles is through linguistic practices, and languages typically have various means to mark such social categories. This is called social deixis, and common illustrations are the presence of informal and deferential second-person pronouns, the T/V phenomenon, the informal T marking solidarity (and, in earlier historical periods, higher status and power), and the deferential V indexing lack of solidarity (or, formerly, lower status and power). Asian languages like Japanese and Javanese have especially complex systems of social deixis, besides expressing solidarity or deference *vis-à-vis* the addressee, they also employed honorifics or humbling expressions to indicate the social rank relative to the speaker of participants in the utterance. The other social categories that can be indexed via social deixis are relative age or kinship relations; in egalitarian societies often these are the only social categories thus indexed. In addition to social deictic forms, languages also often have social markers, forms statistically correlated with one or another social category. Good examples are sociolinguistic variables, such as the variation in pronunciation of /r/ in New York City, which seems closely correlated to economic class, speakers of higher classes using more /r/s than those of lower classes. Other social markers are code switching or diglossia in which whole languages or varieties of languages are shifted to index categories of status or solidarity. One social category commonly marked by such code switching is ethnicity or race, so that the language and its ethnic tie are often interchangeable as a label of social identity; consider the importance of Vernacular Black English as an index of Black ethnicity in America.

Further Reading

Basic sources on social stratification, class, status, and power include Bendix and Lipset (1968), Béteille (1969, 1977), Bourdieu (1984), Flanagan (1989), Giddens (1981), and Tumin (1967); there are also good sections on these topics in introductory textbooks of sociology like Berger and Berger (1976), Giddens (1993), or Worsley (1987). T/V phenomena and honorifics are well covered in Agha (1994), but also see Agha (1993), Beeman (1986), Brown and Ford (1964), Brown and Gilman (1972), Duranti (1992), Errington (1988), Haviland (1979a, b), Hill and Hill (1978), Inoue (1979), Levinson (1982), Martin (1964), and Prideaux (1970). On sociolinguistic variables, the classic source is Labov (1972b), but also have a look at some of the work of other people in this field: Horvath (1985), Macaulay (1977; 1991), Milroy (1987a, b), Sankoff (1980), and Trudgill (1974, 1978). Introductory textbooks in sociolinguistics such as Chambers (1995), Fasold (1990), Holmes (1992), Hudson (1980), Romaine (1994), Trudgill (1983) and Wardhaugh (1992) also tend to cover the topic of sociolinguistic variables in great depth, as well as other topics of this section (the anthologies of articles, Giglioli (1972), Gumperz and Hymes (1972), Pride and Holmes (1972), are also very valuable). For code switching and diglossia have a look at Blom and Gumperz (1972), Ferguson (1972), Gal (1979, 1987, 1989), Heller (1988), Hill and Hill (1986), Myers-Scotton (1993), and Romaine (1995). Work on Vernacular Black English in America is surveyed in Baugh (1988); see also Abrahams (1976), Baugh (1983), Hewitt (1986), Kochman (1972), Labov (1972a), as well as the relevant articles in Ferguson and Heath (1981).

17

Language Socialization

The Acquisition of Communicative Competence: Three Cultures

In the previous chapters of this Part, we have looked at many cases of contrasting uses of language in different contexts and with different inter-locutors. Given the various social roles that people are called upon to assume with their particular class or caste positions and associated status entitlements, appropriate linguistic behavior properly follows as indexes or markers of these social meanings, all part of the expected basic communic-ative competence of any adult native speaker of the language. The question in the chapter is how is this communicative competence acquired? How are children socialized into appropriate linguistic behavior? In other words, how are the dispositions which generate these diverse linguistic practices in social roles and fields inculcated in the habitus and made to seem natural. How do they take on their hegemonic status and seem to be the way the world ought to be? These are the questions I will look at in this chapter.

The basic cultural practices through which children are socialized into being competent users of their native language vary quite widely across the globe; some basic contrasts in three societies are summarized in Ochs and Schieffelin (1984) (spelled out in greater detail in Ochs (1988) and Schieffelin (1990)). They contrast child-rearing practices with respect to language instruction in three societies: white middle-class America, Samoa, and Kaluli of New Guinea. They note that in white middle-class American society, infants from birth are treated as social beings, persons, and potential and actual addressees in verbal interaction. Adults address utterances to infants and in turn interpret infants' vocalizations and gestures as meaningful, ascribing "speech acts" to the infant. In this way, the model for future con-versational turn taking is established. Importantly in this culture, mothers and other caregivers typically try to assume what they believe might be the infant's perspective on the verbal interaction through the use of a special baby talk variety of speaking, in which her own adult language is radically simplified grammatically and takes on many specific lexical items like *poo*, *all gone*, *doggie*, and marked intonation patterns, all with strong intimate emotional overtones.

Samoa could hardly be more different. Until the baby begins to crawl, she is a non-conversational partner; babies are not directly addressed. Their gestures and vocalizations are interpreted only for what they might indicate about the infant's physiological state, not as a meaningful "speech act." When the infant begins to become mobile by crawling, instructions such as "come!" and negative sanctions now begin to be addressed to the infant, who is viewed as willful and headstrong, and needs to be brought into line to know her proper place in Samoan society. The language used is not simplified lexically or grammatically, unlike the American baby talk register. The proper place of the child is where she fits into the overall hierarchical structure of Samoan society, stratified by age and titled versus untitled. Higher ranking people, particularly titled people, act in specific ways, most particularly minimizing their movement and activities. Hence higher ranked caregivers have little active engagement with the child, leaving tasks like bathing and changing to lower ranked caregivers. This stratification has strong linguistic reflexes in the socialization of the child. When a child learns to talk, she soon learns to address her requests to the higher ranked caregivers. This caregiver, however, as befits her rank, will instruct a lower ranked one to meet the child's request. The child learns not to expect a direct response from the person she addresses, so that we find the following type of conversational sequencing (Ochs and Schieffelin 1984:296):

Child appeals to high-ranking caregiver (A → B)
High-ranking caregiver directs lower-ranking caregiver (B → C)
Lower-ranking caregiver responds to child (C → A)

This contrasts markedly with prototypical turn-taking sequencing (ABAB) norms of American English generally, and particularly between caregiver and child. It also provides a straightforward model for the child that conversations in Samoa are multiparty and organized along hierarchical lines, important knowledge in adult communicative competence.

Social hierarchy is important also in ascribing meaning to an utterance. As described in chapter 14, the responsibility of clarification of the meanings of utterances falls on those of lower rank. So if a high-rank speaker produces an unintelligible utterance, he is not expected to clarify it; that burden falls on those of lower rank. If a low-ranking speaker's utterance is unclear, the task of clarifying it, of course, remains with him. Because children are necessarily low ranking in Samoan society, their caregivers generally do not try to determine what they are saying if their speech is unclear, for example, by slow repetition or expansion of the utterance. It is up to the child to make herself understood. Again this is in marked contrast to the behavior of white American middle-class mothers. In that culture, a good mother is one who compensates for the child's linguistic incompetence by making special efforts to interpret the child's utterance and establish her intentions (this may reflect the individualist orientation of this culture: the child is already a "little person" with her own rights). She does this by taking the perspective of the child, for example, using baby talk. In Samoa, on the other hand, good caregivers encourage the child to take on the perspective of others, particular high-ranking persons, in order to show proper respect to them. Thus, using language appropriately in sociocentric Samoa, acquiring communicative competence, requires close attention to social hierarchy, a pervasive fact of Samoan social organization and cultural practices.

Kaluli of New Guinea is yet another story. The Kaluli, like most New Guinea groups, are a strongly egalitarian society, in which networks of obligation and reciprocity are all important. Language is viewed as a means of social manipulation and individual assertion, getting one's desires or rights. Infants who cannot speak are regarded as helpless and lacking understanding; they are not treated as conversational partners. When Kaluli mothers do address their babies, they do not do so directly, but hold them facing outward toward other members of the social group. When other people direct utterances to the infant, the mother responds for it in a high pitched nasalized voice, but in normal Kaluli language, there being no baby talk register. These responses by the mother are not for the infant or to instruct him linguistically (recall infants have no understanding in Kaluli belief, so how could they comprehend these utterances?); rather they are for the older children speaking to the infant, to help forge a proper social relationship between them.

When the child starts to speak (the Kaluli define it by the uses of the words *no* "mother" and *bo* "breast"), the Kaluli believe that now he must be instructed how to speak. This is done with a method of direct instruction, in which the mother models an utterance followed by the imperative verb *ɛlɛma* "say like that." Only assertive types of speech acts, like teasing, requesting, and reporting are done this way; mothers do not teach the names of objects in this manner, as white middle-class American mothers commonly do: "now this is a froggie. What's that? No, that's a turtle." Children are believed to acquire these and the ability to beg for objects naturally, so there is no need to instruct them explicitly. However, the ability to use language for asserting one's needs and staking one's claims is explicitly taught, for it is believed that this is the real role of language. And as society is primarily understood in terms of a network of obligations and reciprocal responsibilities among equals, learning to use language to assert one's needs and entitlements in this network is acquiring communicative competence in this culture. It also accounts for why there is no baby talk register. The desired goal of the mother's explicit instructions in assertive "hard" language is a strong and independent child who claims his just rights like adults, an equal among equals. Clearly, a baby talk register would be counterproductive, for it would make the child sound babyish, exactly the opposite of what is intended.

Linguistic Socialization of Gender Roles

Ultimately, as the above three examples show, language socialization is about learning how to enact in language the range of social roles available to the speaker, whether it be a Kaluli demanding his equal share in a butchered pig or a Samoan commoner puzzling out the obscure words of a titled orator. What these roles are, their range and their relative status entitlements, of course, varies widely from society to society, but common across all of these is the function of the family or core kin relations in providing models for appropriate role behavior, as the child learns to take on the dispositions of these others and their behavior in appropriate fields. The father, uncles, and their friends provide a model for appropriate male behavior, linguistic and otherwise, while the mother, aunts, and friends play the parallel role for appropriate female behavior. In relatively simple egalitarian societies like Kaluli, this may exhaust the list of potential role models. Crucially, it appears that the family is the ultimate source for a very large part of the habitual practices for appropriate gender-differentiated roles across societies. Consider the differences in the use of directive speech acts like commands and orders by young boys and girls in the United States. Remember that such speech acts, in terms of Brown and Levinson's (1987) model, threaten one's negative face, one's right to act freely without undue hindrance. Such speech acts can be performed baldly, i.e. a direct command *get out of here*, or with redressive action to one's negative face (negative politeness), *would you mind leaving; I've got a lot of work to finish*. Gleason (1987) found that fathers and mothers contrasted strongly in this feature. Fathers produced bald imperatives twice as often as mothers, fully 30 percent of the time, and more often to boys than to girls. Further, they often appended threats or insults to their commands when speaking to their sons: *don't go in there or I'll break your head*. Mothers, on the other hand, typically used redressive techniques in their directives and on the whole spoke more and with longer utterances to their children, with no obvious sexual differentiation.

These differences in male and female roles in appropriate linguistic behavior seemed to be well learned by the age of 5. For example, Anderson (1986) studied 5-year-old children in role play situations involving puppets representing the roles within a nuclear family, father, mother and child, and asked them to make up stories, taking on these various roles (this required them to take on the dispositions (habitus) of the other, a crucial step in socialization (Mead 1934)). The results were dramatic: father puppets issued bald commands with little redressive action, while mother puppets typically performed their request with redressive action like giving reasons for the request or stating them indirectly. "Fathers" also used short curt turns and commonly talked about their roles outside the home, such as their job. "Mothers" used endearments and baby talk and had longer turns. Compare the following exchanges (Anderson 1986:155):

Child:	Tell me a story.
Father:	Mommy will.
Child:	No, I want you to –
Father:	All right. Sit down. "Once upon a time. The end."

Child:	Mommy, I'm all done.
Mother:	OK, sweetie. Now it's time for your naptime.
Mother:	Gotta get the baby tucked into beddy bye. She's not a sleepy. [to baby] Go to sleep, sleep, sleep, darling. Go to sleep. [Turns to father] Don't you think it's time to go to bed? It's midnight – we should go to bed.

In giving directives to the child puppet for actions to be carried out, "fathers" statistically used bald imperatives 88 percent of the time, as opposed to "mothers" 46 percent. Also, "mothers" used statements or hints as directives to action 54 percent of time, but "fathers" only 12 percent.

Sachs (1987) is another experimental study of role play situations, in which 5-year-old children were instructed to enact the roles of doctor and patient. She investigated the class of speech acts she labelled "obliges," which is any speech act that obligates the addressee to respond, such as imperatives, questions, prohibitions, etc. Some examples are shown in 17.1 (Sachs 1987:182).

Clearly, most of these belong to the class of directives, some of which are bald without redress (imperatives, prohibitives, etc.) and some with redress (pretend and question directives, tag questions, etc.). Not surprisingly, boys and girls differ quite strongly in their preferences for particular types of obliges as shown in table 17.2 (Sachs 1987:182).

Further, when the obliges without redressive action are grouped together and compared with those with redress, a marked gender asymmetry emerges: boys used 42 percent obliges without redress to girls 17 percent, while girls used obliges with redress 65 percent of the time to boys 34 percent. Clearly, the boys in this experimental study were more assertive, quite often simply telling someone else what to do, without any regard for that person's sense

17.1

Speech Act	Example
Imperative	Bring her to the hospital.
Prohibition	Don't touch it.
Declarative Directive	You have to push it.
Pretend Directive	Pretend you had a bad cut.
Question Directive	Will you be the patient?
Tag Question	That's your bed, right?
Joint Directive	Now we'll cover him up.
State Question	Are you sick?
Information question	What does she need now?
Attentional Device	Lookit.

17.2

Category	Boys	Girls
Imperative	25	10
Prohibition	11	2
Declarative Directive	6	5
Pretend Directive	4	11
Question Directive	0	2
Tag Question	16	35
Joint Directive	3	15
State Question	11	2
Information question	22	16
Attentional Device	2	2

of face, just as their fathers seem to behave toward them. Girls, on the other hand, are much more likely to use redressive action in their directives, reflecting the model of their mother's speech and also perhaps a more general female concern with the other person's cooperation and contribution, ultimately a concern to enhance or at least not offend their sense of face. These 5-year-old children already seem to be well socialized into the behavior expected of them as adults.

The studies thus far have investigated children's production of directives, but what about their response to directives issued to them: do their response patterns also exhibit a gender asymmetry? This was investigated by Ervin-Tripp, O'Connor and Rosenberg (1984), with children of 3 to 4 years of age, and it turns out that while boys and girls comply or fail to comply with directives at about the same rate, their patterns of non-compliance are quite different. Boys more commonly refused directives overtly (boys 54 percent to girls 35 percent), reflecting more openly assertive and defiant behavior, while girls were more likely to follow a pattern of ignoring them (girls 33 percent to boys 16 percent). Not surprisingly, for both sexes, bald directives without redress were more likely to assure compliance than those with redressive action. The high rate of boys' outright defiant refusal is clearly a claim of their autonomy and individualist rights, challenging the authority of the issuer of the directive to control their behavior. The status and power contests of boys (and men!) clearly have very early roots in their linguistic socialization.

Linguistic Socialization of Status Roles

Continuing with the subject of directives, Ervin-Tripp (1977) has demonstrated how young children are keenly aware of the social meaning of various types of directives and use them appropriately to enact linguistic routines with interlocutors of different status entitlements. In earlier work, Ervin-Tripp (1976) demonstrated that directives in adults' speech in American English are differentiated according to the social meanings that they carry. Some examples: need or desire statements, *I need a match*, directed to subordinates mainly; imperatives, *give me a match*, directed to subordinates or solidary equals; embedded imperatives, *could you give me a match*, directed to non-solidary interlocutors or those of different status ranking to speaker; permissive directives, *may I have a match?*, directed to non-solidary interlocutors or possibly those of superior rank; hints, *the matches are all gone*, to solidary interlocutors (Ervin-Tripp 1977:166–70). Ervin-Tripp demonstrates that children as young as 2 are aware of the social meaning of at least some of these variants. She reports a study of a 2-year old, who employed imperatives almost exclusively to her peers, but to adults she used either desire or need statements (56 percent) or permissive directives (38 percent). The child even made subtle status distinctions according to age: in her nursery school she freely gave direct imperatives to her fellow 2-year olds, but employed only questions and permissive directives like *can I have an apple, Nida, please?* to the 4-year old present. At home, she strongly differentiated linguistically between her father and mother. Three-fourths of her directives to her father used repetition and politeness formulas, but the rate for her mother was significantly less. An interesting test of her awareness of the social meanings of the various forms of directives was tried. An empty glass was set at her place next to a bottle of milk; normally her milk was poured for her before she was seated. To her mother, she said *Mommy, I want milk*, but to her father, various indirect strategies were employed, typically hints: C: *What's that?* F: *Milk*; C: *My milk, Daddy.* F:

17.3

Child	Age at onset	Total	Lower	Peer	Higher
Iakopo	2;1	100% (3)	0	100% (3)	0
Matu'u	2;1	100% (22)	73% (16)	0	27% (6)
Naomi	2;10	100% (29)	62% (18)	0	38% (11)
Niulala	2;11	100% (25)	8% (2)	68% (17)	24% (6)
Average		100% (19.75)	46% (9)	25% (5)	29% (5.75)

Yes, it's your milk; C: *It's milk, Daddy*. F: *Yes, it is*; C: *You want milk, Daddy?* F: *I have some, thank you*; C: *Milk in there, Daddy*. F: *Yes*. Clearly, at age 2 this child was already aware of different social roles and their relative status entitlements, and the use of language to recognize and enact these social understandings.

Similar findings have been reported in other cultures. Platt (1986) discusses speech patterns of young Samoan children. Remember that Samoa is a highly stratified society and that a typical feature of higher status is little physical activity or motion and minimal involvement in the activities of others around them. As pointed out earlier, higher ranked caregivers (i.e. older) tend not to become directly involved in the more active caregiving tasks, these being reserved for lower ranked (i.e. younger) caregivers. Because of these cultural understandings, the verb *sau* "come" is properly used only by higher status people to lower, as it expresses the ability for one to direct another person's movement. Because within the household, relative rank in status is based on age, children are always lower ranking than adults, and younger children lower than older children. Hence *sau* "come" is not an appropriate command by young children to adults or older children, in contrast to its ubiquity in the speech of American children. Indeed, 2-year-old Samoan children seem to be quite aware of the social meaning embedded in the imperative *sau* "come," using it mainly to lower ranking children or peers, as table 17.3 (Platt 1986:143) shows.

This is in marked contrast to the distribution of the imperative *'aumai* "give, bring." Reciprocity and exchange is a fundamental value of Samoan culture, even across the status rankings. Anyone, even a young child, has the right to request her fair share from anyone else, regardless of their relative ranking. Obviously, young children are not normally likely to have much in the way of desirable objects, so their directives will most likely be addressed to those older, i.e. of higher status. Hence, *'aumai* "give, bring" has a distribution of usage, roughly opposite to that of *sau* "come," as shown in table 17.4 (Platt 1986:148).

While the distribution of *sau* "come" clearly demonstrates the young

17.4

Child	Age at onset	Total	Lower	Peer	Higher
Iakopo	2;1	100% (112)	0	38% (42)	62% (70)
Matu'u	2;1	100% (28)	18% (5)	29% (8)	53% (15)
Naomi	2;10	100% (161)	1% (1)	0	99% (160)
Niulala	2;11	100% (62)	15% (9)	29% (18)	56% (35)
Average		100% (91)	4% (4)	19% (17)	77% (70)

Samoan child's understanding of social rank in Samoa and its cultural manifestations and normative uses of language, that of '*aumai* "give, bring" probably reflects the simple economic fact that higher ranked interlocutors are generally the holders of desired goods. Nonetheless, Samoan children even at age 2, like American children of the same age, are well aware of status differences and how to use language appropriately to recognize these.

A study by Hollos (1977) demonstrates similar knowledge in somewhat older Hungarian children (ages 7 to 9) by probing their control of the complex T/V phenomena in this language. The adult system is as follows:

T form: *te* plus second-person singular form of verb
V form: *maja* plus third-person singular form of verb
P(olite) form: title plus surname or honorific plus Christian or surname plus third-person singular of the verb *tetszen*; "wish, like, please" plus infinitive of main verb
F(ormal)-P(olite): *on* plus third-person singular form of verb

The norms for adult usage: T is for solidary interlocutors, e.g. between close kin, especially those similar in age and between same-sex friends or opposite-sex intimates. V is for non-solidary interlocutors of same status, e.g. in most opposite-sex interactions, customer/clerk, waiter/customer, or where status differentials are minimized by working together, e.g. boss/worker. P is generally non-reciprocal. Non-reciprocal P/T is exchanged between adults, even kin relations, with a considerable age difference, the older giving T, but receiving P. Persons with considerable status differences, e.g. veterinarian/farmer, exchange P/V, the higher status person giving V, but receiving P. Finally, FP is restricted in use and only rarely used in the rural areas of Hollos's study, but is used non-reciprocally with V in situations of formal applications like in addressing a high functionary.

The children in the study actively control only a reduced variant of the system, using T reciprocally to children and P non-reciprocally to adults, receiving T in return. They do not actively control V, but they are at least passively aware of its social meaning, as brought out by Hollos's study. She presented the children with pictures of different types of people of varying ages and professions engaged in their daily activities. Children were instructed to scrutinize the role of one of the figures in the pictures and asked "How does your mother greet the shopkeeper when she goes shopping? Ask for eggs as your mother would." The address forms the children used were then recorded. In a second task, children were again presented with pictures with the figures but this time with dialog supplied. The children were asked to decide which figure in the picture would be the appropriate addressee of a particular address form, T, V or P. The scenes and figures presented were chosen with a view to presenting all possibilities. For example, the mother in the figure asks "Did you leave the door open?" Possible addressees depicted are: grandfather (P form), child (T form), veterinarian (V form).

All children had no problems with appropriate usage between children (reciprocal T) and between children and adults (non-reciprocal P/T). These mirror their own active competence. Nor was reciprocal T between solidary adults of similar ages much of a problem, again a usage they would observe daily. V, however, did present problems. The children often correctly assigned it when familiar adults like parents were addressing strangers, but were almost completely baffled about when it should be used between unfamiliar adults, generally incorrectly extending reciprocal P to this situation. This, of course, is an extension of their own system for addressing adults to this unfamiliar situation. On the whole, even the youngest children distinguished between the P/V use of familiar adults like parents, but had great difficulties in figuring out what were the appropriate forms in interactions with unfamiliar adults. However, by age 9, most of these errors became ironed out, the number of errors now being very small, but still most of them involving unfamiliar adults using V. The V form clearly seems to be the most difficult for the children, a fact undoubtedly related to its absence in active use from their speech, requiring the children to generalize from other's usage. Still, the fact that most 9-year olds do assign the use of V correctly in most cases does indicate that they are aware of most of its social meaning, and are simply trying to pinpoint it more accurately.

The Acquisition of Communicative Norms

The final case study in this chapter looks at how children acquire what might loosely be called communicative "style," the overall basic normative principles which guide the form and use of languages in different speech communities (see also Scollon and Scollon 1995) (we might regard this as a kind of "linguistic habitus" (Bourdieu 1991)). Clancy (1986) discusses this for Japanese, a language whose norms of usage contrast very strongly with those of American English. Japanese culture is one that sets great store by empathy with others, using language to reinforce emotional ties that bind all together to forge social harmony. Anything that threatens this harmony is avoided, and, rather as with Malagasy, indirectness in speech is highly prized, thoughts and ideas being expressed tentatively, so as not to threaten social harmony. Speakers must always be on guard to protect the feelings of others, to monitor their own speech so that the all important harmonious social interactions will not be harmed. Ambiguity and indirectness, then, are highly prized linguistic features, allowing a wide leeway for interlocutors to negotiate harmonious interactions and relationships.

Clancy studied the language acquisition of three 2-year-old children to see how these linguistic values were imparted to the children by their caregivers, in this case their mothers. She noted a number of distinct methods by which these dispositions were inculcated. First, children were impressed upon to pay attention to the speech of others, never allowed to fail to respond (Clancy 1986:220):

Adult:	*Mahochan wa nanika tabeten no? Koko nani ga haitten no?*
	"Are you eating something? What is in there?"
Child:	[No response]
Mother:	*Nani ga haitteru no ka naa. Oneesan nani ga haitten no tte kiiteru yo*
	"I wonder what could be in there. Older sister is asking 'What is in there?'"
Child:	*Purin*
	"Pudding"

Requests were repeated with even greater insistence; mothers exhibited great concern if the child failed to comply with a request (Clancy 1986:221):

PC:	*Yotchan no shooboojidoosha misete*
	"Show me your fire engine"
Child:	[No response]
Mother:	*Shooboojidoosha da tte.*
	"She said, 'Fire engine'"
PC:	*Shooboojidoosha.*
	"Fire engine"
Mother:	*Sa, hayaku. Patricia-san misete tte yutteru yo. Isoganakucha. Isoganakucha. A! A!*
	"Well, quickly. Patricia is saying, 'Show me it.' You must hurry. You must hurry. Oh! Oh!"

Second, children were taught to respond positively to requests or overtures, regardless of their own individual feelings, again an emphasis on

Japanese norms of empathy for others and overall social harmony (Clancy 1986:223):

> [Child refused to lend toys to younger child]
> *Mother*: *Dame tte yuu no? Hirochan ni mo doozo tte kashite agenakya. Takusan aru kara, hitotsu doozo tte kashite agenakya. Akachan Kawaii deshoo?*
> "Do you say 'No!'? You must lend one to Hirochan, saying 'Help yourself'. The baby is cute/lovable, isn't he?"

Also to facilitate overall social harmony, children are instructed overtly to conform with acceptable social behavior and censured if they do otherwise (Clancy 1986:237):

> [Child pretends to eat one of some toy dishes]
> *Mother*: *Sonna koto shite osara taberu to okashii deshoo? Osara tabeteru hito inai deshoo? Ne? Osara dare ga tabeteru no?*
> "Isn't it strange to do that kind of thing, if you eat a plate? No one eats plates, do they? Who eats plates?"
> *Child*: *Kore Mahochan*
> "Maho (eats) this"
> *Mother*: *Mahochan ga tabeteru no? Kaijuu mitai. Kowai. Iya. Kowai, obake mitai. Mama obake kirai yo*
> "You're eating it? Like a beast. It's scary. I don't like it. It's scary, like a monster. I hate monsters"

Indeed, Japanese often tell a misbehaving child *hito ni warawareru*, "you'll be laughed at by other people," a succinct formula for the importance of overt social conformity in this society and the crucial idea of socialization as internalizing in the habitus the dispositions of the other. This exchange also demonstrates the pivotal role of the mother as the primary agent for teaching this idea to the child and making him properly Japanese in outward demeanor.

Finally, because of the overarching goal of social harmony through attendance to others' needs, direct refusals or rejections of others' requests or overtures are strongly negatively sanctioned. Children are instructed to avoid saying "no" directly, as in the last comment by the mother in the following exchange (Clancy 1986:237):

> *Adult*: *Kore nani iro?*
> "What color is this?"
> *Child*: *Een, dame!*
> "No!"

Mother: *Nani yutten no! Midori tte yuu n deshoo*
           "What are you saying! You should say, 'Green'"
Child: *Midori*
           "Green"
Mother: *Dame nante yuu hito dare mo inai yo*
           "There is no one who says things like 'No!'"

Clearly, Japanese children are given very different models of, and instructions in, language use during their language acquisition than are American children, and this results ultimately in the very different norms of usage or linguistic habitus for adults in these societies. A result, which in the end, is the source for the very serious problems of crosscultural communication commonly discussed in studies of Japanese–American relations (Barlund 1975; Ito 1980; Moeran 1988). The process of acquiring a language of a culture and of becoming a competent person in it are crucially tied together: to be a fully competent Japanese or American person requires knowledge of the norms for the appropriate use of Japanese or American English. Difficulties in communication are not isolatable to linguistic differences alone, but include the understandings of how a person should enact herself across the range of roles society provides for her. Japanese indirectness and reticence and American forthrightness and assertiveness are more than simply linguistic conventions; they go to the heart of what are valued as qualities of persons in these cultures. To return to Gergen (1990), ultimately the kinds of persons these cultures value emerge in the mutual coordination of their actions with others, including linguistic actions. Linguistic socialization is no more and no less than this process of coordination and in this deeper sense continues through life. (Of course beyond the early childhood socialization in the context of the family, nuclear or extended, much crucial socialization in modern societies takes place in the educational system of formal schooling, which, predicated on Western models, does tend to have some similarities crossculturally. Central to this process is the inculcation of the skills of literacy, which I will turn to in chapter 21.)

Summary

The acquisition of normative linguistic practices plays a central role in the socialization of the child into being a competent member of the culture. Because different cultures have different practices and values, linguistic socialization practices vary quite widely: in middle-class American society infants are encouraged to speak and are treated as conversational partners from birth, but in Samoa and Kaluli, this is not the case. Only when the child begins to show social autonomy, either through crawling or the first utterances does the child begin to be addressed, inculcating in her the proper linguistic practices for these cultures, learning proper deference to superiors (Samoa) or the ability to assert one's wants (Kaluli). From an early age, children seem to be aware of gender-determined differences in norms for the use of language. At age 5, boys already clearly see language as a way to assert their dominance and needs, with little redressive action, while girls typically employ redressive strategies and exhibit a concern for the addressee's cooperation and contributions. Young children are also well attuned to differences of status and power; by age 2, they seem able to appreciate status differences among interlocutors and employ proper linguistic uses, although the full complexities of systems like T/V contrasts may elude them until much later. Linguistic socialization also plays a primary role in inculcating in the child various norms for linguistic interactions as they enact proper behavior for a competent person in the culture. Ultimately, Japanese indirectness and reticence and American assertiveness and forthrightness are valued personal characteristics in these two cultures which are primarily enacted in linguistic practices and hence learned by successful linguistic socialization.

Further Reading

On socialization in general, consult Field, Sostek, Vietze, and Leiderman (1981) and Munroe, Munroe, and Whiting (1981). For language socialization, have a look at the survey articles by Ochs and Schieffelin (1984) and Schieffelin and Ochs (1986a). Individual case studies are found in Cook-Gumperz (1973), Cook-Gumperz, Corsaro, and Streek (1986), Ervin-Tripp and Mitchell-Kernan (1977), Ochs (1988), Schieffelin (1990), Schieffelin and Ochs (1986b), and Streek (1983). For more structural approaches to language learning, Bowerman (1981) is an excellent introduction, but also see textbooks on language acquisition like Eliot (1981), Goodluck (1991), or Ingram (1989).

18

Genre: Poetics, Ritual Languages, and Verbal Art

Genres and Framing

In the previous three chapters, I presented differences in linguistic forms or registers as indexes or markers of various social variables centered on the personhood of the various speech event participants, their gender, class, caste, or ethnicity, etc. There is at least one other way that the personhood of a speech act participant can be indexed by a linguistic form, and this is through the concept of *genre*, the different types of speech events themselves and how they are constructed and understood linguistically. Hanks (1996) demonstrates that the social role of the shaman in curing ceremonials in Mayan culture is crucially tied to his ability to possess texts of a particular genre, curing chants, and to enact these unique texts in the ritual contexts of curing, which, to some extent at least, are in fact created by the very enaction of those texts. This indexical marking of social roles through controlling and enacting genre types is, of course, not unique to Mayan shamans; in our own culture, Catholic priests are indexed by, among other features, their enaction of the Church liturgy, and lawyers, by their mastery of legal genres. In fact, mastery of particular genre types may be a crucial defining property of many of the more highly conventionalized and prescribed roles in society.

Genre is a contentious and much written about subject, but Bakhtin's (1981, 1986) work is perhaps the most insightful in its understanding. For Bakhtin, genres consist of historically transmitted, relatively stable frameworks for orienting the production of discourse. While strongly conventionalized and grounded in the social practices of language production and understanding in the community, they are still nonetheless flexible and open to creative manipulation by performers. Thus, while *once upon a time* is a conventionalized opening formula for the production of a text belonging to the fairy-tale genre in English; this need not necessarily be so: a speaker could creatively invoke this formula, for example, to add particular folksy, fairy-tale like or traditionalist nuances to an academic paper (for an example of an academic paper cast in a narrative framework, see Pawley (1993b)). Formulae like *once upon a time* are framing devices in Bateson's (1972) terms or markers of *footing* (Goffman 1974, 1981), that is, indexes of the genres which the speaker is producing or wishes for some reason to invoke. They can also be seen as kinds of *contextualization cues* in the sense of Gumperz (1982, 1993). Such framing/footing devices work, as clearly seen by Bakhtin, to the extent that genres are not so much inherent in the text forms themselves, but in the frameworks and interpretive procedures that verbal performers and their audiences use to produce and understand these texts. (For example, an academic paper remains an academic paper because it invokes most of the framing devices associated with that genre, for example, extensive referencing; it can, however, be related in a narrative-like "key" (Hymes 1972b) by invoking some framing devices characteristic of this genre. This demonstrates that genre classifications are not rigidly definable in terms of formal text types, but are the result of applying (sometimes conflicting) interpretive procedures.)

Intertextuality

As emphasized by Bakhtin, the orienting frameworks and interpretative procedures that constitute genres are historically transmitted, as are other language forms. And like other language forms in Bakhtin's view, genres are strongly *dialogic* in his particular sense, i.e. "a single strip of talk (utterance, text, story) can juxtapose language drawn from, and invoking, alternative cultural, social and linguistic home environments, the interpenetration of multiple voices and forms of utterance" (Duranti and Goodwin 1992:19). Other terms for the same Bakhtinian notion are *polyphony* or *heteroglossia*. The different voices in dialogic texts call up different cultural, historical and personal perspectives, "prior texts" in Becker's (1995) terminology or "intertextuality" in that of Briggs and Bauman (1992). Thus, in the academic paper example mentioned above, the framing devices that invoke the genre of academic papers call into mind the many hundreds of previous academic papers any professional academic must have read, leading her to judge the present one under discussion in terms of the historically situated and professionally transmitted canon for this genre. Whether it is a good or bad academic paper is judged in terms of this canon, and this is not absolute, but is calibrated in terms of the many previous good or bad academic papers (prior texts, intertextuality) the professional academic reader has read. The grounds for determining whether it is a narrative or not are, of course, completely different. The framing devices for this genre call into memory the many narratives or stories that the academic reader knows; these are the prior texts, the source of intertextuality. As a result of this, the reader will have fairly clear ideas of what a narrative should be like; whether the case under discussion succeeds or not will depend on the reader's judgment of how well the author blended the demands of academic exposition with the expectations of this genre.

In essence, it is the prior texts or intertextuality which constitute the dialogic sense of this text, but this text is not unusual, for language, being historically transmitted, is inherently dialogic. Our mouths are full of the words of others, which we apply to our present circumstances. A superb example is the proverb. Proverbs are passed on from generation to generation in a quite fixed form to communicate an important moral or practical truth which pertains to a new situation. They are the words of others, recontextualized in our present now, in order to provide an interesting or important viewpoint on the present situation. They derive their power both from their formal fixed rather poetic structure and from their carrying a kind of folksy received wisdom, a putatively widely shared public opinion. Proverbs like *he who hesitates is lost*; *there's no use crying over spilt milk*; or the proverb from Maninka of West Africa *the lizard and the bat do not eat the same dish* (i.e. *one man's meat is another man's poison*) (Bird and Shopen 1979:190) demonstrate both these properties. This proverb genre can be performed when a speaker finds a context in which their message seems relevant and their abbreviated forms seem to succinctly sum up the situation. So on hearing that one has missed an opportunity to make a significant profit in the stock market, one might respond: "well, you know, *there's no use crying over spilt milk.*" In Maninka culture, the creative and appropriate use of proverbs is a highly valued facet of verbal interaction; one must master this genre well if one is to be a competent speaker of the language, as in the following interchange (Bird and Shopen 1979:99):

Old man:	Ah, you are becoming a Maninka. You speak the language like one of us
Newcomer:	No matter how long a log lies in the water, it never becomes a crocodile (i.e. "as a foreigner I still and always will have a lot to learn")
Old man:	Ah, my son, a log lying in the water is still the cause of fear (i.e. "you are behaving enough like a Maninka to be respected as a member of the group")

Genres do vary to the extent that they involve dialogic expansion and richness, which can be viewed as a scale, ranging from those which are relatively monologic to those which are richly dialogic. Genres like proverbs, charms, and spells (Sebeok 1964) and some types of poetry have highly

stereotypical and constrained forms and do not easily admit the incorpora-
tion of new and multiple dialogic voices, while others like drama, the epic
poem and, most importantly, the novel are formally much more open-ended
and easily allow the addition of new and often conflicting voices, from whence
much of the power of these genres derives. A typical way these genres accomplish just this is through the device of *reported speech* (Vološinov 1986), in
which the quoted speech of one party is embedded in the talk of another
(like *Jane then said "Well, I'm not going to the wedding"*), either that of the
author of the work, as commonly in the novel, or of another character, for
example, in drama. The presence of reported speech distinguishes genres
along a dimension from more monologic to more dialogic. Highly formally
constrained, stereotypical genres like proverbs tend toward the monologic
side of the scale in contrast to some more openly formatted genres like the
novel, which tend to be strongly dialogic. There are also some relatively
more openly formatted genres which tend toward the monologic, for example, scientific writing, especially in the hard sciences. To be an exemplary
member of the genre of the scientific essay, a scientific journal article must
speak in one voice, be cogently argued, and present a single coherent point
of analysis; in this sense it can be viewed as a monologic genre. Of course,
a scientific journal article is historically situated and marked by the pro-
lific citing of the thoughts and statements (i.e. voices) of earlier workers in
the field (documented through references, a salient framing device for this
genre); these are dialogic components in this genre. However, unlike the
typical novel and more notably, the typical drama, these are background
information for this genre, not normally part of its major rhetorical power,
which is to convince the reader of the author's arguments and analysis. It is
in this sense that they are monologic, like proverbs or magic spells.

The Poetic Function

Genres, then, differ along one very salient dimension in how fixed or
stereotypical are the expected formats and interpretive procedures we use
for producing and interpreting them. Of course, these are culturally defined
and will vary, but ultimately these are questions of form, how the generic
performance is formally carried out. In Jakobson's (1960) terms, what is of
concern here is the *poetic function* of language, a reflexive concern with the
actual form of the utterance itself. Form becomes a focus of attention in its
own right, independent of meaning. A good example might be that lines in
much of English poetry rhyme; this is a purely formal constraint for this
type of English poetry, quite independent of other aspects of a poem's
meaning. This formal constraint defines some poetic genres in English,
leading speakers who spontaneously produce rhyme of this sort in their

speech to disclaim "Oh, I'm a poet and I didn't know it." This focused concern with an utterance's form is what Jakobson means by the poetic function, and while perhaps most salient in poetic genres (hence Jakobson's name for it), it is by no means limited to them. All genres have formal constraints salient to them, their own realizations of the poetic function. Narratives in English, as in other European languages, for example, have formal features which act as frames for this genre (for example, see Labov (1972a); Labov and Waletzky (1967)). Among the most noticeable are those associated with the development of the plot. The order of events in the story should be sequential, so that the order of events in the plot is iconic with the order of their narration. Flashbacks, i.e. narrated events which actually occurred earlier in the plot, and jumping ahead to narrate events which have yet to occur in the development of the plot are permissible, but they must be clearly signposted, indicated by a framing device that they are such. These constraints are in marked contrast to Becker's (1995) description of the generic format for the Javanese shadow theatre. In this genre, such linear plot development is not mandated. The plots of Javanese shadow theatre jump around, leading to coincidences of narrative events from different times and places, and it is in the nature of these coincidences that the power of the plot obtains. Coincidence rather than cumulative development is the salient formal constraint, a realization of the poetic function, in the Javanese shadow theatre. The psychological salience of such formal-framing properties is demonstrated in work by Bartlett (1932). In some pioneering experiments, Bartlett had subjects listen to various exotic stories from various cultural traditions and then asked them to recall the plot at various subsequent intervals. He found that they were not able to recall such input accurately and that the inaccuracies exhibited regular patterns. Subjects would revise the plots until they came to resemble standard stories they had heard, a prototypical wild west narrative, for example. This demonstrates the forceful constraining power of framing devices in constructing genres of diverse types; in the case of these exotic narratives, the familiar framing devices of well-known narratives were so salient as to cause the exotic narratives to be reframed in order to fit into standard cultural models of this genre.

Genres like proverbs, spells, poetry and narratives, exist first and foremost in their performance. They may be written down or memorized and thus en-textualized, i.e. turned into relatively stable re-presentable decontextualized versions of themselves as texts (Bauman and Briggs 1990), such as when an oral epic poem like the *Iliad* is offered to readers as a written text (what Hanks (1989) calls "decentering"). But clearly this is a strictly secondary, derivative version of the genre, removed from the circumstances which generated it, first and foremost as a performance with a performer and an audience. The formal constraints which frame the genre, its poetic function, are primarily those which diagnose its performance as a competent, even better, artful one for both the performer and the audience. If the performer varies too much from the appropriate formal constraints, the audience may judge it a poor performance of the genre and may not even recognize it as a performance of the genre. Again this may be most apparent with the more formally fixed genres like proverbs; if the utterance is a completely new expression, the audience will probably not even recognize it as a proverb at all. On the other hand, in some more openly formatted genres like epic poetry, if the performer sticks too rigidly to stereotypical formal constraints, the audience may also judge it a poor performance, due to boredom from repetition and lack of imagination. By and large, a good performance should lie between extreme fixity and unconstrained creativity; skillfully navigating the range between these two poles is the essence of verbal art.

Framing Devices: Lexical Shifts

The poetic function, as realized in various genres, gives the performer and audience a number of formal framing devices for the performance of good instances of verbal art. Bauman (1977:15–24) provides a useful inventory of these different types of framing devices. One type is the use of special introductory formulae which index the genre, such as *did you hear the one about* for a joke or *once upon a time* for a fairy tale. Related to this and, in a sense a global extension of it, is the use of specialized language styles or codes to signal a particular genre. These are the ritual languages so familiar from ethnographic descriptions of cultures around the world. Quite commonly the major differences between these ritual languages and the ordinary languages of the community are found in the lexicon, but there may be grammatical differences as well, especially in relatively short, highly stereotypical genres like charms or magical spells. Thus, Sebeok's (1964) study of Cheremis charms shows them to have a syntactic structure quite divergent from ordinary conversation and narrative, as well as a highly abstruse vocabulary, largely of non-native etymology. In other cases the differences are largely lexical, as in Sherzer's (1983:26) presentation of the special lexical forms of the Kuna *ikarkana* or curing rituals:

Everyday Kuna	Curing Ritual Kuna	
ome	walepunkwa	"woman"
tii	wiasali	"water"
ipya	tala	"eye"
neka	posumpa	"house"
enukke	yatwe	"to wash"

A similar phenomenon obtains in the specialized language of Asmat songs, a language of Irian Jaya (Voorhoeve 1977:27):

Everyday Asmat	*Song Asmat*	
pi	sap	"cassowary"
ew	osama	"crocodile"
pir	manam	"moon"
cowuc	yuwar	"woman"
mu	okom	"water"
amas	mama	"sago"

The most extreme cases of specialized codes or ritual languages to frame a particular genre involve the use of an entirely distinct language, as with the role of Latin in the Roman Catholic ritual of the Mass throughout the world up until the 1960s.

Another typical device is the use of figurative language or literary tropes (see Burke 1941, 1969; Fernandez 1974, 1986; Friedrich 1979, 1986, 1991). These also derive their power as framing devices from their deviation from the uses of ordinary language, directing the audience to attend to the text through the semantic density and suggestiveness of the lexical items used. One of the most common types of figurative language is metaphor, describing one thing in terms of another, by at least sharing some semantic feature(s) (see chapter 9), well known in English poetry. It is also employed in Kuna *ikarkana*, where Everyday Kuna *kwalluleke* "to be born" is replaced by *akteke* "to land," *tuttu* "flower" by *kurkin* "hat," and is pervasive in Asmat songs, in which a word used in a line of a song should not be repeated in later lines, but replaced with a metaphorically related equivalent. So *yow* "sun" will be replaced by *yesir*, which in turn will be replaced by *pir* "moon." Quite long metaphorical chains can be constructed in this way: as "faeces" → *peke* "lump of clay" → *minuk* "hard lump of clay" → *pow* "soft mud"; and *yuwur* "dog" → *sun* "wallaby" → *foc* "possum"→ *nayir* "type of marsupial" → *yiwir* "sugar glider" → *mupir* "water rat" → *poco* "rat" → *pirow* "big mouse" → *pea* "mouse" (Voorhoeve 1977:23–6). Another type of figurative language is metonymy, the linking of words through a part–whole relationship or physical contiguity. Again, Asmat song language provides good examples; *cen* "vagina" is replaced by *men* "sharp edge" or *pim* "edge, rim" and *ser* "fish" by *makpin* "ripples on the surface of the water" (often caused by *ser* swimming close to the surface). One of the most striking types of figurative language use is antonymy, using a specific word or utterance, but actually meaning its opposite. This is a large part of irony in English genres, but plays an important role in many ritual languages, especially those of Australian Aborigines like the Warlpiri (Hale 1971). A good example is provided by specialized languages associated with curing rituals among the

Kewa of highlands New Guinea (Franklin 1975), so that *inumakua*, normally "young unmarried girl" actually means "boy" in the ritual language.

Parallelism

Perhaps the most common framing device is parallelism, stated most generally as recurring patterns in successive sections of the text. Jakobson (1960:358) sees parallelism as the poetic function *par excellence* and defines it as "the poetic function projects the principle of equivalence from the axis of selection into the axis of combination." Unpacking this, what he means is the kinds of choices which constitute the structure of the linguistic system at various levels, phonological (the phonemes /p/ versus /b/, /pɛt/ versus /bɛt/), grammatical (*a quicker runner* versus *one who runs more quickly*) and lexicosemantic (*big* versus *little*, *little* versus *tiny*, *state* versus *government*, *child* versus *flower*), are projected onto recurring successive bits of text, leading to similarities, parallelisms, across units of the text. This is perhaps most apparent in phonology; phonological parallelism is the basis of rhyme for line final syllables in English poetry and recurring metrical patterns in the lines of a verse, as in Shakespeare's Sonnet 29:

> When in disgrace with fortune and men's eyes,
> I all alone beweep my outcast state,
> And trouble deaf Heaven with my bootless cries,
> And look upon myself, and curse my fate,
> Wishing me like to one more rich in hope,
> Featur'd like him, like him with friends possess'd,
> Desiring this man's art, and that man's scope,
> With what I most enjoy contented least;
> Yet in these thoughts myself almost despising,
> Haply I think on thee, – and then my state
> (Like to the lark at break of day arising
> From sullen earth) sings hymns at heaven's gate;
> For thy sweet love remember'd such wealth brings,
> That then I scorn to change my state with kings.

Note the recurring parallel pattern of final rhyme in alternate lines (line 1 /aɪz/, line 2 /eɪt/, and again line 3 /aɪz/, line 4 /eɪt/, and so on) and the common metrical pattern of each line (a unit of unstressed syllable followed by stressed syllable repeated five times, so called iambic pentameter). This is parallelism at the phonological level, and such a rigid parallelistic patterning is indexical for this genre of English poetry, for a sonnet is an alternately rhymed poem in iambic pentameter consisting of exactly 14 lines. Other genres of English poetry may be less rigid, but still rely on phonological parallelism; for example, free verse dispenses with rhyme, but still uses meter, that is rhythmical parallelism, as well as other kinds of phonological parallelisms, as in the opening of Whitman's "Out of the Cradle Endlessly Rocking":

> Out of the cradle endlessly rocking
> Out of the mockingbird's throat, the musical shuttle
> Out of the Ninth-month midnight

The rhythm of each line is built around the same meter, from two to four short unstressed syllables (˘) followed by a strongly stressed syllable (´). The first line is composed of two of these units:

Oŭt ŏf thĕ crádlĕ ĕndlĕsslў róckĭng

The first line contains two of these units, the second line, three, and the third line, two. In addition each line is in parallel by starting with the words *out of the*; this is a kind of alliteration, recurring initial phonemic sequences.

The use of rhyme, alliteration, and meter are framing devices, indexicals, for English poetic genres, and we might expect that, while some other verbal traditions may also make use of these framing devices for poetry, others may not. The study of how other traditions of verbal art frame their performances of oral poetry is the study of ethnopoetics (Hymes 1981; Tedlock 1972, 1983). Tedlock argues that poetry among the Native North American traditions is not characterized by the patterns of phonological parallelism typical of European traditions, but is largely structured by the placement and durations of pauses, and other paralinguistic phenomena such as pitch and loudness, with grouping of words between pauses belonging to a single phonological unit, which is then set up in parallel array to preceding and following units. Conversely, Hymes (1981, 1987) argues that it is grammatical properties which structure Native North American poetry into units, the local equivalent of lines and verses. The use of particular sentence initial particles or adverbials is claimed to signal the beginning of new poetic units. (It is probably unnecessary to choose between Tedlock's and Hymes's views, for quite probably both are operative in these Native North American poetic genres; for a brilliant synthesis of both views plus some very original contributions of his own, see Woodbury (1985, 1987).)

Hymes's understanding of ethnopoetics introduces the idea of grammatical parallelism, recurring morphological or syntactic patterns in a text. Again these are highly noticeable in English poetry; note that each line in the snippet from Whitman's poem cited above begins in a prepositional phrase. Grammatical parallelism often mixed with phonological parallelism as in the Whitman lines above, is highly characteristic of performances of ritual languages. In Kuna (Sherzer 1983), the suffix -*ye*, which signals an optative or vocative mood, occurs with great frequency in the ritual language performances for curing. Further, utterances in Kuna ritual language often conclude with one of a stereotypical class of words, meaning "say," "see," "hear," and "in truth." Note the extensive phonological and grammatical parallelism in the following ritual chant for curing headaches and increasing brain power (Sherzer 1983:54) (*kurkin* "hat" is used metaphorically to mean "brain power"):

> *kurkin ipekantinaye*
> Owners of *kurkin*
> *olopillise pupawalakan akkuekwichiye*
> To the level of gold your roots reach
> *kurkin ipekantinaye*
> Owners of *kurkin*
> *olopillise pe maliwaskakan upoekwichiye*
> Into the level of gold your small roots are placed
> *kurkin ipekantinaye*
> Owners of *kurkin*
> *olopillise pe maliwaskakana pioklekekwichiye*
> Into the level of gold your small roots are nailed
> *kurkin ipekantinaye*
> Owners of *kurkin*
> *olopillipiye apikaekwichiye kurkin ipekantinaye*
> Within the very level of gold you are resisting, owner of *kurkin*
> *olopilli aktikkimakkekwichi kurkin ipekantinaye*
> In the level of gold you weigh a great deal, owners of *kurkin*
> *olopilli kwamakkekwichi kurkin ipekantinaye*
> In the level of gold you are firmly placed, owners of *kurkin*
> *olopilli aktitimakkekwa kwichiye kurkin ipekantinaye*
> In the level of gold you are moving, owners of *kurkin*
> *olopillipiye*
> Within the very level of gold
> *kinakaekwichiye*
> You are accumulating

Note the recurring possessed plus possessor noun phrase structures ("owners of kurkin"), followed by the optative/vocative suffix -*ye*. This is followed by a case marked nominal *ollopillise* "to/into the level of gold," which is then modified by a restrictive relative clause, the verb of which is always suffixed with -*kwichi* "standing" and the optative/vocative suffix -*ye*. Lexicosemantic parallelism is also highly apparent in this Kuna chant. Lexical items are regularly repeated (e.g. *kurkin* "hat," *olopilli* "level of gold"). But lexicosemantic parallelism involves more than simple repetition of the same lexical item(s). Typically it acts in concert with the concerns of figurative language. Thus, the principles operative in Asmat songs produce lexicosemantic parallelism through the replacement of one lexical item by another on the basis of metaphorical relationships (*as* "faeces" → *peke* "lump of clay") or metonymic ones (*ser* "fish" → *makpin* "ripples on the surface of the water").

Lexicosemantic parallelism reaches probably its greatest elaboration in the ritual languages of the eastern islands of Indonesia (Fox 1971, 1974, 1975, 1977, 1988; Kuipers 1990). These ritual languages serve a number of functions: political or marriage negotiations, narrations of clan histories, divination, communicating with spirits, etc., but they are typified by extensive parallelism in all levels. In these languages, words typically form paired sets with other words, so that one replaces a word with its pair in the following line, and the whole couplet forms a structural unit, as in the following couplet from Wanukaka from Sumba (Mitchell 1988:83):

Karei wei   "ask for water"
Karei ohu   "ask for cooked rice"
(meaning "to ask for a wife")

in which *wei* "water" is paired with *ohu* "cooked rice." Other pairings from Rindi, also from Sumba (Forth 1988:148) include:

hiri/aha   "polish/winnow"
ngilu/ngàmba   "blow(away)/shake out"
puri/paita   "sour/bitter"
lunga/ranga   "soul/spirit"

Quite commonly, multiple pairings are possible, as in Rindi *tana* "earth" paired to *wai* "water," *rumba* "grass, weeds," *pindu* "gate," *awangu* "sky," or *watu* "stone" among others; or Rotinese (Fox 1975:112) *ai* "plant, tree" with *batu* "stone," *boa* "fruit," *dae* "earth," *oe* "water," or *naü* "grass," again among others.

The couplets that result from these dyadic sets are highly stylized and their usage is an immediate indexical for ritual language. Ritual language performances may be very long, consisting of thousands of lines, but paired couplets are always the basic organizational principle. Some highly stylized genres like blessings consist entirely of couplets; others like those in divination rituals employ extralinguistic devices to contextualize the couplets to the immediate circumstances (Kuipers 1990). These couplets are often highly figurative, with the conventional meaning quite hidden behind the forms dictated by these constraints of the poetic function. Some examples:

Wanukaka (Mitchell 1988:71, 77):
Katikuku'dingu na penangu　　　"Squeaking of the floor slats"
Karu'uku'dingu na wei ta pajala　"Splashing of water in the water jar"
(conventional meaning: consummation of a marriage)

Angu wihi kamemi　"Eating goat meat"
Angu wihi ahu　　"Eating dog meat"
(conventional meaning: agreement reached in a negotiation)

Korahu kataraku　"The rat-tat-tat of sand"
Ladihu palibungu　"The cross-legged pandanus"
(conventional meaning: the beach)

Weyewa (Kuipers 1990:76):
Ndara ndende kiku　　"Horse with a standing tail"
Bongga mette lomma　"Dog with a black tongue"
(conventional meaning: a good orator)

Kadu nda pa-toda　"Horn that cannot be clipped"
Ulle nda pa-roro　"Tusk that cannot be cut"
(conventional meaning: invincible, irrepressible person)

Paralinguistic Features

The final types of framing device to be considered are those involving special paralinguistic features, such as pausing, speed of delivery, pitch, voice quality, or even musical accompaniment. We have already seen that the Asmat ritual language is typically sung, often accompanied by drums. Musical accompaniments with drums and also gongs is often true as well of performances of ritual languages in eastern Indonesia in certain contexts. In any case, whether performed with musical accompaniment or not, the ritual languages of eastern Indonesia are spoken in a markedly different style than ordinary language, with a slower speed of delivery and a heightened sense of rhythm. During Kuna curing rituals, the language is chanted. These musical properties of ritual language performances are all framing devices which key them as instantiations of particular genres. An especially interesting use of paralinguistics to frame genres is found in the Native South American community Shokleng (Urban 1985, 1991). In this culture, the origin myth can be performed in two ways, either as a narrative, told as other stories might be, or in a special paralinguistic style unique to this legend, termed *wąɲẹklɛn* in the native language. This involves two men, who sit on the ground facing each other. One man begins by uttering the first syllable of the first word of the myth and the second repeats this. The two men go on, uttering and repeating the myth, syllable by syllable, until the performance is complete. Each syllable is of the same length and is produced with the same pitch, and features extreme constriction of the pharynx and a sudden diaphragmic pulse in its production giving a kind of ballistic character to the phonation; *wąɲęklɛn* is in marked contrast to ordinary Shokleng speech and entails the obliteration of a number of phonemic distinctions found in the latter, including vowel length, intonation contours to indicate speech acts, and pauses for word and phrase boundaries. All of these losses make the language of *wąɲęklɛn* extremely difficult to understand unless one is already familiar with the origin myth as narrated in ordinary everyday language. Further, the ballistic phonetic qualities of *wąɲęklɛn* speech index the ideal qualities of Shokleng men, the performers of this genre: bold, gruff, and aggressive warriors.

Genres and Context

Viewing genres from a performance perspective, i.e. enacted by a performer or performers for an evaluation by an anticipated audience, both real and prospective, entails taking any representative text from any genre not as simply an abstract given, but as emergent, and hence contextualized here and now in the social situation of any particular performance. So, the actual text performed will creatively index aspects of the wider ongoing discourse, social relations between performer(s) and audience, or between performers, or within the audience itself, and, finally, wider social or cultural issues. For example, the telling of a fable may be to entertain, but it also may be used to instruct children about proper moral behavior, as in *Aesop's Fables*. The choice of which fable to relate may be prompted by a particular child's misbehavior earlier in the day, so that the performance of the fable indexes both wider sociocultural beliefs about proper moral behavior as well as a currently relevant social relationship between the performer (the father) and the audience (the naughty child). Thus, the fable has been recontextualized (or *recentered*, using another popular terminology) from ancient Greece to a modern interaction between father and child. While the fable may be understood as an idealized sub-type of narrative genres, any entextualized instantiation of it is necessarily contextualized in a given social situation and ultimately recontextualized from earlier performances of it, invoking again, Bakhtin's notion of the dialogic basis of speech.

Of course, for a text to be a recontextualized performance, it must first be decontextualized (or *decentered*) from earlier performances. Decontextualization of a performed genre entails distilling a stable and extractable version of the performed spoken discourse which can be lifted from the given performance. In other words it means coming up with something like a "canonized" text of the performed genre, a *text*, so that, following Bauman and Briggs (1990), we may call this *entextualization*. In the case of *Aesop's Fables* this is straightforward and was done for us two millennia ago; any printed version of *Aesop's Fables* carries texts, entextualized versions of these fables, which once, of course, were just oral performances. The same is true of countless other examples of printed versions of genres of verbal art, from epic poetry to jokes. Examples of performance of verbal art seem relatively easy to entextualize and this is no doubt due to the high reflexive profile of the poetic function in such stretches of spoken discourse. The high regard for attention to the form of the utterances, which is the basis of the poetic function, as played out, for example, in figurative language, speech formulae, parallelism, etc., encourages fixation on the form of the utterances and hence the setting of its text – in a word, entextualization. Of course, entextualization in these terms is a matter of degree, correlated to the openness of format of the genre; proverbs are highly entextualized, allowing almost no formal deviation from the "canonized" text, while narratives are more weakly so, permitting much more improvisation, only, however, within a largely set, overall generic framework.

Intertextual Gaps

When any text, i.e. a decontextualized and entextualized bit of discourse, is enacted in a performance, it is necessarily recontextualized to the social circumstances of that performance. This creates what Briggs and Bauman (1992) call a *intertextual gap* between the idealized generic model that the text invokes and the actual text enacted. This gap is minimized by enacting a text form that carries framing devices prototypical for the generic model invoked, for example starting a fairy tale with *once upon a time*. But it can be maximized by independent and creative improvisation on the part of the performer; for example, an academic who chooses to cast an academic paper with appeal to framing devices characteristic of the fairy tale is maximizing the intertextual gap between the idealized model of the genre of an academic paper and his performance of it. Another way of conceiving the difference between minimizing and maximizing intertextual gaps is in terms of the flexibility of possible recontextualizations of texts. Performances in which the gap is minimal impose strong expectations on the interpretations available to the recontextualized text, so that a text starting *once upon a time*, just as it did in previous versions (earlier entextualizations), is likely to be taken as a fairy tale. On the other hand, performances with a wider gap may admit much more open-ended possibilities of interpretation. A text that begins as an academic paper, but proceeds to *once upon a time* and other framing devices of fairy tales is likely to induce amusement, confusion, or other valiant attempts at interpretation of the performer's purposes. In any case the audience has much wider latitude of interpretation in the latter than in the former. Of course, as this example shows, the choice of minimizing or maximizing the intertextual gap is a strategic one on the part of the performer(s), by which she hopes to achieve certain ends or communicate certain meanings. To see what these ends or meanings might be, it will be worthwhile investigating a few examples in some depth.

Minimizing Intertextual Gaps

As an example of a minimizing strategy, consider Basso's (1984, 1988) wonderful studies of the use of place names among the Cibecue Apache. Place names in this community are complex expressions referring to physical features ("white rocks lie above in a complex cluster"; "big wide juniper tree"), former activities ("men stand out above"), dangerous places ("a porcupine sits"), or historical events ("horse fell down into water"). All of these named places have stories associated with them, for example "big cottonwood trees stand spreading here and there" (Basso 1984:36):

> Long ago, the Pimas and Apaches were fighting. The Pimas were carrying long clubs made from mesquite wood; they were also heavy and hard. Before dawn the Pimas arrived at Cibecue and attacked the Apaches there. The Pimas attacked while the Apaches were still asleep. The Pimas killed the Apaches with their clubs. An old woman woke up; she heard the Apaches crying out. The old woman thought it was her son-in-law because he often picked on her daughter. The old woman cried out: "You pick on my child a lot. You should act pleasantly toward her." Because the old woman cried out, the Pimas learned where she was. The Pimas came running to the old woman's camp and killed her with their clubs. A young girl ran away from there and hid beneath some bushes. She alone survived.
>
> It happened at "big cottonwood trees stand spreading here and there."

This story like other stories attached to place names in Cibecue Apache has a moral: the harmful consequences that come to those who overstep traditional role boundaries. In this it is rather close to our notion of fable. In any case place names are used as a powerful genre in Cibecue Apache to provide moral instruction. The performance of this moral instruction can be done through the mere mention of the relevant place name; it will call up in the mind of the audience the relevant story and its moral. In this way place names in Cibecue Apache function a bit like our genre of proverbs as well. Thus, in one conversation recorded by Basso (1988), a distraught Apache woman is comforted simply by the citation of three place names over a period of some two minutes, each bringing into mind a story which relates to some facet of the worry at hand and its resolution. This "speaking with names" is a genre in Cibecue Apache and one with a minimizing strategy at that. The mere mention of the place name on its own is a performance of this genre that necessarily calls to mind a particular story with a moral message. The performance of this genre is fixed, unambiguously framed, and the audience is in no doubt as to how to interpret the performance.

Another example of a minimizing strategy is provided by Weyewa ritual language, as discussed by Kuipers (1990). Ritual language specialists endeavor to stick close to what they believe is a received version of their texts, "the words of the ancestors" in their performances. Thus, the most highly formalized ritual events that involve ritual language, what Kuipers calls "rites of fulfilment" involve a wholesale reduction in the use of shifters, of those indexical features of language which would tie the performance of the ritual language to the here and now particulars of the social occasion, for example deictics and personal pronouns. Taking blessings as the most highly entextualized performances of ritual language, it is to be noted that per hundred words of text, their frequency of independent personal pronouns is 0.0, and demonstratives, 2.9 (Kuipers 1990:64–5). Being highly entextualized, the ritual language of blessings is also highly parallelistic; the average number of unpaired words per hundred words of text is only 0.12 (Kuipers 1990:72). All of this is strongly diagnostic of a minimizing strategy on the part of the performer(s), tying the actual performance very closely to the idealized generic model, as befits "the words of the ancestors." This is all in marked contrast to the ritual language of divinations, which are employed to ascertain the source of personal or community misfortune and are much less formalized and therefore entextualized. The frequency of personal pronouns and demonstratives per hundred words of text is 5.7 and 7.33 respectively, and the number of unpaired words, 4.2. In other words, in divinations there is more of the individual performer's speech than in blessings. Also, necessarily, any divination ceremony is tied to the particulars of the social occasion that gave rise to the ceremony in the first place, leading to indexical markers of current social circumstances in the performance. Divination, then, permits a greater gap between the text performed and the generic model than do the more traditional ancestor-ordained blessings. Weyewa blessings and Cibecue Apache "speaking with names" also illustrate another point about minimizing strategies: their appeal to traditionalism. A close fit between the performed text and the idealized generic model entails a powerful preordained authority given to those texts (and their holder), indexing their hegemony, and this can be used to buttress traditional social arrangements and ways of acting (this is demonstrated most transparently by the fact that the mere mention of a Cibecue Apache place name can be used to censure a person's inappropriate or non-traditional behavior).

Maximizing Intertextual Gaps

For an example of a more maximizing strategy consider Duranti's (1983, 1994) study of the function of the *lāuga* genre in Samoa. This is an oratorical genre of formal speech making used in a number of different social contexts. As a generic model it is most closely associated with formal ceremonies like the investiture of a new nobility title (*saofa'i*). In these contexts the *lāuga* is subject to strong constraints of the idealized generic model, causing the gap between the performance and the generic model to be minimized. For example, the performer raises his voice so that the *lāuga* can be heard clearly by the large audience present. Further, the speech used is highly stylized, and this highlights its continuities with performances of this genre in previous investitures and other formal ceremonies. In contrast, the use of *lāuga* in village political meetings (*fono*) is quite different. In this situation it is much less a ceremonial, relatively fixed language than it is a strategic use of the formulae of this genre to achieve desired political ends. The first *lāuga* in a *fono* creates the background for the meeting, which the following develop. Such *lāuga* in a *fono* are not necessarily delivered in a louder voice. Further, *lāuga* in a *fono* are used strategically to channel the ensuing discussion; they do not highlight continuities with previous performances of the generic model, but are tied to social and political conditions that gave rise to this particular *fono*. These strategic ends of the performers of *lāuga* in a *fono* sanction a much greater departure from the generic model of a *lāuga* than is found in an investiture ceremony. In investiture ceremonies, the gap between performance and generic model is minimal; the performances of *lāuga* in these ceremonies are examples of *lāuga par excellence*. But in *fono* meetings, the gap is much wider, as the genre is used and manipulated strategically for perceived political ends.

The difference between Samoan *lāuga* in investiture ceremonies and *fono* illustrates recontextualization of a genre in different speech events, but the ideal model of this genre remains the same, that of formal ceremonies like investitures. A more radical example of recontextualization in which the gap between an established genre and performance is widened would be one in which the actual model for the genre shifted, so that what is taken as an ideal exemplar of the genre between two different performance contexts actually changes. Such a process has occurred among the Gayo of Sumatra in their genre of poetic duelling (*didong*) (Bowen 1989). In traditional egalitarian Gayo society these poetic duels are mainly individualized; they resemble formal oratory which involves turn taking between two virtuoso orators (*cêh*) representing different villages or sub-village units. For example, negotiations for marriage partners are carried out using these poetic duels, emphasizing the idea of marriage as a balanced complementary exchange among equal parties. The text of these duels is highly formulaic and parallelistic, recalling the ritual languages of eastern Indonesia. Turns during the duel consist of fixed two-line proverbs of high parallelism, which the other speaker ratifies with words like "true," "like that," "like this." He begins his own turn by acknowledging "you said X; you said Y and it is true," before providing his own contribution. Since the late 1940s the Gayo have been part of the Indonesian nation-state, a large centralizing and modernizing political entity. In order to propagate its nationalist and modernist ideology, the local government administration has off and on encouraged a new type of performance of poetic duels. Unlike the traditional individualist approach, these performances involve teams, consisting of between ten and twenty men and boys, each led by two to four head orators (*céh*). Each team composes songs, many of which provide religious advice or commentary on economic development or current politics, while others attack the moral character or other noteworthy features of the members of the opposing team (team members consist exclusively of persons drawn from one or the other of the two main Gayo social groups). These performances are staged in Takèngën, the main town in Gayo country, merely for local entertainment. Each team takes strictly timed half-hour turns, from about nine in the evening until dawn. These team-based poetic duels are highly prestigious and viewed as more "modern" than traditional individualized duels throughout the Gayo area; one can even buy cassette tapes of these live performances. This is an excellent example of a modern recontextualization of an old and traditional genre. While in traditional times and perhaps in some highly traditional areas even today, the individualized poetic duels, as found in marriage negotiations, were the ideal model of this genre, this has altered with social and cultural changes among the Gayo. Today it is the team-based poetic duels which seem to be the ideal example of *didong* for most Gayo. The genre of poetic duelling and the entextualized forms prototypically linked to it have been radically recontextualized due to the social and ideological forces at work in Gayo country today, as part of the modern Indonesian nation-state. The gap between the texts of traditional individualized poetic duelling and the modern team based ones could hardly be wider and are still seen to be continued instantiations of the same genre.

These studies of recontextualizations and of intertextual gaps of varying widths demonstrate that a genre is not a closed invariant linguistic object like a grammatical sentence, but a set of discoursal practices that link a particular performance or entextualization to previous performances and other bits of discourse; it is a Bakhtinian dialogic exercise in its clearest form. Texts can be linked to genres in multiple ways, leading to a blurring of any proposed sharp distinctions among genres (remember the academic essay cast as a fairy tale), and their recontextualization can be highly innovative (maximizing the intertextual gap) or strongly conservative (minimizing the gap). The choices made are strategic, reflecting ideological and political goals. Genres are not created equally; some, like academic essays or legal drafting carry more social value than others, conferring greater social power and prestige on those who control them. It is no accident that Western schooling is largely about mastering the discursive patterns which prototypically frame and entextualize particularly favored genres. He who masters these skills is rewarded (see chapter 21). Genres, then, reflect a kind of lived history of the discursive patterns of the speech community. As speakers engage each other in mutual linguallaxis, they carry traces and memories of prior texts, prior entextualizations of performances. These are decontextualized and recontextualized through performances in new social conditions for new strategic ends (for example Gayo *didongs*), extending the lived history of these genres and creating still new opportunities for further recontextualizations. Thus, genres exist not as abstract linguistic categories but as lived, remembered, and ultimately embodied (note the importance of music in the performances of various genres) practices of human structural coupling through language, perhaps the paradigmatic example of linguallaxis.

Summary

Genres are historically situated ways for constructing and interpreting texts, an interpretive set of principles linking historically transmitted schemes for framing linguistic performances. These frames for interpreting or framing devices are typically dialogic, juxtaposing language drawn from various historical sources, and it is from this intertextuality that much of the power of individual genres derives. Framing devices are features of the poetic function of language, formal linguistic principles for the enaction of diverse genre types, such as line final rhyme for certain genres of English poetry, like sonnets. Various types of framing devices include special formulae or lexical items, tropes like metaphor or metonymy, paralinguistic features, like drums or singing, and, most importantly, parallelism. This last is recurring patterns in successive sections of text and can be found at all levels of the linguistic system, phonology (rhyme and rhythm), grammatical (repeated phrases or clauses), and lexical (e.g. paired words in the couplets of eastern Indonesia). Genres do not exist as abstract categories, but only as schemes of interpretation which are enacted in particular performances. Thus, genres can be recontextualized from earlier contexts to new ones with a greater or lesser shift in their interpretation. This is called an intertextual gap between the actual performance and the abstract idealized generic model we might have of it from earlier performances. This intertextual gap can be strategically manipulated by performers to minimize the break with earlier performances or maximize it, the point being to communicate certain meanings by such choices, such as adherence to tradition and the importance of the ways of the ancestors (minimizing) or the value of the new in a rapidly modernizing nation-state (maximizing).

Further Reading

The topic of genre (Dubrow 1982) is vast and has obvious overlaps with the field of literary criticism. Bakhtin (1981, 1986) are the basic sources for his important ideas. Bauman (1977) gives a more anthropological slant to the problem, as do the important survey articles by Bauman and Briggs (1990) and Briggs and Bauman (1992), and the anthology of classic articles by Becker (1995). Jakobson (1960) is his most famous statement of the poetic function, and Hymes (1981), Tedlock (1983), and Woodbury (1987) are important milestones in the development of a theory of ethnopoetics. Valuable case studies of genre framing, illustrating minimal and maximal intertextuality, include Abu-Lughod (1986), Bauman (1986), Briggs (1988, 1992), Caton (1990), Duranti (1994), Fox (1988), Gossen (1972), Kuipers (1990), O'Barr (1982), Sherzer (1983), and Urban (1991).

Part VI
Culture and Language Change

19

Contact Induced Language Change

Sources of Cultural Change

Cultures and languages do not exist in isolation, nor are they unchanging. Cultures and languages are constantly in flux, sometimes due to internal forces, i.e. conflicts of interest among groups, and sometimes from contact with other cultures and languages. The end results of these situations of contact are manifold indeed. As Part V argued, no society is homogeneous: all are marked by internal cleavages along lines of sex, age, kinship relations, and often caste or class and ethnicity. Correlated to these societal divisions are differences in cultural attitudes and practices, so that no culture is a homogeneous monolithic system of beliefs and practices. Given their respective positions in society, two individuals may hold quite different systems of beliefs and practices due to their individual histories of communicative routines and structural couplings. This may be most obvious in modern multicultural societies like Australia or the United States, comparing, say, a white middle-class native born male of Anglo-Saxon parentage with an immigrant non-English-speaking female from China, but it is also true in small-scale, seemingly homogeneous, societies like Yimas village. For here, there are very significant differences in meaningful cultural practices between men and women, and also between older initiated men, those with full cognizance of traditional lore and secret knowledge, and younger uninitiated men, who lack such cultural knowledge and are thereby denied participation in and understanding of particular rituals.

All cultures, whether they be those of the vastly complex societies of modern industrialized nation-states or those of seemingly simple, egalitarian traditional "tribal" groups, undergo transformations of various types and degree. The changes typically originate in the fault lines marked by societal divisions along the lines of sex, kin groups, age, caste/class, etc. The interests of these different groups are often not the same: consider the different interests of men and women over a cultural practice of female infanticide and perhaps even more strikingly, the immolation of widows. Cultural beliefs and practices are clearly not value or interest neutral; and those which hold a dominant position in a society, as one might expect, favor the more powerful social groups over others; typically males over females, older over younger, some clans over others (see Harrison (1987) for a case study of the Manambu of the Sepik area in New Guinea in which those clans with the most profitable trade contacts in other villages are clearly becoming dominant politically over those with less advantageous connections; this is occuring in an at least ideologically egalitarian society), high caste Brahman over untouchable, landowner over peasant, and elite industrialist employer over his employees. But such a situation often generates conflict: those less powerful disadvantaged groups will try to improve their social position and this struggle is often played out in terms of competition between different sets of cultural practices. Consider how the cultural matter of a difference in religious practices between Catholics and Protestants in Northern Ireland is the terms for characterizing what is essentially an economic and political struggle for power between the majority disadvantaged poor lower classes and the minority wealthier elite classes. Or the now defunct white Afrikaner regime's claim to be the bearer of "civilization" in Africa against the "chaos" of Black Africa as an excuse for its economic and political dominance over the black majority in South Africa. In both these cases, people have died in the name of cultural practices, but only because of the way culture was tied to wider social, economic, and political divisions. Cultural change often is a direct reflex of changes in a society; changes in the balance of power among the different groupings in the society, such as shifting alliances among clans, lead to a new alternative prestigious evaluation of the cultural practices associated with these groupings. For example, if a violent revolution by a dominated group leads to them being established as the new elite, it will be their dialect or language which becomes the esteemed standard to be emulated by other groups; the dialect or language of the former elite may now become stigmatized. Because any society is a conglomeration of groups with conflicting interests and variable constraints imposed on them, it may be unstable, and over time this translates into cultural change.

No society is truly isolated, no matter how nomadic and seemingly remote its people may be. All societies engage in relations with other societies, no matter how sporadic this may be, and the type of contacts individuals may have with other societies is a major source of social inequality. I already mentioned the case of Manambu (Harrison 1987), in which incipient inequality among clans is being introduced in this ideologically egalitarian society through particularly advantageous economic trading links to other villages, but the principle is general: those with greater economic and political power and higher societal position typically have wider economic links, which permit them to accumulate more wealth and thereby enhance their social position. Because of these economic links with the outside, these individuals also commonly adopt cultural practices from their trading partners. The high social position of these individuals means that the new cultural practices linked to them are likely to be positively viewed by others, and therefore will likely lead to the successful introduction of these imported cultural practices to the society as a whole, especially if the source culture is generally viewed as superior. The ease with which Indian culture was diffused through Southeast Asia or Chinese cultural practices to Korea and Japan amply testifies to this fact. Of course, given the unstable, contested nature of much of societal practices, such adoptions may be successfully resisted, at least for a time, but a second basic mechanism of cultural change through adoption of cultural practices from outside has been established. Finally, of course, change can be imposed from without, by powerful coercive forces like colonialism or missionization. This has been a major force on traditional peoples throughout the world over the last 400 years. In immigrant-settled ex-colonies like Canada, Australia, and the United States the impact this has had on Native peoples has been immense; they have had wholesale cultural and linguistic change imposed on them by governments and their handmaidens, the Christian missions.

Linguistic Change

Linguistic change is commonly a weather vane of cultural change. In chapter 16 we saw how choices in linguistic form, whether they be phonological variables, honorifics, or T/V pronouns, and even whole languages as in code switching or diglossia, are enactments of cultural meanings, statements about the society, and one's and others' position within it. As the society undergoes change, the linguistic forms and the social meanings they enact may also change. For example, in eighteenth-century pre-revolutionary France, the diphthong *oi* had two realizations: the prestigious [oj], associated with the nobility and urban elite, and the stigmatized [wa] of the peasantry and urban poor. Cataclysmic social change in the form of the Revolution occurred, and by the early nineteenth century [wa] emerged as the prestigious standard pronunciation, as it is in French today. In Java at the turn of the century, the *madya* speech level was despised and avoided by the noble elite, viewed by them as indicative of the peasantry and their poor attempt to speak in a high level. Yet, with a gradual shift in Java over the twentieth century to something more like a modern class-based society and a more egalitarian ethic, this has changed, so that *madya* is now properly used reciprocally when speaking with someone outside one's social grouping

(Errington 1988). Actually, in many such encounters today, the national language Indonesian is favored, redolent, as it is, of cultural meanings of a modern unified nation looking forward to a prosperous technological future. This again reflects radical cultural change between the Java of 1900 and that of 2000, ultimately due to wider social changes. Finally, Gal (1979) reports of a complex bilingual situation in Austria, in an area near the border with Hungary. Hungarian is the older language in the area, but it has been bilingual since at least the nineteenth century, when many German-speaking immigrants from the west arrived. These formed the dominant elite group of merchants, craftsmen, government officials, and professionals; the Hungarian speakers were and remain peasants. Since the area was incorporated into Austria in 1921, German was given additional prestige by being the official national language. Still, the peasants have retained Hungarian and are fully German–Hungarian bilinguals. This is beginning to change, however, as the use of Hungarian carries cultural meanings of the traditional agrarian-based peasant life, while German bears that of the modern progressive nation-state of industry and technology, as well as being associated with higher status-bearing social roles like professional jobs. The cultural meanings of speaking German are often viewed more positively, so younger speakers tend to use German more, especially women, for many Hungarian-speaking young women choose to marry German-speaking men over Hungarian speakers, preferring to avoid taking on the hard life of the peasant wife.

Types of Linguistic Change: Borrowing and Interference

As culture contact is perhaps the most common vector of culture change, the nature of this contact is often manifested in linguistic change. This linguistic change is of two types, borrowing and interference, although in specific cases it is often difficult to draw a sharp line between them. Borrowing is the more straightforward: the adoption of features of one language into another. The most common kind of borrowing is lexical items, with the items being borrowed indicative of the nature of the cultural contact. If a society comes into contact with another it views as culturally or technologically superior, it is very likely to borrow from this culture heavily, including lexical forms for many of the cultural items or practices in the language of this culture. English is a particularly good example of this. Early borrowings before the Anglo-Saxon conquest of Britain are *wine* and *street* from Latin *vinum* and *strata* respectively, reflecting the alcoholic cultural practices and the higher technological ability of the Romans. With Christianization came words like *abbot* and *altar* from Latin *abbas* and *altare* respectively. The greatest source of borrowing in English is French, due to the Norman conquest in 1066. Loans are in all semantic domains, but especially concentrated in areas of higher "culture" and technology:

food: *pork, beef, mutton* (note that native English words denote the animal as opposed to the meat: *swine, cow, sheep*)
law: *judge, court, just, marry*
government: *state, power, people*
war: *war, battle, siege, danger*
religion: *saint, pray, save, nature*
sport: *sport, cards, dice, track*
"culture": *glory, honor, art, beauty*
household: *chair, table, serve, soup*
names: *Helen, John, Henry, Luke*

In addition, English has borrowed promiscuously from many other languages over the past centuries when it needed a term for an introduced concept or artifact: Italian (*piano, sonata, cello, virtuoso*), Irish (*brogue, shamrock*), German (*hamburger, pretzel*), Russian (*sputnik, tundra, mammoth*); even exotic languages: Japanese (*Zen, soya*), Malay (*amok*), Hindi (*thug, pundit, jungle, curry*), Tagalog (*boondocks*), Sanskrit (*karma, yoga*), Algonkian (*tomahawk, moccasin*), Luganda (*impala*), Guugu-Yimidhirr (*kangaroo*).

And English is not unusual. For example, in Thai the borrowed lexical items are like a map of the history of culture contact: first, Sanskrit or Pali (the scriptural-written language of early Buddhism) for religious, philosophical, and "high cultural" areas of vocabulary; then, Khmer, for royal and court vocabularies; then, Chinese, for numerals, words for business and commerce, and the culinary arts; and finally, European languages, primarily English, for words denoting items of modern technology, for example words for computer technology. Other languages of Southeast Asia like Tagalog, Malay, or Javanese display similar patterns; in the latter two, the role of Arabic loans is especially pronounced, due to the adoption of the religious tradition of Islam in the sixteenth century, replacing an earlier adopted Indic Hindu–Buddhist tradition (the many Sanskrit borrowings, however, remain indicative of this earlier pervasive cultural adoption).

For reasons not really understood, some languages eschew the wholesale borrowing of lexical items. In situations of cultural contact quite similar to those discussed above, a foreign cultural concept, practice, or technological item may be adopted, but the word for it is hewn out of native elements. These are known as loan translations or calques. This is really an example of interference, one language interfering with the structure or vocabulary of another, rather than strictly borrowing. Native Amerindian languages especially make use of this device as in these examples from Tewa of New Mexico (Dozier 1964:513–14): $ʔòz\grave{e}^h sóyó^h$ "mule" from $ʔòz\grave{e}^h$ "ear" and $sóyó^h$ "big", $b\grave{e}·fó\mathbf{?}~i\mathbf{?}$ "peach" from $b\grave{e}·$ "fruit" and $fó\mathbf{?}~i\mathbf{?}$ "hairy," $w\grave{a}·tc^h$ "automobile" from $w\grave{a}·$ "wind" and tc^h "structure, building," and $f\grave{a}·f\acute{e}^h$ "match" from $f\grave{a}·$ "fire" plus $f\acute{e}^h$ "wood." German, despite its close relationship to English, also commonly makes use of the device: *Fernsehen* "television" from *fern* "far" plus *sehen* "seeing" (note the English term contains loans from Ancient Greek and Latin, but it is analysable in the same way as the German, *tele-* "far" from Ancient Greek and *vision* "seeing" from Latin). And Tibetan, while being the language of a culture at least as deeply Buddhist as Thailand, and one converted to Buddhism over a thousand years ago, largely lacks Sanskrit loan words. Buddhist concepts are simply loan translated by native Tibetan morphemes, for example Sanskrit *sūrya-garbha* sun-womb "essence of the sun" is rendered into Tibetan as *nyi-mai snying-po* sun-of heart-the (Sapir 1921:197).

Interference most commonly makes itself felt in the phonology or grammar of a language, but this typically requires cultural contact of more than a sporadic or transitory nature. In this case the speakers of the language of the importing culture modify its structure toward that of what they perceive as a superior culture. To the extent that this succeeds, it results in the adopting language looking exactly like the source language in the relevant features. This could be viewed as borrowing, as the boundary between borrowing and interference can be very hazy in this area. In phonology a good example of this type of borrowing/interference is found in Javanese. For nearly a thousand years up to the sixteenth century, Java was subject to very intense Indic Hindu–Buddhist influence (Borobudur, the most famous monument in Java, for instance, is a Mahayana Buddhist shrine). As a consequence, Javanese was heavily influenced by Indic languages, specifically Sanskrit, the scriptural language of Mahayana Buddhism and the high literary language of Indic civilization. Old Javanese or Kawi, the Javanese literary language and strongly associated with court literature, is not less than 85 percent Sanskrit in vocabulary. Modern Javanese is unusual among Indonesian languages in having two series of anterior coronal stops, a laminal dental series, and an apical retroflex one; its stop inventory is:

p	t	ʈ	c	k
b	t	ɖ	j	g
m	n		ɲ	ŋ

Because such a contrast is so rare in Indonesian languages, it is plausibly derived from Sanskrit, which like Indic languages generally does have a dental–retroflex contrast:

p t ṭ c k
b d ḍ j g
m n ṇ ɲ ŋ

(It should be pointed out that the contrast is not original to Indo-Aryan languages like Sanskrit either, these being descended from Proto-Indo-European which had no such coronal contrast. Rather the Indo-Aryan languages probably adopted it from the Dravidian languages, as their speakers invaded and occupied northern India, in the process adopting a great deal of the aboriginal culture of the Dravidian language speakers).

Interference or borrowing is also well attested in grammatical systems. There is at least one good example of interference in the grammatical system of English, by French. Germanic languages like Old English form their comparatives and superlatives with suffixes like *-er* and *-est*; German *schwer* "hard," comparative *schwer-er* "harder," superlative *schwer-sten* "hardest." English, of course, does this with monosyllabic adjectives, typically those of native Germanic origin: *strong, strong-er, strong-est*. French, on the other hand, uses particles like *plus* "more" and *le/la plus* "the most" to form comparatives and superlatives: *beau* "handsome" *plus beau* 'handsomer," *le plus beau* "handsomest." By interference from French, English also has this pattern (but using the native words *more* and *most*) with polysyllabic adjectives, again typically of French origin: *interesting, more interesting, most interesting*. The two systems existing in the language, native and French interference, leads to some indeterminacy, especially with disyllables; *lovely, lovelier/more lovely, loveliest/most lovely; happy, happier/?more happy; unhappy, ?unhappier/more unhappy; pretty/handsome, prettier/handsomer, ?more pretty/more handsome*.

In other cases, full paradigmatic systems have been borrowed, morphemic form and all, from the language of a culturally dominant group. Thomason and Kaufman (1988) present the fascinating case of Mednyj Aleut. The Aleuts are a Native Amerindian group inhabiting the islands between Alaska and Russia. In the nineteenth century, Russian fur seal hunters arrived and settled, marrying Aleut women. As a result a population with a certain degree of bilingualism in Russian and Aleut grew up, although generally Aleut remained dominant until relatively recently. On one of the islands, Mednyj, the Russian proportion of the population was significantly larger than on the others, and this has effected the Aleut spoken there. Aleut is a morphologically complex language, with extensive verbal inflection. On Mednyj the system is mostly unchanged, except that the finite inflectional paradigm is borrowed from Russian (interestingly, the non-finite forms are not affected) (Thomason and Kaufman 1988:234).

		Aleut	Mednyj Aleut	Russian	
	1	uŋuči-ku-q	uŋuči-ju	ja sižu	I sit
SG	2	uŋuči-ku-xt	uŋuči-iš	ty sidiš	you(SG) sit
	3	uŋuči-ku-x	uŋuči-it	on sidit	he sits

The Russian inflectional endings -*(j)u*, -*iš*, and -*it* are directly borrowed into Mednyj Aleut as suffixes to the root *uŋuči-* "sit," supplanting the native tense suffix -*ku* and person-number suffixes, -*q*, -*xt*, and -*x*.

Interference in syntactic patterns is also common across languages. In New Guinea a number of genetically Austronesian languages have adopted the syntactic patterns of their Papuan language-speaking trading partners. The Austronesian languages in Oceania are verb initial or medial languages, having prepositions and a word order not too different from English, as in this example from Tolai:

> a   tutuna i   ga   oe   ra   davai livuan ta ta   uma
> DET man   3SG PAST plant DET tree   middle at DET garden
> "The man planted a tree in the middle of the garden"

Note that the subject *tutuna* "man" precedes the verb *oe* "plant" and the object *davai* "tree" follows. The prepositional phrase consists of the preposition *livuan ta* "middle of" followed by its object *ta uma* "the garden." Papuan languages typically contrast in all these features, as the following Watam example demonstrates:

> namot an   padoŋ endau nik   ŋgatki-r
> man   DET wood house inside put-PERF
> "The man put the wood inside the house"

In this language, as in many Papuan languages, the verb typically occurs finally, with all constituents preceding it; further, Papuan languages have postpositions, *nik* "inside" follows its object *endau* "house" in the above example. A number of the Austronesian languages of New Guinea have the syntactic features exemplified by Watam above, rather than their genetic relative, Tolai. This reflects interference from the Papuan languages of their trading partners, as in this example from Motu:

> tau ese   au na   imea bogarai-na i vada   e-hado
> man SUBJ tree DET garden middle-its at PERF 3SG-plant
> "The man planted a tree in the middle of the garden"

Note that in the Motu sentence, as in Watam, the verb is final, while determiners follow their nouns, and postpositions, their objects. The contrast with its relative, Tolai, could hardly be more striking.

Interference and Multilingualism

Perhaps the most pervasive example of language interference is Gumperz and Wilson's (1971) study of the village of Kupwar in India. Kupwar is a village in south-central India of roughly 3000 people in which four languages from two different language families are spoken: two Indo-Aryan languages, Urdu, spoken by the minority Muslim landowners, and Marathi, spoken by the lower caste untouchables and landless laborers, and two Dravidian languages, Kannada, spoken by majority population Jains, who are also landowners and craftsmen, and Telugu, spoken by a small group of local rope makers (this language is rather unimportant in the overall scheme of things in Kupwar and will not feature in the following discussion). Marathi, while a minority language in Kupwar, is the dominant language of the wider area, being the language of surrounding villages and Sangli, the district capital, as well as neighboring markets. It is also the principal written language, with only a few Jain priests being literate in Kannada.

Nearly all men are bilingual, and Marathi is the language one uses in outgroup communication. Kannada-speaking Jains, for instance, use it in speaking to untouchable field hands and also to Urdu-speaking fellow landowners. Bilingualism seems to be of extremely long standing in Kupwar; while Marathi is the indigenous language, Kannada-speaking Jains have been in the area for six centuries, and Urdu-speaking Muslims for three to four centuries. This situation appears to be stable because of the functional specialization of the different languages. Local cultural beliefs require a strict separation between the domestic sphere of home, extended family and close friends, and the public domain of action, such as work. Within the domestic sphere, speech is exclusively in the ingroup language. In the public domain of work, all three languages are used, but with specific social meanings: to address one's coworkers in an ingroup language, say Kannada, is to make an assertion of solidarity; Marathi, the normal language of choice for outgroup communication, specifically avoids making this statement. It is not the domestic language of the vast majority of the village population and certainly not of the dominant castes in the village, the local elite, so its usage is culturally neutral. This explains the long period of stable multilingualism in Kupwar, and as long as it plays this role of communicating vital cultural meanings, it is likely to remain so.

However, this long period of stable bilingualism has had a massive impact on the three languages involved, each of them causing interference in the others. The end result of this is that the Kupwar varieties of these languages are very different from their respective standard languages or varieties found elsewhere in India. Further, the three Kupwar varieties of these languages are remarkably similar grammatically; indeed, it may not be too far off the mark to say that Kupwar residents actually speak just one language, with three different lexicons. Look at the following sentence in the three languages (Gumperz and Wilson 1971:25):

> Kup Urdu:　　o　　gəe t-a　　　　　[bhæs　carn-e-ko]
> Kup Marathi:　tew gel hot-a　　　　[mhæs　car-ayla]
> Kup Kannada: aw　hog id-a　　　　 [yəmmi mes-k]
> 　　　　　　　he　go　AUX-3SG [buffalo graze-to]
> "He went to graze the buffalo"

Let us look in more detail at a few of these patterns of interference. All three Kupwar varieties have a type of natural gender like English, in which the gender of nouns is determined by the sex and animacy of their referents, and have three gender distinctions, masculine, feminine, and neuter. Only standard Kannada has this kind of gender system. Standard Urdu and Standard Marathi have rather typical Indo-European gender systems like German or French: Standard Urdu has two genders, masculine and feminine, but, like French, nouns with inanimate referents are assigned to either gender; Standard Marathi has three genders, masculine, feminine and neuter, but, again like German, inanimate nouns are assigned across the three genders.

The marking of direct objects in the Kupwar varieties follows a typical Indo-Aryan pattern of Urdu and Marathi rather than a Dravidian one. Indo-Aryan languages use the dative postposition to mark animate direct objects, as in this Urdu example (Gumperz and Wilson 1971:161):

> gəriib admi-ko　　dekh-kər　diy-a　　　th-a
> poor　man-DAT　see-having　give-3SG AUX-3SG
> "Having seen the poor man, he gave (it) to him"

All Kupwar varieties do this:

> Kup Urdu:　　gərib manus-ko dekh ke　　 die　　t-a
> Kup Marathi:　gərib mansa-la　bəg　un　　dil　　hot-a
> Kup Kannada: gərib mansya-gə nod　i　　　 kwatt id-a
> 　　　　　　　poor　man-DAT see　having give　AUX-3SG
> "Having seen the poor man, he gave (it) to him"

Finally, yes/no questions in Standard Urdu are marked by a word meaning "what," as in this example (Gumperz and Wilson 1971:264):

> kya　ghocii dii
> what horse give
> "Did you sell the horse?"

Standard Marathi also uses "what" for this function, but puts it at the end of the sentence rather than the beginning, while Standard Kannada has a verbal suffix, which, as the language is verb final, also occurs at the end of a sentence. All Kupwar varieties are like Standard Marathi in this feature (Gumperz and Wilson 1971:264):

```
Kup Urdu:     ghodi di      ya          kya
Kup Marathi:  ghodi dil     əs          kay
Kup Kannada:  kudri kwatt i              yan
              horse give    you(SG)      what
"Did you sell the horse?"
```

Overall, Kupwar Urdu has undergone the most extensive changes from Standard Urdu, Kupwar Kannada, the next most extensive, and Kupwar Marathi is the least altered from the standard language. This may be surprising given its minority status, but this reflects its function as a language of wider intergroup communication, as well as the fact that it is the dominant language of the district. It is interesting to note that the code which carries public meanings of non-solidarity for most residents of Kupwar is the most conservative; whether this is general in cases of bilingualism would be valuable to know, and, if so, why?

Linguistic Areas

Widespread interference patterns of the type just exemplified in Kupwar sometimes spread over a large geographical area, affecting many languages of different genetic groups. These are called linguistic areas, and cases discussed in the literature include India (Emeneau 1964; Masica 1976), Mesoamerica (Campbell, Kaufman, and Smith-Stark 1986), the Pacific Northwest of North America (Sherzer 1976; Thomason 1983), and Arnhem Land in Northern Australia (Heath 1978). I will exemplify with the linguistic area of mainland Southeast Asia. In this region, languages of four different major language families are spoken: Sino-Tibetan, Thai, Mon-Khmer, and Austronesian. The ancestral languages and earlier stages of these languages from the four families were very different from each other, but centuries of mutual interference have reduced this diversity so that they now share many structural features. For example, languages across the four families, typically make a three-way distinction in their oral stops: voiceless unaspirated, voiceless aspirated and voiced, as in this Thai system:

$$p \quad t \quad c \quad k$$
$$p^h \quad t^h \quad c^h \quad k^h$$
$$b \quad d$$

Further, many languages make use of a phonemic distinction of pitch to distinguish lexical items (most dialects of Khmer are a major exception here), again as in Thai: *ná·* (high tone) "aunt," *nâ·* (falling tone) "face," *nǎ·* (rising tone) "thick."

Grammatically, the languages largely lack morphology (typologically isolating), so that independent words and particles signal grammatical functions. They lack inflected tense as a category and use auxiliaries to mark aspectual and modal distinctions: Thai *kamlaŋ pay* PROG go "is going"; Burmese (Becker 1993:81) *we lai'* buy PERF "bought"; Khmer *baan samlap* PERF kill "killed." In addition, serial verb constructions, juxtapositions of verb stems in a single sentence, are heavily used to express complex semantic notions in these languages: Thai (Diller 1993:405) *hay pay ráp* give go receive "pick up"; Burmese (Becker 1993:75) *nei htain* stay sit "reside"; Khmer *ʔaoy cbah* give clear "clarify." Finally, languages throughout the Southeast Asian linguistic area make use of classifiers in quantifying noun phrases, although in some languages they are optional (Khmer, for instance): Thai *dèg khon hâa* boy CLF boy "five boys"; Burmese *nwa lei kaun* cow four CLF "four cows"; Haroi (Austronesian) *thua trii manuʔ* two CLF chicken "two chickens"; Khmer *kruu bəy neaʔ* teacher three CLF "three teachers."

Pidgin Languages

One of the more unusual results of a multilingual contact situation must be pidginization. A pidgin language occurs in a contact situation when one of the languages, typically that of the culturally or socioeconomically dominant group (the superstrate language), undergoes radical simplification and is adopted as a language of wider communication by speakers of languages in a subordinate position (the substrate languages). For some sociocultural reasons, full models of the superstrate language are withheld from the substrate speakers, so that they are unable to learn the true language, and the pidgin language develops instead. The superstrate language provides the bulk of the pidgin's lexicon, with some admixture from the substrate languages. Pidgins develop when a wide cultural or socioeconomic gap separates the speakers of the superstrate and substrate languages. In the prototypical cases, they grew up in the plantation areas of the Atlantic, Pacific and Indian Oceans, where economic conditions and social mores dictated a very wide gulf between the slaves or plantation workers who spoke the substrate languages and their overseers who spoke the superstrate, typically a Western European metropolitan language. In other cases, pidgins have arisen in institutionalized trading situations, but always in cases where there is a clear asymmetry in power and status between the speakers of the languages involved. Pidgins are strictly simple, "make do" languages of economic transactions and are normally little valued by their speakers. They are second languages for all speakers (if a pidgin should become nativized as a first language, it is called a creole, but this normally entails significant elaborations in both its functions and its structure; see Foley (1988)).

I would like to look in some detail here at a case of the latter type – pidginization in a trading situation – and at a pidgin language not from a European superstrate. The case in point is Yimas Pidgin, a pidginized version of the Yimas language that was used until recently by Yimas villagers in their regular trading contacts with their upriver neighbors, the Arafundi, who speak a genetically unrelated language. Within the Sepik culture area, in which trading networks are extensive and culturally highly salient, there is an important distinction between what are called the "water people" and the "bush people" (Gewertz 1983). "Water people" live on the rivers and catch and smoke fish. This they exchange with the "bush people" for sago, the carbohydrate staple. The "water people" occupy a superior position economically and socially *vis-à-vis* the "bush people"; they are the local elites. In this particular trading context, the Yimas are the "water people" and the Arafundi, the "bush people," so it is no surprise that Yimas should serve as the superstrate language for the pidgin and Arafundi, the substrate.

Structurally, Yimas Pidgin is a radically simplified version of Yimas, with some mixture of Arafundi. Yimas is a highly complex polysynthetic language; Yimas Pidgin is morphologically simple, of an almost isolating structure. Lexically, over 80 percent of the vocabulary of Yimas Pidgin is Yimas in origin, the rest is Arafundi or of unknown source. Not a single verb root is Arafundi, although, perhaps surprisingly, some grammatical function words do come from this language. Table 19.1 shows a sample of words in Yimas Pidgin with their parent forms in Yimas or Arafundi.

As mentioned above, grammatically Yimas Pidgin shows massive simplification from Yimas, which is morphologically a very complex language indeed. For example, Yimas has not less than ten major gender classes and a three-way number distinction, singular, dual, and plural. Nouns inherently belong to a particular gender class and are inflected for number; modifying adjectives, possessives, and even the copula must agree with the head noun in gender and number, as in these examples:

patn   ama-na-kn   kpa-n   anak
betelnut V SG 1SG-POSS-V SG big-V SG COP.V SG
"My belelnut is big"

parŋkat   ama-na-ra   kpa-ra   arak
betelnut V PL 1SG-POSS-V PL big-V PL COP.V PL
"My betelnuts are big"

19.1

	Yimas	*Yimas Pidgin*	*Arafundi*
man	payum	payum	
man		nuŋgum	nuŋgum
woman	ŋaykum	aykum	nam
pig	numbran	numbrayn	ya
cassowary	awa	karima	karɨma
dog	yura	tam	taum
yesterday	ŋarɨŋ	arɨŋ	nay
betelnut	patn	patn	kumwɨ
sun	tɨmal	tim	kom
village	num	kumbut	kumbuk
water	arɨm	yim	yem
one	mban	mban	kapunta
two	tɨmbal	kundamwin	kɨndamuɲ
talk	malak-	mariawk-	yaŋ-
hear	andɨ-	andɨ-	eik-

trŋ   ama-na-ŋ   kpa-ŋ   akk
tooth VI SG 1SG-POSS-VI SG big-VI SG COP.VI SG
"My tooth is big"

trŋkl   ama-na-ŋkl   kpa-ŋkl   aklak
tooth VI DL 1SG-POSS-VI DL big-VI DL COP.VI DL
"My two teeth are big"

In Yimas Pidgin all inflection for gender and number is lost. The number of a noun is indicated by *kundamwin* "two" or *manba* "many," both from Arafundi. The forms for gender class V singular (the unmarked class in Yimas with the largest membership) are extended to cover all nouns:

$\begin{cases} \text{patn} \\ \text{trɨŋ} \end{cases}$ ama-nakɨn kɨpan anak
"My betelnut/tooth is big"
trɨŋ kundamwin ama-nakɨn kɨpan anak
"My two teeth are big"
patn manba ama-nakɨn kɨpan anak
"My betelnuts are big"

kɨpan and *anak* are the invariable forms for "big" and the copula respectively in Yimas Pidgin and *-nakɨn* is a general possessive suffix, able to be added to any pronoun to form the corresponding possessive: *mɨn* "he," *mɨ (n)-nakɨn* "his."

Similar simplification applies to Yimas verbs, which, being a polysynthetic language, are extremely elaborate, with up to 13 possible affix positions. Yimas, like many polysynthetic languages, indicates grammatical relations with affixes to the verb:

yura   na-ka-tpul
dog V SG V SG OBJ-1SG SUBJ-hit
"I hit the dog"

tpuk   ku-n-ŋa-ŋa-kt
sago X SG X SG OBJ-3SG SUBJ-1SG IND OBJ-give-RM FUT
"He will give me sago later"

Yimas Pidgin loses all this affixation, except for a much reduced future versus non-future contrast in tense suffixes. Indirect objects are marked with a postposition *namban* from Yimas *nampan* "toward," which extends optionally to mark animate direct objects, a situation in which ambiguity could result, due to indeterminacy between subject and direct object:

ama yura (namban) kratɨkɨ-nan
1SG dog OBJ   hit-NON FUT
"I hit the dog"

mɨn tupwi ama namban   asan anak
3SG sago 1SG IND OBJ give FUT
"He will give me sago later"

Language Death

The most extreme and tragic outcome of a multilingual contact situation is language death. This occurs when all of the speakers in a language community shift to speaking another language. Typically the shift is the language of the culturally and economically elite group, but this is not universally the case, as demonstrated by the story of English, in which the French-speaking Norman overlords gave up French in favor of the English language of their vassals (although the demographic pattern, in which the French-speaking Normans were greatly outnumbered by the native English-speaking population, probably accounts for this anomaly). Language shift can be very slow and gradual, as is the case with Hungarian in Austria (Gal 1979) or Gaelic in Scotland (Dorian 1981), or it can be sudden and swift, as is now occurring with a number of languages of the Sepik region of New Guinea, in which language death is occurring over little more than a single generation (Kulick 1992). In the former cases the languages are dying by being swamped demographically by speakers of the language of the wider nation-state and economically with the national language's elite connections and its importance as a vehicle of communication for technology and education. But in the latter New Guinea cases, this is not occurring to any significant degree, at least not yet. What is crucial here are cultural beliefs, especially those which put a strong premium on the new and the imported as a source of power and status, and it is these which are responsible for this very rapid transition from village-based vernacular languages to Tok Pisin, which is widespread throughout Papua New Guinea and is associated with modernization and the wider world (for further discussion see Kulick 1992). The vernacular languages are associated with the precontact traditional culture, a way of life now seen as backward by their speakers. When a language and its associated cultural beliefs and practices are no longer viewed positively by its speakers (no longer carries sufficient social honor), and it is in competition with one which is, it is doomed (for a contrastive case to the Sepik area of New Guinea, for which Western contact spans less than a century, see Fasold's (1984:231–9) discussion of Tiwa of New Mexico, where even after over 400 years of domination by European languages, first Spanish and then English, Tiwa is still holding strong, a persistence no doubt related to the fact that the language and the traditional culture with which it is associated is strongly positively valued by the people; see also Kroskrity (1993) on Arizona Tewa).

Summary

No culture is homogeneous; all are marked by internal divisions, diverse groupings with competing interests, and as a result cultures continually change as these competing groups strive to advance their interests. Linguistic change largely reflects the struggle for power among these groups; languages typically change to take on features of speech of those groups who are socially favored. One common type of linguistic change is borrowing in which the lexical items of one high prestige language are borrowed into another less prestigious language. Another type is interference in which the structure of a high prestige language imposes itself on that of a language of lower status; this typically requires more intimate contact between the languages, sustained bilingualism. If this obtains over a long span of time, perhaps centuries, this can lead to massive influence of the languages on each other, so that they come to resemble each other in even the smallest details of pattern. Interference patterns diffused over a large geographical area containing languages from diverse genetic families can result in linguistic areas in which all the languages regardless of genetic background come to resemble each other in various features. Multilingual contacts of a more sporadic, economically and politically asymmetrical nature often lead to pidginization, in which the language of the economically dominant group undergoes radical simplification to become a jargon language of trade or economic contacts. Finally, the end result of prolonged contact between two languages of differentially accorded prestige will often be the death of the language of lower status, as the higher prestige one ousts it from active use.

Further Reading

Contact induced language change has long been an area of intense study in historical linguistics, that field of linguistics which studies how languages change over time. Any textbook in historical linguistics will contain chapters on this topic, try Anttila (1972), Bynon (1977), Crowley (1992), or Hock (1986). An excellent treatment of this subject is Thomason and Kaufman (1988); other sources include Cooper (1982), Heath (1984), Masica (1976), and Weinreich (1953). On pidgins see Foley (1988), Holme (1988–9), Mühlhäusler (1986) and Romaine (1988), and, on language death, Kulick (1992) and the articles in Dorian (1989).

20

Standard Languages and Linguistic Engineering

The Concept of the Nation-State and the National Language

One of the most momentous sociocultural changes over the last few centuries has been the emergence of the modern nation-state. Most of us in the industrialized countries of North America, Western Europe, and Australasia tend to take the concept of the nation-state and its associated national standard language for granted, but, in fact, both of these are the outcome of centuries of struggles among competing political and economic groups to advance their own interests.

The nation-state in the form we know it is largely a result of economic and political developments in nineteenth-century Europe, particularly the French and industrial revolutions, and from these, via Europeanized education of local elites, diffused throughout the world. The ideology of the French Revolution played a central role in altering people's sense of identity from being subjects of a monarch, by virtue of being resident in a delimited space under the sovereignty of that monarch, to *citizens* of a nation, a status they have through the rights and duties they can exercise through the institutions of the state, such as voting for elected representatives. In a similar way the industrial revolution broke down traditional local ties of kinship and village life through migration to industrialized areas in search of work, causing masses of people for the first time to come into contact with people of very different backgrounds and with whom were needed means of living together. The end result of both of these sets of changes was a shift in the nature of political communities from what Tönnies (1955) called communities based on *Gemeinschaft* "community" to those based on *Gesellschaft* "association" (Durkheim (1947[1893]) drew a broadly similar distinction in his contrast between communities based on "mechanical" solidarity versus "organic" solidarity). *Gemeinschaft* signifies relationships based on likeness, shared properties of kinship and descent or locality

(Geertz's (1973) notion of "primordial attachments"). The home, farm, or traditional village are examples of communities based on *Gemeinschaft*. *Gesellschaft* communities, on the other hand, are based on willed or ideologically, at least, freely chosen acts of association between members, leading to complex systems of exchange of goods and services. People of quite different backgrounds can and commonly do choose to engage in these contracts of association and exchange; larger units like cities or industrial companies are examples of *Gesellschaft* communities, as is clearly the modern nation-state. Both the French Revolution and the industrial revolution played central roles in the shift from the *Gemeinschaft* of the village and the guild to the *Gesellschaft* of the nation and the corporation by widening the scope of peoples' sense of ties and allegiances, ultimately to something we can call the "nation."

In this sense, the nation-state is clearly what Anderson (1983) calls an "imagined community." For example, an individual Australian will never meet more than a minuscule amount of her 17 million or so fellow cocitizens; yet her understanding of Australia as a political unit is exactly predicated on her imagining herself and them as a bounded community, based on their willed association, of institutionalized rights and duties, such as the right to vote, for example, or to collect social security. Further, this political entity of free association, Australia, is delimited and set off in marked contrast to other such entities with their own institutions of rights and duties, such as Indonesia or New Zealand. Anderson (1983) and Gellner (1983) claim the basis for this sense of association, or at least a powerful force for forming and continuing it, is a shared language. Anderson (1983) argues that the diffusion of nationalist ideology via the print media of local newspapers, novels, or political pamphlets was a *sine qua non* for the formation of modern nation-states, especially those breaking free of colonial powers in the nineteenth and twentieth centuries. But even in the French Revolution the print media via printed proclamations, pamphlets, and newspapers played a major role in the diffusion of the Revolution's ideology. Of course, for such diffusion to be effective it is essential that there be a shared language between the writers and printers of such materials and their readers, clearly favoring the *de facto* development of a standard national language. Indeed, the French Revolution was a watershed period for the development of a conscious and explicitly enunciated policy (Grillo 1989) for the promulgation of Parisian French as the standard language throughout the French nation, in some cases leading to a rather brutal suppression of other minority languages or dialects, like Basque, Breton, or Occitan. Gellner (1983) also points out the effective exercising of one's rights and duties as a citizen requires that we be educated in these rights and duties. Again literacy in a standard national language is commonly seen as the most effective way to deliver this education, especially as part of the wider agenda of a national education system whose mission is to produce technologically competent citizens for the broader interests of the industrialized and technologized state. Gellner provides instructive examples like the following: Yimas village (a *Gemeinschaft* community) can produce a competent Yimas, but only the Papua New Guinea nation-state through its educational institutions is capable of producing an effective Papua New Guinea citizen, one able to engage profitably in the technological and political institutions of the wider Papua New Guinea community (a *Gesellschaft* community). Yimas village on its own is simply too limited in its resources to do this. Ultimately, the effectiveness of this education relies on a shared language between the Yimas villager and other Papua New Guinea villagers, again requiring a *de facto* standard national language. These facts were well recognized by the French revolutionaries and was the reason behind their policy for the aggressive promulgation of Parisian French.

The forces which produce and mold standard national languages are many and various, but revolve mainly around political and economic variables. Essentially, a standard national language is likely to largely reflect the speech of a nation's elite, those who hold political and economic power. (As we have seen there is a very close interconnection between these two, even when there is a perceived or *de jure* separation. Those who wield economic power in the United States, for example, the large shareholders of major corporations, have an enormously disproportionate influence over those who hold political power, the legislators and government executives.) The reason for this, of course, is that it is through the standard national language that we may gain access to wealth and power; many studies on the United States have shown that American Blacks who speak Standard American English are much more likely to be employed in higher paying and higher status jobs than those who only speak Vernacular Black English. Standard languages not only reflect the speech of the elites, but, as we shall see, also their interests.

The Development of Standard English

The story of the rise of Standard English, although taking place well before the nineteenth-century rise of the nation-state, well exemplifies the effect of these variables. Standard forms of English, be they American or British, for example, did not arise spontaneously; they were carefully crafted. The idea of a standardized form of English began to emerge in the London area around the fourteenth century (Shaklee 1980). English at that time was spoken in four main dialect groupings: Northern, above the Humber River; Midland, north of the Thames and Avon Rivers, but south of the Humber;

Southern, south of the Avon and Thames rivers, but west of London; and Kentish, south of the Thames River and mainly east of London (the regional dialects of English in England today are the modern descendants of these Middle English dialect groupings). By the late fourteenth century London had taken on dialect characteristics quite particular to itself, for it had become a main center of trade and commerce, attracting people from all over England, a process set in motion as early as the eleventh century due to the decision of the Norman conquerors to centralize courtly power in this city. In the early fourteenth century, London society was highly stratified: titled nobles, a small minority, over a mass of skilled and unskilled laborers. The dialect of the city was largely that of the Southern grouping. But by the fifteenth century there had been some changes: the city's dialect now had features typical of the Midland grouping. This no doubt reflected that the East Midland area, the most populous in all of England, was also now its economic center, responsible for the exporting of grain and wool. Further, membership in social classes during the course of the fourteenth and early fifteenth centuries in London was more fluid, due in no small part to the demographic collapse resulting from the Black Death, which killed between 30 and 40 percent of England's population and hit the city's population especially hard. Consequently, the demand for labor greatly exceeded the supply, weakening traditional feudal ties and allowing those who travelled to the city to set themselves up in craft leagues and business. The fact that the East Midland area was the least ravaged by the Black Death combined with its economic power to result in the social ascendancy of the people from this area within a few generations and hence features of their dialect finding their way into the London dialect, again the speech of elites setting the pace for everyone else.

Finally, by the sixteenth century, things had changed again; notably the speech of London now exhibited a number of features of the Northern dialect (e.g. third-person plural pronouns in *th*: *th*ey *th*eir *th*em instead of *h*: *h*y *h*ir *h*em; the third-person singular indicative ending -*s* instead of -*th*: *does* instead of *doth*, etc.). This reflected the gradual social ascendancy of speakers of the Northern dialect grouping during the course of the fifteenth century. England's major manufacture and export during the fifteenth century was woollen goods, and the center of production for these goods was the Northern counties. London was the center of this export trade, but the ultimate source of the these goods was the Northern counties. Thus, economically powerful Northern wool growers were drawn to London and gradually rose up to the higher strata of the social hierarchy, i.e. became a major force in the elites, guaranteeing prestige to their dialect and its ultimate effect on the regional dialect spoken in London.

By the late fifteenth and early sixteenth centuries, England was becoming quite centralized, under absolutist Tudor monarchs centered in London.

The elite class maintained dwellings there, and much of England's cultural life was also located there, due no doubt to the concentration of wealth and power in the city (note that Shakespeare, while born in Stratford in the West Midlands, lived and performed his plays in London). Consequently, the dialect of the city associated with the elites' strata, with its mixture of Southern, East Midland and Northern dialect features, was gradually seen as prestigious not only in London, but throughout the entire country. Many of the wealthiest Londoners had extensive land-holdings in the country, aiding the diffusion of the prestige London dialect to new areas. Further, in the latter half of the fifteenth century, William Caxton brought a printing press to England and began printing many manuscripts. He himself acted as editor for these manuscripts and undertook to standardize their language and spelling; he did so in the direction of the prestigious London dialect of his times, that of the elites. Caxton's printing of manuscripts in this dialect reinforced the notion of it being a standard to be emulated. This supports Anderson's (1983) idea of the role of the printing press as a diffuser of standard languages and, ultimately, ideas of an imagined national community. Increased literacy and literary activities (e.g. Shakespeare, Spenser, Marlowe, etc.) during the sixteenth and seventeenth centuries only served to solidify its position as the prestige form of English, so by the beginning of the eighteenth century, the position of the speech of upper strata Londoners as "proper" English was well entrenched. Eighteenth-century scholars of English concerned themselves with further fine tuning of a form of standard "proper" English on the basis of this prestigious London dialect, as spoken by the political and economic elite (Crowley 1989); gentle manners, rationality, and a host of traits of high social honor were equated with control of this language. Inability to control it was equated with boorishness. Finally, with the rise of modern ideas of the nation-state in the late eighteenth and nineteenth centuries, a full-scale attack on the minority languages of the British Isles, Irish, Scots Gaelic, Welsh, Manx, was mounted, with the aim to supplant them with Standard English (Crowley 1989; Grillo 1989). This reflected widespread Romantic beliefs going back to Herder, which tied together national spirit, reason, and language spoken; language was seen as the most fundamental expression of the soul of a people and thus clearly linked to the budding of nationalist ideologies, especially German nationalism. In the British context, a unified British nation and people required acceptance by all of a standard British language, i.e. a standard English based on the usage of the elites of the community, the economically and politically privileged living in London. Standardizing spelling and stigmatizing certain variant forms followed, mainly through the development of prescriptive grammars and dictionaries, such as Samuel Johnson's famous English dictionary of 1755. The end result of all this is the Standard English language we know today, so that a middle-class speaker of English in Britain,

Australia, the United States, or South Africa all speak essentially the same language, in spite of tens of thousands of kilometers which separate them. This Standard English is also the form taught as a second language in many former British colonies, so that middle-class Ghanaians, Solomon Islanders, Burmese, and Jamaicans also speak the same language. These people, however, may have great difficulty in understanding a regional non-standard dialect of English, such as Lowland Scots or Vernacular Black English.

To summarize, the rise of Standard English (Shaklee (1980) and Crowley (1989)) exhibits a number of important general points about the how and whys of language standardization: first, if economic and political power is centralized in a particular area, the language of that area has a strong likelihood of being the basis of the standard, as the center imposes its hold upon the periphery (Standard French based on the Parisian dialect is another example of this); second, the standard is likely to be based on the speech of economically and politically powerful social groups, the elite, as their speech becomes imposed upon or diffused to lower status groups; ability to speak this dialect now becomes emblematic of higher social standing and thus a desirable skill, a kind of symbolic resource further empowering the elite, who may control access to the dialect through the education system, as is clearly the case in most modern nation-states; and third, a language or dialect which is the basis of literate forms and other cultural activities is a strong candidate for an imposed standard (Standard Italian based on the Tuscany dialect of Dante exemplifies this).

The Fate of Dutch as a Standard Language

As an interesting contrast to the development of Standard English, consider the fate of the closely related Dutch in the Netherlands and Belgium (Cooper 1989:140–1). Dutch is spoken in both the countries and is the standard language of the Netherlands, but in Belgium it shares with French the status of one of that country's official languages. Originally, the whole of modern Belgium and the Netherlands spoke regional Dutch dialects of some type, but by the middle of the sixteenth century, under Habsburg rule centered in Spain or Austria, the dialect of the Brussels and Antwerp region, the main commercial and political area of this territory, began to emerge as a kind of standard for the whole Dutch-speaking area. However, by the beginning of the seventeenth century, following a revolt against Habsburg rule, the northern provinces we know now as the Netherlands had become independent and a new standard literary language emerged, this time based on the Amsterdam dialect, the new commercial center. During the seventeenth century, the Dutch "Golden Age," Amsterdam became enormously successful, the commercial and maritime center for all of Europe. The Netherlands became a great trading and maritime power, with a major empire in the East Indies. This economic power was linked to a major cultural and scientific flowering, the time of Rembrandt, Hals, Huygens, Spinoza. From this economic and cultural base in Amsterdam, developed a Standard Dutch, based on the speech of the rich merchants and bankers of Amsterdam.

The story of the rise of Standard Dutch in the Netherlands is not too dissimilar to that of English, but the developments in Belgium are quite different. Habsburg hegemony continued over the southern provinces until the middle of the nineteenth century, when the Kingdom of Belgium emerged. French became the language of its elite, a development aided no doubt by a brief period of French rule under Napoleon (1797–1814), but in fact French was an elite language over much of continental Europe during the eighteenth century; it was the language of courts from Paris to Moscow. The farmers and laboring classes in Dutch-speaking areas of today's Belgium continued to speak regional Dutch dialects; no Belgian standard form of Dutch emerged. This situation more or less continues today. In fact, Dutch in Belgium did not receive official equality in status with French until 1938. French speakers formed and, to a certain extent, still do constitute the bulk of the elite, those with economic and political power, and this has militated against the development of a standard Belgian form of Dutch. The Standard Dutch of the Netherlands, based on the Amsterdam dialect, has been accepted *de jure* by Belgium as well, but this has somewhat been resisted by Belgians, so that fluency in this standard is lower in Belgium than in the Netherlands. The numerous efforts to create a Belgian version of Standard Dutch based on Belgian regional dialects have been failures. This is a reflection, no doubt, of the fact that real economic power in Belgium is not in the hands of Dutch speakers, but rather French speakers. Further, in recent years the prestige of French has been given another boost by Brussels, the capital city of Belgium and officially bilingual in French and Dutch, becoming the administrative center of the European Union. Because France is a major player in the Union and many diplomats and administrators are fluent in French, a major world language, its position *vis-à-vis* Dutch cannot help but be strengthened in Brussels and by extension the whole country (Dutch is clearly a small minority language in the European and world context).

The differing fates of a standardized form of Dutch in the Netherlands and Belgium reinforce the points made earlier about the hows and whys of standard languages. Standard Dutch based on the Amsterdam dialect emerged in the Netherlands, because that city was economically and politically central and had a clear economic and political elite which spoke its dialect. This elite's patronage and wealth made possible a great cultural and scientific efflorescence in the city. Such a standard did not emerge in the Belgian provinces because, while the Antwerp–Brussels area was economically central, real political power lay in the Habsburg monarchy in Vienna and Madrid. Further, the elite did not speak Dutch, but French, and elite cultural activities were carried out in this language, a link to the cultural dominance of the French court of the Ancien Régime, a model for all eighteenth-century European courts, even those of Vienna and Madrid.

Standard Languages in Norway

Standard English and Standard Dutch more or less emerged from the speech of their respective elites well before the nineteenth-century rise of modern nationalist ideologies. An interesting contrastive case is the story of the development of Standard Norwegian, which does exemplify the powerful effects of those ideologies, in particular, the Romantic idea that a nation's unique identity and its distinctive national language are closely intertwined (Haugen 1966). Norway was ruled by Denmark from the fifteenth century until 1814. During this period, the official language was the colonial language Danish, so that when independence occurred in 1814 there was no standard Norwegian language. The informal speech of the urban elite was their regional dialect with a heavy Danish influence; the formal language was Danish with a Norwegian pronunciation. Non-elite town dwellers spoke Norwegian dialects with significant Danish influence, whereas rural people spoke Norwegian dialects largely uninfluenced by Danish.

A first official language, Dano-Norwegian or Bokmål ("book language") was developed on the basis of the speech of the urban elite who spoke Danish influenced Norwegian. This was a straightforward development in terms of the variables discussed above: it was based on the economically and politically powerful towns, especially Oslo; it was spoken by the economically and politically powerful social groups, the elites; and it had close ties to Danish, a language of significant cultural achievements. However, it runs afoul of the Romantic factor just noted; being close to Danish, it carries connotations of the previous imperial power and, in any case, is hardly representative of a unique Norwegian national identity. Consequently, a school teacher named Ivar Aasen suggested a new standard language based on the rural Norwegian dialects of the western part of the country, believed to have had the least amount of Danish influence. This language, now called Nynorsk ("new Norwegian"), was made an official language on a par with Bokmål in 1885, largely as a result of strong nationalist sentiments. Norway now had two official languages, not an insignificant problem in a country of 4 million, if we consider the costs of printing government publications, school books, etc. in the two languages. Over the last hundred years or so successive governments have tried to legislate linguistic reforms to bring the two languages closer together (they are not all that extremely different in the first place, merely dialectal variants). It is not likely that one standard Norwegian language will emerge by this process in the near future, but this example of language planning and standardization by legislation does indicate that this process is only secondarily a linguistic one. It is primarily a political and economic process reflecting the conflicting interests of competing social groups, in this case, urbanized conservative elites versus more radical nationalists with rural power bases (see also Blom and Gumperz 1972). The Norwegian case also conclusively demonstrates the role that ideologies of nationalism and statehood can play in the creation of standard languages. This was not an important factor in the rise of Standard English and Dutch because they were largely fixed before the modern concepts of nationality and statehood emerged. However, these concepts undoubtedly have been central in the imposition, especially in the nineteenth century, of Standard English upon Scotland, Ireland and Wales, for example.

Building National Identities

The interplay among concepts of nation, state, and standard language is especially apparent in the new countries of Asia and Africa which have emerged from the collapse of European colonial empires in the 1950s and 1960s. These countries are often multiethnic and multilingual, and the problems of developing a standard language are viewed by them and others as being especially acute. For reasons that should already be readily apparent from the preceding discussion, constructing a national standard language is commonly seen in these countries as an intrinsic part of building a modern nation-state, as in the catch cry of the Indonesian nationalists of the first half of this century: "one nation, one people, one language"; and this in a country of over 300 regional languages! In turn, building a modern nation-state out of these former colonies is itself highly problematic, as their citizens are often divided by tribe, race, region, custom, religion, as well as language. Much of the civil strife in these ex-colonies in the latter twentieth century was conflict along these lines, for example, the conflict between Bantu versus Nilotic tribes in Uganda in the 1970s and 1980s or the revolt of the outer islands against perceived Javanese domination of the central government in Jakarta in 1950s or the struggle in the 1990s of Bougainville Island to secede from Papua New Guinea on the basis of perceived ethnic differences. In fact, conflicts of this sort can ultimately lead to the collapse of the nation-state, as effectively occurred in Somalia in the 1990s, where regional factionalism *de facto* resulted in the partition of the country (this process, of course, was not limited to recent ex-colonies in the 1990s: the breakup of the Soviet Union, Yugoslavia, and even Czechoslovakia along regional, ethnic, or religious lines demonstrated how widespread this process is).

Geertz (1973:255–310) argues that such civil strife and occasional partition is the result of "integrative failure," the failure to extend citizens ties beyond their immediate social givens of kinship/tribe, religion, language, or dialect (what Geertz calls "primordial attachments" or the basis of *Gemeinschaft* communities) to wider civic connections, ultimately, "routine allegiance to a civil state, supplemented to a greater or lesser extent by government use of police powers and ideological exhortation," a "single sovereignty" (*Gesellschaft* communities) (Geertz 1973:260, 277). Deutsch (1966) makes a similar point employing a more active network model. As people are socially mobilized through nationalist appeals to a unified civil state, they are exhorted to extend the range of their social connections. To the extent that this process succeeds in spreading citizens' ties well beyond Geertz's "primordial attachments," state formation is likely to prosper; to the extent that if it does not, it is likely to flounder. Of course, there are other means available to bind people together into a state, notably the effective use by one ruling elite of the means of repression and terror at its disposal. Whether this is a possible long-term solution on its own remains to be seen; the experience of the Soviet Union suggests it is not. A standardized national language therefore assumes a central role as a vital means of extending these ties beyond "primordial attachments" through centralization of a national media, national school curricula, and a national governmental bureaucracy. It is obviously the aim of any national government to spread its nationalist message through these channels, and this is most effectively done through the medium of a single language. The United States Government, for example, effectively broadcasts its strong nationalist ideology through the written and electronic media and school system, all in the *de facto* national language, Standard American English. Imagine the problems of national integration in the United States, if each state had its own standard language and all media broadcasting and teaching were conducted in that language, and one begins to get an idea why the idea of a standard national language is taken so seriously in the new states which have emerged from the ex-colonies. Having said this, however, it still must be recognized that national integration and the use of the standard language to forge and maintain this integration still largely reflects the interests of the ruling national political and economic elites; it is they who have the most to lose through national disintegration.

The concepts of "nation" and "state," which are found combined in "nation-state," are modern ideas in need of some careful defining. As we have seen, the ideology of nationalism and the rise of the nation-state were the products of the late eighteenth century and nineteenth centuries. States had existed since antiquity, and perhaps nations even before that, but not nation-states. A state is any region governed under a central administration, with its own legal and political institutions, and separated by the administration and its institutions from surrounding regions. Prior to the eighteenth-century states had been city states, e.g. classical Athens or fifteenth-century Florence, or empires, e.g. second millennium BC Egypt, Rome, India under Ashoka, the latter two especially being remarkably multiethnic and multilingual, comprised of many nations. A nation is any community of people who see themselves as an ethnic and cultural (and typically linguistic) unit, and contrast with other communities of people surrounding them (Smith (1994) calls these *ethnie*, but the idea is much the same). Hence the use of the term "first nations" in modern Canada to describe the autochthonous Amerindian population; the same could apply to the Aboriginal groups of Australia. In this sense too the Kurds, spread over parts of modern Turkey, Iraq and Iran, are a nation. One of the major sources of conflict in the current world scene is the struggle of communities who are nations in this sense to become states. The ongoing struggle of the Kurds for their own separate nation-state and the successful struggle of Slovenia and Croatia illustrate this process of forging new nation-states. In a way the struggles of the Kurds and the Slovenes are the opposite of the problems facing the ex-colonies; for these people are nations fighting to be states. The ex-colonies in some ways face a more daunting task: they are states struggling to be nations, i.e. forging a sense of civil unity among their citizens, an identity which distinguishes them from citizens of other nations. While "primordial attachments," *Gemeinschaft* traits, may be disintegrative, it is imperative that these new states forge some new state-wide national, shared cultural traits, beliefs or practices to promote integrative ties and buttress simple *Gesellschaft* links of free association, of cocitizens. It seems clear that the latter in these multiethnic multilingual societies are not enough; we need only to look at the stories of Lebanon, Yugoslavia, Burma, Nigeria, Uganda, Rwanda, etc. in the latter half of the twentieth century years to see the truth of this statement.

Standard Languages and Elite Hegemony

Clearly, one powerful force that can be used to build this sense of common identity for citizens of nation-state X is a shared standard national language. Official languages are also necessary for the functioning of the state and its central institutions; a state in which the judiciary uses one language and the executive bureaucracies another is not likely to work well. Ideally, the national language, the emblem of one's national identity and the official language of state functions should be one and the same. However, many ex-colonies have found this *modus vivendi* difficult to achieve. Throughout much of the British and French ex-colonial Africa, the colonial language English or French continues to function as the official state language and the language of national cultural life, as in the media or school system. There are two main reasons for this situation. First, many of these countries are highly multilingual and if one of the local languages were chosen as the official and national language, it would greatly advantage its speakers and disadvantage others, possibly leading to serious civil strife. Second, and more importantly, in the light of earlier discussion, prior to independence, the political and economic elite of these countries were educated in the colonial languages and, of course, the colonial bureaucracy was conducted in those languages. After independence, these linguistic policies remained in force, and they entrenched the position of the ruling elite who, of course, are hardly likely to espouse policies which weaken their position. In fact, in much of Africa since independence there has been the emergence of a clear class of the linguistic elite. Good active control of the colonial language is possessed by only a small percentage of the population, the elite, and as knowledge of this language is essential to gaining access to power and prestige in these countries, it virtually guarantees their entrenched position. The ruling elite use their wealth to send their children to a selective education system which ensures a high degree of competence in the spoken and written types of the colonial language, a task the state-school system, often starved of funding, cannot hope to match. This linguistic stratification mirrors and perpetuates the social stratification. This pattern, of course, is not limited to ex-colonies. Bourdieu (1991) (see also Grillo (1989)) points out how closely tied, even in developed countries like France, are the differential prestige of linguistic varieties and the relative social status of their speakers, with the highest social honor being awarded to those who control standard language usage most proficiently. It is the role of the educational system to screen individuals for access to high social esteem, largely through restricting access to the most valued norms of usage of the standard language. In this way the elite effectively reproduces itself and bars access to its ranks for all but a select few. If you cannot read and write Standard English, your chances of getting into Harvard College and from there, potentially the elite ranks of American society, are fairly dismal. Of course, if you already come from the elite class, your chances of reading and writing Standard English are pretty high, certainly more so than if your parents are inner-city Haitian Creole speaking immigrant laborers. It is extremely important to note that there is nothing inherently superior about the standard variety of a language over other varieties. It is simply that through its connection with elite groups, it has been granted differential prestige over other varieties, i.e. high symbolic value. Further, it is a hegemonic variety in exactly Gramsci's (1971) sense: through its effective diffusion via powerful and prestigious institutions, most notably educational institutions, people accept its high value as being legitimate in the order of things and view their own control of its norms as essential to their own high status. Hence, the state institutions function in a sense to naturalize the dominance of the standard language, whereas there is absolutely nothing natural about it, simply the effect of power differentials in the society as a whole.

Forging a Standard Language: The Case of Indonesian

Not all ex-colonies have followed the path of adopting ex-colonial languages as national languages, however. Tanzania and Indonesia are two examples of former colonies which have raised regional languages to the status of official national languages, Kiswahili in Tanzania and Indonesian/Malay in Indonesia. I will discuss the case of Indonesian here; for an overview of Kiswahili in Tanzania see Fasold (1984:266–77). Although Indonesia is a highly multiethnic multilingual country (over 300 languages and at least that number of ethnic/cultural/tribal groups), in fact, one ethnic/cultural group does dominate, the Javanese, of central and east Java, with over half the population of the archipelago. Their language, Javanese, might have seemed an obvious choice for an official national language, but the nationalist groups who struggled for Indonesian independence in the first half of the twentieth century were clever enough to foresee a number of shortcomings in this choice. First, the elaborate indication of social status in the Javanese speech levels I discussed in chapter 16 made it somewhat dysfunctional as a carrier of modernist and nationalist ideologies of equal citizens, associating together in the struggle to form a new nation. Second, the Javanese language is intimately linked to the intricate high culture of Hindu–Buddhist–Islamic syncretism in central Java; the values of this syncretism are not largely shared by the more mercantile outer islands like Sumatra or Borneo, and in this sense the Javanese language could be viewed as a carrier of "primordial attachments" rather than nationalist ties. Finally, the groups of nationalists struggling for independence were dominated by Javanese, like Sukarno, Indonesia's first president. Those from outer islands were already suspicious of a Javanese hegemony in an eventually independent Indonesia, and any choice of Javanese as an official national language, further entrenching their dominant position, was bound to spark disintegrative forces in the new nation, which in any case was seriously plagued by these throughout its first two decades.

Hence, the nationalists looked elsewhere for an official national language and they had a good candidate, Malay. Malay had for centuries been spread throughout the archipelago as a lingua franca of trade. The Dutch, the colonial overlords of Indonesia, also used Malay as a *de facto* auxiliary language of administration and also for everyday trading transactions, such as in the markets. Further, the nationalists, young well-educated children of the urbanized Indonesian elite, already spoke it as a second language. Thus, in spite of its being the native language of a tiny fraction of the archipelago's population, Malay was proclaimed by the nationalists in 1928 as the official national language of an independent-to-be Indonesia and renamed Indonesian.

This process was given an enormous boost by World War II and the Japanese invasion of Indonesia. The Japanese smashed the Dutch administrative structure and proscribed the Dutch language, intending, ultimately, of course, to replace it with Japanese. In the meantime out of necessity, Malay/Indonesian was used, so that when final independence finally came in 1949, its position as a national official language was not an issue.

The Malay that had spread over the Indonesian islands over the preceding millennium was by 1950 differentiated into a number of dialects. These ranged from a kind of simplified pidgin-like Malay called Bazaar Malay to a morphologically rich form, closer to the written Malay of the Malay-speaking courts in Sumatra and the Malay peninsula. It was a kind of Malay of the latter type which is the basis of modern standardized Indonesian. The following two sentences illustrate the difference between ordinary colloquial or village Malay and the standardized modern Indonesian (Benjamin 1993:357)

colloquial:	aku	tanam	sayur	di	kebun
	I	plant	vegetables	in	garden

"I plant vegetables in the garden"

standard:	saya	men-(t)anam-i	kebun		dengan	sayur
	I	plant	garden	with	vegetables

"I plant the garden with vegetables"

The colloquial varieties largely employ word order to signal grammatical functions and are morphologically unelaborated. In contrast Standard Indonesian makes great use of derivational morphology: in the above example the prefix *men-* indicates that the sentence is in active voice and the suffix *-i* that the direct object of the verb is semantically a location (the garden is *where* the vegetables are planted). Further, the standard language employs the polite V-form pronoun *saya* "I," contrasting with the familiar T-form *aku*, a contrast the lower colloquial forms typically lack.

Differences between varieties of a language such as these illustrate a fundamental task in any attempt in language planning, what Ferguson (1968) refers to as corpus planning (see also Cobarrubias and Fishman (1983), Cooper (1989), Eastman (1983), Fishman (1974), Fishman, Ferguson and Das Gupta (1968), Laitin (1992), and Rubin and Jernudd (1971)). All languages have internal variation, regional dialects, sociolinguistic variables and register variation. Once a particular local language has been chosen as the official national language, this internal variation is seen as problematic:

what forms are to be used in official government documents, newspapers, radio and television, and school textbooks? Which will constitute the official standard language? The choice of a particular variety over others will obviously politically and economically advantage the speakers of that variety, so it is a potentially explosive question. In Indonesia, this issue was somewhat diffused by the choice for the national language of a numerically insignificant part of the population, but the selection of the morphologically elaborate variety of this language, understandable as it is by virtue of its closeness to the written language of the Malay courts, did in fact advantage those who controlled this variety, namely the urbanized educated native elite. This variety, of course, has been successfully promulgated by publications, the electronic media and the school system, so that today its active control is essential for anyone wishing to participate in the professional life of modern Indonesia. Again, it is the national education system which effectively promulgates this variety and through it screens for individuals who may rise into the more elite circles in the country.

This modern Standard Indonesian, then, has been forged by adopting a particular urban-based variety spoken by elite educated speakers and codifying particular uses and forms within it, and stigmatizing others. This Standard Indonesian is by now far removed from those colloquial and regional forms. Besides the differences in the use of verbal affixes, correct pronunciation has been codified (standard *gulai* instead of *gule* for "soup" and *pulau* instead of *pulo* for "island"), as have lexical items (the standard language has *lezat* and *enak* for "delicious," but the former is lacking in many colloquial varieties) (Moeliono 1986:63–5). Even syntactic rules have been codified. For example, prepositions are required in the standard language, where they might be optional in colloquial varieties (Moeliono 1986:65):

standard: kemarin ia ber-temu dengan wartawan
           yesterday he meet   with   journalist

colloquial: kemarin ia ber-temu wartwan
            yesterday he meet   journalist
            "Yesterday he met with the journalists"

Condensed morphologically complex constructions are selected over periphrastic ones (Moeliono 1986:65):

standard: ia mem-per-besar   gambar-nya itu
           He ACTIVE-CAUSE-big picture-his the
colloquial: ia bikin besar gambar-nya
            He make big   picture-his
            "He enlarged his picture"

(Note also the contrast in English between *enlarge* and *make big*; the former is clearly associated with a higher prestige "more educated" variety of the language, what we might expect well-educated "cultivated" speakers to use.)

standard: majikan-nya men-(n)aik-kan   gaji-nya
               employer-his ACTIVE-climb-CAUSE wage-his
colloquial: majikan-nya kasih naik gaji-nya
               employer-his give climb wage-his
               "His employer raised his wage"

These preferred Standard Indonesian forms have not displaced the colloquial variants. They are largely in a diglossic relationship (Ferguson 1972), with Standard Indonesian serving as a written language and a formal register, and the colloquial varieties, the speech of everyday informal interactions. Again, the standard language is not only a marker of elite speakers, but also elite functions.

Modernization in Language Standardization

As part of its function as a written language and language of formal contexts, such as school or university teaching, professional meetings, etc., Standard Indonesian is under pressure to "modernize" i.e. reflect the technologies, practices, beliefs, of the modern (read largely *Westernized*) world. The elites of Indonesia are clearly tied to those of Europe, North America, and Japan; hence their interests will largely coincide with those of the latter and there will thereby be enormous pressure on the national language to conform to these interests. As pointed out by many local writers on the subject (Alisjahbana 1976; Moeliono 1986), Malay, as the language of traditional peoples and courts, lacks many words for concepts and practices associated with the modern world of technology, bureaucracy, and economy. Like other languages in a similar position, i.e. Hindi, Arabic or Kiswahili, it needs to acquire these in order to carry out its modernizing function, a process regarded by Ferguson (1968), not surprisingly, as modernization, the second wing of his corpus planning, although we should perhaps be wary of the generally positive connotations associated with this word, in Indonesia as well as the West. This process too is not value free, for modernism and its institutions transmit particular understandings and practices toward the world and its people, basically the values and practices of the countries of the industrialized West, so well brought out in Berger, Berger, and Kellner (1973). For all practical purposes, modernization has turned out to be Westernization, with its ideological emphasis on urbanization;

technological fixes to problem solving, leading to secularization; bureaucratic processes for providing services; and constant expanding of one's horizons of consumption, with consequent rapid social change. Such ideas have had a massive impact when transferred to the societies in the new postcolonial nations. In a few, modernization in these terms has met some resistance (Iran/Burma), but in most it has been embraced wholeheartedly. Indonesia is an interesting case. While a strongly modernizing nation, images of its glorious precolonial past of Indicized empires in Java and Sumatra have been successfully manipulated to buttress current nationalist ideologies; the official state creed, the *panca sila* "five precepts," has an Indic name and a claimed precolonial pedigree. These asserted indigenous cultural features (but, of course, ultimately of foreign, Indic derivation!) are used to legitimize current Indonesian state policy by appealing to earlier precolonial Indonesian identities (Sukarno, Indonesia's first president, was especially clever in using the Indic past to legitimize the country's revolutionary present of the 1950s and early 1960s). This legitimizing rhetorical device is rather like the use of *Nynorsk* to rally Norwegian nationalism and aspects of related ideologies like socialism against the colonially derived *Bokmål*, connected, as it is, to conservative urban elites. Consequently, in coining new words for modern concepts, Indonesian language planners first of all look for sources in Indonesian languages, then in Sanskrit, the Indic language associated with the classical empires, and finally in European languages, particularly English. Many abstract nouns are based on Native roots with the circumfixes *ke-* . . . *-an*: *ke-bangsa-an* "nationality" (*bangsa* "people"), *ke-cepat-an* "velocity" (*cepat* "fast") (Alisjahbana 1976:73). Sometimes Native words are extended in meaning: *garam* "salt" to "chemical salt" (Moeliono 1986:70). Sanskrit roots and sometimes affixes are borrowed: *sastera* "literature," *budaya* "culture," *negara* "state," *-wan* "person of" (*warta* "news" + *-wan* equals *wartwan* "journalist"). Sanskrit words particularly dominate in the area of literature and the arts. And finally many European words are borrowed from English or Dutch: *antropologi* "anthropology," *kwalitet* "quality," *rasionalisasi* "rationalization," *politik* "politics," *demokrasi* "democracy." Note loans from European languages dominate in the spheres of politics, economics and technology, the areas in which Westernized elites will have the greatest interests. Note further that in its mixture of Native, Sanskrit, and European sources for words for modern concepts, Standard Indonesian demonstrates the effects that various planks of nationalist ideology can have on the conscious processes of language planning. This may be an important consideration if the state views the standard national language to be useful at least as much as an emblem of an authentic identity for a citizen of a particular nation-state as it is a conduit of the ideas, practices, and institutions of the modern world. Of course, the process forging a standard language cannot be completely controlled: many forms and expressions will come into the language regardless of the wishes of language planners, particularly from high prestige world languages like English.

The Westernization of Standard Thai

In other cases, the process of modernization through Westernization may be an explicit part of the nationalist ideology promulgated by local elites. Thailand in the nineteenth century is a good illustration of this path. The story of the codification of Standard Thai in the nineteenth and twentieth centuries illustrates how pervasive Western norms have been on language standardization and modernization in Thailand. Like Indonesian, Standard Thai and colloquial varieties are highly differentiated. Diller (1993) argues that Standard Thai has many features directly imported from European languages, particularly English, features lacking in the colloquial varieties. These include: overt "tense" markers like *dâ*y PAST, overt prepositions, fixed subject–verb–object word order, a passive with the agent marker *dûay*, subordinated nominalizations, etc. Many of these were promulgated into high styles of Thai by royal proclamations or translations from English prose and poetry (for example, King Rama VI translated Shakespeare into (a highly anglicized form of) Thai). Through their connection to the royal family, the highest grade of Thai elites, these became varieties to emulate, bearing high symbolic value, leading to a high status form of Thai with many diffused European features. Finally, in 1918 a normative grammar of Thai incorporating most of these features was published. For decades, this has remained the main handbook for Thai grammar, taught to millions of school children, so that again the national education system has been the venue through which the speech norms of the local elite have been transmitted to the masses. Examinations for the Thai civil service, a major road to elite power and prerogatives in the country, have always included testing candidates for control of the norms of this codified Standard Thai, insuring its continued hegemony. As a result of these processes, modern Standard Thai can quite fairly be called "Westernized."

Summary

One of the major sociocultural changes over the last 200 years has been the rise of the nation-state and closely correlated with that has been the development of standard languages. Nation-states entail the replacement of community attachments of kin, village, or tribal affiliation with a willed free association of cocitizens. Standard languages play a central role in the promulgation and maintenance of this association of cocitizens, especially through their diffusion via a national education system. Standard languages typically reflect the speech of the local elites, those who have power and prestige. Access to the ranks of the elites is regulated through control of the norms of the standard language, and it is a primary function of the education system to screen for this control of possible access. In the new multilingual multiethnic states of the ex-colonies of Africa and Asia, nation building on the basis of association of citizens has been very problematic, commonly facing challenges from disintegrative forces of tribal or ethnic ties. Languages of the ex-colonial powers have often been adopted as standard languages given the often complex multilingual situation in these countries, but this also has the effect of entrenching the position of the former colonially educated elite and their descendants, creating a new category of the "linguistic elite," that small percentage of the population who controls the colonial language well. Other countries like Indonesia have selected a local language as the standard language, but this has required an active and sustained policy of linguistic engineering, tailoring the local language to the needs of a modern nation-state, its education system and the wider technological world. Often, given the dominance of the industrialized West in technological spheres, this has resulted in the "Westernization" of the language, adoption of European lexical items and even grammatical structures into the local language.

Further Reading

For sources on the rise of the modern nation-state and ideologies of nationalism, see Anderson (1983), Gellner (1983), Seton-Watson (1977) and Smith (1983, 1986, 1991, 1994), and the articles in Tilly (1975). For general introductions to the problems and procedures of language planning see Cooper (1989), Eastman (1983), Joseph (1987), and Laitin (1992); also consult Bourdieu (1990), Bourdieu and Passeron (1977), Grillo (1989), and Woolard and Schieffelin (1994) for the effects of ideology and elite class interests on the process of language standardization. Laitin (1977) is an excellent study of the history of language planning in Somalia, while Alisjahbana (1976) tells the story of Indonesian efforts. The rise of Standard English is set out in Crowley (1989) and Shaklee (1980). Since the end of the colonial era in the 1960s and the rise of so many multiethnic multilingual nation-states, there has been a swathe of anthologies on language planning, the most important being: Cobarrubias and Fishman (1983), Fishman (1974), Fishman, Ferguson and Das Gupta (1968), Marshall (1991), and Rubin and Jernudd (1971).

21

Literacy

The Cognitive Consequences of Literacy

In a seminal study, Goody (1977), building on earlier work (Goody 1968; Goody and Watt 1972) proposed that literacy is a major force for social and cultural change. He proposed to replace earlier contrasts in anthropological writings between prelogical versus logical mentalities or "primitive" versus civilized minds (Lévy-Bruhl 1926), or the Neolithic "science of the concrete" versus our modern "science of the abstract" (Lévi-Strauss 1966) with a contrast between oral versus literate cultures. In other words, the invention of writing, roughly around five thousand years ago, was a watershed event in human history, so that societies possessing this "technology of the intellect" (Goody 1977) are fundamentally different as a result of this invention. Goody followed this work up with subsequent publications (Goody 1986, 1987), and this hypothesis has independently been proposed or enthusiastically taken up by a number of other researchers (Havelock 1963, 1982; Olson 1977, 1994; Ong 1982, 1992). On the face of it, this suggestion might seem relatively uncontroversial. The members of a literate society are clearly different from those of an oral one – they can read and write. But Goody and his fellow researchers mean much more than this; it is their contention that the possession of this skill, this "technology of the intellect," leads to major cognitive changes in the way literates think about themselves and their world. Literacy brings about a major cognitive revolution, a revolution best exemplified, in Goody's view, in the flowering of critical and speculative thought in classical Greece (a view most fully developed in Havelock (1963, 1982)), but a potential outcome wherever literacy takes hold.

Just what are these cognitive changes? Goody is more circumspect than other researchers like Ong (1982, 1992), but he still attributes sweeping cognitive and social effects to the development of literacy. Goody points to the relative permanency of written language, as opposed to oral, which typically fades in memory quickly after being uttered. This fading of oral language allows information transmitted this way to be forgotten or revised.

However, information written down is not so easily altered, and, in fact, different versions of events or beliefs can be more easily scrutinized for alteration or omission. Goody traces the ancient Greek origin of history, the factual recording of events, as opposed to myth, to the scrutinizing of written documents. He also argues that the resulting awareness of contradictions in differing texts led to an attitude of scepticism and critical inquiry, culminating in the Greek philosophy and science of Plato and Aristotle.

Another important cognitive skill that Goody traces to writing is the development of logic and rationality. Scepticism breeds many opposing viewpoints and explanations. A critical problem is how to choose among these, to determine which hypothesis best fits the facts. In many societies myth may be the charter which fills this function, but when myth is ousted by history, it loses its ability to compel. In literate societies logical procedure and reasoning emerge to reconcile contradictions and affirm propositions. Writing is claimed to favor a decontextualized vantage point on language. Oral language is generated in a particular space and time and within a specific social configuration, i.e. sex/class/caste of the speaker, her relationship to the addressee, etc. Written language is free from these exigencies; it is decontextualized, removable from its place and time of composition and freely interpretable, potentially ascribable to a multiplicity of authors and available to readers of diverse social backgrounds. This decontextualization is further mirrored in the actual forms that writing can take. Goody (1977) argues that writing encourages decontextualized kinds of language which are unlikely in oral cultures, for example, lists. Goody notes that lists occur in the earliest forms of writing, e.g. Sumerian and Babylonian, and notes that this is decontextualized language *par excellence*, being just words divorced from normal discourse contexts and sentential structures. Hence, some organizing principle other than the syntactic and textual principles of the language can be evoked to organize lists, so that they are either largely random inventories of items, like our shopping lists, or items organized by overarching cognitive groupings, like lists of types of frogs or clan names, or totemic ancestors. These lists are organized conceptually by abstract categories, taxonomic ("kinds of frogs") or otherwise ("clans of this village" or "totemic ancestors of such and such a clan"), and this brings into the foreground of cognition the concept of classificatory schemas and abstract generalities so crucial to scientific thought and logical reasoning.

Logical reasoning according to Goody is typified by the syllogism, whose origin he ties to the salience of classificatory and abstract cognitive categories made possible through writing. Consider a syllogism like:

All birds have feathers.
Kookaburras are birds.
Therefore, kookaburras have feathers.

Note that this syllogism is dependent on the abstract classificatory concept "bird," the class to which kookaburras belong, and therefore partake of anatomical features of this class. Such logical reasoning is already dependent on decontextualized uses of language typified by lists (e.g. "bird" as a class concept, "kookaburra" a member of this class, etc.), and, as such, is closely associated with the development of written forms of language. Ultimately, then, cognitive activities often ascribed to civilization, such as, the differentiation of fact/history from fiction/myth, logical reasoning to correct and remove contradiction and error, leading to closer apprehensions of the truth, and a consequent belief in progress and development, are traced by Goody to the innovation of literacy and especially its spread in ancient Greece.

In an earlier response to some of Goody's claims, Gough (1968) argues that these cognitive effects cannot be so clearly ascribed to literacy, for the two great literate civilizations of the East, India and China, followed quite different trajectories from the Greek influenced West. Han China (second century BC) and Guptan India (fourth and fifth centuries AD) probably had literacy rates quite parallel to that of classical Greece, but its cultural effects, if any, were markedly different. India never developed a strong tradition of written records until the Muslim period beginning in the sixteenth century, at which point myth and history can be said to have diverged. China, on the other hand, had a strong tradition of written records going back to the Han period (beginning sixth century BC). This contrast seems to have nothing to do with the presence or absence of literacy, but with local cultural traditions, the Indian one emphasizing the supremacy of the orally transmitted Vedic tradition through its Brahman priests versus the secularization and early bureaucratization of the Chinese empire.

Both India and China developed strong logical and philosophic traditions, and probing and sceptical minds were characteristic of both civilizations. But how closely this was tied to literacy in these civilizations remains to be established. For instance, the codification of principles of logical reasoning was developed to an especially high degree in India, surpassing even the Greeks, but this was not done for our scientific purposes, to unlock the secrets of nature, but for otherworldly purposes, to detect doctrinal inconsistencies and contradictions in order to achieve salvation. Indeed, public debates over doctrinal issues according to these codified rules of logic were a pervasive feature of Buddhist schools and continues even today in the Indian-based Buddhist tradition of Tibet. But crucially logic was not in the service of science, but of the divine, and the religious tradition in India was almost exclusively *orally* transmitted, throwing seriously into question the whole contention of Goody in linking logic with literacy. It is interesting to note as well in this connection that Lloyd (1990) argues that it was Greek oral political and legal discourse and its rules of debate and evidence which gave rise to Greek logic, philosophy and science, not widespread literacy.

Written Language as Decontextualized

Perhaps the foremost proponent of the claim that literacy through the decontextualization of language has salient cognitive effects is the psychologist David Olson (1977, 1994). He champions a major cognitive distinction between spoken utterance and written text, and argues that the latter, due to its decontextualized nature, is necessarily more explicit in terms of expressing its meanings in an unambiguous and "autonomous" manner. In spoken language such background meaning can be gleaned from the surrounding context of the utterance, but in a written text, available meanings are basically reduced to what is written, and hence this calls for a much greater degree of explicitness on the part of the author. In terms of Grice's Cooperative Principle, speakers can assume a much higher degree of cooperative participation of their interlocutors, due to various types of shared information, and hence a greater latitude in the employment of conversational implicatures, than can authors. As a consequence of assuming potentially less cooperative readers, authors necessarily invoke implicatures less frequently and are thereby more explicit in their wording so as to make their meanings clear and "autonomous."

As far as this goes, as a description of idealized types of spoken and written language this is probably true (but see below), but Olson wants to go further, to tie this difference in explicitness or "autonomy" to differences in cognition. Olson claims that changes in the style of language actually alter the nature of thought itself, leading to more rational, critical and analytical thinking, outcomes much as those that Goody claims for literacy. Interestingly, Olson (1994) approaches this problem from the viewpoint of a reader, arguing that much as written language is relatively explicit in its intentions *vis-à-vis* spoken language, it also potentially leaves out a lot of information ordinarily carried in spoken language via intonation or paralinguistic features, such as type of speech act. This information has to be supplied by the reader, although Olson points to the enormous increase, since the fifteenth century and the rise of printing, in the number of verbs denoting speech acts, mostly of French or Latin origin and mostly limited to written contexts, as a sign of the increasing will to make all meanings explicit in a written text. However, the ideal of making all meaning explicit in written text is just that, an ideal, and one never fully realized. No matter how carefully crafted and explicit a written text is, the reader still has to interpret it. But because the text is fixed and present before her, the reader can critically reflect on it, and this provides a context for reflecting on language as an object in itself. This metalinguistic awareness abetted by literacy is linked by Olson to the development of traditions of grammar and lexicography and, most importantly, as with Goody, logic. These traditions are then used recursively to guide interpretations of written texts, so as to provide clear criteria for determining what texts meant, leading in turn to still further codifications for how to render written texts logical and explicit. In short, the stylistic criteria for modern essayist prose emerged and were well established by the seventeenth century, as witnessed by the writings of the philosophers Descartes and Locke or the scientists Newton and Pascal. It is in fact this genre that Olson holds as the paragon for exemplifying the cognitive effects of literacy.

Ultimately, Olson argues, modern science emerged in roughly the same period by reading the "book of nature" in parallel fashion. Scientists like Harvey or Boyle took the observable phenomena of nature as signs to be read, but as explicit and literal signs, not the mysterious manifestations of a supernatural otherworld, just as the words of a text should be clear and unambiguous. And the readings should cohere by principles of logic, leading to a final correct explanation of the phenomena, just as a correct definitive interpretation of a text could be arrived at. Canons of proper scientific reasoning through experimentation were developed, again paralleling the conventions of argumentation in essayist prose.

For Olson these innovations are not simply changes in the conventions for using language, but are deeply cognitive, affecting the way literates think. He sees it as a transition from thinking about the world to thinking about representations of the world (this of course is a cognitivist position; see chapter 3). Because our thoughts can be set down on paper and scrutinized, we can literally study representations of what we are thinking. This has a de-anchoring effect from the self, its beliefs, and the present here and now, and leads to thinking in terms of its others, and maybe an objectification of hypotheses and assumptions, which, while representations and models, can be confirmed or disconfirmed as bearing a truth value with respect to the world via the process of experimentation and critical logical reasoning. Again, explicitness in these representations and their careful, deliberate manipulation via logical reasoning is normative. In short, all this leads to thinkers in the mold of Lévi-Strauss's (1966) "science of the abstract," the educational ideal in the modern West.

Literacy as a Social Force

But is all this really due just to literacy, or are there other forces at work? The Russian psychologist Vygotsky (1978, 1986) also claimed that literacy had major cognitive effects on "higher psychological functions," the type of logical scientific thinking discussed above, but he saw it mediated particularly as a *social* force, linked to specific sociocultural conditions, in marked contrast to Olson's (and, more ambiguously, Goody's) view of it as an individual's intellectual tool (this, of course, reflects Vygotsky's overall Marxist position). If literacy's effects are socially mediated and not autonomous to an individual's intellect, then the question becomes one of extracting the effects of literacy, if any, from those of other educational/instructional institutions in the community, especially formal schooling. Vygotsky himself was well aware of this difficulty, and in the 1930s one of his students, Luria, performed some, by now, classic experiments with peasants in a rapidly modernizing section of central Asia, as mechanized farming and collectivization diffused through the area. Not all individuals were equally affected, and Luria could divide the inhabitants into two testable groups, one consisting of traditional farmers with no schooling or literacy skills and another of those who had participated in short teacher-training programs and had acquired vernacular literacy. He administered a number of experimental tasks, but what concerns us here are those associated with logical reasoning. For example, he presented subjects with syllogisms of the following sort (Luria 1976:108–9): In the Far North, where there is snow, all bears are white. Novaya Zemlya is in the Far North and there is always snow there. What color are the bears there? Educated literate subjects drew the expected conclusion: bears there are white, demonstrating reasoning along clear logical lines. But the unschooled non-literate subjects did not, saying things like "I don't know . . . there are different sorts of bears." Luria took such responses as failures to reason along proper logical lines and, in line with the evidence from his other experiments, claimed that their thoughts tended to be concrete and context bound, driven by the tangible properties of perceived objects (note more than a hint of Lévi-Strauss's (1966) neolithic "science of the concrete"), in contrast to the literate schooled population who took a more abstract, logical approach ("science of the abstract"). Following Vygotsky, Luria linked this difference to the sociocultural changes brought about by collectivization and urbanization, with those more affected by these changes demonstrating thinking processes more akin to those generally associated with modernity. Notably, he did not localize the effects in individual thought processes, so he did not try to separate differential effects of schooling as against literacy. A similar study was done 30 years later among the Wolof of Senegal (Greenfield 1966). Children attending school and thereby having acquired literacy skills were tested against unschooled non-literate counterparts, and experiments similar to those of Luria were performed. In one experiment the children were asked to group familiar objects together and then to explain the reasons for their grouping. Greenfield concluded that the schooled, literate children could group the objects according to abstract logical categories, but that the unschooled non-literate children could not, but only on set, concrete, tangible properties. Schooled, literate children were also more verbally explicit in their explanations for their grouping than the unschooled non-literate children.

Greenfield's findings replicate Luria's, but again they fail to disentangle effects of literacy, if any, from those of schooling. This is generally a problem because literacy skills are normally acquired in a school setting, so how could the effects of literacy ever be independently determined?

Cognitive Effects: Literacy versus Schooling

The answer came in a monumental study by Scribner and Cole (1981) among the Vai people of Liberia. In this society literacy and school are not always necessarily connected, for there is an indigenous Vai vernacular script, a syllabary, which is transmitted informally, for example, in households, with no link to formal schooling. There are two other literacies in the society, Arabic, taught in special Koranic schools run by Islamic scholars, and English, which is the language of instruction of the formal school system. Hence, the indigenous Vai literacy is completely distinct from schooling, as opposed to Arabic and English, and therefore Vai society provides an ideal natural laboratory to test for possible cognitive effects of literacy on its own, as opposed to the overall effects of modernizing Westernized schooling. Further, each of the three literacies is associated with different functional domains: English is for official business, for government, and education; Arabic literacy is for religious purposes, especially writing and memorizing of the Koran (in fact, many Vai Arabic literates do not know Arabic, but have memorized and can therefore read and recite sections of the Koran); and Vai vernacular literacy is for practical everyday affairs like making lists, keeping records, or writing letters.

When testing via diverse experimentation for any cognitive consequences of literacy, Scribner and Cole achieved results that cast grave doubts on the strong theorizing of Olson and Goody about the source of reasoning and abstract classification in literacy. Neither Vai nor Arabic literacy seemed to bring about the cognitive changes expected; neither favored decontextualized uses of language, logical syllogistic reasoning, or the elaboration of abstract categories. Only literacy in English did this, but this of course was transmitted through formal schooling, suggesting the cognitive effects are not due to literacy, but to schooling. Interestingly, Scribner and Cole found that English literate schooled individuals did best in tasks involving verbal exposition, giving explicit verbal reasoning for choices, but that this effect was transient. Schooled English literate subjects who had left school a number of years previously did not necessarily *perform* better in classification and abstract reasoning tasks; they merely *talked* about them better, giving more explicit verbal descriptions and explanations.

An extremely important outcome of Scribner and Coles's study was that each of the three literacies was associated with quite specific skills and distinct cognitive effects. For example, Vai script was especially effective in enhancing metalinguistic awareness, putting together syllables to make Vai words and talking about correct Vai grammar. These skills reflect typical practices of the Vai literate community. As the script is a syllabary, literates are skilled in stringing syllables together to form words. Writing of letters in Vai also reinforces metalinguistic awareness because Vai literates commonly discuss whether a letter is written in "good" Vai or not. Arabic literacy had its strongest effects in memory-related tasks, scoring highest in recall of words and word strings. This again is a reflection of everyday practices of Arabic literates in the memorization and recitation of sections of the Koran.

The Practice Approach to Literacy

These findings led Scribner and Cole to reject broad claims for strong and general cognitive skills resulting from literacy. Rather they replaced it with what they call a "practice account of literacy." Each literacy has local cognitive effects due to its social niche and type of practice. The same can be said for English-based literacy and schooling, which imparts particular skills, e.g. logical reasoning, development of abstract categories, explicit expository talk, which are highly practiced and valued in that context, but which at least in Vai country are largely specific to that domain. Even in advanced industrialized societies, there is minimal evidence that many of the skills relevant to solving cognitive tasks in the school domain are generalized outside it (Rogoff and Lave 1984).

Scribner and Cole's findings also point up the inadequacies of the term Goody uses to describe literacy – the "technology of the intellect." Is there any useful notion of a technology that does not include its material basis and uses? And further is the intellect a meaningful concept apart from the practices it engages in, practices which necessarily have a social and material grounding (an important point highlighted in the work of Vygotsky and Luria)? Scribner and Cole (1981:236) think not and for them literacy is:

> a set of socially organized practices which make use of a symbol system and a technology for producing and disseminating it. Literacy is not simply knowing how to read and write a particular script by applying this knowledge for specific purposes in specific contexts of use. The nature of these practices, including, of course, their technological aspects, will determine the kinds of skills ("consequences") associated with literacy.

For Scribner and Cole (1981:236) practices are "recurrent goal directed sequences of activities using a particular technology and particular knowledge." The recurrent coordination of actions blending technology and knowledge that is literacy is nothing more than a type of structural coupling between organism and world mediated through the technology of a script. This structural coupling leads to changes in the state of both organism and world, but these are locally defined by the nature of the structural coupling. Thus, there are no global effects, but only local ones, and whatever broad effects there may be result from histories of repeated diverse types of structural coupling. They do not reside in any one case, nor still less in the nature of the mediating technology. Given that the histories of structural couplings depend on both the organism and its social and material environment, it is clear that literacy is only a part of a much greater range of social practices and that its cognitive consequences cannot be meaningfully separated from this whole range. It follows, then, that literacy and its consequences among the Vai, given their whole range of sociocultural practices, the history of structural couplings which defines them as a culture and society, should be expected to be quite different than that among white urbanized well-educated middle-class Americans.

The Oral/Literate Continuum

A further implication of this position is that there is no unified universal notion of literacy nor a sharp contrast between orality and literacy, but rather a continuum. Finnegan (1988:175) straightforwardly claims:

> "orality" and "literacy" are not two separate and independent things; nor (to put it more concretely) are oral and written modes two mutually exclusive and opposed processes for representing and communicating information. On the contrary they take diverse forms in differing cultures and periods, are used differently in different social contexts, and, insofar as they can be distinguished at all as separate modes rather than a continuum, they mutually interact and affect each other, and the relations between them are problematic rather than self-evident.

Linguists (Biber 1986, 1988; Chafe 1982, 1985; Chafe and Tannen 1987; Tannen 1982a, b, 1985) have probed the formal linguistic differences between different types of oral and written discourse. Writing is claimed to be more detached and more grammatically integrated than speaking, which is more involved and structurally fragmented. Thus, we have two parameters (Chafe 1982, 1985):

writing	*speaking*
detached	involved
integrated	fragmented

Some linguistic reflexes of these parameters in texts are: for writing as detached, the frequency of passives and nominalizations, and for writing as integrated, frequency of subordinate clauses, marked information structure options like *it was rice that Bob ate*, and high numbers of participants per clause, especially those mentioned in prepositional phrases. For speaking as involved, the features include high frequency of first and second person, i.e. speech act centered pronouns, tag questions, and highly expressive or colorful vocabulary like *heaps of money*. For fragmented speaking, as diagnostics, are the high frequency of simple juxtaposition of phrases and clauses, simple coordination using *and* and flow monitoring words like *well, anyhow*, etc. Chafe (1982) studied conversations and the published papers of 20 academics and, indeed, found marked disparities in the frequency of these features between these two genres. But, of course, casual conversation and academic expository prose are genres at opposite ends of any meaningful oral–literate continuum. Casual conversation is unplanned and on the fly, and centered in the present here and now of the speaker and addressee, so should score very high on features of fragmentation and involvement. On the other hand, academic expository prose, such as you are now reading, is typically carefully crafted to present scientific objectivity and flow well in the reading, so again, should score high on detachment and integration. Other genres such as personal letters or academic lectures may be expected to be intermediate in these features. Tannen (1985) argues for the primacy of the notion of involvement, replacing the idea of an oral–literate continuum with a notion of more versus less focus in involvement, with spoken discourse typically scoring high in measures of this feature and written, lower.

Biber (1988) is the most careful and extensive study of spoken and written discourse. Making use of extensive spoken and written corpora, he analyzed the distribution of 67 different grammatical and lexical features in some 20-odd genres. Importantly, he found no single, absolute difference between spoken and written English, but rather a number of parameters of variation among which the different text types could be graded. One of these he termed, "interactive versus edited text," which contrasts texts "produced under conditions of high personal involvement and real time constraints . . . (marked by low explicitness . . .) as opposed to texts produced under conditions permitting considerable editing and high explicitness in the lexical content" (Biber 1986:395). The former will, of course, favor spoken discourse, and the latter, written, but the fit is not perfect, for, while casual conversations do indeed score high in involvement and official documents and academic prose, low, professional letters, a written text type, score higher than oral radio and television broadcasts. Another parameter is "situation versus abstract content," contrasting "concrete content and more informal style" with a "highly abstract, nominal content and a highly learned style" (Biber 1986:295–6). Spoken texts like casual conversations are associated with the former and written ones like academic prose with the latter, but again the fit is not perfect: speeches and interviews, while spoken genres, score closer to academic prose in this feature than does written fiction. Indeed, romantic fiction has about the same score as face-to-face conversations; these findings are no doubt the result of fictional authors trying to create the impression of everyday life in their writings, but they do again point out the impossibility of a sharp oral/literate split or, indeed, even a straightforward oral/literate continuum.

Besnier (1988, 1995) replicates Biber's research strategy with Nukulaelae, an atoll in Tuvalu speaking a Polynesian language. While literate in the vernacular, the inhabitants of Nukulaelae mainly use literacy in a very restricted range of contexts, in writing personal letters and drafting religious sermons. Personal letters are frequently used to regulate exchanges among kin and are heavily affective in content and information poor. Written sermons, on the other hand, are generally directive and accusatory, violating general Nukulaelae norms of circumspection. Rather than affective toward the hearers, they are typically information rich. Besnier investigated 42 linguistic features in seven text types, five spoken and the two written ones discussed. Like Biber, he isolated a number of parameters of variation. The first was "attitudinal versus authoritative discourse," the former associated with text types exhibiting high indexes of the producer's beliefs and attitudes versus those which are more "objective." Interestingly, all spoken text types score positively for this feature, but so do personal letters, with only written sermons having a strong negative score. Another parameter, "informational versus interactional focus" is a restatement of Chafe's and Tannen's high versus low involvement parameter. Contrary to Chafe and Tannen's claims, this completely fails to distinguish spoken and written discourse in Nukulaelae, for the two written text types are at opposite ends of the range of scores for this feature. Written sermons group with radio broadcasts and talk in political meetings, with their emphasis on the presentation of general information, while personal letters group with conversations, on the basis of high scores in affect and interpersonal involvement. This, no doubt, is due to the function of personal letters in Nukulaelae in manipulating inter-kin relations for exchanges, an end for which affective appealing is a useful means, but it does again point out the implausibility of any broad universal characterizations of oral and literate texts.

Literacy, Genres, and Privilege

What Biber's and Besnier's findings do clearly provide is further evidence for Scribner and Cole's claims from yet another domain. Literacy is not a monolithic skill, but consists of a range of diverse practices, practices which are related only to the extent that they are mediated through the same script technology. Literacy consists of several genre linked skills; they are domain specific and not straightforwardly generalizable across domains. English personal letters are not constructed by drawing on the same framing devices, in the form of linguistic (and cognitive) skills, as academic expository prose; the same can be said of Nukulaelae personal letters and religious sermons. Olson holds up expository prose as a paragon of the exercise of literacy, its verbal skills and associated cognitive processes, but this is a value judgment on his part which has no obvious scientific validity, and interestingly is one which privileges his own discoursal resources, as it does those of Western cultural elites more generally. That such a style is generally privileged in Western industrial culture is an important question and one which requires an answer in terms of the distribution of power (see Finnegan 1988; Graff 1979, 1982, 1987; Street 1984), i.e. the way differential control of these discursive genres discriminates for access to power and social esteem – education as the road to upward mobility (but see especially Graff (1979)) – but surely no objective criteria have ever been offered that say that a piece of expository prose from an eminent academic psychologist is a better piece of writing than a Nukulaelae personal letter or, indeed, *Moby Dick*. All of these call on different clusters of linguistic resources and different types of literate practices in Scribner and Cole's sense.

In a sense this whole debate is strangely reminiscent of one in the late 1960s between the work of Basil Bernstein (1970) and William Labov (1972a). Bernstein argued for a distinction between an elaborated versus a restricted code. The former was more explicit in its meanings, relatively decontextualized in its possible interpretations, and characterized by higher syntactic integration and richness of grammatical structures employed. The latter was the opposite in these features. In short the distinction was one we can now recognize as between written versus spoken language. But Bernstein went further and claimed that elaborated codes were a feature of middle-class linguistic repertoires, a resource the working class lacked, being limited to restricted codes. In a further move, remarkably prescient of Olson, Bernstein also held that elaborated codes made what he called "universal" meanings available, which were basically cognitive skills of abstract classification and logical reasoning. Because schooling is associated with the effective use of elaborated codes, working-class children's common failure in school was traced to their lack of control of elaborated codes and the cognitive processes linked to them. This, of course, is also tied to effective control of the norms of the standard language, for skilled use of the standard language entails control of its most highly valued discoursal styles and genres. It is no surprise that working-class children who "succeed" in the educational system do so at least in part by mastering the norms of the standard language.

Labov (1972a) was a stinging attack on this view. He demonstrated that a speaker of Vernacular Black English, by any of Bernstein's metrics, a restricted code, could produce chains of logical reasoning to do honor to any academic. Labov further demonstrates that much of Bernstein's elaborate code is just verbosity that masks confusion and vagueness. There is no necessary link between an elaborated code (or indeed written language) and explicit, clear, logical thinking nor between a restricted code and vague illogical thinking. An elaborated code or academic essay is not necessarily better than a restricted code or personal letter; it is just different. Each is tied to particular social and material contexts in which they developed through diverse histories of structural coupling. Judgments of their respective value reflect the vested interests of particular social groupings, especially the elite classes; their judgments are, of course, transmitted through the educational system (Bourdieu 1991; Bourdieu and Passeron 1977).

Literacy Practices in Three American Communities

These points are elegantly developed in the work of Shirley Brice Heath (1982, 1983). She studied the literacy practices of three communities in the Piedmont area of North Carolina, one, white middle class (Mainstream), another, white working class (Roadville), and a third, black working class (Trackton). Following Hymes's (1972b) notion of speech event, Heath introduces the concept of *literacy event*, which is any activity involving the use of written texts. Heath demonstrates that the way both adults and children participate in literacy events is very different across the three communities.

The residents of Mainstream engage in various literacy events in ways typical of white middle-class Americans (and middle-class citizens of other industrialized societies as well). Focusing on the institution of the bedtime story, Heath (1982) shows how certain ways of dealing with printed texts is taught to Mainstream children. Parent and child engage in a dialog; the parent directs the child's attention to the page and asks various information questions: *What's that? What is it doing?* etc. The child responds to this, and the whole dialog may be repeated in this way for many pages. Note that this dialog style is the basic interactive pattern between teacher and pupil in a classroom, especially in the lower grades. It also encourages the child to see a text as an object that should be scanned and interpreted for meaning. Furthermore, parents encourage children to interpret the real world in terms of categories provided by the fictional world of books; Heath's example is a parent likening a fuzzy black dog seen on the street to a character Blackie in a child's book and asking the child, along the lines of the plot in the book: 'Look, there's a Blackie. Do you think he's looking for a boy?' In turn this practice encourages the children to develop their imagination, ascribing fictional properties to everyday objects, even using the knowledge of events in books to justify their departures from the truth. The creation of fictional texts and their autonomy from the events of the everyday world (their decontextualization) is strongly encouraged for these Mainstream children and is perhaps the most salient feature of Mainstream literacy practices. Note that this way of dealing with printed material is also the norm of the school system.

The white working-class community of Roadville is very different. The reading of books at bedtime also occurs in this community, but strong emphasis is placed on repeating what was said or read by the parents or supplying predictable information, not flights of imagination on the part of the child. Children are discouraged from extending the knowledge they gain from the fictional world of books to the everyday world around them. The habits of literacy events are not extended beyond book reading, in marked contrast to Mainstream. Any attempt to present events of the everyday world in fictional imaginative terms is viewed as a lie: "reality is better than fiction" (Heath 1982:63). Adults coach children in retelling the events of an incident so that it does not diverge from the adult's recall of these events. Hence, children are discouraged from decontextualizing their knowledge of the world, i.e. shifting understandings they have of one domain into another, a skill strongly fostered by the endemic fictionalizing in Mainstream literacy practices. This difference has a strong impact on the success of Roadville's children in school; they find it difficult to take knowledge learned in one context and use it in another or to compare two different objects or events to indicate similarities or differences, both skills vital to school-based literacy practices.

The black working-class community of Trackton is different again. Aside from a few religious texts, there is no reading material in the home; therefore parents do not sit and read to children at bedtime or any other time. The main literacy event in Trackton is the reading aloud of letters or brochures, while the listeners comment on their contents, asking questions and relating the texts' meanings to their experience. The group as a whole synthesizes the oral reading of the text and the associated commentary to arrive at a meaning for the written text. The information and knowledge gained from these literacy events is not decontextualized, but is tied to the particulars of the text under discussion. The creativity of commentary upon the text, however, is unrestrained. Literacy practices in Trackton are public events, not private dialogs, as in Mainstream. This is in keeping with the general tenor of Trackton verbal life. Stories are told by providing a context and asking the audience to join in developing the plots. Trackton is a highly verbal community, and games and competitions through the creative use of language are much in evidence. Fictionalization of events and verbal dexterity are highly encouraged, and children have to compete to get their stories heard. The more verbally skilled they are, the more likely they will be successful. Unfortunately, the group centeredness of verbal performance in Trackton runs strongly counter to the dialogic norms of formal schooling, so that the transition of Trackton's children to school is quite difficult.

Heath's descriptions are good illustrations of practice accounts of literacy. Each of the three communities has different ways of encountering written texts, demonstrating that a simple oral/literate division is untenable. Each of the three communities mixes oral and literate skills in different ways, for example, fictionalization and imaginative storytelling is closely associated with literacy in Mainstream, but orality in Trackton. Further, the literacy practices of Mainstream are those that carry high cultural value in the society in general and practiced in the school system. Having already acquired these practices in the home, Mainstream children are clearly primed for success in school. Conversely, the children of Roadville and Trackton confront unfamiliar literacy practices in school; their eventual success in school is determined largely by their acquisition of these practices in the normal school context. School, then, functions for these children as a socialization device into these literacy practices, often attempting to supplant earlier linguistic practices inculcated in the home (see chapter 17).

Literacy Practices Among the Athabaskans of Canada

That literacy practices are construed differently crossculturally is given further support in the work of Scollon and Scollon (1981), who compare the different perspectives on literacy of white middle-class Canadians (basically the same as Heath's Mainstream residents) and Athabaskan Native peoples of northwestern Canada. Scollon and Scollon argue that learning the mainstream literacy practices of the school involves learning values and social practices and ways of knowing that conflict with local Athabaskan norms. For Athabaskan people in subordinate positions, such as students, do not show off or engage in self displays either verbally or non-verbally; rather they observe the person in a superior position in order to learn. This is in marked contrast to white middle-class Canadian or American children who are expected to demonstrate their abilities, especially verbal abilities. Correlated with this Athabaskan lack of self-display is a reticence to boast, predict the future, or gloat over another's misfortune. Overall, Athabaskans seem taciturn; they avoid conversation except when everyone's point of view is familiar (see also Basso 1972), so that communication is relatively information poor. English speakers, on the other hand, use conversation to get to know one another.

Essayist prose puts Athabaskan children in an impossible situation. The production of an essay requires the child to engage in a major act of self-display, to persuade the reader, typically the superior teacher, of her, the inferior child's, point of view, no less! Further, the normative audience of any essay is an idealized reader about whom the child knows nothing. In the everyday world of the Athabaskan child, this is a situation which calls for silence, not verbal self-display. What counts as good use of language for Athabaskans, i.e. discourse about information already known to the participants without any use of rhetorical devices of persuasion (which would violate norms against self-display), is in fact bad essayist prose by the standards of the school system. The Athabaskan have their own indigenous genre for instructing children, if you like, traditional schooling. A good example would be riddles, which teach children to guess about meanings, resolve ambiguities and speak indirectly, all norms for the use of language highly valued in Athabaskan culture. When these norms are adapted to literacy events, it is clear that literacy practices for Athabaskans must necessarily be fundamentally different from white middle-class North Americans.

Literacy Practices Among the Gapun of New Guinea

For a final example, I want to consider the literacy practices of a small, rural, newly literate village in the Sepik region of New Guinea, called Gapun (Kulick and Stroud 1993). Literacy has been introduced into Gapun through Christian missionization and hence carries some association with religious activities. Traditional religion in Gapun has a strong utilitarian character, the use of religious ritual to achieve desired secular goals, and it is not surprising that Christianity has been taken in the same way, given its clear link in the minds of Gapun villagers with the material prosperity of the European people professing this religion. The literacy skills that were transmitted via missionization also have this utilitarian character; written texts, especially those of the New Testament or other religious tracts, can be used to intercede with God to realize desired outcomes. But this tallies very closely with the traditional Gapun ideological understanding of language. Traditionally, the people of Gapun like many other peoples have viewed language as a way of action to transform the world. Certain words uttered in certain contexts have the power through supernatural sanction to bring about desired outcomes. Hence, what is most striking about Gapun literacy practices is how much they have taken on as norms the uses of language associated with oral discourse, particularly oratory. Although a strongly individualistic and contentious society, egocentric stubbornness is usually publicly condemned in Gapun, and this characteristic of one's fellow villagers is commonly claimed as the reason for the failure of the village to modernize. To countenance these centrifugal, individualistic forces, there are highly valued beliefs about social sensitivity and solidary awareness of social obligations and appropriate social roles. Norms of oratorical language mandate the downplaying of individualistic interests in favor of the import- ance of social obligations and appropriate social behavior to the benefit of the community. Hence oratorical language is marked by self-effacement of the speaker, indirect statement of requests, and conciliatory utterances, such that the speaker is not pronouncing his own views, but information reported to him from elsewhere. All of these norms make their way into literacy practices of Gapun villagers, for example, in personal letters. Writ- ers make requests to the addressee of the note in indirect, roundabout ways; they continually efface their own needs and importance through the use of understatement and so forth; they write in a conciliatory vein, without forcefulness or insistence, leaving the response to the request up to the addressee and his understanding of the importance of his social respons- ibilities over his individualistic self-interests.

The differing norms governing literacy practices among white middle- and working-class North Americans, Black Americans, Athabaskan Native peoples, and Gapun villagers demonstrate the impossibility of any mono- lithic literate technology and simple oral/literate divide. Literacy is not a straightforward "technology of the intellect"; technologies, like intellects (as recognized by Vygotsky), are social and cultural constructions, arrived at by particular histories of engaging with the world and each other through various institutions and events. There are as many literacies as there are ways of engaging the world and ourselves through the written word. Those whose lives are deeply embedded in and lived through the written word could expect some cognitive effects as a result of this, but that is simply the result of their particular lived histories, their trajectories of structural coupling and nothing more. And, of course, what those effects might be will be local, specific to the local literacy practices that they have engaged in and whose understanding they embody. There are no certain or universal effects.

Summary

Recent work in anthropology and cognitive psychology has claimed that literacy as a "technology of the intellect" is a great dividing line that separ- ates modern civilized scientific thought patterns from those of "primitive" traditional peoples. Literacy is claimed to foster scepticism and critical inquiry, leading to development of logic and rationality and ultimately sci- entific methods of investigation, divorcing the subject matter of study from its immediate context. Experimental studies had tended to confirm such cognitive processes among literate peoples, but problematically it has been difficult to extricate the effects of literacy from those of modern Westernized schooling, as the latter is largely the conduit for the former. Scribner and Cole's landmark study of the Vai, who possess their own indigenous tradition of literacy in addition to the school-imposed one, refutes these strong claims for the effects of literacy *per se*, for the proposed universal cognitive effects of literacy were found only among those literate via modern schooling. Indigenous Vai-based literacy had no such global cognitive effects. This work suggests a revised practice approach to literacy, which sees literacy as a set of distinct cultural practices, each requiring different cognitive skills as a result of its role in ongoing social interactions and institutionalized ways of engaging with the world. The oral/literate divide is replaced with an assemblage of skills related to different genres and linked only by virtue of sharing the same script technology. The social value ascribed to literacy is a function of the differential esteem in which different literate genres are held, not a fact intrinsic to the genres themselves, but of the wider social, educational and institutional practices of elite groups, whose values these judgments reflect. Cultural practices and beliefs about literacy are highly variable, demonstrating the impossibility of any simple oral/literate divide or monolithic literate technology. Rather, literate practices of each culture reflect the way they engage with the world through the written word, their lived history of structural coupling via a script technology.

Further Reading

Literacy, as might be expected, has a voluminous literature. For those who view literacy as an autonomous technology of the intellect with consequent cognitive effects, consult Goody (1977, 1986, 1987), Havelock (1982), Olson (1977, 1994), and Ong (1982). For an alternative practice account of literacy see Besnier (1995), Finnegan (1988), Heath (1983), Scollon and Scollon (1981), and Street (1984). Important collections of articles on literacy from both these perspectives include Cook-Gumperz (1986), Goody (1968), Olson, Torrance and Hildyard (1985), Olson and Torrance (1991), Schieffelin and Gilmore (1986), and Street (1993). The important work on cognitive testing for literacy effects is found in Luria (1976), and Scribner and Cole (1981). On literacy and educational success see Collins (1989), Graff (1979), and Meek (1991). Finally, for formal differences between oral and written language, in English at least, have a look at Biber (1988), and Chafe and Tannen (1987).

References

Abrahams, R. (1976). *Talking Black*. Rowley, MA: Newbury House.

Abu-Lughod, L. (1986). *Veiled Sentiments: Honor and Poetry in a Bedouin Society*. Berkeley: University of California Press.

Agar, M. (1972). Talking about doing: lexicon and event. *Language in Society* 3: 83–9.

Agha, A. (1993). Grammatical and indexical convention in honorific discourse. *Journal of Linguistic Anthropology* 3: 131–63.

Agha, A. (1994). Honorification. *Annual Review of Anthropology* 23: 277–302.

Aiello, L. and Dunbar, R. (1993). Neocortex size, group size, and the evolution of language. *Current Anthropology* 34: 184–93.

Alexander, J. and Seidman, P. (eds) (1990). *Culture and Society: Contemporary Debates*. Cambridge: Cambridge University Press.

Alisjahbana, S. (1976). *Language Planning and Modernization: The Case of Indonesian and Malaysian*. The Hague: Mouton.

Andersen, E. (1978). Lexical universals of body-part terminology. In Greenberg, J., Ferguson, C. and Moravcsik, E. (eds), *Universals of Human Language*, volume 3: *Word Structure*, pp. 335–68. Stanford: Stanford University Press.

Anderson, B. (1983). *Imagined Communities: Reflections on the Origin and Spread of Nationalism*. London: Verso.

Anderson, E. (1986). The acquisition of register variation by Anglo-American children. In Schieffelin, B. and Ochs, E. (eds), pp. 153–61.

Anderson, R., Hughes, J. and Sharrock, W. (1986). *Philosophy and the Human Sciences*. London: Croom Helm.

Andrews, A. (1990). Unification and morphological blocking. *Natural Language and Linguistic Theory* 8: 507–58.

Anttila, R. (1972). *An Introduction to Historical and Comparative Linguistics*. New York: Macmillan.

Atkinson, J. and Errington, S. (eds) (1990). *Power and Difference: Gender in Island Southeast Asia*. Stanford: Stanford University Press.

Atran, S. (1985). The nature of folk-botanical life forms. *American Anthropologist* 87: 298–315.

Atran, S. (1987). Ordinary constraints on the semantics of living kinds: a commonsense alternative to recent treatments of natural-object terms. *Mind and Language* 2: 27–63.

Atran, S. (1990). *Cognitive Foundations of Natural History*. Cambridge: Cambridge University Press.

Austin-Broos, D. (ed.) (1987). *Creating Culture: Profiles in the Study of Culture*. Sydney: Allen and Unwin.

Bakhtin, M. (1981). *The Dialogic Imagination: Four Essays*. Austin: University of Texas Press.

Bakhtin, M. (1986). *Speech Genres and other Late Essays*. Austin: University of Texas Press.

Barlund, D. (1975). *Public and Private Self in Japan and the United States: Communicative Styles of Two Cultures*. Tokyo: Simul.

Barnard, A. (1994). Rules and prohibitions: the form and content of human kinship. In Ingold, T. (ed.), pp. 783–812.

Baron, D. (1986). *Grammar and Gender*. New Haven: Yale University Press.

Bartlett, F. (1932). *Remembering*. Cambridge: Cambridge University Press.

Basso, K. (1972). "To give up on words": silence in Western Apache culture. In Giglioli, P. (ed.), pp. 67–86.

Basso, K. (1984). "Stalking with stories": names, places and moral narratives among the Western Apache. In Bruner, E. (ed.) *Text, Play and Story*, pp. 19–55. Washington: American Ethnological Society.

Basso, K. (1988). "Speaking with names": language and landscape among the Western Apache. *Cultural Anthropology* 3: 99–130.

Basso, K. (1990). *Western Apache Language and Culture: Essays in Linguistic Anthropology*. Tucson: University of Arizona Press.

Bateson, G. (1972). *Steps to an Ecology of Mind*. New York: Ballantine Books.

Bauer, L. (1992). *Introducing Linguistic Morphology*. Edinburgh: Edinburgh University Press.

Baugh, J. (1983). *Black Street Speech: Its History, Structure and Survival*. Austin: University of Texas Press.

Baugh, J. (1988). Language and race: some implications for linguistic science. In Newmeyer, F. (ed.), pp. 64–74.

Bauman, R. (1977). *Verbal Art as Performance*. Prospect Heights, IL: Waveland Press.

Bauman, R. (1983). *Let Your Words Be Few: Symbolism of Speaking and Silence among Seventeenth-Century Quakers*. Cambridge: Cambridge University Press.

Bauman, R. (1986). *Story, Performance and Event: Contextual Studies of Oral Narrative*. Cambridge: Cambridge University Press.

Bauman, R. and Briggs, C. (1990). Poetics and performance as critical perspectives on language and social life. *Annual Review of Anthropology* 19: 59–88.

Bauman, R. and Sherzer, J. (eds) (1974). *Explorations in the Ethnography of Speaking*. Cambridge: Cambridge University Press.

Bauman, R. and Sherzer, J. (1975). The ethnography of speaking. *Annual Review of Anthropology* 4: 95–119.

Bauman, Z. (1978). *Hermeneutics and Social Science: Approaches to Understanding*. London: Hutchinson.

Bean, S. (1978). *Symbolic and Pragmatic Semantics: A Kannada System of Address*. Chicago: University of Chicago Press.

Bean, S. (1981). Referential and indexical meanings of *amma* in Kannada: mother, woman, goddess, pox and help! In Casson, R. (ed.), pp. 188–202.

Bechtel, W. and Abrahamsen, A. (1991). *Connectionism and the Mind: An Introduction to Parallel Processing in Networks*. Oxford: Basil Blackwell.

Becker, A. (1975). A linguistic image of nature: the Burmese numerative classifier system. *Linguistics* 165: 109–21.

Becker, A. (1993). The elusive figures of Burmese grammar: an essay. In Foley, W. (ed.), pp. 29–46.

Becker, A. (1995). *Beyond Translation: Essays Toward a Modern Philology*. Ann Arbor: University of Michigan Press.

Becker, E. (1971). *The Birth and Death of Meaning*. New York: Free Press.

Beeman, W. (1986). *Language, Status, and Power in Iran*. Bloomington: Indiana University Press.

Bendix, R. and Lipset, S. (1968). *Class, Status and Power*. New York: Free Press.

Benjamin, G. (1993). Grammar and polity: the cultural and political background of Standard Malay. In Foley, W. (ed.), pp. 341–92.

Benton, R. (1968). Numeral and attributive classifiers in Trukese. *Oceanic Linguistics* 7: 104–46.

Berger, P. and Berger, B. (1976). *Sociology: A Biographical Approach*. Harmondsworth: Penguin.

Berger, P., Berger, B. and Kellner, H. (1973). *The Homeless Mind: Modernization and Consciousness*. Harmondsworth: Penguin.

Berlin, B. (1992). *Ethnobiological Classification*. Princeton: Princeton University Press.

Berlin, B. and Berlin, E. (1975). Aguaruna color terms. *American Ethnologist* 2: 61–87.

Berlin, B., Breedlove, D. and Raven, P. (1973). General principles of classification and nomenclature in folk biology. *American Anthropologist* 75: 214–42.

Berlin, B. and Kay, P. (1969). *Basic Color Terms*. Berkeley: University of California Press.

Berman, R. and Slobin, D. (1994). *Relating Events in Narrative: A Cross-linguistic Developmental Study*. Hillsdale, NJ: Lawrence Erlbaum.

Bernstein, B. (1970). *Class, Codes and Control*. London: Routledge and Kegan Paul.

Bernstein, R. (1983). *Beyond Objectivism and Relativism: Science, Hermeneutics, and Praxis*. Philadelphia: University of Pennsylvania Press.

Besnier, N. (1988). The linguistic relationships of spoken and written Nukulaelae registers. *Language* 64: 707–36.

Besnier, N. (1995). *Literacy, Emotion and Authority*. Cambridge: Cambridge University Press.

Béteille, A. (ed.) (1969). *Social Inequality*. Harmondsworth: Penguin.

Béteille, A. (1977). *Inequality among Men*. Oxford: Basil Blackwell.

Biber, D. (1986). Spoken and written textual dimensions in English. *Language* 62: 384–414.

Biber, D. (1988). *Variation Across Speech and Writing*. Cambridge: Cambridge University Press.

Bickerton, D. (1990). *Language and Species*. Chicago: University of Chicago Press.

Bird, C. and Shopen, T. (1979). Maninka. In Shopen, T. (ed.), pp. 59–111.

Black, M. (1962). *Models and Metaphors*. Ithaca, NY: Cornell University Press.

Blakemore, D. (1992). *Understanding Utterances: An Introduction to Pragmatics*. Oxford: Blackwell.

Blom, J.-P. and Gumperz, J. (1972). Social meaning in linguistic structures: code-switching in Norway. In Gumperz, J. and Hymes, D. (eds), pp. 407–34.

Boas, F. (1966[1911]). *Introduction to the Handbook of American Indian Languages*. Lincoln: University of Nebraska Press.

Bogoras, W. (1922). Chukchee. *Bulletin of the Bureau of American Ethnology* 40(2): 631–903.

Bohannan, P. and Middleton, J. (eds) (1968). *Kinship and Social Organization*. Garden City, NY: Natural History Press.

Bourdieu, P. (1977). *Outline of a Theory of Practice*. Cambridge: Cambridge University Press.

Bourdieu, P. (1984). *Distinction: A Social Critique of the Judgement of Taste*. Cambridge, MA: Harvard University Press.

Bourdieu, P. (1990). *The Logic of Practice*. Stanford: Stanford University Press.

Bourdieu, P. (1991). *Language and Symbolic Power*. Cambridge, MA: Harvard University Press.

Bourdieu, P. and Passeron, J.-C. (1977). *Reproduction in Education, Society and Culture*. London: Sage.

Bowen, J. (1989). Poetic duels and political change in the Gayo highlands of Sumatra. *American Anthropologist* 91: 25–40.

Bowerman, M. (1981). Language development. In Triandis, H. and Heron, A. (eds), *Handbook of Cross-cultural Psychology*, volume 4, pp. 93–187. Boston: Allyn and Bacon.

Bowerman, M. (1993). Typological perspectives on language development: do crosslinguistic patterns predict development? In Clark, E. (ed.), *Proceedings of the Twenty-fifth Annual Meeting of the Child Language Research Forum in Stanford*, pp. 7–15. Stanford: Center for the Study of Language and Information.

Bowerman, M. (1994). From universal to language specific in early grammatical development. *Philosophical Transactions of the Royal Society of London* B346: 37–45.

Briggs, C. (1988). *Competence in Performance: The Creativity of Tradition in Mexicano Verbal Art*. Philadelphia: University of Pennsylvania Press.

Briggs, C. (1992). Generic versus metapragmatic dimensions of Warao narratives: who regiments performance? In Lucy, J. (ed.), *Reflexive Language: Reported Speech and Metapragmatics*, pp. 179–212. Cambridge: Cambridge University Press.

Briggs, C. and Bauman, R. (1992). Genre, intertextuality, and social power. *Journal of Linguistic Anthropology* 2: 131–72.

Bright, J. and Bright, W. (1969). Semantic structures in northwestern California and the Sapir-Whorf hypothesis. In Tyler, S. (ed.), pp. 66–77.

Bright, W. (1952). Linguistic innovations in Karok. *International Journal of American Linguistics* 18: 53–62.

Brown, C. (1976). General principles of human anatomical partonomy and speculations on the growth of partonomic nomenclature. *American Ethnologist* 3: 400–23.

Brown, D. (1991). *Human Universals*. New York: McGraw-Hill.

Brown, K. and Miller, J. (1991). *Syntax: A Linguistic Introduction to Sentence Structure*. Second edition. London: Routledge.

Brown, P. (1980). How and why are women more polite: some evidence from a Mayan community. In McConnell-Ginet, S., Borker, R. and Furman, N. (eds), pp. 111–36.

Brown, P. (1991). *Spatial Conceptualization in Tzeltal.* Working paper number 6. Nijmegen, Netherlands: Cognitive Anthropology Research Group, Max-Planck Institute for Psycholinguistics.

Brown, P. and Levinson, S. (1987). *Politeness: Some Universals in Language Usage.* Cambridge: Cambridge University Press.

Brown, P. and Levinson, S. (1992). "Left" and "Right" in Tenejapa: investigating a linguistic and conceptual gap. *Zeitschrift für Phonetik, Sprachwissenschaft und Kommunikationforschung* 45: 590–611.

Brown, P. and Levinson, S. (1993). "Uphill" and "downhill" in Tzeltal. *Journal of Linguistic Anthropology* 3: 46–74.

Brown, P. and Levinson, S. (1994). *Linguistic and Non-linguistic Coding of Spatial Arrays: Explorations in Mayan Cognition.* Working paper number 24. Nijmegen, Netherlands: Cognitive Anthropology Research Group, Max-Planck Institute for Psycholinguistics.

Brown, R. and Ford, M. (1964). Address in American English. In Hymes, D. (ed.), pp. 234–44.

Brown, R. and Gilman, A. (1972). The pronouns of solidarity and power. In Giglioli, P. (ed.), pp. 252–82.

Brown, R. and Lenneberg, E. (1954). A study in language and cognition. *Journal of Abnormal and Social Psychology* 49: 454–62.

Bulmer, R. (1967). Why is the cassowary not a bird? *Man* 2: 5–25.

Blumer, R. (1968). Worms that croak and other mysteries of Karam natural history. *Mankind* 6: 621–39.

Bulmer, R. (1970). Which came first, the chicken or the egg-head? In Pouillon, J. and Maranda, P. (eds), *Échanges et communications, mélanges offert à Claude Lévi-Strauss à l'occàsion de son 60ème anniversaire,* pp. 1069–91. The Hague: Mouton.

Bulmer, R. and Tyler, M. (1968). Karam classification of frogs. *Journal of Polynesian Society* 77: 333–85.

Burke, K. (1941). *The Philosophy of Literary Form: Studies in Symbolic Action.* Baton Rouge: Louisiana State University Press.

Burke, K. (1969). *A Rhetoric of Motives.* Berkeley: University of California Press.

Burling, R. (1969). Cognition and componential analysis: God's truth or hocus-pocus? In Tyler, S. (ed.), pp. 419–32.

Burling, R. (1993). Primate calls, human language, and nonverbal communication. *Current Anthropology* 34: 25–54.

Burton, M. and Kirk, L. (1979). Ethnoclassification of body parts: a three culture study. *Anthropological Linguistics* 21: 379–99.

Bynon, T. (1977). *Historical Linguistics.* Cambridge: Cambridge University Press.

Calhoun, C., LiPuma, E. and Postone, M. (eds) (1993). *Bourdieu: Critical Perspectives.* Chicago: University of Chicago Press.

Calvin, W. (1983). *The Throwing Madonna: Essays on the Brain.* New York: McGraw-Hill.

Cameron, D. (ed.) (1990). *The Feminist Critique of Language: A Reader.* New York: Routledge.

Cameron, D. (1992). *Feminism and Linguistic Theory.* Second edition. New York: Macmillan.

Campbell, L., Kaufman, T. and Smith-Stark, T. (1986). Meso-America as a linguistic area. *Language* 62: 530–70.

Cann, R. (1988). DNA and human origins. *Annual Review of Anthropology* 17: 127–43.

Cann, R., Stoneking, M. and Wilson, A. (1987). Mitochondrial DNA and human evolution. *Nature* 325: 31–6.

Carrithers, M., Collins, S. and Lukes, S. (eds) (1985). *The Category of the Person.* Cambridge: Cambridge University Press.

Carroll, J. and Casagrande, J. (1958). The function of language classifications in behavior. In Maccoby, E., Newcomb, T. and Hartley, E. (eds), *Readings in Social Psychology*, pp. 18–31. New York: Henry Holt.

Casson, R. (ed.) (1981). *Language, Culture and Cognition.* New York: Macmillan.

Casson, R. (1983). Schemata in cognitive anthropology. *Annual Review of Anthropology* 12: 429–62.

Caton, S. (1990). *"Peaks of Yemen I Summon": Poetry as Cultural Practice in a North Yemeni Tribe.* Berkeley: University of California Press.

Chafe, W. (1982). Integration and involvement in speaking, writing and oral literature. In Tannen, D. (ed.), pp. 35–53.

Chafe, W. (1985). Linguistic differences produced by differences between speaking and writing. In Olson, D., Torrance, N. and Hildyard, A. (eds), pp. 105–23.

Chafe, W. (1994). *Discourse, Consciousness and Time: The Flow and Displacement of Conscious Experience in Speaking and Writing.* Chicago: University of Chicago Press.

Chafe, W. and Tannen, D. (1987). The relation between written and spoken language. *Annual Review of Anthropology* 16: 383–407.

Chambers, J. (1995). *Sociolinguistic Theory: Linguistic Variation and its Social Significance.* Oxford: Basil Blackwell.

Chase, P. and Dibble, H. (1987). Middle Paleolithic symbolism: a review of current evidence and interpretations. *Journal of Anthropological Archaeology* 6: 263–93.

Cheney, D. and Seyfarth, R. (1990). *How Monkeys See the World.* Chicago: University of Chicago Press.

Chodorow, N. (1974). Family structure and feminine personality. In Rosaldo, M. and Lamphere, L. (eds), pp. 43–66.

Choi, S. and Bowerman, M. (1992). Learning to express motion events in English and Korean: the influence of language-specific lexicalization patterns. In Levin, B. and Pinker, S. (ed.), *Lexical and Conceptual Semantics*, pp. 83–121. Oxford: Basil Blackwell.

Chomsky, N. (1968). *Language and Mind.* Expanded edition. New York: Harcourt, Brace, Jovanavich.

Chomsky, N. (1980). *Rules and Representations.* New York: Columbia University Press.

Chomsky, N. (1988). *Language and Problems of Knowledge: The Managua Lectures.* Cambridge, MA: The Massachusetts Institute of Technology Press.

Clancy, P. (1986). The acquisition of communicative style in Japanese. In Schieffelin, B. and Ochs, E. (eds), pp. 213–50.

Clark, H. (1973). Space, time, semantics and the child. In Moore, T. (ed.), *Cognitive Development and the Acquisition of Language*, pp. 28–64. New York: Academic Press.

Clark, H. (1992). *Arenas of Language Use.* Chicago: University of Chicago Press.

Coates, J. (1993). *Men, Women and Language.* Second edition. London: Longman.

Cobarrubias, J. and Fishman, J. (eds) (1983). *Progress in Language Planning: International Perspectives.* Berlin: Mouton.

Cohen, A. (1994). *Self-consciousness: An Alternative Anthropology of Identity.* London: Routledge.

Cole, M. and Scribner, S. (1974). *Culture and Thought.* New York: John Wiley.

Collier, J. and Yanagisako, S. (eds) (1987). *Gender and Kinship: Essays Toward a Unified Analysis.* Stanford: Stanford University Press.

Collins, J. (1989). Hegemonic practice: literacy and standard language in public education. *Journal of Education* 171: 9–34.

Comrie, B. (1989). *Language Universals and Linguistic Typology.* Second edition. Oxford: Basil Blackwell.

Conklin, H. (1964). Hanunoo color categories. In Hymes, D. (ed.), pp. 189–92.

Conklin, H. (1969). Lexicographic treatment of folk taxonomies. In Tyler, S. (ed.), pp. 41–59.

Cook-Gumperz, J. (1973). *Social Control and Socialization.* London: Routledge and Kegan Paul.

Cook-Gumperz, J. (ed.) (1986). *The Social Construction of Literacy.* Cambridge: Cambridge University Press.

Cook-Gumperz, J., Corsaro, W. and Streek, J. (eds) (1986). *Children's Worlds and Children's Language.* Berlin: Mouton de Gruyter.

Cooper, R. (ed.) (1982). *Language Spread: Studies in Diffusion and Social Change.* Bloomington: Indiana University Press.

Cooper, R. (1989). *Language Planning and Social Change.* Cambridge: Cambridge University Press.

Corballis, M. (1991). *The Lopsided Ape.* Oxford: Oxford University Press.

Craig, C. (ed.) (1986). *Noun Classes and Categorization.* Amsterdam: John Benjamins.

Craig, C. (1992). Classifiers in a functional perspective. In Fortescue, M., Harder, P. and Kristoffersen, L. (eds), *Layered Structure and Reference in a Functional Perspective*, pp. 277–301. Amsterdam: John Benjamins.

Craig, C. (1994). Classifier languages. In *Encyclopedia of Language and Linguistics*, volume 2, pp. 565–69. Oxford: Pergamon Press.

Croft, W. (1991). *Syntactic Categories and Grammatical Relations: The Cognitive Organization of Information.* Chicago: University of Chicago Press.

Crowley, T. (1989). *Standard English and the Politics of Language.* Urbana: University of Illinois Press.

Crowley, T. (1992). *An Introduction to Historical Linguistics.* Oxford: Oxford University Press.

Culler, J. (1976). *Saussure.* London: Fontana.

D'Andrade, R. (1981). The cultural part of cognition. *Cognitive Science* 5: 179–95.

D'Andrade, R. (1990). Culture and human cognition. In Stigler, J., Shweder, R. and Herdt, G. (eds), pp. 65–129.

D'Andrade, R. (1995). *The Development of Cognitive Anthropology.* Cambridge: Cambridge University Press.

Danziger, E. (1991). *Semantics on the Edge: Language as Cultural Experience in the Acquisition of Social Identity among the Mopan Maya.* Unpublished Ph.D. dissertation, University of Pennsylvania.

Darnell, R. (1990). *Edward Sapir: Linguist, Anthropologist, Humanist.* Berkeley: University of California Press.

Davidoff, J. (1991). *Cognition Through Color.* Cambridge, MA: The Massachusetts Institute of Technology Press.

Davidson, D. (1980). *Essays on Actions and Events.* Oxford: Oxford University Press.

Davidson, D. (1984). *Inquiries into Truth and Interpretation.* Oxford: Oxford University Press.

Davidson, I. and Noble, W. (1989). The archaeology of perception: traces of depiction and language. *Current Anthropology* 30: 125–55.

Davidson, I. and Noble, W. (1993). Tools and language in human evolution. In Gibson, K. and Ingold, T. (eds), pp. 363–88.

Dawkins, R. (1986). *The Blind Watchmaker.* New York: Norton.

Deacon, T. (1992a). The human brain. In Jones, S., Martin, R. and Pilbeam, D. (eds), pp. 115–23.

Deacon, T. (1992b). The neural circuitry underlying primate calls and human language. In Wind, J., Chiarelli, B., Bichakjian, B. and Nocentini, A. (eds), pp. 121–62.

Denny, J. (1976). What are noun classifiers good for? In Mufwene, S., Walker, C. and Steever, S. (eds), *Papers from the Twelfth Regional Meeting of the Chicago Linguistic Society*, pp. 122–32. Chicago: Chicago Linguistic Society.

Descartes, R. (1951[1641]). *Meditation on First Philosophy.* New York: Liberal Arts Press.

Deutsch, K. (1966). *Nationalism and Social Communication.* New York: Massachusetts Institute of Technology Press.

Devitt, M. and Sterelny, K. (1987). *Language and Reality: An Introduction to the Philosophy of Language.* Oxford: Basil Blackwell.

Diamond, J. (1991). *The Rise and Fall of the Third Chimpanzee.* New York: Harper-Collins.

Diller, A. (1993). Diglossic grammaticality in Thai. In Foley, W. (ed.), pp. 393–420.

Dilthey, W. (1976). *Selected Writings.* Cambridge: Cambridge University Press.

Dixon, R. (1971). A method of semantic description. In Steinberg, D. and Jakobovitz, L. (eds), pp. 436–71.

Dixon, R. (1982). *Where Have All the Adjectives Gone? and Other Essays in Syntax and Semantics.* Berlin: Mouton De Gruyter.

Dorian, N. (1981). *Language Death: The Life Cycle of a Scottish Gaelic Dialect.* Philadelphia: University of Pennsylvania Press.

Dorian, N. (ed.) (1989). *Investigating Obsolescence: Studies in Language Contraction and Death.* Cambridge: Cambridge University Press.

Dougherty, J. (1981). Salience and relativity in classification. In Casson, R. (ed.), pp. 163–80.

Dougherty, J. (ed.) (1985). *Directions in Cognitive Anthropology.* Urbana: University of Illinois Press.

Dougherty, J. and Keller, C. (1985). Taskonomy: a practical approach to knowledge structures. In Dougherty, J. (ed.), pp. 161–74.

Dozier, E. (1964). Two examples of linguistic acculturation: the Yaqui of Sonora and Arizona and the Tewa of New Mexico. In Hymes, D. (ed.), pp. 511–20.

Dubois, B. and Crouch, I. (1975). The question of tag questions in women's speech: they don't really use more of them, do they? *Language in Society* 4: 289–94.

Dubrow, H. (1982). *Genre*. London: Methuen.

Dunbar, R. (1993). Coevolution of neocortical size, group size and language in humans. *Behavioral and Brain Sciences* 16: 681–735.

Duranti, A. (1983). Samoan speechmaking across social events: one genre in and out of a *fono*. *Language in Society* 12: 1–22.

Duranti, A. (1988a). Ethnography of speaking: toward a linguistics of the praxis. In Newmeyer, F. (ed.), pp. 210–28.

Duranti, A. (1988b). Intentions, language and social action in a Samoan context. *Journal of Pragmatics* 12: 13–33.

Duranti, A. (1992). Language in context and language as context: the Samoan respect vocabulary. In Duranti, A. and Goodwin, C. (eds), pp. 77–99.

Duranti, A. (1993). Truth and intentionality: an ethnographic critique. *Cultural Anthropology* 8: 214–45.

Duranti, A. (1994). *From Grammar to Politics: Linguistic Anthropology in a Western Samoan Village*. Berkeley: University of California Press.

Duranti, A. and Goodwin, C. (eds) (1992). *Rethinking Context: Language as Interactive Phenomenon*. Cambridge: Cambridge University Press.

Durkheim, E. (1947[1893]). *The Division of Labor in Society: Studies on the Organization of Advanced Societies*. New York: Free Press.

Eastman, C. (1983). *Language Planning, an Introduction*. San Francisco: Chandler and Sharp.

Eckert, P. and McConnell-Ginet, S. (1992). Think practically and look locally: language and gender as community-based practice. *Annual Review of Anthropology* 21: 461–90.

Edelsky, C. (1981). Who's got the floor? *Language in Society* 10: 383–421.

Ekka, F. (1972). Men's and women's speech in Kūrux. *Linguistics* 81: 25–31.

Eliot, A. (1981). *Child Language*. Cambridge: Camubridge University Press.

Emeneau, M. (1964). *India as a Linguistic area*. In Hymes, D. (ed.), pp. 642–53.

Errington, F. and Gewertz, D. (1987). *Cultural Alternatives and a Feminist Anthropology*. Cambridge: Cambridge University Press.

Errington, J. (1985a). *Language and Social Change in Java: Linguistic Reflexes of Modernization in a Traditional Royal Polity*. Athens, OH: Ohio University Center for International Studies.

Errington, J. (1985b). On the nature of the linguistic sign: describing the Javanese speech levels. In Mertz, E. and Parmentier, R. (ed.), pp. 287–310.

Errington, J. (1988). *Structure and Style in Javanese*. Philadelphia: University of Pennsylvania Press.

Errington, S. (1990). Recasting sex, gender and power: a theoretical and regional overview. In Atkinson, J. and Errington, S. (eds), pp. 1–58.

Ervin-Tripp, S. (1976). Is Sybil there? the structure of American English directives. *Language in Society* 5: 25–66.

Ervin-Tripp, S. (1977). Wait for me, Roller Skate. In Ervin-Tripp, S. and Mitchell-Kernan, C. (eds), pp. 165–88.

Ervin-Tripp, S. and Mitchell-Kernan, C. (eds) (1977). *Child Discourse*. New York: Academic Press.

Ervin-Tripp, S., O'Connor, M. and Rosenberg, J. (1984). Language and power in the family. In Kramarae, C., Schulz, M. and O'Barr, W. (eds), *Language and Power*, pp. 116–35. Newbury Park, CA: Sage Publications.

Falk, D. (1987). Hominid paleoneurology. *Annual Review of Anthropology* 16: 13–30.

Falk, D. (1990). Brain evolution in *Homo*: the "radiator" theory. *Behavioral and Brain Sciences* 13: 333–81.

Falk, D. (1992). *Evolution of the Brain and Cognition in Hominids*. New York: American Museum of Natural History.

Falk, D. (1993). *Braindance: What New Findings Reveal about Human Origins and Brain Evolution*. New York: Holt.

Fasold, R. (1984). *The Sociolinguistics of Society*. Oxford: Basil Blackwell.

Fasold, R. (1990). *The Sociolinguistics of Language*. Oxford: Basil Blackwell.

Ferguson, C. (1968). Language development. In Fishman, J., Ferguson, C. and Das Gupta, J. (eds), pp. 27–35.

Ferguson, C. (1972). Diglossia. In Giglioli, P. (ed.), pp. 232–51. Also in Hymes, D. (ed.) (1964), pp. 429–39.

Ferguson, C. and Heath, S. (eds) (1981). *Language in the USA*. Cambridge: Cambridge University Press.

Fernandez, J. (1974). The mission of metaphor in expressive culture. *Current Anthropology* 15: 119–45.

Fernandez, J. (1986). *Persuasions and Performances: The Play of Tropes in Culture*. Bloomington: Indiana University Press.

Fernandez, J. (ed.) (1991). *Beyond Metaphor: The Theory of Tropes in Anthropology*. Stanford: Stanford University Press.

Field, T., Sostek, A., Vietze, P. and Leiderman, P. (1981). Culture and Early Interactions. Hillsdale, NJ: Lawrence Erlbaum.

Fillmore, C. (1975). An alternative to checklist theories of meaning. In Cogen, C., Thompson, H., Thurgood, G., Whistler, K. and Wright, J. (eds), *Proceedings of the First Annual Meeting of the Berkeley Linguistics Society*, pp. 123–31.

Finnegan, R. (1988). *Literacy and Orality: Studies in the Technology of Communication*. Oxford: Basil Blackwell.

Fishman, J. (ed.) (1974). *Advances in Language Planning*. The Hague: Mouton.

Fishman, J., Ferguson, C. and Das Gupta, J. (eds) (1968). *Language Problems of Developing Nations*. New York: John Wiley and Sons.

Fishman, P. (1983). Interaction: the work women do. In Thorne, B., Kramarae, C. and Henley, N. (eds), pp. 89–102.

Fitzgerald, T. (1993). *Metaphors of Identity: A Culture-Communication Dialogue*. Albany: State University of New York Press.

Flanagan, J. (1989). Hierarchy in simple "egalitarian societies". *Annual Review of Anthropology* 18: 245–66.

Flannery, R. (1946). Men's and Women's speech in Gros Ventre. *International Journal of American Linguistics* 12: 133–35.

Foley, W. (1988). Language birth: the processes of pidginization and creolization. In Newmeyer, F. (ed.), pp. 162–83.

Foley, W. (ed.) (1993). *The Role of Theory in Language Description*. Berlin: Mouton De Gruyter.

Forth, G. (1988). Fashioned speech, full communication: aspects of Eastern Sumbanese ritual language. In Fox, J. (ed.), pp. 129–60.

Foucault, M. (1984). *The History of Sexuality, volume 1: An Introduction.* New York: Random House.

Fox, J. (1971). Semantic parallelism in Rotinese ritual language. *Bijdragen tot de Taal-, Land- en Volkenkunde* 127: 215–55.

Fox, J. (1974). Our ancestors spoke in pairs: Rotinese views of language, dialect and code. In Bauman, R. and Sherzer, J. (eds), pp. 65–85.

Fox, J. (1975). On binary categories and primary symbols: some Rotinese perspectives. In Willis, R. (ed.), *The Interpretation of Symbolism*, pp. 99–132. London: Malaby Press.

Fox, J. (1977). Roman Jakobson and the comparative study of parallelism. In Schooneveld, C. and Armstrong, D. (eds), *Roman Jakobson: Echoes of his Scholarship*, pp. 59–90. Lisse: Peter de Ridder Press.

Fox, J. (ed.) (1988). *To Speak in Pairs: Essays on the Ritual Languages of Eastern Indonesia.* Cambridge: Cambridge University Press.

Fox, R. (1967). *Kinship and Marriage.* Harmondsworth: Penguin.

Frake, C. (1964). The diagnosis of disease among the Subanun of Mindanao. In Hymes, D. (ed.), pp. 192–211.

Frake, C. (1972). How to ask for a drink in Subanun. In Giglioli, P. (ed.), pp. 87–94. Also in Pride, J. and Holmes, J. (eds), pp. 260–6.

Franklin, K. (1975). A Kewa religious argot. *Anthropos* 70: 713–25.

Frawley, W. (1992). *Linguistic Semantics.* Hillsdale, NJ: Lawrence Erlbaum.

Friedrich, P. (1970). Shape in grammar. *Language* 46: 379–407.

Friedrich, P. (1979). *Language, Context, and the Imagination.* Stanford: Stanford University Press.

Friedrich, P. (1986). *The Language Parallax: Linguistic Relativism and Poetic Indeterminacy.* Austin: University of Texas Press.

Friedrich, P. (1991). Polytropy. In Fernandez, J. (ed.), pp. 17–55.

Gadamer, H. (1975). *Truth and Method.* Boston: Seabury Press.

Gal, S. (1978). Peasant men can't get wives: language change and sex roles in a bilingual community. *Language in Society* 7: 1–16.

Gal, S. (1979). *Language Shift: Social Determinants of Linguistic Change in Bilingual Austria.* New York: Academic Press.

Gal, S. (1987). Codeswitching and consciousness in the European periphery. *American Ethnologist* 14: 637–53.

Gal, S. (1989). Language and political economy. *Annual Review of Anthropology* 18: 345–67.

Gamble, C. (1994). Human evolution: the last one million years. In Ingold, T. (ed.), pp. 79–107.

Gardner, H. (1985). *The Mind's New Science: a History of the Cognitive Revolution.* New York: Basic Books.

Gardner, R., Gardner, B. and Van Cantfort, T. (eds) (1989). *Teaching Sign Language to Chimpanzees.* Albany: State University of New York Press.

Geertz, C. (1972). Linguistic etiquette. In Pride, J. and Holmes, J. (eds), pp. 167–79.

Geertz, C. (1973). *The Interpretation of Cultures.* New York: Basic Books.

Geertz, C. (1983). *Local Knowledge.* New York: Basic Books.

Geertz, C. (1984). Anti Anti-relativism. *American Anthropologist* 86: 263–78.

Geertz, C. (1995). *After the Fact: Two Countries, Four Decades, One Anthropologist.* Cambridge, MA: Harvard University Press.

Gellner, E. (1973). *The Concept of Kinship and Other Essays.* Oxford: Basil Blackwell.

Gellner, E. (1983). *Nations and Nationalism.* Oxford: Basil Blackwell.

Gelman, S. and Coley, J. (eds) (1991). *Perspectives on Language and Thought: Inter-relationships in Development.* Cambridge: Cambridge University Press.

Gentner, D. and Gentner, D. (1982). Flowing waters or teeming crowds: mental models of electricity. In Gentner, D. and Stevens, A. (eds), *Mental Models,* pp. 99–129. Hillsdale, NJ: Lawrence Erlbaum.

Gergen, K. (1990). Social understanding and the inscription of self. In Stigler, J., Shweder, R. and Herdt, G. (eds), pp. 569–606.

Gergen, K. (1991). *The Saturated Self.* New York: Basic Books.

Gergen, K. (1994). *Realities and Relationships: Soundings in Social Construction.* Cambridge, MA: Harvard University Press.

Gergen, K. and Davis, K. (eds) (1985). *The Social Construction of the Person.* New York: Springer-Verlag.

Gewertz, D. (1983). *Sepik River Societies.* New Haven: Yale University Press.

Gibson, J. (1979). *The Ecological Approach to Visual Perception.* Boston: Houghton-Mifflin.

Gibson, K. (1988). Brain size and the evolution of language. In Landsberg, M. (ed.), pp. 149–72.

Gibson, K. (1991). Tools, language and intelligence: evolutionary interrelationships. *Man* 26: 602–19.

Gibson, K. and Ingold, T. (eds) (1993). *Tools, Language and Cognition.* Cambridge: Cambridge University Press.

Giddens, A. (1979). *Central Problems in Social Theory.* Berkeley: University of California Press.

Giddens, A. (1981). *The Class Structure of the Advanced Societies.* Second edition. New York: Harper and Row.

Giddens, A. (1984). *The Constitution of Society.* Berkeley: University of California Press.

Giddens, A. (1993). *Sociology.* Second edition. Cambridge: Polity.

Giglioli, P. (ed.) (1972). *Language and Social Context.* Harmondsworth: Penguin.

Gleason, J. (1987). Sex differences in parent–child interaction. In Philips, S., Steele, S. and Tanz, C. (eds), pp. 189–99.

Goffman, E. (1956). *The Presentation of Self in Everyday Life.* New York: Doubleday.

Goffman, E. (1967). *Interaction Ritual: Essays on Face-to-face Behavior.* New York: Doubleday.

Goffman, E. (1971). *Relations in Public: Microstudies of the Public Order.* New York: Harper and Row.

Goffman, E. (1974). *Frame Analysis: An Essay on the Organization of Experience.* New York: Harper and Row.

Goffman, E. (1981). *Forms of Talk.* Philadelphia: University of Pennsylvania Press.

Goldin-Meadow, S. (1992). When does gesture become language? A study of gesture used as a primary communication system by deaf children of hearing parents. In Gibson, K. and Ingold, T. (eds), pp. 63–85.

Gonda, J. (1948). The Javanese vocabulary of courtesy. *Lingua* 1: 333–76.

Goodall, J. (1986). *The Chimpanzees of Gombe*. Cambridge, MA: Harvard University Press.

Goodenough, W. (1964[1957]). Cultural anthropology and linguistics. In Hymes, D. (ed.), pp. 36–9.

Goodenough, W. (1970). *Description and Comparison in Cultural Anthropology*. Chicago: Aldine.

Goodenough, W. (1981). *Culture, Language, and Society*. Second edition. Menlo Park, CA: Benjamin/Cummings.

Goodluck, H. (1991). *Language Acquisition: A Linguistic Introduction*. Oxford: Basil Blackwell.

Goodwin, M. (1980). Directive-response speech sequences in girls' and boys' task activities. In McConnell-Ginet, S., Borker, R. and Furman, N. (eds), pp. 157–73.

Goodwin, M. (1991). *He-Said-She-Said*. Bloomington: Indiana University Press.

Goody, J. (ed.) (1968). *Literacy in Traditional Societies*. Cambridge: Cambridge University Press.

Goody, J. (1977). *The Domestication of the Savage Mind*. Cambridge: Cambridge University Press.

Goody, J. (1986). *The Logic of Writing and the Organization of Society*. Cambridge: Cambridge University Press.

Good, J. (1987). *The Interface between the Written and the Oral*. Cambridge: Cambridge University Press.

Goody, J. and Watt, I. (1972). The consequences of literacy. In Giglioli, P. (ed.), pp. 311–57. Also in Goody, J. (ed.), pp. 27–68.

Gossen, G. (1972). Chamula genres of verbal behavior. In Paredes, A. and Bauman, R. (eds), *Toward New Perspectives in Folklore*, pp. 145–67. Austin: University of Texas Press.

Gough, K. (1959). The Nayars and the definition of marriage. *Journal of the Royal Anthropological Institute* 89: 23–34.

Gough, K. (1961). Variation in matrilineal systems. In Schneider, D. and Gough, K. (eds), pp. 445–652.

Gough, K. (1968). Implications of literacy in traditional China and India. In Goody, J. (ed.), pp. 70–84.

Graburn, N. (ed.) (1971). *Readings in Kinship and Social Structure*. New York: Harper and Row.

Grace, G. (1987). *The Linguistic Construction of Reality*. London: Croom Helm.

Graff. H. (1979). *The Literacy Myth: Literacy and Social Structure in the 19th Century City*. New York: Academic Press.

Graff, H. (ed.) (1982). *Literacy and Social Development in the West: A Reader*. Cambridge: Cambridge University Press.

Graff, H. (1987). *The Legacies of Literacy: Continuities and Contradictions in Western Culture*. Bloomington: Indiana University Press.

Gramsci, A. (1971). *Selections from the Prison Notebooks*. London: Lawrence and Wishart.

Greenfield, P. (1966). On culture and conservation. In Bruner, J., Oliver, R. and Greenfield, P. (eds), *Studies in Cognitive Growth*, pp. 225–56. New York: John Wiley and Sons.

Greenfield, P. (1991). Language, tools and brain: the ontogeny and phylogeny of hierarchically organized sequential behavior. *Behavioral and Brain Sciences* 14: 531–95.

Greenfield, P. and Savage-Rumbaugh, E. (1990). Grammatical combination in *Pan paniscus*: processes of learning and intervention in the evolution and development of language. In Parker, S. and Gibson, K. (eds), pp. 540–78.

Grice, H. (1971). Meaning. In Steinberg, D. and Jakobovitz, L. (eds), pp. 52–9.

Grice, H. (1975). Logic and conversation. In Cole, P. and Morgan, J. (eds), *Syntax and Semantics*, volume 3, pp. 41–58. New York: Academic Press.

Grice, H. (1989). *Studies in the Ways of Words*. Cambridge, MA: Harvard University Press.

Grillo, R. (1989). *Dominant Languages: Language and Hierarchy in Britain and France*. Cambridge: Cambridge University Press.

Gu, Y. (1990). Politeness phenomena in Modern Chinese. *Journal of Pragmatics* 14: 237–57.

Guidon, N. and Delibrias, G. (1986). Carbon-14 date point to man in the Americans 32,000 years ago. *Nature* 321: 769–71.

Gumperz, J. (1958). Dialect differences and social stratification in a North Indian village. *American Anthropologist* 60: 668–81.

Gumperz, J. (1982). *Discourse Strategies*. Cambridge: Cambridge University Press.

Gumperz, J. (1993). Culture and conversational inference. In Foley, W. (ed.), pp. 193–214.

Gumperz, J. and Hymes, D. (eds) (1964). *The Ethnography of Communication*. (*American Anthropologist* 66, Special Publication) Washington: American Anthropological Association.

Gumperz, J. and Hymes, D. (eds) (1972). *Directions in Sociolinguistics: The Ethnography of Communication*. New York: Holt, Rinehart and Winston.

Gumperz, J. and Levinson, S. (1991). Rethinking linguistic relativity. *Current Anthropology* 32: 613–23.

Gumperz, J. and Wilson, R. (1971). Convergence and creolization: a case from the Indo-Aryan-Dravidian border. In Hymes, D. (ed.), pp. 151–69.

Haas, M. (1964). Men's and women's speech in Koasati. In Hymes, D. (ed.), pp. 228–33.

Haegeman, L. (1994). *Introduction to Government and Binding Theory*. Second edition. Oxford: Basil Blackwell.

Haiman, J. (1985). *Natural Syntax: Iconicity and Erosion*. Cambridge: Cambridge University Press.

Hale, K. (1971). A note on a Warlpiri tradition of antonymy. In Steinberg, D. and Jakobovitz (eds), pp. 472–82.

Hallpike, C. (1979). *The Foundations of Primitive Thought*. New York: Oxford University Press.

Hanks, W. (1989). Text and textuality. *Annual Review of Anthropology* 18: 95–127.

Hanks, W. (1995). *Language and Communicative Practices*. Boulder, CO: Westview Press.

Hanks, W. (1996). Exorcism and the description of participant roles. In Silverstein, M. and Urban, G. (eds), *Natural Histories of Discourse*, pp. 160–200. Chicago: University of Chicago Press.

Hardin, C. (1988). *Color for Philosophers: Unweaving the Rainbow*. Indianapolis: Hackett Publishing Company.

Harman, G. (1971). Three levels of meaning. In Steinberg, D. and Jakobovitz, L. (eds), pp. 66–75.

Harré, R. and Mühlhäusler, P. (1990). *Pronouns and People: The Linguistic Construction of Social and Personal Identity*. Oxford: Basil Blackwell.

Harris, C. (1990). *Kinship*. Minneapolis: University of Minnesota Press.

Harris, G. (1989). Concepts of individual, self and person in description and analysis. *American Anthropologist* 91: 599–612.

Harrison, S. (1987). Cultural efflorescence and political evolution in a Sepik River village. *American Ethnologist* 12: 413–26.

Harrison, S. (1990). *Stealing People's Names: History and Politics in a Sepik River Cosmology*. Cambridge: Cambridge University Press.

Haugen, E. (1966). *Language Conflict and Language Planning: The Case of Modern Norwegian*. Cambridge, MA: Harvard University Press.

Havelock, E. (1963). *Preface to Plato*. Cambridge: Cambridge University Press.

Havelock, E. (1982). *The Literate Revolution in Greece and its Cultural Consequences*. Princeton: Princeton University Press.

Haviland, J. (1979a). Guugu-Yimidhirr brother-in-law language. *Language in Society* 8: 365–93.

Haviland, J. (1979b). How to talk to your brother-in-law in Guugu-Yimidhirr. In Shopen, T. (ed.), pp. 161–239.

Haviland, J. (1993). Anchoring, iconicity, and orientation in Guugu-Yimidhirr pointing gestures. *Journal of Linguistic Anthropology* 3: 3–45.

Hawkins, J. (ed.) (1988). *Explaining Language Universals*. Oxford: Basil Blackwell.

Headland, P. (1986). Social rank and Tunebo requests. In Huttar, G. and Gregerson, K. (eds), *Pragmatics in Non-Western Perspective*, pp. 1–34. Dallas: Summer Institute of Linguistics.

Heath, J. (ed.) (1978). *Linguistic Diffusion in Arnhem Land*. Canberra: Australian Institute of Aboriginal Studies.

Heath, J. (1984). Language contact and language change. *Annual Review of Anthropology* 13: 367–84.

Heath, S. (1982). What no bedtime story means: narrative skills at home and school. *Language in Society* 11: 49–76.

Heath, S. (1983). *Ways with Words: Language, Life and Work in Communities and Classrooms*. Cambridge: Cambridge University Press.

Heider, E. (1971). Focal color areas and the development of color names. *Developmental Psychology* 4: 447–55.

Heider, E. (1972a). Probabilities, sampling, and the ethnographic method: the case of Dani colour names. *Man* 7: 448–66.

Heider, E. (1972b). Universals in color naming and memory. *Journal of Experimental Psychology* 93: 10–20.

Heller, M. (ed.) (1988). *Code-switching: Anthropological and Sociolinguistic Perspectives*. Berlin: Mouton de Gruyter.

Hewes, G. (1973). Primate communication and the gestural origin of language. *Current Anthropology* 14: 5–24.

Hewitt, R. (1986). *White Talk, Black Talk*. Cambridge: Cambridge University Press.

Hiley, D., Bohman, J. and Shusterman, R. (eds) (1991). *The Interpretive Turn: Philosophy, Science, Culture.* Ithaca, NY: Cornell University Press.

Hill, D. (1993). *Finding Your Way in Longgu.* Working Paper Number 21. Nijmegen, Netherlands: Cognitive Anthropology Research Group, Max-Planck Institute for Psycholinguistics.

Hill, J. and Hill, K. (1978). Honorific usage in modern Nahuatl. *Language* 54: 123–55.

Hill, J. and Hill, K. (1986). *Speaking Mexicano: Dynamics of Syncretic Language in Central Mexico.* Tucson: University of Arizona Press.

Hill, J. and Mannheim, B. (1992). Language and world view. *Annual Review of Anthropology* 21: 381–406.

Ho, M. and Saunders, P. (1984). *Beyond Neo-Darwinism.* New York: Academic Press.

Hock, H. (1986). *Principles of Historical Linguistics.* Berlin: Mouton de Gruyter.

Hockett, C. (1958). *A Course in Modern Linguistics.* New York: Macmillan.

Hockett, C. (1960). The origin of speech. *Scientific American* 203: 89–96.

Hoijer, H. (1964). Cultural implications of some Navaho linguistic categories. In Hymes, D. (ed.), pp. 142–8.

Holland, D. and Quinn, N. (eds) (1987). *Cultural Models in Language and Thought.* Cambridge: Cambridge University Press.

Holland, D. and Skinner, D. (1987). Prestige and intimacy: the cultural models behind Americans' talk about gender types. In Holland, D. and Quinn, N. (eds), pp. 78–111.

Hollenbach, B. (1990). Semantic and syntactic extensions of Copala Trique body-part nouns. In Cuarón, B. and Levy, P. (eds), *Homenaje a Jorge A. Suárez: Lingüística indoamericana e hispánica*, pp. 275–96. Mexico City: El Colegio de México.

Hollis, M. and Lukes, S. (eds) (1982). *Rationality and Relativism.* Oxford: Basil Blackwell.

Hollos, M. (1977). Comprehension and use of social rules in pronoun selection by Hungarian children. In Ervin-Tripp, S. and Mitchell-Kernan, C. (eds), pp. 211–23.

Holme, J. (1988–9). *Pidgins and Creoles.* Two volumes. Cambridge: Cambridge University Press.

Holmes, J. (1984). Hedging your bets and sitting on the fence: some evidence for hedges as support structures. *Te Teo* 27: 47–62.

Holmes, J. (1992). *An Introduction to Sociolinguistics.* London: Longman.

Hope, E. (1974). The deep syntax of Lisu sentences: a transformational case grammar. *Pacific Linguistics* Series C34.

Hopkins, W., Morris, R., Savage-Rumbaugh, S. and Rumbaugh, D. (1989). Hemispheric activation for meaningful and nonmeaningful symbols in language-trained chimpanzees: evidence for a left hemisphere advantage. Unpublished manuscript. University of Georgia.

Horvath, B. (1985). *Variation in Australian English: The Sociolects of Sydney.* Cambridge: Cambridge University Press.

Hudson, R. (1980). *Sociolinguistics.* Cambridge: Cambridge University Press.

Humboldt, W. (1988[1836–9]). *On Language: The Diversity of Human Language-structure and its Influence on the Mental Development of Mankind.* Cambridge: Cambridge University Press.

Hundius, H. and Kölver, U. (1983). Syntax and semantics of numeral classifiers in Thai. *Studies in Language* 7: 165–214.

Hunn, E. (1985). The utilitarian factor in folk biological classification. In Dougherty, J. (ed.), pp. 117–40.

Hurvich, L. and Jameson, D. (1957). An opponent-process theory of color vision. *Psychological Review* 64: 384–404.

Hymes, D. (ed.) (1964). *Language in Culture and Society: A Reader in Linguistics and Anthropology.* New York: Harper and Row.

Hymes, D. (1966). Two types of linguistic relativity (with examples from Amerindian ethnography). In Bright, W. (ed.), *Sociolinguistics*, pp. 114–67. The Hague: Mouton.

Hymes, D. (ed.) (1971). *Pidginization and Creolization of Language.* Cambridge: Cambridge University Press.

Hymes, D. (1972a). On communicative competence. In Pride, J. and Holmes, J. (eds), pp. 269–93.

Hymes, D. (1972b[1964]). Toward ethnographics of communication: the analysis communicative events. In Giglioli, P. (ed.), pp. 21–44.

Hymes, D. (1981). *"In Vain I tried to Tell You": Essays in Native American Ethnopoetics.* Philadelphia: University of Pennsylvania Press.

Hymes, D. (1986). Discourse: scope without depth. *International Journal of the Sociology of Language* 57: 49–89.

Hymes, D. (1987). Tonkawa poetics: John Rush Buffalo's "Coyote and Eagle's daughter". In Sherzer, J. and Woodbury, A. (eds), pp. 17–61.

Imai, M. and Gentner, D. (1993). Linguistic relativity vs universal ontology: cross-linguistic studies of the object/substance distinction. In Beals, K., Cooke, G., Kathman, D., Kita, S., McCullough, K. and Teston, D. (eds), *What We Think, What We Mean and How We Say It: Papers from the Parasession on the Correspondence of Conceptual, Semantic and Grammatical Representations*, pp. 171–86. Chicago: Chicago Linguistics Society.

Ingold, T. (1986). *The Appropriation of Nature: Essays on Human Ecology and Social Relations.* Manchester: Manchester University Press.

Ingold, T. (1990). An anthropologist looks at biology. *Man* 25: 208–29.

Ingold, T. (ed.) (1994). *Companion Encyclopedia of Anthropology: Humanity, Culture and Social Life.* London: Routledge.

Ingram, D. (1989). *First Language Acquisition: Method, Description and Explanation.* Cambridge: Cambridge University Press.

Inoue, K. (1979). Japanese: a story of a language and people. In Shopen, T. (ed.), pp. 241–300.

Irvine, J. (1974). Strategies of status manipulation in the Wolof greeting. In Bauman, R. and Sherzer, J. (eds), pp. 167–91.

Irvine, J. (1979). Formality and informality in communicative events. *American Anthropologist* 81: 773–90.

Ito, K. (1980). Toward an ethnopsychology of language: interactional strategies of Japanese and Americans. *Bulletin of the Center for Language Studies* 3: 1–14. Yokohama: Kanagawa University.

Jakobson, R. (1957). *Shifters, Verbal Categories, and the Russian Verb.* Cambridge, MA: Harvard University Russian Language Project.

Jakobson, R. (1960). Closing statement: linguistics and poetics. In Sebeok, T. (ed.), *Style in Language*, pp. 350–77. Cambridge, MA: Massachusetts Institute of Technology.

Jakobson, R. (1965). Quest for the essence of language. *Diogenes* 51: 27–37.

Jakobson, R. (1968). *Child Language, Aphasia, and Phonological Universals.* The Hague: Mouton.

James, D. and Clarke, S. (1993). Women, men and interruptions: a critical review. In Tannen, D. (ed.), pp. 231–80.

James, D. and Drakich, J. (1993). Understanding gender differences in amount of talk: a critical review of research. In Tannen, D. (ed.), pp. 281–312.

Johnson, M. (1987). *The Body in the Mind: The Bodily Basis of Meaning, Imagination, and Reason.* Chicago: University of Chicago Press.

Jones, R. (1989). East of Wallace's line: issues and problems in the colonization of the Australian continent. In Mellars, P. and Stringer, C. (eds), pp. 743–82.

Jones, S., Martin, R. and Pilbeam, D. (eds) (1992). *The Cambridge Encyclopedia of Human Evolution.* Cambridge: Cambridge University Press.

Jones, R. and Meehan, B. (1978). Anbarra concept of colour. In Hiatt, L. (ed.), *Australian Aboriginal Cognition*, pp. 20–39. Canberra: Australian Institute of Aboriginal Studies.

Joseph, J. (1987). *Eloquence and Power: The Rise of Language Standards and Standard Languages.* Oxford: Basil Balckwell.

Juntanamalaga, P. (1988). Social issues in Thai classifier usage. *Language Sciences* 10: 313–30.

Kant, I. (1958[1781]). *Critique of Pure Reason.* New York: Random House.

Kaplan, J. (1995). *English Grammar: Principles and Facts.* Second edition. Englewood-Cliffs, NJ: Prentice-Hall.

Kay, P. (1970). Some theoretical implications of ethnographic semantics. In Fischer, A. (ed.), *Current Directions in Anthropology*, Bulletins of the American Anthropological Association, volume 3, no. 3, part 2, pp. 19–31. Washington: American Anthropological Association.

Kay, P. (1975). Synchronic variability and diachronic change in basic color terms. *Language in Society* 4: 257–70.

Kay, P. (1987). Linguistic competence and folk theories of language: two English hedges. In Holland, D. and Quinn, N. (eds), pp. 67–77.

Kay, P., Berlin, B. and Merrifield, W. (1991). Biocultural implications of color naming. *Journal of Linguistic Anthropology* 1: 12–25.

Kay, P. and McDaniel, C. (1978). The linguistic significance of the meanings of basic color terms. *Language* 54: 610–46.

Keeler, W. (1990). Speaking of gender in Java. In Atkinson, J. and Errington, S. (eds), pp. 127–52.

Keenan, E. (1974). Norm-makers, norm-breakers: uses of speech by men and women in a Malagasy community. In Bauman, R. and Sherzer, J. (eds), pp. 125–43.

Keenan, E. (1976). The universality of conversational postulates. *Language in Society* 5: 67–80.

Keenan, E. and Ochs, E. (1979). Becoming a competent speaker of Malagasy. In Shopen, T. (ed.), pp. 113–58.

Keesing, R. (1974). Theories of culture. *Annual Review of Anthropology* 3: 73–97. Also in Casson, R. (ed.), pp. 42–66.

Keesing, R. (1975). *Kin Groups and Social Structure*. New York: Holt, Rinehart and Winston.

Kelley, J. (1992). Evolution of apes. In Jones, S., Martin, R. and Pilbeam, D. (eds), pp. 223–30.

Kempton, W. (1981). Category grading and taxonomic relations: a mug is a sort of a cup. In Casson, R. (ed.), pp. 203–29.

Kiparsky, P. (1973). Elsewhere in phonology. In Anderson, S. and Kiparsky, P. (eds), *A Festschrift for Morris Halle*, pp. 93–106. New York: Holt, Rinehart and Winston.

Klein, R. (1985). Breaking away. *Natural History* 94: 4–7.

Klima, E. and Bellugi, U. (1979). *The Signs of Language*. Cambridge, MA: Harvard University Press.

Kochman, T. (ed.) (1972). *Rappin' and Stylin' Out: Communication in Urban Black America*. Urbana: University of Illinois Press.

Kochman, T. (1981). *Black and White Styles in Conflict*. Chicago: University of Chicago Press.

Kohut, H. (1977). *The Restoration of the Self*. New York: International Universities Press.

Kondo, D. (1990). *Crafting Selves: Power, Gender and Discourses of Identity in a Japanese Workplace*. Chicago: University of Chicago Press.

Kövecses, Z. (1986). *Metaphors of Anger, Pride and Love: A Lexical Approach to the Structure of Concepts*. Amsterdam: John Benjamins.

Krausz, M. (ed.) (1989). *Relativism: Interpretation and Confrontation*. Notre Dame, IN: University of Notre Dame Press.

Kripke, S. (1980). *Naming and Necessity*. Cambridge, MA: Harvard University Press.

Krishnamurti, B. (1979). Problems of language standardization in India. In McCormack, W. and Wurm, S. (eds), *Language and Society: Anthropological Issues*, pp. 673–92. The Hague: Mouton.

Kronenfeld, D., Armstrong, J. and Wilmoth, S. (1985). Exploring the internal structure of linguistic categories: an extensionist semantic view. In Dougherty, J. (ed.), pp. 91–110.

Kroskrity, P. (1993). *Language, History, and Identity: Ethnolinguistic Studies of the Arizona Tewa*. Tucson: University of Arizona Press.

Kuipers, J. (1990). *Power in Performance: The Creation of Textual Authority in Weyewa Ritual Speech*. Philadelphia: University of Pennsylvania Press.

Kulick, D. (1992). *Language Shift and Cultural Reproduction: Socialization, Self and Syncretism in a Papua New Guinea Village*. Cambridge: Cambridge University Press.

Kulick, D. and Stroud, C. (1993). Conceptions and uses of literacy in a Papua New Guinean village. In Street, B. (ed.), pp. 30–61.

La Fontaine, J. (1985). Person and individual: some anthropological reflections. In Carrithers, M., Collins, S. and Lukes, S. (eds), pp. 123–40.

Labov, W. (1972a). *Language in the Inner City: Studies in the Black English Vernacular*. Philadelphia: University of Pennsylvania Press.

Labov, W. (1972b). *Sociolinguistic Patterns*. Philadelphia: University of Pennsylvania Press.

Labov, W. and Waletzky, J. (1967). Narrative analysis. In Helm, J. (ed.), *Essays in the Verbal and Visual Arts*, pp. 12–44. Seattle: University of Washington Press.

Laitin, D. (1977). *Politics, Language and Thought: The Somali Experience*. Chicago: University of Chicago Press.

Laitin, D. (1992). *Language Repertoires and State Construction in Africa*. Cambridge: Cambridge University Press.

Lakoff, G. (1987). *Women, Fire and Dangerous Things*. Chicago: The University of Chicago Press.

Lakoff, G. (1990). The invariance hypothesis. *Linguistics* 1: 39–74.

Lakoff, G. and Johnson, M. (1980). *Metaphors We Live By*. Chicago: University of Chicago Press.

Lakoff, G. and Kövecses, Z. (1987). The cognitive model of anger inherent in American thought. In Holland, D. and Quinn, N. (eds), pp. 195–221.

Lakoff, G. and Turner, M. (1989). *More than Cool Reason: A Field Guide to Poetic Metaphor*. Chicago: University of Chicago Press.

Lakoff, R. (1973). The logic of politeness; or, minding for p's and q's. In Corum, C., Smith-Stark, T. and Weiser, A. (eds), *Papers from the Ninth Annual Meeting of the Chicago Linguistics Society*, pp. 292–305. Chicago: Chicago Linguistics Society.

Lakoff, R. (1975). *Language and Woman's Place*. New York: Harper and Row.

Lakoff, R. (1977). What you can do with words: politeness, pragmatics and performatives. In Rogers, A., Wall, B. and Murphy, J. (eds), *Proceedings of the Texas Conference on Performatives, Presuppositions and Implicatures*, pp. 79–105. Washington: Center for Applied Linguistics.

Lamb, T. and Bourriau, J. (eds) (1995). *Colour: Art and Science*. Cambridge: Cambridge University Press.

Landau, B. and Jackendoff, R. (1993). "What" and "where" in spatial language and spatial cognition. *Behavioral and Brain Sciences* 16: 217–65.

Landsberg, M. (ed.) (1988). *The Genesis of Language: A Different Judgement of Evidence*. Berlin: Mouton de Gruyter.

Lantz, D. and Sefflre, V. (1964). Language and cognition revisited. *Journal of Abnormal and Social Psychology* 69: 472–81.

Laver, J. (1981). Linguistic routines and politeness in greeting and parting. In Coulmas, F. (ed.), *Conversational Routine*, pp. 298–304. The Hague: Mouton.

Leach, E. (1958). Concerning Trobriand clans and the kinship category *tabu*. In Goody, J. (ed.), *The Developmental Cycle of Domestic Groups*, pp. 120–45. Cambridge: Cambridge University Press.

Leach, E. (1962). *Rethinking Anthropology*. London: Athlone.

Leach, E. (1964). Anthropological aspects of language: animal categories and verbal abuse. In Lenneberg, E. (ed.), *New Directions in the Study of Language*, pp. 23–63. Cambridge, MA: Massachusetts Institute of Technology Press.

Leach, E. (1974). *Lévi-Strauss*. London: Fontana.

Leacock, E. (1978). Women's status in egalitarian society: implications for social evolution. *Current Anthropology* 19: 247–58.

Leech, G. (1983). *Principles of Pragmatics*. London: Longman.

Lenneberg, E. (1953). Cognition in ethnolinguistics. *Language* 29: 463–71.

Lenneberg, E. and Roberts, J. (1956). *The language of experience: a study in methodology*. Indiana University Publications in Anthropology and Linguistics, Memoir 13. Baltimore: Waverly Press.

Lévi-Strauss, C. (1963). *Structural Anthropology*. New York: Basic Books.

Lévi-Strauss, C. (1964). *Totemism*. New York: Beacon Press.

Lévi-Strauss, C. (1966). *The Savage Mind*. London: Weidenfeld and Nicolson.

Lévi-Strauss, C. (1969). *The Raw and the Cooked*. Boston: Beacon Press.

Levinson, S. (1982). Caste rank and verbal interaction in Western Tamilnadu. In McGilvray, D. (ed.), *Caste Ideology and Interaction*, pp. 98–203. Cambridge: Cambridge University Press.

Levinson, S. (1983). *Pragmatics*. Cambridge: Cambridge University Press.

Levinson, S. (1992). *Language and Cognition: Cognitive Consequences of Spatial Description in Guugu-Yimidhirr*. Working paper no. 13. Nijmegen, The Netherlands: Cognitive Anthropology Research Group, Max-Planck Institute for Psycholinguistics.

Levinson, S. (1994a). Frames of reference and Molyneaux's questions: cross-linguistic evidence. Paper presented at the Conference on Language and Space, Tucson, March 1994.

Levinson, S. (1994b). Vision, shape and linguistic description: Tzeltal body-part terminology and object description. *Linguistics* 32: 791–856.

Levinson, S. and Brown, P. (1994). Immanuel Kant among the Tenejapans: anthropology as empirical philosophy. *Ethos* 22: 3–41.

Levy, P. (1994). *How Shape Becomes Grammar: On the Semantics of Part Morphemes in Totonac*. Working paper number 29. Nijmegen, The Netherlands: Cognitive Anthropology Research Group, Max-Planck Institute for Psycholinguistics.

Lévy-Bruhl, L. (1921). *Primitive Mentality*. Boston: Beacon Press.

Lévy-Bruhl, L. (1926). *How Natives Think*. New York: Knopf.

Lewontin, R. (1983). The organism as the subject and object of evolution. *Scientia* 113: 65–82.

Lieberman, P. (1975). *On the Origins of Language: An Introduction to the Evolution of Human Speech*. Cambridge, MA: Harvard University Press.

Lieberman, P. (1984). *The Biology and Evolution of Language*. Cambridge, MA: Harvard University Press.

Lieberman, P. (1991). *Uniquely Human: The Evolution of Speech, Thought, and Selfless Behavior*. Cambridge, MA: Harvard University Press.

Lloyd, G. (1990). *Demystifying Mentalities*. Cambridge: Cambridge University Press.

Lounsbury, F. (1965). Another view of the Trobriand kinship categories. In Hammel, E. (ed.), *Formal Semantic Analysis*, pp. 142–185. Washington: American Anthropological Association.

Lounsbury, F. (1969). A formal account of the Omaha- and Crow-type kinship terminologies. In Tyler, S. (ed.), pp. 212–55.

Lucy, J. (1992a). *Grammatical Categories and Cognition: A Case Study of the Linguistic Relativity Hypothesis*. Cambridge: Cambridge University Press.

Lucy, J. (1992b). *Language Diversity and Thought: A Reformulation of the Linguistic Relativity Hypothesis*. Cambridge: Cambridge University Press.

Lucy, J. (1996). The linguistics of "color". In Hardin, C. and Maffi, L. (eds), *Color Categories in Thought and Language*, Cambridge: Cambridge University Press.

Luria, A. (1976). *Cognitive Development: Its Cultural and Social Foundations*. Cambridge: Cambridge University Press.

Lutz, C. (1987). Goals, events, and understanding in Ifaluk emotion theory. In Holland, D. and Quinn, N. (eds), pp. 290–312.

Lyons, J. (1977). *Semantics*. Two volumes. Cambridge: Cambridge University Press.

Macaulay, R. (1977). *Language, Social Class and Education: A Glasgow Study*. Edinburgh: Edinburgh University Press.

Macaulay, R. (1991). *Locating Dialect in Discourse*. Oxford: Oxford University Press.

MacLaury, R. (1987). Color-category evolution and Shuswap yellow-with-green. *American Anthropologist* 98: 107–24.

MacLaury, R. (1991). Exotic color categories: linguistic relativity to what extent? *Journal of Linguistic Anthropology* 1: 26–53.

MacLaury, R. (1992). From brightness to hue: an explanatory model of color-category evolution. *Current Anthropology* 33: 137–86.

MacLaury, R. and Galloway, B. (1988). Color categories and color qualifiers. In Halkomelem, Samish, Lushootseed, Nootsack, and Yakima. *Working Papers of the Twenty-third International Conference on Salishan and Neighboring Languages*. Eugene, WA.

MacNeilage, P. (1989). The postural origins theory of primate neurobiological asymmetries. Unpublished paper, University of Texas.

MacNeilage, P. (1992). Evolution and lateralization of the two great primate action systems. In Wind, J., Chiarelli, B., Bichakjian, B. and Nocentini, A. (eds), pp. 281–300.

MacNeilage, P., Studdert-Kennedy, M. and Lindblom, B. (1987). Primate handedness reconsidered. *Behavioral and Brain Sciences* 10: 247–303.

Malinowski, B. (1923). The problem of meaning in primitive languages. In Ogden, C. and Richards, I. (eds), *The Meaning of Meaning*, pp. 296–336. New York: Harcourt, Brace and World.

Malinowski, B. (1929). *The Sexual Life of Savages in Northwestern Melanesia*. London: Routledge.

Malinowski, B. (1930). Kinship. *Man* 30: 9–29.

Malinowski, B. (1960[1944]). *A Scientific Theory of Culture and Other Essays*. New York: Oxford University Press.

Maltz, D. and Borker, R. (1982). A cultural approach to male–female miscommunication. In Gumperz, J. (ed.), *Language and Social Identity*, pp. 196–216. Cambridge: Cambridge University Press.

Manchester, M. (1985). *The Philosophical Foundations of Humboldt's Linguistic Doctrines*. Amsterdam: John Benjamins.

Marcus, G. and Fischer, M. (1986). *Anthropology as Cultural Critique: An Experimental Moment in the Human Sciences*. Chicago: University of Chicago Press.

Margolis, J. (1986). *Pragmatism Without Foundations: Reconciling Realism and Relativism*. Oxford: Basil Blackwell.

Marsella, A., DeVos, G. and Hsu, F. (eds) (1985). *Culture and Self: Asian and Western Perspectives*. New York: Tavistock.

Marshall, D. (1991). *Language Planning*. Amsterdam: John Benjamins.

Martin, S. (1964). Speech levels in Japan and Korea. In Hymes, D. (ed.), pp. 407–15.

Masica, C. (1976). *Defining a Linguistic Area: South Asia*. Chicago: University of Chicago Press.

Mathiot, M. (1964). Noun classes and folk taxonomy in Papago. In Hymes, D. (ed.), pp. 154–61.

Mathiot, M. (1969). The semantic and cognitive domains of language. In Garvin, P. (ed.), *Cognition: A Multiple View*, pp. 249–76. New York: Spartan Books.

Matsumoto, Y. (1988). Reexamination of the universality of face: politeness phenomena in Japanese. *Journal of Pragmatics* 11: 721–36.

Maturana, H. and Varela, F. (1987). *The Tree of Knowledge: The Biological Roots of Human Understanding*. Boston: New Science Library.

Mauss, M. (1985[1938]). A category of the human mind: the notion of person; the notion of self. In Carrithers, M., Collins, S. and Lukes, S. (eds), pp. 1–25.

Maynard Smith, J. (1986). *The Problems of Biology*. Oxford: Oxford University Press.

Maynard Smith, J. (1989). *Evolutionary Genetics*. Oxford: Oxford University Press.

McBrearty, S. (1990). The origin of modern humans. *Man* 25: 129–43.

McConnell-Ginet, S. (1988). Language and gender. In Newmeyer, F. (ed.), pp. 75–99.

McConnell-Ginet, S., Borker, R. and Furman, N. (eds) (1980). *Women and Language in Literature and Society*. New York: Praeger.

Mead, G. (1934). *Mind, Self and Society*. Chicago: University of Chicago Press.

Meek, M. (1991). *On Being Literate*. London: Bodley Head.

Mellars, P. (1989). Major issues in the emergence of modern humans. *Current Anthropology* 30: 349–85.

Mellars, P. and Stringer, C. (eds) (1989). *The Human Revolution: Behavioural and Biological Perspectives on the Origins of Modern Humans*. Edinburgh: Edinburgh University Press.

Merleau-Ponty, M. (1962). *Phenomenology of Perception*. London: Routledge and Kegan Paul.

Merleau-Ponty, M. (1963). *The Structure of Behavior*. Boston: Beacon Press.

Mertz, E. and Parmentier, R. (eds) (1985). *Semiotic Mediation: Sociocultural and Psychological Perspectives*. New York: Academic Press.

Mervis, C. and Rosch, E. (1981). Categorization of natural objects. *Annual Review of Psychology* 32: 89–115.

Mey, J. (1993). *Pragmatics: An Introduction*. Oxford: Blackwell.

Miles, H. (1990). The cognitive foundations of reference in a signing organgutan. In Parker, S. and Gibson, K. (eds), pp. 511–39.

Miller, G. and Johnson-Laird, P. (1976). *Language and Perception*. Cambridge, MA: Harvard University Press.

Milroy, L. (1987a). *Language and Social Networks*. Second edition. Oxford: Basil Blackwell.

Milroy, L. (1987b). *Observing and Analysing Natural Language*. Oxford: Basil Blackwell.

Minsky, M. (1986). *The Society of Mind*. New York: Simon and Schuster.

Mitchell, D. (1988). Method in the metaphor: the ritual language of Wanukaka. In Fox, R. (ed.), pp. 64–86.

Moeliono, A. (1986). Language development and cultivation: alternative approaches in language planning. *Pacific Linguistics* Series D 68.

Moeran, B. (1988). Japanese language and society: an anthropological approach. *Journal of Pragmatics* 12: 427–43.

Moore, H. (1988). *Feminism and Anthropology*. Cambridge: Cambridge University Press.

Moore, H. (1994). Understanding sex and gender. In Ingold, T. (ed.), pp. 813–30.

Morgan, L. (1871). *Systems of Consanguinity and Affinity of the Human Family.* Washington: Smithsonian Institution.

Mühlhäusler, P. (1986). *Pidgin and Creole Linguistics.* Oxford: Basil Blackwell.

Munroe, R., Munroe, R. and Whiting, B. (eds) (1981). *Handbook of Cross-cultural Human Development.* New York: Garland Press.

Murdock, G. (1949). *Social Structure.* New York: Macmillan.

Myers, F. (1986). *Pintupi Country, Pintupi Self.* Washington: Smithsonian Institute Press.

Myers-Scotton, C. (1993). *Social Motivations for Codeswitching: Evidence from Africa.* Oxford: Oxford University Press.

Needham, R. (1962). Genealogy and category in Wikmunkan society. *Ethnology* 1: 223–64.

Needham, R. (1971). Remarks on the analysis of kinship and marriage. In Needham, R. (ed.), *Rethinking Kinship and Marriage*, pp. 1–34. London: Tavistock.

Newmeyer, F. (ed.) (1988). *Linguistics: The Cambridge Survey, Volume IV. Language: The Socio-cultural Context.* Cambridge: Cambridge University Press.

Newport, E. and Meier, R. (1985). The acquisition of American Sign Language. In Slobin, D. (ed.), *The Crosslinguistic Study of Language Acquisition, Volume 1: The Data*, pp. 881–938. Hillsdale, NJ: Lawrence Erlbaum.

Nichols, P. (1980). Women in their speech communities. In McConnell-Ginet, S., Borker, R. and Furman, N. (eds), pp. 140–9.

Nichols, P. (1983). Linguistic options and choices for black women in the rural south. In Thorne, B., Kramarae, C. and Henley, N. (eds), pp. 54–68.

Noble, W. and Davidson, I. (1991). The evolutionary emergence of modern human behavior: language and its archaeology. *Man* 26: 602–32.

O'Barr, W. (1982). *Linguistic Evidence: Language, Power, and Strategy in the Courtroom.* New York: Academic Press.

Ochs, E. (1988). *Culture and Language Development: Language Acquisition and Language Socialization in a Samoan Village.* Cambridge: Cambridge University Press.

Ochs, E. (1990). Indexicality and socialization. In Stigler, J., Shweder, R. and Herdt, G. (ed.), pp. 287–308.

Ochs, E. and Schieffelin, B. (1984). Language acquisition and socialization: three developmental stories and their implications. In Shweder, R. and LeVine, R. (eds), pp. 276–320.

Olson, D. (1977). From utterance to text: the bias of language in speech and writing. *Harvard Educational Review* 47: 257–81.

Olson, D. (1994). *The World on Paper: The Conceptual and Cognitive Implications of Writing and Reading.* Cambridge: Cambridge University Press.

Olson, D. and Torrance, N. (eds) (1991). *Literacy and Orality.* Cambridge: Cambridge University Press.

Olson, D., Torrance, N. and Hildyard, A. (eds) (1985). *Literacy, Language and Learning: The Nature and Consequences of Reading and Writing.* Cambridge: Cambridge University Press.

Ondling-Smee, F. (1994). Niche construction, evolution and culture. In Ingold, T. (ed.), pp. 162–96.

Ong, W. (1982). *Orality and Literacy: The Technologizing of the Word.* London: Methuen.

Ong, W. (1992). Writing is a technology that restructures thought. In Downing, P., Lima, S. and Noonan, M. (eds), *The Linguistics of Literacy*, pp. 293–319. Amsterdam: John Benjamins.

Ortner, S. (1984). Theory in anthropology since the Sixties. *Comparative Studies in Society and History* 26: 126–66.

Ortner, S. and Whitehead, H. (ed.) (1981). *Sexual Meanings: The Cultural Construction of Gender and Sexuality*. Cambridge: Cambridge University Press.

Ortony, A. (ed.) (1993). *Metaphor and Thought*. Second edition. Cambridge: Cambridge University Press.

Ottoson, D. and Zeki, S. (eds) (1985). *Central and Peripheral Mechanisms of Colour Vision*. London: Macmillan.

Oyama, S. (1985). *The Ontogeny of Information*. Cambridge: Cambridge University Press.

Pace, D. (1986). *Claude Lévi-Strauss: The Bearer of Ashes*. London: Routledge and Kegan Paul.

Parker, S. and Gibson, K. (1990). *"Language" and Intelligence in Monkeys and Apes*. Cambridge: Cambridge University Press.

Patterson, F. and Linden, E. (1982). *The Education of Koko*. London: André Deutsch.

Pawley, A. (1993a). Kalam pandanus language: an old New Guinea experiment in language engineering. *Pacific Linguistics* Series C110: 313–34.

Pawley, A. (1993b). A language which defies description by ordinary means. In Foley, W. (ed.), pp. 87–130.

Peirce, C. (1965–6). *Collected Papers*. Eight volumes. Cambridge, MA: Harvard University Press.

Petersen, M., Beecher, M., Zoloth, S., Green, S., Marler, P., Moody, D. and Stebbins, W. (1984). Neural lateralization of vocalizations by Japanese macaques: communicative significance is more important than acoustic structure. *Behavioral Neuroscience* 98: 779–90.

Petersen, M., Beecher, M., Zoloth, S., Moody, D. and Stebbins, W. (1978). Neural lateralization of species-specific vocalizations by Japanese macaques (*Macaca fuscata*). *Science* 202: 324–7.

Philips, S., Steele, S. and Tanz, C. (eds) (1987). *Language, Gender and Sex in Comparative Perspective*. Cambridge: Cambridge University Press.

Pilbeam, D. (1988). Human origins and evolution. In Fabian, A. (ed.), *Origins: The Darwin College Lectures*, pp. 89–114. Cambridge: Cambridge University Press.

Pinker, S. and Bloom, P. (1990). Natural language and natural selection. *Behavioral and Brain Sciences* 13: 707–84.

Pinxten, R., van Dooren, I. and Harvey, K. (1983). *The Anthropology of Space: Explorations into Natural Philosophy and Semantics of the Navajo*. Philadelphia: University of Pennsylvania Press.

Platt, M. (1986). Social norms and lexical acquisition: a study of deictic verbs in Samoan child language. In Schieffelin, B. and Ochs, E. (eds), pp. 127–52.

Poedjosoedarmo, S. (1968). Javanese speech levels. *Indonesia* 6: 54–81.

Polanyi, M. (1959). *The Study of Man*. Chicago: University of Chicago Press.

Polanyi, M. (1962). *Personal Knowledge: Towards a Post-critical Philosophy*. Chicago: University of Chicago Press.

Polanyi, M. and Prosch, H. (1975). *Meaning*. Chicago: University of Chicago Press.

Poole, F. (1994). Socialization, enculturation and the development of personal identity. In Ingold, T. (ed.), pp. 831–60.

Premack, D. (1986). *Gavagai! Or the Future History of the Animal Language Controversy*. Cambridge, MA: Massachusetts Institute of Technology Press.

Pride, J. and Holmes, J. (eds) (1972). *Sociolinguistics: Selected Readings*. Harmondsworth: Penguin.

Prideaux, G. (1970). *The Syntax of Japanese Honorifics*. The Hague: Mouton.

Putnam, H. (1975). *Mind, Language and Reality*. Cambridge: Cambridge University Press.

Putnam, H. (1981). *Reason, Truth and History*. Cambridge: Cambridge University Press.

Quine, W. (1960). *Word and Object*. Cambridge, MA: Massachusetts Institute of Technology Press.

Quine, W. (1961). *From a Logical Point of View*. Second edition. Cambridge, MA: Harvard University Press.

Quine, W. (1969). *Ontological Relativity and Other Essays*. New York: Columbia University Press.

Quinn, N. (1991). The culture basis of metaphor. In Fernandez, J. (ed.), pp. 56–93.

Rabinow, P. and Sullivan, W. (eds) (1979). *Interpretive Social Science: A Reader*. Berkeley: University of California Press.

Randall, R. (1987). The nature of highly inclusive folk-botanical categories. *American Anthropologist* 89: 143–6.

Randall, R. and Hunn, E. (1984). Do life forms evolve or do uses for life? Some doubts about Brown's universals hypothesis. *American Ethnologist* 11: 329–49.

Read, K. (1955). Morality and the concept of the person among the Gahuku-Gama. *Oceania* 25: 234–82.

Reddy, M. (1993). The conduit metaphor. In Ortony, A. (ed.), *Metaphor and Thought*, pp. 164–201. Second edition. Cambridge: Cambridge University Press.

Reisman, K. (1974). Contrapuntal conversations in an Antiguan village. In Bauman, R. and Sherzer, J. (eds), pp. 110–24.

Reynolds, P. (1983). Ape constructional ability and the origin of linguistic structure. In de Grolier, E. (ed.), *Glossogenetics: The Origin and Evolution of Language*, pp. 185–200. New York: Harwood Academic Publishers.

Reynolds, P. (1993). The complementation theory of language and tool use. In Gibson, K. and Ingold, T. (eds), pp. 407–28.

Richman, B. (1972). Some vocal distinctive features used by gelada baboons. *Journal of the Acoustical Society of America* 60: 718–24.

Richman, B. (1978). The synchronisation of voices by gelada monkeys. *Primates* 19: 569–81.

Richman, B. (1987). Rhythm and melody in gelada vocal exchanges. *Primates* 28: 199–223.

Ricoeur, P. (1981). *Hermeneutics and the Human Sciences*. Cambridge: Cambridge University Press.

Ringo, J. (1991). Neuronal interconnection as a function of brain size. *Brain, Behavior and Evolution* 38: 1–6.

Rivers, W. (1901). Introduction and vision. In Haddon, A. (ed.), *Reports of the Cambridge Anthropological Expedition to the Torres Straits*, volume 2, pp. 1–140.

Rivers, W. (1914). *The History of Melanesian Society*. Two volumes. Cambridge: Cambridge University Press.

Rogoff, B. and Lave, J. (eds) (1984). *Everyday Cognition: Its Development in Social Context*. Cambridge, MA: Harvard University Press.

Romaine, S. (1988). *Pidgin and Creole Languages*. London: Longman.

Romaine, S. (1994). *Language in Society: An Introduction to Sociolinguistics*. New York: Oxford University Press.

Romaine, S. (1995). *Bilingualism*. Second edition. Oxford: Basil Blackwell.

Romney, A. and D'Andrade, R. (1969). Cognitive aspects of English kin terms. In Tyler, S. (ed.), pp. 369–97.

Rorty, R. (1979). *Philosophy and the Mirror of Nature*. Princeton: Princeton University Press.

Rorty, R. (1989). *Contingency, Irony and Solidarity*. Cambridge: Cambridge University Press.

Rorty, R. (1991). *Objectivism, Relativism and Truth*. Cambridge: Cambridge University Press.

Rosaldo, M. (1973). I have nothing to hide: the language of Ilongot oratory. *Language in Society* 2: 193–223.

Rosaldo, M. (1974). Woman, culture and society: a theoretical overview. In Rosaldo, M. and Lamphere, L. (eds), pp. 17–42.

Rosaldo, M. (1980a). *Knowledge and Passion: Ilongot Notions of Self and Social Life*. Cambridge: Cambridge University Press.

Rosaldo, M. (1980b). The use and abuse of anthropology: reflections on feminism and cross-cultural understanding. *Signs* 5: 389–417.

Rosaldo, M. (1982). The things we do with words: Ilongot speech acts and speech act theory in philosophy. *Language in Society* 11: 203–37.

Rosaldo, M. (1984). Toward an anthropology of self and feeling. In Shweder, R. and LeVine, R. (eds), pp. 137–57.

Rosaldo, M. and Lamphere, L. (eds) (1974). *Women, Culture and Society*. Stanford: Stanford University Press.

Rosch, E. (1977). Human categorization. In Warren, N. (ed.), *Advances in Cross-cultural Psychology*, volume 1, pp. 1–49. London: Academic Press.

Rosch, E. (1978). Principles of categorization. In Rosch, E. and Lloyd, L. (eds), *Cognition and Categorization*, pp. 27–48. Hillsdale, NJ: Lawrence Erlbaum.

Rosch, E. and Mervis, C. (1975). Family resemblances: studies in the internal structure of categories. *Cognitive Psychology* 8: 382–439.

Rosch, E., Mervis, C., Gray, W., Johnson, R. and Boyes-Braem, P. (1976). Basic objects in natural categories. *Cognitive Psychology* 8: 382–439.

Rosenberger, N. (ed.) (1992). *Japanese Sense of Self*. Cambridge: Cambridge University Press.

Rubin, J. (1968). *National Bilingualism in Paraguay*. The Hague: Mouton. Excerpt in Pride, J. and Holmes, J. (eds), pp. 350–66.

Rubin, J. and Jernudd, B. (eds) (1971). *Can Language Be Planned? Sociolinguistic Theory and Practice for Developing Nations*. Honolulu: University of Hawaii Press.

Rumsey, A. (1989). Grammatical person and social agency in New Guinea Highland exchange systems. In Music, B., Graczyk, R. and Wiltshire, C. (eds), *Papers from the Twenty-fifth Annual Meeting of the Chicago Linguistics Society. Part 2:*

Parasession on Language in Context, pp. 242–53. Chicago: Chicago Linguistics Society.

Rumsey, A. (1990). Wording, meaning and linguistic ideology. *American Anthropologist* 92: 346–61.

Ryle, G. (1949). *The Concept of Mind*. London: Hutchinson.

Sachs, J. (1987). Preschool boys' and girls' language in pretend play. In Philips, S., Steele, S. and Tanz, C. (eds), pp. 178–88.

Sacks, K. (1979). *Sisters and Wives: The Past and Future of Sexual Equality*. Westport, CT: Greenwood Press.

Sahlins, M. (1976). Colors and Cultures. *Semiotica* 16: 1–22.

Sahlins, M. (1977). *The Use and Abuse of Biology: An Anthropological Critique of Sociobiology*. London: Tavistock.

Sanches, M. and Blount, B. (1975). *Sociocultural Dimensions of Language Use*. New York: Academic Press.

Sankoff, G. (1972). Language use in multilingual societies: some alternative approaches. In Pride, J. and Holmes, J. (eds), pp. 31–51.

Sankoff, G. (1980). *The Social Life of Language*. Philadelphia: University of Pennsylvania Press.

Sapir, E. (1921). *Language: An Introduction to the Study of Speech*. New York: Harcourt, Brace and World.

Sapir, E. (1949). *Selected Writings*. Berkeley: University of California Press.

Sapir, E. (1964). Conceptual categories in primitive languages. In Hymes, D. (ed.), p. 128.

Sapir, J. and Crocker, J. (eds) (1977). *The Social Use of Metaphor*. Philadelphia: University of Pennsylvania Press.

Saunders, B. (1992). *The Invention of Basic Colour Terms*. Utrecht, The Netherlands: Faculty of Social Science, University of Utrecht.

Saussure, F. (1959[1916]). *Course in General Linguistics*. New York: McGraw-Hill.

Savage-Rumbaugh, E. (1986). *Ape Language: From Conditioned Response to Symbol*. Oxford: Oxford University Press.

Savage-Rumbaugh, E. and Rumbaugh, D. (1993). The emergence of language. In Gibson, K. and Ingold, T. (eds), pp. 86–108.

Savage-Rumbaugh, S. and Lewin, R. (1994). *Kanzi: the Ape at the Brink of the Human Mind*. New York: John Wiley.

Schank, R. and Abelson, R. (1977). *Scripts, Plans, Goals, and Understanding: An Inquiry into Human Knowledge Structures*. Hillsdale, NJ: Lawrence Erlbaum.

Scheffler, H. and Lounsbury, F. (1971). *A Study in Structural Semantics: The Siriono Kinship System*. Englewood Cliffs, NJ: Prentice-Hall.

Schieffelin, B. (1990). *The Give and Take of Everyday Life: Language Socialization of Kaluli Children*. Cambridge: Cambridge University Press.

Schieffelin, B. and Gilmore. (eds) (1986). *The Acquisition of Literacy: Ethnographic Perspectives*. Norwood, NJ: Ablex.

Schieffelin, B. and Ochs, E. (1986a). Language socialization. *Annual Review of Anthropology* 15: 163–91.

Schieffelin, B. and Ochs, E. (eds) (1986b). *Language Socialization across Cultures*. Cambridge: Cambridge University Press.

Schiffman, H. (1973). Language, linguistics and politics in Tamilnad. In Gerow, E.

and Lang, M. (eds), *Studies in the Language and Culture of South Asia*, pp. 125–34. Seattle: University of Washington Institute of Comparative Foreign Area Studies.

Schneider, D. (1972). What is kinship all about? In Reining, P. (ed.), *Kinship Studies in the Morgan Centennial Year*, pp. 32–63. Washington D.C.: Anthropological Society of Washington.

Schneider, D. (1980). *American Kinship: A Cultural Account.* Second edition. Englewood Cliffs, NJ: Prentice-Hall.

Schneider, D. (1984). *A Critique of the Study of Kinship.* Ann Arbor: University of Michigan Press.

Schneider, D. and Gough, K. (1961). *Matrilineal Kinship.* Berkeley: University of California Press.

Scollon, R. and Scollon, S. (1981). *Narrative, Literacy and Face in Interethnic Communication.* Norwood, NJ: Ablex.

Scollon, R. and Scollon, S. (1995). *Intercultural Communication: A Discourse Approach.* Oxford: Basil Blackwell.

Scribner, S. and Cole, M. (1981). *The Psychology of Literacy.* Cambridge, MA: Harvard University Press.

Searle, J. (1969). *Speech Acts: An Essay in the Philosophy of Language.* Cambridge: Cambridge University Press.

Sebeok, T. (1964). Structure and content of Cheremis charms. In Hymes, D. (ed.), pp. 356–71.

Senft, G. (1987). Kilivila color terms. *Studies in Language* 11: 313–46.

Seton-Watson, H. (1977). *Nations and States.* London: Methuen.

Shaklee, M. (1980). The rise of standard English. In Shopen, T. (ed.), *Standards and Dialects in English*, pp. 33–62. Cambridge, MA: Winthrop.

Sherzer, J. (1976). *An Areal-typological Study of American Indian Languages North of Mexico.* Amsterdam: North-Holland.

Sherzer, J. (1983). *Kuna Ways of Speaking.* Austin: University of Texas Press.

Sherzer, J. (1987). A diversity of voices: men's and women's speech in ethnographic perspective. In Philips, S., Steele, S. and Tanz, C. (eds), pp. 95–120.

Sherzer, J. and Woodbury, A. (eds) (1987). *Native American Discourse: Poetics and Rhetoric.* Cambridge: Cambridge University Press.

Shibatani, M. (1990). *The Languages of Japan.* Cambridge: Cambridge University Press.

Shopen, T. (ed.) (1979). *Languages and their Speakers.* Cambridge, MA: Winthrop.

Shweder, R. (1990). Cultural psychology – what is it? In Stigler, J., Shweder, R. and Herdt, G. (eds), pp. 1–43.

Shweder, R. (1991). *Thinking Through Cultures: Expeditions in Cultural Psychology.* Cambridge, MA: Harvard University Press.

Shweder, R. and Bourne, E. (1984). Does the concept of the person vary cross-culturally? In Shweder, R. and LeVine, R. (eds), pp. 158–99.

Shweder, R. and LeVine, R. (eds) (1984). *Culture Theory: Essays on Mind, Self and Emotion.* Cambridge: Cambridge University Press.

Sifianou, M. (1992). *Politeness Phenomena in England and Greece: A Cross-cultural Approach.* Oxford: Oxford University Press.

Silverstein, M. (1976). Shifters, linguistic categories, and cultural description. In

Basso, K. and Selby, H. (eds), *Meaning in Anthropology*, pp. 11–55. Albuquerque: University of New Mexico Press.

Silverstein, M. (1979). Language structure and linguistic ideology. In Clyne, P., Hanks, W. and Hofbauer, C. (eds), *The Elements: A Parasession on Linguistic Units and Levels*, pp. 193–247. Chicago: Chicago Linguistics Society.

Silverstein, M. (1981). *The limits of awareness*. Working Papers in Sociolinguistics 84. Austin, TX: Southwestern Educational Laboratory.

Silverstein, M. (1985). Language and the culture of gender: at the intersection of structure, usage and ideology. In Mertz, E. and Parmentier, R. (eds), pp. 219–60.

Silverstein, M. (1987). Cognitive implications of a referential hierarchy. In Hickman, M. (ed.), *Social and Functional Approaches to Language and Thought*, pp. 125–64. New York: Academic Press.

Silverstein, M. (1992). Metapragmatic discourse and metapragmatic function. In Lucy, J. (ed.), *Reflexive Language: Reported Speech and Metapragmatics*, pp. 33–58. Cambridge: Cambridge University Press.

Smith, A. (1983). *Theories of Nationalism*. Second edition. London: Duckworth.

Smith, A. (1986). *The Ethnic Origin of Nations*. Oxford: Basil Blackwell.

Smith, A. (1991). *National Identity*. Harmondsworth: Penguin.

Smith, A. (1994). The politics of culture: ethnicity and nationalism. In Ingold, T. (ed.), pp. 706–733.

Smith-Hefner, N. (1988). Women and politeness: the Javanese example. *Language in Society* 17: 535–54.

Smolensky, P. (1988). On the proper treatment of connectionism. *Behavioral and Brain Sciences* 11: 1–74.

Sohn, H.-M. and Bender, B. (1973). A Ulithi grammar. *Pacific Linguistics* Series C27.

Soja, N., Carey, S. and Spelke, E. (1991). Ontological categories guide young children's inductions of word meaning: object terms and substance terms. *Cognition* 38: 179–211.

Spencer, A. (1991). *Morphological Theory: An Introduction to Word Structure in Generative Grammar*. Oxford: Basil Blackwell.

Sperber, D. and Wilson, D. (1986). *Relevance: Communication and Cognition*. Oxford: Basil Blackwell.

Spiro, M. (1993). Is the Western conception of the self "peculiar" within the context of the world's cultures? *Ethos* 21: 107–53.

Stefflre, V., Castillo Vales, V. and Morley, L. (1966). Language and cognition in Yucatan: a crosscultural replication. *Journal of Personality and Social Psychology* 4: 112–15.

Steinberg, D. and Jakobovitz, L. (eds) (1971). *Semantics: An Interdisciplinary Reader in Philosophy, Linguistics and Psychology*. Cambridge: Cambridge University Press.

Steklis, H. (1988). Primate communication, comparative neurology, and the origin of language re-examined. In Landsberg, M. (ed.), pp. 37–68.

Stigler, J., Shweder, R. and Herdt, G. (eds) (1990). *Cultural Psychology: Essays on Comparative Human Development*. Cambridge: Cambridge University Press.

Stoneking, M. and Cann, R. (1989). African origins of human mitochondrial DNA. In Mellars, P. and Stringer, C. (eds), pp. 17–30.

Strathern, M. (1988). *The Gender of the Gift*. Berkeley: University of California Press.

Streek, J. (1983). *Social Order in Child Communication*. Amsterdam: John Benjamins.

Street, B. (1984). *Literacy in Theory and Practice*. Cambridge: Cambridge University Press.

Street, B. (ed.) (1993). *Cross-cultural Approaches to Literacy*. Cambridge: Cambridge University Press.

Stringer, C. (1992). Evolution of early humans. In Jones, S., Martin, R. and Pilbeam, D. (eds), pp. 241–51.

Sturrock, J. (1986). *Structuralism*. London: Paladin.

Swacker, M. (1975). The sex of speaker as a sociolinguistic variable. In Thorne, B. and Henley, N. (ed.), pp. 76–83.

Talmy, L. (1983). How language structures space. In Pick, H. and Acredolo, L. (eds), *Spatial Orientation: Theory, Research, and Application*, pp. 225–320. New York: Plenum Press.

Talmy, L. (1985). Lexicalisation patterns: semantic structure in lexical forms. In Shopen, T. (ed.), *Language Typology and Syntactic Description*, volume 3, pp. 57–149. Cambridge: Cambridge University Press.

Tambiah, S. (1990). *Magic, Science, Religion, and the Scope of Rationality*. Cambridge: Cambridge University Press.

Tannen, D. (1982a). Oral and literate strategies in spoken and written narratives. *Language* 58: 1–21.

Tannen, D. (ed.) (1982b). *Spoken and Written Language: Exploring Orality and Literacy*. Norwood, NJ: Ablex.

Tannen, D. (1985). Relative focus on involvement in oral and written discourse. In Olson, D., Torrance, N. and Hildyard (eds), pp. 124–47.

Tannen, D. (1989). Interpreting interruption in conversation. In Music, B., Graczyk, R. and Wiltshire, C. (eds), *Papers from the Twenty-fifth Annual Meeting of the Chicago Linguistics Society. Part 2: Parasession on Language in Context*, pp. 266–87. Chicago: Chicago Linguistic Society.

Tannen, D. (1990). *You Just Don't Understand: Men and Women in Conversation*. New York: Morrow.

Tannen, D. (ed.) (1993). *Gender and Conversational Interaction*. Oxford: Oxford University Press.

Taylor, C. (1985a). *Human Agency and Language*. Cambridge: Cambridge University Press.

Taylor, C. (1985b). *Philosophy and the Human Sciences*. Cambridge: Cambridge University Press.

Taylor, C. (1989). *Sources of the Self*. Cambridge, MA: Harvard University Press.

Taylor, C. (1993). To follow a rule. . . . In Calhoun, C., LiPuma, E. and Postone, M. (eds), pp. 45–60.

Taylor, D. (1982). "Male" and "female" speech in Gros Ventre. *Anthropological Linguistics* 24: 301–7.

Tedlock, D. (1972). *Finding the Center: Narrative Poetry of the Zuni Indians*. New York: Dial.

Tedlock, D. (1983). *The Spoken Word and the Work of Interpretation*. Philadelphia: University of Pennsylvania Press.

Templeton, A. (1993). The "Eve" hypothesis: a genetic critique and reanalysis. *American Anthropologist* 95: 51–72.

Thomason, S. (1983). Chinook Jargon in areal and historical context. *Language* 59: 820–70.

Thomason, S. and Kaufman, T. (1988). *Language Contact, Creolization and Genetic Linguistics*. Berkeley: University of California Press.

Thompson, E. (1995). *Colour Vision: A Study in Cognitive Science and the Philosophy of Perception*. London: Routledge.

Thompson, E., Palacios, A. and Varela, F. (1992). Ways of coloring: comparative color vision as a case study for cognitive science. *Behavioral and Brain Sciences* 15: 1–74.

Thompson, J. (1981). *Critical Hermeneutics: A Study in the Thought of Paul Ricoeur and Jürgen Habermas*. Cambridge: Cambridge University Press.

Thompson, J. (1991). Editor's introduction. In Bourdieu, P. (1991), pp. 1–31.

Thorne, B. and Henley, N. (eds) (1975). *Language and Sex: Difference and Dominance*. Rowley, MA: Newbury House.

Thorne, B., Kramarae, C. and Henley, C. (eds) (1983). *Language, Gender and Society*. Rowley, MA: Newbury House.

Tilly, C. (ed.) (1975). *The Formation of National States in Western Europe*. Princeton: Princeton University Press.

Tobias, P. (1987). The brain of *Homo habilis*: a new level of organization in cerebral evolution. *Journal of Human Evolution* 16: 741–61.

Tönnies, F. (1955). *Community and Association*. London: Routledge and Kegan Paul.

Tornay, S. (ed.) (1978). *Vois et Nommer les Couleurs*. Nanterre: Service de Publication du Laboratoire d'Ethnologie et de Sociologie Comparative de l'Université de Paris X.

Toth, N. (1985). Archaeological evidence for preferential right-handedness in the Lower and Middle Pleistocene, and its possible implications. *Journal of Human Evolution* 14: 607–14.

Trudgill, P. (1972). Sex, covert prestige and linguistic change in the urban British English of Norwich. *Language in Society* 1: 179–95.

Trudgill, P. (1974). *The Social Differentiation of English in Norwich*. Cambridge: Cambridge University Press.

Trudgill, P. (ed.) (1978). *Sociolinguistic Patterns in British English*. London: Edward Arnold.

Trudgill, P. (1983). *Sociolinguistics*. Second edition. Harmondsworth: Penguin.

Tumin, M. (1967). *Social Stratification: The Forms and Functions of Inequality*. Englewood Cliffs, NJ: Prentice-Hall.

Turner, M. (1987). *Death is the Mother of Beauty: Mind, Metaphor, Criticism*. Chicago: University of Chicago Press.

Turner, V. (1967). *The Forest of Symbols*. Ithaca, NY: Cornell University Press.

Turner, V. (1969). *The Ritual Process*. Chicago: Aldine.

Tyler, S. (ed.) (1969). *Cognitive Anthropology: Readings*. New York: Holt, Rinehart and Winston.

Uhlenbeck, E. (1978). *Studies in Javanese Morphology*. The Hague: Koninklijk instituut voor taal-, land-, en volkenkunde.

Urban, G. (1985). The semiotics of two speech styles in Shokleng. In Mertz, E. and Parmentier, R. (eds), pp. 311–31.

Urban, G. (1991). *A Discourse Centered Approach to Culture*. Austin: University of Texas Press.

Varela, F., Thompson, E. and Rosch, E. (1991). *The Embodied Mind: Cognitive Science and Human Experience.* Cambridge, MA: Massachusetts Institute of Technology Press.

Vološinov, V. (1986). *Marxism and the Philosophy of Language.* Cambridge, MA: Harvard University Press.

Voorhoeve, C. (1977). *Ta-poman:* metaphorical use of words and poetic vocabulary in Asmat songs. *Pacific Linguistics* Series C 40: 19–38.

Vygotsky, L. (1978). *Mind in Society: The Development of Higher Psychological Processes.* Cambridge, MA: Harvard University Press.

Vygotsky, L. (1986). *Thought and Language.* Revised edition. Cambridge, MA: Massachusetts Institute of Technology Press.

Wainscoat, J., Hill, A., Boyce, A., Flint, J., Hernandez, M., Thein, S., Old, J., Lynch, J., Falusi, A., Weatheral, D. and Clegg, J. (1986). Evolutionary relationships of human populations from an analysis of nuclear DNA polymorphisms. *Nature* 319: 491–3.

Wallace, A. and Atkins, J. (1969). The meaning of kinship terms. In Tyler, S. (ed.), pp. 345–68.

Wallerstein, I. (1979). *The Capitalist World-economy.* Cambridge: Cambridge University Press.

Walsh, M. (1994). Interactional styles in the courtroom: an example from northern Australia. In Gibbons, J. (ed.), *Language and the Law,* pp. 217–64. London: Longman.

Wardhaugh, R. (1992). *An Introduction to Sociolinguistics.* Second edition. Oxford: Basil Blackwell.

Wassman, J. (1991). *The Song to the Flying Fox.* Port Moresby: National Research Institute of Papua New Guinea.

Weber, M. (1968[1922]). *Economy and Society: An Outline of Interpretive Sociology.* New York: Bedminster Press.

Weinreich, U. (1953). *Languages in Contact.* The Hague: Mouton.

White, G. and Kirkpatrick, J. (eds) (1985). *Person, Self, and Experience: Exploring Pacific Ethnopsychologies.* Berkeley: University of California Press.

White, R. (1982). Rethinking the Middle/Upper Paleolithic transition. *Current Anthropology* 23: 169–192.

Whorf, B. (1956). *Language, Thought, and Reality: Selected Writings of Benjamin Lee Whorf.* Cambridge, MA: The Massachusetts Institute of Technology Press.

Wierzbicka, A. (1980). *Lingua Mentalis: The Semantics of Natural Language.* Sydney: Academic Press.

Wierzbicka, A. (1985). *Lexicography and Conceptual Analysis.* Ann Arbor: Karoma.

Wierzbicka, A. (1990). The meaning of color terms: semantics, culture and cognition. *Cognitive Linguistics* 1: 99–150.

Wierzbicka, A. (1992a). *Semantics, Culture and Cognition.* New York: Oxford University Press.

Wierzbicka, A. (1992b). What is a *life form*? Conceptual issues in ethnobiology. *Journal of Linguistic Anthropology* 2: 3–29.

Wierzbicka, A. (1993). A conceptual basis for cultural psychology. *Ethos* 21: 205–31.

Wilkins, D. (1993a). Ants, ancestors and medicine: a semantic and pragmatic account of classifier constructions in Mparntwe Arrernte. Paper presented at the conference,

Back to Basics in Nominal Classification, Nijmegen, The Netherlands: Cognitive Anthropology Research Group, Max-Planck Institute for Psycholinguistics.

Wilkins, D. (1993b). Linguistic evidence in support of a holistic approach to traditional ecological knowledge. In Williams, N. and Baines, G. (ed.), *Traditional Ecological Knowledge*, pp. 77–93. Canberra: Centre for Resource and Environmental Studies.

Wilkins, W. and Wakefield, J. (1995). Brain evolution and neurolinguistic preconditions. *Behavioral and Brain Sciences* 18: 161–226.

Willis, P. (1977). *Learning to Labour*. London: Routledge and Kegan Paul.

Wilson, E. (1980). *Sociobiology: the New Synthesis*. Abridged edition. Cambridge, MA: Harvard University Press.

Wind, J., Chiarelli, B., Bichakjian, B. and Nocentini, A. (ed.) (1992). *Language Origin: A Multidisciplinary Approach*. Dordrecht, The Netherlands: Kluwer Academic Publishers.

Witherspoon, G. (1977). *Language and Art in the Navajo Universe*. Ann Arbor: University of Michigan Press.

Wittgenstein, L. (1953). *Philosophical Investigations*. New York: Macmillan.

Wolpoff, M. (1989). Multiregional evolution: the fossil alternative to Eden. In Mellars, P. and Stringer, C. (eds), pp. 62–108.

Wood, B. (1992). Evolution of australopithecines. In Jones, S., Martin, R. and Pilbeam, D. (ed.), pp. 231–40.

Woodbury, A. (1985). Functions of rhetorical structure: a study of Central Alaskan Yupik Eskimo discourse. *Language in Society* 14: 150–93.

Woodbury, A. (1987). Rhetorical structure in a Central Yupik Eskimo traditional narrative. In Sherzer, J. and Woodbury, A. (ed.), pp. 176–239.

Woods, N. (1988). Talking shop: sex and status as determinants of floor apportionment in a work setting. In Coates, J. and Cameron, D. (eds), *Women in their Speech Communities*, pp. 141–57. London: Longman.

Woolard, K. and Schieffelin, B. (1994). Language ideology. *Annual Review of Anthropology* 23: 55–82.

Worsley, P. (1987). *The New Introducing Sociology*. Third edition. Harmondsworth: Penguin.

Yanagisako, S. and Collier, J. (1987). Toward a unified analysis of gender and kinship. In Collier, J. and Yanagisako, S. (eds), pp. 14–50.

Ziff, P. (1971). On H. P. Grice's account of meaning. In Steinberg, D. and Jakobovitz, L. (eds), pp. 60–5.

Zimmerman, D. and West, C. (1975). Sex roles, interruptions and silences in conversation. In Thorne, B. and Henley, N. (eds), pp. 105–29.

Zvelebil, K. (1964). Spoken languages of Tamilnad. *Archivi Orientalni* 32: 237–64.

Index